Snowboarding the World

Matt Barr, Chris Moran, Ewan Wallace

> " "
>
> For me, snowboarding isn't just about the actual riding. It's just as much about the entire experience of travelling to new places and having a good time with your buddies. I have made it my goal to go on two entirely new trips every season and that's what really keeps me going and motivates me. Although travelling can be very exhausting at times, it's also where I get most of my inspiration from.
>
> *David Benedek*

Snowboarders are, by definition, travellers. Unless you're lucky enough to live at the foot of a mountain, the typical snowboarding trip means planning an overseas journey – and making some important decisions.

So how do you narrow down the options? Unlike surfing, with its rich culture, sophisticated market and detailed guidebooks, snowboarding travel literature lags behind. Such guides as do exist are often poorly researched, badly written and – unforgivably – guilty of propagating the same hackneyed opinions that have been current since the first pioneers decided to descend a hill while standing sideways.

It was for this reason that we wanted to write a guide that reflected the reality of modern snowboarding travel. Together, we've spent seasons in France, ridden secret valleys in Iran, crested virgin peaks in the far northern reaches of Greenland, and hiked glaciers in Iceland under the midnight sun. We've been lost in Russian forests, had the best week hitting rails in Big Bear, and enjoyed night-time powder sessions in Japan. We wanted to use these experiences to help other riders broaden their own particular horizons.

We asked locals, friends, pros, photographers, barmen, chalet staff, park builders and newcomers to snowboarding for their opinions, and these opinions have tempered and informed our own. We've tried to show the resorts in the truest possible light with our choice of photos, and above all, we've tried to depict snowboarding in the way we've been lucky enough to live it – as an incredibly enriching experience that offers everybody who tries it a passport to a new world. Which part of the world you choose to drop into is, of course, down to you, but we hope this guide helps you make some of those key decisions along the way.

Contents

Essentials

Austria

Canada

Eastern Europe & Middle East

France

Italy

Japan

New Zealand

Scandinavia

South America

Spain & Andorra

Switzerland

USA

From the authors

When we first started riding, the snowboarding world was a very different place from the one we know today. Snowboarding was still in its punk phase, and the notion that this rebellious youth culture would ever become so mainstream and accepted as to become an Olympic sport was just plain ludicrous.

For each of us, the decision to do our first winter season was a no-brainer. We loved snowboarding, and all we knew was that we had to do it as much as possible. There wasn't really any choice at all. To not go was unthinkable. True, none of us had even the vaguest idea of the impact it would have on our lives, but then it wasn't something that we gave much thought to at the time.

Over the ensuing years, we've been around the world several times in our quest to find the best riding. Along the way two of us became professional riders, and all three of us began writing about the sport we love. We made a lot of friends and had a lot of great experiences, and it's fair to say our lives would have been poorer without it all.

In addition to all this we've gained a massive amount of knowledge about snowboarding and snowboarding travel, without any real outlet for it. Until now.

The three of us were getting to the point where we'd spent almost half our lives going snowboarding, and it is now intensely satisfying to finally realize a project that puts it all to good use. Now we can kid ourselves that the last however many years haven't been spent frivolously snowboarding our way around the world, but instead conducting the sort of extensive live-the-project research that any method actor would be proud of. Nothing like a bit of retrospective purpose to give meaning to your actions.

About the authors

Between them, Matt, Chris and Ewan have almost half a century of snowboarding experience under their belts. Chris has been riding since the sport first arrived in the country, is generally considered to be one of the early pioneers of professional snowboarding in the UK, and is one of the most successful British riders to date, with several British championship titles to his name. Matt started the first of many winter seasons after completing an English Literature degree, and has spent the last 10 years writing for *White Lines* magazine as well as working as a journalist and travel writer for newspapers and magazines worldwide. Ewan is a professional snowboarder and also writes for *Snowboard UK* magazine. Together, they formed the ACM Writing Group to provide specialist and mainstream media titles with boardsports and travel journalism that reflects the realities of the lifestyle and sports they love. They live in Brighton, UK, and travel the world extensively each winter in the perpetual search for the next best place you've never heard of. For more information, check out acmwriting.com.

R: DAN MILNER P: CHRIS MORAN

A: CHRIS MORAN L: VALLEE BLANCHE, CHAMONIX, FRANCE P: ALEX ASHLEY

A: MATT BARR L: BUENOS AIRES, ARGENTINA P: JAMES MCPHAIL

A: EWAN WALLACE L: ISFAHAN, IRAN P: JAMES MCPHAIL

Acknowledgements

Although this book is the end product of over 30 years of snowboarding and travelling experience, we have been fortunate enough throughout our riding careers to work with many, many talented and inspirational people. For giving us the opportunity to travel the world and indulge our passions, and – laughably – call it work, we'd like to thank the publishers and staff at all the magazines we've worked for over the years. Particular thanks to James McPhail for his help, advice and long hours racked up behind the wheel over the years, and to Chris Nelson and Demi Taylor for their inspiration.

In putting together this book, we have (often quite blatantly) called in every favour and bit of goodwill we've ever accrued over the years. Many people have been browbeaten and electronically doorstepped for information and knowledge, and to show our gratitude for this we would like in particular to acknowledge the contributions of: Posy Dixon, Tam Leach, Jesse Huffman, Annie Fast, Gary Greenshields, Dan Milner, Ed Leigh, Sian Leigh, Adam Gendle, Tim Warwood, Becky Horton, Mary Stewart Miller, Colin Whyte, Richard Dass, Jason Horton, Tash Green Armytage, Marianne Haulkes, Mike Weyerhaeuser, Nick Ivanov, Ste'en Webster, John Matkovic, Thomaz Garcia, Andoni Epelde, Les Seddon Brown, Natalie Mayer, Maria Ferretti, Nick Hamilton, Andy Wright, Anne Pederson, Dan Caruso, Cira Riedel at 7th Sky, Phil and team at Urb Orbis, everyone at BGB, Stu, Spence, Jo, Matt and Pippa from Soulsports and Jay Tierney in Aspen. Lastly – thanks to Andy Pietrasik at the *Guardian* for some great suggestions.

For help with country and resort specifics, we'd like to thank: **Andorra** J McNamara, Marta Rotes and Andrew at Millennium PR. **Argentina** Dan Evans and Richard Dass from Snoventures.com. **Austria** Posy Dixon, James Bryant, the Hungerpain Hotel crew, David Benedek, Friedl Kolar, Beckna, Steve Gruber, Birgit Gruber, Caro at Aesthetiker, Annette Tame, Sue and Rob Freeman, Eva Maria, Martin Muck and the Absolute Park crew, Gogo Gosner and Wilma at St Anton. **Bulgaria** Harriet at Busgang and Ash at Method. **Canada** Posy Dixon, Sara and Wendy at Whistler, Rob Cote at Banff, Becky Horton, Mike at Sunshine, Grant at Lake Louise, George and Brian Rode in Jasper, Christine Grimble at Fernie, Chris Elder at Kimberley, Rachel Grieve at Gosh PR, Air Canada, Andrew Hardingham, Colin Whyte at Future Snowboarding. **Chile** Richard Dass at snoventures.com. **Finland** Martin Robertson, Riine at Finnish Tourism, Becky Horton. **France** Youri Barneoud, Fab Lomboret, Eric Bergeri, Nico Droz, Régis Rolland, Chris Cracknell, Susannah Osborne, Richard Lett and Erica Sivil, Marcus Chapman, Stef Berlioz, Lesley McKenna, Nev from seasonaires.com, Ash Strain, John Bassett, Spencer Claridge, Matt Swann, the Telemark (sorry for the noise). **Iran** Cyrus Shahad, Mahmood Darydel and Leily Lankarni. **Italy** Rita Comi, Dani Milano, Tam Leach, Cath Argyle, Susie, Helen and Megan at BGB. **Japan** Owain Bassett, Matt Fletcher, Rob Tyrell, June Clarke, Kylie and Miyuki at JTO, Jenny, Erin, Josie, Lisa, Sandy, Johno and Phil, Hester, Ed and Rachel at Motorola. **New Zealand** Siân Leigh, Sam and Snow Park crew, Tom Wilmott, Chelsea Gannon, Ste'en Webster, Johnny McCormack, Eddie Spearing, Chris Kirkham, Stephen Scott, John Matkovic at Board The World, David Ovendale, Clare Roach, Dylan Wyn Davies, Kat, Sophia and Christie at Red Bull. **Norway** Jan Prokes, Richard Palmgren, Morten Mymoen, Ulrik Solum, Ski Norway, Preben Stene Larsen, Terje Haakonsen, Geilo Tourism. **Poland** Eric Bergeri, Mark at Zakopane Life. **Russia** Kat at Red Bull, Ivan and his mate from Sochi, Fjodor from Red Bull, Nick Ivanov. **Spain** Thomaz Garcia at Snow Planet, Antxon, Iker Fernández. **Sweden** Caroline Andersson at Swedish Tourism, Anders Neumann at Transition. **Switzerland** Alexeja Pozzoni, Michi Albin, Gian Simmen, Freddie Kalbermatten, Nicolas Muller, Maria Ferreti, Tina Birbaum, Hamish McKnight, James McPhail, Anna at Les Diablerets, Orange AIM Series and Adelboden Tourism. **USA** Nicole at Aleyska, Nate Kern, Christian Stevenson, Wayne Yates, Sunset and Vine, Jim and Paul Wedlake, Carly Nunn and friends, Nick Vine, Kate Osborn at Breckenridge, Randy at Brighton, Kelly Burgdof, Jon Nutting and Mike Basich.

We would also like to the Footprint team for giving us the opportunity to put this book together. They understood what we were trying to do from the moment we approached them and have backed us completely, even when we sailed effortlessly past every deadline we'd set for ourselves. In this respect, thanks to Alan Murphy, Patrick Dawson, Andy Riddle, Rob Lunn and Debbie Wylde.

We'd also like to thank Jim and Chod at *White Lines* for all their fantastic support and for the years we were able to broaden our horizons on the Permanent Publishing account(!) For similar reasons, we'd like to say a huge hello to Eddie, Ian, Carl, Tom, Marcus and Dan – *Snowboard UK* staff past and present.

Finally, thanks to all our friends and family for listening to endlessly tedious discussions about 'the book' and for putting up with our generally antisocial tendencies for the last year.

R: JOSH WOLF L: CANAZEI P: JAMES McPHAIL

Essentials

R: JAMES STENTIFORD L: VAL D'ISERE P: NICK HAMILTON

Powder, face shots, cold air. What it's all about.

Planning a trip

Where to go

Snowboarding has grown up. Yet to read those 'Guide to snow speak' sidebars wheeled out by the newspapers each time the thermometer dips, you'd be forgiven for thinking our sport was some kind of dark art, cloaking itself in strange lingo for the benefit of a few adolescent rebels. This may have partly been true 15 years ago, but today snowboarding is a broad church whose members defy easy categorization. The term 'snowboarder' means different things to many, many different people. For every park rat staring at Sweden's Åre and complaining 'It's not exactly Mammoth is it?', there's a beginner lusting after the gentle undulation of Méribel's Altiport slopes on which to get their turns down. For every semi-professional who thinks snowboarding is about building a powder kicker in the backcountry and wanging yourself off it, there are scores of ordinary riders just as stoked on a good day's riding and who wouldn't know a good powder landing if they sideslipped down it. The point is that snowboarding has evolved in the same way that every sport evolves eventually, so that anybody saying 'that's not real snowboarding' is missing the point rather spectacularly. The entire world now contains some form of 'real snowboarding' in its many shapes and forms and the modern snowboarder's options are in, reality, almost limitless. So how do you choose where to go?

Some 30, 20, even 15 years ago, it was simple. With so few resorts even allowing snowboarders to darken their freshly-cut pistes, riders would simply head wherever they'd receive a warm welcome. Resorts such as Breckenridge, Vail, Avoriaz and Saas Fee are still dining out on this far-sightedness today, each of them woven deeply into snowboarding's fabric as resorts that accepted 'us' when it was unfashionable to do so. Today, with snowboarding having given the entire winter sports industry a much-needed shot in the arm, and resorts the world over clamouring for our business, choosing the place you're going to go to for your annual two-week snowboarding jamboree is a much more inexact science. As we discovered while writing this book, the variables are infinite.

That's why the resorts in this book are, to put it mildly, a diverse bunch, reflecting the wildly varied needs of modern riders themselves. While some need a perfect park, others hanker for a high number of blue runs on which to hone their technique. For everybody who finds the convenience of the United States the perfect foundation upon which to lay a few turns, others yearn for the adventurous travel that only a truly foreign culture can provide. In making our selection, we canvassed as many expert opinions as we could and drew from our own long experience. Some resorts virtually included themselves by dint of their towering reputations, but some rank outsiders made it in simply because we went on holiday there and had an unexpectedly great time. Some people will doubtless be asking why, for example, Marmot Basin in Canada is in at the expense of,

... but where to start?

Even though we've devised a key for each resort, enabling you to compare the merits of each resort at a glance, there are still some classic, tried and tested trips out there. Here are our selections to get you started.

	Week	Month	Season
Party	Soldeu, Andorra ▶▶*p290*	Val D'Isère, France ▶▶*p158*	Méribel, France ▶▶*p146*
	Bansko, Bulgaria ▶▶*p100*	Engelberg, Switzerland ▶▶*p312*	Verbier, Switzerland ▶▶*p330*
Powder	Baqueira, Spain ▶▶*p292*	Las Leñas, Argentina ▶▶*p272*	Niseko, Japan ▶▶*p210*
	St Foy, France ▶▶*p150*	Krasnaya Poliana, Russia ▶▶*p108*	Kicking Horse, Canada ▶▶*p80*
Park	Silvretta Nova, Austria ▶▶*p52*	Zillertal, Austria ▶▶*p56*	Snow Park, New Zealand ▶▶*p230*
	Big Bear, USA ▶▶*p352*	Morzine, France ▶▶*p148*	Mammoth, USA ▶▶*p366*

L: KICKING HORSE P: TASH

say, Hoch Y Brig in Switzerland. But that's what snowboarding can be like sometimes. How often have you been tempted to stay in bed, dragged yourself up in the rain and been treated to the sight of your chair breaking through the clouds into a bluebird sky, before having the best day of your week? Or put your hood up and got in the trees when it's been snowing? Intrepidness can often bring its own rewards.

A good guidebook fulfills two functions: reference and, more importantly in our case, comparison. The first aspect is relatively easy to cover, and most guidebooks stand or fall on the credibility of their recommendations and insider tips. Nobody likes to feel like a tourist, and the best guidebooks let readers have their cake and eat it too by letting them feel like a local while herding them around all the major sites anyway. Less easy to accomplish is a scale of comparison that most readers find useful, especially when, as we've already stated, most of the people reading this book will have highly varied needs. That's why we've devised a key for each resort that allows you to quickly ascertain if a resort is going to be the right one for you, while supporting the actual nuts and bolts information found in each review. Look at the inside back cover flap for a detailed explanation of how to use this 'quick-flick' key.

To me travelling has always been an important part of snowboarding as well as my life. I have had a couple of years with over 300 travelling days a year. For me it's crucial, as Sweden, where I'm from, has limited options for epic snowboarding. The best thing about being able to travel is to go wherever the snow is good at that moment. It is easier said than done though. It takes a lot of research, trustworthy contacts and nowadays a lot of surfing on weather websites checking cloud patterns. Usually it is so worth it once you are there.

Vincent Skoglund

L: BRECKENBRIDGE PIPE P: TIM WARWOOD

How to go

Choosing your destination is only one aspect of planning a riding trip, and the sophistication with which the travel industry has got involved in the snowboarding revolution is matched only by the artfulness of the ski industry. The early days abound with tales of riders sleeping in cars to get to the goods, or ramming apartments with like-minded friends to keep the cost down during hedonistic early snowboarding trips. In contrast, today you can buy a bespoke season online, simply turning up with your kit and having your meals cooked for you for four months. Each approach has its own pros and cons.

Packages

In the past, the idea of booking a snowboarding specific package holiday would have seemed a notion plucked from the realms of fantasy. Not any more. Today, every major tour operator has a winter programme offering complete package deals. Obviously the options vary wildly, with some offering all-inclusive deals (flights, full board, lift tickets, transfers, all meals and reps in resort) and other variations that require the holidaymaker to buy their own flights, lift passes and other details. The advantages of the package are obvious: they're cheap, convenient and are particularly suitable for families looking to get their kids on the snow at the cheapest possible price. The

Snowboard travel has given me some of my richest experiences. I've met great friends, ridden ridiculous powder and experienced places I'd never have imagined otherwise. To me it's about adventure and discovery, getting off the beaten track, finding empty untracked mountains and searching for powder in places most people wouldn't bother to look. I never thought that snowboarding would take me to the places I've been lucky enough to experience like India, Russia, Turkey and Greenland. There are so many unusual places out there waiting to be discovered. After 12 years of snowboard travel I still feel like I've only scratched the surface. Every time I look at the atlas I see new possibilities.

James Stentiford, pro snowboarder

P: CHRIS MORAN/HOTSHITPICTURES.COM

disadvantages are a lack of flexibility if the hotel turns out to be a shocker, and a feeling that you're not actually travelling – more being herded from one familiar environment to another painstakingly recreated in a foreign country. Witness the hordes of UK tourists slowly turning the Bulgarian resorts into English ghettos.

Independents

The huge interest in snowboarding over the last decade has seen a corresponding increase in the number of independent companies promoting snowboarding on their own terms. As a rule, they're run by passionate snowboarders intensely familiar with their local resorts who have looked at the current state of the market and gone out on a limb by deciding to go one better. Once a tiny minority, their numbers are slowly increasing – especially in the European Alps, North America and New Zealand. The advantages for the customer are obvious: you're in the hands of passionate people who know their local area intimately, and have a direct link to the mainline of resort life; and you're also likely to have more in common with fellow guests. The disadvantages of this approach are twofold: smaller companies are less able to keep the prices down and so are generally more expensive than 'stack 'em high, pack 'em in' packages; and there's also the risk that you'll book with a company that is perhaps not quite the slick outfit that's been made out in the advertising or on the internet bulletin boards. It can happen. Word of mouth is probably your greatest ally here, so ask around and do some research.

R: DCP L: NEW ZEALAND SECRET SPOT P: DEAN 'BLOTO' GRAY 2007 BURTON SNOWBOARDS

Explanations

Explanation of terms used

⊖ **Skier's right** The industry standard term meaning to the right-hand side if you're looking downhill.

⊖ **Skier's left** To the left-hand side looking downhill.

⊖ **Looker's right** Industry standard term meaning to the right-hand side if you're looking uphill.

⊖ **Looker's left** To the left-hand side if you're looking uphill.

⊖ **Freestyle** Riding or riders who prefer to ride obstacles, often man-made, that will put them into the air, or get them onto a rail.

⊖ **Freeride** Riding style or riders who prefer to ride powder, off-piste runs, or natural terrain that may include cliffs, rocks and couloirs. In practice most riders blend freeriding and freestyle riding seamlessly throughout the day – often in one run, but we have used these terms throughout the book to give the reader an idea of the conditions he or she might wish to look for or avoid.

DIY

It's still a classic. Get a group together, strap the boards to the roof of a mate's banger and head for the hills. There's just something liberating about it – especially when you round that last bend before the resort and see the mountain hove into view – preferably in the light of the moon. The camaraderie, the flexibility and – perhaps more persuasively – the cheapness are all strong arguments for the DIY approach. For many groups of young riders, the cost-cutting approach is the only feasible way they can go snowboarding which, let's not forget, is an incredibly pricey pastime. The flexibility this approach gives you, both in terms of cost and the weather (if there is no snow, you can always move on until you find some, especially in resort-rich countries such as France or Austria), is invaluable. The feeling engendered by a classic road trip cannot easily be dismissed either. But on the flipside, it's an approach not obviously suited to families with young children, or trips of a more involved nature. Older snowboarders with large disposable incomes are also likely to feel that their slumming-it days are behind them. However, some of the more 'out there' destinations featured in the guide can only be reached by following the DIY method, so choose you resort accordingly if comfort and convenience are your main requirements.

Airlines

As our surfing brethren know, air travel with a board bag is one way to up the cost and stress levels of any long journey. Thankfully, most snowboard bags are designed to allow you to use the bag as your main hold luggage, thus helping to keep the number of bags down as well as protecting your stick. Cost and weight are still a problem though, so research the weight limits of each airline before turning up at the airport. You will in all likelihood be penalized if your bag is over, and the cost can rise rapidly. On a trip to Sydney, for example, **BA** charge up to €44 (US$55) per extra kilo of luggage.

Airlines handle the problem in different ways, and riders should be especially careful when using budget airlines such as **Ryanair** or **easyJet**. The convenience often comes at a (hidden) price. **Ryanair** now charge a flat fee of €30 (US$38) per board on all their flights. Similarly, **easyJet** charge an additional levy per board, and make travellers sign a disclaimer so that any damage incurred is the responsibility of the traveller, not the airline. Check the websites listed in each country introduction to find out more about the specific charges on each route applicable to your planned trip.

JENNY JONES AT ZURICH TRAIN STATION. P: CHRIS MORAN

Snowboarding media

Snowboarding breeds passion, and nowhere is this more evident than in the world of the snowboarding media. Usually run by an unlikely combination of washed-up pros, snowboard geeks who were never good enough to be pros in the first place and, increasingly (and bizarrely), ambitious young journalists looking for a viable entry point into the world of media, snowboard mags usually closely reflect the scenes they represent.

At the centre of the snowboarding magazine universe are the American duopoly of *Transworld Snowboarding* and *Snowboarder*, closely followed by the pan-European magazines *Method Mag* and *OnBoard*. These mags set the trends, decide which riders will become household names and sell the most copies. As is often the case, more interesting things tend to happen at the fringes, and here we find magazines that truly define the term 'labour of love'. These snowboard mags operate at the margins in more ways than one.

Often sustained only by the passion of the staff and the avidity with which their generally low readership devours each issue, they must balance the voracious needs of the advertisers that bankroll each issue with the desire to put out a magazine that the readers are actually interested in reading. Despite such constraints, they usually succeed admirably. Freeriding-oriented mags like *Frequency* and *The Snowboard Journal* take their lead from surf titles such as *The Surfer's Journal* and are slowly upping the standards of shred journalism as the age of their audience slowly increases. In contrast, magazines such as Spain's *Snow Planet*, Sweden's *Transition* and the caustic *White Lines* from the UK eye snowboarding through the lens of their own unique scene. Always funny, sometimes scathing but always passionate they are generally the self-appointed oracles of snowboarding culture. It's good to know that there is still a place for mustard-keen minority interest magazines to thrive despite the fact that they aren't selling a million copies a month. Long may it continue.

Riders' tales
Vegetarianism in the mountains   Dan Milner – photographer, vegetarian

It seems cafés and restaurants in many countries, particularly in continental Europe, still have trouble in the proper translation of the word 'vegetarian'. Heading to a snowboard resort with a veggie appetite needn't be a problem – it's just unfortunate we veggies have to lower our culinary standards. That said, during a decade of shooting snowboard pictures in places as varied as Greenland and Alaska, Turkey and Chile, rarely – if ever – have I had to go hungry. Across Europe it seems almost impossible to avoid cheese getting in on the act, especially in France and Switzerland where being veggie popularly means you eat ham, fish and chicken. Here it's cheese dishes that come to the rescue. While most French resorts harbour an Italian-styled joint or two, the abundant French eateries won't offer much other than the molten cheese dishes of fondues (cook-your-own bread and cheese party), croute (bread soaked in cheese and wine then baked) or raclette (a DIY cheese grill served with potatoes) and a slender selection of meat-free salads. It's good food, but only in moderation. In Switzerland, look for rösti (grated, fired potato-cake with added tomatoes, mushrooms and more cheese) for a slightly different fill up. Italy is perhaps the easiest country for vegetarians, offering the usual pizza (ask for one without cheese, they'll do it no problemo), pasta, gnocchi (potato pasta) with simple arrabiata sauce or paninis (hot filled sandwiches). Austria is probably the vegetarian's worst nightmare, with sausage and mash featuring largely on every menu. It's not all doom and gloom though as they tend to feature more regional dishes and hence more overall variety than the uniform French menus. Dig about and you'll often find a decent veggie dish. The USA and Canada are – of course – where vegetarians are most easily catered for, as you'd expect in a country whose national identity is built on convenience and customer service. Eastern Europe sits at the other end of the spectrum, with unidentified flesh swimming in almost every dish. However, those who do understand the principle of vegetarianism are usually more than happy to help and will often rustle up something satisfactory. Good luck in your efforts to find good veggie food, and I hope this guide goes some way to helping you choose a resort that should satisfy your taste buds as well as your hunger for snowboarding.

SELF PORTRAIT P: DANMILNER.COM

Dan's exceptional European veggie hotspots

Chamonix's Grand Central Café has great bagels and wraps. The **Mojo Café** has brilliant filled sandwiches, and **Belouga** is a decent, alternative takeaway. **Le Delice** in Les Houches is a great little veg-choice restaurant ▶▶ *p128.*

In **Les Deux Alpes** La Spaghetteria has a surprisingly good 'eat all you like' buffet of Italian veggie antipasti ▶▶ *p144.*

Zermatt, Switzerland, has either the **Brown Cow** bar for veggie burgers, or **The Green Dinner** restaurant for organic vegetarian cuisine. For a resort, it is exceptional veggie food ▶▶ *p332.*

Val d'Isère has the **Billabong** café for quick bites ▶▶ *p158.*

Here shown doing a Double Cork 1080, you'll have to check out Blank Paper's new project to see David stomp the Double Cork 1260.
Lifestyle by Hansi Herbig – Action by Christian Brecheis

SCOTTY ARNOLD

JUSTIN BENNEE
JOSH DIRKSEN
WOLLE NYVELT
CHRISTOPHE SCHMIDT

JAMIE ANDERSON
ANNIE BOULANGER
TORAH BRIGHT

LIKE NOTHING BEFORE

DAVID BENEDEK & THE RELAY PRO

Doing things that haven't been done before is what drives David; it is a vital part of who he is. We've been with David since day one because we share the same drive.

To help him land new tricks like the Double Cork 1260, we developed with David the RELAY PRO: A binding built around a soft ankle harness for natural ankle movement, a tensor system for effortless transmission and a smart sole for ultimate absorption. The Relay binding is like nothing before.

Key up salomonsnowboards.com for more about David and the Relay Pro.

SALOMON
SNOWBOARDS

Six of the best

✪ Underground classics

❶ St Foy, France
Bafflingly uncrowded freeriding that everybody ignores in their rush to get to Val D'Isère and Tignes.

❷ Kicking Horse, Canada
Nobody outside Canada seems to have heard of it. That is set to change.

❸ Silvretta Nova, Austria
No, you've never heard of it. Yes, it's got one of the best parks in Europe. How did that happen?

❹ Arcalis, Andorra
The closest you'll get to Alaskan steepness in the Pyrenees.

❺ Baqueira-Beret, Spain
Everyone who's ever experienced the food, snow and friendliness of this Pyrenean classic vows to go back. Fact.

❻ Jurassik Park/Falgaria, Italy
Another resort you've never heard of with an amazing park. Only open on a Saturday though, strangely enough.

✪ Snowboard-friendly places to stay

❶ The Block, Heavenly, USA
MFM's bling-palace extraordinaire, complete with sponsor-designed rooms, plasma screens and more baggy trousers than would seem plausible.

❷ Rider's Palace, Laax, Switzerland
OK, it looks like a multi-storey car park masquerading as a hostel with a fancy lick of paint and no kitchens, but if you like partying, welcome to your fantasy crib.

❸ Dragon Lodge, Tignes, France
Not strictly a hotel, but definitely one of the mellowest, friendliest places you'll stay in. Great food as well.

❹ Chill Chalet, Bourg Saint Maurice, France
A stay here is almost like doing a season in the old days – and look at the resorts on standby.

❺ Shinzenkan, Niseko, Japan
Cheap, down-to-earth lodging in the middle of this powder paradise.

❻ Hotel Belle Vue, Engelberg, Switzerland
Engelberg is a party town on the sly, and the Belle Vue is in the thick of the action.

✪ Snowboard bars

❶ Popcorn, Saas Fee, Switzerland
World-renowned snowboard shop that turns itself into a raging party every night.

❷ The Coffee Shop, Shemshak, Iran
OK, they don't serve booze, but the insanely stoked locals here are out there on their own when it comes to welcoming visiting riders.

❸ The Ice Bar, Niseko, Japan
Built every year entirely from ice (including the glasses), this one is like Niseko itself – unique and unforgettable.

❹ The Cavern, Morzine, France
As local rider Adam Gendle says: "They play snowboarding on the TV and it's where all the seasonaires usually go."

❺ The Rondpoint, Méribel, France
Not strictly speaking a snowboard bar, but the après sessions are rightly legendary – and a quick way of meeting every seasonaire in town.

❻ Jimmy's Bar, Innsbruck, Austria
Has any bar held more legendary shred parties than Jimmy's …?

✪ Must do runs

❶ Valle Blanche, Chamonix, France
Yes, it's a cliché – but for good reason. Once you've got past the precarious *arête*, the run is long and the views will take your breath away.

❷ Night riding in Niseko, Japan
Blasting through knee-deep powder under floodlights? You can't do that at Talma…

❸ Big Bear Express, USA
Any direction you choose from the top will take you through the middle of the world's best maintained all-mountain funpark.

❹ The Marte chair, Las Leñas, Argentina
Not strictly speaking a 'run', this legendary lift accesses the terrain that gives Las Leñas its worldwide renown.

❺ The run to Les Ruinettes, Verbier, Switzerland
The run from Attelas from the top of the Funispace gondola down to Les Ruinettes. Got to catch it mid-morning when it's softening up, before it turns into a mogul field.

❻ Snow Park, New Zealand
Taking on the big kicker line at SP says to the assembled masses 'I have my shit down'. Don't try and blag it – you'll hurt more than your pride.

Six of the worst

Queues

1 Every lift, Krasnaya Poliana, Russia
The antiquated lift system simply can't cope with the increasing numbers, and the queuing system is survival of the fittest.

2 Chamonix, France, in February
Although every French resort gets crowded during the February holidays, Chamonix's creaking lift system is the worst.

4 Zakopane, Poland
You have to pay by the lift. So that's two queues for every run. Great.

3 Canazei, Italy
Chosen for its 'cable car to the base of slopes' access, which causes huge queues in town each morning.

5 Courmayeur, Italy
Same as Canazei, although Courmayeur's popularity mean they really should have sorted this out by now. At the end of the season, downloading is essential – prepare to wait.

6 Shemshak, Iran
The chair at the bottom gets clogged easily, although it does make a good social opportunity when it comes to meeting locals.

Scariest lifts

1 Penkenbahn, Zillertal, Austria
Dog-leg gondola with only one pylon holding it up between town and resort. And it's quite a way up …

2 Aiguille du Midi, Chamonix, France
Take a look at the top station, precariously perched atop the Midi at a height of 3842 m, and ask yourself how those crazy French threw this up back in the '50s.

3 Every chairlift, Krasnaya Poliana, Russia
Not high, but the fact that there are no barriers and they regularly halt for up to an hour while someone turns the power back on lends them an eerie feel.

4 Vanoise Express, La Plagne-Les Arcs, France
Linking La Plagne and Les Arcs – the technology might be new, but this thing still tops out at a whopping 380 m above the valley floor.

5 Freccia, Cortina, Italy
An impossibly sustained vertical rise in a rickety old cabin built when fur was a legitimate fashion item? No, thanks.

6 Nutcrackers, New Zealand Club Fields
See page 222 for a look at the world's most frustrating lift.

Draglifts

1 Levi, Finland
Great hill for beginners – shame the majority of lifts are windswept, icy drags.

2 Saas Fee, Switzerland
In an otherwise exemplary shred resort, Saas Fee's higher than average drag count is the only blot on its copybook.

3 Courchevel and Three Valleys, France
You can avoid them, but if you want to access the goods in this area, you'll have to tackle them sooner or later. Courchevel 1650 is pretty much all drag accessed.

4 Serre Chevalier, France
With 20 chairs and 39 drags, the odds of avoidance are stacked against you in Serre Che.

5 Jurassik Park/Folgaria, Italy
Park? Check. Drags? Just the one. Any other lifts? None whatsoever. Ah.

6 Engelberg, Switzerland
Switzerland is generally T-bar heavy, but Engelberg's high count will put off some beginners.

Transfer times

1 Stryn, Norway
It's a whopping 480 km from Oslo to Stryn – good job the scenery is diverting.

2 Jasper/Marmot Basin, Canada
363 km lie between Edmonton and the town of Jasper, underneath Marmot Basin. Peace, quiet and bear-spotting are the many rewards.

3 Baqueira-Beret, Spain
Yes, it's a long way from Barcelona to Baqueira – but prepare for the 340-km journey with a night on the Ramblas.

4 Mammoth, USA
It's one of the most famous resorts on the planet, but Mammoth – 265 km from Reno – is mightily difficult to get to.

5 Zermatt, Switzerland
Believe it or not, it's 244 km from Zermatt to Geneva.

6 Livigno, Italy
With its weird tunnel, closed valley and 240 km drive from the nearest airport, this place might be the toughest place to reach in Europe.

Riders' tales
Snowboarding and the environment

Respect the Mountain was launched by the Ski Club of Great Britain in 2004 to help safeguard the natural environment and the long-term future of snow sports. The aim of the campaign is to remind people to be aware of the delicate environment we live and play in and advise people to try and follow seven steps to preserve the mountain. To date, the campaign has raised money for the Woodland Trust's 'Tree for All' scheme and other alpine tree-planting schemes, sponsored an environmental research project and provided mountain users with green resort information and advice on travelling by train to resorts. For a full explanation, a seven-step plan and many fantastic links, please visit respectthemountain.com.

For more information on the Respect the Mountain Campaign please visit their website, and generously buy a green Respect the Mountain wristband for £2. Bands can be bought online or by calling T09065 224698 – the price of the call buys the band. All profits from the sales of the wristbands go towards the campaign.

In this guide, each resort has an environmental rating placed in the key on the right-hand side of the page. The rating is a mark out of six. A resort scores a point for every one of the following factors: Recycling, Green Power Use, Traffic Reduction, Sewage Properly Managed, Climate Policy and Green Building Policy. So, if Serre Chevalier offers recycling, green power use and has a climate policy but *does not* practice traffic reduction, sewage management or a green building policy then they would have a rating of three stars out of six.

During the writing of this guide, certain resorts stood out for their environmental policies and are making a concerted effort to become eco-friendly. These resorts are listed in the box below, but it is also useful to note that many resorts are improving their environmental practices all the time, so we apologise in advance if we have missed anyone out.

CHAIRLIFT S/S L: NEW ZEALAND P: JAMES MCPHAIL

SNOW CANNON L: ARE, SWEDEN P: TIM WARWOOD

Environmental

Resorts with good environmental practices

Lech, Austria ▶▶*p46*

St Anton, Austria ▶▶*p48*

Banff/Sunshine, Canada ▶▶*p70*

La Tania, France ▶▶*p140*

Madonna di Campiglio, Italy ▶▶*p186*

Davos, Switzerland ▶▶*p310*

Saas Fee, Switzerland ▶▶*p326*

Aspen, USA ▶▶*p348*

R: DIMITRI FESENKO L: NORDPARK, INNSBRUCK P: CHRIS MORAN/HOTSHITPICTURES.COM

Dimitri Fesenko getting a 540 degree view from Nordpark over Innsbruck.

Austria

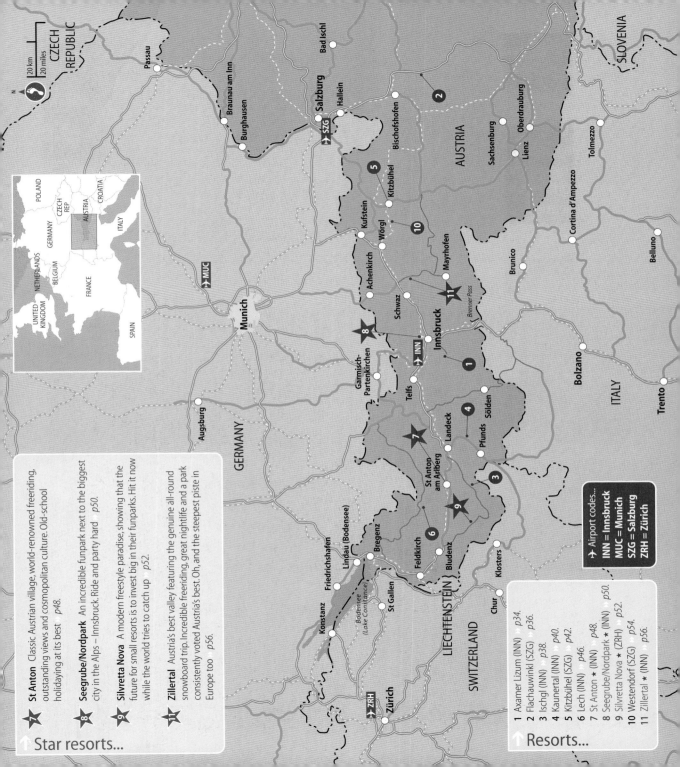

Star resorts...

★7 **St Anton** Classic Austrian village, world-renowned freeriding, outstanding views and cosmopolitan culture. Old-school holidaying at its best ▸ *p48.*

★8 **Seegrube/Nordpark** An incredible funpark next to the biggest city in the Alps – Innsbruck. Ride and party hard ▸ *p50.*

★9 **Silvretta Nova** A modern freestyle paradise, showing that the future for small resorts is to invest big in their funparks. Hit it now while the world tries to catch up ▸ *p52.*

★11 **Zillertal** Austria's best valley featuring the genuine all-round snowboard trip. Incredible freeriding, great nightlife and a park consistently voted Austria's best. Oh, and the steepest piste in Europe too ▸ *p56.*

Resorts...

1 Axamer Lizum (INN) ▸ *p34.*
2 Flachauwinkl (SZG) ▸ *p36.*
3 Ischgl (INN) ▸ *p38.*
4 Kaunertal (INN) ▸ *p40.*
5 Kitzbühel (SZG) ▸ *p42.*
6 Lech (INN) ▸ *p46.*
7 St Anton ★ (INN) ▸ *p48.*
8 Seegrube/Nordpark ★ (INN) ▸ *p50.*
9 Silvretta Nova ★ (ZRH) ▸ *p52.*
10 Westendorf (SZG) ▸ *p54.*
11 Zillertal ★ (INN) ▸ *p56.*

Airport codes...
INN = Innsbruck
MUC = Munich
SZG = Salzburg
ZRH = Zürich

Introduction

In the world of winter sports, Austria has always been regarded as one of the old-world stalwarts. Its chalets are picture perfect, its mountains are beautiful, lederhosen and cows with bells around their necks are plentiful, and its après can be as cheesy – and as fun – as it gets. In some respects, however, it will always rate lower than other Alpine nations. The perception is that Switzerland and France have much bigger mountains, that Austria has fewer ride-in, ride-out resorts and that snow cover can be a problem in the lower resorts. While much of this is true, what is becoming clear is that the country is in the middle of a revolution, with many resorts realizing that to attract a younger clientele, they don't have to have the biggest or the best slopes. As Snow Park in New Zealand and Big Bear in California have already proven, all you really need is a mountain chock-full of interesting features to ride.

For some resorts – mostly ones with a firm, established client base – the transition will take a while. But even here there are exceptions. For example, Kitzbühel, perhaps the ultimate 'oom-pa-pa' resort, has designated one mountain to those interested in funparks and speed courses. It is utterly fantastic. Other resorts, such as Silvretta Nova, Nordpark and Flachauwinkl, might be virtually unheard of around the world, but with their futuristic efforts in building incredible funparks and keeping pristine pipes, they are rapidly moving onto snowboarders' must-visit lists.

Austria has other attractions too. In comparison to Switzerland, it is incredibly cheap, its nightlife is unpretentious, and it is increasing in popularity for foreign seasonaires. Should France ever get round to building funparks half as good, then Austrian resorts would have a problem on their hands, but in the near future this looks very unlikely, and for any rider looking for a serious alternative destination, Austria should be at the top of the European wish-list.

Austria rating

Value for money
★★★★★

Nightlife
★★★★☆

Freestyle
★★★★★

Freeride
★★★☆☆

Essentials

Getting there

Austria's resorts are best served by either Salzburg's WA Mozart International Airport (salzburg-airport.com) or Innsbruck Airport (flughafen-innsbruck.at) in the heart of the mountains. Carriers to Salzburg include **Aer Lingus** (aerlingus.com), **Austrian Airlines** (aua.com), **BMI Baby** (bmibaby.com), **Fly Be** (Flybe.com, KLM (klm.com), **Lufthansa** (lufthansa.com), **Monarch** (flymonarch.com), **Ryan Air** (ryanair.com), **Thomson** (thomsonfly.com) and **Sky Europe** (skyeurope.com), while Innsbruck has **British Airways** (ba.com), **Sky Europe** (skyeurope.com), **Austrian Airlines** (aua.com) and **Welcome Air** (welcomeair.com). Visitors to the Alps also often arrive via Germany's Munich International (munich-airport.de/EN), which has a multitude of international carriers.

Austria's train network (raileurope.com) is very well maintained, while bus services throughout Europe to Austria can be booked through Eurolines (eurolines.com). Austria's road system is also very good with good high-speed links to Switzerland, Germany, Italy and Slovenia. A vignette, or road tax sticker, must be bought if you intend to use the country's motorway network.

Red tape

Austria has been a member of the EU since 1995. Member states require no visas but foreign nationals from the rest of the world need to apply for permission to enter.

Getting around

Driving is standard European (right-hand side). A valid driving licence from your home country is fine. Generally speaking, people drive with care and consideration and tend to obey all signs. Beware that the high speeds you may have enjoyed through Germany cannot be

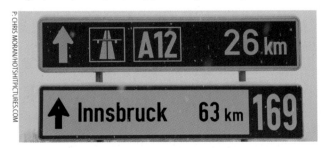

Austria price guide							
In €	1,00	2,50	2,80	0,85	3-4,00	2,00	0,70

Top tips

- Take cash. Credit card machines and ATMs do exist, but rural Austria is still very much a cash society.

- Get up early for breakfast. Guesthouses often stop serving at 0900.

- Nearly 80% of the country is Roman Catholic, so forget about getting any supplies on a Sunday.

- Obey road signs, speed limits, parking signs and no entry signs as the traffic cops are some of the most efficient in the world.

- Avoid seafood if you can – as a landlocked country any *fruits du mer* is unlikely to be fresh.

applied once the border is crossed, and traffic offences are enforced with immediate fines.

Mountain passes   If you're planning on taking a high pass between resorts, it's essential to check whether it is open when planning the route.

Car hire   Most major hire car companies (easycar.com, hertz.com, avis.com, etc) have offices in airports and cities. Usual age restrictions apply.

Public transport

Austria's superb public transport network has been designed from the ground upwards, and is based on the idea that intercity transport is by train, with connections by local bus companies at major stations to complete the local network. There are several discount schemes in operation on the trains, including the VorteilsCard (for around €20), which gives under 26s a discount of 45% for every journey. Most resorts have great train links to their nearest major airport.

What's so good about the Austrian Alps? We also get snow from different directions, which means it's always good somewhere. So we've got all kinds of terrain, many lift options to get on the mountain, nice backcountry, good parks, short distances between one place and another, nice people and epic snow. Yeah, this is Austria and there is a lot to explore. That's why it's so good and the reason why we live here.

Steve Gruber, Aesthetiker and pro snowboarder

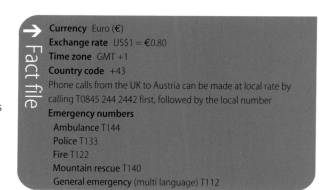

Fact file

Currency Euro (€)
Exchange rate US$1 = €0.80
Time zone GMT +1
Country code +43
Phone calls from the UK to Austria can be made at local rate by calling T0845 244 2442 first, followed by the local number
Emergency numbers
Ambulance T144
Police T133
Fire T122
Mountain rescue T140
General emergency (multi language) T112

Opening hours and traditions

Shops are generally open 0900-1200, before reopening again from 1500 to 1900. For cheap supplies (often with an attached café), the supermarket chain M-Priess is unbeatable.

Eating

Like France, Austria is full of restaurants covering a very narrow area of the culinary spectrum. Happily, they do it well, and traditional Austrian cuisine is the stuff of banqueting legend. Roasted pigs, chicken parts, breaded hams and potatoes abound, and of course there are more schnitzels, strudels and sausage dishes than any sane person could attempt on a week's holiday.

For the modern traveller of course this culinary cul-de-sac can pose a problem and while traditional dishes – possibly served by buxom wenches in lace shirts – are undeniably part of Austria's charm, such a conservative approach to food is also limiting. For those with special dietary needs it might be enough to put you off going at all. As one recent commentator noted, "In Austria, even the vegetarians eat meat."

That aside, a huge part of Austria's appeal for the mainstream eater is its forthright approach to grub. Mountain restaurants are usually filled to bursting point at lunch times, serving stodgy staples such as burger and chips, pizzas and spag bol. What Austria has long since realized is that holidaymakers just need some cheap energy during the day to keep going. For many snowboarders, this truism makes a refreshing change, and means that it is often cheaper to eat on the mountain than to go for an evening meal.

There are, of course, exceptions to this sweeping statement. St Anton has several world-class restaurants, upmarket après ski joints and more than one trendy café, while Austria's M-Preiss supermarket chain – found near most resorts – is well stocked for health food fanatics. But, for the moment, it would be safe to say that while a

R: MARK RUPERELIA L: KITZBÜHEL P: CHRIS MORAN/HOTSHITPICTURES.COM

P: KITZBÜHEL

Key phrases

Key words/phrases		Cheese *der Käse*
Yes *ja*		Help! *hilfe!*
No *nein*		North *nord*
Please *bitte*		South *süd*
Thank you *danke*		East *ost*
Sorry *Entschuldigung*		West *west*
Hello *servos*		
Goodbye *auf*		Days of the week
Wiederschauen/Ciao		Monday *Montag*
I don't understand *ich*		Tuesday *Dienstag*
verstehe Sie/dich nicht		Wednesday *Mittwoch*
I'd like … *ich möchte …*		Thursday *Donnerstag*
How much is it? *was kostet es?*		Friday *Freitag*
Where is…? *wo ist…?*		Saturday *Samstag*
Men *Herren*		Sunday *Sonntag*
Ladies *Damen*		
Left *links*		Numbers
Right *rechts*		1 *eins*
Straight on *gerade aus*		2 *zwei*
Night *die Nacht*		3 *drei*
Room *das Zimmer*		4 *vier*
Shower *die Dusche*		5 *fünf*
Toilet *die Toilette*		6 *sechs*
The bill *die Rechnung*		7 *sieben*
White coffee *Kaffee mit Rahm*		8 *acht*
Beer *das Bier*		9 *neun*
Mineral water *das*		10 *zehn*
Mineralwasser		11 *elf*
Orange juice *der Orangensaft*		20 *zwanzig*
Sandwich *das Sandwich*		100 *hundert*
Ham *der Schinken*		1000 *tausend*

cultural revolution is well underway on the slopes, Austria's kitchens are lagging way behind.

Language

The official language is German, although Austrians speak a version with several everyday words changed. English is widely spoken, especially in the resorts.

Crime/safety

Crime is generally at levels lower than in European cities. Boards and belongings can be left on balconies and outside restaurants, but theft does occur, especially in the bigger, busier resorts. Despite issuing on-the-spot fines (for traffic or street offences), which must be paid immediately, the Austrian police are generally fair. Motorway drivers should be aware that a vignette, or road tax sticker, is essential, as it is difficult to drive too far without meeting an impromptu checkpoint.

Health

As part of the EU, Austria is governed by European health standards. Health insurance is recommended, and EU citizens should carry a European Health Insurance Card (EHIC), which replaces the old E111 form.

Lift chat

Hello, Austria!

Every resort wants to stand out from the crowd. Some resorts, such as Mount Baker with their vintage Banked Slalom event, take a timeless, rootsy approach. Others, such as Mammoth Mountain, have opted for a mascot. In this case, it's 'Woolly the Mammoth' who rides around the resort getting pelted with snowballs by the local snowboarders. Others go even further out on a limb – Nagano hosted the inaugural snowboarding Olympic events, even though at the time they didn't actually allow snowboarders to ride their mountain.

And then there's Ischgl in Austria. This glitzy resort, little known outside central Europe, has hit upon an extremely novel way of standing apart from the herd. They simply hold two hugely extravagant concerts at the beginning and end of each season, and invite the biggest rock stars they can afford to headline.

This is how I found myself singing along to 'All Night Long' with Lionel Ritchie and 12,000 rabid Austrians at the beginning of the 2005-2006 season. It was clear that Lionel didn't have the slightest clue where he was, but it didn't stop him from belting it out along with other Commodores and Ritchie classics. Other presumably bemused rock stars to have shouted 'Hello Switzerland!' to an Austrian crowd include Pink, Elton John, Sting and even Bob Dylan! During my stay, the head of tourist board confidently confided that they expected to secure Robbie Williams for the headline slot within the next few years. Whether it's having the desired effect, and pushing Ischgl as a brand around the world, is a moot point. It sure as hell gives the locals two of the nights of their lives each year.

Check out www.ischgl.com to find out who'll be playing this coming season.

Snowboarding Austria

"Innsbruck's an awesome place to live. It's located really close to most of the good terrain in the region and it's enough of a city not to go crazy if the weather's bad". David Benedek, pro snowboarder

Austria has a strange clientele. There are the foreign visitors: mostly older skiers looking for that rosy-cheeked charm that skiing seemed to possess around the 1950s. Then there is the local contingent, fiercely loyal to the national way of life and totally uninterested in any other Alpine exploration. And then of course there's the third, most interesting breed: the snowboard contingent.

Make no mistake, Austria has a strong, solid and secure snowboarding undercurrent. **Burton Snowboards** heads up a long list of industry HQs based around the granite city of Innsbruck. Local riders Gigi Ruff, Friedl Kolar, Chris Kroll, Sani Alibabic and Steve Gruber have been cover stars the world over. The world's biggest snowboard competition – the Air and Style – wooed crowds for years, with the loudest cheers reserved for Stefan Gimpl's historic home wins. Over the coming years it looks set to build on this heritage, showing clear signs that investment in parks and pipes is high on the agenda for most resorts. In short, it is quietly turning into the most snowboard friendly country in Europe. How this translates into other areas is hard to tell, but though some of the old national stereotypes will be harder to shake off, in some ways, they only add to the intrigue and interest each visit generates.

Conditions

Austria's weather systems come in from all angles. Generally speaking,

Pros ...
- Freestyle centre of Europe? It might well be. Look out for innovative features such as Mayrhofen's bowl.
- Comparatively cheap by European standards.
- Massive competition scene, from open jam formats upwards.
- Densely packed resorts and good ticket sharing systems mean you can easily turn a short visit into a road trip.
- Vibrant, young scene means Austria has great nightlife.

... and cons
- Good vegetarian food is hard to come by.
- Mountain access is normally via cable car from town, often resulting in big down and upload queues.
- Higher than average 'jobsworth' count can lead to difficulties.

weather from the north, and especially from the northwest, brings cold and snowy conditions. Weather from the east can bring snow, while anything straight from the south can bring snow as well. This unique set-up basically means there is always snow to be found.

When to go

Austria has classic Alpine weather. Early snowfalls are common (as in November/December 2005) but it would be foolish to book a trip for the end of November and expect there to be snow. Most resorts gear up to a full opening the week before Christmas. Exceptions are Kaunertal, which opens in October, and Ischgl, which opens at the end of November. The season draws to a close from mid-April onwards, with only Kaunertal staying open through May. Hintertux – part of the

Breakneck Mountain

After working for most of December and January I was stoked to get some time on my board. The board felt good, my body felt good and after having such a good season I couldn't wait to be shredding at full whack again.

The day I hurt myself, I headed up a little late and started riding. I landed a few backside 540s, then decided to try a 720. The second one I tried, my board seemed to get stuck in a rut on the take-off, so instead of the momentum spinning me smoothly, it launched me sideways towards the biggest and iciest death cookies you've ever seen on the side of the landing. I managed to land on them with my back and neck and rag doll down the landing. Once I stopped, everything felt good – except my left arm. So the piste patrol came long and took me down by skidoo to the lift. I went down to the doctor who looked at me and sent me straight down to the specialist in Innsbruck.

Dr Schmid put the fear of God into me straight away by muttering "Du hasst kaput dein neck". Happily, further explanation revealed I had broken the joint between vertebrae fünf and sechs in my neck and twisted my spine for good measure. He went on to say "I will cut you open from here to here", gesturing to my windpipe and explaining that they'd have to cut my neck open, move the windpipe around for two hours, remove the bad joint and replace it with bone from my hip, before sealing it up with metal and pins. Worrying stuff, but my fears were slightly put to rest by the doc telling me he did this kind of thing every day of the week!

Five days after I came out of hospital I started doing physio at Sportmed, a specialist place in Zillertal for ski and snowboard injuries. They're super helpful and now I'm in the gym three times a week getting ready to ride again in the autumn. What have I learned? Ride wearing a back protector! And make sure you have the best insurance possible! If I didn't have a protector I doubt I'd be walking now, such was the impact on my back. The impact happened just where my protector finishes and I am sure it took a lot of the impact for me. I'll never ride without one again!

Jon Weaver, pro snowboarder

R: JON WEAVER L: MAYRHOFEN P: IAN SANSOM

Zillertal chain – has a short closing period then re-opens for summer riding. The best weather is traditionally through early February until the end of March, although clearly this is subject to fluctuation.

Off-piste policy

Austria has a very relaxed policy to off-piste riding. However, follow the resort rules and read the warnings closely. Austria has a high fatality record for avalanches.

Secret spots

With a fierce local scene, secret powder stashes are jealously guarded and some of the more organized local riders insist on having filming rights to their local out-of-bound areas. However, no Austrian crews are ever that aggressive, and any situations can be usually be diffused with some respectful discussion. The Zillertal Valley is particularly well known and guarded, but even here the local snowboard contingent are very open to outside riders. They are, however, unlikely to guide you around. That said, Austria's mountains have been the source of backcountry books for decades now, and a library of secret spots awaits any rider intrepid enough to delve into the local book market.

Freestyle

Austria is rapidly turning into the freestyle capital of Europe. In particular, Nordpark – just above Innsbruck – is one of the best maintained areas around. But with a large local base next door, it can get busy. Flachauwinkl and Silvretta Nova are the current hidden

" **"**

Austria has a big mix of everything. You can find the easy slopes, the crazy hard slopes, sick parks and even really good pipes these days. And the other thing is that in only six hours you can get across the country, so it's easy to find it all. Especially when you think that Austria is affected by three weather systems. We get the east, the south and the west, so we constantly get snow. If there's some system in Europe coming, you know you'll find powder in Austria somewhere.

Friedl Kolar, Aesthetiker and local pro snowboarder.

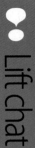
Innsbruck heights

Innsbruck is one of Austria's jewels, mixing a strong local identity with a growing reputation for cosmopolitanism. The same can be said for the town's snowboarding scene, which has an equally thriving mixture of history and vibrancy. There's just a generally baggy-trousered air about the place, from the stickers on the roadsigns to the amount of snowboard branding adorning the clothing of the locals. The Zillertal Valley is just down the road and the city itself is surrounded by quality resorts such as Axamer Lizum and Nord Park. In short, it is the quintessential European snowboarding town.

This trend seems to have begun back in 1985, when Jake Burton bumped into local snowboarder Hermann Kapferer at the SIA tradeshow in Las Vegas in 1985. The two clicked instantly, and a couple of weeks later Jake asked Hermann to help him and his wife Donna to establish Burton Snowboards in Europe. Recognizing Innsbruck as an ideal base, they set up camp and within two years were supplying 30 European countries with Burton Snowboards.

These days, the influence of 'Innsbrooklyn' has grown exponentially in the European snowboarding world. Much of this renown is down to the fact that, for so many years, the city played host to the Air and Style, still Europe's most influential and prestigious snowboarding contest. The International Snowboarding Federation used to have offices in the city, and these days industry powerhouses Method Mag and Westbeach are based there along with Burton, who are still the biggest industry presence in the town. Today, this insidious snowboarding influence permeates the very fabric of the city, from the party scene centred around Jimmy's Bar to the local and worldwide fame of riders such as Sani Alibabic and the local Aesthetiker crew. As Burton's PR Manager Birgit Gruber, a long time Innsbruck local puts it, "Innsbruck is just very centrally located in the hearts of the Alps, and a lot of pro snowboarders pass through town at least once a season either because they are filming in the area or they are on their way to an event. I think its location might be the main reason why companies actually open up offices here. You are close to tons of resorts and from IBK you can easily make it to Germany or Switzerland, Italy and even French resorts without spending too many hours in the car. It's perfect."

gems. Virtually every resort will have a well-stocked local snowboarding shop. Pop in for local happenings and events.

The scene

Austrian riders have always been at the top of the snowboard tree, and the Aesthetikers (see Lift chat on next page) continue to represent Austria at the highest level. Today, serious riders like Germany's David Benedek have made Innsbruck their home, due to close airport links, incredible local mountains, and a very healthy local snowboard scene. Austria probably has more snowboard competitions – from mini jams to huge super-pro TTR events – than all of the other European countries put together.

The industry

Austria, and Innsbruck in particular, is the undisputed centre of the European snowboard industry (see box on this page for more). By far the best website to cover Austria and the eastern Alps is the fantastic snow-parks.com. They also run a printed version of the site in magazine form – called the *Freestyle Yearbook* – which will have a detailed map of each resort covered, including a rundown of each funpark and a study of the best lines. It's usually found at resort kiosks, although every snowboard shop in Austria should have free copies. Currently the site and corresponding mag are in German only (with some of the bigger resorts getting a mini English translation), but an English version is in the pipeline.

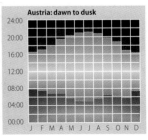

Austria: dawn to dusk

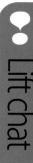
The Aesthetikers and the Zillertal

No matter how death-defying the rails and gaps, how mathematically impossible the spins and tricks, we all know that snowboarding is at its purest when you're ragging it down the mountains with your mates, trying to slash each other with powder snow. Bottle this feeling and distill it and you'd have discovered the Holy Grail of snowboarding credibility. It's just more fun that way.

It's also why, for a sport actually carried out by individuals, snowboarding has such a strong culture of 'scenes'. Everyone is at it: lowly dry slope crews in Britain (the ATV crew), European filming crews (the Pirates) and top-echelon US pros (the 'Gre-nerds'). In Europe, one of the best known crews are the Aesthetikers.

The Aesthetikers are closely associated with the Zillertal in Austria, despite the fact that most of them aren't from there. As Friedl Kolar says, "we're not even local boys. It's just that we've seen the whole world and every time we make the 'where is the perfect spot?' call, we always say here."

These days, Friedl, Steve Gruber, Beckna, Wolle Nyvelt, Chris Kroll and Mone Monsberger are the main Aesthetikers. So how did it start? Friedl explains: "We formed the crew 10 years ago, when snowboarding was small. We wanted to find travel companions to ride with, to work things out. Through riding together, pushing ourselves, we got where we are now and became pro snowboarders. And the idea has stayed the same. Back then, we didn't know snowboarding and even today we're still figuring it out. But for us it's about riding endless powder, riding long runs through the trees, and endless smiles throughout the whole year. Back in the day we came to the Zillertal because you could ride 365 days a year because of the glacier. That was a big thing for us and it meant we had the endless winter. From the age of about 18 to 24, that was all it was about – riding powder in the valley in June while other people were at the beach. Even today, I still ride here 100 days out of 160 a year."

Today the Aesthetikers are some of the best riders on the planet, travelling the globe, filming and shooting. But somehow they've done it by maintaining the feeling they had when they first strapped in as a gang of kids while managing to communicate it to the wider snowboarding world through their many videos, contests and shots in the snowboarding media. The Holy Grail? Maybe these boys have already discovered it.

Austria: a brief history of snowboarding

1914 → Toni Lenhardt from Bruck an der Mur in the east of Austria organizes a race down the local hill. The participants must use only single boards – skis are banned. The idea, unfortunately, doesn't catch on. **1980** → German rider Petra Mussig is one of the first of the modern generation of snowboarders to try out the eastern end of the Alps. **1982** → Tommy Delago from Oberammergau in Germany is building and refining snowboards. By 1983 there are small pockets of riders springing up in St Anton and Lech, using home-made boards after seeing snowboarding in skate mags. **1984** → Burton Snowboards tries getting its boards made in Austria by one of the ski factories. **1985** → Jake Burton Carpenter meets Hermann Kapferer in Las Vegas, USA. Hermann becomes the European distributor of the brand, basing the operation in Innsbruck. **1987** → German hardboot rider Peter Bauer becomes the poster boy for snowboarding in the Germanic world, turning a whole new generation onto the joys of tight carves, flouro suncream and zebra striped suits. Carving boards and plate bindings are the norm. **1989** → Newcomers Martin Freinademetz and Dieter Happ strengthen the hard boot scene. **1990** → Europe's snowboard scene splits into three camps: freestyle, freeride and hardboot. Austria has a good mix of all three but dominates world comps (along with Germany) in the racing divisions. **1991** → *Scream of Consciousness*, a snowboard film featuring freestyle, freeride and hardboot riding, is released and is one of the last films to feature the three disciplines together. **1993** → The first World Championships finals organized by the International Snowboard Federation is held in Ischgl. Terje Haakonsen and Nicole Angelrath are crowned the winners, kick-starting a new European freestyle revolution. **1993** → The first Air and Style contest held in Axamer Lizum attracts 500 spectators. Swiss rider Reto Lamm takes first place ahead of Bryan Iguchi and Shaun Palmer. **1995** → Max Plotzender emerges as the freestyle star of Austria. **1998** → Brigitte Köck wins a bronze medal in the Giant Slalom at the Olympic Games. Austrian summer resorts such as Kaprun, Kaunertal and Hintertux become perfect summer homes for scores of pro riders. Camps like SPC based in Mayrhofen spring up with mega star coaches. **1999** → Five people are killed in the Olympic Stadium, Innsbruck, after the sixth Air and Style, due to icy conditions and overcrowding. 39 people are hospitalized. The event is moved to Seefeld for the following year with riders donating their prize money to the victims and survivors. **2000** → Austrian resorts report 35% of their tickets are sold to snowboarders. **2002** → The Aesthetiker crew, based in Zillertal, start to appear worldwide in snowboard films. **2003-2004** → Austria's freestyle revolution is complete, small resorts starting to invest heavily in park building equipment. **Today** → The Freestyle scene is gathering momentum, with several resorts operating night-time parks and marketing themselves as snowboard friendly areas.

Axamer Lizum boasts modern, well maintained facilities and guaranteed snow thanks to its array of snow cannons and a wide variety of terrain: all just a 30-minute bus ride away from Innsbruck.

🔷 *If you like this …*
… try Westendorf ➤*p54,*
Cardrona ➤*p228, or*
Les Diablerets ➤*p322.*

The Town

Axamer Lizum is merely a handful of hotels and a car park but staying there can guarantee first lifts every day. Alternatively you can stay in one of the quaint villages below the resort, such as Gotzner, Birgitz or Axams, or stay in Innsbruck and catch the free 40-minute ski bus up to the slopes. For more info on Innsbruck see Nordpark/Seegrube.

Sleeping If you'd rather stay in one of the valley villages, Gotzner is a good choice as you can ski out when the snow conditions are good. For a reasonable hotel try **Aparthotel** Gotzens (T523 448010). For accommodation in Axamer try the 4-star **Hotel Lizumhof** (T523 468244).

Eating In Axamer your only eating choices are the hotel restaurants and **Café Liz** at the base of the Olympia Furnicular. In Gotzner the **Gruberwirt Inn** (T523 433020) or the **Klammhutte'n Café** (T523 433155) specialize in traditional hearty fare.

Bars and clubs Again in Axamer nightlife pretty much comes down to a handful of hotel bars. In Gotzner, however, the **Movie Pub** is open until 0400 on the weekends (T523 432223), as is the **Gotzner Disco** (T523 433182).

Shopping No shops at Axamer but the **M Price** (T523 448006) supermarket in Gotzner will cater for all your needs, though not on a Sunday.

Health The **Vital Physiotherapy and Massage Centre** (T523 434127) in Gotzner.

Internet Try **Hotel Lizumerhof** (T523 468244) at the base of Axamer Lizum.

Transfer options Fly directly to Innsbruck and then catch the 'F' bus to the main train and bus station, just a 17-minute ride. From there, catch the free shuttle bus to Axamer Lizum (it also stops at Gotzens, Birgitz and Axams). Alternatively, book a private shuttle on T512 341541.

Local partners Like Nordpark/ Seegrube, Axamer Lizum is included in the 'Olympia Skiworld Innsbruck' ticket which covers a variety of resorts around Innsbruck. The Innsbruck Tourist office (T523 432236) also offers combination ski and hotel packages for various nearby resorts.

R: JAMES STENTIFORD   P: DAN MILNER.COM

P: CHRIS MORAN/HOTSHITPICTURES.COM

⊛ OPENING TIMES
Late Nov to late Apr: 0900-1600

ⓢ RESORT PRICES
Week pass (6 days): €150
Day pass: €27,50
Season pass: €278 (year-long pass also valid for summer season)

ⓘ DIRECTORY
Tourist office: T523 432236
Medical centre: T523 433800
Pisteurs: T523 468240
Taxi: T523 46611
Local radio: None
Website: axamer-lizum.at

The Mountain

Of all of Innsbruck's mountain resorts Axamer Lizum offers the most varied terrain: beginner to advanced slopes, backcountry hikes, tree runs and a small snowpark. The mountain area is easily manageable if you are new to the resort, but big enough to offer endless lines and powder stashes if you're a more adventurous rider looking to get away from the crowds.

Beginners Right from the car park you can catch the Kaserwald tow lift to take you up a short approachable blue run ideal for learning. Once confidence is soaring, head up the Olympiabahn funicular to the peak of the Hoadl. From here you can slowly make your way down Blue Route 1 and back to the car park.

Intermediate From the top of the Olympiabahn funicular you will be free to explore most of the mountain's predominately intermediate red runs. Try your luck on the men's Olympic downhill, Red Route 3, and then make your way across the mountain to the

Easily accessible backcountry, natural kickers, a fun park, excellent and well maintained trails and great snow conditions make it a brilliant place for everyone.

Samantha Hart, snowboard photographer

Pleisen Lift, for less crowded slopes and the friendly **Pleisenhutte** restaurant.

Advanced Head straight up the Birgitzkopfl chair to access some of the steepest terrain on the mountain and check out the ungroomed red ski routes back down to the car park. Once you've exhausted this side of the hill head back up Birgitzkopfl and make your way down to Gotzens for some food and drink. Catch the bus back up to Axamer Lizum and session the super fun snowpark for the rest of the afternoon.

Kids Children under six ski for free.

Flat light days All the lower parts of the mountain have tree areas to provide some visibility on bad weather days.

LOCALS DO
- Ride the 'Birgitzkopfl' mountain.
- Session the mini fun park at the end of the day until the lift closes and it's time to go home!
- Ride out to Gotzens on a powder day.

LOCALS DON'T
- Get lost riding down to Gotzens; clarify the route with someone before you leave!
- Ride the women's downhill (Blue Route 1), on a busy Saturday morning.
- Eat at the very shiny, but very expensive, Hoadlaus restaurant.

PROS
- Great snowmaking facilities mean reliable conditions.
- The mountain offers a wide variety of snowboarding.
- A good choice for groups including non snowboarders as Innsbruck is nearby.

CONS
- Busy with Innsbruck locals on weekends and holidays.
- Axamer Lizum itself has little more than a car park and a few hotels.
- Powder runs get tracked out early in the day.

NOT TO MISS
Locals drop in at the top of the Hoadl and straight line down the piste into the speed track to break world records.

REMEMBER TO AVOID
Attempting to ride down to Gotzens when there is not enough snow.

SNOW DEPTH
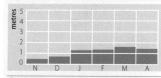

RELIVE A FAMOUS MOMENT
Axamer was the location for 2002's *Extreme Ops* starring Rufus Sewell. So bad it's good.

1580 m	TOWN ALTITUDE
25 km	KM TO AIRPORT
INN	AIRPORT
★☆☆	VEGETARIAN RATING
★★☆	INTERNET CAFES
★★☆	RIDE IN/RIDE OUT
2340 m	HIGHEST LIFT
760 m	VERTICAL DROP
100	RIDEABLE AREA (IN ACRES)
41 km	KM OF PISTES
1	NURSERY AREAS
6/5/2	RUNS: BEG/INTER/ADV
1/0	FUNICULAR/CABLE CARS
0/6	GONDOLAS/CHAIRS
4	DRAGS
no	NIGHT RIDING
1	PARKS
0	PIPE
no	SUMMER AREAS
figures not available	ENVIRONMENTAL RATING
$\$\$\$$	COST INDICATOR
AUSTRIA AXAMER LIZUM	

P: DANMILNER.COM

Flachauwinkl

A low-key snowboarder's paradise hidden in Austria's massive Ski Amade area. A perfect park and amazing chair-accessible freeriding make Flachauwinkl one of Austria's best-kept secrets.

☼ *If you like this…*
… *try Morzine* ▸▸p148.

The Town

Kleinarl, a quaint little Austrian village, is the ride-out base at the bottom of the Flachauwinkl ski area. While it isn't a hot spot for nightlife, it's attractive and family friendly, and you can walk from most hotels straight to the Champion Shuttle in the morning. For those looking for a livelier base for their holiday, Flachau, a free 10-minute bus ride away, has a greater selection of shops, restaurants and bars.

Sleeping In Flachau, **Jugendgastehaus Ennshof** (ennshof.at) provides quality budget youth hostel accommodation, while the **Panorama** (panorama-flachau.at) has self-catering apartments to rent. Both the **Wellness Hotel Gastehaus Keil** (T6418 6218) and **Fritzenwallner**

Appartments (fritzenwallner.at) are right next to the lifts in Kleinarl. For a four-star hotel, check out Flachau's **Tauernhof Hotel** (T6457 2311) which comes complete with its own private ice rink.

Eating It's worth travelling to Flachau for a greater choice of places to eat. The **Schnitzleck** (schnitzleck.at) sells a variety of the national classic, schnitzel. For those looking for a slightly more upmarket feed, the **Schusterhausl** comes highly recommended.

Bars and clubs In Flachau, local snowboarders rate **Ema's Pub**, an Irish bar which makes a point of avoiding the cheesy Austrian après-ski scene. For later night action try the super-trendy **Fire & Ice Lounge**.

Shopping **Penny Market** is best for bargain shopping in Flachau, or try **Sparmarket** which, unusually for Austria, is open on Sundays.

Health Fix up your body and soul at

A great hidden snow hole in Austria, one of the best places for finding new freeride lines on a powder day.

Henry Jackson, snowboarder

the **Biobalance Institute** (T6457 3232) in Flachau.

Internet Café Double Dutch (double-dutch.at) in Flachau.

Transfer options Just 70 km from Salzburg, Flachau and Kleinarl, the resort can be reached via a train to Radstad and then a bus (T6418 0206). Alternatively, book a transfer with **Scherer Taxi** (T6413 7200).

Local partners As a central location in the Ski Amade area, a day pass will give you access to eight ski areas while passes for multiple days cover all 12 ski centres. Check out www.skiamade.com.

R: TADEJ VALENTIN P: NAISI/ABSOLUT PARK

The Mountain

On Flachauwinkl itself, there is a wealth of things to do for snowboarders of every standard. The epic snowpark, wide well-groomed runs, accessible powder hits and a children's funpark make the mountain comparable to a top Canadian resort such as Whistler, only on a much smaller scale. One added bonus is that if you do happen to get bored in Flachauwinkl (unlikely) you can check out the other 860 km of slopes included on your Ski Amade lift pass.

Beginners At the base of both Kleinarl and Flachauwinkl there are small rope tows servicing short mellow runs that are perfect for beginners. You can then work up from the blue run under the Sunshine Shuttle, to the longer blue run from the top of the Family Shuttle all the way to the Fachauwinkl base station. The runs are wide, rolling and perfect for beginners.

Intermediate Warm yourself up by charging the long cruising runs from top to bottom on either side of the mountain into Flachauwinkl and Kleinarl. Once you've worn these out you can start your freestyling career in the small beginner jib park or check out the ungroomed powder run from the Mooskopf summit down to Kleinarl.

Advanced On a powder day head straight to the aptly named Powder Shuttle – it takes you to the summit of the Mooskopf. From here you can pick endless lines down the

face under the chair, choosing between different sized cliff drops and chutes. Finish off the day with a session in the epic snowpark opposite.

Kids For families with three or more children, under-16s ski for free as long as at least one parent buys a pass of the same validity (skiamande.com).

Flat light days On down days checkout **Amade Water World** in Wagrain pools, saunas and slide.

R: RENE BRODER P: NAISI/ABSOLUT PARK

◑ OPENING TIMES

Early Dec to mid-Apr: 0845-1630

ⓢ RESORT PRICES

Week pass (6 days): €196,50
Day pass: €36
Season pass: €415

ⓘ DIRECTORY

Tourist office: Flachau T6457 2214
Medical centre: T6457 2444
Pisteurs: T6452 2072
Taxi: T6457 3000
Local radio: None
Website: kleinarl.com

☺ LOCALS DO

☺ Enter the free competitions in the snowpark throughout the year.
☺ Party at Ema's Pub.
☺ Freeride the safe powder zones under the chairlifts.

☹ LOCALS DON'T

☹ Shop at Spar in Flachau. The Penny Market is far cheaper.
☹ Ride the obvious open powder faces – they are very prone to slides.
☹ Just ride Flachauwinkl. Make the effort to explore the Ski Amade area on a powder day.

✔ PROS

✔ Europe's longest park – worth a visit alone.
✔ Very laid back, low key and friendly resort.
✔ All new shuttle chair lifts are quick and efficient.

✖ CONS

✖ Queues, especially in the park, can get pretty bad in early January.
✖ No black runs – most pistes are fairly mellow.
✖ Not the best venue if you are looking for a crazy party scene.

◉ NOT TO MISS

The Jib King competition in January is free to enter and is held floodlit under the stars.

ⓘ REMEMBER TO AVOID

The powder face to the right of the park – it looks great but tends to avalanche several times a year.

❄ SNOW DEPTH

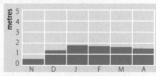

metres | 5 4 3 2 1 0
N D J F M A

♥ RELIVE A FAMOUS MOMENT

Where Eagles Dare was filmed around the Flachauwinkl area.

1000 m	TOWN ALTITUDE
70 km	KM TO AIRPORT
SZG	AIRPORT
★★☆	VEGETARIAN RATING
★★☆	INTERNET CAFES
★★☆	RIDE IN/RIDE OUT
1980 m	HIGHEST LIFT
980 m	VERTICAL DROP
area not measured	RIDEABLE AREA (IN ACRES)
16 km	KM OF PISTES
2	NURSERY AREAS
7/4/1	RUNS: BEG/INTER/ADV
0/0	FUNICULAR/CABLE CARS
0/5	GONDOLAS/CHAIRS
5	DRAGS
no	NIGHT RIDING
1	PARKS
1	PIPE
no	SUMMER AREAS
figures not available	ENVIRONMENTAL RATING
Ⓢ Ⓢ Ⓢ	COST INDICATOR

AUSTRIA
FLACHAUWINKL

Ischgl

The Town ⊖⊘⊖

Ischgl is one of those resorts that has stayed beneath the regular 'snowboard traveller' radar. They've had a thriving local clientele for generations and haven't embraced snowboarding in the same way as some of their nearby counterparts, meaning that those looking for hip, cutting edge freestyle facilities might be disappointed. Freeriders and all-round cruisers, on the other hand, will relish riding around this old fashioned, super efficient resort. It's a marvellously friendly place where the lifts run smoothly, the mountains are great and the après riding scene is a throwback to the old days. Whether of course this a good thing or not, remains a moot point ...

Sleeping The cheapest accommodation here is booked through an operator – try inghams.co.uk for a wide range of options. The **Engadin** (engadin.ischgl.com) is a reasonable boarding house at €50 a night. The four-star **Hotel Solaria** (solaria.at) is quintessentially Austrian and has a spa in the basement.

Eating Try the **Ischgler Einkehr** pub in the village for cheap eats. The on-hill **Panorama** is also reasonable. Slightly pricier options are the **Salz und Pfeffer** and the Steakhouse at the **Hotel Grillalm**.

Bars and clubs Try the Guinness at the **Golden Eagle**, before following everybody else in the immediate area to the **Trofana Arena**, the hugely over-sized nightclub in the **Trofana Royal Hotel** basement.

Shopping Three options: the **Spar**, **Nah and Frisch** and **Billa**.

Health The **Silvretta Center** (silvretta.at) is on hand to knead, pummel and generally grapple with your aches.

Internet Most hotels are wireless enabled. The **Silvretta Center** also has internet terminals and laptop points.

Transfer options If you fly **Swiss Air**, there's a special deal with **Ischgl Taxi** for €44 each way per person. Or take the train to Landecj and catch the **Post Bus** up to Ischgl for €6.

Local partners As part of the Silvretta Arena, Ischgl is connected to Samnaun in Switzerland. Pass also valid in Galtur, Kappl and See areas.

> 66 99
> Due to a lot of alcohol consumption, guests here don't really get the first gondola up each morning. This means that ambitious riders can find perfectly prepared slopes and untracked powder. Even weeks after the last snowfall you can find one or two untracked runs.
> *Karl-Heinz Auer, Ischgl seasonaire*

Old-fashioned, glitzy resort, where designer outlets, fur coats and a serious mountain co-exist quite happily.

☼ *If you like this…*
… try Val d'Isère ▸▸p158, Cortina ▸▸p176, or Verbier ▸▸p330.

⊗ **OPENING TIMES**
Early Dec to early May: 0900-1600

⑤ **RESORT PRICES**
Week pass (6 days): €207,50
Day pass: €36
Season pass: €582,50

ⓘ **DIRECTORY**
Tourist office: T5444 5266
Medical centre: T5444 5200
Pisteurs: T5444 5266
Taxi: T5444 5999
Local radio: None
Website: ischgl.com

The Mountain

Ischgl is a very forward-thinking, efficiently run resort. As well as having great snowmaking and lift facilities, the runs have been well thought out so there's a lot for riders of all standards to do. Linked with Switzerland's Samnaun area to form the Silvretta Arena, the area is absolutely huge. On the Ischgl side, the Idalp is the focal point, and most runs converge on this point. Austria's best-kept secret? Not for the locals, but for the rest of us Ischgl is an extremely impressive surprise.

Beginners There's a nursery area right at the point where the two valley gondolas disgorge everybody at the resort base proper. If you're linking turns, spend the morning on the C4 and C2 lifts lapping the blues that take you back down to the base. After lunch here, take the D1 chair to the summit of Palinkopf and take the meandering blue back to the base.
Intermediate Intermediates will love this place. Start the day by taking the E2 chair and lapping the summit of Hollenspitze down to base area. Have a run through the park before lunch, and then later take the B3 chair that links the Swiss side. Over in the Alp Truda area, there are plenty of mellow cruising runs to get stuck into before heading back over to Ischgl in the late afternoon.
Advanced If there is any fresh snow, take the E2 chair to the summit of the Hollenspitze side and head down the cat track. Off to the left there are a lot of easy chutes and powder fields, although obviously look out for any avalanche danger. In the afternoon, head to the park and pipe for a session.
Kids Those born after September 1999 go free, but check the site for up-to-date details as the various deals are slightly confusing.
Flat light days Due to its height Ischgl is not ideal for flat light riding as much of the resort is above the treeline. Instead, spend the day checking out the surprising number of historical artefacts. The 17th-century Catholic Church is beautiful.

LOCALS DO

- Whoop it up during après and in the Trofana Arena every night.
- Take advantage of the runs on the Swiss side.
- Hike when the snow is getting thin.

LOCALS DON'T

- Bother taking their passport over to the Swiss side – although you're supposed to.
- Appear to have noticed that fur is no longer in fashion.
- Snowboard that much. Still very much a skier's resort.

PROS

- Very up to date resort – 60% high speed lifts make for a slick hill with few queues.
- Crazy nightlife.
- Bustling, busy atmosphere.

CONS

- Expensive.
- Terrible for freestylers – and the après scene will be a definite turn-off for some.
- Might be too busy for some tastes.

REMEMBER TO AVOID

By the end of the day, the run back down to Ischgl gets busy and icy. If you're not too confident, download on the lift.

NOT TO MISS

A night in the Trofana Arena. You could only be in central Europe …

SNOW DEPTH

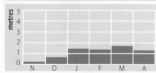

RELIVE A FAMOUS MOMENT

Sting, Tina Turner, Bob Dylan and Lionel Ritchie have bizarrely all opened Ischgl's winter season. See page 28.

R: UNKNOWN P: ISCHGL TOURISM

1377 m	TOWN ALTITUDE
99 km	KM TO AIRPORT
INN	AIRPORT
★☆☆	VEGETARIAN RATING
★★★	INTERNET CAFES
★★☆	RIDE IN/RIDE OUT
2872 m	HIGHEST LIFT
1472 m	VERTICAL DROP
704	RIDEABLE AREA (IN ACRES)
230 km	KM OF PISTES
1	NURSERY AREAS
12/36/13	RUNS: BEG/INTER/ADV
0/2	FUNICULAR/CABLE CARS
3/23	GONDOLAS/CHAIRS
12	DRAGS
no	NIGHT RIDING
1	PARKS
1	PIPE
no	SUMMER AREAS
★★★ ★★★	ENVIRONMENTAL RATING
$ $ $	COST INDICATOR

AUSTRIA
ISCHGL

The Town

Kaunertal is the name of this region, with no town claiming the name as its own. The farming community of Feichten, however, is where most riders stay – little more than a few chalets tied together by a community centre and swimming pool. It is, however, a very forward thinking resort, with a highly efficient tourist office and a very youthful attitude towards snowboarding, enticing people deep into this Austrian valley. It's also a very popular summer spot.

Sleeping In the summer, **Camping Kaunertal** will let you pitch up for €5 per night, while private rooms can be had even in winter for less than €20 per night – try **Haus Sonnenheim**

(sonnenheim.info). There's also the **Tirolerhof** (tirolerhof-feichten.at) for €40 or four-star luxury can be found at the **Larchenhof** (kaunertal.at) for around €80. All accommodation can be found and booked through kaunertal.com.

Eating Most people eat in their hotels or guesthouses or try a different hotel out, but there is also the **Pizzeria Rustica** for a change of scenery or the fantastic **Hotel Post** for some top scran. **Biohof Falkeis** (T5472 2311) is worth finding if you're after good veggie food to cook yourself.

Bars and clubs Again, Feichten is somewhat limited but there is the **Kiwi Pub**, or head to nearby Pfunds to try out the **Highlander**. Afterwards, if you don't like the look of the **Post-Alm** in Pfunds, then it's bedtime. There's nowhere else to go.

Shopping Get groceries at the **Nah and Frisch Parmenn** Grocery store in Fleichten, or follow the locals down

> ❝ ❞
> The place feels like it shouldn't exist. Why doesn't anyone know about it? I love it.
>
> *Mark Ruperelia, pro snowboarder*

the **M-Preis** in Prutz. Health shoppers should head to **Hofladen Organic Foods** in Kauns.

Health The **Kneipp Spa** in Pfunds should cure all your aches and pains with its thermal baths.

Internet The tourist office has wireless, as do some hotels, but there is no dedicated internet café.

Local partners Buy the 'Ski 6' pass and you're entitled to ride at nearby Fendels, Serfaus-Fiss-Ladis, Nauders, and Venet – all classic Austrian terrain – plus the mighty Ischgl area. A total of 340 km of pistes upped to 550 including Ischgl.

Early opening freeriding paradise with one of Austria's best parks and a reputation for often being empty. Basically, a hidden gem, and a very cheap one at that.

☀ *If you like this ...*
... try Hintertux (Zillertal area) in summer ▸p56.

**AUSTRIA
KAUNERTAL**

The Mountain

Kaunertal makes our list of best resorts for three reasons. One is that it lies at the far end of a very inaccessible valley, meaning the slopes are generally empty, the freeriding is left well alone, and the queues are kept to an absolute minimum. The second is that its opening hours are ridiculously long, normally kicking off in early October and staying open until the end of July. Lastly, it boasts one of Austria's best-maintained funparks, which generally stays untouched throughout the day and can see riders hitting corduroy pipe walls in the afternoon. Add in the 'Ski 6' resorts and the terrain is equal to anywhere in the Alps.

Beginners Beginners with 'Ski 6' liftpasses should head to the Serfaus-Ladis-Fiss area, where wide open blue runs, serviced by gondolas, are the order of the day. Start at Ladis, head up to the Fisser Joch, keep heading skier's right until you make it to Fiss, then up the Komperdell, then again skier's right towards Serfaus. From the top of the Scheid, reverse the process until you're back at Ladis, stopping halfway down the Fisser Joch

for a perfect late afternoon lunch.
Intermediate Head straight to the Kaunertal glacial area. After spending the morning in the fantastic funpark (at the top of the Ochsenalmbahn 2), take a trip all the way over to the top of the Karlesspitz drag which will probably be completely empty. Any powder stashes up here will be easy to spot. Head all the way back to the start lift working out which corners of the piste you can cut out.
Advanced Be well aware that everything above the Norderjoch is glacial and, therefore, riddled with crevasses. Kaunertal on a clear day is perfect for cutting off the piste for some exploring. Everything to the skier's right of the Ochsenalmbahn 1 and 2 is north-ish facing, meaning it'll stay fresh for a long time. The restaurant under the park is perfect for cheap food.
Kids Kids under 10 ride or ski for free when one parent buys a full price ski pass. Fendels has Babi-Land, where kids can learn how snow is made as well as learn the ropes in the award-winning ski school. Entry is free with a liftpass.
Flat light days Kaunertal itself lacks trees in all but the lowest slopes, limited to the Ochsenalmbahn 1, but Serfaus or Fendels has plenty of tree-lined slopes for low light visibility.

P: CHRIS MORAN/HOTSHITPICTURES.COM

☺ LOCALS DO
☺ Head to Kaunertal for pre-season training.
☺ Get passes from the road toll at the start of the valley.
☺ Head to Kaunertal for the park, Fendels for a leisurely cruise, and Serfaus for the full day ride.

☹ LOCALS DON'T
☹ Worry about the snow cover. The glacier guarantees good riding.
☹ Forget to get up early – it's a long drive from village to slope.
☹ Ride much in flat light – there are few trees.

✔ PROS
✔ Close to year-round season.
✔ Empty pistes, incredible and easily accessed freeriding.
✔ Great park.

✖ CONS
✖ Lots of T-Bars means beginners might hate it.
✖ Access road prone to deviations.
✖ Long transfer even from nearest airport.

♥ NOT TO MISS
The impressive Kaunertal funpark. It's perfect for intermediate riders.

ⓘ REMEMBER TO AVOID
Going off-piste on the glacier.

❄ SNOW DEPTH
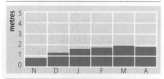

♻ RELIVE A FAMOUS MOMENT
Legend has it that Terje threw down the first ever switch McTwist-revert in Kaunertal, way back in 1992.

1280 m	TOWN ALTITUDE
85 km	KM TO AIRPORT
INN	AIRPORT
★★★	VEGETARIAN RATING
★★★	INTERNET CAFES
★☆☆	RIDE IN/RIDE OUT
3160 m	HIGHEST LIFT
1010 m	VERTICAL DROP
area not measured	RIDEABLE AREA (IN ACRES)
36 km	KM OF PISTES
1	NURSERY AREAS
15/9/2	RUNS: BEG/INTER/ADV
0/0	FUNICULAR/CABLE CARS
0/2	GONDOLAS/CHAIRS
6	DRAGS
yes	NIGHT RIDING
1	PARKS
1	PIPE
yes	SUMMER AREAS
★☆☆ ★☆☆	ENVIRONMENTAL RATING
$$$	COST INDICATOR
AUSTRIA	
KAUNERTAL	

Kitzbühel

Glitzy Austrian über-resort doing the worst job in history of dispelling Austrian stereotypes. Has fantastic architecture, lots of cash-rich patrons and a surprisingly forward-thinking attitude to snowboarding.

❯ If you like this …
…try Chamonix ⇒p128, Cortina ⇒p176, or Verbier ⇒p330.

AUSTRIA
KITZBÜHEL

The Town

The medieval town of Kitzbühel is perhaps the definitive Austrian ski resort, featuring one of the all-time great ski races (the Hahnenkamm race held in January), thigh-slapping nightlife, an older client base, and locals who look like they're on the set of National Lampoon's Austrian Vacation. Fantastic for those looking for over-the-top campness in their choice of resort or those looking for one of the only 'saucy' bars in the Alps (Club Paradise).

Sleeping Most visitors are far from poor, so cheap digs are tough to find, but **Pension Rainhof** (T535 662312) caters from €30 per night. **Hotel Tiefenbrunner** (hotel -tiefenbrunner.at) will house you from €90 upwards and the four-star **Hotel Weisses Rössl**, (weisses -roessl.com) has a pool-bar. Go on.
Eating Hotel Schwarzer Adler (T535 669 1158) has a Michelin star, **Hotel zur Tenne** (T535 664444) does Austrian tradition with a twist, or go all out with the sushi at **Ecco** (T535 671300).
Bars and clubs The Londoner, Flannigans and Brass Monkeys are undoubtedly where you'll end up hanging out.
Shopping There's an **M-Preis** at the start of town, which is easily the best supermarket in town.
Health Fitness For Fun (fitnessforfun.at) has the works.
Internet Café Kortschak, Kitz Video Internet Café and **Internetcafe** are all hooked in, plus many of the big hotels offer wireless.
Transfer options transferbus.net runs transfers for €65 return per person. **oebb.at** has train transfer times and prices.
Local partners Kirchberg and Jochberg make up the main area, plus two-week passes offer discounted services in St Moritz, Gstaad and Arosa. The Kitzbuheler Alpen Season Pass has all manner of twinned resorts including Zillertal and Alpbach to name just two.

"While I was in Kitzbühel I saw possibly the most beautiful sunset I've ever seen – made even sweeter by the amazing run down to the town through the farm fields.

James Thorne, pro snowboarder

P: CHRIS MORAN/HOTSHITPICTURES.COM

P: CHRIS MORAN/HOTSHITPICTURES.COM

☺ **OPENING TIMES**
Early Dec to late Apr: 0830-1700

$ **RESORT PRICES**
Week pass (6 days): €192
Day pass: €36,50
Season pass: €455

◷ **DIRECTORY**
Tourist office: T5356 777
Medical centre: T5456 63009
Pisteurs: T5356 62265 or 140
Taxi: T5356 66133
Local radio: None
Website: kitzbuehel.com

The Mountain

Perhaps by accident, Kitzbühel has discovered that the key to good riding is to give snowboarders their own mountain. While the main area is riddled with black-slope, mogulled nightmare spots that only hardbooters can really enjoy, the separate Kitzbüheler Horn basks in the late sun with its own funpark, cool runs and mellower cat tracks. Add in the fact that it's generally emptier and has a fantastic speed course (with a timed, electronic read-out at the end), and the makings of a perfect mellow break are all there. Have fun on the empty slopes and then go home to a bustling and vibrant town.

Beginners For beginners, intermediate and advanced riders, the Kitzbüheler Horn is a must virtually every day, but for an all-mountain excursion, head to Kirchberg – take the Fleckalmbahn gondola there and the tree-lined blue run back to the village. The views are beautiful and you should have the slope to yourself until about 1430 when people start to head home. At that point, cross the town and have a run on the fantastic toboggan course.

Intermediate Riders wanting a fun challenge should try and complete the area lap. Head up the Hahnenkammbahn and keep following the elephant signs (they say Ski Safari). You'll cross the new 3S Gondola chasm to Wurzhohe, then keep heading to the top of the Zweitausender where you can take a picture of the mighty Grossglockner (Austria's highest peak) to the east. A round trip including a restaurant stop of your choosing should complete your day.

Advanced If you've done the 'Safari', had a go on the speed course (and beaten 75-kph switch!) then head to the back of the Kitzbüheler Horn to the Raintel chairlift. On the way up, note the route down to skier's right of the chair. It usually holds powder for weeks after a storm.

Kids If two older kids buy full ski passes, all juniors ride for free. Plus all beginner lifts are free.

Flat light days Virtually all the mountain is below the treeline so there are few bad visibility areas.

😊 LOCALS DO
- 😊 Build kickers in the gentle off-piste on the Kitzbüheler Horn.
- 😊 Try to ollie all the roads back down to town from the Kitzbüheler Horn.
- 😊 Tuck their baggy kecks in for the speed course! It adds at least 5 kph.

😠 LOCALS DON'T
- 😠 Pay €7 for the gimmicky fold-out 3D map.
- 😠 Pay much attention to the Pengelstein area if it's busy. The Kitzbüheler side is virtually always empty.

✅ PROS
- ✅ The ultimate 'traditional Austrian' resort.
- ✅ Little exploring done by the usual clientele.
- ✅ New lifts have opened up amazing new terrain.

❌ CONS
- ❌ Nightlife and partying aimed at an older market.
- ❌ Many pistes left to their mogully fate to serve the town's bread and butter – hip-wiggling skiers.

🏂 NOT TO MISS
The speed course on the Kitzbüheler Horn is incredible fun if you can straightline.

ℹ️ REMEMBER TO AVOID
Sedlboden, Hochsaukaser and the Barenbadkogel are pistes left to form moguls. And for those lacking confidence, the Streif Race area is a real no go area.

❄️ SNOW DEPTH

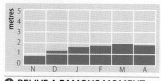

🏆 RELIVE A FAMOUS MOMENT
Visit the grave of mountaineer Peter Aufschnaiter – *Seven Years in Tibet* was based on his life – in Kitzbühel's churchyard.

L: SPEED COURSE, KITZBÜHEL P: CHRIS MORAN/HOTSHITPICTURES.COM

L: SPEED COURSE, KITZBÜHEL P: CHRIS MORAN/HOTSHITPICTURES.COM

761 m	TOWN ALTITUDE
80 km	KM TO AIRPORT
SZG	AIRPORT
★☆☆	VEGETARIAN RATING
★★★	INTERNET CAFES
★★☆	RIDE IN/RIDE OUT
2004 m	HIGHEST LIFT
1600 m	VERTICAL DROP
area not measured	RIDEABLE AREA (IN ACRES)
148 km	KM OF PISTES
2	NURSERY AREAS
22/24/13	RUNS: BEG/INTER/ADV
0/1	FUNICULAR/CABLE CARS
8/28	GONDOLAS/CHAIRS
17	DRAGS
yes	NIGHT RIDING
1	PARKS
1	PIPE
no	SUMMER AREAS
★★★	ENVIRONMENTAL RATING
💲💲💲	COST INDICATOR
AUSTRIA KITZBÜHEL	

Riders' tales
Park and ride

The mid 1970s are responsible for the current state of snowparks around the world. When Dogtown skateboarders Stacy Peralta, Tony Alva and Jay Adams appeared in magazines grinding and airing their way around a variety of empty Californian swimming pools they turned kids around the world onto the possibilities of skating concrete bowls, halfpipes and transitions. Kneepads and helmets were in, and flatland skateboarding was suddenly the boring end of the wedge. At the time, modern snowboarding was in its infancy. A few riders had Wintersticks – the only commercial snowboards available and primarily powder boards for recreating the surf sensation – but there was little of what we would recognize today as freestyle riding.

That changed in 1977 when other snowboard manufacturers broke the Winterstick monopoly. Tom Sims led the way on the west coast, while Jake Burton Carpenter headed up the revolution on the other side of the country. But they weren't alone. Around the US garages were churning out home-made boards as more people caught onto the underground vibe. The result was that pockets of riders with their own unique styles sprang up independently. Perhaps the most influential of these pioneering riders were the freestyle kids of Tahoe city, led by a young man named Terry Kidwell.

Most of the riders were sponsored by Sims – at the time, the biggest skateboard manufacturer in the world. It was only natural that the tricks they learned on their snowboards would be directly inspired by their skate tricks, and there's no question that this scene re-routed the direction of snowboarding. By 1983, the Tahoe crew had learned airs, handplants, spins and grinds. The idea of a snow halfpipe had taken root. What was clear was that snowboarding was all about getting air, grabs, spins and going big. In the US, at least, it was a freestyler's sport. Pipes were built, ramps were made and new tricks were invented by the bucketload each winter.

Throughout the 1980s snowboarding's progression and cultural impact gathered pace. The sport doubled in size each year, attracting more and more converts from skating. By 1990 there were enough riders in Vail, Colorado, to pressure the resort into building the world's first resort funpark. Its success meant other resorts quickly followed suit. By 1992 there were parks on the east coast, in Canada, all over California and around Colorado too. 1993's seminal video New Kids on the Twock saw Colorado riders taking on immense kickers, the likes of which had been beyond the realms of fantasy a mere two years before. While there had never been a shortage of stuntmen taking on natural terrain in previous snowboard videos (as Damien Sanders and Steve Graham proved to glorious effect in Critical Condition and Riders on the Storm), the realization that man-made jumps were the future became apparent. The problem then became one of maintenance. Huge jumps need huge amounts of manpower to keep their shape. To keep a pipe in a rideable state could take 20 shapers digging all day. What was really needed was a machine that could do the job. Several ideas sprung up – Cardrona in New Zealand was one of the first resorts to try and built a pipe cutting machine as far back as 1991, but its experiments were ultimately outshone by an agricultural constructor from Colorado named Doug Waugh, who designed the Pipe Dragon, a fantastically precise arc that cut into the walls with a chainsaw edge and removed the snow with conveyer belt shovels. Its success lay in the fact it could be attached to the Kasbohrer Piste Bashers, snow-moving vehicles, which most resorts already owned. By the mid-90s if a resort wanted a decent pipe it had only to invest in a Dragon.

Of course, resorts with an abundance of natural terrain shunned funparks. They were time consuming, took up room and were a huge initial investment, followed by a high maintenance bill. The Chamonixs of this world could do without them. But for smaller resorts, or those with a more forward thinking outlook, being able to build and maintain a good funpark had obvious advantages in attracting riders. In the late 1990s, several North American resorts, and notably Laax, Saas Fee and Avoriaz in Europe, took the 'if you build it they will come' dictum to heart. And it worked.

In 2002 the next logical step was taken. Snow Summit, just outside Los Angeles, bought its neighbour Bear Mountain and transformed the resort into the world's first 'all-mountain' funpark. Every piste featured a rail, kicker, pipe, quarter or new feature from the creative team behind the project. At around the same time, Snow Park in New Zealand followed suit to dazzling success and infamy around the world. Austrian resorts have also taken this idea and run with it – witness resorts such as Nordpark, Flachauwinkl, Silvretta Nova and Mayrhofen in the Zillertal Valley, attracting freestyle-hungry riders in their droves. It's the same story in Switzerland, where smaller resorts such as Adelboden have followed the lead of trendsetting Laax and Saas Fee and now also promote their parks heavily. Only the French remain stubbornly recalcitrant, save a few noticeable exceptions such as Avoriaz, La Clusaz and Les Deux Alpes.

Wherever it is happening, the successes of these parks has led us to the current situation, in which well designed funparks mean more snowboarders through the lift turnstiles and more revenue for the resort. As every resort manager worth their salt follows the same lead in either establishing or consolidating their own cutting edge facilities, it's an instant way of gauging a resort's snowboarding friendliness. More than this though, it means it's just a terrifically exciting time to be a snowboarder. Let the good times roll …

L: SNOW PARK, NEW ZEALAND P: TIM WARWOOD

Lech

The Town ⊜ ✦ ⊜

With its nude ski calendars, incredible buildings and surplus of private banks, Lech is posh. Built up from the solid base of an old farming community, this small town won European Village of the Year in 2004. This, coupled with its height and easy access to the slopes, have given Lech all the attractions it needs. Although it can't rival neighbour St Anton in nightlife and youth culture, its funpark is much, much better.

:) *If you like this...
... try Courchevel* ▶▶*p130,
or Méribel* ▶▶*p146.*

Sleeping lech-zuers.com has accommodation for most price ranges but there is little in town that qualifies as budget. The **Pension Irmgard** (T5583 2966) should cost under €50, while the **Gasthof Post** (postlech .com) is for Bridget Jones fans (see opposite page) and can cost over €200 a night.

Eating Sniggering aside, **Fux** (T5583 2992) has everything from sushi to crocodile steak in decor that defies pigeonholing. Expensive but recommended. Lighter wallets should head to **Resaurant Charly** (T5583 2339) for classy but straightforward Italian cuisine.

Bars and clubs The **Pfefferkorndl**, the **Sidestep Bar** and the **Tannbergerhof** are the three big bars, while the **Vernissage** is the after-party venue.

Shopping For groceries head to the **M-Preis** below St Anton.

Health The Hotel Montana (T5583 2460) has a pool, sauna and spa but shuts at 1600.

Internet The **Coffeeshop** in the **Ambrosiuspassage** has laptops you can use but no wireless as yet.

Transfer options Eurocity and Orient Express fares and information (seat61.com). Alternatively, **Arlberg Express** (arlbergexpress.com), **Loacker Tours** (T5523 5909) and **Four Seasons Travel** (airport-transfer.com) run transfers from Zurich, Friedrichshafen and Munich respectively.

Local partners Zürs, St Christoph, St Anton.

Beautiful old village with one of the best parks in Austria. Lech shares its runs with Zürs, St Christoph and the mighty St Anton, making a triangle of the coolest Austrian hideouts and is another of the 'Best of the Alps' resorts.

The Mountain

Lech is the Bentley of the resort world, offering unrivalled comfort, speed if you want it, and beautiful curves from every angle. Where else has heated seats on its chairlifts?

Beginners Once beginners have got to grips with the area under the Fluhen lift, it's time to head up the Schlegelkopf chairlift to ride the park and surrounding tree-lined runs. The funpark has a great beginner line though, featuring gentle jumps and ride-on boxes and rails – great for introducing riders to the basics of freestyle riding. Three laps of the park, followed by a hearty lunch at the restaurant at the bottom of the baby park is a great target to aim for over the course of a week's riding.

Intermediate The Zürs/Lech area has had 'Der Weisse Ring' – its own intermediate day route – since 1955. Pick up a free map and pocket book from the tourist office and join a long line of historical mountaineers and skiing pioneers (photos and bios are included in the booklet). The route starts and finishes in Zürs, taking in the viewing platforms at Aussichts-plattform and Naturplattform throughout the day. Watch out for the area between Rufikopf and Shuttboden where plenty of flat spots can prolong the day and lead to a lot of walking, but confident and strategic straight-lining should see you through. If you're feeling really good, break off the 'Weisse Ring' at Kreigerhorn and try some riding under the Hassensprung chair. All routes lead back to the piste and the incline is perfect for those looking to test their new-found powder skills.

Advanced Riding in Lech/Zürs falls into two categories – freestyle fun at the incredible funpark under the Schlegelkopf chair, and awesome freeriding in the area's ample secret spots and off-piste gullies. Since we assume most head straight to the park, a suggested day itinerary would be to go freeriding on the northwest facing slopes above St Christoph. Alternatively, head to the Steinmahder, the furthest lift north in the whole area. Do as many laps as your powder legs will allow you then take the pistes all the way back to Lech, passing through the park to throw down a couple of airs over the biggest kickers. Job done.

Kids Miniclub Lech (T5583 21610) takes kids from three years upwards on day excursions including a minimum 90-minute ski from €50 per day.

Flat light days The Zugerberg lift above Zug has ample tree coverage, as does the area around Oberlech.

P: LECH TOURISM

OPENING TIMES
Early Dec to late Apr: 0900-1600

RESORT PRICES
Week pass (6 days): €136-194
Day pass: €40,50
Season pass: €650

DIRECTORY
Tourist office: T5583 2161
Medical centre: T5583 2032
Pisteurs: T5586 2855 or T140
Taxi: T5583 2501
Local radio: None
Website: lech-zuers.at

LOCALS DO
Ride huge boards off-piste. Strolz (T5583 2361) is the one and only snowboard shop in the town centre with a selection of rental boards that go up to a gigantic 222 cm. Jesus H!
Party in St Anton.

LOCALS DON'T
Throw their stuff away – everything goes to the recycling depot where it's either re-used or burnt to make the town's electricity - including the lifts.
Use freestyle boards in the powder. Huge boards, fish or swallowtails are the order of the day.
Head to St Anton to ride that often.

PROS
Fantastic access to the slopes without being a purpose built resort.
Great funpark.
Massive area.

CONS
Expensive.
Older clientele generally.
Private banks where honest pubs should be.

NOT TO MISS
Have a race (or, if you're really daring, a switch race) down the speed check course under the Weibermahd lift. Your time is shown on the airport timetable-style display at the bottom.

REMEMBER TO AVOID
Zürs' slopes on a flat light day.

SNOW DEPTH

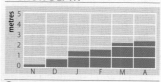

RELIVE A FAMOUS MOMENT
Bridget Jones – Edge of Reason's ski segment was filmed in town, with the Gasthof Post and Schlegelkopf chair featuring heavily.

1450 m TOWN ALTITUDE

110 km KM TO AIRPORT

INN AIRPORT

 ★☆☆ VEGETARIAN RATING

★★☆ INTERNET CAFES

★★☆ RIDE IN/RIDE OUT

2450 m HIGHEST LIFT

1000 m VERTICAL DROP

area not measured RIDEABLE AREA (IN ACRES)

276 km KM OF PISTES

3 NURSERY AREAS

32/79/6 RUNS: BEG/INTER/ADV

1/6 FUNICULAR/CABLE CARS

3/36 GONDOLAS/CHAIRS

29 DRAGS

yes NIGHT RIDING

2 PARKS

2 PIPE

no SUMMER AREAS

★★★ ★★☆ ENVIRONMENTAL RATING

 COST INDICATOR

AUSTRIA
LECH

FIGURES COVER THE ARLBERG AREA

St Anton

Austria's most popular seasonaire hang-out, with huge freeriding potential, a decent enough park, a forward-thinking town and lots of nightlife.

☀ If you like this ...
... try *Whistler* ▸▸*p86*, *Chamonix* ▸▸*p128*, *Niseko* ▸▸*p210*, or *Verbier* ▸▸*p330*.

The Town

St Anton's centre is a mix of high-class hotels, beautiful old buildings, high-end shops and good bars. Built in the first boom of Alpine tourism, the resort is one of the 'Best of the Alps' group, which is a synonym for 'old money'. However, since the early '90s, St Anton has been a Mecca for snowboarders willing to spend all winter riding the famed Arlberg powder. Building on this fame, the town is now perhaps the hippest resort in Austria, rivalling Chamonix and Verbier for its seasonaire community.

Sleeping Any of the guesthouses in the communities of Pettneu, Schnann and Flirsch down the valley. Check out stantonamarlberg.com for a comprehensive list from €25 per night. The **Skihotel Galzig** (skihotel.at) is slightly more upmarket, while the **Stantoner Hof** (st.antonerhof.at) has cheaper digs for those staying longer than a week.

Eating Anton Café does a mean line in upmarket grub, or try the **Underground on the Slopes** for candlelit sophistication.

Bars and clubs For possibly the trendiest après in the Alps, try **Anton Café**, at the bottom of the slopes. People with ID to prove their name has 'Anton' in it (Anthony, Antonia etc…) get a special gift and a chance to join the wall of fame.

> **" "**
> This place rocks. Easily the best in Austria.
> *Jason Horton, editor of* Method Mag

Shopping The **M-Preis** a mile down the valley is where all the locals shop, plus it has a fantastic 'Jetsons'-style café and is one of the coolest buildings in the valley.

Health The **Wellness Centre** has pool, sauna and massage facilities (arlberg-well.com).

Internet Mail Box is on the main street with wireless, cable and machines to use. Many of the hotels and bars also have wireless.

Transfer options Innsbruck and Zurich both have easily accessible train connections direct to St Anton, while Friedrichshafen (a **Ryanair** destination) and Munich are within transfer reach. Even Vienna runs a direct train. For **Eurocity** and **Orient Express** fares and info (it is on the fabled line) visit seat61.com. Alternatively, **Arlberg Express** (arlbergexpress.com), **Loacker Tours** (T5523 5909) and **Four Seasons Travel** (airport-transfer.com) run transfers from Zurich, Friedrichshafen and Munich respectively.

Local partners Lech, St Christoph, Zürs.

P: ST ANTON TOURISM

P: CHRIS MORAN

⊛ OPENING TIMES
Early Dec to early May: 0815-1630

ⓢ RESORT PRICES
Week pass (7 days): €204-219
Day pass: €40,50
Season pass: €650

ⓘ DIRECTORY
Tourist office: T544 622690
Medical centre: T5446 0664
Pisteurs: 140
Taxi: T5446 2315
Local radio: Arlberg TV
Website: stantonamarlberg.com

The Mountain

Austria's flagship resort is situated in the renowned Arlberg area of the country, considered to be one of Europe's best: guaranteed snow, great freestyle facilities and absolutely limitless freeriding possibilities. Part of this reputation is to do with the town itself, which has cultural and historical origins that ensure it transcends its 'ski resort' appellation. The village itself retains that rustic Tyrolean charm that the Austrians cherish, with all the dangling accoutrements of the modern ski resort blended in relatively successfully. But it's the mountain and the outstanding freeriding that has really earned the town its fame. You need a bit of luck to get the conditions right, but when it's good there really is no better freeriding resort anywhere. Beginners and intermediates will also find much to explore. Thanks to links with Lech, Zürs and St Christoph to form the Arlberg Pass, the area is enormous, with a plethora of perfect pistes and staggering views.

Beginners The slopes right next to St Anton town centre are perfect for learning on. When you feel ready, head to the top of the Galzig on the new cable car. From the top back to town is a drop of 1000 m on pistes 8, 9, 4 and 1 – perfect for a morning or afternoon challenge. Reward yourself with a coffee at the **Anton Café**.

Intermediate The Rendl area, separated from the Arlberg area by the town of St Anton, is the place to head for St Anton's funpark. Try and ride back to town cutting off the R1 to skier's right through the numerous paths in the trees.

Advanced The whole Arlberg tour is possible but you'll need to take a bus here and there. Try and reach the peaks of Kappall, Valluga, the Madlock Joch and the Juppenspitze in one day. If you can also make it up the Rendl side, you're doing better than most!

Kids **Children's World** (skischool -arlberg.com) will feed and look after the nippers for around €60 a day.

Flat light days There's an ice skating rink, a decent skiing museum, a toboggan course (with night lights) and plenty of bars!

R: UNKNOWN P: ST ANTON TOURISM

☺ LOCALS DO
- Head to Rendl on Sundays – it's less busy than the main area.
- Go out on Thursday night as it's 'Chef Night' and every other night is normally booked.
- Head to Lech for the best funpark.

☹ LOCALS DON'T
- Bring a car into town.
- Bother with shops – they buy and sell kit, trade jobs and get accommodation from the message board inside the Mailbox cafe.

✔ PROS
- Incredible terrain, easily accessible from the lifts.
- Easy off-piste route finding from available views.
- Huge seasonaire community gives the town a young, vibrant edge.

✘ CONS
- Parking impossible or overpriced in town.
- Powder can get tracked out quickly.
- Will be generally too hectic for some tastes.

☺ NOT TO MISS
The funpark above Lech. Enough said.

ⓘ REMEMBER TO AVOID
The 1 piste is crowded with fast returnees after 1600.

❄ SNOW DEPTH

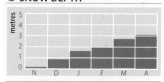

☺ RELIVE A FAMOUS MOMENT
The Jamiroquai video *Light Years* was filmed on the slopes above St Anton. Also, *Die Weisse Rausch* (from 1931) was one of the first ever ski films. Footage can be found at the Ski Museum in town.

1304 m	TOWN ALTITUDE
100 km	KM TO AIRPORT
INN	AIRPORT
★★☆	VEGETARIAN RATING
★★★	INTERNET CAFES
★★☆	RIDE IN/RIDE OUT
2450 m	HIGHEST LIFT
1000 m	VERTICAL DROP
area not measured	RIDEABLE AREA (IN ACRES)
276 km	KM OF PISTES
3	NURSERY AREAS
32/79/6	RUNS: BEG/INTER/ADV
1/6	FUNICULAR/CABLE CARS
3/36	GONDOLAS/CHAIRS
29	DRAGS
yes	NIGHT RIDING
2	PARKS
2	PIPE
no	SUMMER AREAS
★★★☆	ENVIRONMENTAL RATING
$$$	COST INDICATOR

FIGURES COVER THE ARLBERG AREA

AUSTRIA
ST ANTON

Seegrube/Nordpark

Cosmopolitan snowboarding at its best. Ride Nordpark's infamous Skyline snowpark all day and then head down to Innsbruck for sushi and drinks at one of the city's fine restaurants and bars .

If you like this ...
... try *Chamonix* ➠*p128, or Mammoth* ➠*p366.*

AUSTRIA
SEEGRUBE/NORDPARK

The Town

Seegrube/Nordpark is located a short drive away from the centre of Innsbruck on the north side of the city. Innsbruck is a lively compact city buried in the Tyrolean Alps. Having hosted the Olympics in both 1964 and 1976 Innsbruck offers visitors all the culture, shopping and nightlife of a modern European city, with the added bonus of excellent snowboarding facilities. Also home to Burton Europe and *Method Mag* snowboard magazine, Innsbruck is a hive of snowboarding culture, competitions and events.

Sleeping The Jugendherberge Innsbruck is well located for accessing Nordpark by public transport (jugendherberge -innsbruck.at). Slightly more upmarket is the **Best Western Hotel Goldener Adler** (T512 571111), located right in the middle of the pedestrian Old Town district. Alternatively, **The Gasthof Innbrucke** is a great central welcoming base for your stay (T512 28193).
Eating For a budget filling meal, **Magic Pizza** on Herzagfriedrich

Strasse in the Old Town. The **Stiftskeller** (T512 583490) offers well priced traditional Austrian fare while vegetarians can eat at **Restaurant Philipine** (T512 589157).
Bars and clubs Favourites for local snowboarders include **Jimmy's Bar** and the aptly named **Couch club**.
Shopping There are a number of supermarkets such as **Billa, M-Price** and **Spar** located around Innsbruck.
Health Visit the **Alpine Heath Spa**, just 5 km out of Innsbruck.

Internet Free internet station in the tourist office, and a **Telecome** office with Internet at the main Post Office opposite the train station.
Transfer options Fly directly to Innsbruck and then catch the 'F' bus to the main train and bus station: a 17-minute ride.
Local partners The Innsbruck Tourism Board have an 'Olympia Skiworld Innsbruck Pass' allowing access to eight resorts, 75 lifts and 270 km of slopes nearby to Innsbruck.

☻ ⚡ ⊖

⊕ OPENING TIMES

Dec to Apr: 0900-1600

⊖ RESORT PRICES:

Week pass (6 days): €126,50
Day pass: €26,40
Season pass: €238

⊕ DIRECTORY

Tourist office: T512 59850
Medical centre: T512 55040
Pisteurs: T512 36045
Taxi: T512 5311
Local radio: Freies Radio Innsbruck – 105.9 MHz
Website: nordpark.at

R: JAMES THORNE P: CHRIS MORAN/HOTSHITPICTURES.COM

50

The Mountain

Although not a massive area, the terrain is truly breathtaking. Perched above the city of Innsbruck at 2330 m, the resort offers predominately steep runs from the top of the Hafelekar peak to the base of the Hungerburg Bahn. With some serious freeriding, powder field and tree runs, as well as one of the best maintained snow parks in Austria, Seegrube/Nordpark is an advanced snowboarder's heaven.

Beginners With only one small nursery slope really kitted out for kids, and one blue run that snakes through the snow park, beginner snowboarders in Innsbruck will do much better to head to the nearby Axamer Lizum.

Intermediate Spend the day lapping the lower section of the mountain from Seegrube to the base of the Hungerburg Bahn. Several choices of routes down the mountain combine steep sections with long, tree-lined cat tracks perfect for racing

Small but perfectly formed – there's something magic about riding Seegrube on a powder day whilst the city hurries along below you.

Samantha Hart, snowboard photographer

your closest friends and rivals down. **Advanced** On a clear day head straight for the peak of the Hafelekar and make your way down either of the advanced extreme routes through steep gullies to the Seegrube base below. Then either jump on chairlift D and session the perfect pipe and snowpark for the afternoon or take the unpisted 'Tobel' route down the back of the park for more freeriding. This route is really only for the avalanche savvy.

Kids There is a small children's area at the top of the Hungerberg Bahn.

Flat light days The trees under the Hungerberg Bahn are the place to be on a cloudy day, as the top of the mountain can be a white-out during bad conditions.

☺ LOCALS DO
⬤ Race the home run through the trees, pretending to be in a video game!
⬤ Go to the night sessions and check out the view of Innsbruck's city lights.
⬤ Eat huge helpings at Magic Pizza.

☹ LOCALS DON'T
✖ Ride the back 'Tobel' bowl when avalanche danger is high.
✖ Take unconfident riders up to Seegrube.
✖ Take the car on the weekends. Buses from the city centre are free to those wearing ski gear.

✔ PROS
⬤ In the city riding for locals and visitors.
⬤ Seriously good snowpark.
⬤ Really good value for money. A halfday pass is under €20.

✖ CONS
✖ Not a resort for families and beginners.
✖ When the weather comes in the top half of the resort becomes fairly inaccessible.
✖ Expect to see queues for first powder lines from 0800 on weekend powder days.

ⓘ REMEMBER TO AVOID
Avoid the various Hafelekar to Seegrube routes during bad conditions. It gets icy and route finding can be dangerous.

❄ SNOW DEPTH

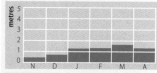

✪ RELIVE A FAMOUS MOMENT
Ice-T got the entire crowd at Innsbruck's Bergisel to shout 'Ice Motherfucking T Bitch!' during his concert at the 1999 Air and Style. Lovely!

575 m	TOWN ALTITUDE
4 km	KM TO AIRPORT
INN	AIRPORT
★★☆	VEGETARIAN RATING
★★★	INTERNET CAFES
★★☆	RIDE IN/RIDE OUT
2269 m	HIGHEST LIFT
1400 m	VERTICAL DROP
area not measured	RIDEABLE AREA (IN ACRES)
15 km	KM OF PISTES
0	NURSERY AREAS
1/4/6	RUNS: BEG/INTER/ADV
0/2	FUNICULAR/CABLE CARS
0/2	GONDOLAS/CHAIRS
0	DRAGS
yes	NIGHT RIDING
1	PARKS
1	PIPE
no	SUMMER AREAS
figures not available	ENVIRONMENTAL RATING
$ $ $	COST INDICATOR

AUSTRIA
SEEGRUBE/NORDPARK

Silvretta Nova

The Town

The village of Gaschurn is picturesque and low key, and a convenient place to stay while riding Silvretta Nova, though you can choose from the handful of villages in the Montafon Valley. The Versettlabahn telecabin runs out of the village centre so mountain access is a short walk or bus ride from your hotel and you can ride home at the end of the day. None of the Montafon villages are hives of late night party action, but there are plenty of restaurants, bars and hotels to choose from.

Sleeping For a cheap stay check into the hostel **Jugendferienhaus Hammer** (T5558 8353). If you're not on such a tight budget the **Nova Hotel** provides a great location – near the town centre but still ride in, ride out (T5558 8293) and good value for money.

Eating For a decent pizza try the **Ristorante La Taverna VIII** at the Nova Park (T555 820015), or if you are a fan of fish try the fresh trout at the **Illstobli Restaurant** (T5558 8107).

Bars and clubs After riding, head to the caffeine-fuelled **Red Bull Apres Ski Bar**. Later in the evening the most happening bar in town is the **Muhle Local Bar/Club** – popular with local snowboarders and holidaymakers.

Shopping The **Sparmarket** at the Nova Park.

Health Brave a trip to the vitality planet that is the **Cure and Health Centre** (T555 886170) complete with thermal and healing baths.

> 66 99
>
> The resort is cool because everyone gets his runs … no matter if it's freeriding, backcountry, kickers or park. It is pretty big and if you're into hiking, there's even more stuff to do.
>
> *Ludschi, photographer and Silvretta local (Ludschi.com/Pirates)*

Internet Free internet access at the Gaschurn tourist office.

Transfer options From Zurich airport catch a train to Gaschurn (bahn.at) or book a transfer with **5 to 12 Shuttles** (airport-montafon.com).

Local partners You can buy a pass for the entire Montafon region – and explore 62 lifts and 222 km of runs. (montafon.at).

The largest ski area of the Montafon Alpine region, Silvretta Nova boasts a variety of mountain terrain, a good snowpark and a handful of traditional, atmospheric Austrian villages to stay in.

⊙ *If you like this …*
… try Flachauwinkl ⇥p36, *Les Arcs* ⇥p142, *or Méribel* ⇥p146.

P: SILVRETTA NOVA TOURISM

⊛ **OPENING TIMES**
Mid-Dec to late Apr: 0815-1600

💲 **RESORT PRICES**
Week pass: €192,50
Day pass: €36
Season pass: €372

🕐 **DIRECTORY**
Tourist office: T5557 6300
Medical centre: T5558 8325
Pisteurs: T5557 6300
Taxi: T5558 8222
Local radio: None
Website: silvrettanova.com

P: SILVRETTA NOVA TOURISM

AUSTRIA
SILVRETTA NOVA

The Mountain

A key benefit of the area is that many slopes of different levels of difficulty start and end at the same place. This makes it a great location for groups of mixed abilities as it is easy to ride different routes and stick together. The mountains seem to be dominated by families, although snowboarders do have an increasing presence due to the impressive park. On a powder day Silvretta is a playground, and, due to the large number of visiting families, the lines don't get tracked out too quickly.

Beginners Start your day on the short Vallua tow located right next to the Versettla gondola. Learn your turns on this wide beginner run (with the help of several snow cannons) before heading up the Versettla gondola to try Blue Piste 1, which will take you all the way back to town at the end of the day.

Intermediate Session the blue runs under the Nova chair to warm up for the day ahead, before heading down towards Garfrescha, where you can ride the Vermielbahn and Grandau chairs finding new routes through the trees below on each run. During the afternoon head to the top of the Rinderhutte chair to enjoy the views from the highest point of the ski area, before wending your way home for a well-earned beer.

Advanced If you are lucky enough to be blessed with fresh snow rise early and catch the first Versettla gondola of the day. From the summit you can take several different routes back down to the mid station, which provides seriously fun and challenging powder riding. Once you've worn out this side of the mountain head to the top of the Rinderhutte chair and session the epic snowpark for the afternoon.

Kids Children are well provided for at the newly developed 'Noviland' next to the Versettla gondola base station.

Flat light days The Garfrescha chair and the subsequent chairs above it provide a quiet spot for fun sheltered tree riding in flat light.

☺ LOCALS DO
● Explore the Montafon valley and its smaller resorts on a powder day.
● Party at the Muhle bar in Gaschurn.
● Ride with an iPod to entertain you on the long chairlift that services the park.

☹ LOCALS DON'T
✗ Just ride park – the valley offers some amazing freeriding.
✗ Eat too much local cuisine at lunch.
✗ Drive around the valley on a Saturday – too busy.

✔ PROS
● There are powder stashes to be found days after a snow dump.
● Excellent park for all abilities.
● A down to earth good value resort.

✗ CONS
✗ Bad party scene.
✗ Need a car to best explore the area's potential.
✗ Slow chair means long lap times in the park.

⦿ NOT TO MISS
On a powder day you've got to check out the unbelievable 9 km run of pure joy from the top of the 'Golm' ski area to the base of the Golmerbahn gondola in Vandans.

ⓘ REMEMBER TO AVOID
If the snow is patchy it is best to take the gondola from the top station back to Gaschurn at the end of the day.

❄ SNOW DEPTH

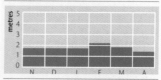

★ RELIVE A FAMOUS MOMENT
Absinthe Productions new film *More* was filmed on location at Silvretta Nova. For literary types – Ernest Hemingway wrote several books there.

1000 m	TOWN ALTITUDE
175 km	KM TO AIRPORT
ZRH	AIRPORT
★☆☆	VEGETARIAN RATING
★★☆	INTERNET CAFES
★☆☆	RIDE IN/RIDE OUT
2298 m	HIGHEST LIFT
1298 m	VERTICAL DROP
area not measured	RIDEABLE AREA (IN ACRES)
114 km	KM OF PISTES
1	NURSERY AREAS
15/10/7	RUNS: BEG/INTER/ADV
0/0	FUNICULAR/CABLE CARS
4/11	GONDOLAS/CHAIRS
11	DRAGS
yes	NIGHT RIDING
1	PARKS
1	PIPE
no	SUMMER AREAS
★★☆	
★☆☆	ENVIRONMENTAL RATING
$ $ $	COST INDICATOR

AUSTRIA
SILVRETTA NOVA

Westendorf

Part of Europe's third largest ski area, Westendorf is a traditional Austrian Alpine resort, best for families, intermediate piste cruising and park riding.

⊃ If you like this . . .
. . . try *Winter Park, Big White* ▸▸p72, *or Morzine* ▸▸p148.

The Town ⊟ 🏂 ⊟

Westendorf is everything you would expect from an Austrian Alpine Village: low-rise wooden chalets lining the main street and housing bars, with restaurants and a selection of food and gift shops catering for visitors. The central village is fairly compact with the 'Alpenrosenbahn' gondola a short walk away, although some hotels are spread out along the sprawling valley. Nursery runs come right into the town centre and are the location for après tobogganing, creating a real winter wonderland atmosphere.

Sleeping Reasonably priced self-catering apartments are available through www.skiwelt.at. More upmarket is the **Vital Land Hotel Scheermer** (T5334 6268), while the **Maierhof** (T5334 6412) sits just under the Alpenrosenbahn mid station.

Eating The cheap and cheerful **La Vita** (T5334 20019) stays open at lunch, while the snow-buried **Aunerhof** (T5334 6333) is the romantic option.

Bars and clubs Gerry's Inn is the après hot spot, although you'll surely regret not checking out **The Wunderbar**, the main disco in town.

Shopping There are two large supermarkets in the town centre, **Spa** and **Billa**, both closed on Sundays.

Health Massage, physiotherapy and a range of alternative treatments are available at the **Therapiezentrum Westendorf**.

Internet There are internet stations at **Friends** bar, the **Wunderbar** and at the tourist office.

Transfer options Get the train to Worgl and catch the OEBB train up to the resort – railway information (T5334 051717).

Local partners For an extra €20 you can add the Kitzbuhel ski area to a seven-day lift pass.

66 99

The most fun I've had riding piste in ages, and the park is amazing.

Roland Morley-Brown,
pro snowboarder, New Zealand

☺ **OPENING TIMES**
Dec to Apr: 0830-1600

💲 **RESORT PRICES**
Week pass (6 days): €168
Day pass: €34,50
Season pass: €455

🕐 **DIRECTORY**
Tourist office: T5334 6230
Medical centre: T5334 6390
Pisteurs: T5334 2000
Taxi: T533 430044
Local radio: None
Website: westendorf.net

The Mountain ☺☺☺

Buy a week pass – you'll have access to the whole SkiWelt area including nine different resorts, 90 lifts and 250 km of piste. The runs at Westendorf are immaculately maintained and over two-thirds of them are covered by snow cannons, meaning snow shortages are never a major problem. The massive, wide slopes rarely feel busy and are ideal for beginners, intermediate riders and families as they are safe, predictable and well groomed. There is a distinct lack of steep and black runs, so those looking for an advanced adrenaline trip will do better to head to the impressive 'Boarders Playground' snowpark, where jumps, hips and rails of varying sizes are open to the public.

Beginners Westendorf is an excellent place for beginners. Start the day off on the Schneebergbahn, a short four-man chairlift coming right out of the centre of town, before heading to mid station on the Alpenrosenbahn gondola and taking the long, cruising blue run down to the bottom at your own pace.

Intermediate Choose one of the 'SkiWelt Routes' to explore the whole area on your week pass. Marked on the piste with different coloured arrows, first have a try at the 11.5-km long Salven Route, and if you're still feeling strong take on the epic 22.65-km long Westendorf Route by the end of the week. Both tours are based on red and blue runs and provide a day-long circuit tour around the vast ski area.

Advanced Check out the most challenging runs in the SkiWelt area by catching the free shuttle bus from Westendorf to Brixen Im Thale. Take the Hochbrixen gondola and head for the peak of the Hohe Salve, choosing one of many steep, rolling runs down towards Hopfgarten or Itter. When your legs have had enough you can take one last black run all the way back down the Brixen and catch the shuttle bus back.

Kids Westendorf is a great family friendly resort, with children under seven going free and numerous other offers (skiwelt.at).

Flat light days Take the bus to the nearby Aquarena at Kitzbühel, for a day of swimming, water slides, saunas and spas.

☺ LOCALS DO
☺ Après at Gerry's Inn – wilder then a night on the town.
☺ Ride the North Side of the Choralpe Mountain on a blue bird powder day.
☺ Eat at the Alpenrosenhutte.

☺ LOCALS DON'T
☒ Head to the lift at 1000 when the queues are at their biggest.
☒ Take the gondola home – the ride out run to Westendorf is one of the best on the mountain.
☒ Get stuck in the Talkaser four man lift queues during busy weeks.

✔ PROS
☑ Amazing wide empty runs allow for some serious high-speed cruising.
☑ Good facilities for families and kids.
☑ Really good snowpark for all standards.

✖ CONS
☒ In the Westendorf riding area, steep pistes are limited for advanced riders.
☒ Few trees on the hill so whiteout days can be tricky.
☒ Good après but the late night partying really only kicks off on the weekends and special events.

☻ NOT TO MISS
Wednesday is 'Ladies Day' meaning day passes for women are priced at child rate!

ⓘ REMEMBER TO AVOID
Avoid getting stuck on the Fleiding Mountain at the end of the day. The only chair lift back gets busy.

❄ SNOW DEPTH
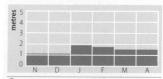

☺ RELIVE A FAMOUS MOMENT
Down the road towards Salzburg is where *The Sound of Music* was filmed.

R: GOGO GOSNER P: RENILLA

FIGURES COVER THE SKIWELT AREA	
790 m	TOWN ALTITUDE
100 km	KM TO AIRPORT
SZG	AIRPORT
★☆☆	VEGETARIAN RATING
★★★	INTERNET CAFES
★★☆	RIDE IN/RIDE OUT
1865 m	HIGHEST LIFT
1092 m	VERTICAL DROP
617	RIDEABLE AREA (IN ACRES)
250 km	KM OF PISTES
6	NURSERY AREAS
62/50/8	RUNS: BEG/INTER/ADV
0/0	FUNICULAR/CABLE CARS
12/38	GONDOLAS/CHAIRS
45	DRAGS
yes	NIGHT RIDING
2	PARKS
1	PIPE
no	SUMMER AREAS
★★★	ENVIRONMENTAL RATING
$$$	COST INDICATOR
AUSTRIA WESTENDORF	

Zillertal

The Town ⊖ ⊘ ⊖

Like Chamonix, the Zillertal Valley has several different areas linked by a bus/train system and an all-encompassing Zillertal Superskipass. Accommodation can be found at Fugen, Ramsau, Kaltenbach, Hintertux and Zell am Ziller – tiny villages with a lift station to their respective higher slopes – but the majority stay in Mayrhofen, a busy hub of large, ornate Tyrolean hotels, chalets and tasteful though uninspiring apartment blocks. It has a healthy snowboard scene and as such is one of the country's youngest and hippest resorts.

Sleeping Ludwigs (opposite Scotland Yard pub, ask in the bar for Ludwig, no phone or website and he only speaks German) for €8-10 per night. Once in your life you must stay at the **Hotel Strass** (hotelstrass.com) for around €70 per night – the most central hotel in town, or else try the **Elisabeth Hotel** (elisabethhotel.com).
Eating In Mayrhofen, **Mama Mia's** does pizza and pasta, **Mo's** has Tex Mex, or try **Café Tirol** for authentic Austrian schnitzel. For cheap but filling grub The **Sports Bar** at the

Hotel Strasse works.
Bars and clubs In Mayrhofen, **Scotland Yard** and **The Ice Bar** are institutions. Kaltenbach's **Après-Ski** is worth visiting purely for the incredible thumping Euro house. You'll also end up at the **Arena** and the **Speakeasy**.
Shopping Spar in Mayrhofen town centre has ubiquitous high prices, while real locals head to the **M Preis** next to Kaltenbach.
Health Melissa at Solarice Wellness Centre and Spa (solarice.com) is a keen snowboarder herself.
Internet The **Tirol Café** has computers to use, while the hotels

Strass, Kramerwirt, and Eberhater have wireless for around €4 an hour.
Transfer options A regular train service runs from Innsbruck, Salzburg and Munich to Mayrhofen (T528 562362, zillertalbahn.at). All three airport websites (munich-airport.de, innsbruck-airport.com and salzburg-airport.com) have info on coach and train transfers.
Local partners The Zillertal Superskipass links, in order, Fugen, Hochfugen, Kaltenbach, Zell am Ziller, Ramsau, Mayrhofen, Finkenberg, Landersbach and Hintertux. However, little of it is actually linked by runs.

R: TOBIUS THOMASSON P: CHRIS MORAN/HOTSHITPICTURES.COM

Austria's best valley: the freestyle Mecca of Mayrhofen lies at the end of a wide valley littered with freeriding gems.

If you like this …
… try *Chamonix* ▶p128, *Squaw* ▶p374, *or Vail* ▶p376.

⊙ **OPENING TIMES**
Early Dec to late Apr: 0830-1630

⑤ **RESORT PRICES**
Week pass (6 days): €268
Day pass: €33,50
Season pass: €484

⊙ **DIRECTORY**
Tourist office: T528 56760
Medical centre: T528 562550
Pisteurs: T140
Taxi: T0664 250 0250
Local radio: None
Website: mayrhofen.at

AUSTRIA
ZILLERTAL

Last year the last powder day in the valley was on 16 June, and sometimes you can get the first powder in September. So you can ride 10 months of powder a year. Sure, you need to check and find the good spots. But you can find it.

Friedl Kolar, Zillertal local and Aesthetiker

R: LOUIS PURUCKER P: CHRIS MORAN/HOTSHITPICTURES.COM

The Mountain

Most snowboarders head here for either the incredible Mayrhofen snow park – one of Austria's best – or the freeriding that the valley is famous for. The areas are actually separated so expect to do a little travelling. At the entrance to the valley lie Fugen and Kaltenbach, areas popular with day visitors from nearby Innsbruck and Munich. Most of those visitors, however, come for the pistes and the après (which does little to dispel any Austrian stereotypes) meaning that the incredible amount of off-piste is often left untouched for days after a storm. Highly recommended.

Beginners The Zillertal Superskipass handily comes with suggested runs for all experiences, but we think beginners should spend a day or two finding their feet on the blues of the Rastkogel area, then head to Zell am Ziller for the day. It's possible to ride all the way to Gerlos and back without hitting anything too difficult, plus there are plenty of good lunch spots on the way.

Intermediate Head to Kaltenbach, then schlep all the way to the far end of Hochfugen. On the way back, pay close attention to the route down the north face of the Marchkopf (you can see it on your right as you go up the return gondola). Here, powder stashes lie untouched for weeks. Just be prepared to hop over the stream at the end of the run and possibly walk a little way back down the cross-country ski track.

Advanced The newly installed Tux150 cable car now makes it possible to ride powder on the Penken face, right down to the funpark at the bottom. Surely the dream run for most snowboarders. And with a high-speed chairlift and endless lines to try out, plus the café at the bottom serving spag bol for €6, the dream lap is complete.

Kids Wuppy's Kinderland (mayrhofen.at) takes the youngest kids from three months old for around €30 per day or €16 for a half day.

Flat light days Erlebnisbad, Mayrhofen's swimming pool, has a chute and river rapids to tackle on inflatable tubes. It's almost worth taking a day off to try out.

😊 LOCALS DO
- Eat up the hill. The restaurants at the funpark are really cheap.
- Ride down under the Hohbergbahn if it's powder or spring slush. Any other conditions make it a nightmare.
- Stay late at the park for afternoon sessions. Make the most of the sun!

😞 LOCALS DON'T
- Get scared on the ludicrously high Penkenbahn lift.
- Follow tracks under the Tux 150. It's a dangerous area unless you know it, or are very happy at route finding.

👍 PROS
- Easily found, world class off-piste.
- Unpretentious and budget.
- Great park, voted Austria's best.

👎 CONS
- Cable car access and download can cause bottlenecks.
- Huge amounts of drunken après-ski action.
- High season queues.

❤ NOT TO MISS
Opposite the Mayrhofen park lies the 'Harikari', the fabled steepest run in Austria. It's nowhere near its boasted 78 degrees (how could it be?) but is worth a shot just for a laugh.

ℹ REMEMBER TO AVOID
From 0900 to 1000 the Penkenbahn can get clogged so take the bus to the Hohbergbahn and go up from there. If downloading is fully queued up, have a beer at the top of the Penken before reversing your route.

❄ SNOW DEPTH

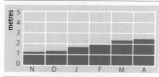

✪ RELIVE A FAMOUS MOMENT
In *Last Holiday*, LL Cool J and Queen Latifah drive their Hummer down Mayrhofen high street.

630 m	TOWN ALTITUDE
75 km	KM TO AIRPORT
INN	AIRPORT
★★☆	VEGETARIAN RATING
★★★	INTERNET CAFES
★★☆	RIDE IN/RIDE OUT
3286 m	HIGHEST LIFT
2656 m	VERTICAL DROP
area not measured	RIDEABLE AREA (IN ACRES)
625 km	KM OF PISTES
3	NURSERY AREAS
45/90/22	RUNS: BEG/INTER/ADV
0/3	FUNICULAR/CABLE CARS
18/62	GONDOLAS/CHAIRS
74	DRAGS
yes	NIGHT RIDING
1	PARKS
1	PIPE
yes	SUMMER AREAS
★★★	ENVIRONMENTAL RATING
💲💲💲	COST INDICATOR
AUSTRIA ZILLERTAL	

P. CHRIS MORAN/HOTSHITPICTURES.COM

Canada

R: MARCUS CHAPMAN   L: KICKING HORSE   P: TASH

Untouched powder as far as the eye can see ... not that uncommon in Canada.

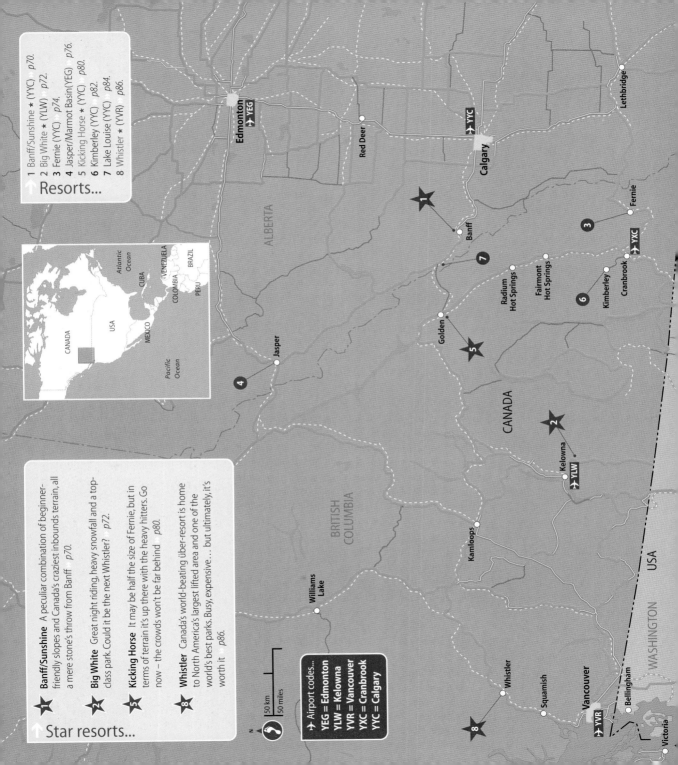

↑ Resorts...

1 Banff/Sunshine ★ (YYC) ↑ p70.
2 Big White ★ (YLW) ↑ p72.
3 Fernie (YYC) p74.
4 Jasper/Marmot Basin (YEG) p76.
5 Kicking Horse ★ (YYC) p80.
6 Kimberley (YYC) p82.
7 Lake Louise (YYC) p84.
8 Whistler ★ (YVR) p86.

↑ Star resorts...

★ 1 **Banff/Sunshine** A peculiar combination of beginner-friendly slopes and Canada's craziest inbounds terrain, all a mere stone's throw from Banff. ↑ p70.

★ 2 **Big White** Great night riding, heavy snowfall and a top-class park. Could it be the next Whistler? p72.

★ 5 **Kicking Horse** It may be half the size of Fernie, but in terms of terrain it's up there with the heavy hitters. Go now – the crowds won't be far behind. p80.

★ 8 **Whistler** Canada's world-beating über-resort is home to North America's largest lifted area and one of the world's best parks. Busy, expensive... but ultimately, it's worth it. ↑ p86.

✈ Airport codes...
YEG = Edmonton
YLW = Kelowna
YVR = Vancouver
YXC = Cranbrook
YYC = Calgary

50 km
50 miles

N

For non-North Americans, a snowboarding trip across the Atlantic has usually been the preserve of the very rich, those with more time on their hands, or both. But now that transatlantic travel is easier and more affordable than ever before, Canada has become a very viable option.

If you are used to Europe, why go to the trouble of making that long flight? Well, maybe you're bored of poorly kempt pistes, antiquated lift systems, shoddy funparks or being barged around in lift queues. Or maybe you're bored of being treated like an impostor in France and would prefer to ride somewhere that actually appreciates your business. Whatever your reasons, Canada takes the winter sports culture of Scandinavia, the service industry of America, the mountains of Western Europe, the snowfall of Japan and the friendliness of New Zealand, adds a healthy dose of its own Canuck flavour, and combines the lot into one incredibly attractive package. It really is one of the best places on the planet to go snowboarding.

Just look at the terrain: from the epic pillow lines of Whistler to the groomers of Lake Louise, Canada has the lot. Add to this a more relaxed off-piste policy than the US, a generally high standard of parks, incredibly beautiful mountains and some of the politest people in the world and you start to see the appeal.
So really the question ought to be, why *not* go to Canada?

Introduction

Canada rating

Value for money
★★★☆☆

Nightlife
★★★★☆

Freestyle
★★☆☆☆

Freeride
★★★☆☆

Essentials

Getting there
There are two main points of entry for the featured Canadian resorts – Calgary and Vancouver. Carriers include **Air Canada** (aircanada.com), **Zoom** (flyzoom.com), **British Airways** (ba.com) and **American Airlines** (aa.com). For resorts such as Fernie and Kimberley flying into Cranbrook is a great option, if you can afford it. Internal flights from Vancouver are available from **Air Canada**.

Red tape
In the case of the US, New Zealand, Australia and the vast majority of European countries, a valid passport is all that's required for entry to Canada. Other nationalities may require a Temporary Resident Visa (TRV) – visit canadainternational.gc.ca for more information. As with the US, avoid making flippant remarks about bombs or terrorism while travelling though airports – it won't be appreciated.

Getting around
Driving The huge distances involved mean that travel between major cities such as Toronto, Vancouver and Calgary is best done by plane. Check **Air Canada** (aircanada.com), **WestJet** (westjet.com) and **CanJet** (canjet.com) for domestic flights. Otherwise, car is by far the best way to get about. Resorts are much more spread out than they are in the Alps, so if you're planning a road trip then be prepared for some long (though typically stunning) drives. Though Canada is the world's second largest country after Russia, it's very sparsely populated so happily the roads are relatively empty. Speed limits are nonetheless quite strictly enforced. Beware of the phenomena of 'freezing rain' that you often find in the Rockies, which can turn the roads to sheet ice – heed any local weather warnings. Note that right turns at red lights are allowed in all provinces except Quebec.

Car hire Canada recognizes all valid foreign driving licences, so an international driving permit is not necessary. The minimum age for renting a car is 21, and drivers of 21-24 years are normally subject to an additional 'young driver fee'. You'll find all the major car hire companies (hertz.com, avis.com) at major airports and in city centres.

Public transport
Canada's rail service is quite expensive and doesn't score highly on convenience, but if nothing else it's a great way to take in the scenery.

Top tips

- Explore. There are a multitude of resorts in BC and Alberta, and a road trip is the perfect way to visit a few of them whilst taking in some magnificent Rocky Mountain scenery.

- Don't go to Whistler just because it's the place you've heard of. There are plenty of other top-class Canadian resorts that are worth looking into as well.

- Wrap up warmly. It gets blisteringly cold here in winter, particularly on the east of the Rockies.

- Don't mistake Canadians for Americans – this is likely to be met with a frosty response.

- Talk to people. Canadians are friendly people and they love chatting to foreigners, particularly the Scots and the Irish.

There are often cheaper fares to be had for those who book in advance – check viarail.ca for more info. Those on a tight budget could try **Greyhound** (greyhound.ca). It's cheap but the typically huge distances to be covered in Canada can make for a gruelling journey.

L: ICE CLIFFS NEAR SUNSHINE P: MATT BARR

I strongly believe that Canada, especially on the west coast, has some of the best mountains to ride in the world; it seems limitless but yet quite accessible. The snow is usually deep and very good from below tree level up to the alpine. I love Canadian pow... it's my favourite!

DCP, Canadian pro snowboarder

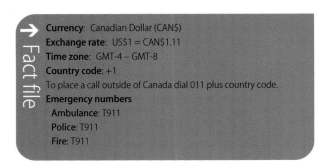

→ **Currency**: Canadian Dollar (CAN$)
Exchange rate: US$1 = CAN$1.11
Time zone: GMT-4 – GMT-8
Country code: +1
To place a call outside of Canada dial 011 plus country code.
Emergency numbers
  Ambulance: T911
  Police: T911
  Fire: T911

Fact file

Opening hours and traditions

Most shops are open Monday to Saturday 0900-1730, though in larger cities malls and supermarkets may open a bit earlier and stay open as late as 2100. Some stay open round the clock. Shops are generally closed on Sundays, though this won't apply in more touristy areas. Note that prices quoted in shops are usually without tax (one exception being fuel), and **GST** (Goods and Services Tax) of 7% will be added to most purchases. Most provinces charge an additional **PST** (Provincial Sales Tax), which varies from region to region: in British Columbia it's 7%, whereas in Alberta there's no PST. The legal drinking age varies from province to province, standing at 18 in Alberta and 19 in BC.

Eating

Canadians have a very broad ethnological background, and aside from obvious dishes like *poutine* (chips served with cheese curds and gravy) it's quite difficult to define what Canadian food actually is. There's a

L: WHISTLER WINTER P:WHISTLER TOURISM

very strong Asian influence, and most towns will have at least one Chinese restaurant, if not a Thai and a Japanese one too.

On the whole, breakfasts tend to be very similar to those in the US, with eggs, bacon, toast, cereal, coffee, orange juice and pancakes making a regular appearance at the table. Waffles and maple syrup, that most quintessentially Canadian of things, are also very popular. Like in the US, meat is a primary ingredient in Canadian meals, and the portions tend to be very large compared with what most Europeans are used to. On the whole, the Canadian tooth is sweeter than the European one, and it's quite difficult to avoid sugar being added right the way across the culinary board. However, like the US, it's a country of extremes, and whilst there's a huge array of fast food joints serving the least healthy food imaginable, these seem to coexist happily with small independent establishments selling good, wholesome food. Milk allergies are also very well catered for, and it's a rare coffee shop indeed that doesn't have soya milk.

European visitors, particularly those from the UK and France, may be puzzled to find that sandwiches in petrol stations are often quite good. Rather than the pre-packed variety, they're often fresh and locally made, with interesting filling ingredients and unusual kinds of bread. Of course,

BC snowboarding is a full experience of its own; starting from the valley floor at sea level, the mountains access all the way up high alpine glaciers. Having that elevation difference creates a huge variety of riding with pillows and insane tree runs in the lower mountains, to huge endless alpine ice fields with ridges full of features and all the rest of the lovin'. Yes the backcountry is endless, but mountain resorts offer great terrain, with huge skiable areas and access to backcountry riding. Every mountain is worth a visit because of the great snowboarding, but also for the good old BC chill lifestyle... The people, the mountains, the beer and ehh, the greens... The land is wild and untouched in many areas, makes you want to become a full-time hippie.

Phil Tifo, photographer and BC resident

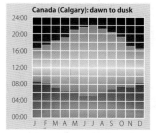

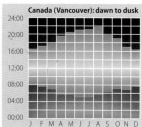

you'll also find those typically North American items such as beef jerky and huge bags of jalapeno and cheese flavoured crisps, along with chocolate bars hell bent on containing peanut butter.

What this all means for the visiting snowboarder is that it's pretty easy to get by in Canada, even if you have particular dietary

Lift chat

Cliff drops in Canada

Ask any keen snowboarder what riding in Canada means to them and you'll get a range of answers. These will invariably include epic parks, bone-chillingly cold blue sky powder days, high-speed charging on perfectly groomed pistes, and endless pillowlines in the misty west coast of British Columbia. What they're also bound to include is cliff drops, and if there's one aspect of riding in which Canadians excel, it's this.

Look at any of the leading Canadian riders and you'll see that they're all masters of the art. Any movie section from the likes of Devun Walsh, DCP or JF Pelchat will consist of tech tricks being done off massive cliffs and stomped into deep, Canadian-style powder. This is also something that the average Canadian rider tends to be noticeably more adept at than the average European one. So what makes Canada such a good place for dropping cliffs?

Simple. It's the combination of heavy snowfall, climate and terrain features. The nature of the terrain in Canada tends to provide much steeper landings than the terrain in the Alps (it's anyone's guess why), and whereas the greater altitudes of the Alps mean that high winds often bedevil the chance of a soft landing, the heavy snowfall and treeline elevation of Canadian ones mean that they're often well on.

Consequently, in resorts such as Tignes and Chamonix, large cliff drops are the preserve of the brave riders who are unfazed by heavy landings with questionable snow cover. In Canada, they're safer, they're more fun, so they're simply what people do.

R. S/BRASS P: JAMES MCPHAIL

---

requirements. It's a service culture and most people in restaurants will be happy to help out. Food on the mountain tends to be of a high standard, and good coffee is very easy to come by. It's not unusual to find Starbucks franchises in resort cafés, which will no doubt horrify and delight people in equal measure.

Language

English and French are the two official languages, with around 61% of the population counting English as their mother tongue. English is the main language in every province except Quebec, where French is dominant.

Crime/safety

The rate of violent crime in Canada is vastly less than that of its more bellicose neighbour to the south. There are restrictions on handguns, and permits are required. The use of firearms for hunting is very common, yet gun related crime remains very low, even in the major cities. As with most other countries petty crime such as handbag theft does occur in populated centres, but on a much lower level than in most other countries. The threat of international terrorism in Canada is low.

Health

As with the US, fully comprehensive health insurance is absolutely essential for any trip to Canada. The standard of healthcare is very high, but it's also very expensive. Make sure you specify this when taking out your insurance as most companies charge extra for cover in North America.

Snowboarding Canada

"Since the earliest days of snowboarding, Canada's riders have contributed to both the sport's progression and its culture. This is no surprise when you think about it: Canada is a cold, sparsely populated, mountainous country founded by adventurous souls. Whether you're enjoying a 200-plus day season at Whistler, becoming a terrain park technician in central Canada, or braving frostbitten digits for a taste of the Alberta Rockies' cold smoke, the riding in Canada is raw, real and almost always worth it." Colin Whyte, editor, Future Snowboarding
futuresnowboarding.com

Unlike some other nations, Canada never really put up a fight when it came to accepting snowboarding. It embraced the sport in the early days and has been a steadfast supporter ever since. Perhaps this is due to the generally mellow temperament of the Canadian people, or perhaps it's simply a natural progression for a country with such harsh winters and such a history of winter sports culture. Whatever the reason, it's this acceptance that has led Canada to become the snowboarding superpower that it is today.

'Progressive' is the word that springs to mind when describing the Canadian approach to snowboarding. Throughout the country, resorts cater for the needs of snowboarders in a way that much of the rest of the world would do well to learn from, and the parks and pipes leave most of Europe looking pale by comparison. And that's not just the big resorts either – we all know that Whistler has long laid a valid claim to the coveted *world's best park* title, but there are many resorts in Canada that are hot on its heels, Big White being just one example. Then there's the Rocky Mountains, which must rank as one of the most beautiful of all the world's mountain ranges. Though the terrain can't match the Alps for scale, it lends itself to snowboarding very well, and the quality and quantity of the snowfall means they're a much

more reliable proposition for those who want to ride powder.

A good way to gauge the riding in a particular country is to look at the sort of riders to come out of there. Canadians can ride park, pipe and rails pretty well, but above all they excel at backcountry freestyle: cliffs, natural gaps and pillow lines. In short, powder; and virtually guaranteed powder is Canada's real trump card. But don't take our word for it, go there and see for yourself …

Conditions
The resorts in this book are all in British Columbia and Alberta, and

JASPER PITSTOP

WHISTLER PIPE TAKING SHAPE

Sledding in Whistler BC

British Columbia is a province populated by pioneers. The Canadians that settled its cold wintry reaches must have been a hearty and slightly disjointed lot. Can you imagine the tenacity of these proto-adventurists, lured by the biblically-proportioned beauty of the Howe Sound, travelling on foot north past present day Vancouver and into the rugged reaches of the Whistler/Blackcomb mountains?

Their intrepidity has certainly been bred into the BC people. The modern reincarnation can be seen in the zeal of snowboarders who penetrate the depths of Whistler's immense, mountainous backcountry, not so much relying on beaver-skin boots and foot trails as gas-guzzling machines that belch out two-stroke smoke. The snowmobile is their tool, and these riders go to ridiculous lengths, distances, and removes to film snowboard movies/take pictures/and just plain get their powder fix.

Snowmobiling has become a raging scene in Whistler due to the unprecedented access to terrain. Within a 30-minute drive from town, there are at least a dozen different areas to park your truck and snowmobile into the wilderness. The second reason is the unparalleled quality of the terrain. Again, just a 30-minute snowmobile tour up the trail delivers the cliffs, spines, peaks, pitches, cornices and other formations that consistently land photos labelled 'Whistler Backcountry' in the glossy pages of snowboard magazines. The terrain is ideal for snowboarding on an epic scale: the landings are all steep, and because elevation is just

a matter of snowmobiling further, the powder is almost always good.

Which is why the place has come to be a bit of a professional circus. The production line quality of snowmobiling in Whistler means that on any given sunny mid-winter day, you could find seven different film crews in the same backcountry spot, all trying to get their piece of the rad. What would those original fur-trapping settlers think? Their adventures were of a more primal variety, but their motives were similarly tinged with capital: they were traders, and they too had a product to create and sell. Regardless, standing atop Whistler Resort mountain, gazing east at the expansive white-peaked reaches of the Whistler backcountry, it's comforting to know some half-crazed and adrenaline-soaked individuals, have, with almost all certainty, been there and shredded that.

Jesse Huffman

P: CHRIS MORAN/HOTSHITPICTURES.COM

being the Rocky Mountains the weather is unpredictable. Of the two, BC has the milder climate thanks to its proximity to the Pacific Ocean. Along with prevailing westerly winds, this gives resorts such as Whistler their famously heavy snowfall, but it also gives the snow its equally famous high water content meaning that the powder can be quite heavy. Moving further east into the Rockies, the winter temperatures get much colder and the snow gets drier – here's where you'll find the dry, fluffy snow known as *champagne powder*. There tends to be a further decline in temperature as you continue east across the Rockies, and if you thought Fernie was chilly then just wait till you get to Banff and Lake Louise. And as if that's not enough, their high altitude means that sunburn is also a problem.

When to go

These resorts follow the general North American pattern of opening from December through April, though Sunshine opens from early November right through into May, making it the obvious choice for early- or late-season riding. Whistler also stays open into May, and it's

a great spot for some end of season park riding. Canadian winters tend to be very cold, with the peak times for powder being January and February, though snowfall is such that you can often get great powder into the middle of March. Slush is usually pretty well established by late March or early April.

Off-piste policy

Canadians take avalanche hazards very seriously, and their patrollers are among the best in the world. As with all North American resorts there are no hard and fast rules to out of bounds access, though in general the policy is more relaxed than that of the US and you may well be allowed to go if you're prepared with the proper safety gear. While people used to the 'do what you like' attitude of the French may find this overzealousness patronizing, it's comforting to know that they err on the side of caution in their concerns for your safety.

Secret spots

Despite what the resorts might claim, the fact that you're not allowed

R. NELSON PRATT L: KICKING HORSE P: TASH

The scene

Snowboarding is massive in Canada, and Canadian riders such as Jon Cartwright, DCP, Devun Walsh, Chris Dufficy, Jonaven Moore, JF Pelchat and Kevin Sansalone are at the forefront in the world snowboarding scene. Whistler is the main focal point and it's where many Canadian and international pros base themselves, though there are also vibrant scenes around Banff and Quebec too.

The industry

Fittingly, Canada has a large industry with several major snowboarding brands such as Option and Westbeach hailing from British Columbia. *Snowboard Canada* (snowboardcanada.com) is the major magazine, but there's a massive amount of crossover and Canadian riders feature heavily in the top US magazines such as *Transworld Snowboarding* and *Snowboarder*. Canada's most famous crew of snowboarders are the Wildcats (Devun Walsh, JF Pelchat, Dionne Delasalle, Chris Dufficy, Gaetun Chanut and honorary Finn Paavo Tikkanen among others), and they've made some highly influential movies such as *Nine Lives*. Other Canadian scene movies are very common, with the riding being of a predictably high standard. *FourPlay*, *Positron* and *Sandbox* are other examples.

R: JON CAULFIELD L: WHISTLER P: LUKE SP

to ride out of bounds means that the extent of the rideable terrain doesn't compare with that of the Alps. Consequently, there's much more competition for secret spots, particularly in busier resorts such as Whistler. Locals solve this problem simply by buying snowmobiles and heading deep into the backcountry to get away from the crowds (see Lift chat). In quieter resorts, befriending a local may prove to be your ticket to the goods.

Freestyle

Most resorts have excellent parks and pipes, with jumps and jibs nicely graded for beginners up to advanced riders. They're also very well maintained. As with Scandinavia, the standard of riding of the average Canadian is very high, as anyone who has spent any time watching nameless riders quietly ripping up the Whistler park will have noticed. Unlike in Scandinavia, they actually have proper mountains so many of the leading Canadian riders are either big mountain types such as Jonaven Moore, or backcountry freestyle rippers such as Devun Walsh and JF Pelchat.

Canada: a brief history of snowboarding

1979 → Canadian brewing company Labatt run a beer commercial featuring the snurfer pro Paul Graves. The advert runs for four years, and is the first instance of a mainstream company using snowboarding to sell its products. **1980** → Ken Achenbach opens the legendary Snoboard Shop in his mum's Calgary garage. **1985** → North American Snowboarding Championships held at Sunshine Village. **1986** → Barfoot TwinTip board developed in Calgary by Neil Daffern and Ken Achenbach and it raises the bar in freestyle snowboarding. **1987** → Westbeach becomes one of the first companies in the world to offer a line of snowboarding specific outerwear. The clothing features a much looser fit designed to facilitate the heavily tweaked airs that are in vogue at the time. With its instantly recognizable maple leaf logo, Westbeach goes on to become the brand most associated with Canadian riding. **1988** → Calgarian Dave B Achenbach scores the first *Transworld Snowboarding* cover. Canadian legend Alex Warburton graces another early cover. Calgary/Banff riders Achenbach, Warburton, Jon Boyer and Don Schwartz all figure heavily in the freestyle and mogul contests of the day. **1988** → Ken Achenbach starts Camp Of Champions, one of the world's first summer snowboarding camps. It has taken place on a yearly basis ever since. **1989** → Blackcomb, BC becomes synonymous with late season riding with the infamous Blackcomb 'windlip' and a natural quarterpipe. *Transworld* print shots of Damian Sanders and Doug Lundgren launching 50-ft airs off the windlip and the magazine receives dozens of letters claiming they're fake. Whistler-Blackcomb becomes the centre of the universe for Canadian snowboarding. **1990** → The rise of the French Canadians begins. Martin Gallant takes a four-day bus trip across the country from Quebec to Whistler, and arrives with a fearless spirit that will help define myriad other French Canadians such as Marc Morisset, JF Pelchat, Gaetan Chanut, Mike Paige, Alex Auchu and others in the years to come. **1994** → Canadian beer company Molson uses snowboarding footage in a beer ad premiering on *Monday Night Football*. **1995** → Sean Johnson and Sean Kearns start the *Whiskey* series of snowboarding movies. The three movies are widely considered some of the most influential snowboarding movies ever made, (*Jackass* would be unimaginable without the *Whiskey* movies). Kearns and Johnson still figure prominently in the snowboard industry. **1996** → Whistler filmmaker Murray Siple releases *The Burning* and, later, *Cascadia*, both now cult classic shred flicks. **1996** → The all-Canadian Shortys team of Devun Walsh, Chris Brown, Kevin Young ('KY') and friends is in full effect and leading the zeitgeist of snowboarding. **1997** → Victoria Jealouse, who has already been around for 'quite a while' by '97, continues to cement her reputation as the preeminent female freerider in the world, a title she holds to this day. **1998** → Ross Rebagliati wins the first ever snowboarding gold medal in the Olympics at Nagano, but is stripped of it three days later after testing positive for marijuana. The case goes to appeal on the arguments that marijuana is not a performance-enhancing drug, and Rebagliati wins the appeal and is allowed to keep his medal. **1998** → Allan 'Cartons' Clark and Greg 'GT' Todds start the superpipe camp in the Whistler backcountry. Unfortunately, Todds died in an avalanche near Revelstoke in 2005. The big guy brought a lot of heart to Canadian snowboarding and was a true innovator who pushed park and pipe design. **1999** → The hugely influential Wildcats crew comes into being, taking its name from a signature backflip cartwheel thing popular with the group. It originally comprises Devun Walsh, Chris Dufficy, Dionne Delesalle, Rob Dow, Dave Cashen and Jake 'the bottle' McEntire, but expands over the years to include many more riders (including Finns and Japanese). They go on to release a series of movies including *Nine Lives*. The Wildcats are often confused with another Vancouver crew, The Seymour Kids, but they are separate entities. **1999** → Mike Michalchuk explodes onto the scene with his incredibly powerful pipe riding and a distinctive new trick that he names the 'heave ho'. The trick, essentially a backside rodeo done on the backside wall of the halfpipe, soon becomes widely known as the 'Michalchuk'. Michalchuk dominates US and Canadian pipe comps for a couple of seasons, but just when his form appears to be world beating (including a 'doublechuck') and he's on the road to becoming one of snowboarding's greats, a severe knee injury knocks him to the sidelines. **2001** → Marc-André Tarte lands a Cab 1080 off the 30-m Megaroller in Hintertux, Austria. He's travelling at over 60 mph as he hits the jump. **2003** → Marc-Andr Tarte lands the first competitive 1440 off a straight kicker at the Innsbruck Air & Style. **2004** → Whistler has one of its worst winters ever and the entire northwest goes crazy. **2005** → Everything's OK now. The snow came back. Canadian riders continue to kill it.

Banff/Sunshine

A heady mix of big town nightlife, family friendly pistes and crazy big mountain riding, nicely rounded off with the highest snowfall in Alberta.

❄ If you like this ...
... try Ishgl ➨p38, Kicking Horse ➨p80, or Lake Louise ➨ p 84.

CANADA
BANFF/SUNSHINE

The Town 😐🚴🏂

Named after the Scottish town near Aberdeen, Banff is a former frontier town on the main trans-Canada route. It was first established as a service centre for visitors to the national park, but these days it's a bustling year-round town that provides an ideal base for the surrounding resorts of Lake Louise, Sunshine and Mount Norquay. The town's facilities are up there with the best, and there are quick and easy links by shuttle bus with Sunshine (8 km, CAN$14 return) and Mount Norquay (5 km). Note that the shuttle bus is free if you buy a Tri-Area lift pass. See skibig3.com for more info.

Sleeping If you're on a tight budget try the **SameSun Backpacker Lodge** (T403 762 5521). It's a two-minute walk from the town centre and has a hot tub, sauna and internet access. **Brewster's Mountain Lodge** (brewstermountainlodge.com) is also very central, and all rooms come with a continental breakfast. A more upmarket service can be had from the **Rimrock Resort Hotel** (rimrockresort .com), which has its own restaurant, spa service and a heated indoor pool.

Eating There's masses of choice, with most major international cuisines

Sunshine has opened up some of the biggest mountain inbounds riding I'm familiar with. It truly is the place to learn how to take down a mountain. It's close to town and has the best snow in Banff.

Andrew Hardingham,
pro snowboarder and Banff resident

being well represented. **Japanese Restaurant Miki** (T403 762 1909) is good, as is **Typhoon** (T403 762 2000) which offers a range of Asian cuisine. **Michaels Café** (T403 762 9339) has tasty vegetarian meals. **Old Spaghetti Factory** (T403 760 2779) is good for a cheap fill up. **Evelyn's Coffee Bar** (T403 762 0352) offers speciality coffees, homemade pastries and desserts as well as a good lunch menu, or for swanky Canadian cooking try the **Maple Leaf Grille** (T403 760 7680).

Bars and clubs For a rowdy evening head to the **Rose and Crown** pub. It has pool tables, frequent live music and is usually rammed. For later nights there's the **Hoodoo** and the **Aurora** nightclubs – they're both comfortable, not outrageously priced and usually play good music. For a mellower vibe try the **Saltlick**. It's a martini bar with good beats most nights.

Shopping Banff has very good shopping facilities. **Rude Boys** (rudeboys.com) in the Sundance mall is the town's best snowboard shop, and there are several supermarkets.

Health Try **Pleiades Massage & Spa** (T403 760 2500).

Internet There are several internet cafés. Try **Cyberweb** on Banff Avenue.

Transfer options Rocky Mountain Sky Shuttle (rockymountainskyshuttle.com) for transfers from Calgary. Note that if you're driving you'll need a National Park pass. These are available from the National Parks authority who will invariably stop you to check.

☺ OPENING TIMES

Mid-Nov to late May:
0900-1600 (1630 from spring)

💲 RESORT PRICES

Week pass (5 out of 7 days):
CAN$310.75
Day pass: CAN$64.95
Season pass: CAN$599

ℹ DIRECTORY

Tourist office: T403 277 7669
Medical centre: T403 762 4595
Pisteurs: T403 762 6500
Taxi: T403 762 4444
Local radio: Radio Banff 96.3 FM
Website: skibanff.com

Local partners Banff (Norquay & Sunshine). See skibig3.com for details.

OPEN GATE WITH TRANSCEIVER P: BECKY HORTON

L: BANFF MAIN STREET P: BANFF TOURISM

The Mountain

Sunshine Village, to use its full title, is made up of three distinct but interconnected mountains: Goat's Eye Mountain, Mount Standish and Lookout Mountain. It receives over 30 ft of powder snow every year – that's more than double that of any other resort in Alberta. It also has the world's fastest eight-seater gondola, and it's open from early November through to mid May making its season the longest in the Canadian Rockies. As if all that wasn't reason enough to go there, it's home to Delerium Dive, the most ridiculous inbounds freeride terrain you'll find this side of the Atlantic. Add to this a decent park and a great setup for beginners and you begin to get the picture.

Beginners Mount Standish is the best area for beginners. Find your feet on the mellow green runs accessible from the Strawberry chair, then when confidence is peaking head up the Angel Express and tackle the array of blue and green runs to the skier's left.
Intermediate Warm up with a few laps on the Angel Express chair. There's an array of good pistes to cruise right underneath. Next, head to the Sunshine park – though it's not up to much by Canadian standards, there are some mellow rails which are good for learning on. After lunch, head up the Mount Standish Express lift and spend the afternoon finding natural hits. The undulating terrain of the Banff Avenue homerun provides some good jib possibilities, so don't be tempted to download on the gondola.
Advanced If you get the snow then Delerium Dive is the place, provided it's open (T403 762 6511 to check). A transceiver is mandatory to make it past the check in gate, though you're also required to have a shovel and probe, and be accompanied by at least one other person. Failing this, head to the Wild West area of Goat's Eye Mountain, which is the next best thing.
Kids Kids under six years of age get a free lift pass and free access to the Banff shuttle bus.
Flat light days Head up the Wolverine Express – the runs are entirely within the treeline and there is some serious stuff.

R: UNKNOWN P: SEAN HANNAH

LOCALS DO
- Get good at freeriding.
- Go to Mount Norquay for night riding.
- Ride Delirium Dive.

LOCALS DON'T
- Queue. The world's fastest eight-seater gondola and several high speed quads take care of that.
- Ride the park. The one at Lake Louise is far superior.
- Ride with an unwaxed board. The home run is littered with flat spots.

PROS
- Great for families, beginners and advanced riders alike.
- Alberta's biggest vertical drop.
- Very reliable snowfall. And it's not called 'Champagne powder' for nothing.

CONS
- When the snow's not great there's not a huge amount for more experienced riders to do.
- If you're staying in Banff as most people do, it's hardly ride in/ride out snowboarding.

NOT TO MISS
A run on 'Freefall' at Goat's Eye Mountain – there's an 83 degree pitch which will have your heart in your mouth.

REMEMBER TO AVOID
Rocking up at Delirium Dive without a transceiver – you won't be allowed past the gate.

SNOW DEPTH
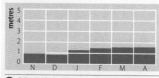

RELIVE A FAMOUS MOMENT
Stanly Kubrick's *Dr Strangelove*, starring Peter Sellers, was filmed on location in Banff.

1660 m	TOWN ALTITUDE
113 km	KM TO AIRPORT
YYC	AIRPORT
★★★	VEGETARIAN RATING
★★★	INTERNET CAFES
★☆☆	RIDE IN/RIDE OUT
2730 m	HIGHEST LIFT
1070 m	VERTICAL DROP
3358	RIDEABLE AREA (IN ACRES)
runs not measured	KM OF PISTES
1	NURSERY AREAS
21/59/27	RUNS: BEG/INTER/ADV
0/0	FUNICULAR/CABLE CARS
1/9	GONDOLAS/CHAIRS
2	DRAGS
no	NIGHT RIDING
1	PARKS
1	PIPE
no	SUMMER AREAS
★★★ ★★★	ENVIRONMENTAL RATING
	COST INDICATOR

CANADA
BANFF/SUNSHINE

Big White

The Town

Unpretentious, laid-back and family friendly, Big White's location right in the heart of the mountain and status as home to North America's largest night-riding terrain means you can fully immerse yourself in snowboarding 24 hours a day. Runs, chairlifts and a gondola snake through the small village centre ensuring you need never catch a bus in the morning.

Sleeping Same Sun Backpacker Ski Lodge (samesun.com) is the place for sociable long- and short-term budget accommodation, while the **Whitefoot Lodge** (whitefootlodge .com) offers a range of accommodation to suit all budgets. The **Inn at Big White** is a pricier option. All accommodations in Big White can be arranged through the central booking system (bigwhite.com).

Eating Stave off the early morning munchies at **Beano's Coffee Parlour**, also good-value meals at **Carvers**. If you feel like splashing out try The **Copper Kettle Grille** in the **White Crystal Inn**.

Bars and Clubs Snow Shoe Sams and **Raakels Ridge Pub** for après-ski and night-time action for locals and visitors alike.

Shopping Get groceries at the **Mountain Mart** in the village centre.

Health The **Spa Beyond Rapture** at the **Big White Chateau** has an extensive variety of massage treatments.

Internet Three cafés, with most of the big hotels being wireless connected.

Transfer options Big White run their own shuttle service between the resort and Kelowna Airport seven times a day for a reasonable CAN\$64.95 return. You must book; shuttles don't run if they are not reserved (T1800-663 2772).

Local partners None.

> Big White is the province's up-and-coming ski resort. More commonly known for dry interior powder and acres of diverse freeriding terrain, the resort's park has also become a big drawing point …
>
> *Russell Dalby*, Snowboard Canada

Affordable ski in/ski out riding in BC's second biggest resort: 7.5 m of annual snowfall, varied alpine terrain and an ever-expanding progressive snow park.

If you like this …
… try *Courchevel* ▸▸p130, or *Verbier* ▸▸p330.

R: UNKNOWN P: BIG WHITE TOURISM

The Mountain

Recent extensions to Big White's terrain and a massive effort to improve the mountain's park and event facilities mean the resort is rapidly becoming an impressive winter sports destination. A variety of open runs make it ideal for families, while any number of chutes and bowls mean experienced riders are also well catered for. Big White is now fighting for recognition as a destination comparable to Whistler, providing speciality attractions such as a massive snowpark that's rapidly making its mark on Canada's freestyle map. Overall, Big White is pitching itself to be the next big thing and they're going the right way about it. Impressive indeed.

Beginners For those total beginners there's a special learning area next to **Happy Valley Lodge** complete with handle tow and magic carpet. Those more confident beginners can take the Ridge Rocket Chair and check out the super smooth summer groomed Highway 33 or the epic top to bottom Serwas run.

Intermediate Start your day with warm up runs on the Black Forest Chair: the mellow runs and easily accessible glade skiing providing a great introduction to those tighter tree runs to come. In the afternoon, session the Bullet Chair to explore some steeper and more challenging runs, scattered with natural hits and trees to push your skills as far as you wish. End the day with a session in the Telus Park.

Advanced Head straight to the Alpine T-Bar and the Cliff Chair on a powder day. Once up on the ridgeline, there are a wealth of chutes and cliffs to pick your line through, a freeriders' playground through which you can do fast laps without hiking all day long. On the left-hand side of the mountain, the Falcon Chair and the Powder Chair are your gateways to some of the resorts more gnarly gullied terrain.

Kids Head for the award-winning Kids Centre in the village. Kids aged six and under get a free pass when accompanied by an adult. Free helmets are available for three- to 12 year-olds from the Kids Centre, T205 765 3101 (ext 233).

Flat light days Head to the trees – the Black Forest and the area around the Moonlight Run are two low-altitude, sheltered areas perfect for all abilities in bad weather.

P: BIG WHITE TOURISM

☺ LOCALS DO
- Ride the trees: ask a local about Easter Trees.
- Drive down to Kelowna to do a big grocery shop.
- Ride the park at night (it's quieter).

☹ LOCALS DON'T
- Dress up all gangsta style. Big White is a very mellow resort.
- Shred the mogul hills off Ridge Rocket.
- Wear flashing 'Big White' caps – even though they're really cool.

✔ PROS
- Many of the benefits of Whistler riding in a more low-key, relaxed environment.
- Good value for money.
- Lots of light, cold powder.

✘ CONS
- Shops, bars and clubs in the village are limited.
- Full mountain terrain often not open until mid-January.
- The trade-off for all the snow is a fair amount of 'white-out' days.

☺ NOT TO MISS
Ride two resorts in one day – a morning in Big White followed by a helicopter shuttle to Silver Star for an afternoon on the slopes and dinner! T205 491 4244.

❶ REMEMBER TO AVOID
On busy days, Perfection, Goat's Kick and Dragon's Tongue become treacherous icy mogul fields – avoid at all costs!

❄ SNOW DEPTH

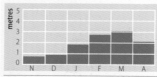

☺ RELIVE A FAMOUS MOMENT
The Canadian backcountry riding is now one of the most popular filming locations for the big films. Big White has too many famous lines to mention.

1509 m to 1755 m TOWN ALTITUDE	
56 km KM TO AIRPORT	
YLW AIRPORT	
★★☆ VEGETARIAN RATING	
★★★ INTERNET CAFES	
★★★ RIDE IN/RIDE OUT	
2319 m HIGHEST LIFT	
777 m VERTICAL DROP	
905 RIDEABLE AREA (IN ACRES)	
runs not measured KM OF PISTES	
3 NURSERY AREAS	
47/19/19 RUNS: BEG/INTER/ADV	
0/0 FUNICULAR/CABLE CARS	
1/10 GONDOLAS/CHAIRS	
2 DRAGS	
yes NIGHT RIDING	
1 PARKS	
2 PIPE	
no SUMMER AREAS	
★★★☆ ENVIRONMENTAL RATING	
💲💲💲 COST INDICATOR	

CANADA
BIG WHITE

Fernie

The Town

Like many of the Canadian resorts, Fernie consists of two distinct towns: the old mining town of Fernie where all the locals live, and the newly built resort at the riding area. As is the norm, the two are just a short drive apart. Fernie town is what you'd describe charitably as functional rather than attractive. It's fairly large and pretty well set up in terms of amenities, but the nightlife's not up to much. Fortunately, it's rescued by the lively après scene up at the resort.

Sleeping The Same Sun (T250 423 4492) hostel in Fernie town has hot tubs, a pool, table tennis, a large common room and friendly staff. There's also the **Raging Elk** (ragingelk.com) directly opposite.

The **Stanford Inn** (T250 423 5000) is a pretty good mid-priced place. It's comfortable, well appointed and has a water slide so it's ideal for kids. **Lizard Creek** (lizardcreek.com) up in the resort is the best place to stay if you've got a bit of money to spend. It's luxurious and right on the slopes.

Eating On the mountain, the **Day Lodge** is good for a cheap, canteen style lunch, though **Slopeside** is far better and it does Starbucks coffee. In Fernie town, **The Curry Bowl** (T250 423 2695) is very popular with the locals – it peddles freshly cooked Thai food with massive portions. **Mojo Rising** (T250 423 7750) in the **Royal Hotel** is very popular with the younger crowd.

Bars and clubs All the bars are on the 1st and 2nd avenues. **Eshwigs** and **The Corner Pocket** (in **The Central**) are popular local hangouts.

"Fernie's sick! It has everything a rider wants, from steep chutes, cliffs, trees, open bowls to nice groomers and a decent terrain park."

Paul McMahon, Fernie Snowboard Instructor

The **Pub** does CAN$9 pitchers on Mondays and Tuesdays, and 10 wings for CAN$3. Also check out the **Art Place Lodge**, **Phat City** and the **Brickhouse**. There are no late clubs in Fernie – everywhere shuts at 0200.

Shopping There are a number of supermarkets and snowboard shops in Fernie town. There's also a repair service in the rental shop up the mountain.

Internet Many hotels and lodges have high speed internet access, often wireless.

Transfer options Rocky Mountain Sky Shuttle (rockymountainskyshuttle.com) for transfers from Calgary.

Local partners Kimberley.

With an average annual snowfall of almost 9 m, there's no doubting that Fernie packs the clout to justify its 'Legendary Powder' tagline.

☼ If you like this ...
... try *Kicking Horse* ➤p80, *Niseko* ➤p210, *or Jackson Hole* ➤p362.

R: RYAN DAVIS P: TASH

⊚ OPENING TIMES

Early Dec to mid-Apr: 0900-1600

⑤ RESORT PRICES

Week pass (6 days): CAN$434 (CAN$469 peak)
Day pass: CAN$64 (CAN$69 peak)
Season pass: CAN$859

❶ DIRECTORY

Tourist office: T250 423 4655
Medical centre: T250 423 4442
Pisteurs: T250 423 2426
Taxi: T250 423 4409
Local radio: The Drive 99.1 FM
Website: skifernie.com

CANADA
FERNIE

The Mountain

The mountain is subdivided into what locals call the 'old side' and the 'new side', though there's not much to distinguish between them. The crazy 'headwall' at the top of the mountain is Fernie's most visually defining feature, and it's where you'll find the most challenging terrain – it's also visible from the whole resort so it has a high Hollywood factor. Famously high snowfall and frigid weather conditions virtually guarantee that if you come here, you're going to ride some powder. Just make sure you bring that goose down jacket.

Beginners The Mighty Moose drag is the ideal place to learn. Once you can turn, head up to the mellow greens on the Deer chair.

Intermediate Head to the Fernie park. It's pretty long with tables ranging from small to medium, and there's plenty of rails and some interesting features such as a step-up. The downside is that the run out ends with a long, flat track and it's not easy

to do laps on, but the first half of it is littered with good hits and a couple of fun cat tracks. Fernie is a great place for cruising around – there are loads of natural hits, many excellent pistes (always well groomed), plenty of great cat tracks and some very easy access in bounds freeriding. Go explore!

Advanced If you get the snow then go straight to the headwall. You can hike up either far skier's left or far skier's right. We recommend the skier's left spot, because there are some nice obvious lines and some good drops. It gets steeper and more involved near the middle of the headwall. As is the norm in Canada the Fernie ski patrol are on it, so check with them before you go. Spend the remainder of the day checking out the Cedar Bowl, or if you're feeling more adventurous drop into the Fish Bowl on the other side. It's out of bounds and the avalanche risk is high, so be careful.

Kids The Mighty Moose drag at the bottom of the hill is the spot. Under fives get a free liftpass.

Flat light days Most of the resort is within the treeline, including the park, so it's pretty good.

☺ LOCALS DO
- Dress warmly. A neck warmer is essential.
- Hike the kickers in the park. Chair laps take too long.
- Ride the trees. Fernie is a great place to get into tree riding.

☹ LOCALS DON'T
- Use warm wax on their boards – the snow gets so cold you'll want low temperature wax.
- Stay in resort – there are far cheaper options down in Fernie town.
- Mind hiking the headwall on powder days. It's not as far as it looks.

✓ PROS
- Fantastic resort with something to offer everyone.
- That 'Legendary Powder' they're always talking about.
- Pretty large by Canadian standards.

✗ CONS
- Shame you weren't here 10 years ago – it can get tracked out pretty quickly these days.
- Nightlife's not amazing.
- The cold can bother some people.

☺ NOT TO MISS
A freezing cold blue sky powder day in the trees. It pretty much epitomizes Fernie.

ⓘ REMEMBER TO AVOID
If your board is very slow then steer clear of the Falling Star run out of the bottom of the park. The lower section is very flat.

❄ SNOW DEPTH

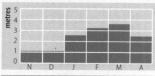

☺ RELIVE A FAMOUS MOMENT
Adam Horowitz, aka Ad-Rock of Beastie Boys' fame, spent a season in Fernie and was regularly visited by his bandmates out for a quick ride.

1068 m	TOWN ALTITUDE
303 km	KM TO AIRPORT
YYC	AIRPORT
★★☆	VEGETARIAN RATING
★★★	INTERNET CAFES
★☆☆	RIDE IN/RIDE OUT
1925 m	HIGHEST LIFT
857 m	VERTICAL DROP
2504	RIDEABLE AREA (IN ACRES)
runs not measured	KM OF PISTES
4	NURSERY AREAS
32/43/32	RUNS: BEG/INTER/ADV
0/0	FUNICULAR/CABLE CARS
0/6	GONDOLAS/CHAIRS
4	DRAGS
no	NIGHT RIDING
1	PARKS
1	PIPE
no	SUMMER AREAS
★★★ ★★★	ENVIRONMENTAL RATING
$$$	COST INDICATOR

CANADA
FERNIE

R: CHRIS MORAN P: NICK HAMILTON

Another side to the Canadian Rockies: old-fashioned rootsy snowboarding in the middle of Alberta's logging heartland, well off the beaten track.

If you like this …
… try Zillertal ▶▶p56, Baqueira Beret ▶▶p292, or Les Diablerets ▶▶p322.

CANADA
JASPER/MARMOT BASIN

The Town

Three hours north of Banff and its attendant resorts, Jasper is remote and retains some of the atmosphere of its old frontier days as a logging town. Staying here feels a little like peeping round the curtain into another era. It's an impression underlined by the mighty scenery that envelops the town, and the welcome afforded to you by the locals. Elk and mountain goats really do wander the streets round these parts. This narcoleptic atmosphere also extends to nearby Marmot Basin, the resort that sits about half an hour's drive outside the town. Its remoteness means the slopes are generally uncrowded, and the riding unfolds at a nicely unhurried pace. Although it doesn't have the steepest terrain in Alberta or British Columbia, and the riding is best suited to intermediates and families, we think this, combined with the chance to stay in the time capsule that is Jasper, makes Marmot Basin worthy of inclusion in the guide.

Sleeping Inghams (inghams.co.uk) run packages to Jasper from the UK, and this is the easiest way of making the trip. Check the site for more. Easily the priciest and grandest place in town, the **Fairmont Jasper Park Lodge** (fairmont.com/jasper) is once in a lifetime, but worth it! The **Astoria Hotel** (astoriahotel.com) is a microcosm of Jasper history, owned by the same family for generations.

Eating Papa George's restaurant (T780 852 3351) is the finest in town. **Truffles and Trout** (T780 852 9676), Jasper Pizza Place (T780 852 3225) and **Mountain Foods Café** (T780 852 4050) are also popular. **Coco's Café** (T780 852 4550) is a really good vegetarian.

Bars and clubs Without doubt, the **De'd Dog Bar and Grill** is the social hub of the town with a thriving local crew. **O'Sheas** and **Pete's** are also popular.

Shopping The Jasper Marketplace and **Robinson's** for food and other essentials.

Health Ashton's Massage Studio (T780 852 5799) and **European Beauty and Wellness Centre** (T780 852 3252).

Internet Two well-appointed cafés: **Digital Den** and **Internet Jasper**.

> "Jasper is laid-back and relaxed. There are no big crowds, lift queues are virtually non-existent and the locals are friendly, easy-going and helpful."
>
> *Brian Rode, long-time Jaspar local*

Transfer options Most stays with hotels or operators include transfers. Try **Sundog Tours** (sundogtours.com) or **Jasper Taxis** (jaspertaxi@yahoo.ca) for more.

P: BECKY HORTON

P: SKIMARMOT.COM

🕐 **OPENING TIMES**

Early Dec to early May: 0900-1600

💲 **RESORT PRICES**

Week pass (6 days): CAN$422
Day pass: CAN$62
Season pass: CAN$579-829 (family discount available)

ℹ️ **DIRECTORY**

Tourist Office: T780 852 3858
Medical Centre: T780 852 3344
Pisteurs: T866 952 3816
Taxi: T780 852 3600
Local radio: FOX 95.5 FM
Website: skimarmot.com

P: SKIMARMOT.COM

The Mountain

Like most North American ski areas, Marmot Basin is an extremely well planned riding area. Although it isn't huge, there's enough to do to keep most standards happy. The majority of runs in the resort are basically arrayed around the circumference of a huge bowl, with the steeper terrain at the top and the mellower slopes near the base. It makes navigation easy, as the bottom lifts and the top slopes all converge at the bottom of the Chalet Slope area. As with most resorts over there, each lift has an easy route down, making it a particularly fun resort for beginners and intermediates as they won't be confined to a certain part of the hill.

Beginners The slopes at the bottom of Marmot Basin are as perfect as it gets for beginners, so get straight on the Eagle Express chair and take a green down to the Tranquilizer. Once confident is up, take the Paradise Chair and lap the runs coming back down to the central Chalet Slope point. Then do it all again after lunch. Save Knob Chair till the end of the week.

Intermediate With a bit of snow and sun, it could be the ultimate mid-shredders paradise. The pistes off each chair are great fun, there's a mellow park in which to cut your teeth, and there are even some obvious, basic hikes to try if you're feeling confident. Take Knob Chair and cut off skier's left to try some more challenging terrain, and end the week by taking on some of Eagle East and Eagle Ridge's steeper stuff

Advanced You've really got two options: Knob Chair and Eagle Ridge. The trees of Eagle East are surprisingly involved, and will keep everyone happy if the snow is good. Later, try the hike up the ridge from the Eagle Ridge Quad, and head hard skier's left along the obvious traverse off the Knob Chair for some good steeps. Finally, hike the peak, but don't duck the rope – it's a nature reserve, and you will have your pass pulled.

Kids Kids under fives get free passes, while kids aged six to 12 get a substantial discount. There's also a magic carpet lift at the base, adjacent to the nursery, that's a great places for kids to take their first turns.

Flat light days Lower down there are plenty of trees but the terrain is flatter. Eagle East is where you want to be.

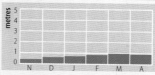
P: MICKE GERE

☺ LOCALS DO
☺ Rip. This is a classic winter town, with locals that eat, sleep and breath the mountains.
☺ Extend quite a welcome to visitors.
☺ Hang out at the De'd Dog Bar and Grill. It goes off.

☹ LOCALS DON'T
☹ Remember to turn off their engines while waiting in the car park.
☹ Forget to explore Jasper and Jasper National Park. It's a UNESCO World Heritage site and Canada's largest Rocky Mountain National Park.
☹ Rush! The pace of life here is decidedly slow.

✓ PROS
◉ Rustic Canada *in excelsis*.
◉ Almost perfect for intermediates, beginners and families.
◉ Wildlife.

✗ CONS
✗ No on-slope accommodation means a long drive each day.
✗ Those craving steeps will be disappointed.
✗ Long flight followed by long transfer.

◉ NOT TO MISS
The hikes up Eagle Ridge and the peak – easily the most challenging and fun terrain in the resort.

ⓘ REMEMBER TO AVOID
The car park at the end of the day. With hordes of SUVs, coaches and hire cars leaving their engines running, it's smoggy chaos.

❄ SNOW DEPTH

metres	N	D	J	F	M	A
5						
4						
3						
2						
1						
0						

◉ RELIVE A FAMOUS MOMENT
Sir Arthur Conan Doyle and HM Queen Elizabeth II are Jasper Park Lodge regulars. Well, they've been there at least once …

1636 m
TOWN ALTITUDE

363 km
KM TO AIRPORT

YEG
AIRPORT

★★★
VEGETARIAN RATING

★★☆
INTERNET CAFES

★☆☆
RIDE IN/RIDE OUT

2601 m
HIGHEST LIFT

914 m
VERTICAL DROP

1675
RIDEABLE AREA (IN ACRES)

runs not measured
KM OF PISTES

1
NURSERY AREAS

13/18/53
RUNS: BEG/INTER/ADV

0
FUNICULAR/CABLE CARS

0/7
GONDOLAS/CHAIRS

2
DRAGS

no
NIGHT RIDING

1
PARKS

0
PIPE

no
SUMMER AREAS

★★☆
★★★
ENVIRONMENTAL RATING

COST INDICATOR

CANADA
JASPER/MARMOT BASIN

Riders' tales
Making holidays a lifestyle

Snowboarding can be very addictive. But what happens when you save up for one, two or maybe even three snowboard holidays, and you end up getting bad conditions every time? How gutted would you be? And how long would it be before you really gave some thought into doing a season?

Ah – three words to send any respectable snowboarder into a swivel-eyed daydream. For many it's a reality. The idea of spending up to six months living in a resort either eking out a living or simply riding on cash you've saved up is – often – a temptation much too powerful to ignore. And one of the most commonly heard phrases from the mouths of ex-seasonaires is 'I didn't realize how easy it was to do. I wish I'd done it earlier.'

There are two ways of spending your winter in the mountains. You either work or you don't. The obvious difference is money. Jobs in resort tend to be incredibly low paid – more often than not way below national pay barriers. They can often be hard to find, and most likely will have no safety net should you fall ill or become unavailable to work. All of these factors are due to one inescapable truism – the ratio of jobs to people is ludicrously weighed in the favour of the employer.

That said, many people have had a great time working in resort. Natives.co.uk, scuk.co.uk, seasonworkers.com and coolworks.com are four great websites for finding and advertising jobs. But working in a resort throws up several problems, not least of which is this: what if your job keeps you off the mountain during the day? Because of this, many riders find it more appropriate to save up during the summer and then live throughout the winter on a strict budget, thus earning the dubious accolade of 'bums'. In reality, this is by far the best option, and here there are two routes to go down. One is the DIY path, well trodden by generations of riders and skiers. It involves finding an apartment or chalet (the internet can help, especially sites such as natives.co.uk, but nothing beats visiting your chosen resort in late summer to check the local agencies and supermarket corkboards), then filling it with double the amount of people it was intended for and having the time of your lives.

The second option is to buy your season outright from one of the many companies currently offering long-term package holidays. Here, seasonaires.com have been the European leader since the idea began back in the late '90s, but planetsubzero.com, chillchalet.com, dragonlodge.com, chaletchardons.com and alpineelements.co.uk – amongst many others – all have similar deals.

When they first launched, the idea of paying outright for the entire season had the hardcore up in arms, but today it seems to be generally accepted. However, it is worth pointing out that for a well-organized group of friends who wish to spend a few months riding the world's best terrain, such companies can often be little more than an unnecessary middle man, adding costs to what is likely to be an expensive time. Yes, they're convenient – but people have been organizing seasons quite happily for decades without any outside help, so think about it carefully before you take the plunge.

MIKE WEYERHAEUSER BRUSHING UP HIS MINI POOL SKILLS IN CHAMONIX ON A BAD WEATHER DAY P: CHRIS MORAN

GIVEN A SEASON YOU CAN EVEN BUILD YOUR OWN TOBAGGAN TRACK R: CHRIS MORAN L: MERIBEL P: NICK HAMILTON

Kicking Horse

Though little developed as yet, Kicking Horse boasts Canada's best inbounds terrain and an infrastructure that ought to see it live up to its promise. The Canadian super resort of tomorrow? Maybe.

If you like this …
… try Fernie ▸▸p74, or Jackson Hole ▸▸p362.

The Town

Kicking Horse may not be a name you've heard before, but it's steadily beginning to pervade the general snowboarding consciousness in the way that Fernie did some 10 years ago. It's only a few years old and currently there's not much to speak of at the resort itself, with most of the action taking place in the base town of Golden, a 10-minute drive away and linked to the resort by a regular shuttle bus. However, Kicking Horse is five years into a 15-year development plan and there are huge amounts of money being spent. Get in there and experience it now so that you're one of those who can say 'I was there before …'

Sleeping In resort, the **Glacier** and **Mountaineer** lodges offer luxury self-catering apartments. Book online at kickinghorseresort.com. Down in Golden you'll find a range of motels, motor inns, hostels and B&B. **Kicking Horse Hostel** (kickinghorsehostel .com) and **Packer's Place Inn** (T250 344 5951) are both cheap and cheerful. **Ramada Limited** (ramadagolden.com) is a bit pricier, with an indoor pool and hot tub and high speed internet. **A Quiet Corner** (aquietcorner.com) is a good B&B. There's extensive info on all accommodation on the resort's website.

Eating The **Horse Thief Café** for snacks and coffee, **Extreme Peaks** for drinks, burgers and salads etc, or **Sushi Kuma** for some Japanese flavour (evening reservations required), all at the base of the resort right in front of the gondola. **The Local Hero** (T250 344 7220) pub lays on a buffet curry night on Thursdays.

You can splash out on lunch at the **Eagle's Eye Restaurant** (T250 349 5424) at the top of the gondola, but you'll need to book in advance. Self-catering is a good option, and you can get pretty much everything you'd need at the **Kicking Horse General Store** or at **Overwaitea Foods** in Golden.

Bars and clubs **Extreme Peaks** and **The Local Hero** pubs are the town's watering holes. **Extreme Peaks** is great at après, whilst **The Local Hero** is Scottish themed and has a good selection of malt whiskies. **Packers Place Inn & Pub** in Golden puts on live music and DJs, and opens until 0200.

Shopping The general store in resort is surprisingly well stocked, if a little pricey. **Darkside Snowboards & Skateboards** (darksidegolden.com) in Golden is the best place for snowboarding related paraphernalia.

Health The **Glacier** and **Mountaineer** lodges have their own fitness rooms and outdoor hot tubs. **Kutenai Massage Therapy** (T250 344 6770) in Golden for a range of massage services.

Internet **Kicking Horse General** store has a couple of terminals.

Transfer options Rocky Mountain Sky Shuttle (rockymountainskyshuttle.com) for transfers from Calgary.

Local partners None.

R: EWAN WALLACE P: TASH

The Mountain

Were it not for the three ridges (Redemption, CPR and Terminator) at the top of the hill, Kicking Horse would simply be a very good Canadian treeline resort. Throw the ridges into the mix and it becomes hands down the best freeriding resort in Canada. There are a multitude of marked (but unpisted) runs coming off down the length of the ridges into three bowls (Bowl Over, Crystal Bowl and Feuz Bowl) with terrain that's simply out of this world. Go there and see for yourself.

Beginners Kicking Horse is perfect for beginners. The Pony Express magic carpet lift will take care of first timers, while the greens and blues in the Slow Skiing Zone in the lower section of the mountain (up the Catamount chair) are perfect for those who can already turn.

Intermediate Head up the Golden Eagle Express and drop down into the Crystal Bowl. If you stick skier's right there are some brilliant hits on the side of the piste, and a couple of good cat tracks to launch off. There are some nicely spaced trees on the lower half of the mountain on the way back down to the Golden Eagle Express,

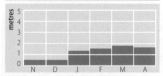

I moved to Kicking Horse for the unbelievable big-mountain terrain. The big alpine, steep trees, backcountry and dry snow all make Kicking Horse one of the best places on earth.

Mike McPhee, photographer and Golden resident

but be careful not to head to far skier's left or you'll end up out of bounds.
Advanced On a powder day, take the Stairway To Heaven lift and hike to the top of Redemption Ridge. Drop into the Feuz Bowl and huck yourself off every drop you can find, just like the locals. Whether they land or not doesn't seem to be the issue, it's the hucking that counts. It's infectious, as is the whooping – everyone in Kicking Horse whoops. You should also head down CPR Ridge and drop in skier's left, where you'll find lines and drops aplenty. There are a total of 70 inbounds chutes in Kicking Horse, and they're all fair game – go kitted up with all the avalanche safety gear.
Kids Get them up and running on the Jelly Bean run, off the Pony Express magic carpet.
Flat light days The entire lower section of the mountain is awash with trees, so stay low and take your pick.

P: EWAN WALLACE P: TASH

☺ LOCALS DO

- Ride very fast.
- Like dropping cliffs.
- Whoop a lot on powder days.

☹ LOCALS DON'T

- Live in Kicking Horse – Golden is much cheaper and there's way more going on.
- Seem to have an unfriendly bone in their bodies.
- Mind making huge bomb holes. It adds to the fun!

✓ PROS

- Some of the best inbounds terrain in Canada.
- Good snowfall.
- More good drops and cliffs than you can shake a stick at.

✗ CONS

- Lacks a decent park.
- Quite far from any major airports.
- Small.

◉ NOT TO MISS

Lunch in the excellent Eagle's Eye restaurant, the highest restaurant in Canada at 2347 m. Locally caught salmon is the speciality.

ⓘ REMEMBER TO AVOID

Straying into one of the permanently closed avalanche areas. There are several, all clearly marked on the piste map, and they're closed for a reason.

❄ SNOW DEPTH

metres	N	D	J	F	M	A
5 4 3 2 1 0						

☺ RELIVE A FAMOUS MOMENT

Kicking Horse featured in one of the first ever moving pictures – a 1901 picture entitled *Panoramic View: Kicking Horse Canyon*.

1190 m	TOWN ALTITUDE
264 km	KM TO AIRPORT
YYC	AIRPORT
★★☆	VEGETARIAN RATING
★★☆	INTERNET CAFES
★☆☆	RIDE IN/RIDE OUT
2450 m	HIGHEST LIFT
1260 m	VERTICAL DROP
2750	RIDEABLE AREA (IN ACRES)
runs not measured	KM OF PISTES
1	NURSERY AREAS
32/0/74	RUNS: BEG/INTER/ADV
0/0	FUNICULAR/CABLE CARS
1/3	GONDOLAS/CHAIRS
1	DRAGS
no	NIGHT RIDING
1	PARKS
0	PIPE
no	SUMMER AREAS
☆☆☆ ☆☆☆	ENVIRONMENTAL RATING
⑤⑤⑤	COST INDICATOR
CANADA KICKING HORSE	

Kimberley

The Town

Given the company it's keeping in this book, the decision to include Kimberley might seem a strange one. True, it doesn't have the majesty of Chamonix, the scale of Verbier or the 'out there' factor of Shemshak, but as a family resort we think it's second to none – small, friendly and well situated at only 20 minutes' drive from Cranbrook airport. Kimberley proper (a former mining town turned Bavarian theme town, five minutes' drive from the resort) is a viable alternative for accommodation and offers more in the way of services and entertainment.

Sleeping Those on a budget should plump for one of the many B&Bs or motels in Kimberley town. Staying in resort is a bit more costly but the service and facilities are excellent. The **Purcell Rocky Mountain Condo Hotel** (purcellrocky.com) is good value, from CAN$85 per night, or if you fancy splashing out then opt for the stately **Trickle Creek Residence Inn** (T250 427 5175).

Eating The Stemwinder Bar & Grill or Slopeside Coffee & Deli for snacks (the latter serves Starbucks coffee). **Kelsey's Bar & Grill** in the Trickle Creek Marriot Hotel is good for evening meals if you want to stay in resort, though Kimberley town offers plenty of choice. Try **The Old Bauernhaus Restaurant** for authentic German cuisine. The building is a 350- year-old Bavarian structure that was taken apart, shipped to Canada and rebuilt in Kimberley. The **Snowdrift Café** (Bavarian Platz) has tasty vegetarian meals.

Bars and clubs Possibilities are limited in resort, but The **Stemwinder Bar & Grill** is your best bet. You'll find regular live entertainment at **McBee's**, The 'Brook and The Ozone Pub in Kimberley town.

Shopping Sports Alpine in the resort plaza will take care of all your snowboarding needs, and Kimberley town has three supermarkets.

Health Try Denai Bell (T250 427 0756) for hot stone massage, shiatsu, reflexology, raindrop therapy and reiki.

Internet Most hotels have wireless broadband access.

Transfer options It's best to get a domestic flight into Cranbrook airport, which is a short taxi ride from

Kimberley is some of the best fun you could ever have in a whiteout. It's totally within the treeline so flat light is never a problem.

Nelson Pratt, pro snowboarder

Kimberley. Otherwise you can get a **Greyhound** (greyhound.ca) from Calgary, but it takes around six hours.

Local partners Fernie.

Good snowfall, beginner friendly snowpark and great tree runs – Kimberley is British Columbia's premier family destination.

🌒 *If you like this . . .*
. . . try Banff/Sunshine ▶▶*p70, or Bansko* ▶▶*p100.*

CANADA
KIMBERLEY

R. MARCUS CHAPMAN P. TASH

The Mountain

Small, relatively flat and perfectly suited to learners and families it may be, but don't be put off – Kimberley has plenty to offer the more experienced snowboarder too. The pistes are immaculately well groomed, and since it's almost entirely within the treeline, on a powder day – frequent thanks to the resort's good snowfall – there's a huge range of really fun gladed tree runs to explore, without the worry of getting into too much trouble. There's also a well maintained funpark replete with nicely shaped small-to-medium kickers and an array of rails.

Beginners First timers can find their feet on the Owl Learning Area right at the base of the resort. There's a magic carpet and two draglifts to practice on. Next port of call will be the North Star Express chairlift, which offers a large selection of easy blue runs and a couple of greens back down to the resort.

Intermediate The back side of the resort is where all the steeper terrain is

to be found. There are a large number of short black runs and some great trees to explore, accessible from the Tamarack Double and Easter Triple chairs. Make sure you catch the Pine Flats or Ridgeway tracks at the bottom, which mark the boundary of the ski area. Also make sure you have a few runs in the park – there's nothing too challenging here, so it's ideal for learning new tricks.

Advanced On a powder day the whole resort turns into one long tree-lined playground, but in average conditions advanced riders will exhaust Kimberley's possibilities fairly quickly. There are a number of natural hits to be found on the steeper backside of the resort, but the patrol don't like any kicker building antics and will tell you to knock them down. There are some tasty looking steeps to the skier's right of the North Star Express chair which you can see from the bottom, but these are out of the resort boundary and are hence unpatrolled. Make sure you check with a ski patroller before you go.

Kids Kimberley Kruisers kids program will take six-12-year olds off your hands from 1130-1530. The programme includes specialist instruction and lunch.

Flat light days Not a problem here!

⊚ OPENING TIMES

Mid-Dec to early Apr: 0900-1600
(Thu-Sat also 1730-2100)

⊖ RESORT PRICES

Week pass (6 days): CAN$329
Day pass: CAN$49
Season pass: CAN$659-779

① DIRECTORY

Tourist office: T250 427 4881
Medical centre: T250 427 4861
Pisteurs: T250 427 4881
Taxi: T250 427 4442
Local radio: Radio 102.9 FM
Website: skikimberley.com

R: RYAN DAVIS R: TASH

☺ LOCALS DO

- Ride the trees in between the pistes.
- Covertly slide the blue handrail beside the Purcell Condo Hotel by night.
- Become very good at jibbing and riding trees.

☹ LOCALS DON'T

- Build kickers – the ski patrol veto them quick.
- Get too het up about anything – it's a mellow place.
- Mind showing visitors the best spots.

✔ PROS

- Perfect for beginners and families.
- Nicely spaced out trees.
- Very friendly atmosphere.

✖ CONS

- No proper steeps.
- In the absence of powder, advanced riders will tire of the place quickly.
- Small.

◉ NOT TO MISS

Night riding under the Northstar Express chair. It's open 1730 till 2100 Thursday to Saturday night.

① REMEMBER TO AVOID

Missing the tracks back from the backside of the resort.

❄ SNOW DEPTH

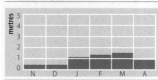

◉ RELIVE A FAMOUS MOMENT

Kim Cattrall (Samantha from *Sex in the City*) is a regular visitor to the resort, and has been known to take part in celebrity fundraisers.

1230 m	TOWN ALTITUDE
20 km	KM TO AIRPORT
YYC	AIRPORT
★★★	VEGETARIAN RATING
★★★	INTERNET CAFES
★★★	RIDE IN/RIDE OUT
1982 m	HIGHEST LIFT
752 m	VERTICAL DROP
1800	RIDEABLE AREA (IN ACRES)
50 km	KM OF PISTES
1	NURSERY AREAS
34/0/45	RUNS: BEG/INTER/ADV
0/0	FUNICULAR/CABLE CARS
0/4	GONDOLAS/CHAIRS
4	DRAGS
yes	NIGHT RIDING
1	PARKS
0	PIPE
no	SUMMER AREAS
★★★	ENVIRONMENTAL RATING
$$$	COST INDICATOR

CANADA
KIMBERLEY

Lake Louise

The Town

Lake Louise epitomizes the rugged natural beauty of the Banff national park, a 2564-square mile region of the Canadian Rockies encompassing the Canadian Continental Divide and an awful lot of Douglas Fir trees. Though the name looms large in the world of winter sports, Lake Louise is in fact a hamlet on the edge of the lake, itself pretty small. Though don't let that put you off – the mountain is amazing, and it really is picture postcard Canada at its finest.

Sleeping Options are very limited. The most cost effective way is to go with one of the major tour operators such as **Inghams** (inghams.co.uk). Medium priced possibilities include **Baker Creek Chalets** (T403 522 3761) and **Deer Lodge** (T403 522 3747), the latter having a very scenic rooftop hot tub. For proper blow-out style opulence try Lake Louise's landmark **Fairmont Chateau Lake Louise** (fairmont.com/lakelouise). Good enough for Marilyn Monroe, good enough for you.

Eating For a value self-service lunch on the mountain head to **The Great Bear Room** (T403 522 3555). Also try **Sawyers Nook** (T403 522 3555) (upstairs at the **Temple Lodge**) and **Kokanee Kabin** (T403 522 3555). Many of the hotels in town have good restaurants, notably the **Post Hotel** (T403 522 3989), the **Deer Lodge** (T403 522 3747) and the **Fairmont Chateau Lake Louise** (T403 522 3511) which has four. Also try **Timber Wolf Pizza** (T403 522 3791) at the **Lake Louise Inn**.

Bars and clubs For après-riding beers and snacks head to the **Powder Keg** or the **Sitzmark Inn**. For evening drinks there's the **Walliser Stube Wine Bar** (in the **Fairmont Chateau Lake Louise**). The party scene in Lake Louise is non-existent so follow the locals' lead and head into Banff if you're after a lively night out.

Shopping The shopping scene in Lake Louise is dead, so the 45-minute drive into Banff is well worthwhile.

Health Check out the **Banff Upper Hot Springs** (parkscanada.gc.ca /hotsprings).

Internet Hotels in Lake Louise have internet access, and there are numerous internet cafés in Banff.

> The Lake has in my opinion some of the most easily accessible backcountry in Canada. You can get crazy back there or just take it easy. If it's on hill you want, Lake Louise's long runs and inbounds features make it one of the most fun mountains in Canada. They make a damn good caesar there too …
>
> *Andrew Hardingham, pro snowboarder, Banff resident*

Transfer options Rocky Mountain Sky Shuttle (rockymountainskyshuttle.com) for transfers from Calgary.

Local partners Banff (Norquay & Sunshine). See skibig3.com for details.

Canada's most stunning resort also has one of the largest areas of all North American resorts. Along with three good funparks, this makes up for the somewhat soporific nightlife.

If you like this …
… *try Banff/Sunshine* ▶p70, *or Engelberg* ▶p312.

☺ **OPENING TIMES**

Early Nov to early May: 0900-1600

💲 **RESORT PRICES**

Week pass (6 days): CAN$384 (CAN$414 peak). Prices drop by CAN$2 per day on passes of seven or more days.
Day pass: CAN$64 (CAN$69 peak)
Season pass: CAN$939

☺ **DIRECTORY**

Tourist office: T403 256 8473
Medical centre: T403 522 2184
Pisteurs: T403 522 3555
Taxi: T403 522 3833
Local radio: 106.5 Mountain FM
Website: skilouise.com

The Mountain

In terms of high speed piste cruising, you won't find many resorts in Canada to better 'the Lake', as it's locally known. There's also an extensive variety of inbound freeride terrain on the backside of the mountain, and some easily accessible backcountry for the more intrepid. This place really is massive, and you'd be hard pressed to find a more picturesque resort. There are three excellent parks with the area's best shaped jumps and a regular shuttle bus links the town with the slopes.

Beginners The Sunnyside beginner centre at the base area is the best starting point – it has an easy draglift and two magic carpets. Next, head to the Glacier Express quad and have a few runs on the beginners-only green run to the base. When you're ready to move on try the green and blue runs off the Grizzly Express gondola. More confident riders could head to the Larch area and try out the Marmot beginner park.

Intermediate Head to the Larch area on the backside of the mountain,

and spend the morning lapping the Larch Express quad. There are some great pistes through the trees, and a fun little park. Take the Ptarmigan quad then drop back down to the base area for lunch at the **Ten Peaks Lodge**. In the afternoon, take the Top Of The World chair then have a few runs on the Summit Platter drag, then spend the remainder of the day getting to grips with the Eagle Plains park under the Glacier Express quad.

Advanced If the snow is good then head over to the backside and check out the bowls. There are some obvious drops to be had in Paradise and East bowls, and some good lines down the E-R Face. If conditions aren't great then warm up with a cruise on the Top Of The World chair then spend the day in the Juniper park. It's set up for experienced riders, so there are some fairly large jumps with lots of pop, as well as plenty of rails, a couple of hips and a quarterpipe.

Kids Under fives get a free lift pass. Bring proof of age.

Flat light days The Lake is great on flat light days due to all those trees. All three parks are totally within the treeline so they stay on during whiteouts, and there are plenty of pistes on the front side that retain good visibility.

☺ LOCALS DO
- Go for an ice skate on the frozen lake behind Chateau Lake Louise.
- Enjoy an après-riding beer at Wild Bill's in Banff.
- Enjoy a swim in the Upper Hot Springs.

☹ LOCALS DON'T
- Feed the wildlife.
- Sleep in on a powder day.
- Let friends go to Whistler.

✔ PROS
- Long winter season with reliable snow.
- The perfect place for learning to ride park.
- Stunningly beautiful scenery.

✖ CONS
- Quiet. The town is essentially an expensive hamlet servicing the resort, and the nearest civilization (Banff) is a 45-minute drive away.
- Some of the inbounds off-piste terrain remains frustratingly closed. La Grave this ain't…
- Granted, the area is large, but not nearly as large as the marketing campaign would have you believe.

☀ NOT TO MISS
A powder day on the fabled backside. Get there before it gets tracked.

ⓘ REMEMBER TO AVOID
Driving behind a snowplough.

❄ SNOW DEPTH

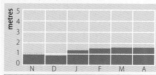

☺ RELIVE A FAMOUS MOMENT
Stay at the Fairmont Chateau Lake Louise like Marilyn Monroe did during the filming of *River Of No Return*, starring herself and Robert Mitchum.

R: CHRIS MORAN P: NICK HAMILTON

1646 m	TOWN ALTITUDE
185 km	KM TO AIRPORT
YYC	AIRPORT
★★☆	VEGETARIAN RATING
★★★	INTERNET CAFES
★☆☆	RIDE IN/RIDE OUT
2637 m	HIGHEST LIFT
991 m	VERTICAL DROP
4200	RIDEABLE AREA (IN ACRES)
runs not measured	KM OF PISTES
1	NURSERY AREAS
28/51/34	RUNS: BEG/INTER/ADV
0/0	FUNICULAR/CABLE CARS
1/5	GONDOLAS/CHAIRS
2	DRAGS
no	NIGHT RIDING
2	PARKS
1	PIPE
no	SUMMER AREAS
★★★☆	ENVIRONMENTAL RATING
	COST INDICATOR

CANADA
LAKE LOUISE

Whistler

The Town

Whistler/Blackcomb (everyone refers to the twin mountain resort as simply 'Whistler') looms like a giant. Along with a few other ski resort superpowers, its very name conjures up images of the best of everything that winter sports have to offer: abundant light powder, flawless snowboarding parks, a huge accessible backcountry area and a kick-ass town to match.

Sleeping Cheap accommodation can be found at the **Shoe String Lodge** at **Nesters**. **Seasonaires** (seasonaires.com) can help you out in arranging a variety of shared houses and properties for seasonal lets. For families or those looking for hotel accommodation, the **Holiday Inn** is in the middle of the village.
Eating For food on the move, the **PitaPit** above the Royal Bank offers exceptional burgers, sandwiches and wraps. For a sit down affair try **The Brewhouse** in the village or **The Alpine Café** out of town. Vegetarians should try the excellent **Ingrid's Village Café** (T403 932 7000).

Bars and clubs The clubbing options are endless in Whistler – every night is party night. For big name DJs up from Vancouver check out **Garfunkels**. **The Boot** comes highly recommended from the recently visiting British Snowboard Team.

Shopping For snow related gear, **The Circle**. Those on a real budget take the bus down to **Function Junction**.

Internet There are seven internet cafés and wireless access.

Health Try Melissa, a keen snowboarder at **Solarice Wellness Centre and Spa**.

Transfer options You can get a direct transfer from Whistler to Vancouver Airport with **Perimeter** (perimeterbus.com).

Local partners None.

The King of North American resorts – Whistler strives to be the world's best snowboard destination and many would argue it succeeds.

*If you like this ...
... try Big White ▸▸p72, Aspen ▸▸p348, Mammoth Mountain ▸▸p366, or Vail ▸▸p376.*

☺ OPENING TIMES
Late Nov to late Apr:
0830/0900-1500/1600
Early Jun to late Jul: 1100-1500

⊙ RESORT PRICES
Week pass (6 days): CAN$317-426
Day pass: CAN$73-75 (CAN$47 summer)
Season pass: CAN$1639

ⓘ DIRECTORY
Tourist office: T604 932 3434
Medical centre: T604 932 4911
Pisteurs: T604 932 4211
Taxi: T604 938 1515
Local radio: 102.1FM Mountain Radio
Website: whistlerblackcomb.com

The Mountain

The mountains of Whistler and Blackcomb cater to each and every need, with the same high speed quads delivering families to wide rolling runs and extreme thrill seekers to ridges and cliff drops that provide some of the world's most accessible freeriding. The people at Whistler Blackcomb have really thought of everything. Three immaculately maintained snowparks for the park rats, avalanche controlled bowls for the powder junkies and speed managed 'Family Zones' for those taking their tentative first turns in their sliding career. There's simply too much to do in a week, a season or a lifetime which explains why so many professional snowboarders choose Whistler as their home and playground.

Beginners Master those turns and gain some confidence on the super friendly Magic Chair at the bottom of Blackcomb. When you've dialled the falling leaf in the safety of the speed controlled Yellow Brick Road hop, on the Whistler gondola all the way to the top. Reward yourself with lunch at the **Round House** and finish up your day on the mellow runs around the Emerald Chair, Marmot, Sidewinder and Lower Whiskey Jack.
Intermediate Head up the Blackcomb gondola and explore the variety of intermediate runs stemming from the Solar Coaster and Jersey Cream chairlifts. Finish your day by ascending Peak Chair to the top of the world, before cruising Highway 86 all the way from the Peak to Creekside.
Advanced If there is snow, explore the wonders of the Flute and Whistler Bowls. If you've got your helmet,

> Simply the most obvious choice for people looking for an alternative to any of the European super resorts.
>
> *Elliot Neave, pro Snowboarder*

advanced pass and balls packed in your backpack, go check out the advanced Blackcomb Park for some truly state of the art jumps and rails.
Kids Kids six and under get a free pass when accompanied by an adult. Whistler Kids (T877 932 0606) provides a variety of different on mountain lessons and childcare services.
Flat light days Staying away from the Peak/Glacier areas and sticking to the alpine/lower areas of the mountain is the obvious option. Due to the huge amount of tree terrain on both Whistler and Blackcomb there's a wealth of stuff to ride on bad weather days. Crystal Chair on Blackcomb is always a favourite.

P: WHISTLER TOURISM

☺ LOCALS DO
◉ Get up early on powder days and queue for Peak Chair to open up for untracked bowls of pow.
◉ Know how to get into the 'Bear Proof' bins without making a scene.
◉ Wear a helmet in the park – no lid and you can't ride.

☹ LOCALS DON'T
✗ Snake lift lines.
✗ Share knowledge of their secret powder stashes.
✗ Throw out their beer cans and bottles – they can be recycled to pay for… MORE BEER! Genius.

✓ PROS
◉ Mind-blowing terrain.
◉ Trees ensure you can ride in all weather.
◉ Incredible customer service on and off the hill.

✗ CONS
✗ It's not cheap!
✗ Proximity to coast means powder is fairly heavy – not that light-as-air sparkly stuff.
✗ Lack of affordable seasonal accommodation.

◐ NOT TO MISS
Whistler Heli-Skiing Canada offer heli-boarding trips catering for various levels of ability (T604 932 4105).

ⓘ REMEMBER TO AVOID
At peak times, central chairs such as Emerald on Whistler become exceptionally busy – check out some alternative terrain to avoid the queues.

❆ SNOW DEPTH

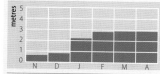

☺ RELIVE A FAMOUS MOMENT
Adam Sandler's *Happy Gilmore* was filmed extensively at the Furry Creek Golf and Country Club in town. Take a running tee-off in his honour.

653 m to 675 m	TOWN ALTITUDE
120 km	KM TO AIRPORT
YVR	AIRPORT
★★★	VEGETARIAN RATING
★★★	INTERNET CAFES
★★☆	RIDE IN/RIDE OUT
2284 m	HIGHEST LIFT
1609 m	VERTICAL DROP
8172	RIDEABLE AREA (IN ACRES)
runs not measured	KM OF PISTES
3	NURSERY AREAS
40/110/50	RUNS: BEG/INTER/ADV
0/0	FUNICULAR/CABLE CARS
3/18	GONDOLAS/CHAIRS
12	DRAGS
yes	NIGHT RIDING
3	PARKS
3	PIPE
yes	SUMMER AREAS
★★☆	ENVIRONMENTAL RATING
$$$	COST INDICATOR
CANADA	
WHISTLER	

Eastern Europe & the Middle East

R: EWAN WALLACE L: SHEMSHAK, IRAN P: JAMES

Ewan Wallace reaping the sweet rewards of far-flung travel in Dog Valley, Shemshak.

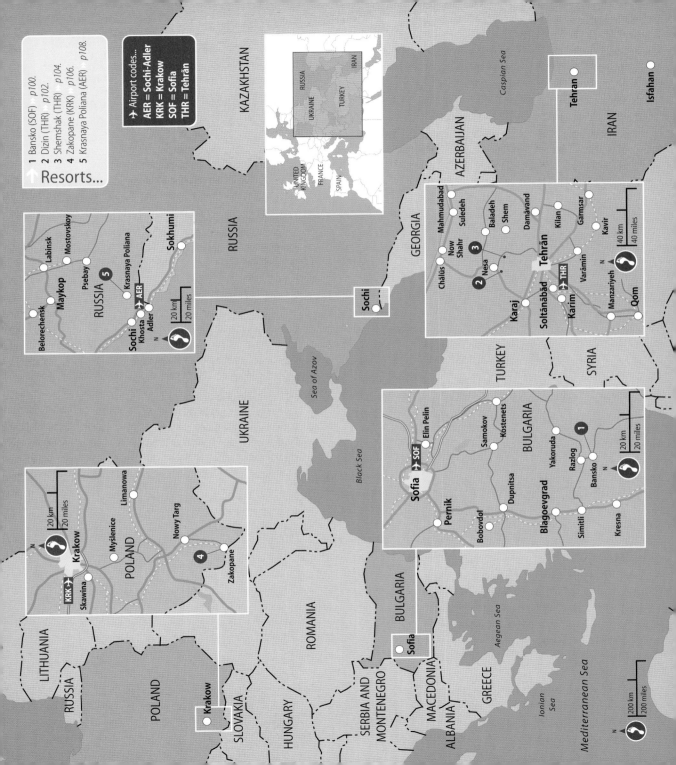

Resorts...

1 Bansko (SOF) → p100.
2 Dizin (THR) → p102.
3 Shemshak (THR) → p104.
4 Zakopane (KRK) → p106.
5 Krasnaya Poliana (AER) → p108.

✈ Airport codes...
AER = Sochi-Adler
KRK = Krakow
SOF = Sofia
THR = Tehrān

KAZAKHSTAN

RUSSIA

Caspian Sea

GEORGIA

AZERBAIJAN

Tehran

IRAN

Isfahan

Mahmudabad
Suledeh
Baladeh
Shem
Damāvand
Kilan
Garmsar
Now Shahr
Chālūs
3
2 Nesa
Tehrān
Kavir
✈ THR
Varāmin
Karim
Manzariyeh
Qom
Karaj
Soltānābād

40 km
40 miles

Labinsk
Mostovskoy
Maykop
Psebay
Krasnaya Poliana
5
Belorechensk
RUSSIA
AER
Sokhumi
Sochi
Khosta
Adler

20 km
20 miles

Sochi

TURKEY

SYRIA

Elin Pelin
Samokov
Kostenets
✈ SOF
Sofia
Yakoruda
Razlog
1
Bansko
BULGARIA
Pernik
Bobovdol
Dupnitsa
Blagoevgrad
Simitli
Kresna

20 km
20 miles

Limanowa
Myślenice
Nowy Targ
✈ KRK
Krakow
Skawina
POLAND
4
Zakopane

20 km
20 miles

UKRAINE

Sea of Azov

Black Sea

Krakow

LITHUANIA

RUSSIA

POLAND

SLOVAKIA

HUNGARY

ROMANIA

SERBIA AND MONTENEGRO

BULGARIA

Sofia

MACEDONIA

ALBANIA

GREECE

Aegean Sea

Ionian Sea

Mediterranean Sea

200 km
200 miles

Introduction

As snowboarding broadens its horizons, new areas are gradually opening up as intrepid riders seek to escape the mainstream. That's why Bulgaria, Iran, Poland and Russia are highlighted here. As snowboarding destinations, each offers something slightly different to the essentially homogenized riding experience that is snowboarding in Europe or North America.

Another interesting point about this collection of resorts is that they are little microcosms of their respective societies. As a new member of the EU, Bulgaria is trying to match its EU counterparts in terms of tourism, and in their day-to-day dealings with tourists they put a country such as France to shame. Poland is similar, though slightly further behind the Bulgarians in terms of how much the tourist industry has developed. In Russia, there's no central government controlling tourism so, very much like the rest of the country, it's a free-for-all. Krasnaya Poliana reflects the black market economy of Russia as a whole, so expect to get ripped off, and expect to pay bribes. Meanwhile, the Iranian government's attitude to tourism could be described as disinterested at best. But as appears to be the case in much of Iran, governmental opinion doesn't reflect that of the masses, and the private sector is awash with individuals who recognize the country's potential and are doing what they can to promote it.

The irony is that it's these idiosyncrasies that make these destinations more appealing for snowboarders. Fifteen years ago people were just happy to go riding where they could. As resorts became more crowded, the travelling habits of snowboarders correspondingly became more sophisticated as people began to look further afield for something new. Underdeveloped towns and antiquated lift systems – things that in the past would have seemed like massive failings in any resort – just add to the experience. It's a trend that will no doubt continue as people venture further and further away from the mainstream.

Eastern Europe & the Middle East rating

Value for money
★★★★★

Nightlife
★★★☆☆

Freestyle
★★★☆☆

Freeride
★★★★☆

Essentials

"Travelling is an integral part of snowboarding for me. Stepping off the beaten track and leaving familiarity behind can add an entirely different dimension to a snowboard trip. Experiencing new environments and different ways of living brings rewards all of its own. The most important thing that snowboarding has given me has been the opportunity to expand my horizons. It's hard to forget the feeling of cranking a turn in bottomless powder but when I'm too old to strap in anymore the memories that I'll hold tightest will be the places I've been and the people that I've met along the way." James McPhail, snowboarding photographer.

Getting there

Bulgaria Sofia is the nearest airport to Bansko, and carriers include **Bulgaria Air** (bulgaria-air.co.uk), **British Airways** (ba.com) and **Alitalia** (alitalia.com).

Iran Iran's major international airport is Tehran. Carriers include **British Airways** (ba.com), **Aeroflot** (aeroflot.co.uk), **Air France** (airfrance.com), **Gulf Air** (gulfairco.com) and **Lufthansa** (lufthansa.com).

Poland The nearest airport to Zakopane is Krakow, and carriers include **Lot** (lot.com), **Lufthansa** (lufthansa.com), **British Airways** (ba.com), **Swiss** (swiss.com) and **Alitalia** (alitalia.com).

Russia Sochi-Adler is the nearest airport to Krasnaya Poliana, so you'll need to get an internal flight from Moscow. Carriers to Moscow include **British Airways** (ba.com), **Swiss** (swiss.com), **KLM** (klm.com), **Transaero** (transaero.com) and **Aeroflot** (aeroflot.co.uk). Aeroflot operate flights from Moscow to Sochi-Adler.

Red tape

Visitors to Iran require visas, which are available from the Iranian Embassy. It's a good idea to apply well in advance. All passports must be valid for a minimum period of six months after arrival. If you overstay your visa you may be required to remain in Iran until the

Top tips

- Think seriously about getting a package deal. English is not widely spoken and having someone take care of all your travel and accommodation arrangements can make life much easier.

- If you're going to Iran, make sure you take enough cash to cover your entire stay as ATMs and credit cards are not useable.

- Take all your snowboarding kit with you. Many of the resorts lack the sort of facilities that might be taken for granted elsewhere.

- If you're going to Iran or Russia, take some interesting things to give to the locals – T-shirts, magazines, CDs etc. In Iran this will stoke people out; in Russia it'll come in handy when trying to bribe someone.

- Learn some local phrases. People won't expect you to speak their language, but they'll be delighted that you bothered to try. A little effort goes a long way.

situation has been resolved. Women should wear a headscarf in visa application photos.

All visitors to Russia require a visa, which must be registered with the local branch of the Ministry of Internal Affairs within three working days of arrival in Russia, though most major hotels will do this automatically. Visa applications are normally processed within 15 working days. In addition, you must fill in a migration card. Note that if your passport has less than six months to run, you may be refused entry to Russia. British nationals do not require a visa to enter Bulgaria or Poland.

Getting around

Thanks to the difficulties in reading road signs, getting around can present a whole new set of problems. Getting some sort of package deal with a native speaker to sort out your travel arrangements is by far the easiest option. If driving, note that there's a zero tolerance policy on drink driving in Poland and Russia, and of course alcohol is strictly off limits in Iran. Each of the four countries drive on the right, and all but Poland require an International Driving Licence (IDP). It's also a legal requirement that you carry original vehicle registration papers, ownership documents and insurance papers at all times (this also applies to rental cars). In Russia, visiting motorists who have held a driving licence for less than two years must not exceed 70 kph. Beware of traffic police, who are generally corrupt and issue fines on the slightest pretext.

Car hire Most major hire car companies (europcar.com, e-sixt.co.uk, hertz.com) have offices in airports and cities in Poland, Bulgaria and Russia. **Europcar** (europcar.com) have offices in central Tehran and Tehran airport. Usual age restrictions apply.

Eastern Europe & Middle East price guide (in €)

	☕	🍴	💳	📞	@	📰	🥫
Bulgaria	1,18	1,80	1,80	0,50	2,50	1,55	N/a
Iran	0,20	N/a	0,45	0,45	0,35	0,60	N/a
Note: tourists are likely to pay up to three times these prices							
Poland	1,50	1,30	1,50	0,60	1,30	1,30	N/a
Russia	1,35	0,85	1,60	0,50	1,45	4,30	N/a

Public transport

In all cases the language barrier (both spoken and written) means that using public transport can be trying. In Russia, for example, public transport workers may be on the hunt for bribes, while security on internal flights is not high. The metro in Moscow, however, is recommended: it's cheap, simple to navigate and beautiful. Taxis are cheap and easy in Iran, but make sure you use official ones and accept that you'll pay around three times as much as an Iranian. Also steer clear of internal flights here. Poland has a decent public transport network. Make sure you validate tickets for buses, trams and the metro before travelling (punch them at the yellow machines in the entrance to metro stations or on board buses and trams). If you're caught without a valid ticket you'll be fined around PLN 120. Tickets can be bought at most newspaper stands and kiosks. Taxis are the best way to get about Bulgaria – they're cheap and plentiful but beware of getting overcharged. There are cheap and extensive public transport networks in the larger cities.

Opening hours and traditions

Of all the countries here, it's Iran that's likely to prove the most different for foreign visitors, though it's fairly easy to steer clear of

→ Fact file

Bulgaria
Currency: Leva (BGN)
Exchange rate:
  €1 = BGN 1.95
Time zone: GMT +2
Country code: +359
Ambulance: T150
Police: T166
Fire: T160

Iran
Currency: Iranian Rial (IRR)
Exchange rate:
  €1 = IRR 11,603
Time zone: GMT +3.5
Country code: +98
Ambulance: T115
Police: T110
Fire: T125

Poland
Currency: Zlotych (PLN)
Exchange rate:
  €1 = PLN 3.95
Time zone: GMT +2
Country code +48
Ambulance: T999
Police: T997
Fire: T998

Russia
Currency: Ruble (RUB)
Exchange rate:
  €1 = RUB 34.35
Time zone: GMT +2-+12
Country code: +7
Ambulance: T03
Police: T02
Fire: T01

Lada money

It's a funny thing, drinking alcohol; you never know where you'll end up at the end of it. Russia, whether it be in a bar or on a domestic flight, is a place where it is almost rude and nigh on impossible to refuse a shot of vodka when offered. Needless to say, by the time the three-hour flight had landed in Sochi, a Black Sea town at the edge of the Caucasus, several bottles of spirits had been consumed. I was having difficulty standing up unassisted, let alone leaving the plane. That didn't seem to bother anyone else though; the plane remained half full of drunk Russians long after landing and the doors were opened.

Once out of the safe haven of the plane however, a foreigner is at the mercy of the authorities. A passport spotcheck by a couple of perambulating uniformed officers was their excuse to single me out from the crowd of inebriated locals waiting by the baggage claim. I was soon in a small holding room somewhere deep in the belly of the airport with a heavy-set policeman pushing a newspaper towards me. To one side of the car adverts -mostly for Ladas - was US$100 scrawled in black biro. The cop raised his eyebrows, pointed at me then the "fine notice" and left me to my thoughts, or perhaps to find my wallet.

Being a foreigner in a foreign land where you don't speak the language and they don't speak English can have its moments. In places like this, money is often the international language, and that's what they wanted to hear. They'd got a nice little earner going and I had, by being nice and sociable with a Russian called Dimitri, landed in their trap. Luckily the friends I had on the outside bailed me out for the bargain price of US$40. Whether it was the booze or a deep-rooted disrespect for authority that was stirred within me I don't know, but there was no way I was paying them US$100. Dimitri and all the other drunk Russians were, I noticed, not being fined. On my own in that little cell, I did learn how much it cost to buy a used Lada.

Dan Milner

P: DANMILNER.COM

trouble. Take care not to offend Islamic codes of behaviour – both sexes should dress conservatively with long trousers and sleeves, and women should wear headscarves in public. Alcohol is strictly forbidden to all save some religious minorities (such as Armenian Christians). Foreigners are not exempt. Relationships between non-Muslim men and Muslim women are illegal, as is adultery and homosexuality, the latter carrying a potential death sentence.

Drugs are treated very seriously by the authorities in Iran, Russia and Bulgaria, and there are severe penalties for possession which are strictly enforced. It's not a good idea to take photographs in airports in Iran, Bulgaria or Russia.

Office hours in Russia are 0900-1800, and this includes banks. Shops are open 1000-1900 Monday to Saturday, though in the larger cities they're often open on Sundays too. Poland runs on a slightly earlier programme of 0800-1600. In Bulgaria shops are usually open until 1900 Monday to Saturday and closed on Sunday, though there are an increasing number of 24-hour shops.

Eating

Bulgaria Bulgarian food is characterized by the national practice of cooking food slowly and at a low temperature. This gentle cooking brings out the unique flavours. Expect to eat plenty of fresh vegetables, eaten raw or stewed with meat in terracotta pots. There's also a lot of grilled meat, served with piquant sauces. A popular Bulgarian speciality is *banitsa*, a kind of cheese pie. You'll also find dishes like *sarmi*, vine leaves stuffed with minced meat, spices and rice. Salads are very popular, as are soups such as *Bob Chorba*, a traditional bean soup with herbs. *Rakiya* is a traditional Bulgarian spirit, often served with a salad to start a meal. There are plenty of vegetarian dishes but choice is often limited on restaurant menus. It's worth noting that the Bulgarians are valiantly trying to hide any trace of their national cuisine in the resorts. A major selling point is that the food here is cheap, and Bulgaria seems to attract the sort of clientele who are more interested in eating what they're familiar with, but at a fraction of the cost, rather than being adventurous.

Iran Iran is a huge country with an ancient and enormously diverse cuisine, but in Shemshak and Dizin it's pretty likely that you'll subsist on a diet of *chelow kabab* (literally 'rice and kebabs'). These are often served with a side dish of sliced raw onion and pieces of fresh orange. Iranians drink *doogh* with most main meals, a fermented, slightly fizzy yoghurt drink served with chopped mint, sometimes referred to as 'Iranian wine'.

A typical Iranian breakfast will consist of various flatbreads (such as *sangak*, *lavash* or *barbari*), honey, boiled eggs, cucumber, milk and a cheese very similar to feta called *panir*. Iranians drink a lot of hot, fragrant tea – *chai* – throughout the day, typically immediately before and after every meal. Outside of meal times it's usually served with a selection of sweet pastries on the side. Iranian food is often very spicy and fragrant, with saffron, cinnamon, dried limes and parsley being particularly popular ingredients. The concept of vegetarianism is uncommon.

Poland Polish cuisine is a mixture of Slavic and foreign influences. On the whole, it's hearty and relatively high in fat, protein and starch. Staples include red meat, potatoes, cheese and bread as well as various pies and dumplings. There are a lot of ingredients that foreigners will find unusual, such as sour cabbage, dried mushrooms, curdled milk and sour rye. Pickling is a very common practice in Poland – vegetables and fish such as herring from the Black Sea are all fair game, the latter being a massively popular national dish. The famous *kielbasa* sausages are also very popular.

Russia Russia is a vast country with a correspondingly vast range of culinary influences, and there are various ingredients which are not commonly found outside its borders. One example is *kvass*, a non-alcoholic or mildly alcoholic drink made from the fermentation of various products such as birch sap, berries, fruits, wheat, rye, barley and – most bizarrely – rye bread. Soups have traditionally played an important part in the Russian diet, and there are many different types: fish soups; *kvass*-based cold soups such as *okroshka* and *botvin'ya*; cabbage-based soups such as *shchi*; thick, salty and sour broths such as the spicy *solyanka*; grain- and vegetable-based soups and noodle soups with meat, mushrooms and milk. Sturgeon, salmon and freshwater crayfish are frequently used ingredients. Common main dishes include *pelmeni* (a sort of dumpling containing minced meat), *syrniki* (fried curd fritters served with sour cream, jam, honey, and/or apple sauce) and *katlyeti* (small pan-fried meat loaves normally made from pork or beef). A typical Russian breakfast might consist of *blini*, a type of thin pancake, served with sour cream.

Russia's most famous export, vodka, is of course very popular. It's usually drunk neat with meals, and there are several high quality brands that are difficult to come by outside Russia, most notably the delectable and massively popular *Standard*.

Language

Bulgaria Bulgarian is the national language. It uses the Cyrillic alphabet, so getting around can be tricky. English is widely spoken, particularly in the more tourist areas.

Iran Farsi (also known as Persian) is the national language in Iran, and uses a form of the Arabic alphabet, so unless you're a native speaker or an Arabic scholar then you can forget about reading the road signs. A surprising number of people speak English in Iran, particularly in larger cities such as Tehran and Isfahan.

Poland Polish is the national language. Poland is actively trying to develop its tourism industry so English is quite widely spoken.

Russia Russian is the main spoken language in the Russian Federation, and is written using the Cyrillic alphabet – including road signs and other travel information. This means that getting around can be a problem. English is not widely spoken.

Bulgaria is shaping up to be the next 'undiscovered' collection of resorts and they are not as basic as you think. It reminds me of Andorra six or seven years ago. A wicked little resort where everyone knew everyone and you always had a good time no matter what because everything was so reasonable. I think we have all got used to paying £4 a pint in resorts and £200 a week for a lift ticket. This brings it all back to being able to afford to go riding again.

Ash Newnes, snowboard instructor and Bansko resident

Crime/safety

Of the four countries here, Russia has had the most recent terrorist activity.

Petty crime occurs in all four countries, with pickpockets, robbery and mugging being a threat in Poland, Bulgaria and Russia. Pay particular attention in busy railway stations in Poland and Russia. Car theft is not unheard of in all the countries, but it's very common in Bulgaria. Violent crime is rare in all cases.

In Russia, it's not a good idea to leave drinks unattended in case they are spiked. Racially motivated attacks by groups of skinheads are not unheard of, particularly in the larger cities. Those of Asian or Afro-Caribbean descent should take extra care.

Driving in Poland can be hazardous. Most roads are narrow and poorly surfaced. The rate of deaths is 2½ times as high as it is in Britain. Driving in Iran can be downright frightening – according to the Iranian News Agency, Iran has one of the highest rates of road accidents of any country in the world.

Very few police and local authority officials will speak any English in any of the four countries.

Health

Comprehensive medical and travel insurance is recommended across the board here. British nationals are entitled to emergency medical treatment in Poland – obtain a European Health Insurance Card (EHIC) before leaving the UK. The EHIC is available free of charge through most UK post offices or through the UK Department of Health. In Iran, medical facilities are reasonable in the major cities but fairly poor in more remote areas. British nationals are entitled to free treatment in Russian hospitals. Tap water is not drinkable throughout the country – seek local advice or just stick to bottled water. Note that hospital staff in Bulgaria are unlikely to speak English.

Snowboarding Eastern Europe & the Middle East

"It's just booming. The snow is the best snow you can get here for powder. There aren't many people at the moment. There are going to be a lot more. And because Sochi has made an official bid for the 2014 Winter Olympics at the federal level, you've got a lot of money being allocated into developing the resort. Within the next two years I think there are going to be at least a dozen brand new lifts going in all around the resort and it's just exploding." Tom Rawlins, Krasnaya Poliana local

To pin down accurately the various different attributes of snowboarding in these four countries in such a small space is an impossibility. The region spans a massive distance both from north to south and east to west, and there are various mountain ranges and

Pros & cons

Pros …

- Cheapest snowboarding available to man. Well, save for Russia which is quickly becoming as expensive as Western Europe.
- Rewarding cultural experience, particularly in the case of Iran and – to a slightly lesser extent – Russia.
- Friendly and approachable people. With snowboarding being relatively young in most of the countries, people haven't had the chance to become jaded.
- Resorts are all less busy, particularly in Russia and Iran.
- The food. Opportunities for unusual gastronomic experiences are rife.

… and cons

- Mountains in Bulgaria and Poland are a poor man's Alps.
- Underdeveloped lift systems and resort infrastructure.
- In the case of Iran and Russia, the complications and expense of getting a visa can be a bane.
- The 'winter Ibiza' cliché could hardly be wheeled out to describe Iran's nightlife. Though this will undoubtedly delight some people.
- Communication difficulties – English isn't nearly as widely spoken as in other countries.

numerous seas in between. The difference in character is just as vast, ranging from the former Soviet Bloc starkness of Bulgaria and Poland, to the slight wackiness of Russia right up to the sheer otherworldliness of the Islamic Republic of Iran, a place which, at least for most of us, is likely to produce more than a mild culture shock. You won't find many state-of-the-art lifts, there's no one to hand you little bars of chocolate as you get on, and no one will tell you to have a nice day unless they genuinely want you to have one. And there are certainly no fun parks to compete with those of even the most mediocre of Western European resorts (or in the case of the Iranian and Russian resorts

R: MATT BARR L: SHAMSHAK P: JAMES MCPHAIL

R: ADAM GENDLE L: SHEMSHAK P: JAMES MCPHAIL

If you're looking for some proper riding along with a healthy bit of adventure thrown in, then heading east can provide what you're after. The added challenge of communicating with people who speak a language you've never heard before is more than compensated for by their eagerness to help out. Throw in a healthy snow record and the rewards of immersing yourself in a completely different culture and you've got a trip you won't forget.

Dan Milner, snowboarding photographer

selected here, simply no fun parks at all). What you will find though, is an unusual and memorable snowboarding trip, with uncrowded pistes, friendly people and some interesting culinary experiences, all set in some of the most beautiful mountains on the face of the earth. Every adventurous snowboarder should visit all of these resorts at least once. Chances are, though, once just won't be enough.

Conditions

The region is so large that conditions vary greatly from one area to the next. Bulgaria and Poland are lower in altitude than the Alps, with the result that snowfall tends to be less and it doesn't stick around as long. The weather in the Alborz Mountains of Iran is so strange that in Tehran's wealthier districts to the north of the city it can be dumping while the rest of the city enjoys bluebird conditions. Hence, Shemshak and Dizin frequently get great snow, but Iran's southerly latitude and warmer climate means that it can melt very quickly. Krasnaya Poliana is an altogether different affair. When it comes to tales of limitless powder, it's up there with Japan.

When to go

The seasons are the same as in Western Europe. Opening times of the Iranian resorts are more variable thanks to their less predictable snowfall. In all cases, January and February are the coldest and most reliable months for snow, so they're the best bet.

Off-piste policy

In all four countries, you can generally go where you like, but make sure you're self-reliant as you can't expect the speedy rescue service you'd get in Switzerland or the US. Iran doesn't really have ski patrollers in the normal sense of the world, and they're certainly not versed in the ways of the avalanche transceiver. Iranian riders don't venture off-piste much.

Secret spots

Because snowboarding is a novelty, the locals will be only too happy to show visitors around. This applies particularly to Iran, thanks in part

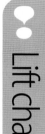

Lift chat

Shemshak reception

About two hours' drive north of Tehran, Shemshak is where we spent the most time and where we discovered the beating heart of the Iranian snowboarding scene. In all my years riding, the snowboarders we met in Shemshak were the keenest, most stoked and funniest snowboarders it has yet been my pleasure to meet. Their enthusiasm and stoke factor ticked every box, and put the anguished debates western snowboarders have about style, 'bookend' video parts and the correct way to wear your baggy trousers into welcome perspective. We met the crew within five minutes of arriving in town at the coffee shop they all used as a main hang out, and they joyously told us about the huge amount of off-piste to be accessed on the mountain and where we could find it. The next day, we went up to check for ourselves.

COFFEE SHOP. P: MATT BARR

to its relative isolation from the rest of the snowboarding world and the good nature of its people.

Freestyle

Freestyle riding hasn't really taken off in this part of the world as it has in the more fashionable snowboarding locations, again particularly in the case of Iran. There are no parks of any kind in Krasnaya Poliana or any of the Iranian resorts. Bulgaria and Poland have more of a scene with a few parks, but don't go there expecting the sort of facilities you'll find in resorts in Western Europe.

The scene/industry

There are no Iranian riders of note, though that's not to say the Iranian snowboarding scene isn't alive and kicking. Scores of people regularly come from Tehran to ride at Dizin and Shemshak, and they're keen as mustard and have all the latest gear. There are various snowboards imported, and there's a **Burton** dealership in Tehran.

There are some good riders in Russia, and some of them, such as Dimitri Fesenko, are world class. However, they're centred around the Moscow street rail scene, which in terms of standard and levels of courage is amongst the best in the world. Riders and film crews are beginning to show up in Krasnaya Poliana, filming for local and international movies.

Freestyle riding is beginning to take off in Poland and Bulgaria, with massive ongoing investments in lifts and facilities at many of the resorts. A case in point is the new park in Bansko, which was designed and built by the same people behind the park in Saas Fee. Thanks to this, it seems pretty likely that a Bulgarian rider of international renown won't be long in coming.

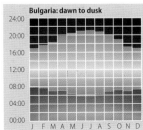

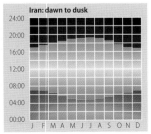

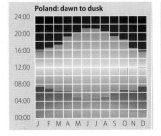

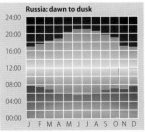

Bulgaria: dawn to dusk

Iran: dawn to dusk

Poland: dawn to dusk

Russia: dawn to dusk

Zakopane is the Whistler of Poland when it comes to the size of the town, the restaurants, the discos and the numerous areas. It's set in a gorgeous national park and big, Alpine-style mountains.

Eric Bergeri, snowboard photographer.

Lift chat

Laughing all the way to the Bansko?

In the old bastions of Eastern European communism, capitalism's final victory had particularly seismic consequences. Countries such as Bulgaria, which had been so closely tied to the old communist economic system, were faced with particularly stark choices. After 1989, a 40% drop in the standard of living was recorded, while it is estimated that 600,000 people, most of them professionals, emigrated. How to join the international marketplace and compete with the west and the rest of the world?

Tourism is an obvious answer, and one reason why Bulgaria, Poland and Slovenia, among others, are suddenly the winter sports destinations of choice among clued-up western punters. Of course, this leads to more local choices. Cheap and cheerful, or classy and cultural? These are important decisions with short- and long-term consequences, and perhaps explains why British package holiday companies are currently shipping out record numbers of Brits to enjoy the Bulgarian take on winter sports. And why Borovets, an old Bulgar resort established in 1896, currently has eight strip bars on its main street.

Over in Bansko, a town of 10,000, they're taking full advantage of the resulting boom, and the place is now rapidly gaining a reputation as a real estate hotspot for those with an eye for a bargain. Do a Google search on the town and as many property developer websites come up as those of tourism companies. The talk among the crowds milling around the luggage carousel at Plovdiv airport is of second homes and money to be made. Which perhaps explains why Bankso has the bustle of a building site, with apartments and houses being slung up as quickly as the locals can erect the scaffolding.

For British tourists, the attractions of this approach are obvious. On every level, it's cheap, whether you're taking the kids to learn to ski or buying a second home. The incredulous talk on the transfer buses up to the Bansko hill each day is of nothing else: of cheap packets of crisps and two-litre bottles of coke for £0.20 - manna for impecunious Brits.

But not everyone is so positive about the boom. According to some, it is in reality a classic South Sea Bubble situation, with people pouring money into the town without worrying if the infrastructure is in place. As one local put it, "Sure you get a cheap flat. But what use is that if you can't flush your toilet every day?"

And what about the effect on the local area? Is it right that Bulgaria becomes merely a warehouse providing cheap booze, food and strip bars for westerners? Do the locals care about the pools of vomit that are staining their streets with increasing regularity? Or are such questions a little quaint when measured against the real poverty suffered by many Bulgarians? As a bar manager in Borovets put it, "…most people here are fine, but there are always some who are rude, and expect to get things cheap or who want to fight us just because we're Bulgarians. Myself, I work here in the winter, make enough money and then return to my real life in Sofia."

Bansko, Bulgaria

The Town

The European Union's newest member finds itself at an important crossroads, reflected perfectly by the rapid development of its winter sports industry – attract bargain-crazed UK punters and erode any remaining local identity as rapidly as possible or attempt to a strike a subtle balance between the two? Over in Borovets, with its seedy strip clubs and Magaluf-on-snow vibe, the battle has already been lost. But in Bansko things are more promising, thanks to the best hill in the country and a resort managing to balance the needs of the tourists (basically, cheap prices and English pubs 'n' clubs) without ruining the original town's heritage and identity. How long they manage to sustain this is anybody's guess, but here's hoping it doesn't end up like its neighbours.

Sleeping Balkan Holidays (balkanholidays.co.uk) are a good option for ultra cheap packages to Bulgaria, with flights and accommodation included. The **Method** snowboard shop (see below) will arrange mid-range accommodation – prices include hot tubs, sauna, gym and airport transfers. Check the website. The more expensive four-star **Hotel Pirin** (T7443 8051) is right by the town square, has a nice pool and bar and a shuttle to the gondola.

Eating There are plenty of local 'mehana' restaurants in Bansko (the **Mehana Bansko** is one of the best), and the food is good, cheap and plentiful. Look out for the bargain snack bars dotted around town.

Bars and clubs The **Happy End** is good for après at the bottom of the gondola, while in town there's the **Buddah Bar**, the **Lion's Pub**, **Amnesia**, the **No Name**…

Shopping One of the main reasons the Brits seems to love it – the supermarkets around town are dirt cheap. A new snowboard shop and school, **Method** (methodsnowschool.com) is opening during the 2006-2007 season.

Health There's a spa centre in many of the hotels, with excellent facilities in the **Pirin** in particular.

Internet Many of the hotels have wireless access and there are internet cafés around town.

Transfer options Bus transfers run from Sofia and also Plovdiv. **Balkan Holidays** also run regular services.

Local partners No local partners.

R: ELLIOT NEAVE P: JAMES MCPHAIL

…y viva Bulgaria! New winter sports giant combines quality snowboarding with cheapness and UK-style nightlife.

If you like this …
… try Dizin ▶▶p102, Zakopane ▶▶p106, or Queenstown/The Remarkables ▶▶p224.

EASTERN EUROPE & MIDDLE EAST
BANSKO

OPENING TIMES
Early Dec to early Apr: 0830-1600

RESORT PRICES
Week pass (6 days): €141,50
Day pass: €26
Season pass: €675

DIRECTORY
Tourist office: T7443 8048
Medical centre: T7443 8388
Pisteurs: T7443 8911
Taxi: No tel number
Local radio: None
Website: banskoski.com

The Mountain

There's no question that Bansko is the best resort in Bulgaria. But does that mean it's any good? Happily, the answer is yes, extremely good. For a start, it has the best infrastructure, with modern quick lifts and good on-hill facilities. Secondly, it's a veritable Alaska compared to its Stratton-like counterparts, and this steepness means some great freeriding. Thirdly, it gets good snow and the pistes are in top nick. Finally, it even has a decent park run by riders who know what they're doing. If they ever sort that pipe out, it'll be even better.

Tantalizingly, there are plans to open up the skier's left side of the mountain with a new chairlift due to be installed. If it does open, some mouth-watering terrain will be opened up.

Beginners Complete beginners should book a lesson with the **Method** school. Confident newcomers want to take the left hand chair in front of the gondola entrance and drop down to the skier's right side of the resort. Over here, there are more wide open blue runs accessed by chairlifts. Be warned: the ones at the very top are draglift accessed. Stop at one of the tent bars and grab a hot dog and coffee for lunch.

Intermediate This is pretty much a perfect resort for intermediates, with swooping pistes aplenty and loads of easily accessible off-piste stuff at the sides. Start by heading straight to the very top and head right towards the obvious right-hand route down. Trees to the side provide potential fun. At Shiligarnika, take the chair to the top and take some runs through the park.

> *You will have a blast riding in Bulgaria. It is a very interesting country in transit to something...*
>
> Vincent Skoglund, photographer

Head down to the base for lunch, and do the lot again.

Advanced Really advanced freeriders will be hiking. But start the day with some runs through the trees over on the far skier's left of the resort. Drop the front of the obvious ridge for some fun, steep tree gulleys being careful to head hard right through the trees back to the resort before it cliffs out. There's a similar cliff band over on the other side of the resort, obvious from the far skier's right chair. To really explore, consider the hikes across the valley or from the top, but be careful of avalanche danger.

Kids There's a ski kindergarten with three baby drags and other facilities.

Flat light days The tree cover means much of it is on, but the tree gullies are the main draw.

P: JAMES MCPHAIL

P: JAMES MCPHAIL

☺ LOCALS DO
- Ride the park. Bansko has a better park than most French resorts.
- Hike. Those lines you can see on skier's left in particular.
- Welcome visitors. Bansko has a great vibe.

☹ LOCALS DON'T
- Stay in much. It's all about the nightlife here.
- Take all the powder. There's plenty to be had after a storm.
- Seem to have much of a plan for the future of the town in the face of mass development. It could go either way.

✔ PROS
- Cheap.
- Surprisingly good mountain for all levels.
- Bulgarian culture still just about intact.

✖ CONS
- Brit lager culture influence is growing massively, not boding well for the future. This might be positive for some.
- Some accommodation long distance from the slopes.

☺ NOT TO MISS
The Amnesia club, complete with 'No handguns' sign by the cloakroom.

ⓘ REMEMBER TO AVOID
The home run – it's too flat for riders.

❄ SNOW DEPTH

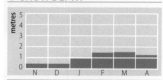

✪ RELIVE A FAMOUS MOMENT
Relive a famous moment? *The Weather Girls* played in Bansko last season. Relive their concert in your own time. Hen parties should need no encouragement.

960 m	TOWN ALTITUDE
150 km	KM TO AIRPORT
SOF	AIRPORT
★☆☆	VEGETARIAN RATING
★★★	INTERNET CAFES
★☆☆	RIDE IN/RIDE OUT
2560 m	HIGHEST LIFT
1600 m	VERTICAL DROP
area not measured	RIDEABLE AREA (IN ACRES)
65 km	KM OF PISTES
1	NURSERY AREAS
4/11/1	RUNS: BEG/INTER/ADV
0/1	FUNICULAR/CABLE CARS
0/7	GONDOLAS/CHAIRS
6	DRAGS
yes	NIGHT RIDING
1	PARKS
1	PIPE
no	SUMMER AREAS
☆☆☆ ☆☆☆	ENVIRONMENTAL RATING
$$$	COST INDICATOR

Dizin, Iran

Iran's answer to Méribel? Not quite, though the country's biggest and busiest resort is more suitable for families and children than its neighbour Shemshak.

If you like this . . .
. . . try *Shemshak* ▸▸*p104,*
or *Las Leñas* ▸▸*p272.*

The Town

Iran's busiest resort opened for business in 1969. Development ground to a halt after the 1979 revolution, and these days it's looking a little rough around the edges. There's not much going on in the town – a few buildings, a couple of hotels, and don't even *think* about getting online from your laptop. For most of us though, a visit to Iran is going to be more about the cultural experience than the riding. It's a far cry from the homogenized world of snowboarding that we've all become familiar with, and this more than makes up for the lack of up-to-date facilities.

Sleeping The town has two hotels, so you're not exactly spoiled for choice. Both are right at the bottom of the pistes. Try **Hotel Dizin** (T215 607 814) on Karaj-Chalus road. Foreigners are always charged a higher rate than Iranians, but it's still cheap. Alternatively, **Persian Voyages**

R: MATT BARR P: JAMES MCPHAIL

(persianvoyages.com) can make all your arrangements for you, including accommodation and travel.

Eating There are five restaurants in Dizin, two of them in the resort's two hotels. On the mountain you can choose from the **Chalet** restaurant (at the top of the gondola) and **Chaman** restaurant (top of the Chaman chair), and there are delicious hot dogs from the stand at the bottom of the hill.

Bars and clubs Being an Islamic Republic, alcohol is strictly off limits hence there are no bars. People socialize in cafés over tea and shishes.

Shopping Facilities aren't good. Make sure you bring all the spares you might need.

Health Work out with a few games on the Dizin tennis courts. There's also an outdoor ice skating rink.

Internet Consider a visit to Dizin a welcome break from the hustle and bustle of the information super-highway.

Transfer options Taxis from Tehran are cheap and easy. Via the Shemshak road Dizin is 71 km from Tehran, but the road is often closed during the winter. In this case you'll need to come by the Chalous road (123 km), which takes about 2½ hours and ups the taxi cost correspondingly.

Local partners None.

OPENING TIMES
Late Nov to late May: 0900-1630

RESORT PRICES
Week pass: No discount
Day pass: €5
Season pass: No discount

DIRECTORY
Tourist office: T212 256 9595
Medical centre: No tel number
Pisteurs: No tel number
Taxi: No tel number
Local radio: None
Website: skifed.ir

102

The Mountain

In terms of lifts Dizin is more developed than Shemshak – there are more of them, and they're more modern. Something that might shock the western visitor to Dizin is that – unlike in Shemshak – some lifts have separate queues for men and women and Islamic rules mean that women must wear headscarves. It's the second highest of all the Iranian resorts, with terrain that's markedly more mellow than Shemshak.

Beginners Dizin is relatively flat so it's great for beginners. Happily, it's possible to get down right from the top of the mountain without encountering a single steeper piste, so steer clear of the black runs and you'll be fine. Total beginners would be best off sticking to the Chaman chair until they get their linked turns down.

Intermediate It's far too easy to have a good day in Dizin. There's nothing steep or challenging here, but the whole place is wide open for exploration and it never gets tracked out. You can ride pretty much everywhere you see, but it's definitely worth checking out the gullies which

you can find by taking the gondola, then the chair, then traversing hard skier's left. There are also some good cruisey pistes around too.

Advanced If you fit into this category, then in a resort such as Dizin you're going to come across like Terje. The locals will be delighted to hook up with you and show you about, particularly if they can learn a thing or two in return. In fact, they're so friendly and so amped on snowboarding that you'd actively have to try *not* to befriend at least one person. The whole area is yours to explore.

Kids There are no real facilities for children, though the gradient of the resort makes it an ideal place to learn.

Flat light days There are no trees in Dizin, so the mountain's a write-off on flat light days. Bring your own entertainment.

P: JAMES MCPHAIL

P: JAMES MCPHAIL

> **" "**
> Dizin is where ordinary Iranians escape the slings and arrows of growing up in the Islamic Republic - and who can blame them? Sure, the lifts are outdated, the roads often closed and amenities virtually non-existent, but this is one of the most unexpected winter wonderlands on earth: friendly, culturally rewarding and beautiful beyond all expectation.
>
> *Cyrus Shahad, journalist*

☺ LOCALS DO

⚐ Come in summer for the grass skiing – it's massive here. Iran is president of the East-Asian Grass Skiing competitions.
⚐ Mob Western visitors.
⚐ Fling themselves off anything they can find.

☹ LOCALS DON'T

⊗ Venture far off piste. Baffling, but true.
⊗ Queue together – those rumours about separate lift lines for men and women are all true here.
⊗ Have snow tyres. You can count on being called on to help push someone's car out of the parking lot.

☺ PROS

⚐ Iran's largest resort.
⚐ Real travelling experience.
⚐ Extremely cheap.

⊗ CONS

⊗ Lack of steep terrain.
⊗ No trees.
⊗ It's a long way to go if there turns out to be no snow.

☺ NOT TO MISS

The views of the magnificent Mount Damavand (5671 m) Iran's highest.

❶ REMEMBER TO AVOID

There's more of a military presence in Dizin than Shemshak, so don't attempt to chat with Iranian women, and if you must wear a T-shirt make it a long sleeved one.

❄ SNOW DEPTH

Figures not available

(metres 0–5, months N D J F M A)

✪ RELIVE A FAMOUS MOMENT

Dizin was supposedly built under orders from the Shah, who was said to have been a fanatical skier. Relive this moment by telling your friends whilst standing in your gender-specific lift queue.

2650 m	TOWN ALTITUDE
123 km	KM TO AIRPORT
THR	AIRPORT
★☆☆	VEGETARIAN RATING
★☆☆	INTERNET CAFES
★★☆	RIDE IN/RIDE OUT
3600 m	HIGHEST LIFT
900 m	VERTICAL DROP
area not measured	RIDEABLE AREA (IN ACRES)
runs not measured	KM OF PISTES
0	NURSERY AREAS
12/6/0	RUNS: BEG/INTER/ADV
0/0	FUNICULAR/CABLE CARS
3/2	GONDOLAS/CHAIRS
8	DRAGS
no	NIGHT RIDING
0	PARKS
0	PIPE
no	SUMMER AREAS
figures not available	ENVIRONMENTAL RATING
$$$	COST INDICATOR

EASTERN EUROPE & MIDDLE EAST
DIZIN

Shemshak, Iran

Cheap, uncrowded and with a wealth of epic terrain. Who could have guessed that the Islamic Republic of Iran would be hiding one of the world's best freeride resorts?

☽ *If you like this* ...
... *try Krasnaya Poliana* ▸▸*p108, Las Leñas* ▸▸*p272, or Baker* ▸▸*p350.*

The Town

Shemshak opened in 1958, and not much appears to have changed since then. As ski resorts go it's very underdeveloped, so don't expect modern facilities. However, if you're coming here then it's likely you're doing so in the spirit of adventure, and on that count the place won't disappoint. The people are a mix of Shemshaki mountain folk, wealthy people from Tehran, bears and intrepid foreigners, often Scandinavians. You also find people from the Arab countries such as Lebanon, and there's even a refugee settlement from Afghanistan which occupies an unfinished building at the upper end of the town. Due to economic sanctions, you can't use credit cards or ATM machines, so bring sufficient cash for your stay.

Sleeping In a place like this, your best bet is to turn up in town and sort it out from there. There are two hotels in town, though by chatting to the locals you can often find other, cheaper options, such as renting an apartment or villa. Try **Hotel Darban** (T2165 1986) – it's clean, cheap and the service is good. Alternatively, **Persian Voyages** (persianvoyages.com) can make all your arrangements for you, including accommodation and travel.

Eating There are various small restaurants, and the town's two hotels serve up some pretty decent food. There are no mountain restaurants as such, but there's a little shack at the top of the main chairlift where you can buy drinks and snacks at inflated prices. It's still cheap though.

Bars and clubs Being an Islamic republic, alcohol is strictly off limits hence there are no bars. As a substitute Iranians gather in cafés where they drink a lot of strong, fragrant tea, eat delicious pastries and smoke endless shishes. The café is a good spot to mingle with the locals

Shopping Shemshak has no decent snowboard shops, so it's a good idea to stock up on any spares before you leave. Make sure you take your own servicing and repair kit.

Health In the world of health tourism, Iran is renowned for its quality dentists, but it's also very cheap to get an MRI scan done here if you've knee or ankle trouble. This can cost as little as €80 from hospitals in Tehran.

Internet None.

Shemshak is one of the most amazing resorts I've ever been to. It's a truly memorable snowboarding experience.

Adam Gendle, pro snowboarder & film maker

Transfer options Tehran is about an hour's very scenic (and at times hair-raising) taxi ride away. This should cost around €24.

Local partners None.

R: EWAN WALLACE P: JAMES MCPHAIL

⊛ OPENING TIMES
Late Nov to early Apr: 0900-1630

⊖ RESORT PRICES
Week pass: None issued
Day pass: €5
Season pass: None issued

☺ DIRECTORY
Tourist office: T212 256 9595
Medical centre: No tel number
Pisteurs: No tel number
Taxi: No tel number
Local radio: None
Website: skifed.ir

P: JAMES MCPHAIL

The Mountain

Shemshak is situated in the Alborz Mountains, just north of Tehran. Although it's not the highest of Iranian resorts, it has by far the best terrain. The pisted area is pretty small, but the runs are fun and there's a wealth of good stuff to be found in between them. There are few lifts, so finding your way around is easy. Contrary to what many people expect, snowboarding is popular in Iran, and around a third of the people you'll see on the slopes are snowboarders. Puzzlingly, none of them seems to venture too far off-piste, meaning that the most obvious of lines that wouldn't last two minutes in Tignes or Chamonix remain untracked indefinitely. For serious freeriders, this alone make it worth the trek.

Beginners You'll probably want to steer clear of those drag lifts for a bit, so spend the morning doing laps on the first section of the main chairlift – it's split station, and the bottom half accesses less challenging slopes. Once you're feeling more confident then head right to the top.

Intermediate Spend the morning riding the main chairlift – the pistes are just the right gradient to open up on without the need for checking your speed the whole time. This is a bit of a leg burner so you'll need a good break for lunch. Afterwards, head into the first valley on the skier's left of the main chair, arriving at the main road and hitching back up to town, and repeat this as many times as you're fit to. Be careful not to stray too far skier's left – some of the further valleys cliff out near the bottom.

Advanced With a short hike up the ridge from the main chairlift you can ride fresh lines all week, snow allowing, and there's plenty to explore by dropping down into the valleys to the skier's left of the hut at the top of the chair. There's no ski patrol though, so if you do venture off-piste you're on your own. It's imperative to come prepared with transceiver, shovel and probe, and make sure you and your group know how to use them effectively.

Kids There are no distinct facilities for kids, and no discount on lift passes. But imagine the kudos they'll get from being able to tell their friends they learned in Iran…

Flat light days There are no trees in Shemshak, so flat light halts play. You'll find some colourful characters hanging out in the café by the road at the base of the resort, and befriending some of them makes for an entertaining stay.

☺ LOCALS DO

● Smoke shishes at every given opportunity.
● Show extraordinary interest in foreigners – they're a very inquisitive and hospitable people.
● Drink *doogh*, a slightly fizzy fermented yoghurt drink often described as 'Iranian wine'.

☹ LOCALS DON'T

● Venture far from the pistes – it's all there for the taking.
● Know how to use avalanche transceivers – make sure you and your group are self-reliant.
● Drink alcohol. It's banned in Iran.

✓ PROS

● Incredible terrain.
● Epic and uncrowded freeriding.
● The friendliest locals on the planet.

✗ CONS

● Slow lifts.
● Unreliable snow.
● No booze! Though this might count as a plus for some people.

☺ NOT TO MISS

Sharing a shishe with some of the locals.

ⓘ REMEMBER TO AVOID

Jumping the lift queues. They can be quite long, and if you're caught you'll get sent right to the back.

❄ SNOW DEPTH

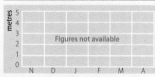

✪ RELIVE A FAMOUS MOMENT

Since most of the world has never even heard of Shemshak, it oughtn't come as a surprise that nothing famous has happened here. Put in the obvious lines on the top ridge and you'll quickly become the local celebrity in the area.

P: JAMES McPHAIL

The Town

Architecturally, Zakopane may well have the most clashing styles of any resort in the world. Staggering old buildings (some listed with UNESCO) are dotted around the town, often restored back to their original 19th-century wooden splendour while the main street is a beautiful cobbled and car-free area. In contrast, out of town sees classic, bleak Eastern Bloc high-rise flats in massed ranks, while in the parks sit incredible statues with strong Soviet undertones. Everywhere retains a look associated with the communist era Zakopane recently lived through. The mountain backdrop adds to the surreal feel.

Sleeping The **Hotel Szarotka** (T18 2064050) is a 1930s wooden hostel from €18 per night. **Sabala** (sabala.zakopane.pl) has had a recent renovation and rooms are around €45 per night. Try **Belvedere** (belvederehotel.pl), a genuine luxury spa in the town centre.

Eating **Nosalowy Dwor** (T18 201 1400), **Staro Izba** (T18 201 3391) and **Little Switzerland** (T18 201 2076) are undoubtedly the best in town, with plenty of antlers on display and hearty meats for all.

Bars and clubs There are too many to list, but for a good starting point, try **Ampstrong** (T50 164 5464) then head to the nearest Vodka bar afterwards. Beware: a 'Discoteque' is for dancing while a 'Nightclub' is where long-distance truck drivers go.

Shopping The **Le Clerc** supermarket, 9 km away in Nowy Targ, should sort you out for supplies and fulfil any 'Allo 'Allo! pun urges too.

Health **Belvedere** is the best spa in town with all the usual massage, mudpack and spa suspects.

Internet The **Granet Internet Café**, and **The Internet Café** are both in town. Many hotels have wireless.

Transfer options The train is the best option with direct lines (intercity.pl/en/main) from Krakow to Zakopane.

Local partners None.

> It's got great restaurants and discos and some funky lifts. It's also full of Russians which makes for great partying!
>
> *Eric Bergeri, photographer*

Culturally different resort with great slopes for beginners and a nightlife scene perfect for stag or hen parties.

⊃ *If you like this* . . .
. . . *try Shemshak* ▸▸*p104, or Krasnaya Poliana* ▸▸*p108.*

R: ELLIOT NEAVE P: JAMES MCPHAIL

The Mountain

Zakopane is split into a few areas: Nosal, Gubalowka Szymoszkowa and – by the far the biggest – Kasprowy Wierch just outside of town. Here, a fantastically old cable car waits to take you to up the mountain. Elsewhere, there are a few chairs and even a funicular train to get you to the slopes, but most of the terrain is accessed by T-bears or pomas. In addition, you pay per lift rather than a day pass, so be aware that you may have to queue more than is usual in most other European resorts. However, for its freeriding potential and for its overall cultural appeal, it's worth a visit.

Beginners Either Nosal or Polana Szymoszkowa (both accessed by local bus service) are the best beginner areas, with fantastic nursery slopes and a decent enough main slope to practice on.

Intermediate Head up to Kasprowy Wierch, all the way up the cable car (both stations) and then do laps all the way to the bottom down the No 2 piste. The whole run takes in some wild terrain with some cool, flatter sections at the bottom that are aching to be straightlined.

Advanced Again, get to the top of Kasprowy. From the top, most of the Tatras Mountains are visible. Budding freeriders will be well aware of the potential of the area. Off-piste gullies, cornices, secret routes and amazing cliffs can be viewed from either the cable car on the way up, or by some short hikes from the top. We're sworn to secrecy as to exactly which directions, but if you head in the direction of the No 1 black run you won't go too far wrong.

Flat light days Head up to Gubalowka after dark on the funicular to get some night riding done.

⏱ OPENING TIMES
Early Dec to late May: 0830-1600

💲 RESORT PRICES
Week pass: No discount
Day pass: €15 for 15 rides or €2,50 for 1.
Season pass: No discount

ℹ DIRECTORY
Tourist office: T18 201 2211
Medical centre: T18 201 2021
Pisteurs: T18 206 1550
Taxi: 919
Local radio: None
Website: go-zakopane.com

☺ LOCALS DO
● Hike from the top of the Kasprowy.
● Shop at the local market – and haggle!
● Drink straight vodka like it's going out of fashion.

☹ LOCALS DON'T
⊗ Worry about the age of the cablecar.
⊗ Leave valuables in the car in the rougher areas of town.
⊗ Get confused by the men/women signs for the bathroom. Men's is a triangle, women's a circle. Don't ask why…

👍 PROS
● You get a lot for your money.
● You're snowboarding in Poland.
● Score it right and you'll get great powder with few freeriding competitors to share it with.

✗ CONS
⊗ Town can be filled with groups of lads – very stag heavy.
⊗ Old lifts and ridiculous ticket system where you pay per lift.
⊗ When it's on, the queue system can be frustrating.

☺ NOT TO MISS
If there's a ski jumping session on the go, definitely check it out.

⚠ REMEMBER TO AVOID
Pre-book your ticket up Kasprowy to avoid the horrendous queues that can build up.

❄ SNOW DEPTH

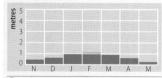

★ RELIVE A FAMOUS MOMENT
Chopin wrote a great deal of his piano concertos at his holiday home in Zakopane. Relive his creative output by taking a recorder.

800 m
TOWN ALTITUDE

110 km
KM TO AIRPORT

KRK
AIRPORT

★☆☆
VEGETARIAN RATING

★★★
INTERNET CAFES

★☆☆
RIDE IN/RIDE OUT

1960 m
HIGHEST LIFT

800 m
VERTICAL DROP

area not measured
RIDEABLE AREA (IN ACRES)

50 km
KM OF PISTES

3
NURSERY AREAS

6/8/6
RUNS: BEG/INTER/ADV

1/1
FUNICULAR/CABLE CARS

0/3
GONDOLAS/CHAIRS

8
DRAGS

yes
NIGHT RIDING

1
PARKS

0
PIPE

no
SUMMER AREAS

figures not available
ENVIRONMENTAL RATING

COST INDICATOR

EASTERN EUROPE & MIDDLE EAST
ZAKOPANE

P: CHRIS MORAN/HOTSHITPICTURES.COM
P: CHRIS MORAN/HOTSHITPICTURES.COM

The Town

Krasnaya Poliana is an unlikely looking boomtown, but that's exactly what it is. It's at the frontline of the transition from communism to capitalism that is taking place right across this huge continent and, with nearby Sochi bidding for the 2014 Winter Olympics, is set to explode in the next few years. At the moment, it combines an edgy, frontier feel with an antiquated lift system that accesses some incredible terrain.

Sleeping Try reinfo-sochi.ru for cheap rents or 377333.ru if you want to get in early and buy somewhere! **The 4 Peaks** (4peaks.ru) is a good local three-star option. Symptomatic of Krasnaya's imminent expansion, the **Radisson Peak** (radisson.ru) off the main road is the hotel with the most 'western' standards of accommodation.

Eating Don't be fooled – the **Petrol Station** on the main road is the best local café in the area, while **Atmosphere** is popular, just on the main road out of town. Up the hill, try the goulash and blinis in the restaurant at the bottom of the top chair.

Bars and clubs UK riders should have a pint in the double-decker bus at the base, while the **Munchausen** café next to the lift station has a nice vibe and a good vegetarian. There are no clubs, but the **Heineken tent** gets lively for the après.

Shopping You'll have to go down into Sochi or Adler for groceries, but there is a good snowboard shop, **Freeride**, stocking Burton spares on the main road into the resort.

Health The **Radisson** has the best facilities in town when it comes to massages and gyms.

Internet There is wireless access at the **Munchausen**, although you have to pay a few roubles to get the access codes and it's currently only for PCs.

Transfer options Hire cars cost up to €80 a day, so arrange a transfer from Sochi-Adler with a local firm. Try Ivan Ivanisovich on T891 8308 1890.

Local partners All going well, a resort will open in the adjacent valley by 2008. There are none at present.

> Krasnaya is in my top five resorts. Outside Alaska, you just don't get such easily accessible steeps and such a high standard of snow. I'm going back!
>
> *James Stentiford, pro snowboarder*

P: JAMES MCPHAIL R: ADAM GENDLE

World-class freeriding in Russia's remote Caucasus region. As wild and adventurous as snowboarding gets.

☼ If you like this . . .
. . . try *Bansko* ⇒*p100*, *Shemshak* ⇒*p104*, or *Las Leñas* ⇒*p272*.

⊛ OPENING TIMES

Early Jan to early Apr: 0830-1545/1600

⑤ RESORT PRICES

Week pass (6 days): €161
Day pass: €29
Season pass: No discount

ⓘ DIRECTORY

Tourist office: No tel number
Medical centre: No tel number
Pisteurs: No tel number
Taxi: T891 8308 1890
Local radio: None
Website: None

The Mountain

Krasnaya's incredible terrain helps to explain why so many people make the trip to this tiny, out of the way Russian resort. It is a serious mountain with serious dangers, but the rewards and scope for exploration for those with enough experience to handle it are limitless. At the moment, an antiquated lift system means much of the best terrain can only be accessed by hiking but this makes the riding all the more rewarding. The top lift accesses a wealth of chutes, spines and steeps, while further down the sparse trees that make up the higher lift line mean the resort stays on during bad weather.

Beginners Krasnaya is definitely not a resort for beginners, although if you do find yourself here and can negotiate the sketchy (and, for the uninitiated, slightly scary) lifts you'll spend most of the day on the lower slopes leading back down to the base.

Intermediate Slightly better for intermediates, but still not really recommended due to big queues and a limited number of pistes. On the plus side, there is much easy freeriding to access after a storm.

Advanced Head straight to the top chair and work your way skier's right along the ridge, taking advantage of the many, many possibilities

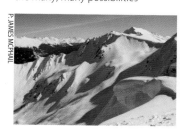

afforded by the wealth of tight chutes and steep terrain. As it gets tracked out, it's possible to access the next valley along, picking off lines as you find them before hiking back into Krasnaya, but this is really only for the extremely confident. On the far skier's right of the ridge, there's an easy (if steep) hike to access the trees that snake down the side of the resort.

Kids The distance to Krasnaya means it's not really suitable for kids, although there are plenty of young Russian shredders on the hill.

Flat light days The trees here put Krasnaya into the same league of Niseko in Japan and make for incredible flat light riding. If conditions are good, head skier's left from the top and work your way down through the woods here. Over on skier's right of the main resort bowl, there are great pillows and spaced trees to be found parallel to the second chair, albeit requiring a hike out.

P: JAMES MCPHAIL

☺ LOCALS DO
- Get there early to avoid the lift queues.
- Hike.
- Always wear full avalanche kit.

☹ LOCALS DON'T
- Ride Saturdays. It's when lift queues are busiest.
- Hike skier's left from the top lift straight after heavy snow. Dangerous.
- Expect to get anything during the national holidays.

✓ PROS
- One of the best freeriding resorts in the world.
- Plenty of trees for flat light riding.
- Great heliboarding facilities.

✗ CONS
- Not a resort for beginners or intermediates.
- Antiquated lift system means big queues.
- Very susceptible to bad weather due to its proximity to the Black Sea.

☼ NOT TO MISS
Krasnaya's heliboarding facilities are world-class and make use of decommissioned Russian military helicopters. If you make the effort to come here, spend the extra cash. heliski.ru

ⓘ REMEMBER TO AVOID
KP's outdated lifts simply cannot cope with crowds, making the Russian national holidays during February nightmarish. Avoid Feb 23rd, 'Man Day', like the plague!

❄ SNOW DEPTH

Figures not available

↻ RELIVE A FAMOUS MOMENT
Vladimir Putin regularly closes all aircraft activity in the region so he can go heli-skiing with his mates in safety.

780 m	TOWN ALTITUDE
35 km	KM TO AIRPORT
AER	AIRPORT
★★★	VEGETARIAN RATING
★★☆	INTERNET CAFES
★★☆	RIDE IN/RIDE OUT
2238 m	HIGHEST LIFT
1458 m	VERTICAL DROP
area not measured	RIDEABLE AREA (IN ACRES)
runs not measured	KM OF PISTES
0	NURSERY AREAS
0/4/4	RUNS: BEG/INTER/ADV
0/0	FUNICULAR/CABLE CARS
0/4	GONDOLAS/CHAIRS
0	DRAGS
no	NIGHT RIDING
0	PARKS
0	PIPE
no	SUMMER AREAS
figures not available	ENVIRONMENTAL RATING

COST INDICATOR

EASTERN EUROPE & MIDDLE EAST
KRASNAYA POLIANA

Huge open faces, the perfect powder, crazy light ... it could only be France.

R: WILL HUGHES. L: TIGNES. P: JAMES MCPHAIL

France

Star resorts...

★1 **Avoriaz** The funpark capital of France and home to the strangest architecture on the planet. ➤ p124.

★3 **Chamonix** The grand old dame of ski resorts. Still has world-class slopes, the best views ever and the longest run in the world – the 22-km Vallée Blanche. p128.

★6 **La Grave** Only the French could come up with a resort like this. One lift, a million crevasses. Take a guide, and leave the kids at home. ➤ p134.

★12 **Méribel** Picture-perfect mountain village with a pumping seasonaire scene and access to the Three Valleys, the world's biggest interlinked lift system ➤ p146.

Airport codes...
GNB = Lyon-Grenoble
GVA = Geneva
TRN = Turin

N 10 km
   10 miles

SWITZERLAND

ITALY

FRANCE

Lake Geneva

Mont Blanc

Fréjus Tunnel

Turin

Lyon

Grenoble

Chambéry

Annecy

Albertville

BELGIUM
GERMANY
SWITZERLAND
ITALY
FRANCE
SPAIN

Chivasso
Settimo
Moncalieri
Carmagnola
Racconigi
Pinerolo
Rivoli
Lanzo Torinese
Susa
Oulx
Sestriere
Briançon
L'Argentière-la-Bessée
Le Monetier
La Grave
La Bourg-d'Oisans
Les Deux Alpes
La Mure
St-Jean-de-Maurienne
St-Michel-de-Maurienne
Modane
Val Thorens
Les Menuires
St Martin-de-Belleville
Méribel
La Tania
Moûtiers
Aime
Bourg St Maurice
La Rosière
Sainte Foy
Val d'Isère
Tignes
Courmayeur
Morgex
Argentière
Chamonix
Les Houches
Megève
La Clusaz
La Fayet
Sallanches
Ugine
Cluses
Bonneville
Taninges
Morzine
Avoriaz
Monthey
Bex
Martigny
Montreux
Lausanne
Renens
Morges
Aubonne
Nyon
Gex
Vernier
Lancy
Annemasse
Geneva
Evian
Thonon
Bellegarde
Dortan
Oyonnax
Rumilly
Belley
Aix-les-Bains
La Tour-du-Pin
Les Abrets
Volvon
Montmélian
GVA
TRN
GNB

Introduction

With huge mountains, that classic laissez-faire attitude to danger, and great weather, it's not hard to see why France has always had a special place in our hearts. Resorts such as Les Arcs and Avoriaz were instrumental in snowboarding's early days, accepting riders when it was far from fashionable to do so, while Chamonix, Val d'Isère, Méribel and Morzine are now home to some of the largest seasonaire communities in the Alps.

You don't have to be a pro to enjoy the best of France. Most resorts try to cater to every taste, offering great beginner runs, great cat tracks to cruise down and often easy access to fantastic off-piste. In the past, while France has suffered from not building good enough funparks – certainly not to US, Canadian and New Zealand standards – some resorts (Avoriaz, Serre Chevalier, Les Arcs, Tignes) are trying to catch up. It's easy to see why they were neglected: the natural terrain is more often than not enough to entice riders.

There are few countries to rival the French when it comes to pride in their culture. And as for food, well, the French will never concede that any other national cuisine could rival their fish and meat dishes, garnished with rich sauces and accompanied by more fine wines than you could shake a corkscrew at. If it flies, crawls or walks, it will go well with garlic and lemon …

France rating

Value for money
★★★☆☆

Nightlife
★★★★☆

Freestyle
★★☆☆☆

Freeride
★★★★☆

Essentials

Getting there

France's main alpine airports are Lyon and Geneva, which is actually in Switzerland. **British Airways** (ba.com) and **easyJet** (easyjet.com), **Air France** (airfrance.com) and many others fly to both. From the UK, if you don't fancy Dover-Calais by sea, you can always hop on the Eurotunnel train (T08705 353535, eurotunnel.com) with your car or van at Folkestone, which will deposit you just south of Calais 35 minutes later. This can, however, be double the price of a ferry crossing, unless you look out for special offers. Alternatively, as a foot passenger, you can hop on the **Eurostar** (T08705 186186, eurostar.com) at London Waterloo and be transported straight through to Moutiers, Chamonix, Aix-les-Bain or Bourg St Maurice. Returns can cost anything from €140 upwards depending on time of travel and can often be a more expensive option than flying. Check connections, or journeys across Europe, with **Rail Europe** (raileurope.com).

Red tape

France is a member of the EU. Member state nationals don't require a visa, but do need a valid passport. A visa is not required for stays of up to 90 days in France and Monaco.

Getting around

Driving (right-hand side) A full driving licence or International Driving Permit is required plus adequate insurance and ownership papers. Roads are generally of a high standard, although the driving experience is different, especially when locals overtake. They'll come up behind, lights flashing until they can speed past.

Motorway (autoroute) France has a great network of toll roads (*peages*) that speeds up the journey but ups the overall journey cost – autoroutes.fr has up to date prices. The speed limit is 130 kph.

Routes nationales and **other roads** Cheaper than the *peages*, but slower and often busier – the choice is yours. The speed limit is 110 kph on dual carriageway, 90 kph single and 50 kph in urban areas.

Mountain passes If you're planning on taking a high pass between resorts, it's essential to check whether it is open.

Car hire Most major hire car companies (easycar.com, hertz.com) have offices in airports and cities. Usual age restrictions apply.

France price guide							
In €	2,00	2,00	5,00	0,80	3,00	4,00	1,50

Top tips

- Learn a few words of French. Though they might answer you back in English, the effort will be appreciated.

- Avoid the larger resorts during the French holidays (early February – early March), when they're exceptionally busy. If you must go then pick a smaller, lesser known resort.

- Don't rely on finding a decent park, unless you're going to one of the ones we've mentioned.

- If you go early season, don't take your brand new board! An old rock-hopper is the best bet.

- Make sure you're well versed in the ways of avalanche safety. The French will pretty much let you ride where you want, but this is entirely at your own risk. Make sure you're prepared.

Public transport

France's SNCF (train network) is fast, efficient and used often. TGVs are the fastest; autotrains tend to stop a lot more. Stamp your ticket before boarding.

Opening hours and traditions

As lunch is generally the most important meal of the day, banks and businesses tend to open Monday to Saturday 0800-1200 and 1400-1700. For most businesses Sundays are a day of rest (which can often stretch into Monday as well).

Eating

Food is to the French what technology is to the Japanese – not just a necessity but an art form. Even a McDonald's in France is more civilized and has a *patisserie* section. *Pain au chocolat*, buttery *croissants* or even a bit of last night's *baguette*, washed down with *une*

L-ANNECY P: CHRIS MORAN/HOTSHITPICTURES.COM

France has the advantage that you can ride two distinct ranges: the Alps and the Pyrenees. Resorts in the French Alps expanded extremely fast with the result that there are many ugly buildings on the mountain. Les Arcs was one of the first resorts in Europe to see a snowboarder – pioneer Regis Rolland – and that's where the main part of the French scene is living and riding, mainly between Grenoble and Avoriaz. All in all, this is one of the biggest riding countries in the world in term of the number of lifts – around 4000 in total.

Youri Barneoud, French editor, Onboard Magazine

→ Currency Euro (€)
Exchange rate £1 = €1.44
Time zone GMT +1
Country code: +33
Emergency numbers
  Ambulance: T15
  Police: T17
  Fire: T18
The Pan-European emergency number T112 works in any EU country from any telephone. It's also the number to call for any emergency services if you're using a mobile.

Fact file

grande café au lait or *chocolate chaud* – this is, quite simply, breakfast heaven. Lunch can be a simple affair involving a *pain* (a fatter bread stick than a *baguette*) and a wedge of your favourite *fromage* (cheese) – be it a creamy Camembert or a salty Roquefort. If you want something more serious, try an *'American'* – a *baguette* stuffed with hamburger patties, salad and french fries – or a *croque monsieur* – a cheese and ham toastie, French-style – at a café.

Language

French, as spoken by about 122 million people worldwide, is the official language of France. Although English is understood in cities and many resorts, it is really important to try out your linguistic skills, even if it is just for the amusement of the French. They will either correct your appalling pronunciation, look bored and pretend they don't understand or, worse still, reply in fluent English to your best efforts.

Crime/safety

Outside the big cities, France is a relatively crime-free country. The biggest problem is with car break-ins – especially tourist cars, which are generally thought to be packed with holiday goodies, passports etc. Leaving anything visible in your car or hidden in the boot will

P: CHRIS MORAN/HOTSHITPICTURES.COM

P: CHRIS MORAN/HOTSHITPICTURES.COM

P: CHRIS MORAN/HOTSHITPICTURES.COM

Key phrases

Key words/phrases		Help!	*au secours!*
Yes	*oui*	North	*nord*
No	*non*	South	*sud*
Please	*s'il te plaît*	East	*est*
Thank you	*merci*	West	*ouest*
Sorry	*pardon*		
Hello	*bonjour*	**Numbers**	
Goodbye	*au revior*	0	*zero*
Good	*bon*	1	*un*
Bad	*mauvais*	2	*deux*
I don't understand	*je ne*	3	*trois*
comprends pas		4	*quatre*
I'd like…	*je voudrais…*	5	*cincq*
Do you have?	*avez vous..?*	6	*six*
How much is it?	*c'est*	7	*sept*
combien?		8	*huit*
Where is..?	*où est..?*	9	*neuf*
Mens	*hommes*	10	*dix*
Ladies	*femmes*	11	*onze*
Left	*gauche*	12	*douze*
Right	*droite*	13	*treize*
Straight on	*tout droit*	14	*quatorze*
Night	*nuit*	15	*quinze*
Room	*chambre*	16	*seize*
Pitch	*emplacement*	17	*dix-sept*
Shower	*douche*	18	*dix-huit*
Toilet	*toilettes*	19	*dix-neuf*
The bill	*l'addition*	20	*vingt*
White coffee	*café au lait*	21	*vingt et un*
Beer	*bière*	22	*vingt-deux*
Red wine/white wine	*vin*	30	*trente*
rouge/vin blanc		40	*quarante*
Mineral water		50	*cinquante*
(sparkling)	*l'eau minéral*	60	*soixante*
(gazeuse)		70	*soixante-dix*
Orange juice	*jus d'orange*	80	*quatre-vingts*
Sandwich	*sandwich*	90	*quatre-vingt-dix*
Ham	*jambon*	100	*cent*
Cheese	*fromage*	200	*deux cent*
Cheese and ham toastie		1000	*mille*
croque monsieur			

make it an easy target. If you do need to report anything, head for the Police Nationale or Gendarmerie Nationale (same but different). Out and about, the police do have amazing powers of search and are happy to use them.

Health

As part of the EU, France is governed by European health standards. Health insurance is recommended, and EU citizens should carry a European Health Insurance Card (EHIC), which replaces the old E1-11 form. If you do need treatment, or to call out an ambulance, be aware you'll be charged (although you can claim this back later). For minor ailments head to the local *pharmacie* – there will always be a local 24-hour chemist open on rotation.

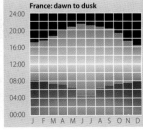

France: dawn to dusk

Snowboarding France

L: TIGNES FINGERS P: CHRIS MORAN/HOTSHITPICTURES.COM

"Snowboarding in France is good because we have a lot of diversity. You can find steep freeriding, easy slopes, cold weather, slushy snow... There are a lot of different spots. Everybody can have fun here, and freeriding is allowed anywhere, anytime! You just have to be careful because the avalanche risk is often high. For the freestylers, parks in France aren't the best in Europe. We are a little bit behind the rest of the world. Except for resorts like Avoriaz and Les Deux Alpes. These resorts are my favourite – you'll find really good parks, great slopes with good backcountry and funny après!" Sylvain Bourbousson, French pro snowboarder

Fittingly for the first country in Europe to embrace the sport, France is now widely regarded as the continent's snowboarding epicentre. Snowboarders of every stripe flock there each winter, from the families and couples that enjoy the wide motorway pistes of the Three Valleys, to the serious freeriders challenging the steeps of La Grave and Chamonix. And after the riding has finished for the day, hedonistic nightlife and après antics are equally strong attractions.

The sublime, ridiculous and the outright dangerous co-exist quite peacefully here, usually within the boundaries of each single resort. True, the number of foreign seasonaires, usually Scandinavian and British, who make the country their home each winter make for a real melting pot feel. But most of the time, the surprisingly antiquated lift systems and uniquely Gallic approach to service culture mean you couldn't really be anywhere else. Denizens of slick North American ski resorts, in particular, are in for a rude awakening. But for great terrain,

Pros & cons

Pros ...

- Much of the world's best lift-accessed freeriding.
- Several huge, interlinked lift areas.
- Laissez-faire attitude to going off-piste.
- Extensive choice of resorts, many of them concentrated in a very small area.
- North America? Pah! In terms of vertical drop, France thumbs its Gallic nose at the rest of the world.

... and cons

- Like Switzerland, it's expensive when compared to its European counterparts such as Austria, Italy or Spain.
- Can become very crowded during peak times.
- Generally unprogressive (haughty, some might say) attitude, particularly when compared to the US or Canada.
- On the whole, the parks leave a lot to be desired.
- Gets tracked out very quickly.

Snowboarding in France is just great because there is tons of different terrain to ride. Every aspect of snowboarding can be found, from big resorts like Avoriaz, Les Arcs, Chamonix, Val d'Isère and Tignes to small unknown resorts with good backcountry features. You just have to go on the search! Plus there are now a lot of good snowparks everywhere. For me Avoriaz is the place to be because the parks are good, so is the superpipe, and the backcountry is easy to access with lots of fun little zones. And of course the town on top of the cliff with no cars makes it different. But be careful when you come up there – respect the locals' spots or they will tell you how it works ...

Nicolas Droz, pro snowboarder

incredible food, fun nightlife and the high-octane atmosphere of a genuine snowboarding culture, France is hard to beat.

Conditions
Thanks to the mighty swathe the Alps cut across the southeast of the country, France is almost embarrassingly rich in fantastic snowboarding resorts. This, coupled with their existing winter sports heritage, meant that the French were quick to see the possibilities inherent in snowboarding, and the sport has enjoyed exponential growth there ever since. Above all, the Alps are diverse, and offer a wide variety of different terrain and challenges as the winter evolves each year.

When to go
French resorts traditionally open at the beginning of December, depending on how much early season snow has fallen. This is a great time to go to avoid crowds and enjoy a cheaper trip – although you'd be wise to take a beaten up old board if the snow-base is still thin. By January, cold temperatures and deep snowfalls mean powder days and flat light are the norm, and with crowds still manageable this can be a great time to visit. February in France means one thing – the infamous French holidays, signalling bigger lift queues and less snow for all. March can be a good compromise, with snowfall still consistent and the overall temperature still rising. By April, powder has generally given way to slush and goggle tans, although late season dumps are fairly regular.

Off-piste policy
Fittingly for the nation that bequeathed the phrase 'laissez-faire' to the world, the French guidelines to ducking under the ropes are

Lift chat

Will I die in Chamonix?

Well, it's a good question, and one to which the most obvious answer is 'maybe'. However, that's no more true than it would be for any other resort, and not because Chamonix is necessarily any more dangerous than anywhere else (at least if you steer clear of glaciers), though from the hardware on display in the town you'd be forgiven for thinking otherwise.

Walking around Chamonix can be a bewildering, even intimidating experience, particularly in the queue for the *Aiguille du Midi*, Chamonix's gnarly freeriding hotspot. Grim-faced Scandinavians jingle around with karibiners and various unidentified bits of metal affixed to their harnesses, ice axes lashed on to their backpacks, looking like they mean business. Where are they going with all that stuff attached to them? And what are they going to do with it when they get there?

Think of it as a fashion parade for backcountry types. You're no one in Chamonix without a harness and an ice axe, and you don't even have to put them to use to enjoy the kudos – fortunate, since it's a very scary place up there in the high mountains and people disappear off cliffs or down crevasses all the time. Much better to cruise about town showing people that you could go up there and get gnarly if you wanted to.

Of course, we're being highly flippant here, as there are thousands of genuine freeriders in Chamonix who head up the Midi every day without giving a hoot who's impressed by it. And being a town full of strange juxtapositions, they'll occasionally find themselves standing next to an Italian tourist in high heels heading up to check out the view, like UK pro freerider Jess Venables here.

And in any case, we shouldn't mock – you never know when you might need your rope, harness and belay to pull some poor random rider out of a crevasse, as happened to an acquaintance of ours last winter.

admirably adult. Resort boundaries are clearly defined and you won't be penalized for heading further afield. Get yourself a Carte Neige when you buy your pass – it's a basic accident insurance policy that will get you off the mountain if you do get in trouble, although subsequent medical bills are not covered. Due to a depressingly high number of incidents, French off-piste recovery is among the best in the world. Transceivers, probes and shovel are absolutely essential.

Secret spots

With such a strong culture of Alpinism, the French backcountry has been zealously mapped and there are plenty of guidebooks detailing potential routes. Within such a setting, and with such a high number of mountain users, secret spots are jealously guarded by resort locals. Don't expect any seasonaires or locals to readily volunteer where all the best powder is. If powder is your thing, go to one of the smaller, less crowded resorts.

Freestyle

Although the French quickly allowed snowboarders to ride within their resorts back in the eighties, they were generally slow to develop funparks within their resorts. Even today, very few French resorts go to the lengths their US, Canadian and Austrian counterparts in providing top-class facilities for freestylers. Most snowboarders are surprised to hear that Chamonix, for example, still doesn't have a world-class funpark.

This is partly because the freeriding in French resorts is usually so good and partly because business is generally always booming in France. While other resorts use funparks to try and attract the snowboarding market, the French generally don't need to. The result is a 'like it or lump it' attitude that somehow adds to the whole Gallic snowboarding experience. Things are changing though, and resorts such as Val d'Isère, Avoriaz and Les Deux Alpes are developing their facilities.

The scene

The French snowboarding scene is one of the most vibrant in the world. Les Arcs local Regis Rolland is generally credited with pioneering the sport in Europe with his *Apocalypse Snow* series of films in the mid-eighties. Regis also started **A-Boards**, a hugely influential board brand. Since then, riders such as David Vincent, Yannick Amevet and Mathieu Crepel have kept French snowboarding at the top echelon.

The industry

As Youri Barneoud, *OnBoard*'s French editor says of the French industry, "In the Alps, the main point of attraction is Grenoble I would say, with the big French mag *Snowsurf* and another one that's gonna come out this year based there. The **Psykopit** crew (psykopit.com) – Pacome Allouis, L'Arrogs, Sylvain Bourbousson – is based there and it's one of the most active crews in France. Another important part of the scene is based around the Annecy, Chamonix and Geneva area. The French industry is pretty much between Grenoble and Annecy. **7TB4** crew (Nicolas Droz) is originally from Thonon (close to Annecy) and they make things happen in Avoriaz. That's probably the most active resort in France when it comes to snowboarding. Nico and crew have now opened a shop in Thonon (goldencircle.fr). There's also the **Advita** (advitawear.com) crew in the same area, who are another important French crew – Sylvain Monney, Aymeric Thonin, Thomas Maxheim. Lastly, things are also starting to happen a bit more in the south (Briançon, Serre Chevalier, Risoul) – my area! Those resorts are now giving snowboarding a big push as well."

Lift chat

The gap

The first time I heard of the jump, I was flicking through an issue of *Onboard* and saw a shot of Romain de Marchi spinning a 360 over it. I remember thinking "That's big". I didn't see it again until the film *Pop*, when Gigi Ruff and Romain again sessioned it. That time, Romain scored the 2005 Burton catalogue cover.

I happened to be in Morzine that season, so I decided to go check it out. I rode past and thought, "You could jump that with that landing". The people I was with were thinking, "He's all talk, he'll never do that". So I went home and watched video footage of it to try and imagine myself flying off it!

Every time I rode past the jump after that I got more and more nervous. It got to the point that I was scared even being near it! So I decided to go up and have a look. I looked over and I knew I could do it because I was scared but 'good' scared. Nervous, but I could picture myself doing it. Being scared like that is kind of enjoyable.

Soon after I was out shooting with my photographer friend Andrew 'Ribs' Hingston and we decided to go and see if the snow was good enough to do it. Someone had bombed the hell out of the landing and jumped it maybe four or five times. So I decided to have a shot and try a 360, like de Marchi. It went kinda OK. I went too big but I nearly landed it. I had one more go at a backside 540 and nearly landed it but the same thing happened. So we decided to wait until the snow was a little better.

Two weeks later I wake up and there is powder everywhere. The phone goes and it's my filmer and photographer. Next thing I know, we're building a run-in and take-off. The sun is out, and snow is good and everything is perfect. I'm on my own at the top, and I'm going "This is it! This is the time to do it! Go fast but not too fast! Spin slowly but make sure you get round". I dropped in, picked up speed, hit the lip, popped and spun round grabbing. I looked under myself and I could see people on the track below, 40 ft under me. I looked to the landing, landed and I kept riding. And I'm thinking, "Yes! I just landed a trick on the gap! Yeah! Yeah!"

As I got back to the landing, I'm suddenly approached by a big guy. I won't name him but he's a well-known pro and I'd looked up to him. He starts shouting at me "What are you doing? This is my place, my jump! What the f*** are you doing, jumping my jump?" I'm like "OK, OK, take it easy", and he cools down, says he's sorry. "I've been waiting to jump that for years!" In the end he shook my hand and respects the fact that I did it, but it was pretty crazy.

What happened after that? A year later we returned – me and Tyler Chorlton and Danny Wheeler. We knew where to go for speed and that the snow was good. In the end I landed a cab 720, and Danny landed a cab 540 underflip. Tyler got a backside 720 off it. We tried a few more tricks off it but we were done – good day, good tricks, good friends... the end. Until next year, of course …

Gary Greenshields

R. GARY GREENSHIELDS L. AVORIAZ P. ANDREW HINGSTON

France: a brief history of snowboarding

1980 → Alain Gaimard, PR director for Les Arcs, invites Australian Winterstick rider Paul Loxton to perform a publicity stunt, becoming the first person to snowboard in France. **1981** → With the opening of the new Les Arcs 2000 village, Alain invites the whole Winterstick team over. The 22 year-old local French mountain guide Regis Rolland sees the team in action and quickly gets hooked on the sport. **1982** → Gaimard commissions film-maker Didier Lafond to make *Ski Espace* in Les Arcs. Regis on his snowboard becomes the star. **1983** → The same production crew returns to Les Arcs to shoot *Apocalypse Snow*, a huge success which is later taken on a theatre tour of Europe, turning thousands onto the new sport. **1984** → French snowboard company *DEA* forms, making a range of swallowtail boards. Meanwhile, the first snowboard shops appear in Paris and Tignes. **1985** → *Hot Snowboards* starts up and introduces the first board with sidecut. **1986** → La Plagne organize the Euro Cup, the first major comp in France, while over in Chamonix, extreme alpinism meets snowboarding when Bruno Gouvy makes many first descents including Mont Blanc itself. **1989** → Hardboots rule. Serge Vitelli unveils the 'Vitelli Turn' ("When you take crazy angles until you get your face in the snow') and Jean Nerva becomes the poster boy for the new carving sensation. He has a pro model on *Burton* snowboards (The PJ, made in conjunction with Peter Bauer). The first *Mondial du Snow* – later turned into a yearly board test – is organized in Les Deux Alpes. High jinx there blamed for subsequent denouncing of snowboarding in the press. **1990** → The second *Kebra Classic*, a freestyle comp in Tignes, is won by newcomer Terje Haakonsen. **1992** → *Snowsurf*, the first French snowboard magazine launched. **1993** → Peter Bauer and Dieter Happ win first inner-city parallel slalom in Paris. Meanwhile, David Vincent is getting all the shots in European mags with his crazy French style and over tweaks. He signs to Regis' newly formed company A Snowboards along with Belgian rider Axel Pauporte. **1995** → Freestyle eventually eclipses hardboots in terms of sales. **1998** → Karin Ruby wins gold medal in Giant Slalom at Nagano Olympics. **Today** → French riders like Mathieu Crepel (winner of the first year *TTR World Snowboard Rankings*) spearhead a freestyle generation.

The Town ⊖ⓕ⊜

Avoriaz is famous for its bizarre architecture and town planning, first proposed by French Olympian Juan Vuarnet in the 1970s. Perched high above Morzine and built to blend in with the surrounding cliffs, most buildings are futuristic in concept, have odd, eclectic shapes and are crammed with apartments that wouldn't look out of place on *The Jetsons*. Virtually all apartments have incredible access to the slopes. The town is odd enough to play host to an annual 'Futuristic' film festival. It's car free, with horse-drawn sledges flying around, and can be reached by either road or cable car from Morzine.

Sleeping Maeva (maeva.com) are the largest apartment agency in town, offering deals as low as €20 per person per night. **Club Med** (clubmed.com) has catered accommodation for around €40 per person per night. **Les Dromonts** (T450 740811) has perhaps the best views in town for €140 a night.
Eating La Falaise (T450 741048) is perhaps the only pizza restaurant in the world next to a 300-m cliff, or try Le Chalet d'Avoriaz (T450 741273).
Bars and clubs Shooters, Le Tavaillon and Pub Le Choucas are all worth a punt. For a big night out, though, get the Prodain lift down to Morzine town.
Shopping There is a supermarket island, between two pistes, in the middle of town but it's heavily overpriced. Morzine offers better competition but an out-of-town shop is very difficult from Avoriaz.
Health Try the Galarie du Baraty (T450 791068) in Morzine for spa, massage and sauna.
Internet Surprisingly for such a futuristic place it lacks a true internet café, but the tourist office and the bowling alley have machines (€2 for 10 minutes), while wireless can be found at the **Manie Brioche** bakery.
Transfer options From Geneva airport, bus transfers (T450 384208) take around an hour. Or for the terminally flash, **Mont Blanc Helicopters** (T450 927821) make the same trip in 10 minutes for around €1000 per person.
Local partners The Portes du Soleil lift pass covers Morzine, Les Gets, Chatel, Les Crosets and Abondance to name a few.

R: MARK KENT P: ANDREW HINGSTON

Affordable ride in/ride out resort at the heart of the Portes du Soleil, one of the two areas in the world battling it out for the title of 'biggest linked lift system'.

🔅 *If you like this* …
… *try Val Thorens* ▸▸p160.

FRANCE
AVORIAZ

⊚ **OPENING TIMES**
Mid-Dec to late Apr: 0830-1630

⊗ **RESORT PRICES (PORTES DU SOLEIL)**
Week pass (6 days): €179
Day pass: €37
Season pass: €706

ⓘ **DIRECTORY**
Tourist office: T450 740211
Medical centre: T450 740542
Pisteurs: T450 741113
Taxi: Avoriaz is car-free
Local radio: Radio Morzine 97.9 FM
Website: avoriaz.com

The Mountain

The Portes du Soleil spreads over the border between France and Switzerland and offers an unbelievable amount of riding. In amongst this ludicrously large area are several world-class parks, and many other mini features and purpose-built boarder cross tracks. Avoriaz alone has the baby park, its main park, plus a permanent halfpipe in town. In addition, the Les Crosets park is considered to be one of the best in Switzerland – home to the likes of Romain de Marchi – while the area obviously has incredible freeriding potential.

Beginners Open your front door and ride towards the eight-man Tour chair that goes back up through town. From there, head down the Proclou run until you hit the area known as Super-Morzine (it is above the Super-Morzine gondola), perhaps the best beginner's area in France. Ride around the whole area and back to Avoriaz and you've done a decent lap.
Intermediate From Avoriaz head to the top of the Chavanette where

you'll encounter 'The Wall', a ludicrously steep mogul run. Don't worry – you can take the chair down. At the bottom keep heading for Les Crosets, when you get there find the park and try out the fantastic gully run. A return lap to Avoriaz via Point de Mossett and the Brocheaux lift is a big day out.
Advanced If there is powder, the home run from Avoriaz to Les Prodains offers some incredible cat tracks to shred. Otherwise, the Avoriaz park should offer any rider a week of decent challenges.
Kids Le Village des Enfants (T450 740446) feeds and looks after the kids for around €40 per day.
Flat light days The Prodains home run offers the best trees nearby.

> **"** Perched high upon a cliff, Avoriaz is one of the best piste accessed resorts around, and has a funpark to rival anywhere in the world – when they can be bothered to shape it. **"**
>
> *James McPhail, photographer*

P: JAMES MCPHAIL

LOCALS DO
- Get the Prodains cable car down to Morzine for a knees-up.
- Head to the Les Crosets park for a sun-filled day of shredding.
- Know some of the best terrain can be found at lower spots – the Mossettes chair in particular.

LOCALS DON'T
- Walk uphill too much. Most buildings have public access elevators and top floor bridges to higher ground.
- Head into Switzerland after 1500 and risk getting stuck.
- Ride down 'The Wall'. Unless they're showing off.

PROS
- Great selection of parks from beginner to expert. There's even a snowskate park!
- Ride straight from your doorstep.
- Snow until late in the season.

CONS
- Can get busy during the holidays.
- Can be a bit of a mission to get your bags to the apartments.
- Crazy architecture people either love or hate.

NOT TO MISS
The Avoriaz funpark. World class.

REMEMBER TO AVOID
Getting stuck in Switzerland after 1630. Make sure you've got enough time to get home as taxis can cost upwards of €100.

SNOW DEPTH

metres	N	D	J	F	M	A

RELIVE A FAMOUS MOMENT
Luc Besson started his film career by entering – and winning – the Avoriaz Film Festival in 1983, later going on to make *The Big Blue* (see Tignes RAFM) and *The Fifth Element*.

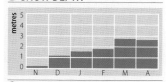

1800 m	TOWN ALTITUDE
88 km	KM TO AIRPORT
GVA	AIRPORT
★★☆	VEGETARIAN RATING
★★☆	INTERNET CAFES
★★★	RIDE IN/RIDE OUT
3200 m	HIGHEST LIFT
2200 m	VERTICAL DROP
area not measured	RIDEABLE AREA (IN ACRES)
659 km	KM OF PISTES
3	NURSERY AREAS
150/110/28	RUNS: BEG/INTER/ADV
0/3	FUNICULAR/CABLE CARS
11/82	GONDOLAS/CHAIRS
110	DRAGS
yes	NIGHT RIDING
10	PARKS
3	PIPE
no	SUMMER AREAS
★★★☆☆	ENVIRONMENTAL RATING
$$$	COST INDICATOR

FIGURES COVER THE PORTES DU SOLEIL AREA

FRANCE
AVORIAZ

Bourg St Maurice

R: CHRIS MORAN P: NICK HAMILTON

As the biggest town in the Tarantaise, sitting at the end of the train line, Bourg has easy access to St Foy, La Rosière, the Espace Killy (Tignes and Val d'Isère) and a direct funicular up to Les Arcs and the Paradiski area.

⊙ If you like this...
... try *St Anton*   p48, *Méribel*   p146, or *Serre Chevalier*   p152.

The Town

Bourg is a classic valley town, sitting grumpily on the valley floor with the sparkling ski resorts up above. It was never intended to be a tourist destination, so while it does have one old cobbled street, there is very little inspiring architecture. Bourg is instead a functional entity, supplying the economic needs of the Tarantaise community. In the 1990s, however, Les Arcs installed a Funicular railway from the town centre in an attempt to ease the traffic on the access road to the resort: tourists could leave their cars in Bourg and holiday in peace. The upshot of course was that seasonaires could find cheap digs in Bourg and use the Funicular to access Les Arcs. By 1998 the community had swelled to several groups and today there is a community of hundreds of Europeans, Antipodeans and Americans who call Bourg home. There are other attractions too: great supermarkets, a skatepark, an express train to Paris, outdoor pools, great climbing and a lovely river when the snow melts. A word of warning though – it is a

☺ **OPENING TIMES**
See Les Arcs, page 142

💲 **RESORT PRICES (PARADISKI)**
Week pass (6 days): €233
Day pass: €46
Season pass: €895

DIRECTORY
Tourist office: T479 071257
Medical centre: T479 070988
Pisteurs: T479 078566
Taxi: T686 242383
Local radio: Radio Les Arcs 93.4 FM
Website: lesarcs.com

Gendarme training centre, with two huge barracks in town. Ratios of men to women are laughably sausage heavy.

Sleeping The Chill Chalet (T614 611437, chillchalet.com) has a new chalet in Bourg from €25 per person with breakfast and optional evening meal. For a longer stay, seasonaires.com have a selection of long-term lets online.

Eating Most people here eat out infrequently, but if you do try Le Refuge and Le Savoyarde.

Bars and clubs The Zoom Bar is the most modern bar in Bourg, although everybody also goes to 'The Spot' as the Centrale Bar is universally known. For clubbing, forget it – take a trip up to the discos of 1800.

Shopping There are two huge supermarkets on the outskirts of town next to the Les Arcs access road. The Super U is generally considered to be the cheapest.

Health The Hotel du Golf (T479 414343) in Les Arcs 1800 is one of the few places to cater for the health market, otherwise there's a pool in town. Warning: as with the rest of

If you want to do a season in a cool town and imagine what the Chamonixs and Morzines of this world were like 20 years ago, then Bourg's the place to head. It's the back door to Les Arcs, my favourite resort in the world.

Scalp, photo editor of OnBoard

France, they insist on men having to wear Speedo-type swimming trunks. We have no idea why.

Internet The versatile Zoom Bar – an art gallery, clothes shop and restaurant, as well as an internet café – is the only place to check those mails.

Transfer options Try Coolbus (thecoolbus.co.uk) or the scheduled bus services Altibus (altibus.com) or Satobus (satobus.com)

Local partners Buy a Paradiski pass and get discounts to La Rosière/La Thuile and St Foy.

▶▶ *For locals do/locals don't …*
… See Les Arcs, page 142.

P: CHRIS MORAN/HOTSHITPICTURES.COM

850 m	TOWN ALTITUDE
120 km	KM TO AIRPORT
GVA	AIRPORT
★★☆	VEGETARIAN RATING
★★★	INTERNET CAFES
★★☆	RIDE IN/RIDE OUT
3250 m	HIGHEST LIFT
2000 m	VERTICAL DROP
34,000	RIDEABLE AREA (IN ACRES)
425 km	KM OF PISTES
6	NURSERY AREAS
144/66/29	RUNS: BEG/INTER/ADV
1/3	FUNICULAR/CABLE CARS
12/66	GONDOLAS/CHAIRS
58	DRAGS
yes	NIGHT RIDING
5	PARKS
1	PIPE
no	SUMMER AREAS
★★★ ★★☆	ENVIRONMENTAL RATING
💲💲💲	COST INDICATOR
FRANCE BOURG ST MAURICE	

FIGURES COVER THE PARADISKI AREA

Chamonix

The Town

Situated at the base of Mont Blanc – Western Europe's highest mountain, at 4807 m – Chamonix is arguably the world's most famous resort. However, it's actually very different from the typical notion of a resort, in that it's a self-contained 'proper' town with thousands of inhabitants. There are a number of populated areas that come under the Chamonix banner, but the two main focal points are Chamonix itself, and the satellite town of Argentière, 10 km further up the valley.

Sleeping Board 'n' Lodge (boardnlodge.com) offer a range of services from accommodation to catered and self-catering snowboarding holidays. **Coldfusion** (coldfusionchalets.co.uk) provide a similar service, for individuals only (ie, no families). **McNab Snowboarding** (mcnabsnowboarding.com) offer catered snowboarding holidays with instruction and guiding from ex-British champion and qualified high mountain guide Neil McNab.
Eating Mojos (T450 891226) in Chamonix town square is a good choice for snacks. **Grand Central** (T450 535609), directly opposite McDonald's, is also very popular, with excellent vegetarian meals, homemade cakes and fresh juices and smoothies. For a top-class meal try **Le Delice** (T450 915206) in Les Houches, or **Munchie** (T450 534541) in the Rue du Moulin.
Bars and clubs The Jekyll does a great pint of Guinness and also serves excellent food. **MBC** brews its own beer, and often puts on live music for après. **Goophy** (also an excellent restaurant) and **Elevation** next door are both very popular. **Le Garage** is Chamonix's main after-hours drinking den.
Shopping As resorts go, Chamonix's shopping facilities are up there with the best. **Zero G** (T450 530101) is the place for all your snowboarding needs.

> Get it on a bad day and you'll spend hours standing in lift queues wondering why you didn't go somewhere else. Get it at its best, and you'll be treated to the best snowboarding you'll find anywhere in the world.
>
> *James Stentiford, pro snowboarder*

Health Angie Wardle (T619 576000) offers a comprehensive mobile massage service including aromatherapy massage.
Internet Le Bureau, on edge of the river on the Rue du Moulins.
Transfer options ATS (a-t-s.net) operate a shared transfer service from both Geneva and Lyon. Try **Alpybus** (alpybus.com) for scheduled bus transfers to Geneva.
Local partners Les Houches, St Gervais, Les Contamines, Megève, Courmayeur, Les Portes du Soleil, Verbier.

The original winter sports Mecca, home of the inaugural 1924 Winter Olympics.

If you like this . . .
. . . try *Krasnaya Poliana* ▸▸p108, *La Grave* ▸▸p134, or *Verbier* ▸▸p332.

P: CHRIS MORAN/HOTSHITPICTURES.COM

The Mountain

Chamonix is made up of five distinct areas. These are all fairly well spaced out and travel between them is by bus or car. The sheer variety of terrain on offer is impressive, and on its day the place boasts some of the world's best freeriding, no question. Les Grands Montets is busy, and its north-facing aspect means that the pistes are often pretty firm. Aiguille du Midi has no pistes, but from the top you can access La Vallée Blanche and various other famed Chamonix glacier spots. Le Brévent and La Flégère offer the largest overall area thanks to the link, but it's the mellow, rolling terrain of Le Tour that often proves most popular with snowboarders.

Beginners Le Tour is the most beginner-friendly of the Chamonix areas thanks to its wide, open pistes and mellower gradient. Spend the morning lapping the chair on the front face, then spend the afternoon exploring the fabled back side serviced by the Tête de Balme chair. For absolute beginners, the learner's slope at Le Vormaine (bottom of the Le Tour area) should be the first port of call. It's also much cheaper than buying the full Le Tour pass.

Intermediate The 22-km trip down the Vallée Blanche is a must-do.

Though it's not that steep or challenging, you'll need a guide as it's a glacier, and tales of the unwary falling down crevasses are not uncommon. If your legs are still up to it, spend the afternoon cruising the frequently sunny north-facing slopes of Le Brévent, marvelling at the sight of the Aiguille where you've just been on the other side of the valley. Madness.

Advanced Get the first bin up from Les Grands Montets, then head straight to the 'top tickets' cable car to beat the queues. Drop into the itinerary on the left, and follow it back down to the mid station. Next, have a couple of runs on the Bochard, then after lunch head up to Le Tour and spend the afternoon cruising the back side and jibbing gullies to the skier's right of the main chairlift on the front face.

Kids There are various family discounts available. The Cham'Baby pass is valid for kids of 4-11 years on six consecutive days, and costs €70.

Flat light days Head up the Grands Montets, then stick on the lower chairlifts on the right as you look up the mountain. Here's where you'll find the fabled Dream Forest.

⊘ OPENING TIMES

Early Dec to early May: peak times 0800-1700; off-peak 0830-1630

🅢 RESORT PRICES

Week pass (6 days): €214 Cham'Ski, €248 Ski Pass Mont-Blanc
Day pass: €44
Season pass: €670 Cham'Ski, €690 Ski Pass Mont-Blanc

ⓘ DIRECTORY

Tourist office: T450 530024
Medical centre: T450 558055
Pisteurs: T450 532275
Taxi: T450 531914
Local radio: Radio Mt-Blanc 97.4 FM
Website: chamonix.net

☺ LOCALS DO

⊘ Take great care when riding the back bowls at Le Tour – avalanche risk is high.
⊘ Take advantage of the proximity of Courmayeur – it often has great snow when Chamonix is lacking.
⊘ Take avalanche safety pretty seriously. At the very least, people are kitted out with a shovel, transceiver and probe.

☹ LOCALS DON'T

⊗ Eat in the mountain restaurants – they're pricey.
⊗ Leave boards on the balcony in Chamonix Sud.
⊗ Ride Les Grands Montets until March, except on powder days. It's in the shade so it's almost always icy.

✓ PROS

⊘ Great range of terrain.
⊘ Vibrant town centre.
⊘ Very near Geneva airport.

✗ CONS

⊗ Unlinked ski areas.
⊗ Lift queues.
⊗ No park.

☺ NOT TO MISS

A trip to the top of the Aiguille du Midi, for breathtaking views of Mont Blanc and the Chamonix Valley.

ⓘ REMEMBER TO AVOID

The download queue at La Flégère during peak times.

❄ SNOW DEPTH

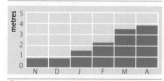

☺ RELIVE A FAMOUS MOMENT

Check out famously Mohicaned skier Glen Plake's infamous drop-in off the bridge at the top of the top tickets cable car, as featured in 1989's legendary *Blizzard of Ahhs* movie. Recreation not recommended.

1035 m	TOWN ALTITUDE
88 km	KM TO AIRPORT
GVA	AIRPORT
★★★	VEGETARIAN RATING
★★★	INTERNET CAFES
★☆☆	RIDE IN/RIDE OUT
3842 m	HIGHEST LIFT
2807 m	VERTICAL DROP
area not measured	RIDEABLE AREA (IN ACRES)
170 km	KM OF PISTES
4	NURSERY AREAS
41/25/13	RUNS: BEG/INTER/ADV
0/6	FUNICULAR/CABLE CARS
6/17	GONDOLAS/CHAIRS
12	DRAGS
yes	NIGHT RIDING
0	PARKS
0	PIPE
no	SUMMER AREAS
★★☆	ENVIRONMENTAL RATING
🅢🅢🅢	COST INDICATOR

FRANCE
CHAMONIX

Courchevel

The largest of the Three Valleys resorts, Courchevel offers something for everyone. Its glitzy reputation keeps the majority of the snowboard crowd away, leaving it wide open for those in the know.

» *If you like this* …
… *try St Moritz* »*p330, or Aspen* »*p350.*

The Town ⊟ ⊘ ⊟

Courchevel is made up of five widely spaced out, populated centres at differing altitudes, each with their own distinct character. This ranges from chic 1850 with its preponderance of fur coats and wealthy Parisians to the low-key and homely feel of Les Praz and St Bon at 1300 m and 1100 m respectively. Though 1850 is the most central in terms of ski area access, many people prefer the vibe of 1650, the latter having seen huge development over the past few years.

Sleeping If you're on a tight budget plump for B&B at the two-star **Edelweiss Hotel** (courchevel-edelweiss.com), or if cost isn't such an obstacle then **La Seizena** (T479 014646) is worth a look. Both are in 1650. Alternatively **Pleisure** (pleisure.co.uk) offer a variety of chalet accommodation around the valley.
Eating For snacks on the go try **S'no Limit** (T479 083844) in 1850's Place du Forum or for a sit down meal 1650's **Bel Air** (T479 080093) is justifiably popular. **Petit Savoyard** (T479 082744) in 1650 is the best spot

for traditional Savoyarde faire.
Bars and clubs The Bubble Bar or Rocky's in 1650, after which you can head to the **Space Bar** til 0400. If you're after a suitably chic late-night establishment try 1850's **Le Kalico**.
Shopping Courchevel is well set up for shoppers, be it high fashion or snowboarding kit. There are also numerous supermarkets in the valley.
Health Pamper Off Piste (pamperoffpiste.com) for mobile massage treatments.

Internet Cybercafé in 1850 and Bubble Bar in 1650.
Transfer options ATS (a-t-s.net) for shared transfers from Geneva and Lyon. Geneva costs around €79 return. Alternatively try **Aerosko Bus** (T227 178275) for Geneva transfers and **Altibus** (altibus.com) for Lyon.
Local partners Les Trois Vallées, Espace Killy (Val d'Isère and Tignes), Paradiski (La Plagne, Peisey Vallandry and Les Arcs), Pralognan-la-Vanoise and Les Saisies.

⊙ **OPENING TIMES**

Early Dec to late Apr: 0900-1630 (1700 end of season)

⑤ **RESORT PRICES (THREE VALLEYS)**

Week pass (6 days): €215
Day pass: €42
Season pass: €935

⊙ **DIRECTORY**

Tourist office: T479 080029
Medical centre: T479 083213
Pisteurs: T479 080091
Taxi: T479 082346
Local radio: Radio Courchevel 93.2 FM
Website: courchevel.com

R: TOM WILLMOTT P: JAMES MCPHAIL

The Mountain

Why Courchevel isn't up there in the ranks of the world's super resorts is something of a mystery. Its reputation may lead you to believe that it's little more than a fashion parade for the French elite, but when it comes to the mountains nothing could be further from the truth. From mellow nursery slopes to funparks, to beautifully kempt high-speed groomers, this place has it all. It offers a greater variety of terrain than its Three Valleys counterparts including plenty of steep north-facing freeride possibilities and an abundance of good tree runs.

Beginners Courchevel is idea for absolute beginners – there are two learner areas in 1850, one in 1650 and one in Le Praz. There is also a variety of good green runs to be found in the trees in the Pralong sector of 1850, accessible from the Jardin Alpin gondola.

Intermediate Start with a blast down the Saulire, then head up the Vizelle chair. From here it's down to

> *Courchevel is an ideal all-round resort. You've got some really sick terrain for more advanced riders, super-fun mellow runs for learners, and everything in between.*
>
> *Johno Verity, professional snowboarder*

Chanrossa and over into 1650 for a few runs on the Pyramides drag. After lunch, make your way back over to 1850, head up to Col da la Loze, then cruise down through the trees into La Tania – particularly good fun if it's a powder day.

Advanced The terrain in the Creux Noirs area will keep you busy for most of the day. Much of it is accessible by a short hike down the ridge off the top of the chair. It's largely north-facing so the snow stays good. After this, head up the Chanrossa chairlift and cruise down into 1650, where you'll find plenty of natural hits and jibs to play around on.

Kids Kids under five get a free lift pass. Bring proof of identity.

Flat light days Head to La Tania and Les Praz where you'll find the valley's best tree runs.

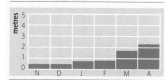

😊 LOCALS DO
- Ride the chutes under the Creux Noirs on a powder day.
- Go to Méribel to ride the parks.
- Hang out in 1650 – it's the more down to earth option.

😠 LOCALS DON'T
- Buy a Courchevel only pass – the extra cost of the Three Valleys pass is well worthwhile.
- Complain about whiteouts – there's plenty of good tree runs.
- Leave for the Belleville (Val Thorens) Valley too late in the day.

✅ PROS
- Huge variety of terrain.
- Enormous area.
- Great for families and beginners.

❌ CONS
- The individual resorts are very widely spaced apart, making a night out in one of the other resorts difficult.
- Gets very busy during peak times.
- Some truly appalling mogul fields.

⊙ NOT TO MISS
A high-speed charge down to 1850 from the top of La Saulire cable car on the immaculate early morning pistes.

ⓘ REMEMBER TO AVOID
Getting stuck in one of the other valleys after the lifts close – it's an expensive mistake.

❄ SNOW DEPTH

metres	N	D	J	F	M	A

☺ RELIVE A FAMOUS MOMENT
David and Victoria Beckham regularly visit the resort. Pictures of Victoria emerging from her chalet were front page news in the UK press. To relive that moment, you'll need a dressing gown and some serious shades.

1100 m to 1850 m	TOWN ALTITUDE
128 km	KM TO AIRPORT
GVA	AIRPORT
★★☆	VEGETARIAN RATING
★★★	INTERNET CAFES
★☆☆	RIDE IN/RIDE OUT
3230 m	HIGHEST LIFT
2130 m	VERTICAL DROP
28,000	RIDEABLE AREA (IN ACRES)
600 km	KM OF PISTES
12	NURSERY AREAS
183/119/33	RUNS: BEG/INTER/ADV
3/3	FUNICULAR/CABLE CARS
34/69	GONDOLAS/CHAIRS
71	DRAGS
no	NIGHT RIDING
5	PARKS
3	PIPE
no	SUMMER AREAS
★★★	ENVIRONMENTAL RATING
⑂⑂⑂	COST INDICATOR
FRANCE COURCHEVEL	

FIGURES COVER THE THREE VALLEYS AREA

The Town

La Clusaz mightn't seem an obvious choice for inclusion in the top 100, but where else in France can you get away from the bustle and experience an unspoilt French mountain town, all merely an hour's drive from Geneva airport? La Clusaz is both pretty and unassuming. It's long been the preserve of the Gallic and thus retains a very French feel. You won't find much in the way of rowdy nightlife, but if you're looking for a good place to take the family or to learn to ride, look no further.

Sleeping The three-star **Hotel Beauregard** (hotel-beauregard.fr) is very central and has its own excellent restaurant, along with a jacuzzi, sauna, steam room and an 18-m swimming pool. The two-star **Hotel Les Sapins** (T450 633333) is also well situated. Various tour operators such as **Crystal** (crystalski.co.uk) operate in La Clusaz – give them a try for late package deals or self-catered accommodation. **Eating** La Calèche (T450 024260) or **Au Cochon des Neiges** (T450 026262) for traditional Savoyarde

cuisine. **La Bergerie** (T450 026340) serves pizzas and local specialities, and though a bit cheaper the food is still excellent.

Bars and clubs Le Salto is great for après, and they also serve food. Popular bars include **Le Pressoir**, **Les Caves du Paccaly** and **Le Grenier** – the latter two frequently put on live music and DJs. **L'Ecluse** is the town's nightclub, replete with glass dancefloor over the river.

Shopping There are two **Marche U** supermarkets in La Clusaz; one in Le Solémont and one in La Perrière.

Health Espace Aquatique des Aravis (T450 024301) have swimming pools, sauna, steam room and a gym. There are also massage services available. Try **Beauvoir Wellness Institut** (T450 648615, beauvoir-institut.com) for osteopathy, physiotherapy and a range of massage services, including ayurvedic, Thai and reflexology.

Internet You can get online at **Arvimedia** (T450 323805) and **Service Academie** (T450 326589) at the **Sno Académie** ski and snowboard school.

Transfer options ATS (a-t-s.net) for transfers from Lyon and Geneva. There is also a regular (three times daily) bus service from Geneva.

Local partners Le Grand Bornand.

R: UNKNOWN P: LA CLUSAZ/F MARIE

Gallic resort par excellence, with a short transfer time thanks to its proximity to Geneva airport.

:D **If you like this** ...
... try *Soldeu* ▸▸*p292*, or *Grindelwald* ▸▸*p318*.

⊙ OPENING TIMES

Mid-Dec to late Apr: 0900 - 1700

⊙ RESORT PRICES

Week pass (6 days): €156
Day pass: €27,50
Season pass: €570

⊙ DIRECTORY

Tourist office: T450 326500
Medical centre: T450 024022
Pisteurs: T450 326515
Taxi: T663 513258
Local radio: Radio Aravis Europe 2 92.0 FM
Website: laclusaz.com

The Mountain

Granted, La Clusaz is pretty low. It's also pretty flat, with around 60% of the pistes being suitable for beginners. But there is a wealth of good riding to be had for those who look a little deeper, including some amazing trees and some perfect kicker building spots. Candide Thovex, one of the world's best freeskiers, snowboards here on powder days. Experience one for yourself to find out why.

Beginners La Clusaz is an ideal place to learn to ride. You'll find some good mellow pistes at the Beauregard and L'Etale areas that are perfect for making your first turns. The drawback is that they're largely serviced by draglifts, but the sooner you take on that challenge the better! Once you can link your turns then it's chocks away, as the vast majority of pistes are beginner-friendly.

Intermediate Thanks to its predominantly mellow gradient, charging around the place is a real blast – there's no need to be constantly checking your speed as you would in steep resorts like Chamonix. The tree-lined Beauregard area is very mellow but fun to explore, and there are fun jibbing possibilities

❝ ❞

La Clusaz is French legend Candide Thovex's local resort, and is the perfect get away from the busier resorts in the area, like Chamonix or Avoriaz. There are loads of good tree runs and a pretty decent park. If it's good enough for Candide, it's good enough for me!

James Stentiford, pro snowboarder

around the nearby Domaine de L'Etale. You'll find better snow up the L'Aiguille, thanks to its higher elevation, so if it's patchy lower down then this might be your best bet.

Advanced The Col de Balme is the highest point in the resort so it usually has the best snow. There's some interesting terrain to explore up here, with plenty of natural hits and a few decent drops. In a place like this, creative thinking is the key – play around on the sides of the pistes and see what air you can get. Any day is well rounded off with a good session in the park.

Kids It's free for children under five years of age. A photo and proof of age are required.

Flat light days Much of La Clusaz is within the treeline, so stick low and you should be okay.

😊 LOCALS DO
- Take day trips to nearby Annecy, one of the most stunning towns in France.
- Have frequent days riding at other nearby resorts, such as Morzine, Chamonix and Flaine.
- Know how to build good kickers.

😐 LOCALS DON'T
- Expect to get by speaking only English.
- Complain about flat pistes – follow one to see why…
- Come here late in the season, particularly if there's not much snow around. Avoriaz and Flaine are both nearby, and their much higher elevation ensures better snow cover.

✔ PROS
- Great for families.
- Very near Geneva airport.
- Beautiful, unspoilt French village.

✘ CONS
- Low altitude means snow cover can be a problem.
- Not great late season.
- Busy at the weekends.

☺ NOT TO MISS
A night out rounded off with a dance above the river on the glass dancefloor at the L'Ecluse nightclub – a strange yet strangely compelling experience!

❗ REMEMBER TO AVOID
At weekends in February it gets pretty manic.

❄ SNOW DEPTH

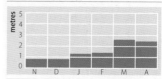

☺ RELIVE A FAMOUS MOMENT
Candide Thovex's *French Toast* was filmed almost exclusively in La Clusaz. It might be a ski film, but it's Candide, and he's enough of a French madman to warrant inclusion.

1100 m	TOWN ALTITUDE
50 km	KM TO AIRPORT
GVA	AIRPORT
★★☆	VEGETARIAN RATING
★★★	INTERNET CAFES
★★☆	RIDE IN/RIDE OUT
2600 m	HIGHEST LIFT
1500 m	VERTICAL DROP
988	RIDEABLE AREA (IN ACRES)
132 km	KM OF PISTES
2	NURSERY AREAS
53/24/7	RUNS: BEG/INTER/ADV
0/2	FUNICULAR/CABLE CARS
4/14	GONDOLAS/CHAIRS
35	DRAGS
yes	NIGHT RIDING
1	PARKS
1	PIPE
no	SUMMER AREAS
★★★	ENVIRONMENTAL RATING
$ $ $	COST INDICATOR
FRANCE	
LA CLUSAZ	

The Town

🖥️ 📷 🖨️

The moment you drive into La Grave you sense you're somewhere special. It's a small village in the Massif des Ecrins, situated along the road running between Briançon and Le Bourg d'Oisans. It has plenty of quiet, rustic French charm, and though small it has pretty much everything you need during your stay. As you walk around the village it's hard not to be awestruck by Le Meije towering above you at 3983 m, its endless glaciers and crevasses offering stark reminders that this is not your average resort.

Sleeping Self-catering is a good option in La Grave. **Le Chalets de la Meije** are really well equipped. They're right by the Jandry lift and have their own spa facilities. Book through peakretreats.co.uk. The two-star **Hotel Edelweiss** (hotel-edelweiss.com, (T476 799093) offers en suite half-board and B&B accommodation. It also has a jacuzzi and sauna, and free internet.
Eating The crêpe selection at **Alp Bar** (T476 799667) will take care of your snacking needs, and the popular **Le Bois des Fées** (T476 110548) bar serves good simple food such as

pizzas. Be sure to try the set menu at **Hotel Edelweiss**, or for local specialities try **Au Vieux Guide** (T476 799075).
Bars and clubs La Grave isn't exactly Ibiza but there are a couple of great places to get a beer. The main hang-out is the **Bois des Fées** bar, which is always full of locals. The bar at the **Edelweiss** is also very popular, and often has live music.
Shopping As well as a supermarket, deli and bakery you'll find numerous snowboard and mountaineering shops.
Health The **Hotel Edelweiss** has a sauna and jacuzzi.
Internet Again, you'll find this at the **Edelweiss**.
Transfer options VFD (vfd.fr) for bus

> 66 99
>
> For me this is how ski resorts should be – one lift, a huge mountain and endless lines to be had. No matter what your level it's essential that you hire a guide though. It's far too easy to end up on top of a monstrous cliff or in a crevasse to take the risk.
>
> *Marcus Chapman, former editor*
> *Snowboard UK*

transfers from Grenoble town and St Geoirs airport. From Lyon Saint-Exupéry, get a bus to Grenoble with **Satobus** (satobus.com) then take a VFD transfer to the resort.
Local partners Les Deux Alpes.

A wild and stunning place that could deliver your best ever day's snowboarding, or a trip down a bottomless crevasse.

⊃ If you like this ...
... try Kicking Horse ▸▸p80, or Chamonix ▸▸p128.

⊕ OPENING TIMES
Mid-Dec to early May: 0900-1650

⊙ RESORT PRICES
Week pass (6 days): €135
Day pass: €32
Season pass: €605

ⓘ DIRECTORY
Tourist office: T476 799005
Medical centre: T476 799803
Mountain rescue: T492 222222
Taxi: T476 799287
Local radio: None
Website: lagrave-lameije.com

R: UNKNOWN P: OT LA GRAVE-LA MEIJE

R: UNKNOWN P: OT LA GRAVE-LA MEIJE

The Mountain

Simply put, there is no other resort like La Grave on earth. There are no marked runs, no ski patrol and it's full of crevasses and massive cliffs to catch out the unwary. The very *idea* of a resort like this even existing in North America is laughable. There are only four lifts in La Grave, but the top elevation is very high and there's over 2 km of vertical drop to cover. The terrain is mind blowing and at times very challenging. Add to this the fact that it's practically deserted compared to every other resort in France. In short, La Grave is freeriding at its very best.

Beginners If you're a beginner then La Grave quite simply isn't the place for you. Go elsewhere.

Intermediate In La Grave, a guide is absolutely essential. Contact the **Bureau de Guide** (T476 799021, guidelagrave.com). To ride here at all you'll want to be totally comfortable in powder, both on steeps and through the trees. The best thing to do is be totally honest with your guide about your level of ability, so that they can accurately gauge where they can take you. This way you won't spend the day digging yourself out of tree wells.

Advanced Have your guide take you straight up the Jandry gondola to the top station. From here the choices are endless, though one common route is Vallons de la Meije. Next is a long ride down to the mid-station (P2) taking in cliff drops and natural gullies. If the snow's good the trees from P2 to P1 are epic – with countless different lines you'll be lapping this until your legs can't take anymore. A great spot for lunch is the mountain restaurant at the top station called **Les Ruillans**, where the food and views are superb.

Kids La Grave is possibly the last resort on earth you'd want to take your kids. Don't bother.

Flat light days Get out of the gondola at P2 and shred the trees back down to P1. You'll still need a guide to do this though as there are some huge cliffs waiting for you in the forest, which requires the correct traverse on exit.

🙂 LOCALS DO
- Wear all the essential avalanche gear: transceiver, shovel and probe.
- Respect the mountain and always know their route.
- Check the weather conditions before going to the top station.

☹ LOCALS DON'T
- Forget their avalanche safety gear.
- Go out on the mountain by themselves.
- Have wide stances and gangsta headphones.

✔ PROS
- A powder day in La Grave is a once in a lifetime experience.
- Some of the best tree runs in the world.
- As unspoilt as it gets.

✖ CONS
- Can be extremely cold until March.
- Snow cover can be thin lower down. Check the conditions before you book.
- The necessity for having a guide means that it can work out quite costly.

☺ NOT TO MISS
The *Derby De La Meije* competition, a kamikaze race from top to bottom of Le Grave. A €10,000 first prize encourages some mental lines and also a fair share of carnage.

ⓘ REMEMBER TO AVOID
Getting lost in a whiteout at the top station.

❄ SNOW DEPTH

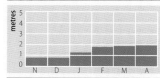

♻ RELIVE A FAMOUS MOMENT
Take part in the legendary *Derby De La Meije*. It's not exactly reliving someone else's favourite moment, but you may want to relive it with your friends if you win.

R: UNKNOWN P: OT LA GRAVE-LA MEIJE

1450 m	TOWN ALTITUDE
77 km	KM TO AIRPORT
GNB	AIRPORT
★☆☆	VEGETARIAN RATING
★★☆	INTERNET CAFES
★★☆	RIDE IN/RIDE OUT
3550 m	HIGHEST LIFT
2150 m	VERTICAL DROP
area not measured	RIDEABLE AREA (IN ACRES)
runs not measured	KM OF PISTES
0	NURSERY AREAS
not measured	RUNS: BEG/INTER/ADV
0/0	FUNICULAR/CABLE CARS
1/1	GONDOLAS/CHAIRS
2	DRAGS
no	NIGHT RIDING
0	PARKS
0	PIPE
no	SUMMER AREAS
figures not available	ENVIRONMENTAL RATING
💲💲💲	COST INDICATOR

FRANCE
LA GRAVE

The Town

La Plagne is made up of six high-altitude stations, along with a further four village resorts. The first thing that visitors driving up the road to La Plagne will notice is the shocking architecture of the complex in Aime la Plagne, cunningly placed right on the skyline for maximum visual impact. The town planning committee that agreed that one must have been on drugs. If you can forgive this blunder, La Plagne is very passable in most respects, and the village resorts have plenty of traditional French charm.

Sleeping Most accommodation in La Plagne is in the form of apartments. Book through the central reservation service (T479 097979, reservation@la-plagne.com). Belle Plagne's **Les Balcons de Belle Plagne** (T479 557655) is one of the best hotels in town, with its own bar/restaurant, sauna, pool and fitness room.

Eating Bar La Cheminée (T479 090550), inside the shopping centre in Plagne Centre, is recommended for snacks on the go. **Chalet de Colosses** (up the drag lift to the top of the pipe, then follow the little path) is arguably the best restaurant in Plagne Bellecôte, or if you're in Belle Plagne then try **Le Matafan** (T479 090919). Hit up **Blu Noir** in Plagne Centre to take care of the late-night munchies.

Bars and clubs Belle Plagne has the most choice. The **Cheyenne** is a decent bar that doubles as a great Tex-Mex restaurant, and there's also the **Tête Inn**, well worth checking out at après (confusingly enough, it's also known as **Matt's Bar**). Once the pubs have shut then the **Saloon** club is the only real place to go. **No Blem Café** is the main bar in Plagne Centre, though you could also try the **Luna Bar**.

Shopping You won't struggle for supermarkets here (for example Plagne Centre has two), and there are numerous spots for snowboarding needs.

Health There are three relaxation centres offering services such as sauna, jacuzzi, massage, spa treatments and physiotherapy. They're in Belle Plagne (T479 092688), Plagne Centre (T479 090345) and Bellecôte (T479 092248). There's also a sports centre in Plagne Centre, and a heated, open-air swimming pool in Bellecôte.

Internet No Blem Café in Plagne centre.

Transfer options Transports **Berards** (T479 097227) for bus transfers from Geneva. **Satobus** (satobus-alps.com) for buses from Lyon. The **Eurostar** (eurostar.com) stops at Aime, La Plagne's base town.

Local partners Paradiski (Les Arcs, La Plagne, Peisey-Vallandry), Val d'Isère, Tignes, La Rosière, St Foy, Three Valleys.

R: STEFAN ROUTIN P: E SIRPARANTA

Extensive pistes, high-altitude riding and access to the Paradiski area – La Plagne has a huge amount going for it. Just don't expect great architecture.

☽ If you like this . . .
. . . try *Lake Louise* ▸▸*p84*, *Val Thorens* ▸▸*p160*, or *Engelberg* ▸▸*p314*.

FRANCE
LA PLAGNE

☺ OPENING TIMES

Late Dec to late Apr (for village resorts and the Grande Plagne and Paradiski ski area): 0900-1700

⑤ RESORT PRICES (PARADISKI)

Week pass (6 days): €233
Day pass: €46
Season pass: €895

ⓘ DIRECTORY

Tourist office: T479 097979
Medical Centre: T479 090466
Pisteurs: T479 096700
Taxi: T479 090341
Local radio: Radio La Plagne 101.5 FM
Website: la-plagne.com

The Mountain

It may be characterized by numerous flat spots and mellow pistes, but with a little exploring you can find some brilliant terrain in La Plagne, and thanks to a largely recreational clientele it stays relatively untracked. There's also some good high-altitude runs on offer up the Bellecôte if you're willing to hike, and there are three parks to choose from. To top it all off, the Paradiski has a whopping 425 km of pistes to explore, so if you can't find anything to please you here then you're doing something wrong.

Beginners The majority of the pistes in La Plagne are blue runs, so it's a good place for beginners. Be prepared to push though, as there are a lot of flat spots. The free draglift at Montalbert is ideal for first timers, though each of the stations has easily accessible nursery slopes.

Intermediate In terms of pistes, intermediate riders won't find much to challenge them, but the mountain is a fast and easy cruise, with plenty of rollers and hits to play around on. A day in the Cappella park in Plagne Centre is highly recommended –

La Plagne is just the ideal playground, and every time I'm out there's a new spot to unveil.

Stephane Routin, professional snowboarder, La Plagne local

there's a six-seater chairlift that deposits you right at the top for easy circuits, and local legend Stephane Routin has a hand in shaping it so expect something at least half decent.
Advanced Some of the best terrain in La Plagne is to be found up the Bellecôte and La Roche de Mio. The north face of the Bellecôte has some great lines, but take care. La Roche de Mio has a few mellow couloirs (known as the Rosset couloirs), which are found by ducking under the rope just below the restaurant. Also spend some time exploring the Trevasse and Rossa chairlifts, then head to the pipe in Bellecôte for a proper workout.
Kids Kids under six go for free. There are six magic carpet lifts in the ESF areas to get them up and running.
Flat light days La Plagne has some OK trees, but the best are to be had by heading across to Villaroger (on the other side of Les Arcs) on the Vanoise Express link lift.

☺ LOCALS DO

- Ride the parks. There are three in the La Plagne area and a very good one in Les Arcs.
- Take advantage of the Vanoise Express link lift.
- Know how to keep their speed up to cruise over the flat spots.

☹ LOCALS DON'T

- Ride with unwaxed boards – see above.
- Give a hoot about the architecture.
- Ride the north face of the Bellecôte if the risk of avalanche is high.

✔ PROS

- Great, uncrowded terrain.
- The bobsleigh…

✖ CONS

- Lots of flat spots.
- Depressing architecture in Aime la Plagne and Bellecôte.
- Limited nightlife in most of the individual resorts.

☺ NOT TO MISS

A run on the bobsleigh course. It's the one they built for the 1992 Albertville Olympics, and it's open between December and mid-March. Book through bobsleigh.net (T479 091 273).

ⓘ REMEMBER TO AVOID

Riding the north face of the Bellecôte in sketchy conditions – it's prone to sliding.

❄ SNOW DEPTH

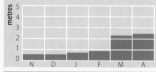

☺ RELIVE A FAMOUS MOMENT

Relive the moment from Christmas Day 2004 when the Paradiski link opened connecting La Plagne to Les Arcs. Simply jump on the Vanoise Express and shout 'Sacre bleu – c'est incroyable!' for the full experience as you go over the 380-m chasm.

1200 m to 2100 m
TOWN ALTITUDE

149 km
KM TO AIRPORT

GVA
AIRPORT

★★☆
VEGETARIAN RATING

★★☆
INTERNET CAFES

★★★
RIDE IN/RIDE OUT

3250 m
HIGHEST LIFT

2000 m
VERTICAL DROP

34,000
RIDEABLE AREA (IN ACRES)

425 km
KM OF PISTES

6
NURSERY AREAS

144/66/29
RUNS: BEG/INTER/ADV

1/3
FUNICULAR/CABLE CARS

12/66
GONDOLAS/CHAIRS

58
DRAGS

no
NIGHT RIDING

5
PARKS

1
PIPE

no
SUMMER AREAS

★★☆
ENVIRONMENTAL RATING

$$$
COST INDICATOR

FRANCE
LA PLAGNE

FIGURES COVER THE PARADISKI AREA

P: CHRIS MORAN/HOTSHITPICTURES.COM

La Rosière

Small, quiet and purpose built it may be, but thanks to the link with La Thuile and its attendant heli-boarding possibilities, La Rosière manages to hold its own among its illustrious neighbours.

☾ *If you like this* ...
... *try Ishgl* ▸▸*p38, or Courmayeur* ▸▸*p178.*

The Town

La Rosière is a small resort situated high in the Tarantiase Valley on the Petit St Bernard Pass. It's a stone's throw from the Italian border, and is linked with La Thuile to form the San Bernardo area. Though it's purpose built, many of the buildings are quite attractive and it's a far cry from the horrors of La Plagne. La Rosière is popular with two very different groups of people: families, and freeriders who come to take advantage of the link with La Thuile, where Italian legislature allows heliboarding. It's a strange mix, but it seems to work.

Sleeping The two-star **Le Relais du Petit St Bernard** (petit-saint-bernard.com) is reasonably priced and offers easy access to the slopes. Also try the family-run two-star **Le Solaret** (hotelsolaret.com) and the two-star **Le Plein Soleil** (T479 068043). **Snow Crazy** (snowcrazy.co.uk) offer excellent private catered chalets.
Eating **Le Yeti** (T479 068317) for pizza, pasta, and Savoyard specialities. **Le Turia** (T479 061365) is one of the best restaurants in town and serves Lebanese cuisine. **The Chalet** (T479 068079) is also very good.

⊙ OPENING TIMES

Mid-Dec to late Apr: 0900-1700

⊜ RESORT PRICES (SAN BERNARDO)

Week pass (6 days): €151
Day pass: €32
Season pass: €609

⊙ DIRECTORY

Tourist office: T479 068051
Medical centre: T479 068909
Pisteurs: T479 411200
Taxi: T626 459416
Local radio: RFM La Rosière 99.2 FM
Website: larosiere.net

Bars and clubs **Le Pub** is very popular, and it's the only place to go once all the other bars shut. **Le Yeti** is small, though also very popular. **Le Petit Danois** and **Le Petit Relais** are the best après spots.
Shopping There aren't any decent snowboard shops in town, so it's best to bring everything you need.
Health The **Espace Forme** (T479 068695) fitness centre offers a sauna and jacuzzi to take care of aches and pains. There's also a gym and weight training room. You'll find it in the **Les Terrasses** shopping centre.
Internet Get online at **Le Petiti Danois** and the **Office du Tourisme**.
Transfer options ATS (a-t-s.net) for shared transfers from Geneva and Lyon. You can also take the **Eurostar** (eurostar.com) to Bourg St Maurice then get a taxi.
Local partners La Thuile.

R: DAVE CRACKNELL P: ANDREW HINGSTON

The Mountain

La Rosière sits back down the valley on the way from Bourg Saint Maurice to Val d'Isère and essentially back onto the Italian side of the Mont Blanc range. This curious position endows the resort with two unique characteristics – half of it is in Italy, and it gets the weather that comes in over the pass from Month Blanc. For freeriders, this is a double boon, as it means the resort gets blasted with some serious weather and – crucially – you can go heliboarding. It's the only place in France from which you can, and unsurprisingly it's pretty popular. For less confident riders, La Rosière is still great fun, and being able to ride in two countries is something everybody is going to enjoy. The views from the fort at the top, where the two countries meet, is of particular note. The only note of caution to be sounded concerns beginners, who might be put off by La Rosière's T-bar heavy lift system.

Beginners Absolute beginners can learn the basics on three free beginner lifts at the main lift area. After this, head up the Roches Noires chairlift where there's a number of decent blue runs to tackle. As the week goes on, work up to that trip into Italy. You'll need to take on some drag lifts, mind.

Intermediate La Rosière isn't very steep, but the pistes are of the sort that you can really blast around, with plenty of rollers. The snow park is worth a look – it's serviced by the Poletta drag for easy circuits. Set aside at least one day to do the classic La Rosiere day out though: head over to La Thuile for lunch in one of the Italian restaurants, stopping at the fort at the

> **" "**
> La Rosière might be small but it's well worth checking out. Where else in the world can you ride two countries within one day, and go heliboarding on the cheap?
>
> *James McPhail, photographer*

top along the way for some photos; in the afternoon, come back over to the French side, heading all the way down to Seez if there's enough snow cover. Don't forget to slap that border sign on your way past!

Advanced Any advanced rider is going to be itching to get over to La Thuile for a crack at one of those helis. The main spots are Mont Miravidi and Mont Ouille, and both have a large vertical drop and some very nice – if not massively challenging – terrain. The heli operations are very strictly regulated here and you're obliged to have a guide. Contact **Evolution 2** (evolution2.com) for details.

Kids La Rosière is great for kids, and has a *Petit Montagnards* award to prove it. There are various crèche and kindergarten facilities, and the ESF have a magic carpet for four-year-olds. Kids under five get a free liftpass.

Flat light days It's pretty high, so you'll find the best trees over in La Thuile.

☺ LOCALS DO
- Go to Le Petit Danois for live bands.
- Go heliboarding as frequently as funds allow.
- Head over to Italy to eat – the mountain restaurants are way better over there.

☹ LOCALS DON'T
- Queue. They're non-existent here.
- Stress about the draglifts. There are a lot of them, but you can get around without them.
- Hit the run down to Seez late in the season – there'll be no snow. It's great when it's on though.

✔ PROS
- Great family resort.
- The only resort in France to offer heliboarding.
- Large area, thanks to the link with La Thuile.

✘ CONS
- Not much steep terrain.
- Lots of draglifts.
- Frequent high winds.

☺ NOT TO MISS
A day's heliboarding. It's the only resort in France to offer it, so get involved while you have the chance.

ℹ REMEMBER TO AVOID
If it's windy, don't bother with the top draglifts.

❄ SNOW DEPTH
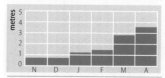

☺ RELIVE A FAMOUS MOMENT
You'll need a few elephants to recreate this one, but head over to La Rosière (on the Petite St Bernard Pass) with 26,000 men and a few African pachyderms and you'll be following in the footsteps of the Carthaginian general Hannibal who came this way in 247BC en route to Rome.

1850 m	TOWN ALTITUDE
170 km	KM TO AIRPORT
GVA	AIRPORT
★★☆	VEGETARIAN RATING
★★☆	INTERNET CAFES
★★☆	RIDE IN/RIDE OUT
2641 m	HIGHEST LIFT
1465 m	VERTICAL DROP
area not measured	RIDEABLE AREA (IN ACRES)
150 km	KM OF PISTES
3	NURSERY AREAS
32/29/12	RUNS: BEG/INTER/ADV
0/1	FUNICULAR/CABLE CARS
0/17	GONDOLAS/CHAIRS
19	DRAGS
no	NIGHT RIDING
1	PARKS
0	PIPE
no	SUMMER AREAS
★★★	ENVIRONMENTAL RATING
$$$	COST INDICATOR
FRANCE	
LA ROSIERE	

FIGURES COVER THE SAN BERNARDO AREA

La Tania

The Town

Situated in the forest right on the cusp of the Courchevel and Méribel valleys, La Tania might just be the perfect base from which to ride the Three Valleys. It's small, cosy and the architecture ranges from attractive wooden chalets to relatively inoffensive apartment complexes. It was originally built to provide on-hill accommodation for the 1992 Albertville Olympics, but has seen considerable development over the last 10 years. There's a strong local community of British and Dutch people, and a very welcoming atmosphere.

Sleeping The Mountain Centre (themountaincentre.com) is cheap and offers great flexibility. **Hotel Telemark** (hoteltelemark.com) is stylish, well appointed and doubles as one of the best restaurants in the area. Those seeking to treat themselves should contact **Icicles** (icicles.org), who offer en suite luxury catered chalet accommodation.

In bad weather La Tania is by far the best place in the Three Valleys to ride. The tree runs are amazing, and you can still ride whilst the rest of the Three Valleys are stuck in a white-out.

Johno Verity, professional snowboarder

Eating Try Snow Food (T479 084899) for quick snacks, or alternatively grab something at the bakery. Head to **The Ski Lodge** (T479 088149) for good value pub food, or **Hotel Telemark** (hoteltelemark.com) for the full gourmet experience.

Bars and clubs The Ski Lodge is the La Tania's main bar, and it often puts on live bands. If you want a slightly more sedate night out try **La Taïga**, or the bar at **Hotel Telemark**. For late nights make your way to **Dick's T-Bar** in Méribel – although you'll need to take a taxi there and back.

Shopping Not much goes on in La Tania in this respect, though there are a couple of snowboard shops and one supermarket.

Health Pamper Off Piste (pamperoffpiste.com) for mobile massage treatments. There are also twice-weekly aqua gym sessions in the **Hotel Montana** (T479 088039) pool.

Internet You can get online at **The Ski Lodge** and the **Tourist Office**.

Transfer options ATS (a-t-s.net) for shared transfers from Geneva and Lyon. Geneva costs around €79 return. Alternatively, try **Aeroski Bus** (T227 178275) for Geneva transfers and **Satobus Alpes** (satobus-alps.com) for Lyon.

Local partners Les Trois Vallées, Espace Killy (Val d'Isère and Tignes), Paradiski (La Plagne, Peisey Vallandry and Les Arcs), Pralognan-la-Vanoise and Les Saisies.

R: CHRIS MORAN P: GRAHAM LAWRENCE

Nestled quietly on the edge of the Three Valleys, La Tania offers affordable access to the world's largest ski area.

☼ If you like this . . .
. . . try Bansko ▸▸p100, St Foy ▸▸p150, Hemsedal ▸▸p252, Vail ▸▸p378.

The Mountain

Though it's reasonably small in itself, a La Tania pass is good for the whole Courchevel Valley meaning you can access a staggering amount of terrain. The pistes in La Tania are excellent, and it's home to some of the Three Valleys' best tree runs, which are at a premium on bad weather days. There's no park, but there are several in the area, including two good ones in Méribel, and the terrain really lends itself to charging around and finding natural hits. There are no real steeps to speak of, but for a taste of this simply get a Three Valley pass and head to Val Thorens or Les Menuires.

Beginners Complete beginners are in luck – there's a learners' area right in the town centre, serviced by an easy drag. Those who can already turn should head up to La Loze and make their way to the flatter pistes down towards 1850. Once you're feeling confident, head up to La Loze and try to make it down the home run through the trees.

Intermediate Spend a few runs lapping the Plantrey and Bouc Blanc lifts, where you'll find some steep pistes which are great for high speed cruising. You'll also find loads of natural hits around here to experiment with. After lunch, head up valley and go for a tour of 1850 and 1650, before heading back over to La Loze and dropping back down the rolling homerun piste for après at **The Ski Lodge**.

Advanced There's some

P: GEORGE BONE

great terrain to the looker's right of the Dou les Lanches chair, though extreme caution should be exercised on powder days. Be sure to veer back skier's right to catch the piste to avoid a long walk out. Pretty much every run down to the town is great on the morning of a powder day, but once the obvious ones have been tracked, check out some of the drops to the skier's right of the Dou les Lanches chair.

Kids The Troïka piste in the centre of the resort is the best place to learn. Kids under five get a free lift pass. Bring proof of identity.

Flat light days Stick on the lower slopes and you'll be just fine.

☺ OPENING TIMES

Mid-Dec to late Apr: 0900-1630/1700

ⓢ RESORT PRICES (THREE VALLEYS)

Week pass (6 days): €215
Day pass: €42
Season pass: €935

ⓘ DIRECTORY

Tourist office: T479 084040
Medical centre: T479 084354
Pisteurs: T479 080409
Taxi: T479 086510
Local radio: Radio Courchevel 93.2 FM, Radio Méribel 97.9/98.9 FM
Website: latania.co.uk

☺ LOCALS DO

⊘ Ride the trees off to the sides of the pistes and draglifts.
⊘ Go to Meribel to ride the parks - they're always much better.
⊘ Like to party! The Ski Lodge is an experience…

☹ LOCALS DON'T

⊗ Buy a La Tania/Courchevel only pass.
⊗ Complain about whiteouts – there are plenty of good tree runs.
⊗ Shop in resort – it's much cheaper to buy your essentials down in Moutiers.

☑ PROS

⊘ Excellent tree runs.
⊘ Cheap way to ride the Three Valleys.
⊘ Great for families and groups.

☒ CONS

⊗ Not much choice in the way of nightlife.
⊗ Town lacks much direct sunlight early season.
⊗ Only one main lift up the mountain.

☺ NOT TO MISS

A high speed run down the tree-lined homerun piste is a must.

ⓘ REMEMBER TO AVOID

Venturing into Méribel without a Three Valleys pass.

❄ SNOW DEPTH

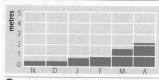

☺ RELIVE A FAMOUS MOMENT

Caught between the glitz of Courchevel and the glamour of Méribel, La Tania is the natural hunting ground for the French C-list celebrity. Funnily enough, it's where the winners of the French reality dating show *Bachelor* headed on their love ski.

FIGURES COVER THE THREE VALLEYS AREA

1400 m	TOWN ALTITUDE
128 km	KM TO AIRPORT
GVA	AIRPORT
★☆☆	VEGETARIAN RATING
★★★	INTERNET CAFES
★★★	RIDE IN/RIDE OUT
3230 m	HIGHEST LIFT
2130 m	VERTICAL DROP
28,000	RIDEABLE AREA (IN ACRES)
600 km	KM OF PISTES
12	NURSERY AREAS
183/119/33	RUNS: BEG/INTER/ADV
3/3	FUNICULAR/CABLE CARS
34/69	GONDOLAS/CHAIRS
71	DRAGS
no	NIGHT RIDING
5	PARKS
3	PIPE
no	SUMMER AREAS
★★★	ENVIRONMENTAL RATING
ⓢⓢⓢ	COST INDICATOR
FRANCE	
LA TANIA	

Les Arcs

The Town

Les Arcs consists of several villages: 1600, 1800, 1950, 2000, Vallandry and Villaroger, with several smaller hamlets making up the area. Each has its own vibe, but all are well serviced with chairlifts, varying nightlife, restaurants, shops and facilities. Though none of them are what you'd call pretty, 1800 does have a certain charm, and the newly built 1950 gives the area a touch of much needed architectural zeal. The valley town of Bourg St Maurice is well linked to the mountain via a quick and easy funicular ride into Arc 1600.

Sleeping For the cheapest, best value option, **Chillchalet** (chillchalet.com) in Bourg St Maurice offers great accommodation in contemporary surroundings. Good food too. For a longer stay, **Seasonaires** (seasonaires.com) is the place. Up in the resort, there are plenty of apartments available through the tourist office's central booking system (lesarcs.com) but try the new snowchateaux.co.uk if you want some snowboard friendly luxury. It's a 23-person, 10-room old-style number with sauna, log fires and amazing views.

Eating Lunch at **Benji's** (T479 074520) in 1800 and dinner at the **Mountain Café** at the other end of 1800. There are also plenty of more traditional restaurants in every village, the best ones being **Le Refuge** and **Le Savoyarde** in Bourg.

Bars and clubs **Café Sol** in 1600, **Before Café** (T479 073647) and **Benji's** (T479 074520), both in 1800, will serve you well for a night out, before heading to the **DC** (T479 063793) or the **Apokalypse** (T479 074377) nightclubs, both in 1800.

Shopping There are plenty of small supermarkets. If you have a car, stock up at **Super U** in Bourg St Maurice, as the prices are often 50% cheaper.

Health Try the **Hotel du Golf** (T479 414343) in 1800 for massages and other pampering.

Internet Most bars have wireless access, as do the post offices.

Transfer options Several bespoke services operate in the area. Try **Coolbus** (thecoolbus.co.uk) or the scheduled bus services **Altibus** (altibus.com) or **Satobus** (satobus.com).

Local partners Val d'Isère, Tignes, La Rosière, St Foy and La Plagne are all with half an hour and offer a free day with a six-day Les Arcs pass.

> ❝ ❞
>
> Les Arcs remains underrated by anyone who hasn't been here, which means that the good stuff remains good. Now joined with La Plagne to form the Paradiski, the area is massive with something for everyone. Plus, it's the closest you'll get to Alaska in Europe.
>
> *Chris Cracknell, snowboarder, founder of chillchallet.com*

The birthplace of alternative snow sports in Europe.

☼ *If you like this...*
... *try Morzine* ▶▶*p148, or Serre Chevalier* ▶▶*p152.*

P: NICK HAMILTON

The Mountain

The recent link with La Plagne to create the Paradiski, the world's second largest area, has brought a lot of investment to the resorts. Most of the old chairlifts have been replaced with new high speed quads (or even sixers!), meaning queues are kept to a minimum, even during busier periods. Although the Les Arcs area is massive, it is relatively easy and quick to get from one sector to the next, meaning you can spend more time on your favourite runs and less time getting to them. Superb piste maintenance means moguls are kept to a minimum.

Beginners The free lifts at 1600 and 1800 are ideal places to make your first turns, with big wide pistes and close proximity to the villages. From there, make your way over to the pistes around chairlift 69, an ideal place to improve your technique amongst peaceful tree-lined pistes.

Intermediate Head over to Vallandry for a morning of high-speed fun on the perfect pistes, hitting natural rollers and banks. Once warmed up, take a long lap of 2000, down to the Comborcière chairlift, into the Malgovert forest for some small rock drops, then back via 1600 to the funpark, situated under the Clair Blanc chairlift, where you'll find kickers and rails of all sizes.

Advanced Hire a guide then head up to the Aiguille Rouge, one of France's highest peaks. After admiring the view, drop down the back in to Villaroger, hitting some serious off-piste, then over to the Grand Col for more of the same. Be warned – these runs are not recommended without a guide. But they are amazing and should be experienced to get the best out of this resort!

Kids Kids under six get a free pass when accompanied by an adult. Check out the Milka Forest above 1800 and even the baby jumps in the park!

Flat light days Head to the trees in 1600 off the Mont Blanc chairlift. There are endless lines to be had. If it's open, make your way to the amazing trees in Villaroger.

R: JAMES PHILLIPS P: CHRIS MORAN/HOTSHITPICTURES.COM

OPENING TIMES
Mid-Dec to late Apr: 0900-1700

RESORT PRICES (PARADISKI)
Week pass (6 days): €233
Day pass: €46
Season pass: €895

DIRECTORY
Tourist office: T479 071257
Medical centre: T479 070988
Pisteurs: T479 078566
Taxi: T686 242383
Local radio: Radio Les Arcs 93.4 FM
Website: lesarcs.com

LOCALS DO
- Live down in Bourg St Maurice.
- Ride very fast (it seems to be a local trait).
- Use the whole mountain – it really is a massive area.

LOCALS DON'T
- Drive up to the resort from Bourg; use the funicular.
- Shred the mogul hills under the Comborcière chairlift.
- Try going anywhere by road on a Saturday – the traffic can be terrible.

PROS
- World-class resort that feels compact and homely.
- Good value for money throughout the resort.
- Some of the best terrain in Europe.

CONS
- Shops, bars and clubs in some of the villages are limited.
- Busy during French holidays in mid-February.
- There can be bottlenecks on some of the main lifts at peak times.

NOT TO MISS
The view from the Aiguille Rouge on a clear day is guaranteed to put a smile on your face.

REMEMBER TO AVOID
The piste under the Comborcière chairlift, roughly 2 km of mogulled hell – long, steep and awful!

SNOW DEPTH

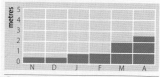

RELIVE A FAMOUS MOMENT
The *Apocalypse Snow* series was filmed around the slopes of Les Arcs. They remain *the* seminal snowboard films. At the bottom of Chair 69 lies the start of the forest paths that are a large part of the first film.

FIGURES COVER THE PARADISKI AREA

1600 m to 2000 m
TOWN ALTITUDE

135 km
KM TO AIRPORT

GVA
AIRPORT

VEGETARIAN RATING

INTERNET CAFES

RIDE IN/RIDE OUT

3250 m
HIGHEST LIFT

2000 m
VERTICAL DROP

34,000
RIDEABLE AREA (IN ACRES)

425 km
KM OF PISTES

6
NURSERY AREAS

144/66/29
RUNS: BEG/INTER/ADV

1/3
FUNICULAR/CABLE CARS

12/66
GONDOLAS/CHAIRS

58
DRAGS

yes
NIGHT RIDING

5
PARKS

1
PIPE

no
SUMMER AREAS

ENVIRONMENTAL RATING

COST INDICATOR

FRANCE
LES ARCS

Les Deux Alpes

The Town

Located in the Oisans area in the southern French Alps, Les Deux Alpes is a fairly large town strung out along the length of a narrow valley. Though it isn't the prettiest of resorts, its magnificent and unusual geographical setting gives the place a certain charm. There are a few populated centres in the valley, but the vast majority of people will stay in 1650, the resort proper. A welcoming vibe and lively nightlife with a broad selection of bars and restaurants further ensure its enduring popularity.

Sleeping Les Deux Alpes has a daunting range of hotels, B&B and self-catering accommodation to navigate. Most accommodation can be booked through the resort's central reservations service, but you might also find **Peak Retreats** (peakretreats.co.uk) helpful. Most of the large tour operators (**Crystal, Inghams**) go there – shop around for good package deals.

Eating The pasta dishes and set menus at **La Spaghetteria** (T476 790577) are excellent value, it also has a great buffet salad bar and is one of the best vegetarian restaurants in the area. Also try **Thai Alloi** (T618 583924). **Smokey Joe's** (T476 792897) does good value pub food (till 2300) and a cracking English breakfast. Ditto **The Red Frog** (T476 792897).

Bars and clubs Smokey Joe's is the main hang-out, and it's right next to the main lift area for easy après-ski. Also check out **The Red Frog** at the Venosc end of town, and **Smithy's** in Venosc. For late nights it's the **Avalanche** and **Bresilien** all the way.

Shopping There is a good selection of snowboard shops in town, and two supermarkets.

Health There's a heated outdoor swimming pool, and access comes free with your lift pass. There are also two sports centres, **Le Club Forme** (T476 792564) and **Le Tanking Centre** (T476 790088) and an outdoor climbing wall.

Internet Smokey Joe's has several terminals.

Transfer options VFD (vfd.fr) for transfers from Grenoble St Geoirs. The best option is flying to Lyon St Exupery, taking a bus to Grenoble with **Satobus** (satobus.com) then getting a **VFD** transfer to the resort. Grenoble town is about 70 km away, and the bus takes roughly 45 minutes.

Local partners La Grave, Alpe d'Huez, Puy St Vincent, Voie Lactée, Serre Chevalier.

Friendly, super resort in the southern Alps, with one of France's best parks and banging nightlife to boot.

P: JAMES THORNE P: JAMES MCPHAIL

P: CHRIS MORAN/HOTSHITPICTURES.COM

If you like this ...
... try, *Zillertal* ▶p56, *Les Arcs* ▶p142, or *Laax* ▶p322.

The Mountain

As its name suggests, Les Deux Alpes consists of two distinct mountains, on either side of the valley. Each is well serviced by lifts, with the bulk of the rideable terrain on the side accessed by the speedy Jandri Express gondola. The overall ski area is massive, and though it's largely featureless and lacking in trees there's a good variety of terrain to suit most levels of rider. The resort is notable for its progressive attitude to snowparks, and each summer the place transforms itself into one of the main European focal points for freestyle riding. Thanks to its altitude and the glacier, you're virtually guaranteed to get some good snow there.

Beginners Unfortunately the runs back down to the resort are amongst the steepest in the valley, which often proves problematic for beginners. The trade-off is that since all the flatter runs are at the top of the mountain, snow conditions are typically good. There's one winding green run that takes you back down to town if you can't face the mogulled hell of the main home run, but for less confident beginners downloading can be the best option.

Intermediate Head to the park to hone your freestyle skills. The jumps typically range from tiny to reasonably large, so there should be something for all levels of ability. There's also a decent selection of rails to get stuck into, a boarder-x track and an excellent halfpipe. Once you've had enough, spend the rest of your day charging the pistes off the top of the glacier.

Advanced There's plenty of challenging terrain in Les Deux Alpes.

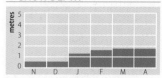

Having scoured French Alpine resorts for a suitable venue to host the Orange British Snowboard Champs, we felt there was nowhere better than Les Deux Alpes. They have made it their primary goal to be regarded among the premier European freestyle arenas, and they're not doing a bad job.

Spencer Claridge, organizer of the Orange British Snowboarding Championships

You can pretty much ride everywhere you can see in resort, but make sure you thoroughly explore the Clot de Chalance area in the centre of the mountain. Serious freeriders will want to spend at least a day in nearby La Grave with which it's partly linked. It's covered by your lift pass.

Kids Les Deux Alpes is ideal for kids. There are three nursery areas and one kids' snowpark. Under fives get a free lift pass.

Flat light days Thanks to the lack of trees, Les Deux Alpes isn't up to much in bad weather.

☺ OPENING TIMES
Late Oct to early May: 0900-1700

⑤ RESORT PRICES
Week pass (6 days): €168,50
Day pass: €35,50
Season pass: €750

① DIRECTORY
Tourist office: T476 792200
Medical centre: T476 792003
Pisteurs: T476 797502
Taxi: T476 800697
Local radio: Radio 2 Alpes 96.2 FM
Website: les2alpes.com

☺ LOCALS DO
● Keep their boards well waxed for good glide across the flat spots.
● Snake a run on the air bag jump when they're feeling mischievous.
● Learn to ride bumps well – they've no choice!

⊗ LOCALS DON'T
⊗ Ride many trees.
⊗ Waste any time getting up the hill on a powder day.
⊗ Ride at La Grave without a guide.

✔ PROS
● Good park.
● Large, wide open area.
● Best and biggest summer riding in France.

✗ CONS
⊗ Runs back down to town get very busy and mogulled at the end of the day.
⊗ Lots of flat spots.
⊗ Lack of tree runs.

◉ NOT TO MISS
A few goes on the air bag kicker – great for those double backflip attempts you always dreamed of!

① REMEMBER TO AVOID
Slowing down while coming along the track past the bottom of the Bellecombes chair.

❄ SNOW DEPTH

(metres)

	N	D	J	F	M	A

☺ RELIVE A FAMOUS MOMENT
Remember the opening section in *Lame*, where Christoph Weber jumps out of a cable car with the camera in his hand? That's the 142-m bungee jump out of the Jandri II lift.

1650 m	TOWN ALTITUDE
120 km	KM TO AIRPORT
GNB	AIRPORT
★★★	VEGETARIAN RATING
★★☆	INTERNET CAFES
★★☆	RIDE IN/RIDE OUT
3568 m	HIGHEST LIFT
2298 m	VERTICAL DROP
1915	RIDEABLE AREA (IN ACRES)
200 km	KM OF PISTES
3	NURSERY AREAS
44/15/14	RUNS: BEG/INTER/ADV
1/2	FUNICULAR/CABLE CARS
4/20	GONDOLAS/CHAIRS
30	DRAGS
no	NIGHT RIDING
2	PARKS
1	PIPE
yes	SUMMER AREAS
★★★	ENVIRONMENTAL RATING
⑤⑤⑤	COST INDICATOR

FRANCE
LES DEUX ALPES

Méribel

The Town ⊟🔾⊟

Originally established by British pioneer Peter Lindsay in 1938, Méribel has long been a favourite amongst British winter sports enthusiasts. Thanks to strict architectural guidelines, the town has a very traditional feel and is vastly more picturesque than its other Trois Vallées counterparts. The main town is at 1450 m, though there are other centres at 1600 m and at Méribel Village, a nearby hamlet that has seen massive development over the past 10 years. A free bus service links these up with each other and with Méribel-Mottaret, the more modern satellite resort at 1700 m, some 5 km further up the Méribel valley.

Sleeping Self-catered accommodation is the cheapest way to go in Méribel. Try **Le Grand Chalets de Pistes** (T479 086083). **Hotel du Moulin** (T479 005223) in Mussillon is affordable and only five minutes' walk from the slopes. For those on a larger budget the four-star **Hotel Grand Couer** is sumptuous and also very central.

Eating La Belle Savoie in Mottaret for lunch, or **Le Rond Point** (T479 003751) if you're feeling a little flusher. Try **Evolution** (T479 004426) for a great English breakfast, or **La Fromagerie Chez Fromton** (T479 085548), a great vegetarian noted for traditional Savoyarde fare. **Hotel Telemark** (T479 088032) in La Tania (a short taxi ride away) is the best restaurant in the area.

Bars and clubs Try **Le Rond Point**, the town's best après spot. **Jack's Bar** and **La Taverne** are good for both après and evening drinks, and **Dick's T-Bar** stays open until 0400.

Shopping There are numerous supermarkets in town. For snowboarding essentials try **Boardbrains** (T479 085296).

Health Parc Olympique La Chaudanne (T479 005821) offers packages including sauna, jacuzzi, steam room and swimming pool.

Internet The town has several internet cafés. **Evolution** is a good spot for wireless access.

Transfer options ATS (a-t-s.net) offer a shared transfer for €79 return.

Local partners Three Valleys, Espace Killy (Val d'Isère and Tignes), Paradiski (La Plagne, Peisey, Vallandry and Les Arcs), Pralognan-la-Vanoise and Les Saisies.

Spiritual home of the French chalet holiday, Méribel is quite rightly known as 'The Heart Of The Three Valleys'. Vast, varied terrain and easily accessible freeriding make it a worthwhile stop for the entire snow-boarding spectrum.

❂ *If you like this ...*
... try Val d'Isère ▸▸p158, or Verbier ▸▸p332.

P:CHRIS MORAN P:NICK HAMILTON

P:DAVE JORDAN

The Mountain ❄☁☺

Méribel sits right at the centre of the massive Three Valleys ski area, which claims to be the largest interlinked ski area in the world. There are over 600 km of pistes to explore, and a whopping 200 lifts to get you there. Méribel offers little in the way of genuine steeps (head to Courchevel and Val Thorens for that), but there's plenty of great terrain to keep all but the most extreme of riders occupied for a season or two. The lift system is efficient, the pistes are well looked after and there are two good funparks and two halfpipes to play with.

Beginners Head up the Rhodos gondola to find your feet on the mellow Altiport green run, doing laps on the draglift. The run is wide, and long enough that you won't get bored in a hurry. Spend the afternoon on the Altiport chair (it takes you much higher than the drag), or if you're feeling more confident then head right down to La Chaudanne and have a run or two on the Burgin-Saulire gondola. Get out at the mid station to avoid the steeper section at the top.

Intermediate Take the Rhodos gondola then the Col de la Loze chair. There's a flat boulevard you can ride down and drop in wherever you like, accessing some fun off-piste runs back down to the chair. Next, head to La Chaudanne and take the Tougnete gondola, then drop down into Mottaret and jump on the Plattieres gondola – here's where you'll find the Mottaret park. Once the sun has gone head back across the valley and spend the remainder of the day lapping the Burgin-Saulire gondola or Adret chairlift.

Méribel is pretty much the perfect resort. It caters well for beginners to advanced riders, with really good lift access and two good snowparks.

Scott Nixon, professional snowboarder

Advanced Head to Mottaret, then take the Platieres gondola up to the second station. Drop down to Mont Vallon and Côte Brune, where you'll find the steepest terrain in the valley. Once you're done, take the Plan des Mains chair then head to the top of the Plattieres gondola. You'll find some fun terrain on the side of the pistes and – on a powder day – some of the best cliff drops in the valley. Take the Pas du Lac gondola then finish up with a cruise down the Saulire to **Le Rond Point**.

Kids Kids under five get a free lift pass. Bring proof of identity.

Flat light days The Combes and Table Verte chairs in Mottaret offer the best tree runs in the Méribel valley. If you have a Three Valley pass then head to La Tania.

☺ OPENING TIMES

Early Dec to early May: 0900-1630

$ RESORT PRICES (THREE VALLEYS)

Week pass (6 days): €215
Day pass: €42
Season pass: €935

ℹ DIRECTORY

Tourist office: T479 086001
Medical centre: T479 086041
Pisteurs: T479 086532
Taxi: T609 527852
Local radio: Radio Meribel 97.9/98.9 FM
Website: meribel.net

☺ LOCALS DO

● Spend sunny afternoons lapping the Adret chairlift (known locally as 'the six man') punctuated with frequent pit stops at Le Rond Point.
● Avoid La Chaudanne (the main lift area) during peak times.
● Head to Courchevel or Val Thorens in search of steeper terrain.

☹ LOCALS DON'T

⊗ Drink the locally popular lager *Mutzig* in anything but a *demi* (half) measure. It's potent!
⊗ Ride the face under the Olympic Express chair in unstable snow conditions – it's an avalanche hotspot.
⊗ Spend much time on black runs – the predominance of skiers mean they quickly become mogul fields.

✓ PROS

● Efficient lift system.
● Easy access to pistes.
● Refreshingly uncrowded freeriding.

✗ CONS

⊗ Very busy in peak season.
⊗ Lack of genuinely steep terrain.
⊗ Expensive.

☺ NOT TO MISS

The legendary Méribel après-ski at Le Rond Point as the sun goes down.

ℹ REMEMBER TO AVOID

Getting stuck in one of the other valleys after the lifts close. It's an expensive taxi ride back.

❄ SNOW DEPTH

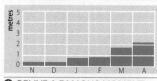

☺ RELIVE A FAMOUS MOMENT

Pick up a guitar and play a gig in any of Méribel's bars and you're standing on the same stages that *The Feeling* used to play on when they did their snowboard seasons.

FIGURES COVER THE THREE VALLEYS AREA	
1400 m to 1700 m	TOWN ALTITUDE
128 km	KM TO AIRPORT
GVA	AIRPORT
★★★	VEGETARIAN RATING
★★★	INTERNET CAFES
★★★	RIDE IN/RIDE OUT
3230 m	HIGHEST LIFT
2130 m	VERTICAL DROP
28,000	RIDEABLE AREA (IN ACRES)
600 km	KM OF PISTES
12	NURSERY AREAS
183/119/31	RUNS: BEG/INTER/ADV
3/3	FUNICULAR/CABLE CARS
34/69	GONDOLAS/CHAIRS
71	DRAGS
no	NIGHT RIDING
5	PARKS
3	PIPE
no	SUMMER AREAS
★★★☆	ENVIRONMENTAL RATING
$$$	COST INDICATOR

FRANCE
MERIBEL

The Town ⊜⊕⊜

Morzine is surprisingly large, but cut by a deep river gorge at the centre with the two sides of the valley connected by a beautiful pedestrian suspension bridge. Whilst the town centre is pleasantly cobbled, it is not the prettiest village in the Alps, with sprawling hotels, chalets and apartment blocks spreading up the three valleys that converge at its centre. But with access to the Portes du Soleil and a huge, youthful seasonaire community, there is always something going on.

Sleeping The Chill Chalet (T614 611437, chillchalet.com) has a perfect base in town from €25 per person per night with breakfast and optional evening meal. Le Dahu (T450 799292 dahu.com) offers three-star half-board from €60 per night and is highly recommended for families. Le Coin du Feu (T450 747521, chillypowder .com) should be around €100.

Eating The Auberge La Chalande (T450 791969) in Ardent (above Montriond) serves exquisite French grub and well worth a trip round the lake to get to it.

Bars and clubs Dixies is probably the favourite foreign hang-out, with a strong football presence. The **Boudha** café is much more chilled, while the **Cavern** bar is probably where the seasonaires are if they're not at the Hotel Ridge.

Shopping The brilliantly named Shoppi is 100 m from the Super-morzine gondola station in the opposite direction from town. Or there's a bigger (and cheaper) **Champion** supermarket in St Jean d'Aulps.

Health Try the Galarie du Baraty (T450 791068) in Morzine for spa, massage and sauna.

Internet Dixies sells internet cards for its wireless computers downstairs. The **Hotel Ridge** has free wireless if you buy a drink.

Transfer options From Geneva airport, bus transfers (T450 384208) take around an hour. Or for the terminally flash, Mt Blanc Helicopters (T450 927821) make the same trip in 10 minutes for around €1000 per person.

Local partners The Portes du Soleil lift pass covers Morzine, Les Gets, Chatel, Les Crosets and Abondance to name but a few.

P: ANDREW HINGSTON

Biggest and liveliest town tagged to the Portes du Soleil, possibly the world's largest rideable area.

◐ *If you like this…*
… try St Anton ⇒*p48,* *Méribel* ⇒*p146, or* Serre *Chevalier* ⇒*p152.*

R: DANNY WHEELER P: ANDREW HINGSTON

The Mountain

The Portes du Soleil spreads over the border between France and Switzerland offering an unbelievable amount of riding. In amongst this ludicrously large area are several world-class parks, and many other mini features and purpose-built boarder cross tracks. Avoriaz, directly above Morzine and accessed by the Supermorzine gondola, has the fantastic baby park, its main park, plus a permanent halfpipe in town. In addition, Les Crosets park is considered to be one of the best in Switzerland – home to the likes of Romain de Marchi – while the area obviously has incredible freeriding potential. The run back to Prodains from Avoriaz can be one of the best powder cat tracks in the world, with endless fly-off potential.

Morzine has always played second fiddle to places like Chamonix. But with more and more seasonaires heading there, plus the incredible parks that Cham has yet to build, Morzine has clawed back a lot of rider respect.

Ed Leigh, broadcaster

Beginners Take the Supermorzine Gondola, then the chair above it, and keep heading in the same direction until you hit the area also known as Super-Morzine, perhaps the best beginner area in France. Ride around the whole area and back to Avoriaz and you've done a decent lap.

Intermediate Head to the top of the Chavanette where you'll encounter

R: SI BRASS P: CHRIS MORAN/HOTSHITPICTURES.COM

OPENING TIMES

Early Dec to late Apr:
0900-1630/1700

RESORT PRICES (PORTES DU SOLEIL)

Week pass (6 days): €179
Day pass: €37
Season pass: €706

DIRECTORY

Tourist office: T450 747272
Medical centre: T450 740542
Pisteurs: T450 741113
Taxi: T450 796454
Local radio: Radio Morzine (97.9 FM)
Website: morzine-avoriaz.com

'The Wall', a ludicrously steep mogul run. Don't worry – you can take the chair down. At the bottom keep heading for Crosets, when you get there find the park and try out the fantastic gulley run. A return lap to Avoriaz via Point de Mossett and the Brocheaux lift is a big day out.

Advanced If there's powder, the run from Avoriaz to Les Prodains offers some incredible cat tracks to fly off, otherwise the Avoriaz and Les Crosets park should offer any rider a week of decent challenges.

Kids Le Village des Enfants (T450 740446) feeds and looks after the kids for around €40 per day.

Flat light days The Prodains home run offers the best trees nearby.

LOCALS DO

- Use the free Internet at the Hotel Ridge.
- Head to the Les Gets area for some relaxed tree runs.
- Use either the Prodains cable car or the Ardent gondola to access the area during busy times.

LOCALS DON'T

- Drive into town. Even off season parking is a nightmare.
- Head into Switzerland after 1500 and risk getting stuck.
- Ride down 'The Wall' – unless they're showing off.

PROS

- Great selection of parks, from beginner to expert. There's even a snowskate park!
- Always a good atmosphere in the bars and clubs.
- Close to Geneva airport.

CONS

- Can get busy during the holidays.
- Bus system could be better.
- Big place – can be a walk to the slopes if you choose the wrong part of town.

NOT TO MISS

The Avoriaz funpark. World class.

REMEMBER TO AVOID

Getting stuck in Switzerland after 1630.

SNOW DEPTH

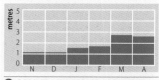

RELIVE A FAMOUS MOMENT

Nicolas Droz, Romain de Marchi, Gary Greenshields and Gigi Ruff have all made the 'road gap' infamous in Morzine. Ride back towards Avoriaz from the Chavanet (over the tunnel) and it's at the end of the track just before Avoriaz comes into view. See page 121 for more details.

1000 m	TOWN ALTITUDE
70 km	KM TO AIRPORT
GVA	AIRPORT
★★★	VEGETARIAN RATING
★★★	INTERNET CAFES
★★☆	RIDE IN/RIDE OUT
3200 m	HIGHEST LIFT
2200 m	VERTICAL DROP
area not measured	RIDEABLE AREA (IN ACRES)
659 km	KM OF PISTES
3	NURSERY AREAS
150/110/28	RUNS: BEG/INTER/ADV
0/3	FUNICULAR/CABLE CARS
11/82	GONDOLAS/CHAIRS
110	DRAGS
yes	NIGHT RIDING
10	PARKS
3	PIPE
no	SUMMER AREAS
★★★	ENVIRONMENTAL RATING
★★★	
	COST INDICATOR
FRANCE MORZINE	

FIGURES COVER THE PORTES DU SOLEIL AREA

St Foy

The Town

St Foy is a traditional French village, unspoilt by the ugly modern developments that plague many of its counterparts in the Tarantaise Valley. It sits nestled in the trees just off the main road from Bourg St Maurice to Val d'Isère and Tignes, very close to the Italian border. It's a very sleepy town with little in the way of nightlife, but it has a real rustic charm that sees many people returning year after year, including day-tripping seasonaires from nearby resorts like Tignes and Les Arcs who know all too well how good it is. A free bus connects St Foy Village with the ski station proper.

Sleeping Try Snow Shacks (snowshacks.com) for a wide range of apartments and catered/self-catered chalets in resort. **Chalet Marigold** (chaletmarigold.com) for the fully catered chalet experience. Contact Dirk and Jeannette at **Gîte De Sainte Foy** (T479 069718) for a luxury gîte/chalet complete with outdoor hot tub and easy access to the pistes.

Eating Try **Les Brevettes** at the top of the first chairlift. It serves rustic, traditional Savoyarde food, and is good for hot chocolate after a morning run. Also try **La Maison de Colonnes** (T479 069480) at the top of the nursery slopes, and **Chez Leon** (T479 069083). **Le Bec de l'An** (T479 069245) does good pizzas – takeaways available. **La Bergerie** (T479 062551) is a nice, traditional restaurant with an open fire.

Bars and clubs **Chez Alison** and **La Pitchouli** for après-ski and evening drinks and with live entertainment. The **Ice Bar** is great for a more local flavour.

Shopping There's a **Sherpa** supermarket for all your grocery needs.

Health **Les Ballons de Sainte** Foy offers packages including swimming pool, saunas, steam room, jacuzzi and fitness facilities.

Internet Le Pitchouli offers wireless facilities.

Transfer options Coolbus (thecoolbus.com) offer a shared transfer service from surrounding airports. Take the **Eurostar** (eurostar.com) to Bourg St Maurice (about 20 minutes away), from where there's a regular bus service to St Foy throughout the day.

Local partners Tignes, Val d'Isère, La Rosière, Les Arcs, La Plagne (Paradiski).

> 66 99
>
> When we turned up no one was on the lift and we pretty much had the whole mountain to ourselves with fresh powder everywhere. Think Terje in *Notice to Appear*, or at least that's what it felt like to me hitting all those natural bumps and drops.
>
> *Ed Blomfield, editor,* White Lines

St Foy is a small, family-friendly resort with some of the best freeride terrain in the Alps. It won't be the Tarantaise valley's best-kept secret for much longer.

⟩ *If you like this . . .*
. . . try Shemshak ⟩⟩*p104, Krasnaya Poliana* ⟩⟩*p108, or Verbier* ⟩⟩*p332, Baker* ⟩⟩*p352.*

R: SCOTT NIXON P: JAMES MCPHAIL

The Mountain

Amongst those in the know, St Foy has the reputation as a freeriding big-hitter, so it may come as a surprise to find out how small the place actually is. There are only six lifts (and two of those are magic carpets), but when you see the terrain you can access you begin to get the picture – extended steep pitches, perfectly graded rollers, trees aplenty and drops everywhere you look. Because of its predominantly northwest-facing aspect the snow tends to stay in good condition. Why it's not more popular is a mystery, but that's not something you hear many of the locals complaining about.

Beginners Take the Grande Plan lift to access the relaxed Plan Bois (a green run), or continue on the L'Arpettez lift to access the Cret Serru du Bas and Les Combes blue runs.

Intermediate The Aiguille piste from the top of the L'Arpettez lift offers a mix of steep and mellow sections. To avoid the steeper sections take Creux de Formeian piste, another red run accessed from the same lift. Make sure you take in the view from the top of the resort on the Aiguille lift (you can see right across to Les Arcs and over to Tignes). Exploration is key here – there are plenty of fun things to do even just on the edge of the pistes for those with a creative eye.

Advanced St Foy is absolutely littered with fun little natural hits, so it really lends itself to charging around popping off everything you can find. With a bit of exploring you can work out some great little circuits that will keep you amused for days. If conditions are good then take the 45-minute hike from the top of the Col de l'Aiguille to the infamous Le Fogliettaz – an amazing 1700-m descent that ends in the village of La Mazure. It's north facing so the snow stays good. It's essential that you go kitted up with full avalanche safety gear.

Kids It's free for children under seven (with proof of age). There are two nursery slopes and some good green runs.

Flat light days It's a joy. Keeping on the lower two lifts is the best option in low visibility.

R: TINA BIRBAUM P: JAMES MCPHAIL

☺ OPENING TIMES

Mid-Dec to mid-Apr: 0900-1630

⑤ RESORT PRICES

Week Pass (6 days): €112
Day pass: €19
Season pass: €330

ⓘ DIRECTORY

Tourist office: T479 069519
Medical centre: T479 069222
Pisteurs: T479 069515
Taxi: T607 411153
Local radio: None
Website: saintefoy.net

☺ LOCALS DO

● Spend sunny mornings and afternoons at Le Brevette, at the top of the first chair, admiring the views.
● Get up early on good snow days, and hike from the top of the mountain to access the Fogliettaz.
● Avoid public holidays – lift queues can become snarled up at peak times.

☹ LOCALS DON'T

⊗ Spend too much time on-piste.
⊗ Ride under the Morion chairlift during times of high avalanche risk.
⊗ Tell too many other people how good it is here.

✔ PROS

● Quiet, uncrowded resort.
● Easy access to off-piste terrain.
● Family friendly.

✖ CONS

⊗ Small.
⊗ Basic lift system.
⊗ Limited pistes.

✪ NOT TO MISS

A powder day in the trees – it's the defining characteristic of this resort.

ⓘ REMEMBER TO AVOID

Ending up in the village out of resort after the bus has stopped.

❄ SNOW DEPTH

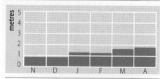

♻ RELIVE A FAMOUS MOMENT

Legendary mushroom-obsessed French pro David Vincent lives in St Foy. Dress yourself in Kana Beach clothing and ride an APO board and you're paying homage to the great man.

1070 m TOWN ALTITUDE

130 km KM TO AIRPORT

GVA AIRPORT

★☆☆ VEGETARIAN RATING

★★☆ INTERNET CAFES

★★☆ RIDE IN/RIDE OUT

2620 m HIGHEST LIFT

1550 m VERTICAL DROP

20 RIDEABLE AREA (IN ACRES)

25 km KM OF PISTES

2 NURSERY AREAS

5/10/4 RUNS: BEG/INTER/ADV

0/0 FUNICULAR/CABLE CARS

0/4 GONDOLAS/CHAIRS

2 DRAGS

no NIGHT RIDING

0 PARKS

0 PIPE

no SUMMER AREAS

★★★ ENVIRONMENTAL RATING

Ⓢ Ⓢ Ⓢ COST INDICATOR

FRANCE
ST FOY

Uncrowded, tree-lined freeriding in the southern French Alps.

If you like this . . .
. . . try Zillertal ▸▸p56, or Engelberg ▸▸p314.

The Town 🛏️🍴🚠

Serre Chevalier is the collective name used to describe several villages stretching out along the main road through the Guisane Valley, which runs from the major town of Briançon up to Monêtier before climbing the Col du Lauteret and on into Italy. The main ski stations are at Briançon (1200 m), Chantemerle (1350 m), Villeneuve (1400 m) and Monêtier (1500 m). They're quite widely spread out and each has their own distinctive feel. They're linked together and with Briançon by a regular shuttle bus.

Sleeping High Rock Chalet (highrockchalet.co.uk) in 1350 is family run and offers flexible catered or self-catering options. Also try **Snow Monkeys** (T1457 861646). The **Plein Sud** (hotelpleinsud.com) is one of the most central hotels and is situated in Chantemerle. It's nice and not too expensive.

Eating Plenty of choice in Serre Chevalier. Up on the mountain, **Le Troll** (T492 242847) and **Café Soleil** (T492 241739) are both good. In Villeneuve, **Mojos** (T492 248393) is fantastic, with a varied international menu. **La Grotte du Yetti** (T492 249019) is a great place for fry-ups and burgers. In Chantemerle, **Le Crystal** (T492 240309) does great French cuisine at a good price, and **La Cabasa** (T492 240683) is a very nice family restaurant. Also try **L'Antidote** (T492 440974) in Monêtier.

Bars and clubs The Grotte Du Yetti in Villeneuve is the resort's liveliest bar, and it has live music most nights. The **Extreme Bar** in Chantemerle is also good with live music once or twice a week, or if you're in Monêtier head to the **Alpen Bar**. In Briançon, try the **Central Bar** and the **Eden Bar**. The

resort's best nightclub is **La Baita** in Villeneuve. It's open until 0600.
Shopping There are five supermarkets in the resort. Try **Generation Snow** (generation-snow.com) in Chantemerle for snowboarding supplies.
Health Relax in the natural hot springs at **Les Bains du Monêtier** (T492 245597). Various indoor and outdoor pools are cooled to 36°C.
Internet Alpen in 1500, **Le Frog** in Villeneuve, **Le Bruno's** in Chantemerle. You can also get online at the **Office du Tourisme**.

Transfer options ATS (a-t-s.net) for shared transfers from Lyon St Exupéry (160 km), Turin Caselle (108 km) and Grenoble St Geoirs (140 km). You can also take the TGV (raileurope.com) from Paris to Oulx in Italy, from where there are regular transfers to the resort. This takes around 40 minutes. Serre Che is well serviced by rail – Briançon station is 6 km away and there is a regular bus service.
Local partners A six-day pass gives you access to Les Deux Alpes, Montgenevre, Puy-St-Vincent and Alpes d'Huez.

R: BUD GALLIMORE P: MIKE WEYERHAEUSER/JDP

The Mountain

Serre Chevalier is the home of the massive Grand Serre Che area, the fourth largest in France. There are 250 km of pistes to get stuck into, and some of the best freeriding in the southern Alps, particularly when it comes to trees. Like the resort, the mountain is made up of several distinct areas, all well linked by lifts. Of these, Monêtier is often the least crowded, being at the far end of the valley from Briançon.

Beginners Serre Chevalier is very beginner friendly, with plenty of green runs for getting you up and running. The slopes at the bottom of Villeneuve and Monêtier are best for first timers. More confident riders can get stuck right in up Chantemerle and Villeneuve without too much trouble.

Intermediate Intermediates will find the whole area a dream. As well as an abundance of great pistes, it's an ideal place to get into riding trees – they're not overly steep, but they're nicely spaced out. If you're lucky enough to get a powder day then it's worth venturing deep into the trees at Villeneuve or Chantemerle, though it's best to get a guide or a local to take you about as you can get stuck pretty easily.

OPENING TIMES

Early Dec to late Apr: 0845-1645

RESORT PRICES

Week pass (6 days): €170
Day pass: €35
Season pass: €693 (25% discount if you buy before opening date)

DIRECTORY

Tourist office: T492 249898
Medical centre: T492 241856
Pisteurs: T492 255500
Taxi: T687 822121
Local radio: Fun Radio 106.5 FM or Radio Zinzine 101.4 FM
Website: serre-chevalier.com

Advanced The park's not up to much, so if you're after jumps then you'll need to find your own. Fortunately, the place caters for that very well. Explore the areas around the La Balme, Prorel and Yret chairs – this is the kind of freeriding terrain for which Serre Che is renowned and there are loads of natural hits. There's also some good and more open terrain off the Cucumelle chair in between Villeneuve and Monêtier, and on La Montagnole in Monêtier.

Kids It's free for under fives. There are several dedicated kids' areas.

Flat light days Plenty of trees here, so stick to the tried and tested 'stay low' formula.

LOCALS DO

Spend afternoons jibbing up above Briançon – this area gets the most afternoon sun.
Ride a lot of trees, and learn the best routes through them.
Get to know each other – it's quite a small and friendly community.

LOCALS DON'T

Give away the whereabouts of all their best powder stashes.
Ride without avalanche safety gear, as the area is prone to avalanche.
Ride the park. The one at Les Deux Alpes (a short drive away) is miles better.

PROS

Uncrowded by French standards.
Caters well for riders of all abilities.
Great for families and beginners.

CONS

The town is widely spaced out along the valley.
Shuttle bus stops running at night, which can make getting around a hassle.
Poorly maintained park.

NOT TO MISS

Heliboarding. It's illegal in France, but you can easily nip over the border into Italy. Contact Oisans Guides Company (guides-serrechevalier.com) for info.

REMEMBER TO AVOID

Getting stuck in the trees. It can be a day-wrecking walk to get yourself out.

SNOW DEPTH

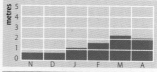

RELIVE A FAMOUS MOMENT

Classic custom swallowtail brand Swell Panik are based near Briançon. Grab one and shred the rad in the manner of an '80s neon postcard!

P: SERRE CHEVALIER TOURISM

Serre Chevalier's main appeal is that it is a freeride heaven. There are plenty of accessible off-piste spots stretching from Briançon to Monêtier. Seek and you will find!

Ash Strain,
High Rock Chalet proprietor

1200 m to 1500 m	TOWN ALTITUDE
180 km	KM TO AIRPORT
TRN	AIRPORT
★★☆	VEGETARIAN RATING
★★☆	INTERNET CAFES
★★☆	RIDE IN/RIDE OUT
2830 m	HIGHEST LIFT
1630 m	VERTICAL DROP
10,984	RIDEABLE AREA (IN ACRES)
250 km	KM OF PISTES
3	NURSERY AREAS
55/44/16	RUNS: BEG/INTER/ADV
0/3	FUNICULAR/CABLE CARS
6/20	GONDOLAS/CHAIRS
39	DRAGS
yes	NIGHT RIDING
1	PARKS
1	PIPE
no	SUMMER AREAS
★★★	ENVIRONMENTAL RATING
$$$	COST INDICATOR
FRANCE SERRE CHEVALIER	

Tignes

The Town ⬛🎯🎵

The first thing visitors notice about Tignes is that, with its experimental architecture and over-reliance on concrete, it is not a pretty place. The resort centre is really made up of five small towns: Les Boisses, Le Lac, Val Claret and Lavachet at the higher end, and the quaint town of Les Brévières underneath the dam. In recent years, Tignes has had quite a makeover: the town centre at Le Lac has been revamped to provide a genuine focal point, and a huge all weather leisure complex has just been finished right next to the lake. It means that while the place can't quite escape the legacy of that initial concrete frenzy, it is moving forward.

Sleeping Dragon Lodge (T479 063297) in Le Lac is an independently owned snowboard specific chalet with friendly staff, great food and lift access. **The Alpaka Lodge** (T479 064530), also in central Le Lac, is more luxurious for families and those with more cash. **Seasonaires** (seasonaires.com) also offer cheap self-catering apartments in the Home Club complex, down in Le Lavachet.

Eating Tignes Cuisine (T479 064444) in Le Lac is a must for after-riding snacks, followed by a beer in the **Loop Bar** (theloopbar.com) next door. This also serves good food. **The Mover Café** (T479 063264) in Val Claret is a snowboarding friendly hang-out, while **La Pignatta Pizzeria** (T479 063297), also in Val Claret, serves great Italian. For local raclettes and tartiflette, try **Brasserie du Petit Savoyard** (T479 063623).

Bars and clubs The Crowded House in Val Claret is Tignes' 'snowboard bar'. Also try St Jacques for the *Kwak* beer. Down in Le Lavachet, **TC's Bar** is popular with locals. They also visit the **Loop Bar** and the **Alpaca**. **The Blue Girl** and the **Melting Pot** are the main nightclubs in Tignes.

Shopping There are various supermarkets in town. **Black Cats** in Val Claret (near the **Crowded House** bar) will cater for all your snowboarding needs.

Health Damn Fine Massage (T667 034056) offer a mobile massage and reiki service.

Internet Lavachet Lounge (next to **TC's Bar**) for wireless access.

Transfer options Try thecoolbus. co.uk, or **ATS** (a-t-s.net) for transfers from Lyon and Geneva to Tignes.

Local partners Espace Killy (Tignes and Val d'Isère). A week pass will also get you one day's riding at St Foy.

Huge purpose-built über-resort with something for everyone.

⏺ *If you like this* . . .
. . . *try La Plagne* ▶▶*p136, or Val Thorens* ▶▶*p160.*

R: ELLIOT NEAVE P: CHRIS MORAN/HOTSHITPICTURES.COM

FRANCE
TIGNES

The Mountain

Tignes' height and the proximity of the Grand Motte glacier ensures that it is one of the few resorts in the world to boast 365 days snowboarding a year. Every snowboarder, no matter what their standard or riding preference, is going to find something here to make them happy. Tignes' links to Val d'Isère means that the sheer amount of terrain is enormous – way more than anyone could hope to cover during a week's holiday. Then there's the variety of terrain: world-class freeriding, a choice of two high-quality snow parks and every pitch and standard of piste in between.

Beginners Absolute beginners should head to the five free lifts around Le Lac and Val Claret. Those who can turn should head to the Palafour lift and take a couple of laps in the morning. In the afternoon, try and make it down to the dam and back via the beautiful Lac piste.

Intermediate Take the funicular from Val Claret, followed by the main cable car to the top of the Grand Motte Glacier. Take in the incredible view, then follow the Genepe run all the way back to your starting point. The whole run should take an hour and a half. Watch out for a few flat sections around halfway down.

Advanced Take the Aeroski lift from Le Lac, then ride down the Tommeuses piste and the Women's Downhill piste to La Daille. From here, get the funicular to the top of Rocher de Bellevarde and then ride the Face Olympique de Bellevarde piste to Val d'Isère. Take

> *I've spent five winters in Tignes, and I keep going back because in five years I still haven't exhausted the huge variety of terrain on offer.*
>
> *James McPhail, photographer*

⊙ OPENING TIMES

Late Sep to early May: 0845-1630/1700

$ RESORT PRICES (ESPACE KILLY)

Week pass (6 days): €226
Day pass: €41
Season pass: €957

⊙ DIRECTORY

Tourist office: T479 400440
Medical centre: T479 065964
Pisteurs: T479 063200
Taxi: T479 004737
Local radio: Radio Tignes 92.2FM
Website: tignes.net

the Solaise lift, then the Glacier Express, followed by the Up and Over chair. Once in the Fornet Valley, ride all the way back down to Fornet for lunch. Reverse in the afternoon to get you home and you've just completed the infamous Killy dash.

Kids Kids under five get a free lift pass.

Flat light days Palafour is a good lift for bad weather days, thanks to rocks that give definition to the slopes. Experts should head straight for Les Brévières trees, although extreme caution is required.

P: CHRIS MORAN/HOTSHITPICTURES.COM

⊙ LOCALS DO

⊙ Make endless laps jibbing the Palafour lift.
⊙ Take the Les Lanches chairlift instead of the funicular to avoid the queues in Val Claret.
⊙ Ride the Val d'Isère park, shaped by local legend Gumby.

⊗ LOCALS DON'T

⊗ Go up the north face of the Grands Motte in the afternoon due to avalanche hazard.
⊗ Mind dropping large cliffs. There are plenty of good ones around, snow conditions allowing.
⊗ Mind hiking – you can access some great freeriding away from the crowds.

⊘ PROS

⊘ Vast area.
⊘ Guaranteed snow.
⊘ Lots of cheap accommodation.

⊗ CONS

⊗ Ugly, purpose-built concrete resort.
⊗ Busy at Easter and Christmas.
⊗ Lack of trees.

⊙ NOT TO MISS

The view from the top of the Grand Motte Cable Car. On a clear day, you can see the Matterhorn and Mt Blanc.

⊙ REMEMBER TO AVOID

The queues for the Tommeuses lift taking riders from Val to Tignes. By 1600 it's a bottleneck. Miss the link, and you'll have to get the bus!

⊛ SNOW DEPTH

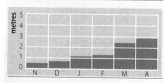

⊙ RELIVE A FAMOUS MOMENT

Visit the lake next to the Genepe run where Luc Besson filmed Jean-Marc Barr and Rosanna Arquette for the winter diving scenes in *The Big Blue*.

1400 m to 2100 m
TOWN ALTITUDE

165 km
KM TO AIRPORT

GVA
AIRPORT

★★☆
VEGETARIAN RATING

★★☆
INTERNET CAFES

★★★
RIDE IN/RIDE OUT

3450 m
HIGHEST LIFT

1900 m
VERTICAL DROP

12,355
RIDEABLE AREA (IN ACRES)

300 km
KM OF PISTES

3
NURSERY AREAS

80/35/16
RUNS: BEG/INTER/ADV

2/4
FUNICULAR/CABLE CARS

4/45
GONDOLAS/CHAIRS

36
DRAGS

no
NIGHT RIDING

2
PARKS

1
PIPE

yes
SUMMER AREAS

★★★
★★★
ENVIRONMENTAL RATING

$ $ $
COST INDICATOR

FRANCE
TIGNES

FIGURES COVER THE ESPACE KILLY AREA

Riders' tales
The genesis of Tignes

Tignes today is a new town – one look at the concrete apartment blocks tells you that. Less well known is that its heritage goes back a long way – back to the Middle Ages, when the secluded village of Les Breniers (it translates literally as 'where the goats are reared') was renowned for its blue cheeses and lacework. By the early 1800s, Les Breniers existed in relative seclusion, faintly notorious for the produce the villagers exported to the rest of France via nearby Bourg Saint Maurice (the major town in the region – situated at the bottom of the valley from Tignes). But in the mid-20th century, two things had a dramatic effect on the hamlet. The first was in 1937, when the Iseran Pass connecting nearby Bourg St Maurice with Italy opened. Its immediate effect was to inflate the importance of Tignes' neighbour Val d'Isère. When the pass opened, Val had two hotels. By 1966, there were 62. To say it hasn't looked back is to flirt dangerously with understatement. Although at the time Tignes, a few kilometres off the beaten track, couldn't compete, the local die had been cast. Tourism would be the new lifeblood of the area.

The second event took place in the early fifties. Rumours of a dam had been doing the rounds in the Alps as far back as 1928, but the local communities had always vehemently – and often violently – opposed any construction work, often making raids on those undertaking evaluation work. But with so many of those against the project killed in the Second World War (it is estimated that three in four men of working age did not return to Tignes after the conflict), the French government moved in on Tignes and announced plans to build a dam across the Isère river at a natural rock bottleneck half a mile downstream from Les Breniers.

According to legend, only the local priest had any understanding of the consequences of building the dam, so with sly timing the authorities waited for him to pass away before announcing their plans. He died in 1952, and according to one source had only just been put in the ground when the first bulldozers moved in. Over the next five years, some 5000 workers lived, breathed and toiled on the ambitious dam project. Local factions, having regrouped after the losses in the war, put up a fight, disrupting the building and resisting the might of the project. But inevitably the 'Barrage de Tignes' went up, opening with the impressive boast that it would soon supply up to 10% of France's electricity needs with its hydroelectric generators.

But what about the ensuing local havoc caused by such a huge engineering project? Les Breniers was buried as the lake rose, never to be seen again. Though furious at this outcome, the locals did recognize the economic benefits. Workers had injected enough cash into the region over the previous five years to enable bars, restaurants and hotels to flourish. Almost by accident, the infrastructure had been laid for tourism to take hold. With a donation of cash from the government, they did a remarkably forward thinking thing: they built a ski lift. Tignes as we know it now was up and running.

Of course, it helped that next door in Val d'Isère they were one step ahead of the game. But while their growth was slow, steady and based on traditional housing, Tignes embraced (some people would say a little too eagerly) the modernist architecture movement prevalent at the time. The ensuing development gave birth to the modern towns of Les Boisses, Le Lac, Val Claret and Lavachet at the higher end, and the smaller, quainter town of Les Breviers underneath the dam at the bottom of the valley, where the bulk of the construction workers lived. But if they got the style of building wrong, one thing is certain – the hills around the place couldn't have been better designed had Wren, Gaudí and Rennie Mackintosh all sat down and designed them specifically with snowboarding in mind. And when the bulging network of lifts from Tignes and Val d'Isère was finally combined to form the outstanding Espace Killy (named in honour of Jean Claude Killy, the region's 1968 Olympic downhill gold medallist), the previously ridiculous concept of this unassuming French hamlet idea being one of the world's finest winter sports destinations suddenly didn't seem so stupid. Killy's

notoriety also brought untold publicity to the valley. What these new visitors discovered was an area boasting some of the best runs in the world and catering for every conceivable budget. From the 1970s onwards, Tignes and Val d'Isère attracted everyone from King Juan Carlos of Spain to the lowliest ski bum in his camper van. Tignes had made it.

These days Tignes is enjoying a brilliant rebirth. With a glacier guaranteeing snow, a longer season than most resorts can offer and a newer, more responsible approach to its architecture, Tignes is now considered one of the resorts of the millennium. And the best part about the whole story is that at its heart is the most delicious of ironies: the dam, the unwanted catalyst behind the changes wrought to the valley, has never actually been used to generate electricity.

P: JAMES MCPHAIL

Val d'Isère

The Town

Val d'Isère is pretty much your archetypical ski resort town, immensely (some would say notoriously) popular with British people. If you're after the quaint and rustic French vibe then look elsewhere. Val has a reputation both for its hedonism and its costliness, and as far as we can see both counts are pretty well justified. The town itself is pretty large and quite attractive, with some interesting architecture in evidence. On the whole it has much less of a low-rent feel than your average French resort.

Sleeping The two-star **Hotel Kandahar** (hotelkandahar.com) is very central with a lively tavern downstairs. If you're feeling a bit flusher try the four-star **Blizzard** (hotelblizzard.com) – it has its own bar and restaurant, as well as a pool, Jacuzzi and Turkish bath. If your budget basically means self-catering, try the **Alpina Lodge** (T479 416000). The main tour operators all go to Val as well.

Eating There are numerous snack bars for quick bites. **The Lodge** (T479 060201) is cosy and great value. **Chez Paolo** (T479 062804) is the best Italian in town, or if you fancy Tex-Mex opt for **Bananas** (T479 060423). **Taverne d'Alsace** (T479 064849) does good rustic fare. It's a bit more costly, but worth it. The **Billabong Café** (T479 060954) does a good English breakfast, has tasty burgers and is a pretty good vegetarian as well.

Bars and clubs **Café Face** gets pretty lively at après-ski, or for a proper on-hill booze up, hit **La Folie Douce**. The **Petit Danois** is very popular with the Scandinavian contingent and serves the very pokey

Red Eric beer. It has pool tables, and is usually rammed. Hit up **Dick's T-Bar** when the other bars shut, although be prepared to queue.

Shopping Val has several supermarkets and an abundance of good snowboard shops.

Health The swimming pool (T479 060590) is open every day from 1400-1700 except Saturday. It also has a sauna and steamroom.

Internet There are numerous internet cafes. Try **Powdermonkey** (in the Gallerie des Cimes next to the Melting Pot restaurant), **Petit Danois** or **Absolute Zero**.

Transfer options ATS (a-t-s.net) for transfers from Geneva. Alternatively, take the **Eurostar** (eurostar.com) to Bourg St Maurice and get a bus or taxi from the train station.

Local partners Espace Killy (Tignes and Val d'Isère).

Enduringly popular French super resort that lives up to all the hype.

☼ If you like this . . .
. . . try *Méribel* ▸▸*p146*, or *Verbier* ▸▸*p332*.

R: SPENCER CLARIDGE P: JAMES McPHAIL

The Mountain

Ultimately, it's the quality of the mountain on which a resort's status stands or falls, and Val d'Isère is up there with the very best. The lift system is on the whole fast and efficient, with a huge and varied spread of terrain: trees, steeps, cliffs, couloirs, endless backcountry and some of the best pistes in France. And all this before you even *think* about the link with Tignes. To top it all off, the park is excellent – well maintained, suitable for all levels of rider from beginner up to pro and easy to lap thanks to the adjacent draglift. In short, Val is a snowboarder's dream.

Beginners The Village green runs in the main lift area are perfect for making your first turns. Next, head to the Solaise area, a plateau with lots of mellow runs suitable for beginners. The run back down to Val is a red, but you can download on the Solaise cable car if you're not feeling up to it.
Intermediate Jump on the Funival from La Daille, which will take you up to the Col De l'Iseran. Take the Orange piste back down to Val right past the park – it's long, varied and so good that many people spend all day just doing laps. There's a variety of other pistes to explore up here, as well as the renowned Val d'Isère bowls (looker's left of the Tommeuses chair) and the Val park.
Advanced Head up the Rocher de Bellvard and ride the Banane, a long off-piste section which takes you back down to the centre of Val. There's a veritable smorgasbord of drops, chutes and convex rollers. In short, classic avalanche terrain – be very careful. Also try La Spatule, over the other side of the Rocher de Bellvarde, where you'll find some steep chutes.

> Val d'Isère has got everything you could ever want in a resort: huge open faces and Alaskan-style descents, one of the highest treelines in Europe for bad weather days, great social scene, incredible backcountry routes and refuges, an amazing park and a link to Tignes for a pipe, oh and the rest of the off-piste in Tignes. My favourite resort hands down.

Ed Leigh, pro snowboarder and TV presenter

When it comes to runs like these, it's imperative that you heed the avalanche warnings. People regularly die here.
Kids Kids under five get a free ski pass. Bring proof of age.
Flat light days Val has some great trees. Take your pick from Le Fornet, Le Lavancher and the Super L.

P. CHRIS MORAN

OPENING TIMES
Late Nov to early May:
0845-1630/1700

RESORT PRICES (ESPACE KILLY)
Week pass (6 days): €226
Day pass: €41
Season pass: €957

DIRECTORY
Tourist office: T479 060660
Medical centre: T479 060611
Pisteurs: T479 060210
Taxi: T479 410125
Local radio: Radio Val d'Isère 96.1FM
Website: valdisere.com

LOCALS DO
Take the funicular from La Daille to avoid the queues.
Ride very fast, thanks to the abundance of classic motorway pistes.
Build kickers in the bowls to the looker's left of the Tommeuses chair.

LOCALS DON'T
Hit the bowl jump at the top of the park with too much speed. It's a short gap, but it drops away pretty steeply.
Ride the open faces off the top of the Solaise chair after a new snowfall.
Get lost in the Solaise or Fornet trees – there's some massive cliffs in there that you won't see until it's too late.

PROS
Huge area.
Good park.
Great kicker building spots.

CONS
Gets very busy.
Expensive.
Full of drunken Brits.

NOT TO MISS
A good session in the Val park. It's maintained by local legend Gumby.

REMEMBER TO AVOID
Getting caught in the bus queue at La Daille at the end of the day.

SNOW DEPTH

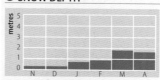

RELIVE A FAMOUS MOMENT
Bono and The Edge recently stayed at the impressive 'Eagle's Nest' house looming over Val d'Isère. Recreate their visit by heading down to Dick's T-Bar and make a right old night of it with the Val seasonaire crew.

1850 m	TOWN ALTITUDE
180 km	KM TO AIRPORT
GVA	AIRPORT
★★★	VEGETARIAN RATING
★★★	INTERNET CAFES
★★☆	RIDE IN/RIDE OUT
3450 m	HIGHEST LIFT
1900 m	VERTICAL DROP
12,355	RIDEABLE AREA (IN ACRES)
300 km	KM OF PISTES
3	NURSERY AREAS
80/35/16	RUNS: BEG/INTER/ADV
2/4	FUNICULAR/CABLE CARS
4/45	GONDOLAS/CHAIRS
36	DRAGS
no	NIGHT RIDING
2	PARKS
1	PIPE
yes	SUMMER AREAS
★★★☆	ENVIRONMENTAL RATING
$$$	COST INDICATOR

FIGURES COVER THE ESPACE KILLY AREA

FRANCE
VAL D'ISERE

The Town

Being the highest resort in Europe, Val Thorens' inclusion in this book was a foregone conclusion. Though it's a purpose-built resort and hardly pleasing to the eye, it's still a far cry from the architectural horror of its neighbour, Les Menuires, a short way down the valley. It has quite a cosmopolitan feel – the clientele consists of Scandinavian, French and English in equal measure, and all the groups mix well. This results in a friendly and welcoming vibe, with the nightlife frequently becoming boisterous, in the nicest possible way.

Sleeping Self-catered accommodation is the cheapest option here – try **Erna Low** (T8707 506820), **Le Cheval Blanc** (T479 000814) and **Residance La Montana** (T479 002101), they are right on the slopes. Hotels such as the **Val Thorens** (T479 000433) and **Le Sherpa** (T479 000070) offer more complete packages and for the deluxe option the four-star **Fitz Roy** (T479 000478), c'est très chic.

Eating Swedish restaurant **Tango** (T479 000270) offers an alternative to the standard Savoyarde option with a great international menu. **John's Restaurant** (T479 000515) makes exceptional burgers – try 'John's Favourite Burger', it won't disappoint. **Les Saint Pere** (T479 000292) in the Gallerie Peclet is great for pizzas and local DIY food. Don't forget the highly acclaimed **L'Oxalys** (T479 001200) near the entrance of the resort, but

> When you're done riding fresh lines from chairlifts three days after a dump, it's time to get down to some serious late-night fun…
>
> *Matt Swann, bar manager*

you'll need to book 48 hours in advance so they can tailor the menu to your taste.

Bars and clubs Tango and Café Sne Sko have great bands during après ski. Next, head to **Le Viking** for big screen sports, free pool and Internet access as well as live music. It's also a great late night drinking venue. **L'Eclipse** in the Gallerie Caron is open till 0400 and is a great French alternative. For clubbing go to the **Underground** for cheese and disco classics and **Malaysia** for a large London-style club with international DJs.

Shopping There are two main areas in Val Thorens: **Gallerie Caron** in the lower part of town and **Gallerie Peclet** at the top of the resort. Both have every shop imaginable, including supermarkets.

Health The sports centre in VT has a 50-m pool and spa/sauna facilities, as well as squash, basketball and tennis courts. There are also over 30 table tennis tables to waste time on bad weather days.

Internet Le Viking offers cheap access and wireless. Also try the **Office de Tourisme**.

Transfer options Altibus (altibus.com) for transfers from Lyon, Geneva and Chambery airports. The **Eurostar** (eurostar.com) stops at Moûtiers, from where Val Thorens is 37 km. There are regular buses from here, which can be booked through valthorens.com or **Altibus**.

Local partners Three Valleys.

The highest resort in Europe, with more good terrain and après-ski action than you can shake a stick at.

➔ *If you like this …*
…try Tignes ▸▸*p154, Val d'Isère* ▸▸*p158, or Verbier* ▸▸*p332.*

⊙ OPENING TIMES
Mid-Nov to early May: 0900-1630

⊙ RESORT PRICES (THREE VALLEYS)
Week pass (6 days): €215
Day pass: €42
Season pass: €935

⊙ DIRECTORY
Tourist ofice: T479 000808
Medical centre: T479 000037
Pisteurs: T479 000180
Taxi: T479 006341
Local radio: Radio Altitude101.0 FM
Website: valthorens.com

The Mountain

Val Thorens' status as Europe's highest resort means that good snow conditions are virtually guaranteed. The flip side of this is that it can suffer from adverse weather, and since it's entirely above the treeline, cloud often halts play. That aside, this is a top class mountain with a wealth of good pistes and great freeriding on offer. Though it's part of the Three Valleys, the VT valley itself takes in Les Menuires and St Martin de Belleville, and most people would be hard pushed to exhaust the possibilities in a week. Rounding things off are a fast and efficient lift system and a pretty decent park and pipe.

Beginners Get started on the green runs around the village and cruise around the Deux Lac chairlift. The more adventurous could try the Plein Sud chair, which offers access to the Méribel Valley.

Intermediate Val Thorens is an intermediate rider's playground.

There are plenty of pistes where it's possible to open it up with some high speed carves, and there are some great cat tracks to jump off in good snow. Cime de Caron is a likely spot for these. If you fancy trying your hand at some creative jibbing then head to the Boismint area, where there are some interesting features to be found. Likewise the area around the Grand Fond Funitele.

Advanced A bit of exploring up Cime de Caron and La Masse will soon open your eyes to the jaw-dropping amount of terrain on offer here – it simply beggars belief. A lot of the best runs are closely guarded secrets, so the best way to go is befriend a local or hire a guide. A trip down to Orelle is highly recommended, especially for its kicker building potential.

Kids Kids under five get a free lift pass. Bring proof of identity.

Flat light days There has to be a flip side to the 'highest resort in Europe' coin, and it's this: there are no trees in Val Thorens. Your only hope is to head over to the Méribel Valley and play around on the Combes and Table Verte chairs in Mottaret.

☺ LOCALS DO

✔ Join in the Scandi après-ski at Tango and Café Sne Sko.
✔ Avoid Caron Village area (the main lift area) during peak times.
✔ Enjoy great spring snow right to the end of the season.

☹ LOCALS DON'T

✘ Drink in Dutch bars during après – you can't get to the bar!
✘ Worry about the off-piste getting tracked out too quickly – there's plenty for everyone.
✘ Forget to check out La Masse in Les Menuires.

✔ PROS

✔ Multicultural resort, with a friendly vibe.
✔ Car-free resort.
✔ Steep and challenging terrain.

✘ CONS

✘ Very busy in peak season.
✘ Poor transport within the resort.
✘ Frequent high winds.

❂ NOT TO MISS

A trip to Orelle, the fourth valley: great terrain and never that busy.

ⓘ REMEMBER TO AVOID

Getting stuck in one of the other valleys after the lifts close. It's an expensive taxi ride back.

❄ SNOW DEPTH

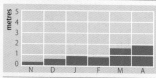

★ RELIVE A FAMOUS MOMENT

Head to the L'Oxalys restaurant and recreate the moment when the Michelin tester had the finest dish in the Trois Vallées and awarded the place a Michelin star. Doing the scene from *When Harry Met Sally* is optional.

2300 m	TOWN ALTITUDE
159 km	KM TO AIRPORT
GVA	AIRPORT
★★☆	VEGETARIAN RATING
★★★	INTERNET CAFES
★★★	RIDE IN/RIDE OUT
3230 m	HIGHEST LIFT
2130 m	VERTICAL DROP
28,000	RIDEABLE AREA (IN ACRES)
600 km	KM OF PISTES
12	NURSERY AREAS
188/119/33	RUNS: BEG/INTER/ADV
3/3	FUNICULAR/CABLE CARS
34/69	GONDOLAS/CHAIRS
71	DRAGS
no	NIGHT RIDING
5	PARKS
3	PIPE
no	SUMMER AREAS
★★★☆	ENVIRONMENTAL RATING
$$$	COST INDICATOR

FIGURES COVER THE THREE VALLEYS AREA

FRANCE
VAL THORENS

P: VAL THORENS TOURISM

R.SHAUN WHITE L: TURIN OLYMPICS 2006 P: MIKE WEYERHAUESER/JDP

There's style, and then there's Shaun.

Italy

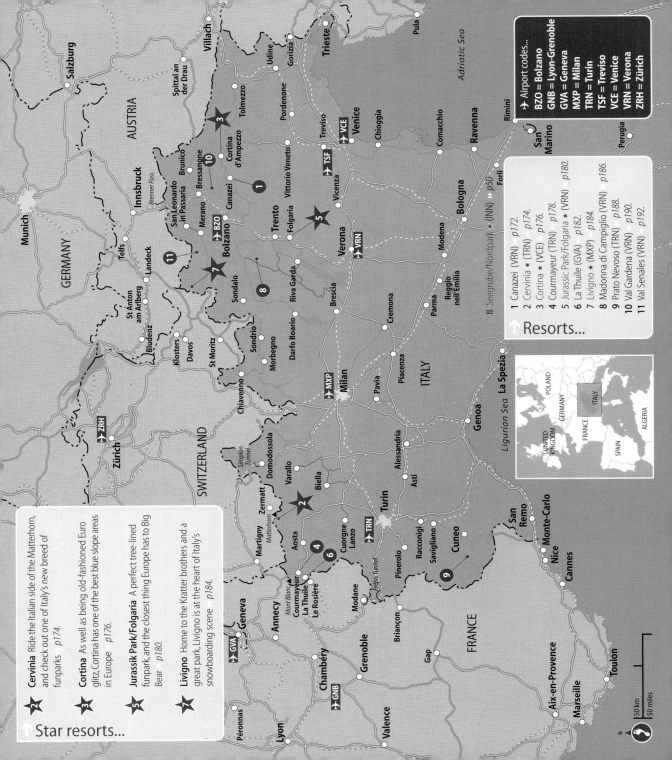

Airport codes...

→ = Airport codes...
BZO = Bolzano
GNB = Lyon-Grenoble
GVA = Geneva
MXP = Milan
TRN = Turin
TSF = Treviso
VCE = Venice
VRN = Verona
ZRH = Zürich

↑ Resorts...

1 Canazei (VRN) p172.
2 Cervinia ★ (TRN) p174.
3 Cortina ★ (VCE) p176.
4 Courmayeur (TRN) p178.
5 Jurassic Park/Folgaria ★ (VRN) p180.
6 La Thuile (GVA) p182.
7 Livigno ★ (MXP) p184.
8 Madonna di Campiglio (VRN) p186.
9 Prato Nevoso (TRN) p188.
10 Val Gardena (VRN) p190.
11 Val Senales (VRN) p192.

8 Seegrube/Nordpark ★ (INN) p50

↑ Star resorts...

2 **Cervinia** Ride the Italian side of the Matterhorn, and check out one of Italy's new breed of funparks p174.

3 **Cortina** As well as being old-fashioned Euro glitz, Cortina has one of the best blue slope areas in Europe p176.

5 **Jurassik Park/Folgaria** A perfect tree-lined funpark, and the closest thing Europe has to Big Bear p180.

7 **Livigno** Home to the Kratter brothers and a great park, Livigno is at the heart of Italy's snowboarding scene p184.

50 km
50 miles
N

It's hard to think of the quintessential Italian resort, perhaps because the country has a very divided mountain industry. The resorts on the eastern side – the Dolomite region – are so different to those in the western end of the Alps as to be almost different countries. There is, however, a uniform feeling – especially in the more traditional resorts – of being in a bit of a timewarp. As most people note after driving from Chamonix through the Mont Blanc tunnel, although only separated by one mountain, Courmayeur might as well be another world. In under 40 km you've gone back in time by 20 years.

Perhaps this is due to the style and culture of the nation. Certainly, in Italy, eighties chic is still very much in, with one-piece suits and serious posing very much irony-free. And while St Moritz and Val d'Isère are often touted as ultra-rich playgrounds, neither come close to the fur-coat count of Cortina d'Ampezzo and its neighbours. If Austria is bad for vegetarians, then Italy's top resorts are a no-go area for PETA supporters.

On the positive side, there are huge pluses: the food is delicious, every café in the country serves coffee a million times better than anywhere else in Europe and – even though the terrain is incredible – there are surprisingly few freeriders in evidence. Italy's best asset is that it can be spectacularly cheap if you search for the right deals, with genuinely quality rides to be had in every one of our featured resorts. Italy makes a great snowboard trip for anyone who fancies broadening their horizons. There are plenty of great parks opening up, and if you hit it right, the chances are you'll be able to ride some incredible powder, followed by some runs in a perfect park. What more do you want?

Italy rating

Value for money
★★★★☆

Nightlife
★★★☆☆

Freestyle
★★★★☆

Freeride
★★★☆☆

Essentials

Getting there

For the shortest transfer times, the Dolomites are best accessed by Bolzano airport. However, it's a small airport and its services change regularly. There's a downloadable list of carriers and times at abd-airport.it. Alternatively, Venice has Treviso airport (trevisoairport.it) which **Ryan Air** (ryanair.com) fly to, while Marco Polo Airport is serviced by **easyJet** (easyjet.com) which is a little further from the mountains and closer to the city of Venice. Milan's main airport is Malpensa (malpensaairport.com), with regular services from **British Airways** (ba.com), **Austrian** (austrianairlines.com), **KLM** (klm.com), **Lufthansa** (lufthansa.com), **SAS** (sas.se), **Swiss** (swiss.com), **American Airlines** (aa.com) and many more major carriers as well as low budget airlines.

Turin airport (aeroportoditorino.it) has **BA**, **Austrian**, **American Airlines**, **easyJet**, **Alitalia** (alitalia.com), **KLM**, **SAS**, **SkyEurope** (skyeurope.com) and **Lufthansa** among others.

Alternatively, the Dolomites can be reached via Innsbruck airport (see page 26) while Courmayeur is within reach of Geneva Airport (see page 300).

Italy also has fantastic road links to France, Switzerland, Austria and Croatia, although it is advisable to check that the mountain passes are open. Most, including the Brenner Pass, the Mont Blanc Tunnel and the Frejus Pass, are motorway trade routes for lorries, which mean they're unlikely to be shut unless a serious accident or severe weather has hit.

Red tape

As an EU state there are no major hassles. Italy now has a no-smoking policy in all public places including restaurants and bars.

Getting around

Driving (right-hand side) A valid driving licence from your home country is fine. Generally speaking, Italy has a terrible reputation for aggressive drivers and it is not without good reason. However, stricter police controls are in evidence these days. If you're used to driving in big cities you should have no problems.

Motorway Italy's motorways are reliable and direct. There is a toll system in operation and several mountain passes and tunnels charge to cross.

Car hire Most major hire car companies (easycar.com, hertz.com, avis.com etc) have offices in airports and cities. Usual age restrictions apply.

Public transport

Italian trains are divided up into Eurostar, Intercity, Interregionale and Regionale services. All are complicated, have unnecessary validation

P: NATALIE MAYER

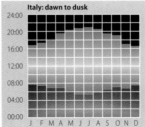

Italy: dawn to dusk

P: JAMES MCPHAIL

Italy price guide

	☕	🍴	📰	🍺	@	🚬	🥤
In €	1,00	2,50	2,80	0,77	3,00	2,50	1,00

Take a look at a map of Italy: what you see are mountains everywhere, from north to south – yes, Sicily included. From the world-class slopes of the Alps (Dolomites and the Monte Rosa are the first two names that spring to mind) to the sweeter steepness of the older Apennines, the whole Italian country has hundreds of resorts. That not only means an incredible variety of terrain and a jaw-dropping backdrop, but it also gives more chance to find fresh, deep snow: lately the south has seen precipitation increasing like never before in the past 20 years. And where else in the world could you go riding in 2 m of pow and then spend the night in a place like Rome? Besides being gifted with mountains and history, Italians are really working at making their parks better in order to make their offer more complete. And, worst-case scenario, if it's a bad day and riding isn't possible, you can always enjoy real Italian cuisine and wines – so worth it!

Rita Comi, professional snowboarder

Fact file

→ Currency Euro (€)
Exchange rate US$1 = €0.80
Time zone GMT +1
Country code: +39
Emergency numbers
  Ambulance: T118
  Police: T113
  Fire: T115

Opening hours and traditions

Shops have long opening hours. Restaurants are often open well into the night, and most clubbing goes on very late. Siestas aren't uncommon and visitors often swing with the Mediterranean vibe very quickly.

Eating

Italy has successfully exported its cuisine to the rest of the world, so it's unlikely you'll be confronted with unfamiliar dish or an incomprehensible menu. However, real Italian food is often a little simpler than dishes found at home, with staples such as gnocchi and polenta (both savoury tastes circling the pasta/potato/cous-cous arena) being much more popular than the export variety. Breads are often spiced with all manner of interesting flavours and breadsticks are pretty much obligatory at every meal.

Even in the Alps, you'll find that each valley or region has its own

stamping on tickets and have huge price fluctuations depending on seasons and times of day. To use the trains you will need patience and you'll have to have your wits about you. The website trenitalia.com is translatable into English and is the national train website.

P: MADONNA TOURISM

Key phrases

Key phrases			
Yes	si	tomorrow	domani
No	no	day	giorno
Please	per favore		
Thank you	grazie (mille)	**Numbers**	
Sorry	scusi	0	zero
Hello	buon giorno	1	uno
Goodbye	ciao	2	due
Good	buono/ buona	3	tre
Bad	cattivo	4	quattro
I don't understand	non capisco	5	cinque
I'd like...	potrei...	6	sei
Do you have..?	avete..?	7	sette
How much is it?	quanta costa?	8	otto
Where is..?	dove è il..?	9	nove
Mens	uomini	10	dieci
Ladies	donne	11	undici
Left	sinistra	12	dodici
Right	destra	13	tredici
Straight on	dritto	14	quattordici
Night	notte	15	quindici
Room	stanza	16	sedici
Shower	doccia	17	diciassette
Toilet	bagno	18	diciotto
The bill	conto	19	diciannove
White coffee	il caffe bianco	20	venti
Beer	birra	21	ventuno
Red wine/white wine	vino	22	ventidue
bianco/rosso		30	trenta
Mineral water (sparkling)	l'acqua	40	quaranta
(gasata)		50	cinquanta
Orange juice	succo d'arancia	60	sessanta
Sandwich	panino	70	settanta
Ham	prosciutto	80	ottanta
Cheese	formaggio	90	novanta
Grilled cheese/ham	prosciutto e	100	cento
formaggio cotti		1000	mille
Help!	aiuto!		
North	nord	**Days of the week**	
South	sud	Monday	lunedì
East	est	Tuesday	martedì
West	ovest	Wednesday	mercoledì
yesterday	ieri	Thursday	giovedì
last night	ieri sera	Friday	venerdì
today	oggi	Saturday	sabato
		Sunday	domenica

sophisticated palate, it would be crazy to go to Italy and not get a few pizza and pasta dishes under the belt.

Language
Italian is the lingua franca. English is spoken by many of the younger generation, so you shouldn't have too many problems in snowboard-friendly areas. Elsewhere a rudimentary grasp of basic sayings will serve you well.

Crime/safety
Smaller Italian resorts are pretty much crime-free, but in the bigger resorts it's worth keeping your snowboards off the balcony, and avoid leaving valuables in cars. Leaving boards outside restaurants is generally fine, but again, it's worth keeping an eye on them.

Health
Italy is a member of the European Union. Health insurance is recommended, and EU citizens should carry a European Health Insurance Card (EHIC), which replaces the old E1-11 form.

L: MADONNA DI CAMPIGLIO P: NATALIE MAYER

L: CERVINIA PARK P: DANI MILANO

speciality, which most restaurants will push, so why not try going local now and again? Livigno, for example, has *bresaola* – a fat-free aged beef carpaccio, as well as a local specialty called *pizzoccheri* – a buckwheat pasta with potato, cheese and chard, then seasoned with butter: the perfect carb-loaded after-riding meal.

It's worth noting that, like Austria, international cuisine is generally hard to find, although the choices for vegetarians are greatly increased by the fact that Italian food has a solid base of tomato, herbs and carbohydrates and meat-free options are many. And while we're all for resorts to start catering for a more

Snowboarding Italy

"Riding in Italy should be an amazing and unique experience. From east to west, from north to south, you'll find the biggest and most beautiful mountains in Europe. The main courses of our Alpine menu are Monte Bianco, Monte Rosa, Marmolada, Gran Sasso and the best terrain park in Europe, the Mottolino fun area in Livigno. Not so many riders in Europe take the time to enjoy our country, so come over and check it out for yourself." Andrea Giordan, Italian editor, Method Mag

If we were to draw a Venn diagram of the Alps, with France depicted as a freeride circle and Austria as a freestyle circle, then Italy would occupy the oval shape in the middle. Like Austria, several Italian resorts have had the foresight to attract riders by building great parks. Livigno stands out as the best of the bigger resorts to take the lead, but the fact that smaller resorts such as Folgaria and Prato Nevoso are building all-mountain terrain parks points to an interesting future for Italian snowboarding. The country also has mountains to rival anything in France. Courmayeur, for example, is linked with Chamonix via the Hellbronner gondolas and a shared lift pass, and several of the Dolomite resorts boast unbelievable

Pros & cons

Pros …
- Food, food and more food.
- Friendly people.
- No smoking in all public places.
- Off-piste is often left untouched.
- Cheap by European standards.
- Easy links to many airports.
- Great for visiting a romantic city during your holiday.

… and cons
- Older style resorts with antiquated lifts.
- Can be rammed with poseurs and old-fashioned winter sporters during holidays.
- Atrocious amount of fur on display.
- Driving to the resort can often be a dangerous affair.

terrain accessed by cable car. Heading to Italy after a huge storm is an amazing experience. There are, however, a few drawbacks that are worth noting. In general terms, the lift systems are older than elsewhere in Europe; T-bars and poma lifts are plentiful and there's a pretty good chance you'll encounter some serious moguls on steeper pistes. There's

R: HAMISH MCKNIGHT L: CANAZEI P: JAMES MCPHAIL

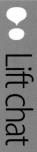
Piste, love and undertsanding

Picture the scene: you've just scored the partner of your dreams but, bafflingly, she/he doesn't know how to snowboard. Keen to include them in the joys of sideways sliding, you book a trip to Chamonix, France, and unwisely vow to spend the week teaching your new love how to ride on the gentle beginner slopes at Le Tour. Impressed at your thoughtfulness, your new belle/beau looks forward to a joyful week of gazing into each other's eyes over hot gluhwein and hand-in-hand adventures on the nursery slopes. And in your head, so do you.

But then you arrive in Cham to find that the dump of the season is in full fury. Suddenly your new partner begins to look less like the girl/man of your dreams and more like a rusty ball-and-chain, intent on keeping you away from the fresh powder that is your birthright. The mantra 'There are no girl/boy friends on a powder day' begins to seep into your head like the ruinous floods that destroyed the fair city of Prague a few years ago.

The next day, you force your bewildered love out of the cosy bed at half past seven. At the base of the Grands Montets area, you 'accidentally' bump into your mates and, stopping only to say, 'That's your toe edge, that's your heel edge. You need to switch from one to the other and stop on your heels. Just point it downhill, and don't forget to use your shoulders', you gleefully leap into the cable car and head for the top. Heading down later to brag about your day to the him/her indoors, you return to your hotel to find the wardrobe empty and a Polaroid of your now ex-love giving you the finger while hobbling around on crutches stapled to the pillow. Burying your head in your hands, you begin to sniffle and laugh at the same time in a deranged manner. Yet again, your snowboarding addiction has sabotaged your love life.

But it doesn't have to be like this. Why not take them on a combined snowboarding and city break instead?
Here's our pick of the best:
▶▶ Venice/Cortina
▶▶ Barcelona/Baqueira
▶▶ LA/Mammoth
▶▶ Portland/Baker
▶▶ Salzburg/Zillertal

P. SALLY FENNER

even a good chance you'll be one of the few snowboarders on the mountain if you head to the classier Dolomite resorts (there are also plans to ban snowboarding in parts of the country, but so far this hasn't come to anything). Note also that under 14s are required by law to wear a helmet on the slopes, and riding off-piste is governed by rules (see below).

Conditions

Italy's weather comes from the north, the northeast and the northwest. Generally speaking, it can be more temperate than other Alpine nations. The treeline can often reach well over 2000 m – great for flat light days – and there is often a very different look to the mountains due to the different species of vegetation in evidence. That said, the higher reaches of the mountains mean it can often be extremely cold – as anyone who has taken the cable car to the top of Cortina can testify – so be well prepared for wild fluctuations in temperatures in the resorts with big vertical drops. It's easy to forget that the mountains are as foreboding as anywhere in Switzerland and France.

When to go

Italy's season traditionally gears up for a grand opening just before Christmas, followed by a peak of cold weather throughout January and February. March and April are traditionally warmer months, with plenty of slush to ride. By May there's hardly anything open.

Off-piste policy

One of the reasons Italy's freeriding scene is disproportionate to the accessibility and quality of its terrain is that going out of bounds often can be an arrestable offence. Get caught by the *carabinieri* riding off-piste in a forbidden area (and they have a ski and snowmobile division) and you're likely to incur a fine of around €50. It is also illegal to ride off-piste without an avalanche transceiver and rescue equipment, which is clearly a sensible idea. While we think imposing restrictions on

P. JAMES MCPHAIL

P. HAMISH MCKNIGHT L: CANAZEI P. JAMES MCPHAIL

out-of-bounds riding is clearly ludicrous (especially when neighbouring France has such a relaxed attitude with virtually identical terrain), we can't suggest breaking the law and urge any freeriders to exercise even more caution in Italy than they would normally.

Secret spots

Because of the off-piste policy, secret spots are well guarded. However, find the nearest snowboard shop, and if they're cool enough, they should be able to give you some sound advice.

Freestyle

As mentioned elsewhere, many of the smaller Italian resorts have come to the same conclusions as those in Austria – well-maintained funparks are the key to attracting the snowboard crowd. The main resorts to have worked this out include Livigno, which is consistently voted the best park in Italy, closely followed by the fantastic Indian Park in Cervinia. Further east, Madonna di Campiglio leads the pack in the best freestyle category, while Cortina is getting there if you use your pass and head to the nearby park at Alleghe. Prato Nevoso and Folgoria are clearly freestyle heaven, and should their ideas work, expect Italy to be awash in small resorts with big funparks over the coming years.

The scene

Italian riders have been at the forefront of European snowboarding since the mid-1990s. Though still essentially a skiing nation, adverts of Alberto Tomba and pasta-loving American Bodie Miller are plastered around resorts: evidence of a very strong underground snowboarding movement. Top riders include halfpipe guru Giacomo Kratter, who placed fourth in the 2002 Olympic games, and Rita Comi, one of the best female riders in the world.

The industry

Like Austria, the fantastic snow-parks.com and accompanying publication *The Freestyle Yearbook* (which should be available for free from most resort snowboard shops) covers the best of the Italian funparks and the burgeoning scene.

Lift chat

Two countries in one day

Among all the talk about tricks, freeriding, pipes and kickers, the humble snowboard's ground-covering abilities are almost always overlooked. But think about it. How far do you travel in a typical day's riding? Travelling from, say, Courchevel to Val Thorens in France's Trois Vallées, probably entails riding hard for much of the day and covering a distance of over 20 km each way. And let's face it, motoring as quickly as possible down a piste is one of snowboarding's simplest pleasures, whether you're on the way to the park, Val Thorens or just racing your way home. In snowboarding the journey often really is the destination.

Maybe the French resort of La Rosière and the Italian resort of La Thuile had this in mind when they linked their mountains back in the day to make one Franco-Italian whole. Whatever the reason, it's easily possible to spend the morning munching on croissants in France, head up the hill, blast your way over to Italy (slapping a 'Welcome to Italy' sign as you cross the 'border'), enjoy pizza and coffee for lunch and leg it back by nightfall. You can't do *that* on a surfboard. Have snowboard, will travel indeed...

L: LA ROSIERE/LA THUILE BORDER P: ANDREW HINGSTON

Italy: a brief history of snowboarding

1981 → The first swallowtailed boards are ridden in Courmayeur and Livigno by early Swiss and French riders. Local instructors and seasonaires quickly catch on. Surf shops in Milan and Rome stock the first few boards and undoubtedly several home-made rides make it to the slopes. **1985** → The first competition featuring international riders is organized in the resort of San Sicario. **1986** → The Italian Snowsurf Association (AISN) is formed, becoming the country's governing body for snowboarding. **1989** → Freestyle riding gains popularity thanks largely to Italian rider Max Perotti who wins several world cups and is a regular in international magazines. **1990** → Italy forms its own snowboard instructor course, which is quickly swamped with enquiries. **1994** → Italy hosts its first world cup in San Candido featuring mainly race-based events. Italy's national snowboard team is founded. **1995** → The country is divided into hardboot riders (influenced heavily by the Austrian scene) and freestyle riding. **1998** → At the first Olympics in Japan, Thomas Prugger wins a silver medal in the men's Giant Slalom, proving that hardboot riding in Italy is still on the rise. **2002** → Lidia Trettel wins a bronze medal in the Parallel Giant Slalom at the 2002 Olympic games in Salt Lake City. Italian rider Giocomo Kratter narrowly misses the podium with a fourth place finish in the men's halfpipe event. Freestyle riding also fights back with the first European Open organized in Livigno in the same year. Nicolas Muller, David Carrier Porcheron and David Benedek take top honours in the HP, SS and QP only event. **2004** → Livigno and Cervinia invest heavily in their funparks, creating a strong freestyle scene in resort. **2005** → Prato Nevoso (translated as 'Snow Field') becomes the first all-mountain park in Italy. Today 100 snowboard clubs and an estimated half a million riders hit the slopes every year. Freestyle riding is by far the most popular side to the sport, but pockets of hardboot riders still exist in the Dolomites.

Canazei

Affordable gateway to the stunning Sella Ronda and the vast cruisers' paradise of the Dolomite Superski area.

If you like this ...
... try *Courchevel* ▸▸p130, *La Plagne* ▸▸p136, *Leysin* ▸▸p324, or *Keystone* ▸▸p364.

The Town

Bustling and attractive, this is the most popular spot in the Val di Fassa: a stand-alone resort from which to explore the valley's many hills and hamlets. A cable car from the village whisks you straight up into the Sella Ronda circuit, with easy descents into swanky Alta Badia and Val Gardena, while a free ski bus serves the quieter, family-oriented areas of the local valley. In atmosphere, the South Tyrol is a little like stepping back into the winter sports universe of yesteryear, where fur is still coveted, snowboarders are viewed with quizzical interest and the locals speak a mixture of German and Italian – a lasting nod to the way the area was carved up in the past. Yet there's something strangely compelling about this time capsule feel.

Sleeping There's a huge range of accommodation here. The fassa.com website has a great accommodation finder for rentals, apartments, guesthouses and hotels so have a look at that first. A good, cheap option in Canazei is the **Campagnolo** (xoomer.alice.it/la.campa/), while the **Garni Serena** (T0462 601340) is pretty reasonable. You can also stay in nearby Campitello.

Eating All the restaurants here put most other countries to shame, but try the **Melester** (T0462 602077), the **Wine and Dine** (T0462 601111) or the **Astoria** (T0462 601302) if you're feeling up for the full maitre'd treatment.

Bars and clubs The **Melester** has a good bar favoured by the locals, while **Huskies** is the classic resort bar – loud house music and posing locals. Head to the **Speckeller Disco** afterwards. **Esso Bar** also gets the thumbs up and is a little more chilled.

Shopping Rent equipment or ogle new gear at **Detomas** (T0462 602447). For food shopping, there are a couple of supermarkets on the main drag.

Health Calm down in the Camomile Cave at the **Eghes Wellness Center** (T0462 601348), the only spa in the area not attached to a hotel, and a very nice one at that. Massage and other treatments available.

Internet Don't forget to bring your ID to the comfy, arty **Dot.Com** café (T0462 600280); thanks to homeland security-type measures in Italy, it's a legal requirement.

Transfer options Ski buses run on Saturdays from Verona and Brescia airports, for a reasonable €40 return. Tickets must be booked in advance (trentinoviaggi.net).

Local partners Twelve areas come under the Dolomite Superski umbrella, and each of those areas comprise more lifts and valleys than you could get round to in a mere week. Closest to Canazei are those of the Sella Ronda, the neighbouring Tre Valli and the Val di Fiemme, to the south.

Flat light days Recreate *The Big Lebowski* (meets *Heidi*) in the bowling lanes of the **Hotel Alpe** (T0462 601357).

> ❝❞
> For cruisers, families and big groups of mixed experience, this place is pretty perfect. It's cheap as well.
>
> *Steve Bailey, pro snowboarder*

☺ OPENING TIMES

Early Dec to early Apr: 0900-1630

⑤ RESORT PRICES

Week pass (6 days): €158
Day pass: €28
Season pass: €390

ⓘ DIRECTORY

Tourist office: T0462 609600
Medical centre: T347 7745793
Pisteurs: T0462 601110
Taxi: T0462 601574
Local radio: 100 FM, Radio Studio Record
Website: fassa.com

P: JAMES MCPHAIL

R: STEVE BAILEY · PP: JAMES MCPHAIL

The Mountain

Don't let the local stats guide you. Right beside Canazei are the lifts of Col Rodella and Passo Pordoi, doubling both vertical and access. The vast Dolomite Superski area is on your doorstep, but a local or valley pass may be all you need. And good value for money doesn't translate to poor facilities: the locals are hot on reinvestment, so that lifts here are generally modern and speedy, the pistes well-groomed, and natural snow shored up by snowcannons. This is primarily cruising terrain, but there's plenty of accessible backcountry for those who know what they're doing.

Beginners Val di Fassa's dedicated snowboard school is based in Canazei (T462 600304). There's one small drag-served nursery slope in town, but you're better off hopping on the bus and heading downvalley to Pozza di Fassa's Vajolet and Pian Peccei-Pramartin lifts, which access blues and mellow reds.

Intermediate Take the gondola up to Pecol and warm up on the long cruisers on Belvedere. After some laps through the park, drop down to Pian Fratacer; if conditions are good, you can nip off-piste and into the trees. In the afternoon, head up to the wide open bowls of the Sella Pass.

Advanced Visiting Canazei can be frustrating for advanced riders. The terrain here is undoubtedly full of potential, and there are huge, eerie cliffs and off-piste itineraries as far you can see. But there are problems with accessing the goods, with riders having been arrested in the past for ducking the rope. Use caution. Some locals also use the passes above Canazei to build kickers and hike away from the crowds.

Kids Drop them at Kinderland (T0462 601211), where kids get their own restaurant, indoor and outdoor games areas and ski school. Under eights ride free with an adult on a Superski pass; note that in Italy, all children under 14 have to wear helmets.

Flat light days Most lifts are above the treeline, but in deep, fresh powder try the trees below Pecol, or above Pozza di Fassa.

🙂 LOCALS DO
● Ride down the Lupo Bianco piste to get back to Canazei, and have a drink in the Rose Garten at the bottom.
● Get drunk before they hit town.
● Speak Ladino, the local mountain language.

😠 LOCALS DON'T
● Let riding get in the way of partying.
● Take it all that seriously – this isn't Snow Park.
● Forget to eat up the hill.

✓ PROS
● Lots of different areas to explore.
● Generally good snow conditions, with lots of sun.
● Good value for money and great food.

✗ CONS
● Terrain parks on the small side.
● Skiers in one-pieces still vastly outnumber riders.
● Considerable on-piste travel.

☺ NOT TO MISS
A late-afternoon trip to the top of the Sass Pordoi, the summit of the rose-coloured rocky fortress that is the heart of the glowing Gruppo del Sella.

ⓘ REMEMBER TO AVOID
The queues in the morning. Everybody takes one gondola from Canazei up to the slopes, and it gets predictably busy at peak times.

❄ SNOW DEPTH
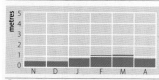

★ RELIVE A FAMOUS MOMENT
The *Italian Job* 2003 remake starring Mark Wahlberg and Charlize Theron has several scenes filmed in Canazei town.

P: JAMES MCPHAIL

1460 m	TOWN ALTITUDE
170 km	KM TO AIRPORT
VRN	AIRPORT
★☆☆	VEGETARIAN RATING
★★☆	INTERNET CAFES
★★☆	RIDE IN/RIDE OUT
2423 m	HIGHEST LIFT
963 m	VERTICAL DROP
area not measured	RIDEABLE AREA (IN ACRES)
40 km	KM OF PISTES
1	NURSERY AREAS
5/25/0	RUNS: BEG/INTER/ADV
0/1	FUNICULAR/CABLE CARS
3/7	GONDOLAS/CHAIRS
2	DRAGS
no	NIGHT RIDING
1	PARKS
0	PIPE
no	SUMMER AREAS
★★★ ★★☆	ENVIRONMENTAL RATING
	COST INDICATOR

ITALY
CANAZEI

173

Cervinia

Better known as Zermatt's ugly sister, Cervinia boasts 150 km of slopes, an efficient lift system and access to one of Europe's highest peaks.

☀ **If you like this** ...
... try *Seegrube/Nordpark* ▸▸*p50, or Avoriaz* ▸▸*p124.*

The Town

Cervina's real weak spot is its architecture. It was first developed as a ski area in 1936 during Mussolini's era when the building of state-of-the-art lifts and hotels commenced, but since those bright beginnings the town hasn't had a real development plan – and it shows. Despite the bizarre architectural mix, access to the slopes is fast and easy from almost every part of the town, and a central main street with plenty of shops offers ample opportunity for a very pleasant after riding stroll.

Sleeping The apartments at **Studio Breuil Cervinia** (T0166 940238) are the cheapest in town. For a real bargain ask for accommodation in the Cielo Alto area: it's about 800 m from the main street but it's connected to the centre with a shuttle and taxi service. The **Hotel Miravidi** (hotelmiravidi.com) is the snowboarders' favourite, while also popular is **La Maison de Vacances** (T0166 948381).

Eating Try the pastries (especially the Chatilly Bignet) at the **Samovar Tea Room** located at the beginning of main street – amazing. The **Black Hole** is the place for hamburgers, made from local beef.

Bars and clubs Everyone starts off in the **Yeti** bar and then heads to the **Discoteca Banconiglio** until the lights come on.

Shopping The cheapest supermarket in town is the **Crai** at the beginning of the village. In the same area **Claudio Salto** sells local Aosta valley produce in his shops.

Health Club Med (T0166 944600) has the best sporting facilities in town, including an Olympic-sized swimming pool, hammam and sauna. Unfortunately it's only open for public use in the mornings.

Internet If your hotel doesn't have Internet access, you can get online at **Lino's** or the **Yeti** bar.

Transfer Options Cervinia is a short drive from Milan (about two hours) and Turin (about 90 minutes). A bus service runs daily from St Vincent.

Local partners Cervinia's lift pass also gives access to Valtournenche. Buy the pricer international ticket to get access to Zermatt as well.

⊛ **OPENING TIMES**

Late Oct to early May: 0900-1700
Late Jun to early Sep: 0700-1330

⑤ **RESORT PRICES**

Week pass (6 days): €211
Day pass: €32
Season pass: €890

ⓘ **DIRECTORY**

Tourist office: T0166 949136
Medical centre: T0166 940175
Pisteurs: T333 664 3244
Taxi: T348 312 3036 (mob)
Local radio: None
Website: cervinia.it

The Mountain ⛰❄😊

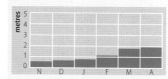

Three interlinked valleys give a wide range of terrain, with plenty to suit all levels of ability. Choose from tree runs in the lower area of Valturnanche, Goillè's off-piste, the perfectly groomed slopes up on the glacier or two snowparks; all overlooked by the distinctive outline of the Cervino (or Matterhorn, as the Swiss call it).

Beginners Head to the new Crétaz four-man chairlift right in the middle of the village – it scoops you up gently and accesses a mellow, short slope. The main station, Plain Maison, also has some beginner-friendly slopes, including the Crétaz blue run accessible by the Vielle beginner lift.

Intermediate There are plenty of good pistes to challenge intermediate riders: check out Plain Maison, Fornet and Bontadini to name but a few. The real must-do is the Ventina: take an afternoon to enjoy this 11.5-km slope, which leads from the glacier area straight to the village. There are several lifts on the way down so that you can ride your favourite sections again. If a bit of mellow off-piste riding is what you're after then head to the Cielo Alto

We've been running the Indian Park here since 2003 and it's been going from strength to strength. Next winter we're going to bring in a lot of new obstacles and really try to up things.

Dan Milano, ex-editor Snowboard Italy, head of Cervinia's Indian Park

and Bardoney chairlifts.

Advanced Test your skills with the Porta Nera glacier on the Zermatt side, where you'll find challenging slopes and breathtaking backdrops. Freeriders can take the Chamois lifts and ride all the way down to Cheney in the Valtournenche area – just remember that the only way back to Cervinia is by car or bus. Freestylers are going to find themselves heading straight to the Indian snowpark. It's got a 15-m kicker, a kinked rail, a wall ride and a chair (the Fornet) that enables easy laps.

Kids Kids are best suited to Plain Maison, a massive plain area situated at 2250 m with vast, gently inclined slopes.

Flat light days All the locals head to the Cielo Alto and Bardoney tree runs, where you can have a great day even when it's a total whiteout.

😊 LOCALS DO

🏂 Carry valid ID when riding to Zermatt.
🏂 Stop for a drink in the many bars and pubs of the village after a long day of riding.
🏂 Always wear a high SPF: the sun rays on the glacier are strong and hit your skin even if there's bad weather!

😠 LOCALS DON'T

❌ Use their cars to get around the village.
❌ Take the Laghi Cime Bianche-Plateau Rosà gondola in high-peak season: the queue can be over an hour long.
❌ Leave the town between 1600 amd 1800 on Saturday and Sunday: there's only one road that reaches Cervinia and it gets jammed quite often during the weekends.

✅ PROS

✔ Reliable snow all year long.
✔ The 11.5-km Ventina is one of Europe's longest slopes.
✔ Wide, perfectly groomed slopes: ideal learner's spot.

❌ CONS

❌ The village is plain ugly.
❌ Can get busy in holiday periods.

😎 NOT TO MISS

The park: it's shaped everyday and has a free barbie. Nice touch.

😟 REMEMBER TO AVOID

Getting stuck in Switzerland. The last ride back is at 1530.

❄ SNOW DEPTH

metres	N	D	J	F	M	A
5						
4						
3						
2					▇	▇
1					▇	▇
0	▇	▇	▇	▇	▇	▇

😊 RELIVE A FAMOUS MOMENT

The nearby Grand St Bernard Pass was used for the opening sequence of Michael Caine's 1969 classic *The Italian Job*.

2050 m	TOWN ALTITUDE
140 km	KM TO AIRPORT
TRN	AIRPORT
★★☆	VEGETARIAN RATING
★★☆	Internet CAFES
★★☆	RIDE IN/RIDE OUT
3489 m	HIGHEST LIFT
1439 m	VERTICAL DROP
1144	RIDEABLE AREA (IN ACRES)
150 km	KM OF PISTES
8	NURSERY AREAS
18/33/16	RUNS: BEG/INTER/ADV
0/0	FUNICULAR/CABLE CARS
7/13	GONDOLAS/CHAIRS
13	DRAGS
no	NIGHT RIDING
7	PARKS
0	PIPE
yes	SUMMER AREAS
★★★	ENVIRONMENTAL RATING
💲💲💲	COST INDICATOR
ITALY	
CERVINIA	

P: DANI MILANO

Cortina

The Town ⬭🏂♨

Cortina was clearly built in the same Victorian boom-time that gave us Chamonix and a million other spa towns. Architecturally it is impressive. But although there is a clear wealthy undercurrent to the town, there seems to be a strange lack of youthful vibrancy around, resulting in a division between the rich, older hotels, and some derelict buildings. That said, the ice rink is a marvel to look at, and the main church tower dominates the town.

Sleeping The **Montana** (cortina-hotel.com) has rooms from €30 upwards. The **Impero** (hotelimpero cortina.it) for around €40 per person. The **Hotel de la Poste** (delaposte.it) is the classic old-school place from €100 upwards.

Eating There's a huge panini selection at the **Lago da Poste** including a Sunday roast panini! **Croda Cafe** is fast and busy, with real Italian food, while **Villa Argentina** in the beginner area has great 'olde world on the slopes charm'.

Bars and Clubs **Enoteca** or the **Villa Sandi** are good from 1700 onwards, then try the **VIP Rooms** after 2300.

Shopping **Kangaru** just before the railway bridge – now a pedestrian walkway – has standard resort supermarket wares. There's also a **General Store** next to the Hotel Royal on the Corso Italia (the main street).

Health The **Corte Spa** (cortespa.it), 10 minutes from Cortina is world clas.

Internet The **Multimedia Centre** (next to the Hotel Alaska) has computers to use. For wireless, head to the **Hotel Impiro** and buy a beer.

Transfer options Cortina operates a free transfer system to Venice for some hotels, with reduced rates for others; dolomiti.org has details but beware – it's a complicated system.

Local partners The Dolomiti Superskipass (dolomitisuperski.com) encompasses an exhausting number of local partners.

A glimpse of what ski resorts were like 20 years ago: very few snowboarders, older cable cars, some incredibly challenging terrain, and beautiful architecture from a different era.

⟁ If you like this . . .
. . . try Courchevel ▶▶p130, Verbier ▶▶p330, or Aspen ▶▶p348.

P: NATALIE MAYER

The Mountain

Perhaps the reason Cortina hasn't ever caught up with its contemporary resorts is that its mountain lacks the same punch that Chamonix has. However, it does have some fantastic pluses. Firstly, the beginner area is absolutely perfect, being far from the main area, so no-one comes charging through. Secondly, the views are staggering, with magnificent granite towers at every turn. It does, however, have older style cable cars, often cruising 1000 ft over the cliffs and undoubtedly putting people off. And although part of the enormous Dolomiti Superskipass, the areas are far from joined up, so we're only including the Cortina Valley in the key. It makes our guide for two reasons: we think you'll enjoy its quiet beginner area, and because it has a certain unchanged charm and seems to be stuck in another era. However, for freestyle riders, nearby Alleghe (included in the pass) has a fantastic team of shapers and is set to open in 2006-07 as an all-mountain funpark. Well worth checking out.

Beginners Beginners should head straight to the top of the Olympia chairlift, where the best blue run area in the Alps lies. There are so many lovely runs through the gentle forest, most of them totally uncrowded, that you should have no problems exploring the area for a whole week.
Intermediate Head up the incredible Faloria cable car, then straight to the top of the Vitelli lift (it'll go over the Faloria funpark). From the top, keep working your way skiers right until you reach the Rio Gere restaurant and car park. There's a

secret green run that heads back to Cortina and will take you through gardens and over roads. It's a fun circuit for the adventurous.
Advanced Head to the top of the Pomedes: the run down the front face back to the start of the chair is possibly the steepest piste in the world. If that doesn't scare you, just have a ride on the Col Druscie cable car next, but don't look down. Need more? Head to Alleghe nearby for their new all-mountain park.
Kids Kids up to eight years old are entitled to a free liftpass from April onwards. For conditions, see dolomitisuperski.com.
Flat light days The runs from the Pomedes down through the forest to the Olympia chair are perfectly lined with trees.

P. CHRIS MORAN/HOTSHITPICTURES.COM

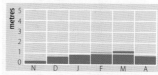

⊙ OPENING TIMES
Late Nov to mid-Apr: 0845-1600
⊙ RESORT PRICES
Week pass (6 days): €175
Day pass: €36
Season pass: €600
⊙ DIRECTORY
Tourist office: T0436 3231
Medical centre: T0436 883111
Pisteurs: T0436 868505
Taxi: T0436 860888
Local radio: Radio Cortina, 103.8 FM
Website: cortinaevents.com
For Alleghe:
dolomiti.it/consorzioalleghe/eng/

☺ LOCALS DO
● Head out after 2300. The town only kicks off after midnight.
● Wear an incredible amount of fur. Seriously.
● Often look like Donatella Versace!

☻ LOCALS DON'T
⊗ Pose for photos – you could end up on the Cortina website in their 'Beauties' section!
⊗ Ski or ride off-piste too much. It's all yours.
⊗ Expect to get a table after 2000 with ease. Later than 1930 and you might go hungry.

✔ PROS
● Proximity to airport – and the chance to visit Venice.
● Varied terrain and chance to relive what it was like to be a snowboarder 20 years ago.
● Fantastic beginner area.

✗ CONS
⊗ Not a great amount of youth culture. It's a very 'old' town.
⊗ Anti-fur campaigners should definitely stay away!
⊗ Terrible traffic means accidents are inevitable.

☺ NOT TO MISS
A trip to the Chinque Torri – beautiful granite peaks a bus ride out of town.

ⓘ REMEMBER TO AVOID
The home run down from the Col Druscie can get busy after 1500, especially the bridge at the end.

❄ SNOW DEPTH

metres

	N	D	J	F	M	A

☺ RELIVE A FAMOUS MOMENT
The Pink Panther (1963) starring Peter Sellers and David Niven, was filmed in and around Cortina. Watch the film and see how little the decor has changed since!

1220 m	TOWN ALTITUDE
150 km	KM TO AIRPORT
VCE	AIRPORT
★☆☆	VEGETARIAN RATING
★☆☆	INTERNET CAFES
★☆☆	RIDE IN/RIDE OUT
2950 m	HIGHEST LIFT
1730 m	VERTICAL DROP
area not measured	RIDEABLE AREA (IN ACRES)
140 km	KM OF PISTES
2	NURSERY AREAS
41/25/12	RUNS: BEG/INTER/ADV
0/6	FUNICULAR/CABLE CARS
0/31	GONDOLAS/CHAIRS
10	DRAGS
no	NIGHT RIDING
1	PARKS
1	PIPE
no	SUMMER AREAS
★☆☆ ★☆☆	ENVIRONMENTAL RATING
$ $ $	COST INDICATOR
ITALY	
CORTINA	

Courmayeur

Imposing scenery, varied terrain and the best restaurants in the Alps, both on and off the mountain. Courmayeur is perhaps the king of Italian resorts.

🌙 *If you like this* …
… *try Big White* ▶▶*p72, or Chamonix* ▶▶*p128.*

The Town

Originally a bustling market town, Courmayeur was well established long before the advent of skiing and snowboarding as winter pursuits, so it still retains a good dose of its traditional Italian charm. It's renowned for its food, and with good reason – it's all but impossible to get a bad meal here. It's not uncommon for people to make the journey through the tunnel from Chamonix primarily to enjoy lunch at one of the mountain restaurants, which put those of other resorts the world over to shame.

Sleeping For budget accommodation try **Chetif** (T0165 846080) or **Bon Souvenir** (T0165 842880). If you're not on such a tight budget the three-star **Hotel Berthod** (T0165 842835) is both affordable and very central. Alternatively, splash out on **Le Grand Hotel Cour Maison** (T0165 831400).
Eating For a quick bite try **Snackbar** (at the bottom of the Dzeleuna chairlift) or have a languid lunch at **Chateau Branlant** (T0165 846584). The town is awash with good restaurants – **Al Camin** (T0165 843442) is amongst the best.
Bars and clubs Café Roma for après with free buffet, and the **American Bar** for late-night action and cocktails in the sumptuous lounge upstairs. **Poppy's Pub** is also very popular.
Shopping There are several supermarkets in the town.
Health Try the **Wellness Centre** (T0165 842666) at the **Forum Sports Centre**.
Internet The town has four internet cafés.
Transfer options The best option is a shared transfer from Turin or Geneva with **ATS** (a-t-s.net). They'll also do a private transfer for a lot more money.
Local partners La Thuile, Chamonix and all the Aosta Valley resorts.

Courmayeur is a pleasant surprise. It's a family-friendly resort, yet it has some amazing big mountain terrain that doesn't get tracked out too quickly, unlike Chamonix only 40 minutes away through the Mont Blanc tunnel.
James Stentiford, pro snowboarder

R: UNKNOWN P: DANMILNER.COM

⊛ **OPENING TIMES**
Early Dec to late Apr: 0900-1630

💲 **RESORT PRICES**
Week pass (6 days): €195
Day pass: €39,50
Season pass: €670

ⓘ **DIRECTORY**
Tourist office: T0165 842060
Medical centre: T0165 841113
Pisteurs: T0165 842060
Taxi: T0165 842960
Local radio: Radio Valle d'Aosta 96.4/100.8/101.1 FM
Website: courmayeur.com

The Mountain

There's plenty of good freeriding to be had in Courmayeur, including steeps, trees, cliffs, open powder faces and some pretty long itineraries off the top of the Cresta d'Arp. For the more intrepid there's also the Funivie Monte Bianco lift (known as the Helbronner), from which you can access some steep and challenging glacier terrain on the Courmayeur side or drop into the Valley Blanche taking you down to Chamonix. The resort is pretty steep – there are no green runs in Courmayeur – and the average red run is in fact nearer a black by most people's ratings. There's also a small snow park where helmets are compulsory.

Beginners For total beginners there's a fenced-off learners' area serviced by a magic carpet lift right outside the Val Veny lift station. After this the Chiecco drag is a good place to find your feet. Move on to the mellow Pra Neyron blue run, then head up the Maison Vieille chair and spend the afternoon lapping the Peindeint chair.

Intermediate Warm up with a high-speed cruise off the top of the Youla cable car. Next, take a few runs on the Checroiut piste, a fairly steep red with fun jibbing possibilities off to each side. After lunch head up the Maison Vieille chair and drop over into the back side of the resort, where you'll find some fun pistes through the trees. Spend the remainder of the afternoon playing around in the park or popping off the fun little rocks and lumps you'll find underneath the Maison Vieille chair.

Advanced On a powder day, turn right out of the top of the Youla cable car and follow the valley all the way down to where it comes out at the bottom of the Zerotta chair. Next, head back up to the top and explore off the sides of the pistes on the way down to Plan Checrouit. Finish up by taking the Arp cable car and following the itinerary back down to Dolonne, after which it's a short walk or a ride on the free shuttle bus back to Courmayeur.

Kids Kids under six go for free, and kids under 130 cm in height get a 50% discount. Crash helmets are compulsory for under 14s.

Flat light days There's plenty of terrain below the treeline, so flat light isn't a massive problem here. Head over to the back side of the resort and lap the Peindeint and Zerotta chairs.

P: DANMILNER.COM

☺ LOCALS DO
- Drink lots of very strong espressos.
- Ride at lunchtime, when the mountain is practically empty.
- Object strongly to the amount of trucks going through the Mont Blanc tunnel.

☹ LOCALS DON'T
- Venture off-piste as much as you'd think.
- Drink to excess.
- Mind having a friendly chat with strangers – it's a welcoming place.

✓ PROS
- Great variety of terrain to suit all abilities.
- The best restaurants in the Alps.
- Very close to Turin airport.

✗ CONS
- Busy at the weekends.
- You have to download.
- Slow lifts.

☺ NOT TO MISS
A relaxed meal followed by an Italian-style hot chocolate in one of the many excellent mountain restaurants.

ⓘ REMEMBER TO AVOID
Getting caught up the mountain after the cable car closes. If the Dolonne piste is bare, it's a long walk down.

❄ SNOW DEPTH

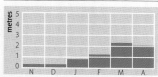

✪ RELIVE A FAMOUS MOMENT
The 1981 Bond movie *For Your Eyes Only*, starring Roger Moore, has ski sequences filmed above Courmayeur.

1224 m	TOWN ALTITUDE
147 km	KM TO AIRPORT
TRN	AIRPORT
★★☆	VEGETARIAN RATING
★★★	INTERNET CAFES
★★☆	RIDE IN/RIDE OUT
3470 m	HIGHEST LIFT
2246 m	VERTICAL DROP
250	RIDEABLE AREA (IN ACRES)
100 km	KM OF PISTES
3	NURSERY AREAS
6/14/4	RUNS: BEG/INTER/ADV
0/4	FUNICULAR/CABLE CARS
2/10	GONDOLAS/CHAIRS
7	DRAGS
no	NIGHT RIDING
1	PARKS
0	PIPE
no	SUMMER AREAS
★★★ / ☆☆☆	ENVIRONMENTAL RATING
⑨⑨⑨	COST INDICATOR

ITALY
COURMAYEUR

Jurassik Park/Folgaria

Once a private resort, it's a one-lift spot that has become one of the best parks in Italy.

If you like this ...
... try *Snow Park* ▸▸p230, *Talma* ▸▸p246, or *Big Bear* ▸▸p352.

The Town

Right in front of the park the only thing you will find is a bar and a small chalet. The rest is trees, trees and more trees. The closest village to Jurassik Park is Folgaria, a traditional resort of the Trentino area, located only 7 km away from the park's area. Folgaria is a big resort, so if you're into hitting up the park it's best to stay here although there are a couple of local options. All in all, a great chance to combine the two by riding Folgaria and the park during the same week.

Sleeping Hotel Fiorentini (T0445 749 201) is five-minute walk from the park. It's open all year long and costs about €20 per person. If you choose to stay in Folgaria try the family run **Antico Albergo Stella d'Italia** (anticoalbergostelladitalia.it). Those with larger budgets should check out the **Golf Hotel** (golfhotelfolgaria.it), about 1.5 km from the centre. It has the lot – pool, gym, spa and nine-hole golf course.

Eating Hotel Fiorentini has a restaurant open to outside guests: for €10 you can feast on the traditional meals of the region.

OPENING TIMES
Early Dec to mid Apr: 0845-1645

RESORT PRICES
Week pass (6 days): €154,50
Day pass: €25-29
Season pass: €390

DIRECTORY
Tourist office: T0464 721133
Medical centre: T0464 721111
Pisteurs: T0464 721133
Taxi: T0464 721172
Local radio: None
Website: folgariaski.com

Bars and clubs Although there are some clubs and bars in Folgaria, most riders at the Jurassik Park usually party up around the park with the locals. As Italian pro rider Rita Comi puts it, 'the party starts right on the slopes and never moves far away from where it started!'

Shopping Folgaria is the place to go for all kinds of shopping. If you're a meat-eater try the *luganega*: it's the traditional sausage from the Trentino area. Vegetarians will like other local delicacies including porcini and cheese.

Health Folgaria's main sporting facility is the **Palazzetto dello Sport** (T0464 720277), replete with pool and basketball court. There's also the Palaghiaccio ice rink.

Internet The **Golf** has wireless access, but try the library as well.

Transfer options Jurassik Park is 25 minutes' drive from Trento, one of the biggest cities in the Trentino region. You can also take the train to Folgaria, from where there's a shuttle that will take you the remaining 7 km to the park.

Local partners Folgaria.

> **" "**
> It's like an American park!
> *Marco Concin, pro rider*

The Mountain

Arriving at Jurassik Park is like stepping into another world. It may be easily accessible from the motorway, but the park is located in an isolated area, surrounded only by trees and mountains. It's a beautiful setting. The mountains themselves resemble hills rather than the usual jagged Alpine peaks, and though most people will come here simply for the park, there are some pretty decent tree runs to be had – ideal for those quiet treeline powder days.

Beginners The park is well thought out and has obstacles for all standards of rider. Beginners may enjoy the small kicker, the tiny box and the 2-m double tube rail – all close to the ground to gain more confidence with tricks.

Intermediate Beside all the boxes, there's a line of kickers ranging in size from 3 m to 10 m, so you can build up as your skills progress. If you're looking to develop your freestyle foundations, you're going to love this place, as you can step up a level when you're feeling strong, and play safe when you need to get some confidence.

Advanced Most of the kickers are in a line, making it challenging for even the more experienced riders. Plus, there are plenty of obstacles to work on, including an 18-m kicker, a kinked rail, a double box, a 9-m double rail and a wall ride.

Kids The Fiorentini area offers kids and beginners a slope serviced by a magic carpet lift.

Flat light days Tree runs! Befriend the locals and ask them to take you to the best ones.

😃 LOCALS DO

- Hang out at the Fiorentini Hotel.
- Stick around at the end of the day for a BBQ at the chalet.
- Go sledding in the backcountry. Ask for approval from the Folgaria County first, as sledding in Italy requires a special permit.

😦 LOCALS DON'T

- Go to Folgaria to party: Hotel Fiorentini is the main hang-out.
- Do much freeriding – although there is some on hand.
- Ride during the week. Jurassik Park is only open on weekends and during Italian holidays. Strange but true.

✔ PROS

- Being very cold and very isolated means it has good snow conditions.
- Great for improving your freestyle skills.
- Lack of queues.

✖ CONS

- There aren't a great variety of slopes to choose from if you're not into park.
- Long commute if you're staying in Folgaria.

👍 NOT TO MISS

The wall ride – brilliant fun.

❗ REMEMBER TO AVOID

Taking on anything you're not ready for. Build yourself up slowly.

❄ SNOW DEPTH

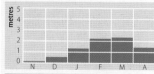

★ RELIVE A FAMOUS MOMENT

Jurassik Park is so new that nothing of note has gone down here… yet. Expect to see it featuring in magazines and videos near you soon.

1400 m	TOWN ALTITUDE
96 km	KM TO AIRPORT
VRN	AIRPORT
★★☆	VEGETARIAN RATING
★★☆	INTERNET CAFES
★★★	RIDE IN/RIDE OUT
1500 m	HIGHEST LIFT
area not measured	VERTICAL DROP
runs not measured	RIDEABLE AREA (IN ACRES)
1 km	KM OF PISTES
0	NURSERY AREAS
1/1/0	RUNS: BEG/INTER/ADV
0/0	FUNICULAR/CABLE CARS
0/0	GONDOLAS/CHAIRS
2	DRAGS
no	NIGHT RIDING
1	PARKS
0	PIPE
no	SUMMER AREAS
figures not available	ENVIRONMENTAL RATING

COST INDICATOR

ITALY
JURASSIK PARK/FOLGARIA

La Thuile

The Town

La Thuile is a fairly nondescript Italian village situated near the top of the Petit St Bernard pass, running from Bourg St Maurice in France to Aosta in Italy. The pass is closed in winter, during which La Thuile is linked by lifts to the adjacent French resort of La Rosière on the other side of the col. This constitutes the Espace San Bernardo, which boasts 150 km of pistes. In winter you access La Thuile via a twisting mountain road up from Aosta, and it's an impressive drive. The town has seen some development over the years so there are a few fairly incongruous new buildings that mingle uneasily with the charming and traditional Italian architecture.

Sleeping The three-star **Chalet Alpina** (T0165 884187) is charming and very close to the lifts. Also try the three-star **Chalet Eden** (T0165 885050) and the two-star family owned **Entrèves** (T0165 884134). A few tour operators have a presence here, so it's worth shopping around for a bargain. Try **Inghams** (inghams.co.uk).

Eating There are some good mountain restaurants in La Thuile, particularly **Rifugio Lo Riondet** (T0165 884006) where you can get an amazing lunch. It's not cheap, but it's well worth the expense. In town, **Le Rascard** (T0165 884999) is famed for its local specialities, or you can get pizza and pasta at **La Grotta** (T0165 884474).

Bars and clubs There are a few places to have a quite drink such as **La Bricole**, **Bar La Buvette** and **La Cage aux Folles**, but don't come to La Thuile in search of rowdy nightlife.

Shopping There's a respectably stocked supermarket in town. There are also a couple of sports shops but you'd be well advised to take all your snowboarding kit with you.

Health Check out the spas at Pré-Saint-Didier (termedipre.it), a short drive down towards Courmayeur.

Internet Facilities aren't great, but you can get online at the library, open Monday-Saturday. There's a one off fee of €5 and it's free thereafter.

Transfer options ATS (a-t-s.net) for transfers from Turin, and Geneva via the Mont Blanc tunnel.

Local partners Le Rosière, Courmayeur and the Aosta valley resorts.

> 66 99
>
> Riding between France and Italy is a really fun experience. The freeriding is also really good and it's way less busy than Val d'Isère.
>
> *James McPhail, photographer*

Ride to France and back, or try some affordable heli-boarding in the shadow of Mont Blanc.

❂ If you like this ...
... try La Clusaz ➽*p132, or Courmayeur* ➽*p178.*

R: GRAHAM MACVOY P: JAMES MCPHAIL

The Mountain

Though La Thuile isn't the most exciting mountain in the world, it's certainly not the dullest either, and with the link to La Rosière there's easily enough to keep you amused, particularly if you take advantage of the possibilities for kicker building, which are pretty good. However, La Thuile's trump card is that it's one of the few places in the Alps to allow heliboarding, and it's for this reason that it enjoys real popularity. It can get pretty busy during peak season with daytrippers from nearby resorts such as Chamonix, Courmayeur and Les Arcs.

Beginners There are a couple of learner areas right at the bottom of the hill. The next step is a trip up to Les Suches on the gondola, where you'll find some easy pistes. Avoid riding down to town until you're feeling confident, as all the runs are pretty steep and challenging. Downloading is advised.

Intermediate If the snow's good then get up early and spend some time exploring the Chaz Dura and Gran Testa areas. The terrain around the San Bernardo chair is also well worth checking out. Next, head over to La Rosière and up to Le Roc Noir, where there's enough fun stuff going on to keep you amused for a while. Make sure you save yourself enough for the run back down to town at the end of the day – it can be a real leg burner.

Advanced La Thuile is all about the heliboarding. It's very strictly regulated and you're obliged to have a guide (**guidemonterosa.com** T0165 884123). Book a couple of early drops up Mont Miraidi or Mont Ouille, then head down to **Lo Riondet** to celebrate a good day's riding with a languid Italian-style lunch.

Kids Kids of under six years of age get a free lift pass.

Flat light days Conveniently, all the tree runs are on the way back down to town from Les Suches, accessible from either of the two lifts out of the resort.

OPENING TIMES
Late Nov/early Dec to 25 Apr (closes on the same day every year regardless of snow): 0830-1630

RESORT PRICES (SAN BERNARDO)
Week pass (6 days): €151
Day pass: €32
Season pass: €609

DIRECTORY
Tourist office: T0165 884179
Medical centre: T0165 884041
Pisteurs: T0165 884563
Taxi: T0165 809840
Local radio: None
Website: lathuile.net

LOCALS DO
- Go heliboarding as often as they can afford.
- Keep their boards in tip-top condition to lessen drag on the flats.
- Eat in the mountain restaurants. Unlike in France, they're excellent.

LOCALS DON'T
- Ride park. La Thuile is more about the freeriding and – more specifically – the heliboarding.
- Give a hoot about the whole badass gangsta style thing.
- Try to venture over to La Rosière in high winds.

PROS
- Well set up for good, affordable heliboarding.
- Great dining, Italian style.
- Cheap.

CONS
- Quite a few flat spots.
- Sluggish nightlife.
- Lack of a decent park.

NOT TO MISS
A bit of heliboarding. It's one of the few places in the Alps where it's allowed, and it's so affordable that you'd be mad to come here and not take advantage of the fact.

REMEMBER TO AVOID
Taking on the horrendously flat and long No 7 piste without a well serviced board.

SNOW DEPTH

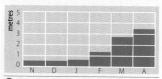

RELIVE A FAMOUS MOMENT
Head to Redoute Ruinee, a Napoleanic fort, along the pass and recreate a shoot out. It's pretty easy as the place is riddled with bullet holes and canon.

ANDREW HINGSTON

1441 m	TOWN ALTITUDE
150 km	KM TO AIRPORT
TRN	AIRPORT
★★☆	VEGETARIAN RATING
★★★	INTERNET CAFES
★★☆	RIDE IN/RIDE OUT
2641 m	HIGHEST LIFT
1465 m	VERTICAL DROP
area not measured	RIDEABLE AREA (IN ACRES)
150 km	KM OF PISTES
3	NURSERY AREAS
32/29/12	RUNS: BEG/INTER/ADV
0/1	FUNICULAR/CABLE CARS
0/17	GONDOLAS/CHAIRS
19	DRAGS
no	NIGHT RIDING
1	PARKS
0	PIPE
no	SUMMER AREAS
★★★ / ★★★	ENVIRONMENTAL RATING
	COST INDICATOR
ITALY / LA THUILE	

FIGURES COVER THE SAN BERNARDO AREA

The Town 📖🔧🍴

Set deep into the end of the Valtellina Valley, Livigno's isolated geographical position doesn't prevent it from being a lively and vast mountain community. It's popular too, with tourists from all over the world making the trek through the tunnel that leads into the valley. They come for the snow, but also to shop, as Livigno's tax-free policy makes it something of a shopping paradise. The village maintains the traditional Valtellina appearance and it stretches all along the road crossing the valley. A free shuttle system running all day guarantees freedom of mobility and easy access to all Livigno's ski areas.

Sleeping Livigno doesn't really have any low budget options. The best thing to do is to check the website for any last-minute deals. Worth checking out are **Hotel Concordia** (T0342 990200), **Hotel Spol** (T0342 996105) and **Hotel Compagnoni** (T0342 996100) – all have spas.

Eating Almost every restaurant in town is good for the local delicacies of the valley. For a classier night out try the **Chalet Mattias** (T0342 997794). It has a higher standard of cuisine and a very exclusive ambience.

Bars and clubs Echo's bar (Via Pontìglia 37) is renowned for its beer, which is brewed on the premises and is apparently Europe's highest brewery. The **Kokodì** (Via Fréita 22) is a late night club that keeps the party going on until 0500.

Shopping Shopping is one of the pleasures of Livigno, especially when it comes to designer brands. For more info on the items you can buy in Livigno check lungolivigno.com. The many snowboard shops and supermarkets are also very cheap.

Health Almost every hotel has a spa area or a gym accessible to non-residents. Try the **Hotel Touring** (T0342 99613) or the **Albergo Meublè Francesin** (T0342 970320).

Internet Wi-Fi access is not very common. A public internet access is available for a reasonable price at the public library (T0342 997275), at the **Bar Jpioca** (T0342 970870) and at the **Roxy** bar (T0342 996980).

Transfer options Fly to Milan's Orio al Serio airport and there'a transfer four days a week (mtbus.it).

Local partners None.

⊙ OPENING TIMES
Early Dec to early Apr: 0900-1700

💲 RESORT PRICES
Week pass (6 days): €175,50
Day pass: €33
Season pass: €515

ⓘ DIRECTORY
Tourist office: T0342 052200
Medical centre: T0342 978107
Pisteurs: T0342 996915
Taxi: T0342 997400
Website: info@livignoweb.com

Livigno has long been Italy's most forward-thinking snowboard resort, and is still setting the pace today.

☽ If you like this …
… try Avoriaz ▸▸p124, or
Laax ▸▸p320.

The Mountain

Livigno has a worldwide rep on the snowboarding scene thanks to its high altitude, long winter season (typically, it starts in December and ends in April), cold temperatures and amount of snow. The riding area itself is spread over six different areas which means a variety of riding conditions and the chance to ride in the sun throughout the day. For freestylers, the jewel is the Mottolino park, with its three different kicker lines, good selection of rails, quarterpipe, half pipes and hip. But everybody who rides here, from beginner to expert, is going to go home happy.

Beginners Beginners' areas are located all over Livigno: many choose the one right in the town centre or the Pemont on the Mottolino. Livigno has a snowboard school where you can get lessons from some of the Italy's best riders – such as Alberto Clement, who paved the way for local legends the Kratters to shine on the international snowboard scene. For more info, contact madnessnow.com.

Intermediate After a few warm up runs on the wide slopes of the Mottolino, you can start practising your freestyle skills in the Livigno Fun courses, located at the side of the slope. These are safe, patrolled off-piste areas full of natural and easy jibbing obstacles like quarterpipes and little jumps, and they are a lot of fun. After gaining some confidence you're ready to hit the easy line of kickers in the snowpark or the small pipe.

> " Livigno is the place where tradition and innovation meet: renowned for its history, vast ski area and jaw-dropping mountains, it also hosts the best snow park in Italy. "
>
> *Rita Comi, Italian pro snowboarder*

Advanced The biggest attraction of Livigno is the Mottolino park but when snow conditions allow, the backcountry terrain is perfect for building kickers. The Carosello area is one of the locals' favourite and good snow conditions last until April.

Kids Top Club (T0342 970025) organizes miniclub and babyclub for kids' first time on snow.

Flat light days Head to the trees between the Mottolino and Degli Amanti slopes is where to keep riding in complete safety when the light is bad.

R: JOHNO VERITY P: DANMILNER.COM

☺ LOCALS DO
- Kick off après-ski at the Tea del Vidal.
- Jump the road tunnels in the area surrounding Livigno.
- Build a lot of backcountry kickers – it's easy to find good spots.

☹ LOCALS DON'T
- Go riding during the winter without wrapping up warmly. Livigno is a very cold place.
- Get caught riding off-piste – there's an €80 fine. Ask Romain De Marchi!
- Ride the park before 1100. It's bulletproof.

✔ PROS
- The park has a great range of obstacles for all levels of ability.
- It also has a great vibe and good local standard of riding.
- Even petrol is tax-free.

✘ CONS
- Getting to the resort can be a bit of a mission.
- Prone to avalanches.
- Can get busy during holidays.

☺ NOT TO MISS
The park. It's a cracker.

ⓘ REMEMBER TO AVOID
Driving to the resort without bringing snowchains (compulsory on the pass from the south) or without checking the peculiar opening schedule of the Munt La Schera tunnel (on the route from the north).

❄ SNOW DEPTH

metres	N	D	J	F	M	A
5						
4						
3						
2						
1						
0						

✪ RELIVE A FAMOUS MOMENT
Drop into the pipe and recreate Nicolas Muller's legendary 2002 Burton European Open win. You'll have to bust out the McTwist Japan to do it right though.

1800 m	TOWN ALTITUDE
240 km	KM TO AIRPORT
MXP	AIRPORT
★★☆	VEGETARIAN RATING
★★☆	INTERNET CAFES
★★☆	RIDE IN/RIDE OUT
3000 m	HIGHEST LIFT
1200 m	VERTICAL DROP
area not measured	RIDEABLE AREA (IN ACRES)
115 km	KM OF PISTES
1	NURSERY AREAS
28/36/10	RUNS: BEG/INTER/ADV
0/3	FUNICULAR/CABLE CARS
0/14	GONDOLAS/CHAIRS
16	DRAGS
no	NIGHT RIDING
10	PARKS
6	PIPE
no	SUMMER AREAS
★★★ ★★★	ENVIRONMENTAL RATING
$ $ $	COST INDICATOR
ITALY	
LIVIGNO	

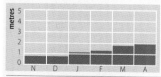

Madonna di Campiglio

Stylish and supremely Italian, yet with a quiet charm, this well-known resort boasts the best park in the Dolomites, sunny, snowsure conditions and lashings of *la dolce vita* – all at a price.

If you like this …
… try Ischgl ▶▶p38, Cortina ▶▶p176, or Leysin ▶▶p324.

The Town

Tucked into a secluded nook in the Val Rendena, with slopes tumbling down into town from both sides of the valley, the pedestrianized village has an intimate atmosphere. It's exclusive but understated rather than ostentatious. Popular with wealthy Italian families and relatively well known outside Italy, this party town is never quiet. That said, it only really gets crowded at Easter, Christmas and New Year, mainly thanks to its relative isolation when compared to the rest of the Dolomite resorts.

Sleeping Campiglio hotels are generally family-run and usually excellent and though on the pricey side, dinner is typically included. Best option for those on a budget is to book an apartment through the tourist office (campiglio.to), although B&Bs like the **Bucaneve** (bucaneve.net) are good value outside peak season.

Eating On the mountain, stop for lunch at the **5 Laghi refuge** (T465 443270) at the top of the village cable car for an inexpensive introduction to the wonders of Italian mountain dining; you'd have to be very unlucky to eat badly here. Try cake and cocktails at **Pasticceria Pasquini** (T0465 441138), and pizza and pasta in the rustic **Antico Focolare** (T0465 441686).

Bars and clubs Italians party late, but the stylish **Cliffhanger** (T0465 446129) and **Ober-One** (T0465 446507) are good places to get the night started, as they also serve food. **Zangola** (T0465 441253) is the classic Italian superclub, located in an old dairy on the outskirts of town.

Shopping Buy local produce from the **Famiglia Cooperativa** (T0456 441030), and pick up an Ursus snowpark belt at **Sport 3 Tre** (T0465 442353).

Health Most of the larger hotels have spas with massage therapists, and take day guests on a discretionary basis.

Flat light days Work on your safety skills at the **Madonna di Campiglio Avalanche Training Center** (T349 869 2508)

Internet The library has an internet point, although you'll need ID.

The best snowboarding resort in the Dolomites.

Tam Leach, snowboarding journalist

Transfer options Unlike many of the Dolomite resorts, Campiglio now has a speedy, inexpensive shuttle bus, with departures from Verona and Brescia airports every Saturday and from Bergamo and Milan airports every Sunday. Book through the tourist office; return fares start at just €47.

Local partners Just south of Campiglio is the quiet hamlet of Pinzolo; to the north is less expensive Val di Sole, less snowsure but popular with package operators.

P: MADONNA TOURISM

P: NATALIE MAYER

☺ OPENING TIMES

Mid-Dec to late Apr: 0900-1630

💲 RESORT PRICES

Week pass (6 days): €180
Day pass: €35
Season pass: €500

ⓘ DIRECTORY

Tourist office: T0465 447501
Medical centre: T0465 443315
Pisteurs: T118
Taxi: T0465 735467
Local radio: Radio Dolomiti, 93.6 FM
Website: campiglio.to

The Mountain

Italians take their eating, shopping and strolling at least as seriously as their mountain use, so Campiglio's sheltered, treelined slopes are seldom too busy – and by late afternoon can be practically empty. Pistes are primarily intermediate, but the park is the best in the Dolomites and the mellow, rolling off-piste terrain ideal for kicker construction and general mucking around. Though not as well-connected as the eastern Dolomites, lifts link to Folgaria and Marilleva in the Val di Sole, with a bus service to neighbouring Pinzolo.

Beginners Take the bus up to the wide nursery meadows at Campo Carlo Magno. Once you're turning, take a couple of laps on the Argento lift before taking the Groste gondola all the way to the summit: more wide open slopes, but this time with a view.
Intermediate Head up the Pradalago gondola and lap the rolling pistes under the Zeledria and Genziana chairs; if conditions are good, there are patches of shrubby off-piste to dip into. When the Italians go in for lunch, ride down and across the valley to the Groste gondola. Jib the baby park right off the summit, then head to the mellow gullies and drops of the lower slopes.
Advanced Campiglio's not known for its steeps, but in powder the slopes off the Patascoss lift will do the trick. Across the valley, the off-piste is mellower but with plenty of possibilities. However, the real star here is the large, well-maintained Ursus snowpark at the summit of Groste. Spend the afternoon lapping the Groste Express and kicking back in the sun.
Kids Smaller kids may have more fun at quieter Pinzolo; there's a 'miniclub' with inflatables, kids' ski school and regular discount promotions. But eager shredders will be stoked on the Ursus beginner park (note that all kids up to 14 years old must wear helmets). Kids under eight ski free when a family member purchases a pass of five days or more.
Flat light days Stick to the sheltered lower slopes, particularly the gentle glades off Mont Spinale.

☺ LOCALS DO
- Ride in the afternoon, when the slopes are quieter.
- Buy a park-access only lift pass.
- Party late. Clubs close at 0600.

☹ LOCALS DON'T
- Bother over Christmas or Easter, when the crowds descend.
- Take their riding too seriously.
- Abbreviate to 'Madonna'. It's 'Campiglio'.

✔ PROS
- High for an Italian resort, with a good snow record and eight days of sun out of every 10.
- Best park in the Dolomites.
- Party town, Italian style.

✖ CONS
- Not easily accessible.
- Expensive for an Italian resort.
- Mostly intermediate pistes.

♥ NOT TO MISS
Typically tourist fodder, but in this case worth the hype: a snowcat trip at night up to the Cascina Zelebria refuge and gastronomic romance.

❶ REMEMBER TO AVOID
The valley floor Groste/Pradalago crossover in the middle of the day: hectic with families attempting to meet up for lunch.

❄ SNOW DEPTH
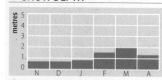

☀ RELIVE A FAMOUS MOMENT
Visit during the classic car Winter Marathon and there's a high chance you'll see Michael Schumacher and all the other famous Ferrari and Ducati celebs.

P. NATALIE MAYER

1550 m	TOWN ALTITUDE
150 km	KM TO AIRPORT
VRN	AIRPORT
★★☆	VEGETARIAN RATING
★★☆	INTERNET CAFES
★★☆	RIDE IN/RIDE OUT
2443 m	HIGHEST LIFT
923 m	VERTICAL DROP
area not measured	RIDEABLE AREA (IN ACRES)
150 km	KM OF PISTES
2	NURSERY AREAS
29/23/10	RUNS: BEG/INTER/ADV
0/1	FUNICULAR/CABLE CARS
4/12	GONDOLAS/CHAIRS
2	DRAGS
no	NIGHT RIDING
2	PARKS
1	PIPE
no	SUMMER AREAS
★★★☆	ENVIRONMENTAL RATING
$$$	COST INDICATOR

ITALY
MADONNA DI CAMPIGLIO

Prato Nevoso

Prato Nevoso is a classic example of playing to one's strengths. Though it lacks steep freeriding terrain, it makes up for it with great beginners' facilities and an excellent floodlit park aimed squarely at the freestyle market. Bigger resorts beware...

◗ If you like this ...
... try *Folgaria* ⇒p180, *Snow Park* ⇒p230, or *Big Bear* ⇒p352.

The Town ⊜⊘⊜

Prato Nevoso was built in 1965 to capitalize on the abundant snowfall of the Malanotte and Prell mountains. The architecture of the village reflects its origins – it doesn't have the same flair as other more traditional Italian resorts but, surprisingly, it holds a certain sense of local community. Being a purpose-built resort, access to the slopes is good. A long gallery with shops, bars and restaurants faces directly onto the slopes making the transition from riding to partying particularly easy.

Sleeping The Residence Stalle Lunghe (T0174 334048) is the cheapest accommodation you'll find, with apartments that can be rented for stays of a weekend and upwards. Hotel Mondolè (T0174 334121) and the Galassia Hotel (T0174 334183) are the two biggest hotels in town and it's very easy to find a room. The pricier **Piccolo Laghetto Hotel** (T0174 334008) is literally right on the slopes.
Eating Il Gallo (T347 3755841) is a town favourites. For a more romantic night out, Le Stalle (T0174 334032) is highly recommended. Book in advance a table in the little room upstairs.
Bars and clubs Probably because of its position (right in front of the snowpark), the **Sporting Bar** is the local snowboard hang-out.
Shopping There are two supermarkets in town but they have only limited supplies. The 20-minute drive down to Villanova is a good option.

❝❞

In the next few years, Prato should have one of the best parks in Italy. It's at the front of the new breed of Italian resorts.
Rita Comi, Italian pro snowboarder

Health Hotel Mondolè (T0174 334121) and the **Hotel Galassia** (T0174 334183) both have swimming pools and saunas.
Internet Most hotels have internet access, but the town has no internet cafés.
Transfer options Get the train to Mondovi (on the Turin/Savona line) then take the bus up to Prato Nevso. It runs twice daily.
Local partners Artesina.

P: RITA COMI

The Mountain

First impressions of Prato Nevoso are that it's pretty flat and featureless. Though there is some steeper and more interesting terrain on the Frabosa side of the mountain, regrettably this is an impression that is borne out by the reality, so those looking for challenging freeriding should unequivocally look elsewhere. But rather than competing in a field where it's noticeably out of its depth, Prato Nevoso has wisely gone for a different and lamentably overlooked angle: beginners. Mellow terrain, easy lifts and well groomed pistes make this the ideal place to learn, and the provision of an excellent floodlit park is indicative of an accommodating attitude that many larger and better-known resorts lack.

Beginners Beginners will be in their element here. Start your week on one of the two slopes served by the two magic carpet lifts close to the ski-school meeting point: 100 m of gently sloping pistes ideal for making your first turns. When you feel up to tackling a real slope you can take the four-man chairlift to the top. Head skier's right for the mellow green.

Intermediate Start the day with the four-man chair, taking the left fork to access more challenging terrain. This is also the slope that takes you to the park. The first obstacles you'll hit are ideal for getting to grips with a bit of freestyle riding: an 8-m box raised 30 cm off the ground, an 8-m flat rail and two easy kickers.

Advanced The lower section of the park is aimed towards more proficient riders, with a well shaped 18-m kicker, a kinked rail and a kinked box. Prato's pipe isn't massive, but is usually in a decent state of repair being used often for junior competitions. Head to the connection with Artesina for a bit of freeride action.

Kids Prato Nevoso has an excellent dedicated kids' area called **Pratolandia**, replete with games, inflatables, a sledge run and instructors. There's a small fee for entry, with supervision available.

Flat light days The trees of the Frabosa side provide better visibility, but if you decide to stay in the park all takeoffs and landings are highlighted with high visibility paint meaning you can still see what you're jumping off. Sometimes they even turn the lights on during the day, which is admirably forward thinking of them.

☺ LOCALS DO
- Have BBQs in the snowpark during the holiday season.
- Respect the snow park rules.

☹ LOCALS DON'T
- Ride the connecting area within the resort when there's no visibility: it's very easy to get lost!
- Use their cars to get around town during peak season or times of heavy snowfall – there are few parking lots in town.

✓ PROS
- Perfect for children and beginners.
- Great night riding.
- High snowfall.

✗ CONS
- Lack of challenging terrain for more advanced riders.
- Not a great variety of nightlife.

◉ NOT TO MISS
Head to Surf Shop Prato Nevoso (T0174 334734) to visit the first and only snowboard museum in Italy. With more than 100 boards on show, it's an interesting look at the evolution of snowboarding.

ⓘ REMEMBER TO AVOID
Getting stuck in Artesia and Frabosa: you'll need to take a taxi back.

❄ SNOW DEPTH

☺ RELIVE A FAMOUS MOMENT
Future celebrity spotters take note: the Junior World Championships took place in Prato in 2005.

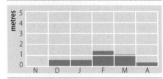
PHOTOGRAPHER: ANNE FLORE MARXER PHOTOGRAPHER: RITA COMI

1500 m	TOWN ALTITUDE
80 km	KM TO AIRPORT
TRN	AIRPORT
★☆☆	VEGETARIAN RATING
★☆☆	INTERNET CAFES
★★☆	RIDE IN/RIDE OUT
2085 m	HIGHEST LIFT
755 m	VERTICAL DROP
area not measured	RIDEABLE AREA (IN ACRES)
100 km	KM OF PISTES
1	NURSERY AREAS
16/11/3	RUNS: BEG/INTER/ADV
0/0	FUNICULAR/CABLE CARS
0/7	GONDOLAS/CHAIRS
17	DRAGS
yes	NIGHT RIDING
7	PARKS
1	PIPE
no	SUMMER AREAS
figures not available	ENVIRONMENTAL RATING
Ⓢ Ⓢ Ⓢ	COST INDICATOR
ITALY	
PRATO NEVOSO	

At the heart of the stunning 'Sella Ronda' area in the Dolomites, Selva is an ideal destination for those who enjoy burning around an extensive mountain range while taking in breathtaking views and beautiful unspoilt scenery.

☼ If you like this ...
... try Avoriaz ▸▸p124, La Plagne ▸▸p136, or Méribel ▸▸p146.

The Town

Right in the middle of the Dolomites, Val Gardena is surrounded by some of Europe's most breathtaking scenery, and is steeped in history and tradition. You get the feeling you're stepping into a winter universe that hasn't changed much for the last century, making it a great place for a family adventure or a romantic weekend in the snow. The town itself is lively, and dominated by large hotels and après cafés. It's not party central, but that's OK.

Sleeping The **Sun Valley Hotel** (T0471 795152) is a comfortable and friendly three-star hotel with great food and an excellent ski-in location. For a basic but well located guesthouse try the **Desiree** (T0471 795107).

Eating For early morning pastries and afternoon pizza munchies the **Costa Bakery** is a great stop for hungry snowboarders. For an evening meal the **Stubele Pizzeria** (T0471 771508) below the **Sun Valley Hotel** is highly recommended by locals.

Bars and clubs Val Gardena isn't exactly Mèribel, but **Café Saltos** (T335 684 9031) is a great stop for evening

drinks and the **Dali Disco Dance** (T0471 795 5069) provides cocktails to fuel clubbers into the early hours during peak season.

Shopping Take any spares you need, and stock up on groceries at the **Gardena Centre Supermarket**.

Health Call **Hagen Kasslatter** (T0471 795510).

Internet Head to the **Café Aaritz** (T0471 795155) or the tourist office (T0471 777900) to check your mail.

Transfer options Fly to Innsbruck and organize a transfer with **Autosella Bus and Taxi** (T0471 790033). Otherwise take a train to Bolzano (trenitalia.it) and then a bus to Val Gardena (sii.bz.it).

⊙ OPENING TIMES
Early Dec to mid-Apr: 0830-1630

⑤ RESORT PRICES
Week pass 7 days): €175
Day pass: €33
Season pass: €470

ⓘ DIRECTORY
Tourist office: T0471 777900
Medical centre: T0471 794111
Pisteurs: T0471 271177
Taxi: T0471 790033
Local radio: None
Website: val-gardena.com

It's not going to keep obsessive freestyle devotees or freeriders happy, but for a family cruise, or groups of beginner and intermediate riders, it's the perfect spot – good food, great vibes and a lot of runs to tick off.

James McPhail, snowboarding photographer

Local partners The Val Gardena ski area is part of the Dolomite Super Ski area, you can buy a pass for this area and enjoy a ridiculous 450 ski lifts and 1200 km of pisted riding.

R: CHRIS CHATT P: JAMES BRYANT

The Mountain

With only a very small and limited snowpark, the Val Gardena area is all about touring the massive amount of terrain on offer. Runs vary from wide steep faces to mellow paths winding through the trees, while the scenery around is nothing short of dramatic as huge craggy cliffs hang high above. The mountain also has many accessible freeriding routes that tend not to get tracked out due to the large numbers of families that frequent the resort.

Beginners Head to the selection of beginner tows at the entrance of town where you can gain confidence on a variety of short user friendly runs. Once those first turns are perfected take the bus through town to the Costabella chair, where you can try the blue run all the way back to your hotel doorstep.

Intermediate From the top of the Ciampinoi Gondola boost down the long red to Plan de Gralba lift area to warm the legs up. From here take the big cable car to the super-fun Piz Sella area, where tows and a chairlift access gladed tree runs, a mini funpark and two highly entertaining boarder cross tracks. A true playground for snowboarders.

Advanced Start your day by tackling the long black run from the top of the Ciampinoi Gondola down to Santa Cristina. From here head up the quiet Santa Cristina-Monte Pana chair and make your way to the peak of Mout Se Seura. You'll find many steep tree runs and powder stashes to be had. At the end of the day take the Tramans chair to make your way back to Val Gardena.

Kids Passes are free for under nines.

Flat light days With endless trees, flat light is rarely a problem. If it's really terrible, check in with **Gardena Mountain Adventures** (T335 684 9031) where you can organize an adrenaline fuelled day of ice climbing and canyoning .

☺ LOCALS DO
- Ride the Costabella chair in icy conditions – this side of the valley gets the most sunshine.
- Check out the nude ski instructors on the walls of Café Saltos.
- Speak 'ladino', like their neighbours in Canazei.

☹ LOCALS DON'T
- Start heading back to Val Gardena any later than 1500.
- Hit the Champinoi gondola on peak season mornings; queues are known to snake down the road.

☺ PROS
- Huge variety of pistes to please all.
- Great food on the mountain and a restaurant on nearly every run.
- Friendly international resort, with visitors from all over Europe.

✖ CONS
- Some very flat runs that are a pain for snowboarders.
- Ride out runs from the Ciampinoi are too steep for beginners.
- The funpark revolution has yet to take hold here!

☺ NOT TO MISS
One of the 'Dolomite Super Tours' that lead you on a themed journey throughout the resort.

ⓘ REMEMBER TO AVOID
Getting stuck in a different valley from where you stay. It's an expensive taxi ride home.

❄ SNOW DEPTH

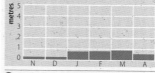

☺ RELIVE A FAMOUS MOMENT
Giorgio Moroder, '80s pop genius behind *I Feel Love* by Donna Summer and the *Top Gun* soundtrack, lives in Val Gardena. Highway to the Danger Zone, indeed.

1563 m	TOWN ALTITUDE
40 km	KM TO AIRPORT
VRN	AIRPORT
★★☆	VEGETARIAN RATING
★★☆	INTERNET CAFES
★★☆	RIDE IN/RIDE OUT
2284 m	HIGHEST LIFT
721 m	VERTICAL DROP
area not measured	RIDEABLE AREA (IN ACRES)
176 km	KM OF PISTES
7	NURSERY AREAS
32/23/3	RUNS: BEG/INTER/ADV
0/2	FUNICULAR/CABLE CARS
7/44	GONDOLAS/CHAIRS
30	DRAGS
yes	NIGHT RIDING
1	PARKS
1	PIPE
no	SUMMER AREAS
★★★	ENVIRONMENTAL RATING
$$$	COST INDICATOR
ITALY	
VAL GARDENA	

P: JAMES BRYANT

Val Senales

The Town

Small and compact, the town of Maso Corto at the base of the Val Senales lifts is a pedestrian conglomeration of apartment blocks, hotels, bars and restaurants. Although not the most aesthetically pleasing resort, it has a lively buzz and the bonus of being at bottom of the ski slopes, so you can ride till the last lift and never worry about catching a bus during your stay.

Sleeping Real mountain lovers should try the **Hotel Grawand** (T0473 662118), perched on top of the glacier at 3228 m, or for a reasonable room in Maso Corto try the **Piccolo Hotel Gurschler** (T0473 662100). If you're looking for something cheaper and have a car to drive to the lifts try one of the guesthouses in Madonna di Senales down the valley such as **Pension Café Helen** (T0473 669647).

Eating Good pizza – hard to avoid in Italy – is available at the **Pizzeria Sport Hotel** (T0472 662166). For a gourmet meal try the restaurant in the **Hotel Piccolo Gurschler** (T0472 662100).

Bars and clubs Après kicks off at the **Bussl Bar** at the bottom of slopes. From there, the crowds move to the laid-back **Platzl Bar** before heading for some serious dancing at the **Disco K2**.

Shopping Supermarket in Maso Corto.

Health Masseuse at **Apparthotel Zirm** (T0473 662188) in Maso Corto.

Internet No internet cafés in Maso Corto but many of the big hotels have wireless that you can pay to use.

Flat light days Visit the **Archeoparc Project** (T0473 676020) in Unser Frau – an indoor/outdoor museum inspired by 'Ortzi' the preserved body of a Neolithic man found in the Val Senales mountain range in 1991.

Transfer options Fly to Bolzano and then catch a train to Merano (trenitalia.it), from there you can take a frequent bus up to Maso Corto (sii.bz.it). For cheaper flights try landing in Innsbruck and taking the train to Merano – this takes about three hours (oebb.at).

Local partners Val Senales is part of the Ortler Skiarena (o2rtlerskiarena.com) comprising 15 resorts in the surrounding Sud Tirol area. Buy an Ortler pass if you want to visit several resorts, although you'll need a car.

> "It's like December up there in the middle of April – a wicked place to pretend winter is never going to end.
>
> *James Bryant, snowboard photographer*

A high-altitude, small, purpose-built resort with year round glacier riding, excellent for first-rate snow conditions.

If you like this …
… try *Avoriaz* ▶▶p124, or *Les Deux Alpes* ▶▶p144.

P: JAMES BRYANT

The Mountain

With two parks and a selection of both beginner and advanced runs there's something to entertain everyone at Val Senales. At the top of the Gletscherbahn Cable Car the glacier forms a massive snow bowl full of mellow wide runs. The pistes that run back into Maso Corto are steeper and more challenging, as are the runs on the other side of the valley under the Lazaun chair. Overall, an easy mountain to navigate with something to satisfy riders of all abilities. The Val Senales glacier is also open through much of the summer.

Beginners The Glocken tow at the base of the mountain is a perfect location to learn to ride within a short walk of Maso Corto. Once the basics are under control, head up the Gletscherbahn to the glacier plateau, where you can ride a selection of wide mellow blue runs. Download in the cable car at the end of the day as the run down can be a bit hairy for beginners.

Intermediate Head straight up the Gletscherbahn first thing in the morning to enjoy any fresh snow on the glacier. Most of the runs in the glacial bowl have accessible off-piste areas on either side that are great for taking those first few powder turns. End your day by heading up the Hintereis two-man chair and tackling the fun red underneath before enjoying one last run back to Maso Corto for a beer.

Advanced Head up to the peak of the Teufelsegg chair at the start of the day and enjoy the challenging runs all the way back to the Maso Corta base. Spend the afternoon doing quick laps in the pipe and park at the base of the mountain.

Kids Passes are free for under sixes.

R: CHRIS CHATT P: JAMES BRYANT

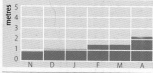

OPENING TIMES

Late Nov to early May: 0830-1720
Mid-Jun to mid-Aug: 0730-1300

RESORT PRICES

Week pass (6 days): €189,50
Day pass: €56
Season pass: From €390

DIRECTORY

Tourist office: T0473 678148
Medical centre: T0473 669770
Pisteurs: T0473 662171
Taxi: T338 2735082
Local radio: None
Website: valsenales.com

LOCALS DO

- Ride the trees under the Lanzun lift.
- Hike the snowpark until it gets dark!
- Play in the mellow powder fields around the Finail tows on the glacier.

LOCALS DON'T

- Ride the open faces under the Teufelsegg chair when avalanche risk is high.
- Leave in summer. You can ride here nearly all year around.
- Park outside the designated car parks – parking ticket guaranteed!

PROS

- Glacier riding means winter snow conditions right into summer.
- Snowpark at the bottom of the hill enables riding until the end of the day.
- Compact village perfect for sports geeks.

CONS

- Not the most attractive of villages.
- Limited choice for eating out and shopping.

NOT TO MISS

The annual Snowboard Opening celebrates Val Senales' early bird park in mid-October. Snowboard competitions, a well-groomed park and killer parties make a great excuse for an autumn snowboard get away.

REMEMBER TO AVOID

The queues to download in the Gletscherbahn at the end of the day. Head down earlier, or stay for a drink at the top until they die down.

SNOW DEPTH

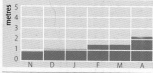

RELIVE A FAMOUS MOMENT

Sylvester Stallone's *Cliffhanger* was filmed in the area around the Val di Fassa.

2011 m	TOWN ALTITUDE
55 km	KM TO AIRPORT
VRN	AIRPORT
★★☆	VEGETARIAN RATING
★☆☆	INTERNET CAFES
★★☆	RIDE IN/RIDE OUT
3212 m	HIGHEST LIFT
1201 m	VERTICAL DROP
123	RIDEABLE AREA (IN ACRES)
35 km	KM OF PISTES
1	NURSERY AREAS
6/6/4	RUNS: BEG/INTER/ADV
0/1	FUNICULAR/CABLE CARS
0/7	GONDOLAS/CHAIRS
4	DRAGS
no	NIGHT RIDING
2	PARKS
2	PIPE
yes	SUMMER AREAS
★★★ ★★★	ENVIRONMENTAL RATING
$$$	COST INDICATOR

ITALY
VAL SENALES

Japan

R: ANTON JENSONS L: NISEKO P: MATT FLETCHER/YAMAPHOTO.NET

Anton Jansens following in a long line of riders to have ridden perfect powder under the volcano at Niseko.

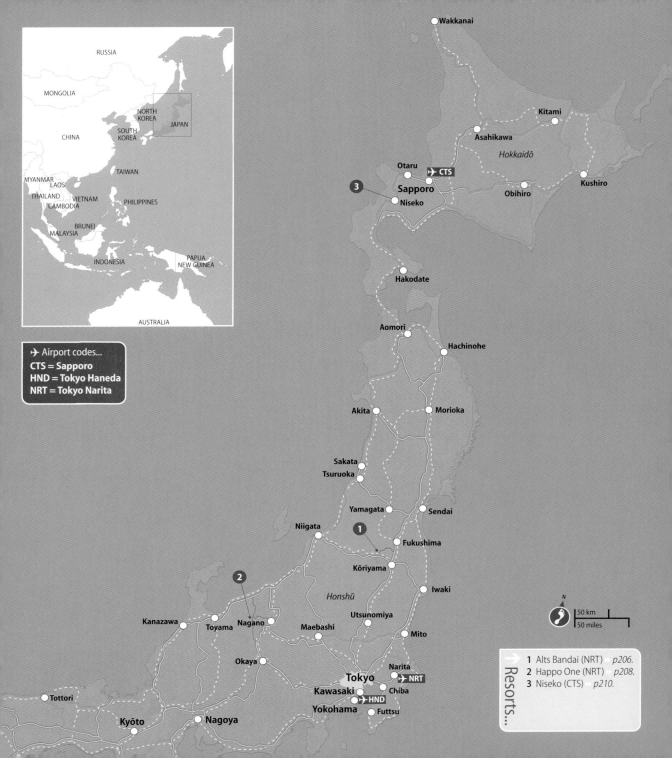

RUSSIA

MONGOLIA

NORTH KOREA

JAPAN

CHINA

SOUTH KOREA

MYANMAR
LAOS
TAIWAN

THAILAND
CAMBODIA
VIETNAM

PHILIPPINES

BRUNEI
MALAYSIA

INDONESIA

PAPUA NEW GUINEA

AUSTRALIA

✈ Airport codes...
CTS = Sapporo
HND = Tokyo Haneda
NRT = Tokyo Narita

Wakkanai

Kitami

Asahikawa

Hokkaidō

Otaru ✈ CTS

3 **Sapporo**

Niseko

Obihiro

Kushiro

Hakodate

Aomori

Hachinohe

Akita

Morioka

Sakata

Tsuruoka

Yamagata

Sendai

Niigata

1

Fukushima

Kōriyama

Iwaki

2

Honshū

Kanazawa

Toyama

Nagano

Utsunomiya

Maebashi

Mito

Okaya

Narita ✈ NRT

Tokyo

Chiba

Kawasaki ✈ HND

Tottori

Yokohama Futtsu

Kyōto

Nagoya

N

50 km
50 miles

Introduction

Japan is slowly but surely coming to the attention of the outside snowboarding world – and for good reason. Its mountains are big enough to offer serious freeriding potential, its parks are cut to precision, its pipes are well maintained, its trees are strange and perfectly spread out and – most importantly – from November to April, it snows like nowhere else in the world.

It means that there's something for everyone here. Most resorts are built to entice even the most timid of riders, with great beginner runs and well-marked trails. But for good riders the off-piste is easily some of the best on the planet. When you factor in the long opening hours of most resorts (floodlit areas mean after-work riders still get their kicks), the clean, efficient and friendly nature of the Japanese people and the sheer cultural diversity, it's a wonder Japan isn't the world's number one snowboard spot. Perhaps one day it will be. But for now, it plays host to a huge home market as well as a hardcore of foreign riders who visited once and have vowed to return each year since.

Few countries rival Japan when it comes to pride in their food. While the world knows about sushi, there remains a palette of food beyond comprehension to those who have not yet visited. From their love of hot vending machines to the odd dry-rolled squid snack, any adventurous visitor will be thrilled by the opportunity to expand their gastronomic horizons.

Niseko, Happo and Alts Bandai have been highlighted as we believe they offer the best 'all round' Japanese experience. However, as is often written, Japan has the highest number of resorts per capita of any country in the world, and most of them are incredibly snowboard-friendly. Put simply, if you want to ride untracked powder, and want a cool, culturally different experience, Japan has to be your number one destination.

Japan rating

Value for money
★★★☆☆

Nightlife
★★★☆☆

Freestyle
★★★★☆

Freeride
★★★★★

Essentials

Getting there

Japan's international gateway is Tokyo's Narita airport. From the US and Canada, **All Nippon Airways** (fly-ana.com), **Japan Airlines** (jal.co.jp/en), **United Airlines** (unitedairlines.com), **Northwest** (nwa.com) and **Korean Air** (koreanair.com) have regular serviced routes. From Europe, **Air France** (airfrance.com), **JAL**, **British Airways** (ba.com), **Virgin** (virgin-atlantic.com), **Finnair** (finnair.com), and **ANA** all fly direct to Tokyo.

In addition, **Cathay Pacific** (cathaypacific.com), **Austrian** (aua.com), **Emirates** (emirates.com), **Alitalia** (alitalia.com), **Korean Air**, **Asiana Airlines** (flyasiana.com), **Thai Air** (thaiairways.com), **Qatar** (qatarairways.com), **Singapore Airlines** (singaporeair.com), **Malaysian Air** (malaysianairlines.com), **KLM** (klm.com) and **Aeroflot** (Aeroflot.ru/eng) also offer connecting flights from mainland Europe.

Lastly, **Cathay Pacific**, **Garuda** (garuda-indonesia.com), **Qantas** (qantas.com), **Air New Zealand** (airnewzealand.com) and **JAL** fly to and from Australia, while **Malaysian Airlines** and **Thai Airlines** also serve the New Zealand route.

Internally, the main flight network is through **ANA**. Niseko, which is on a different island (Hokaidō) than Tokyo, is reached via Chitose airport just outside of the city of Sapporo, while Happo is on the same island (Honshū) as Tokyo and can be reached by train.

Those unwilling to fly to Japan can try the fantastic seat61.com for sea links to the Orient.

Red tape

Visas required, but can be filled out on the flight over.

Getting around

Driving (left-hand side) All foreign nationals need an International Driving Permit (which you can get from you local driving authority – often without a re-test). The road standard in Japan is high, and easy

Top tips

- Take cash. Credit cards and ATMs do exist, but most villages are still very much a cash society.

- Write the name of your destination, hotel, etc in Japanese characters on some paper in order to ask for help with directions.

- Don't tip – the Japanese prefer a sincere thank you and a polite bow.

- Smile and say hello. You'll find the Japanese to be the friendliest nation on Earth. Join in.

- Try at least one new food per day. You may find something you'll love forever.

for Australian, UK, Kiwi drivers and others used to driving on the left-hand side of the road. People drive with care and consideration and generally obey all signs.

Japan's motorway network is not as good as its rail network, which is easily one of the best in the world. As a consequence, most longer trips are generally taken on the train. If you're planning on taking a high pass between resorts, it's essential to check whether it is open while planning the route.

Car hire Most major hire car companies (easycar.com, hertz.com, avis.com, etc) have offices in airports and cities. Usual age restrictions apply.

Public transport

The Japanese 'Bullet' Train is an institution in itself – fast, efficient, cool and surprisingly good value. Most signs and machines have

Japan price guide

In US$	3.60	5.85	2.25	1.30	3.60	0.90	1.35

instructions in English, or station guards will be willing to help. Note that all queue lines and seat numbers are strictly adhered to by the Japanese, and confusion will result if you disregard these rules. Tokyo also has a fantastic underground and mono-rail system from its airports. For all rail info try **Japan Rail** (T33423 0111, japanrail.com).

Opening hours and traditions.
Shops have long opening hours in Japan. Most businesses open around 0800 and close around 1900.

Eating
The main topic of conversation for travellers returning from Japan is usually the food. While sushi, sake, noodles and soy sauce have all been successfully exported from the country, a whole world of taste sensations awaits those who dare to enter the mysterious world of real Japanese cuisine. Thankfully, most restaurants print pictures of their dishes, enabling visitors to see what their food actually looks like. Whether that helps however, is another matter, as what counts as edible foods in Japan is clearly different from other cultures around the world. Generally speaking, if it can't be eaten raw (and there aren't many things, including squid, whole fish, most meats and vegetables that don't fit into this category) then the Japanese will usually try to pickle it. Rice is obviously very popular, but noodles are probably a close second. Fish and seafood are sold virtually everywhere (the Japanese equivalent of crisps would be dried, rolled fish parts sold on every street corner), while vending machines are happy to sell cans of hot corn soup or any of the many drinks that fall under the 'tea' division. If you have an adventurous palate, you'll relish the exciting challenge that Japan presents. You may even find a whole new world of tastes encompassed in one Bento Box.

Language
Japanese is the official language, although English is the first language of the Australian and Kiwi contingent – the people who will likely be

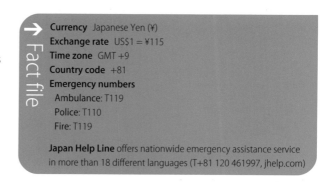

P: MATT BARR

P: ADAM GENDLE

P: CHRIS MORAN/HOTSHITPICTURES.COM

Key phrases

Key words/phrases		Help!	tasukete kudasai!
Yes	hai	North	no-su
No	iie	South	roppou
Please	onegai shimasu	East	azuma
Thank you	arigato gozaimasu	West	nishi
Sorry	gomennasai		
Hello	konnichiwa	**Days of the week**	
Goodbye	sayonara	Monday	getsuyou
I don't		Tuesday	kayoubi
understand	wakarimasen	Wednesday	suiyoubi
I'd like…	kore o kudasai…	Thursday	mokuyoubi
How much is it?	ikura desu	Friday	kin'youbi
	ka?	Saturday	doyou
Where is..?	...wa doko desu ka?	Sunday	nichiyoubi
Mens	(always a sign)		
Ladies	(always a sign)	**Numbers**	
Left	hidarigawa	1	ichi
Right	zen	2	ni
Straight on	maichimonji	3	san
Night	yabun	4	shi
Room	yutori	5	go
Shower	shawa	6	roku
Toilet	toire	7	nana
The bill	kukunin shite kudasai	8	hachi
White coffee	mirukuko-hi-	9	ku
Beer	beero	10	ju
Mineral water	mizu	20	ni-ju
Orange juice	orenjiju-su	100	hyaku
Sandwich	sandoicchi	1000	sen
Ham	hamu	10000	man
Cheese	chi-zu		

organizing your trip to either Happo or Niseko. English is not well spoken by local businesses such as ticket desks, bus companies or lift operators. However, many signs are in English (including all road signs), and with patience, most transactions can be achieved using sign language and ingenuity. Numbers are the same as in western fonts, which helps enormously. If you do have problems, you'll find the Japanese only too willing to help.

Crime/safety

Japan is perhaps the safest country in the world. Most foreigners are amazed to see the staggering number of Japanese people asleep in public places. While this would be unthinkable in most western countries, the idea of stealing someone's belongings while they're grabbing forty winks is clearly not widespread. Leaving boards outside restaurants is generally fine.

Health

Japan has no health risks or dangerous animals to speak of. Standard travel insurance is essential as in most western countries. Hospitals and medical centres are well distributed with interpreters available at both Happo and Niseko.

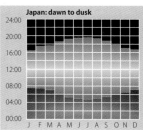

Japan: dawn to dusk

P: CHRIS MORAN/HOTSHITPICTURES.COM

P: CHRIS MORAN/HOTSHITPICTURES.COM

R: ADAM GENDLE P: MATT BARR

P: CHRIS MORAN/HOTSHITPICTURES.COM

Snowboarding Japan

"For any snowboarder, from the absolute beginner to the world's best riders, a trip to Japan will always stand out as one of the most memorable holidays ever. If I had only one week to go riding every year, I'd choose Japan over anywhere else." Johno Verity

There are more resorts per person in Japan than anywhere else in the world. Since the 1960s, Japan's winter snow market has been expanding at an incredible rate. Snowboarding is huge here, with massive competitions going off in the city centres and a huge demand for snowparks in most resorts. It's not uncommon to see around 80% of the slopes taken up by riders rather than skiers.

That said, most of the market is taken by keen amateur Japanese riders – mostly workers going for a ride after office hours – with very few foreign snowboarders on show, especially in the smaller areas. Niseko is arguably the most famous resort in the country, with a strong Antipodean presence due to similar time zones (although opposite seasons) and the abundance of powder, which Australian and NZ resorts often lack. Seasonaires are now, if not common, at least existent. Slowly the world is becoming aware of the incredible terrain the country has to offer, and it will certainly take a revolution in travel before the country is saturated with powder seekers from around the world.

Conditions
Cold, Siberian air is sent across the Sea of Japan where it absorbs moisture and forms perfect snow crystals just in time to catch the volcanic mountains of Japan. As such, Japan's mountains are blessed with some prolific snowfalls, with the northerly island of Hokkaidō hit more than most. Piles of snow higher than local buildings are a common site in many Hokkaidō towns. It is generally very cold too, with night temperatures often below minus 10°C. Add to this the thermal effect of the local volcanoes (*onsen* baths – the local name for hot springs) and you've got very different conditions to most other resorts around the world.

When to go
Japanese resorts traditionally open at the beginning of November, depending on how much early season snow has fallen. This is a great time to go to avoid crowds and enjoy a cheaper trip – although it's best to check conditions before travel. November and December 2005 had the best snowfall in Japan for 80 years, following an upward trend that is hoped to continue. By January, cold temperatures and deep snowfalls mean powder days and flat light are the norm, and with crowds still manageable this can be a great time to visit. February is the most popular month for visitors, but generally speaking, the months vary little as most of the clientele is made up of local riders coming after work. March should still have snowfalls but the decline to

Pros & cons

Pros ...
- The most reliable powder in the world? It might well be ...
- Great and unusual food.
- Tokyo – one of the world's great cities. Spend a few nights.
- Friendly people.
- A genuine cultural experience.
- Futuristic consumer goods.

... and cons
- Huge language barrier – can be a problem when travelling.
- Long, expensive journey. Jet lag takes two days out of every trip.
- Difficult to get direct flights to Sapporo.
- The food can be too exotic for some people.
- Japanese culture being eroded as popularity grows.

R: YUYA NAKAYAMA L: ALTS BANDAI P: CHRIS MORAN/HOTSHITPICTURES.COM

Twisting my melons, man

Any group of British snowboarders travelling in Japan is likely to spend a great deal of time marvelling at the cultural differences between Japan and the West. But what you might also begin to consider is exactly what the Japanese must make of a place like Britain.

What might a travel guide for Japanese people actually say about the place? Maybe something like 'don't be alarmed by how rude people are to you – they're this rude to each other too,' and 'avoid public toilets at all costs' would probably get a mention too. But maybe also a chirpy 'but never mind, the melons are so cheap!'

Yes, the melons. The Japanese have a peculiar relationship with fruit (all strictly legal) – specifically melons and apples. It's possible to spend an inordinate amount of money on a melon or an apple, the latter being a typical gift that one might bring someone when visiting their home. Large, red, shiny and perfectly formed apples are available to buy at huge expense, but don't try eating them – they taste of nothing. This, of course, is hardly the point.

As for the melons, it seems that their round shape is inconvenient enough for Japanese farmers to have spent the last 20 years working out how to grow cuboid ones. Grown with the aid of a glass box, these square watermelons fit nicely in a refrigerator, are easy to cut up and fetch around ¥10,000 each. Expensive maybe, but if it cuts out the problem of those pesky melons rolling around all over the place then surely it's worth US$85 of anyone's money? In any case, don't worry – for the more fiscally challenged among us, melon flavoured chewy sweets are widely available at a fraction of the price.

slush can hit midway through the month. As with most northern hemisphere resorts, the season ends in April, though late snowfalls are not uncommon.

Off-piste policy

It used to be the case that local riders would never dare to ride in the trees, but most of the bigger resorts have now realized that this is their main attraction, and attitudes are changing fast. But it's best to observe local rules – if a resort truly wants you to stay in bounds, we're not going to encourage anyone to break the law. Pretending you didn't understand local custom is becoming harder to get away with. The opening of previously banned tree runs is making that less of an issue.

Secret spots

Japan is probably one of the few places on Earth where riders will happily share their secret spots. Look for someone with a powder board and ask their advice. That said, most resorts don't even need secret spots – their visible powder fields are often perfect.

Freestyle

Most younger Japanese riders are obsessed with following and copying the antics of the Shaun Whites of this world, so the market for freestyle riding has gone through the roof. In addition, many smaller resorts that have little freeriding to offer have cottoned on to the idea

P: CHRIS MORAN/HOTSHITPICTURES.COM

that perfect funparks are the key to drawing in custom. As such, most resorts have very well maintained parks, perfect pipes and interesting features for all standards of riders.

The scene

Japanese riders are now in the upper reaches of the snowboard world. Tadashi Fuse led the way over the last five years, and has been followed by innovative pipe and park destroyers like Yuya Nakayama, Kazuhiro Kokubo, and Takahura Nakai.

The industry

Their national scene is covered by several websites and a version of *Transworld Snowboarding* specifically made for the Japanese public. However, due to the inherent difficulties in reading characters, there is little help for the outside traveller who cannot read Japanese script. Sites such as snowjapan.com offer English advice and links to English speaking resort websites. American writer Neil Hartmann (neilhartmann.com) has good recommendations and info on the local Niseko scene.

Japan: a brief history of snowboarding

1980 → It is uncertain who the first riders were, but by 1980 snowboards had been brought to Japan. **1982** → Kijimadaira, in the Shiga prefectory, becomes the first Japanese resort to officially welcome snowboarders. **1983** → The Japan Snowboard Association is founded. **1984** → First foreign seasonaires realize the potential of the northern island of Hokkaido. Niseko in particular has Australian and American riders staying all winter. **1987** → Japan's 'miracle economy' feeds huge investment in new resorts. **1990** → There are over 600 resorts in the country, more per capita than anywhere else in the world. **1994** → The first Nippon Open is held. US riders Jimi Scott and Michelle Taggart take gold in the halfpipe event. **1995** → First Japanese competitors appear on the World Cup circuit. **1996** → World Snowboard films regularly feature the country in their freeriding sections, pushing the idea that it is a freeriding paradise. **1998** → Yuri Yoshikawa becomes first Japanese rider to win World Cup, coming first place in halfpipe at San Candido, Italy. Nagano hosts the Winter Olympics. **1999** → Several homegrown brands start to make powder board models. **2000** → Katsuya Tahara becomes first Japanese rider to win the Nippon Open. **2003** → Japan becomes the first country in the world to have more snowboarders than skiers. **2006** → Today, Japanese riders are a world force in snowboarding and their competitions are among some of the most anticipated of the season. Nissan X-Trail Jam at the Tokyo Dome regularly gets a crowd of up to 75,000 people, eclipsing even the Air and Style in audience size alone.

Riders' tales
Lucky to be alive

Pro rider Graham MacVoy found himself in the middle of every snowboarder's worst nightmare when an avalanche swept him away in France.

To snowboard in the backcountry, away from resorts and lifts, I think you need to be a calm person, and make sure you don't panic. You need to deal with the situations that are put in front of you. Obviously snowboarding is dangerous, but it's all part of the appeal. I suppose the danger of being away from the resort is what provides that. If it was safe, you wouldn't get that rush. I love being in the mountains. I love the silence. I love everything about it, and hiking to where we're going to ride is almost as good as riding itself.

Everyone has a healthy fear of avalanches. I'm always scared; always on edge, trying to be ready for anything. That's no exaggeration. You know it could happen anywhere, any time. You need to keep your wits about you. So I always think about avalanche stuff while I'm out there.

It was right at the end of the season – about 20 April I think. I'd already been out riding and went out to do some more filming – which is what I have to do as a pro snowboarder – and to see if we could find anything else worth riding. It was then that I saw a perfect untouched powder run with a couple of cliffs which I knew would be perfect for filming. All I needed to do was to hike about an hour and half to get to it, while the others set up to film.

The face I was looking at had a northeasterly aspect, which meant that it'd been in the sun for quite a lot of the day. I actually said to my mate that I thought it looked a bit 'slabby'. He assured me "Nah mate, it'll be fine". So I went to the top and dropped in.

Almost as soon as I made the first turn somebody shouted "Avalanche!" I didn't hear it crack, it just went. Usually you think you'll have some warning to find a way out but this was a really big slide. An area of snow about 200 m wide cracked, perhaps 10 m above where I was. Before I knew it, I was knee deep in snow and sliding with the avalanche. A grumbling noise started to grow. Then it became deafening.

I seemed to tumble and flip over and the only thing going through my mind was to stay upright. I knew that I was going over the cliff and I

really didn't want to be upside down and land on a rock, even though I had a helmet on. I got myself into an upright position, then I felt myself going over the cliff.

I do remember this bit. All I was doing was trying everything in my power to make it as safe as possible and keep the injuries to a minimum. I guess it's like a survival reaction, but I was just trying to stay above the snow, and I knew I had to stop tumbling. I just got this feeling of weightlessness, which was kind of like being in a waterfall. You're falling through the air but at the same rate as everything around you, so actually it feels like nothing is moving. I couldn't see anything – no rock, nothing. It was completely white. No one watching could see me either. So, yeah, the fall through the air was a strange one. It must have lasted only about half a second but it felt like an eternity. I was thinking 'where am I gonna land? Am I gonna be impaled on a spiky rock?' It's a serious concern when you're plummeting towards the ground!

Anyway, as luck would have it, a huge volume of snow had already fallen off the cliff and it seemed to aerate the snow, and I landed OK. To be honest with you, considering I'd fallen off a pretty high cliff and come to a dead stop, it wasn't that bad. Everything stopped for a split second. Then the roar started and I was moving again. It really was quite deep by this time, so I was trying to swim, to stay on top of the snow and to keep my board up. If your board sinks underneath the snow, you're screwed. At the same time I was wondering if I should dump my pack, or try and take my board off – that kind of thing. But in the end I was lucky. Under the cliff there was 60 m of slope and then I flattened out, so I came to a natural stop. When it stopped dead, I was only buried to just above my knees. If the same thing had happened on a 500-m face, it'd have been all over. In that way, the cliff didn't really do me any harm because it put me back on top of the snow. If I'd have slid that distance straight down a wide slope, I think I'd have been in trouble.

When I came to a stop I was still on top of the snow. I was spaced out. I didn't have a bruise or even a dent on my board. I couldn't believe how lucky I'd been. It was nuts. I suppose I was hugely relieved, 'cos it was a traumatic experience, but I didn't panic once. I just concentrated on trying to do it right. I wasn't really in my right mind. I was spun out. I really didn't appreciate how bad it could have been until I saw the pictures. Then I thought 'Holy shit! I was lucky there'.

Alts Bandai

A train ride from Tokyo and yet a world apart, Alts Bandai bills itself as having the best funparks in Japan. It certainly is a freestyle heaven for beginners through to pros, with some incredible freeriding and empty tree runs for those with a penchant for powder riding too.

🔆 *If you like this* ...
... *try Silvretta Nova* ▸▸p52, *Snow Park* ▸▸p232, *or Mammoth* ▸▸p368.

The Town

Alts Bandai is a purpose-built resort that comprises little more than a huge hotel and amenities complex. Containing a pool, several shops, restaurants, a karaoke room, several bars and drinks machines, and a huge reception area with ample space for people to lounge and take in the views, it's got pretty much everything you need. The nearest town and train station, Inawashiro, is a 35-minute bus ride away, but transfers are infrequent and few visitors stay in the town.

Sleeping There are three options at the **Bandai Hotel** (T242 745100): the cheapest digs are at the 'Lodge', standard rooms are the most popular choice, while family-style 'maisonettes' are the higher priced option. Prices vary but expect to pay at least ¥10,000 per person per night.
Eating There are three restaurants on site, plus several mountain cafés and a buffet-style eatery in the hotel.
Bars and clubs The main drinking area is undoubtedly the hotel reception. There is no nightclub, but the hotel often puts on events, which run till late. It sounds rubbish but is

⊙ **OPENING TIMES**
Mid-Dec to early Apr: 0730-2100
⑤ **RESORT PRICES**
Week pass (6 days): ¥23,000
Day pass: ¥4,500
Season pass: ¥40,000
ⓘ **DIRECTORY**
Tourist office: T242 745000
Medical centre: T120 461997
Pisteurs: No tel number
Taxi: T0088 224800
Local radio: None
Website: alts.co.jp/en

actually good fun. Otherwise, the karaoke room is the place to head after hours.
Shopping There are two shops on site that have emergency groceries, but with no cooking facilities in any of the rooms, everyone eats in the restaurants and cafés.
Health The hotel offers one floor dedicated to relaxation, with an indoor pool, jacuzzi, onsen-style hot rooms and massage. It is strictly single sex with well-divided areas. There's a real *onsen* bath around three minutes' drive – get the hotel to find a taxi transfer.
Internet The whole hotel complex is

P: CHRIS MORAN/HOTSHIPPICTURES.COM

P: CHRIS MORAN/HOTSHIPPICTURES.COM

66 99

I love this place. It's got the coolest atmosphere ever. The people are amazing.
Shaun White

wireless, with best reception in the main foyer.
Transfer options The hotel lays on a free shuttle bus from Inawashiro train station. Taxis can be picked up outside station for around ¥5000, or ordered by the receptionists for the return leg.
Local partners None.

The Mountain

Alts Bandai likes to claim it has the best snowpark in Japan. Strictly speaking it has four parks: one fantastically good baby park, which meanders through the trees on a hidden side of the mountain; another main park tucked away at the far end of the resort; a third close to the lifts; and then the main, gigantic park which is pumped up for the Nippon Open – the biggest mountain competition in Japan (usually held in February). On top of this, the resort boasts the usual heavy snowfall, perfect freeriding in the trees and a genuine cultural experience.

Beginners Head to the top of chair 1. From the top turn and face back down towards the resort. The baby park is directly to skier's right, so traverse the piste and then head straight downhill. Here you'll find perfect, small jumps for practising your first freestyle moves. This part of the mountain is normally pretty empty too.

Intermediate Intermediates should head straight to the main park. Take high speed quad 4, then ride straight off and down towards the back bowl chairs. You'll cut straight over the intermediate park and be greeted with a pipe at the bottom. The chair next to the pipe will take you straight back to the start of the long funpark. When you're done riding this all day, take a few cheeky runs through the trees next to it.

Advanced Head past the intermediate park and keep making your way across the mountain using the chairlifts. From the last lift, each area between the runs back towards the pipe is littered with tree-riding gems. Oh and when you're done there, head back to the base hotel, then take chair 1 up to the baby park. On your way up you'll see the main advanced pipe and park to your left. A few laps through that should cap the day.

Kids There's a permanent nursery area for kids and the baby course is perfect for budding freestylers.

Flat light days On flat light days, the trees are perfection. And if it's really bad, just wait until 1700 and they'll turn the floodlights on. There's a wooden halfpipe next to the restaurant for those with skateboards.

☺ LOCALS DO
- Make sure they've got a clear lens for night riding.
- Head to the far end of the resort to get empty pistes.
- Ride the lifts with the Perspex hoods down. It keeps the wind and snow out.

☹ LOCALS DON'T
- Do that much hiking. Most off-piste is lift access.
- Party hard. There's not much call for it.
- Pay for Internet. It's all free.

✔ PROS
- Fantastic park, often perfect powder too.
- Empty. Especially on weekdays.
- Long opening hours. Ride all day and then again in the early evening.

✖ CONS
- Bit of a trek to get to. Four trains from Tokyo at least.
- Wind and unpleasant weather coming off the lake.
- Hotel can induce cabin fever.

☺ NOT TO MISS
The view from the top of lifts 1, 2, 3 and 4 of Lake Inawashiro is spectacular.

ⓘ REMEMBER TO AVOID
Don't try and ride off-piste further than lift 1 or you'll have to get a cab back to the resort. Oh and you'll have to walk across flat snow to the get to the road too. And it's miles.

❄ SNOW DEPTH

metres	N	D	J	F	M	A	M

↻ RELIVE A FAMOUS MOMENT
Put down the best run you've got in the pipe and claim victory like Terje, Shaun White, Torah Bright and Peter Line have all done in this very resort.

R: JONI MALMI · P: CHRIS MORAN/HOTSHITPICTURES.COM

700 m	TOWN ALTITUDE
160 km	KM TO AIRPORT
NRT	AIRPORT
★★☆	VEGETARIAN RATING
★★★	INTERNET CAFES
★★★	RIDE IN/RIDE OUT
1280 m	HIGHEST LIFT
580 m	VERTICAL DROP
1932	RIDEABLE AREA (IN ACRES)
30 km	KM OF PISTES
3	NURSERY AREAS
10/12/7	RUNS: BEG/INTER/ADV
0/0	FUNICULAR/CABLE CARS
1/10	GONDOLAS/CHAIRS
0	DRAGS
yes	NIGHT RIDING
4	PARKS
2	PIPE
no	SUMMER AREAS
★★★☆	ENVIRONMENTAL RATING
💲💲💲	COST INDICATOR

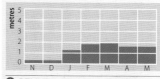

JAPAN
ALTS BANDAI

Happo One

The Town

If Niseko is the premiere resort on Japan's northern Hokkaidō prefecture (area), the Hakuba Valley provides the definitive snowboarding experience on the main island of Honshū, in the Nagano prefecture. Many quality resorts sit outside this major city – around 90 minutes journey time from Tokyo – including Happo One, Hakuba 47, Sanosaka and Goryu. But thanks to a huge riding area, proximity to the valley town and great lift system (a legacy from the 1998 Olympics), we think Happo One has the edge over its neighbours. True, the valley might not be as world-famous as Niseko – but there are fewer foreigners around as a result. Which is why we think that those looking to really experience snowboarding Japanese-style should do so before it inevitably changes.

Sleeping Snowbeds (snowbedsjapan.com) has

It just keeps snowing. Every morning we'd wake up and look in amazement at how much more it had snowed. That's my memory of Happo.

James McPhail, photographer

backpacker-style accommodation in the middle of Hakuba and is within easy reach of each major resort in the valley. Similarly well-appointed, if a little further away, is **Yamago Snow Lover's Club House** (5yama5 .com), another Japanese backpackers. Situated across the valley from Happo One, the **Hotel Viola** (hotel-viola.com) is a comfortable, friendly Japanese hotel with an *onsen*.

Eating Discounting the **McDonald's** at the mid-station up the hill, **Gravity Worx** (gravityworx.com) is a snowboard shop as well as café and bar. Also popular is **Non Jays** (T261 725566), a traditional Izakaya serving Japanese food and drinks.

Bars and clubs Hakuba has a surprising amount of nightlife, but

⊙ **OPENING TIMES**
Mid-Nov to early May: 0830-2130

⊛ **RESORT PRICES**
Week pass: No discount
Day pass: ¥4,600
Season pass: ¥70,000

⊙ **DIRECTORY**
Tourist office: T0261 723066
Medical centre: T0261 722008
Pisteurs: No tel number
Taxi: None
Local radio: None
Website: hakuba-happo.or.jp/

keep an eye out for **Unn Bar** (T261 725775), another Izakaya, and **The Wave Bar** and **Velvet**.

Shopping Hakuba has plenty of amenities, including a couple of supermarkets, fast food joints and snowboard shops in the centre of town.

Health You must try an *onsen*, a Japanese-style public hot tub. There are several public and hotel facilities. Try www.evergreen-outdoors.com for a massage.

Internet Snowbeds and other hotels have wireless and internet access, and there is one internet café – **Studio 902** in Hakuba.

Transfer options Get the bullet train to Tokyo, then to Nagano. Buses up to Hakuba take about an hour and leave from Nagano station east exit – check grace.hyperdia .com/ for up-to-date times.

Local partners Prices quoted here are for a Happo One pass, although you can buy a Hakuba Alpine pass that covers Happo One, Iwatake and Norikura Kogen. Check snowjapan.com for more details.

Just a couple of hours from Tokyo, Nagano's Hakuba Valley has a multitude of epic, powder-filled resorts. Happo One is the best.

⊙ *If you like this* . . .
. . . *try Bansko* ▸▸*p100,*
Shemshak ▸▸*p104,*
Niseko ▸▸*p210, or*
Las Leñas ▸▸*p272.*

JAPAN
HAPPO ONE

P: JAMES MCPHAIL

The Mountain

Happo One is the biggest resort in the Hakuba Valley. Like every riding area in Japan, it gets blasted with snow, so riding the pistes becomes a different proposition for snowboarders used to North American or European conditions. You'll soon notice that the majority of locals are loath to venture out of bounds. The classic dilemma for the foreign visitor confronted by all this powder is whether or not to transgress this local custom, but note that rumours of arrests are rife. As well as all that powder to play in, there's also a good little park and a very well maintained pipe for freestylers. Better still, Happo One is another resort to have regular floodlighting, meaning dusky powder and pipe sessions are another must-do during your visit.

Beginners Although it's steeper than other Nipponese resorts, Happo One still has some pretty perfect beginner terrain. Best bet is to take the gondola (watch for queues – it's a notorious early morning snarl-up) and then head hard skier's left towards the Saka area of the hill. Here, chairs access mellower beginner terrain. After lunch in the village, head back over to the chairs on the Nakiyama side for some more cruisy runs through the trees.

Intermediate You're going to have a blast here wherever you ride. Start at Nakiyama and take each chair to the top. You'll see the obvious routes down, with plenty of trees to swoop through and powder stashes to explore.

Later, head across the resort to the quieter Saka area. There are lots of gullies to explore and tracks to boost off. Finish early, then head back up in the evening for some more powder runs next to the pipe.

Advanced You'll either have the best or most frustrating day of your life, depending on how carefully you choose where to go off-piste. Make no mistake – there is some epic, dangerous terrain here, and the authorities are still very strict when it comes to marshalling access. Over on skier's right at the very top, there are some open fields and cliffs – but it means ducking the rope and risking fines. Ask a local for the best ways to explore Happo's bounty, and use your judgement. A good place to start would be evergreen-outdoors.com who offer guiding trips into the backcountry and avalanche courses.

Kids A children's *gelende* – a special area separated by safety net – is provided for kids, as is a special room called Yuki Daruma where kids can play. The **Snow Bee** school offers lessons everyday as well.

Flat light days The lower slopes hold plenty of trees, meaning the resort is just as viable when it snows (which it does, a lot!) The cognoscenti recommend the trees around the Sakakitaone chair.

R: TINA BIRBAUM P: JAMES MCPHAIL

☺ LOCALS DO
- Get their receptionist to book a taxi – no local firms speak English.
- Wear full avalanche kit if they're going off-piste.
- Ride the weekend – it's the busiest time.

☹ LOCALS DON'T
- Go off-piste, despite all the snow. It's crazy.
- Wear board shorts in the *onsen*!

✔ PROS
- Ridiculous amounts of snow.
- Easiest riding area to get to in Japan.
- Busy town with many amenities.

✘ CONS
- High avalanche danger.
- Much off-piste banned.
- Busy with locals – especially at weekends.

NOT TO MISS
Checking out the ski jumps used in '98 – massive!

ⓘ REMEMBER TO AVOID
Off-piste control is strict here so be aware that people have been arrested for riding off-piste.

❄ SNOW DEPTH

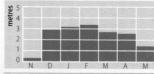

RELIVE A FAMOUS MOMENT
Snowboarding first became an Olympic sport in Nagano in 1998.

760 m	TOWN ALTITUDE
374 km	KM TO AIRPORT
NRT	AIRPORT
★★☆	VEGETARIAN RATING
★★★	INTERNET CAFES
★☆☆	RIDE IN/RIDE OUT
1831 m	HIGHEST LIFT
1071 m	VERTICAL DROP
494	RIDEABLE AREA (IN ACRES)
19 km	KM OF PISTES
0	NURSERY AREAS
3/6/4	RUNS: BEG/INTER/ADV
0/0	FUNICULAR/CABLE CARS
1/33	GONDOLAS/CHAIRS
0	DRAGS
yes	NIGHT RIDING
1	PARKS
1	PIPE
no	SUMMER AREAS
★★★ ★★☆	ENVIRONMENTAL RATING
$$$	COST INDICATOR

JAPAN
HAPPO ONE

Niseko

Japanese freeriding paradise with a strong western influence due to a heavy presence of Antipodean holidaymakers. Incredible snowfall and night-time floodlit riding make this a unique resort.

◑ If you like this . . .
. . . try *Shemshak* ▶▶*p104, Krasnaya Poliana* ▶▶*p108, Alyeska* ▶▶*p346.*

The Town

Confusingly, the town is actually named Hirafu, and sits underneath the Niseko lift area overlooking the impressive Yotei-san volcano. Architecturally, the town is a mish-mash of Japanese and western buildings, giving the place a haphazard, but interesting look. It is, however, very small, with no actual 'centre' to speak of. That said, the bars and restaurants that do exist are very cool; often little more than basements, garages and sheds attached to regular houses. One – the Ice Bar – is simply an igloo built next to a bus stop. It's amazing.

Sleeping Shizenkan (niseko-backpacker.com) has the cheapest digs. **Uranaka Lodge** (niseko.or.jp/uranaka/en) has full Japanese-style lodging, while **Log Log** (niseko-hirafu.com) is a cool, comfortable pension.

Eating For good Yakitori, **Bang Bang** or **The Big Cliff** are perfect. For a quick fix, the **100-yen Noodle Shop** is great while for real sashimi and sushi try Sencho.

Bars and Clubs Yummy's, Fatty's or the (real) **Ice Bar** are all amazing. Walk through the coke fridge door to **Guy's** (but people call it the **Fridge Bar**). For a real local hang-out, check out the **Jam Bar** then head for an after-hours drink to **Red Bar**.

Shopping Seicomart is pretty much the centre of town and the only real place to get groceries. You'll have to jump on a bus and head to Kutchan for the biggest supermarket in the area.

Health *Onsen*, Japanese natural spas, are all over. Try **Niseko Ground Service** (T136 212503) for an English-speaking intro.

> ❝❞
> I've been in Niseko for three winters now and I haven't sharpened my edges once.
>
> *Owain Bassett, seasonaire and founder of Dragon Lodge in Tignes*

Internet Wireless spots can be found in **Yummy's**, the **A-Bu-Cha** bakery (next door to the Seicomart), **Paraiso** pizza place and plenty of other bars. If you need a computer try **Pow Pow** opposite the supermarket.

Transfer Options Chou (T112 310500) or **Donan** (T123 465701) bus companies both have counters at Chitose Airport. Expect to pay around ¥4000 for a return fare. Or there's a train from Chitose to Kutchan but only a few direct per day.

Local partners Your pass works at the next-door resorts of An'nupuri and Higashiyama.

⊕ OPENING TIMES

Mid-Nov to early May: 0830-2130

Ⓢ RESORT PRICES

Week pass (6 days): ¥28,800
Day pass: ¥4,800
Season pass: ¥87,000

ⓘ DIRECTORY

Tourist office: T136 582080
Medical Centre: T120 461997
Pisteurs: No tel number
Taxi: T0088 224800
Local radio: None
Website: niseko.ne.jp

P: MATT FLETCHER/YAMAPHOTO.NET

P: CHRIS MORAN

P: CHRIS MORAN

R: AOYAMA P: MATT FLETCHER/YAMAPHOTO.NET

The Mountain

Little of the mountain is above the trees, which is a blessing because with such heavy snowfall it's almost always a flat light day. But the tree cover is perfect – beautifully spaced, funky trees whose angular branches collect little snow but give great definition in the dim conditions. The mountain is open until 2100 every night, with virtually the whole area floodlit. Because the lights are underneath the cloud, the visibility is usually much better at night – so don't forget to bring a clear lens.

Beginners Take the Prince Gondola then head off down the only run that leads from it. The middle section runs next to the mini funpark and has a jump with a tunnel you can ride through. The pistes are super-wide with incredible views of the volcano opposite. Perfect for practising wide turns and traversing on.

Intermediate You've probably come to Japan to ride powder, so spend a few hours on a freestyle board during the day, hit one of the noodle bars around 1700 – don't get changed – then head back up the hill with a powder board on the Higashiyama Romance Lift. The sparse trees on the face to Skier's Right (underneath the chair) are perfect. Just don't ruin your legs for the next day.

Advanced Where to begin? You can literally hike anywhere on the mountain and you'll get incredible, world-class powder rides through the trees. For a simple but brilliant introduction, take the Prince Gondola, exit the top station and turn immediately right. Walk the 50 m to the top of the small incline and then ride anywhere to the left. It'll bring you out into a gully that leads back to the piste.

Kids Niseko Base Snowsports has a kids club (T136 21500).

Flat light days Flat light? That's why you've come…everywhere has trees. On real, real flat light days they put the floodlights on during the day. How rad is that?

☺ LOCALS DO
- ☺ Make sure they've got a clear lens for night riding.
- ☺ Ride powder boards.
- ☺ Have snowshoes and collapsible poles – they're almost essential.

☹ LOCALS DON'T
- ☹ Wear anything in the *onsen* baths!
- ☹ Get up too early. Party late and ride afternoon and night-time powder.
- ☹ Bother with the park.

✔ PROS
- ✔ Powder. It's as close to guaranteed as you'll ever get.
- ✔ Empty. But it is starting to become well known.
- ✔ Culturally different.

✘ CONS
- ✘ Need a car if you want flexibility.
- ✘ Wind. Not much else to do if it the snow's not great.
- ✘ Cash culture – not many places, accept credit cards. And the nearest cash machine is in Kutchan.

⊙ NOT TO MISS
Views of the Yotei-san Volcano from anywhere on the mountain.

ⓘ REMEMBER TO AVOID
The Chinese New Year (18 February in 2007) is the busy season with more queues than usual but still not that bad. They won't let you on the lift after it's shut, then you'll have to get a taxi back (around ¥4000).

❄ SNOW DEPTH
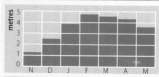

⊙ RELIVE A FAMOUS MOMENT
Nicolas Muller's legendary section in *Pop* was filmed in Niseko – look for the pillow lines.

650 m	TOWN ALTITUDE
110 km	KM TO AIRPORT
CTS	AIRPORT
★★★	VEGETARIAN RATING
★★★	INTERNET CAFES
★★☆	RIDE IN/RIDE OUT
1308 m	HIGHEST LIFT
658 m	VERTICAL DROP
area not measured	RIDEABLE AREA (IN ACRES)
runs not measured	KM OF PISTES
2	NURSERY AREAS
22/0/17	RUNS: BEG/INTER/ADV
0/0	FUNICULAR/CABLE CARS
3/24	GONDOLAS/CHAIRS
0	DRAGS
yes	NIGHT RIDING
4	PARKS
1	PIPE
no	SUMMER AREAS
★★★ ★★☆	ENVIRONMENTAL RATING
$$$	COST INDICATOR

JAPAN
NISEKO

New Zealand

R: SHAUN WHITE L: SNOW PARK P: JAMES MCPHAIL

A high white cloud in the land of the long white cloud – Aotearoa.

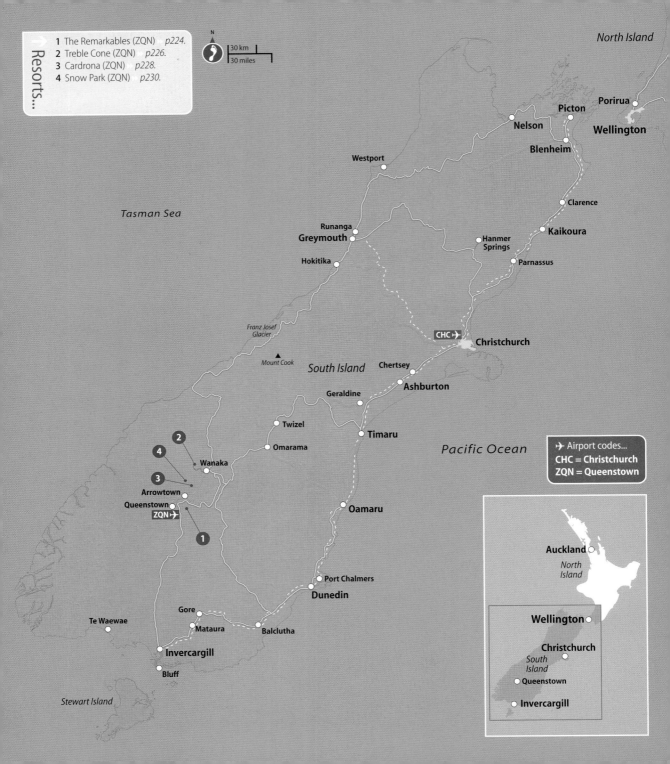

N

30 km
30 miles

North Island

Porirua

Picton

Nelson

Wellington

Blenheim

Westport

Tasman Sea

Clarence

Runanga
Greymouth

Hanmer
Springs

Kaikoura

Hokitika

Parnassus

*Franz Josef
Glacier*

CHC ✈ Christchurch

Mount Cook

South Island

Chertsey

Ashburton

Geraldine

Twizel

Timaru

Pacific Ocean

Omarama

2
4
Wanaka

✈ Airport codes...
CHC = Christchurch
ZQN = Queenstown

3
Arrowtown
Queenstown
ZQN ✈

1

Oamaru

Port Chalmers

Dunedin

Gore

Te Waewae

Mataura

Balclutha

Invercargill

Bluff

Stewart Island

Auckland

*North
Island*

Wellington

Christchurch

*South
Island*

Queenstown

Invercargill

For so long a tantalizingly unknown combination of the foreign and the extremely familiar, New Zealand has enjoyed an explosion of interest over the last four years, both among snowboarders and the world at large. The success of a certain film trilogy has meant that Aotearoa, the 'Land of the Long White Cloud', has now been unofficially rebranded as Middle Earth, while the huge exposure that the Snow Park resort has enjoyed across the entire snowboarding media spectrum has meant a one-off trip to NZ is now a must-do for the serious travelling snowboarder – despite the huge journey time involved.

NZ has it all: amazing surfing, a rich and diverse local history, vibrant cities, an awe-inspiring landscape and, of course, great snowboarding. Above all, though, what New Zealand has is space – and lots of it. With a landmass roughly the same size as the UK shared between only 4 million inhabitants, there's a lot of room to kick around in here; particularly on the South Island, where the main resorts are situated. The result is an appealingly laid-back lifestyle that will snare everybody who visits in some way.

The other aspect that makes a trip to New Zealand extremely viable is that culture shock, despite the long journey from most other western countries. A lingering colonial hangover means New Zealand retains a very British feel. This and the world-class riding on offer mean it isn't difficult to see why some riders are so smitten they never leave.

While there are many resorts on New Zealand's South Island (and some on the North), most foreign visitors tend to base themselves in Wanaka and Queenstown and explore the surrounding resorts. Of these, we picked the Remarkables, Snow Park, Cardrona and Treble Cone but other locations equally worthy of investigation include Coronet Peak, Mount Hutt and Temple Basin and the Club Fields (see page 222).

New Zealand rating

Value for money
★★★★☆

Nightlife
★★★☆☆

Freestyle
★★★★★

Freeride
★★★★☆

Essentials

Getting there

For most snowboarders, New Zealand is so far away to make it a once-only option. From Europe and the US, expect a 30-hour total journey time. Christchurch is the usual point of entry, and carriers to 'Ch-Ch' include **Air New Zealand** (airnewzealand.com), **Qantas** (qantas.com), **British Airways** (ba.com), **Cathay Pacific** (cathaypacific.com), **American Airlines** (www.aa.com) and **United** (united.com). Once in Christchurch, most hire a vehicle and drive to the resorts, although it is possible to catch an internal flight to Queenstown from Christchurch with **Qantas** and **Air New Zealand**.

Red tape

New Zealand's immigration rules are strictly enforced. Most visitors can enter for periods of up to six months without a visa, although Australians citizens are exempt from this. Onward tickets are required, and passports should be valid for at least three months beyond the period of your visit. Those intending to work must have a work visa. Customs regulations here are also strict, so beware of bringing in foodstuffs or even mud on boots or running shoes.

Getting around

Hiring a car or camper is the best way of getting around the South Island, particularly if you plan a road trip of any description. Distances between valley towns and resorts are fairly substantial. Roads in rural areas also tend to be of a basic standard, increasing journey times further. Cars drive on the left, and drivers turning left must yield to those approaching from the right. Another important local idiosyncrasy to consider is that motor insurance is not a legal requirement in New Zealand, meaning that private accident insurance is essential. According to the Foreign and Commonwealth Office, 'New Zealand law has removed the right of accident victims to sue a third party in the event of an accident'. Make sure you're insured.
Car hire The major hire companies operate in New Zealand, but a better option might be to use a local company such as apexrentals.co.nz, ezy.co.nz, acerentals.co.nz or omegarentalcars.com. Most have a huge fleet of campers, modern rentals and 4WDs.

Public transport

Public transport isn't amazing here, which is why cars are really the way forward. Coach and bus services tend to be privately run and

there are plenty making the trip from Christchurch down to Wanaka and Queenstown. Check out **Wanaka Connexions** (wanakaconnexions.co.nz), **Scenic Pacific** (scenicpacific.co.nz) and **Atomic Travel** (atomictravel.co.nz). Train travel around New Zealand is a little more limited and is run by **Tranz Scenic**, NZ's only passenger rail company – www.tranzscenic.co.nz. Hitchhiking is very popular here (a testament to the safety of the country) and a good way to get around the Wanaka and Queenstown areas.

Opening hours and traditions

New Zealand opening hours are common to most first world countries, with shops and businesses open Monday to Friday 0900-1700. In the major cities and tourist centres, many shops are open at the weekends as well.

Never shall I forget the utter loneliness of the prospect – only the far away homestead giving sign of human handiwork, the vastness of mountain and plain, of river and sky; the marvellous atmospheric effects – sometimes black mountain against a white sky, and then again, after the weather, white mountains against a black sky.

Samuel Butler, author of Erewhon

New Zealand price guide							
In US$	2.46	3.08	4.32	0.65	1.23	3-6.00	0.85

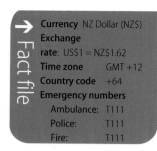

→ **Fact file**

Currency NZ Dollar (NZ$)
Exchange rate: US$1 = NZ$1.62
Time zone GMT +12
Country code +64
Emergency numbers
  Ambulance: T111
  Police: T111
  Fire: T111

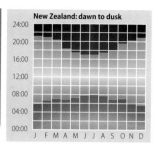

New Zealand: dawn to dusk

Eating

One of the main pleasures of a trip to New Zealand is the chance to sample the local food. As in nearby Australia, food here is simple, plentiful and very reasonably priced; even the humble sandwich is transformed into a delicately flavoured feast. NZ's most famous culinary export to the rest of the world is probably lamb, but the amazingly fresh seafood is held in equally high regard – particularly the mussels and other shellfish. The largely outdoor nature of Kiwi life

Lift chat

'You're going to Arrowtown? You've got to go to the pie shop!'

Back in the early 1990s, when I was a young grommet and the limit of my snowboarding universe was the local dryslope and the pages of well-thumbed snowboarding magazines, Queenstown held a magical allure. Later, early Steve Graham shred films and, notoriously, *Subjekt: Haakonsen* turned the whole snowboarding world onto its possibilities. By the time *The White Album* was released, with its section filmed solely at Snow Park, the South Island had become one of the most famous snowboarding destinations on the planet.

Such popularity comes at a price though, and today Queenstown is a different place: new apartments are springing up each year; and, for some, the recent arrival of Starbucks signifies the beginning of the homogenized era for the town. The fact is that this place is world famous and destined only to get busier. With this in mind, it's perhaps understandable that the tiny village of Arrowtown, 23 km away, is gradually becoming an alternative base for clued-up riders.

Even for a country that takes its pastries as seriously as New Zealand, Arrowtown's bakery enjoys a far-flung renown. Tell anybody you're going to visit and it's the first thing that they mention. There's a lot more to this ex-gold mining community than great pies, however, even if the Gourmet Steak and Cheese puts most other pastries to shame. Nestled in a shady, temperate corner of the Southern Alps, encircled by the foothills of the Crown Range and the river from which it takes its name, it's more akin to a historical exhibit than a real

community, almost unchanged since the discovery of a new seam of gold by William Fox in 1862 put it on the map and led to it becoming a boomtown. And as Queenstown has become somewhat passé since its discovery by hordes of modern-day pleasure prospectors, so Arrowtown has again begun to thrive. But will it go the same way as Queenstown? It was the decision five years ago of then little-known director Peter Jackson to film some of the *Lord of the Rings* trilogy in the area that will probably have the most seismic repercussions on the area. It means that guided Middle Earth tours are now rivalling bungee jumping and snowboarding in popularity – and that the numbers of coach tourists making the trip from Queenstown are rising inexorably. Even the casual visitor can sense a place poised on the brink of change, and it would be a shame indeed if a village which has survived the tumult of the gold rush was permanently changed by this latest invasion.

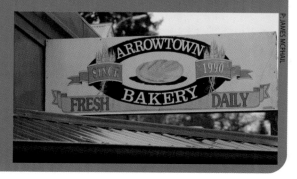

is also reflected in the country's fondness for elaborate, social barbecues and in the huge number of local wines available. There are 10 main wine producing regions here, and they deserve a book treatment of their own.

That said, there's a colonial influence at work in New Zealand, and UK riders in particular will be right at home with the way that the Kiwis have taken home country dishes and improved upon them immeasurably. And then there is the unique Australasian sweet tooth, represented by Lamingtons, Anzac biscuits and Pavlova, the national dessert. Riders should also try to sample some local Maori cuisine if they get the opportunity, particularly the *hangi*, a speciality in which a pit lined with meat, fish, vegetables is covered with red-hot stones and left to cook for hours – as much an extended social ritual as simple meal.

Overall, food is venerated as one of life's simplest, most important pleasures. Certainly, any riding trip to New Zealand would be incomplete without trying an after-riding pie from the garage on the outskirts of Queenstown, or sampling chips, battered mussels and a beer from the local chippie.

Language
English and Maori are the official languages of New Zealand, with English used for most everyday communication.

Crime/safety
In rural areas, crime is almost unheard of, although the usual precautions should be taken in busy resort centres such as Queenstown, and the major cities. Generally, boards on balconies are safe, although theft from outside restaurants is not unknown.

Health
No vaccinations are needed to enter New Zealand, and the standard of health care is of the highest standard. Health insurance is

New Zealand is a special place to ride. Our Southern Alps are as expansive as the European Alps with only a fraction of the population and development; 'space' is the feeling you are left with. This is emphasized with most snow levels above treeline, leaving massive, wide-open expanses as far as you can see. While the snow conditions may sometimes leave much to be desired, the terrain and vibe more than make up for it. And for a unique experience that you'll find hard to replicate anywhere else in the world, try one of the smaller Club Fields. If you score any of these on a powder day you wouldn't want to be anywhere else on the planet!

Ste'en Webster, editor, NZ Snowboarder

strongly advised for every visitor, as health care is not free to visitors. For more information of New Zealand's health care system, call Accident Info Services on T9529 0488. A particular health concern across New Zealand and the rest of Australasia is skin cancer. Sunlight here is far more damaging than in the northern latitudes, so take care to avoid cases of sunburn, no matter how minor – especially while high up in the resorts. Most locals will be vocal about making sure foreign visitors are aware of this seemingly innocuous problem. Listen to them.

P: JAMES MCPHAIL

P: SNOW PARK

Snowboarding New Zealand

"NZ has it all. For such a small country, it boasts six major resorts and over a dozen Club Fields. If you're after a wide open playground, steeps, chutes, parks or pipes, you'll find it in NZ. That's without even mentioning the affordable heliboarding operations in the huge backcountry terrain available out of Queenstown and Wanaka. The only downside is that there is no tree riding in NZ – all the snow is above the treeline. But hey, you can't do everything. As if that wasn't enough, Queenstown is one of the adventure capitals of the world and the nightlife will leave you nursing some serious hangovers." John Matkovic, www.boardtheworld.com

There's no doubt about it, New Zealand snowboarding is going through a boom time right now. True, riders have been making the trip since the late eighties, when the likes of Shawn Farmer scored the first NZ filmed video parts. Later, Terje Haakonsen's legendary *Subjekt: Haakonsen* was partly filmed in New Zealand. But in recent years, the country's reputation had been steadily cranking its way through the notches with each passing winter. It's now firmly established as the summer stop-off *du jour* for most of the world's top northern hemisphere pro riders, while locals such as Dylan Butt are regulars at top contests. As is mentioned often in this guidebook, Snow Park has a worldwide influence that belies its tiny riding stature, and magazines such as *Manual* and *NZ Snowboarder* are representing the scene with great creativity and insight. And that's without even mentioning the natural riding terrain in resorts such as Treble Cone and Cardrona, and the amazing, affordable heliboarding. And how about the towns Wanaka and Queenstown as bases to access all this? Few shred towns

Pros & cons

Pros ...
- At the forefront of modern freestyle snowboarding.
- Cheap heliboarding.
- No culture shock, despite long journey time for most.
- Friendly locals, fresh food and great party scene.
- Among the most beautiful countries in the world. Great surf too.

... and cons
- Actual resorts are tiny compared to Europe and even North America.
- Jetlag means anything less than a three-week trip really isn't viable.
- A lot of driving to get to resorts and between resort centres. Ride in/ride out this isn't...
- Snow conditions are not that dependable, so if you're screaming for freeriding and powder you'll need to get lucky. For park though it's perfect.

can match this pair for location, atmosphere, facilities and sheer ambience. Even when the snow is bad, there's a lot to do.

Each of these disparate elements combine to form the Kiwi snowboarding experience, so is it any wonder that hordes of riders are making the trip each year? Understandably, some locals have expressed gentle concern at the changes being wrought by and on behalf of this traffic: particularly in Queenstown which, being world famous, is destined only to get busier. But perhaps these worries are premature. As has been pointed out, compared to its glitzy European counterparts, Queenstown is still a village.

Conditions
New Zealand weather is dictated by its southerly latitude and isolation

L: SNOW PARK P: JAMES MCPHAIL

P: ADAM GENDLE

The story of Snow Park

Few resorts in the world have as high a profile as Snow Park right now. But how did an area no bigger than four football pitches lined up side by side become one of the most famous resorts in the world?

As General Manager Sam Lee attests, the whole story is a classic example of making the most of what you've got. The Lee family have been synonymous with winter sports in the Crown Range for years, and have owned land in the valley since Sam's grandfather was given a plot for service during the First World War. For years, the family farmed the land until a fateful meeting at a local rugby match. Sam's mum was propping up the scrum when his dad – who was refereeing that day – realized that as well as being a great prop, she'd be a great catch for the farm. A keen skier, she convinced him to buy the land where Cardrona sits today, develop it and sell it on for a tidy profit back in 1987.

The family sat on their remaining land until 2000, when Sam spotted a potential gap in the market and decided to take on the task of creating a world class funpark for the southern hemisphere.

It hasn't been easy, that's for sure. A lack of natural snow thwarted the first attempt in 2001; and 2002 proved to be even more challenging. The snow guns didn't arrive on time, the in-ground infrastructure was installed way behind schedule and all the season ticket passes had to be refunded. It meant 2003 was make or break, but finally, using money from the sale of the land, Sam and his team succeeded in creating a park that isn't just wowing the locals but filmers and pro teams alike. The Burton team were the first to huck themselves around in 2003, and since then Snow Park has taken a unique position on the world scene, offering pros the chance to ride the best stuff in the world and everybody else to ride with the pros in an environment basically designed to aid progression. As we're beginning to see in other countries, this model is being taken up by more and more resorts keen to cash in on the snowboarding dollar. Perhaps the era of the resort funpark is upon us.

Siân Leigh

R: FREDDIE KALBERMATTEN P: JEFF CURTIS/BURTON

out in the southwest Pacific. Westerly winds come in from across the Tasman Sea, cooling and rising as they pass over the Southern Alps to create storms. These fronts are followed by periods of clear weather, a cycle which usually lasts six to 10 days. The other important system is the southerly, passing up the east coast and causing temperatures to drop and snow to fall. Systems from the southeast in particular bring heavy snowfalls. Again, these storms will be followed by periods of calm, clear weather. Temperatures in the NZ winter are also generally chilly; as low as -10°C has been recorded, although a low of around 0-2°C is more usual. The main feature of New Zealand's weather is its unpredictability, meaning days featuring snow, sun, wind and even rain are not uncommon.

When to go

The very fact that New Zealand's winter coincides with the northern hemisphere's summer largely accounts for its popularity. In today's 365/12 snowboarding universe most pros ride for up to 10 months a year, chasing the snow where they can, making two months in NZ during July and August a far more appealing proposition than, say, two months hitting the same park on a French glacier.

Resorts generally open at the end of June, with the season in full swing by July. August conditions roughly conform to March in the north, while by September spring slush is firmly established. Most resorts close by the beginning of October. Time to go surfing at one of the country's many surf spots then…

Off-piste policy

Off-piste riding, either in the main resort centres, the Club Fields or via heliboarding, is huge in New Zealand. Riders are left to make their own decisions, and are expected to be equipped with full avalanche equipment. Take the usual precautions – don't ride on your own, let the patrol know where you're going and follow all local advice.

Secret spots

The locals here are generally very friendly. They're used to foreign riders coming in and riding their areas and are generally pretty forthcoming. Kiwi ski areas are small though, so it can happen. The solution? Spread out. This is a big, big place and if you're lucky enough to hook up with a local expect, you'll be taken to spots you wouldn't normally stumble across. Another thing to be aware of is that some areas of the backcountry are owned by the Department of Conservation. If you end up here you could be fined for trespassing.

NZ is still relatively untouched by the outside world, especially the South Island, which is where most of the snow fun is to be had. Locals talk about Wanaka becoming overpopulated and overdeveloped, and sure, it has in the last 10 years – there's a mall, of sorts, there now. But even with this increase in urbanization, the whole Southern Alps area maintains a remote feel. The roads to all the mountains are still gravel, you can't stay on any of the mountain resorts, and there are still nutcracker lifts from the fifties in some of the Club Fields.

Sian Hughes, NZ local and head of Shed Distribution
(www.sheddistribution.com)

Freestyle

As most resorts here have pretty small in-bounds riding areas, New Zealand was quick to catch on to the importance of funparks. Tiny resorts such as Cardrona and The Remarkables both have amazingly well put together parks and locals who absolutely rip. For many riders, it's this that makes the long schlep south worthwhile.

The scene

New Zealand locals such as Quentin Robbins, Dylan Butt, Kendal Brown, Will and Tim Jackways, Juliane Bray and Nick Hyne are riding to an incredibly high standard, both at the national and international level. One great indication of this progression was at the 2005 Burton NZ Open (itself firmly established as one of the world's premier competitions), where six out of the 15 male Slopestyle finalists were Kiwi, and Nick Hyne and Juliane Bray won the male and female categories.

The industry

Kiwi locals document their place in the snowboarding world pretty passionately, through magazines such as *Manual*, *Australian and New Zealand Snowboarder* and *NZ Snowboarder*. There are also some great online snowboarding resources, particularly boardtheworld.com, snow.co.nz, boarderzone.com and chillout.co.nz. 540s.com is New Zealand's leading clothing outerwear company.

P: JAMES MCPHAIL

New Zealand: a brief history of snowboarding

1980 → First locals begin to experiment with board design, including Grant Skinner in Queenstown. **1982** → Jim Hoare and Craig Harris make and ride their own boards at Turoa, while Nick and Martin Tansley make their own 'Frostbite' boards. **1986** → Craig Harris sets up Drift Snowboards and becomes NZ's first importer. **1987** → Challenger Sports become first Burton importers in the country. **1988** → *Future NZ Snowboarder* editor Ste'en Webster heads to South Island and hooks up with Dave Partridge, who's been designing and riding his own boards for five years already. Together they rebrand the boards from 'Stix' to 'Snostix'. The first American pros visit NZ that season: Brad Reeser, Zach Bingham, Tony Bouzaid and Shawn Farmer. Reeser opens Yanks, NZ's first snowboard store, which is later sold to locals Jeremy Northcote and Ewan Straight; they change the name to NZ Shred. **1988** → First snowboard comp held at Remarkables, which Brad Reeser wins. A week later, Reeser, Webster and an Austrian rider become first to go heliboarding in NZ. **1988** → First snowboard instructor's clinic in Treble Cone. Locals Ewan Straight and Graham Dunbar in attendance. They go on to form New Zealand Snowboard Instructor's Alliance. **1988** → First NZ halfpipe event held in Treble Cone organized by Henry Van-Asch. **1989** → Craig Harris opens The Boardroom store, while Boarderline shop opens in Ohakune. **1990** → The NZ Nationals take shape in Cardrona and become the traditional focal point for seasons to come. Ste'en Webster becomes the first National Champion, a title he holds for two years running. **Early '90s** → Dani 'Kiwi' Meier is NZ's most successful snowboarder of the period, scoring contracts with Rad Air, Level and Oakley). **1991** → Burton team visit NZ. **1992** → Jon Malcolm-Smith wins Nationals. Later he will start Rib Cage snowboards, the only surviving NZ board manufacturer. **1992** → Dave Partridge is now designing for Apocalypse Snowboards. **1992** → Crighton Bone produces *Tube Retreat*, New Zealand's first snowboard video. **1992** → Jason Ford and Ken Achenbach visit, as do Trevor Graves, Matt Goodwill, Nick Perata and Shawn Farmer. **1993** → Pamela Bell wins Nationals and goes onto dominate NZ snowboarding. **1993** → Burton hands distribution back to local riders after ski distributors Snoworld had taken over. **1993** → *NZ Snowboarder* established. **1993** → Aaron Bolt opens Wide Load in Christchurch.

Riders' tales
The Nutcracker experiment

Names such as Craigieburn, Broken River and Temple Basin form the basis of New Zealand boarding folklore and legend. Mythical tales have been passed down from generation to generation, making these almost primitive Club Fields the holy grail of NZ snowboarding. But do these slopes fit the legend? Are these tall tales or true? Hell yeah!

The adventure begins in Christchurch, the gateway to New Zealand's South Island. Sixty minutes on from Christchurch, you will pass through the town of Darfield, before heading further up the highway to Springfield, where, by now, Simpsons' jokes will be met by locals with a stony silence and murderous glare. At this point it's wise to drop into Chill HQ in front of the Springfield Café, where you can sort all your gear, check on the local conditions and regroup for your assault on the famous Club Fields.

As a word of warning, the success of your assault will then depend on how you deal with the Nutcracker, your mode of transport up the hills in the Club Fields. First impressions may be that it would be easier taking on a bunch of Orcs with a shovel: quad chair, this ain't. The Nutcracker is attached to a harness which you strap on around your waist and thighs. It is basically a clamp which you must use to swing over the rope so that you connect onto the pulley driven rope tows in order to get up the mountain. You'll soon realize that the name is in no way connected to the famous ballet: it pretty much does what it says on the label. The Nutcracker is not only difficult and physically demanding, but also responsible for keeping crowds to the bare minimum.

On leaving Springfield drive another 30 minutes up Highway 73 where you will find the sleepy village of Castle Hill. This is a great base for operations for the days' riding ahead. From here you can access Broken River, which is hidden away in the Craigieburn National Park. The turn-off is 10 minutes beyond Castle Hill and when driving through the dirt road switchbacks, cutting back and forth through treelined slopes, you really do feel that you are about to experience something special and unique. Pulling into the car park you immediately notice the goods lift towering up into the snow-covered trees.

Here you load your boards and backpacks into the goods lift which

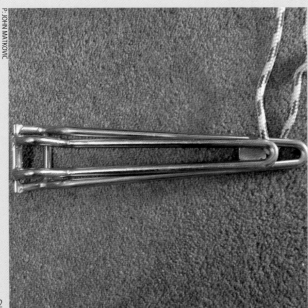
P: JOHN MATKOVIC

L: CRAIGIEBURN P: JOHN MATKOVIC

takes your gear slowly up the hill while you head off up the dark tracks to start a hike through the snow tunnel of trees. After 30 minutes of hiking you suddenly break through the trees and the views are nothing short of spectacular. High above, Broken River beckons… as does your first Nutcracker. For the inexperienced there will be a few humorous failures, much frustration and volleys of expletives. But success is driven both by pure stubbornness and by the knowledge of the delights that lie above.

These delights include two huge bowls (Broken River Basin and Allan's Basin) which have plenty of rollers and kickers just waiting to be hit. There are also the steep chutes of Margaret's Gulch off the peak of Nervous Knob (1815 m) and the many ridge lines off Allan's Basin to drop into. These provide the fun powder face of Sunny Peak, which is off to the left of the Main tow.

There are tons of options and, I kid you not, few people. On some days you might not even see another posse which, considering the NZ$30 day lift ticket, is incredible. There is great cover, wicked terrain, the ski patrol are friendly and more than willing to share a tale or two; the

overall vibe is very casual and relaxed. It's a world away from the crowds and modernization of the commercial resorts.

The next closet resort is Craigieburn, which has a similar set up to Broken River and has a well-earned reputation for its very steep, wide open powder bowls. It is located only another few minutes up

past the Broken River turn off on Highway 73.

From the base, make your way up to the top of the very originally named Top Tow. From there you can stand and look down on the bowls and across the ridge lines that have formed the legend of Craigieburn.

A lot of this legend is based around the magnificent Middle Basin, a massive powder bowl with 600 m of vertical down to the road below the car park. As an indication of its quality, Middle Basin is often compared to a heli run by those who know.

Furthest away from Castle Hill is Temple Basin ski area. It is located 4 km up from Arthur's Pass, and is about a 45-minute drive from Castle Hill on Highway 73. From the car there is a 45-minute hike up through the national park to the first tow rope.

Transworld Snowboarding has been quoted as saying, "If I had to stay in one area, on one mountain to snowboard the rest of my life, it would be Temple Basin, it's that good." That's high praise indeed, but with four separate basins with incredibly diverse terrain and an average of 11.5 m of snow per year, you can see why Temple Basin is spoken in hushed, reverent tones by those that have experienced it.

The whole Club Field 'Nutcracker' experience is truly unique and a very special one in the snowboarding world. While a lot more work is required than what you may be used to, the rewards far, far outweigh the exertion. Take the Nutcracker on. You won't be disappointed.

Check out the following websites for more information:
▶▶ chillout.co.nz
▶▶ brokenriver.co.nz
▶▶ craigieburn.co.nz

R: ALEX SLACK L: BROKEN RIVER P: JOHN MATKOVIC

John 'Ziggy' Matkovic, boardtheworld.com

Queenstown/ The Remarkables

The Town

Less a town and more a winter sports brand name, Queenstown is New Zealand's answer to Chamonix, Whistler and Niseko in that it is a town that has transcended its roots to become a byword for everything 'extreme'. For a certain type of snow traveller, the very name conjures up images of deep, light powder, bungee jumping and a town with a reputation for nocturnal hedonism. Even if you're not interested in snowboarding, Queenstown ranks as an absolute must-see on any South Island itinerary.

Sleeping The central **Discovery Lodge** (gobeyond.co.nz) is the cheap option, though if you want to push the boat out, sample **Brown's Boutique Hotel** (brownshotel.co.nz), Queenstown's take on the boutique hotel trend.

Eating For lunch at a beautiful lakeside location, **Vesta** (vestadesign.co.nz) is the best place in town. No trip to QT would be complete without trying a **Fergburger** (fergburger.co.nz) at 0300 and a pie from the local garage on the outskirts of town. **Dux Delux** (T3442 7745) is the best vegetarian in town.

Bars and clubs Popular with the snowboarding crowd is **Tardis** on Cow Lane. Later, head to **The Bunker** (thebunker.com). Drinks are pricey, but the ambience makes up for it.

Shopping Snowboarders on a budget head to **Fresh Choice Supermarket** on George Street.

Health Queenstown Massage Therapy (messagetherapy@ queenstown.co.nz) is used to dealing with snowboarders.

Internet Budget Communications, above McDs, is a good place to check mail.

Transfer options Get a taxi from Queenstown airport.

Local partners Multi-day passes bought here get you access to Coronet Peak, Mount Hutt and The Remarkables when you want it.

> "Queenstown never stops growing! But it's still a far cry from any of its European counterparts when it comes to the rich 'ski town' feel and is definitely the place to go for nightlife."
>
> *Steven Scott, local rider and heli pilot*

Queenstown is the tourist epicentre of the South Island – for snowboarders and backpackers – and the valley town accessing The Remarkables resort.

⟐ If you like this …
… try Whistler ▸▸p86, Chamonix ▸▸p128, or Niseko ▸▸p210.

⊙ **OPENING TIMES**

Late Jun to mid-Oct: 0900-1600

⊛ **RESORT PRICES**

Week pass (6 days): NZ$355
Day pass: NZ$79
Season pass: NZ$909

ⓘ **DIRECTORY**

Tourist office: T3442 4100
Medical centre: T3441 0500
Pisteurs: T3442 4615
Taxi: T3442 6666
Local radio: Q92 (92 or 92.8 FM)
Website: nzski.com

R:LAURA BERRY P:JAMES MCPHAIL

The Mountain

One of the two main resorts in close proximity to the valley town of Queenstown, The Remarkables reflects New Zealand snowboarding perfectly: relaxed, welcoming and with a healthy interest in high-end freestyle. About 40 minutes' drive out of Queenstown, up one of the hairiest unsealed access roads in the world (let alone New Zealand), the resort consists of three mellow bowls surrounded on all sides by the jagged peaks of The Remarkables range. In aspect, each bowl leads to a central base area indicated by a large, cheerful restaurant; meaning it's impossible to get lost and a great place to go riding with a group of friends. Most riders spending the day here will head unerringly towards the funpark, with its well thought-out blend of kickers, pipes and rails. The locals rip, and after a day here you'll soon understand why. The other great thing about The Remarkables is that it's perfect for beginners and families. The natural geography of the place makes the base restaurant a great spot to meet and watch while others shred, and the beginner slopes are serviced by a centrally located and simple chairlift.

Beginners Complete newcomers will find themselves spending most of the time sessioning the Handle Tow underneath the Base station. Those with a little more experience should start the day by lapping the Alta Chair and sessioning the Turquoise and Alta Green runs before heading over to the Sugar Bowl during the afternoon.

Intermediate The Remarkables funpark is the perfect spot to hone your fledgling freestyle skills, but start the day by taking the Shadow Basin chair and taking the Cat Walk down to the base. Then head to the park, and session the intermediate rails and kickers during the afternoon.

Advanced There is some serious freeriding to be had in The Remarkables, snow conditions allowing. Take the Sugar Bowl chair, and as you do look up to the Anzac Trail that snakes its way along the top of the ridge to the right. From there, the trail accesses two obvious chutes: Gallipoli being the furthest along. Later, hit the park and take the skier's left line to hit the bigger jumps.

Kids Under-10s ride for free. The Handle Tow is the spot to teach them.

Flat light days Take the bus to sleepy Arrowtown, which featured heavily in *Lord of the Rings*. Buses cost NZ$18 and leave three times daily from outside McDonald's in the centre of town.

P: REMARKABLES

P: TIM WARWOOD

P: TIM WARWOOD

🙂 LOCALS DO
- Call it 'The Remarks'.
- Stop to watch the planes land as you drive back into Queenstown.
- Hike to get the good lines.

🙁 LOCALS DON'T
- Drive up at peak times – big queues!
- Forget to check redbullridetoreel.nz for local films made in the resort.
- Feed the parrots.

✅ PROS
- Good park.
- Easy runs for beginners and intermediates.
- Good base restaurant and friendly staff makes it perfect for families.

❌ CONS
- Tiny area.
- Will be tracked quickly after a storm.
- Long journey time from Queenstown.

🌟 NOT TO MISS
Almost as famous as the riding itself are the native Kea parrots.

ℹ️ REMEMBER TO AVOID
The queues on the road at peak times. Getting there half an hour earlier than you think and leaving before the rush starts should save you from getting stuck behind the shuttle buses on the long ride back to QT.

❄️ SNOW DEPTH

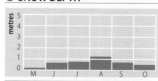

🔁 RELIVE A FAMOUS MOMENT
Go gold panning in Arrowtown and try to find one bigger than 'Honorable Roddy', a 3.1 kg nugget found in 1909.

1943 m	TOWN ALTITUDE
9 km	KM TO AIRPORT
ZQN	AIRPORT
★★★	VEGETARIAN RATING
★★★	INTERNET CAFES
★☆☆	RIDE IN/RIDE OUT
2300 m	HIGHEST LIFT
357 m	VERTICAL DROP
544	RIDEABLE AREA (IN ACRES)
runs not measured	KM OF PISTES
1	NURSERY AREAS
16/0/21	RUNS: BEG/INTER/ADV
0/0	FUNICULAR/CABLE CARS
0/3	GONDOLAS/CHAIRS
1	DRAGS
no	NIGHT RIDING
2	PARKS
1	PIPE
yes	SUMMER AREAS
★★☆ ★★☆	ENVIRONMENTAL RATING
💲💲💲	COST INDICATOR

NEW ZEALAND
THE REMARKABLES

Relaxed, friendly and laid-back, Wanaka is Queenstown's little sister and accesses the resorts of Treble Cone, Snow Park and Cardrona.

)) *If you like this*…
…*try Zillertal* ⇥*p56, La Grave* ⇥*p134, or Las Leñas* ⇥*p272.*

The Town ⊟ ⊘ ⊟

Wanaka is the resort base for Treble Cone, Snow Park (see pages 230-231) and Cardrona (see pages 228-229). Compared to Queenstown, a couple of hours down the road, Wanaka has a sleepy, frontier town feel. It's possible to walk around the centre in five minutes, and this somnolent feel extends to its surroundings, nestled up against Lake Wanaka with the wilds of the South Island on its doorstep. It might only be a matter of time before it succumbs to the commercialization of Queenstown, but for now it really is a must-visit destination for the travelling snowboarder.

Sleeping You can rent houses (basic to plush) from **accommodation-wanaka.com**. In town, **Purple Cow Backpackers** (purplecow.co.nz) is world-renowned for clean, cheap rooms. The **Edgewater Resort** (edgewater.co.nz) has a premium location on the Wanaka lakefront.
Eating Kai Whakapai (kaiwanaka.co.nz) is pricey but does great eggs benedict. Try the

⊛ **OPENING TIMES**
Late Jun to early Oct: 0900-1600

⑤ **RESORT PRICES**
Week pass (6 days): NZ$299
Day pass: NZ$89
Season pass: NZ$1299

① **DIRECTORY**
Tourist office: T3443 1233
Medical centre: T3443 1226
Pisteurs: T3443 7443
Taxi: T3443 7999
Local radio: Wanaka National Radio 91.4 FM
Website: treblecone.co.nz

Doughbin Bakery for more legendary NZ pies and sandwiches, while locals rate **Tuatara Pizza Co** as an absolute must.
Bars and clubs **Red Rocks** is the local snowboarding hangout, while **Slainte** is the obligatory Irish bar in town. **Shooters** enjoys a great view of the lake and nice deck on which to sit and watch the sunset.
Shopping Visit **New World Supermarket** for cheap food or head up Helwick Street for snowboard gear (BASE, Quest, Cheapskates).
Health Wanaka Physio (Wanaka.Physio@xtra.co.nz) is owned by NZ Olympic coach Gin Bush.
Internet **Wanaka Web Ltd** (3 Helwick Street) has many terminals

❝❞

Wanaka is relaxed, closer to the better resorts, and has some stunning scenery to enjoy after a day's riding.

Tom Wilmott, pro snowboarder and local heli guide

and a couple of laptop points.
Transfer options Regular buses run from Wanaka and Queenstown, as well as most of the large NZ towns. Try wanakaconnexions.co.nz.
Local partners Separate passes are needed for Treble Cone, Cardrona and Snow Park, but deals are available at any of Wanaka's many adventure centres.

P: TREBLE CONE RESORT

P: JAMES MCPHAIL

The Mountain

In an area of ski resorts that struggle for area, 'TC' likes to shout about the fact that it is the South Island's biggest resort. The onus here is on freeriding, and terrain particularly well suited to intermediate and advanced riders. Set around the three large bowls, the runs are longer, steeper and more varied, and there is some challenging freeriding to be accessed easily from the lift system. That said, some of the other common themes of the archetypal Kiwi ski area are present and correct here: a sketchy access road and excellent beginner facilities being among them. Those looking to do some actual snowboarding will also find much to keep them occupied at Treble Cone. And how about the views? Even in an area with a heart-stopping aspect around every corner, the vista across Lake Wanaka from the car park will warm the heart of even the most unsentimental rider.

Beginners Treble Cone's beginner facilities are extremely well designed. Situated next to the base, complete beginners will spend most of their time lapping the bottom 'platter' list as they get the basics. Later, the lengthy Triple Treat run criss-crosses the front of the resort and offers a good opportunity to work on turning technique.

Intermediate Get some metres under your base by heading to the lengthy Main Street piste. At 2 km it's a good, steepish run that loops down back to the base of the resort. If the snow is good, head to the top of the front chair and err skier's left towards the Matukituki Bowl. The terrain is good, but be quick: on powder days it

is very popular. In the Saddle (back) bowl, take the Saddle Quad and sample the new Upper High Street piste.

Advanced TC is famed for its freeriding, and snowboarders who have made the NZ trip wondering where all the *Subjekt: Haakonsen* terrain is might have their question answered here. It's generally excellent, but keep a special eye out for the new Mototapu Chutes off the back of the Saddle Basin. These hold extremely involved, yet enjoyable terrain, and are recommended for confident freeriders. Beware of dropping too low, as you'll need to walk out. It's worth exploring though.

Kids Some kids facilities at TC, including a Junior Ski School and a minded crèche, although locals recommend Cardona as a more suitable resort for young kids.

Flat light days It's still possible to have a fun day during flat light at TC, with the front pistes in particular challenging during low visibility.

R: UNKNOWN P: TREBLE CONE RESORT

😊 LOCALS DO
- ✅ Call it 'TC'.
- ✅ Ride Treble Cone when the light is bad.
- ✅ Hike to the summit ridge and look at the views of Mount Aspiring.

😠 LOCALS DON'T
- ❌ Forget their skateboard – Wanaka has a park.
- ❌ Get too excited about the funpark rumoured to be opening in 2006 – although it could be amazing.
- ❌ Forget to enter the Mount Baker style Natural Slalom race held every September.

✅ PROS
- ✅ Interesting steep terrain.
- ✅ Very good for backcountry hiking.
- ✅ No jibbers – for once!

❌ CONS
- ❌ Expensive.
- ❌ Piste patrollers. They will have your pass at the merest blink.
- ❌ That access road!

⭐ NOT TO MISS
Backcountry Heli located at Sun 'n Snow Business on Ardmore Street in Wanaka (heliskinz.com).

ℹ️ REMEMBER TO AVOID
Driving up the access road in anything but a 4WD. Chains are a pain!

❄️ SNOW DEPTH

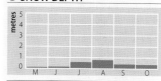

🎬 RELIVE A FAMOUS MOMENT
Lord of the Rings, starring Orlando Bloom, Ian McKellan, Ulggo Mortensen, Sean Bean, Liv Tyler, Cate Blanchett and more …

300 m	TOWN ALTITUDE
76 km	KM TO AIRPORT
ZQN	AIRPORT
★★★	VEGETARIAN RATING
★★★	INTERNET CAFES
★☆☆	RIDE IN/RIDE OUT
1960 m	HIGHEST LIFT
833 m	VERTICAL DROP
3358	RIDEABLE AREA (IN ACRES)
runs not measured	KM OF PISTES
1	NURSERY AREAS
not measured	RUNS: BEG/INTER/ADV
0/0	FUNICULAR/CABLE CARS
0/2	GONDOLAS/CHAIRS
2	DRAGS
no	NIGHT RIDING
1	PARKS
0	PIPE
yes	SUMMER AREAS
★★★ ★★☆	ENVIRONMENTAL RATING
💲💲💲	COST INDICATOR

NEW ZEALAND
TREBLE CONE

Cardrona

> ❝❞
> Cardrona has the best terrain in terms of long, drawn-out runs, because you can actually get some riding in before having to stop again!
>
> *Adam Gendle, pro snowboarder*

Known primarily as a family resort, Cardrona has a huge commitment to providing excellent snowboarding facilities and is the best single option in the Wanaka region for a good mix of everything.

◗ *If you like this* …
…*try Les Arcs* ▸▸*p142, or Keystone* ▸▸*p364.*

R: JAMES CARR P: JAMES McPHAIL

The Mountain

Cardrona is probably the most well-rounded of the NZ resorts. The terrain is spread out over a couple of mellow bowls, and there's enough to keep snowboarders of every standard happy. The runs are practically European in length, and there is a diverse amount of terrain within the resort boundaries. Off the back you'll find serious terrain for those willing to explore and hike, while well-maintained park and pipe facilities help to explain why Cardrona is competing with Snow Park for the local freestyle market.

Beginners Cardrona has plenty of mellow terrain on which to build confidence. There are three magic carpet lifts for beginners and, in the MacDougalls Quad chair, a lift that leads to easy, wide, learner pistes. First-time packages are available – check the website for more.

Intermediate Head to the Playzone park, specifically designed for mid-level riders. Equally as much fun are the pistes of Captain's Basin, so warm up there before heading to the park. If there's powder, cruisey turns await in Powderkeg and Scum Valley.

Advanced From park to pow, 'Cards' has the lot. Freeriders who score it well want to head to the steep chutes of Arcadia, or look for the secret chute accessed via Captain's chair. If it's not on, head over to the Heavy Metal terrain park under the Whistle Star Express chair. And then there's the pipe . . .

Kids Excellent crèche facilities and a snowboard school help to explain Cardrona's family friendly rep.

Flat light days Check out the fighter pilot museum on the edge of town.

Local partners None.

P: JAMES MCPHAIL

⏱ OPENING TIMES
Late Jun to early Oct: 0845-1600

💲 RESORT PRICES
Week pass (6 days): NZ$330
Day pass: NZ$74
Season pass: NZ$1140

ℹ DIRECTORY
Tourist office: T3443 1233
Medical centre: T3443 1226
Pisteurs: T3443 7411
Taxi: T3443 7999
Local radio: Q92 (92 FM or 92.8 FM)
Website: cardrona.com

😎 LOCALS DO
- Eat the pies from Hammer'n'Nail in Wanaka's industrial area. Best in town.
- Stop for a beer at the legendary Cardrona Hotel.
- Eat at the Noodle bar on the hill.

🚫 LOCALS DON'T
- Just shred the park – check the whole hill out before heading straight there.
- Call it Cardrona. It's 'Cards' round here.

👍 PROS
- Higher, drier: the snow quality tends to be the best in the region.
- Excellent park, pipe and SBX course.
- High-speed quad means many runs.

👎 CONS
- Driving up the access road
- Often busy, especially during school holidays.
- If it's a whiteout, visibility is seriously limited.

⭐ NOT TO MISS
A hike up to the summit to enjoy the incredible views back down towards Lake Wanaka, and the best freeriding if it has snowed.

ℹ REMEMBER TO AVOID
NZ school holidays: end of June to mid July and end of September.

❄ SNOW DEPTH

⭐ RELIVE A FAMOUS MOMENT
Head to Stuart Landsborough's *Puzzling World* to see this local celebrity's strange theme park.

1669 m TOWN ALTITUDE

58 km KM TO AIRPORT

ZQN AIRPORT

★★★ VEGETARIAN RATING

★★★ INTERNET CAFES

★☆☆ RIDE IN/RIDE OUT

1990 m HIGHEST LIFT

390 m VERTICAL DROP

790 RIDEABLE AREA (IN ACRES)

runs not measured KM OF PISTES

0 NURSERY AREAS

5/13/7 RUNS: BEG/INTER/ADV

0/0 FUNICULAR/CABLE CARS

0/3 GONDOLAS/CHAIRS

0 DRAGS

no NIGHT RIDING

2 PARKS

1 PIPE

no SUMMER AREAS

★★★☆ ENVIRONMENTAL RATING

$ $ $ COST INDICATOR

NEW ZEALAND
CARDRONA

Snow Park

More like a skate park than a snowboarding resort, Snow Park might just be ushering in a new era of snowboarding-specific riding areas.

If you like this . . .
. . . try Avoriaz ▸▸ p124,
Hemsedal ▸▸ p250, or
Mammoth ▸▸ p366.

66 99

This one lift freestyle hotspot is the dream of every snowboard park monkey worldwide. It does exactly what it says on the tin: jumps rails and the best pipe in the southern hemisphere. It's perfect!

Tim Warwood, pro snowboarder

R: KAZUHIRO KOKUBO P: JEFF CURTES/BURTON SNOWBOARDS

The Set-up ⛰❄☺

It might be one of the smallest, but New Zealand's Snow Park is easily one of the most forward-thinking resorts in the world. True, other resorts such as Big Bear and Mammoth have embraced the possibilities of freestyle snowboarding, but with its welcoming atmosphere, non-stop tunes and lift queue of super-pros rubbing shoulders with beginners, Snow Park is unique.

The first time you arrive at Snow Park it can be overwhelming, as you struggle to take in the sheer number of rails, jumps, hips and halfpipes being endlessly sessioned by hordes of tiny riders. Once you're used to the video-game-like spectacle though, you begin to make out the endless lines available for riders of every standard, from beginner to expert.

Beginners With jumps not much bigger than moguls, and ride-on straight and rainbow rails, it's the perfect set-up to start developing your freestyle skills.

Intermediate Warm up on the beginner-line while the snow softens up. Then head over to the medium kicker lines, before sessioning the pipe in the afternoon, finishing the day by taking on the step-up.

Advanced Get the pipe in the morning while it's at its quickest, then spend the afternoon hitting the big kicker line on skier's left. Finish the day with a quarterpipe session.

Kids Small kids probably shouldn't really be riding here, but confident kids with a yen for freestyle should take on the beginner kicker and rail lines.

Flat light days If the light is really bad, Snow Park isn't really an option.

Local partners None.

◎ OPENING TIMES

Late Jun to late Oct: 0900-1600

⑤ RESORT PRICES

Week pass (6 days): NZ$279
Day pass: NZ$66
Season pass: NZ$1099

● DIRECTORY

Tourist office: T3443 1233
Medical centre: T3443 1226
Pisteurs: T3443 9991
Taxi: T3443 7999
Local radio: Wanaka National Radio 91.4 FM
Website: snowparknz.com

☺ LOCALS DO

● Stay late at the park to see if the lovely girls at the café are giving away any free cakes.
● Talk to the world's best pros. Well, they're all there riding anyway…
● Head to the local spa at Oakridge to sample one of the 10 hot pools under the stars.

☹ LOCALS DON'T

✗ Ride the park without a pass. You'll get caught, and it'll make the papers.
✗ Try the access road with dodgy brakes – it's pretty common for people to get stuck.
✗ Lie in. When Frank Wells is shaping the pipe, it's worth getting first lift.

✔ PROS

● Freestyle heaven.
● Lines for all standards.
● Pro-watching.

✗ CONS

✗ Little accommodation – most stay in Wanaka or Queenstown.
✗ Not for freeriders.
✗ Lift queues.

ⓘ REMEMBER TO AVOID

Lunch gets busy in the café, so pack some sandwiches or get there a little early to maximize riding time.

☺ NOT TO MISS

Snow Park is great for more imaginative lines, so keep an eye out for innovations like the step-up jump!

❉ SNOW DEPTH

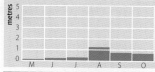

☺ RELIVE A FAMOUS MOMENT

Shaun White's climactic section in *The White Album* was filmed at Snow Park on specially devised kickers and rails.

R: UNKNOWN P: JEFF CURTES/BURTON SNOWBOARDS

1550 m	TOWN ALTITUDE
60 km	KM TO AIRPORT
ZQN	AIRPORT
★★★	VEGETARIAN RATING
★★★	INTERNET CAFES
★☆☆	RIDE IN/RIDE OUT
1530 m	HIGHEST LIFT
110 m	VERTICAL DROP
80	RIDEABLE AREA (IN ACRES)
runs not measured	KM OF PISTES
0	NURSERY AREAS
0/0/0	RUNS: BEG/INTER/ADV
0/0	FUNICULAR/CABLE CARS
0/1	GONDOLAS/CHAIRS
0	DRAGS
yes	NIGHT RIDING
1	PARKS
1	PIPE
no	SUMMER AREAS
★★★ ★★☆	ENVIRONMENTAL RATING
⑤⑤⑤	COST INDICATOR

NEW ZEALAND
SNOW PARK

R: MITCH REED L: HEMSEDAL, NORWAY P: DEAN 'BLOTO' GRAY 2007 BURTON SNOWBOARDS

Mitch Reed heavily involved in a classic Hemsedal late season session.

Scandinavia

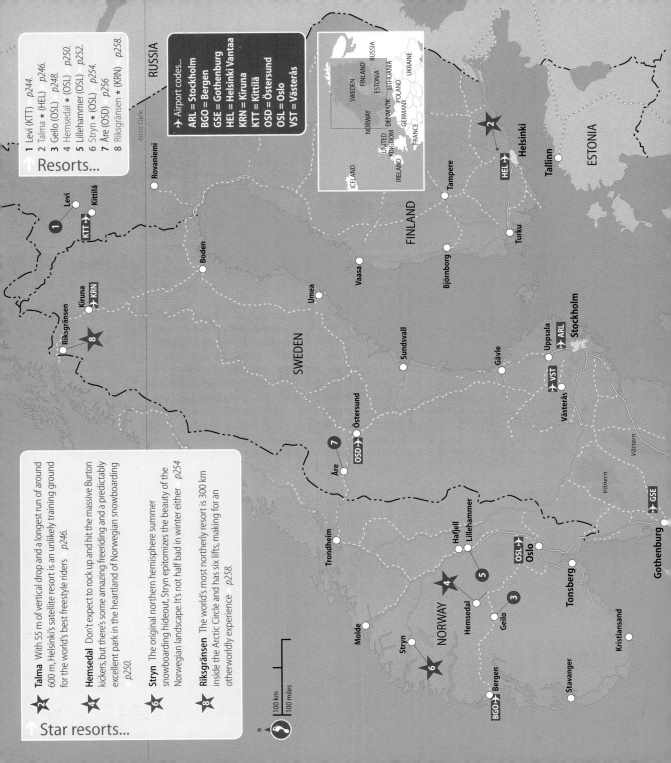

Resorts...

1 Levi (KTT) ► p244.
2 Talma ★ (HEL) ► p246.
3 Geilo (OSL) ► p248.
4 Hemsedal ★ (OSL) ► p250.
5 Lillehammer (OSL) ► p252.
6 Stryn ★ (OSL) ► p254.
7 Åre (OSD) ► p256
8 Riksgränsen ★ (KRN) ► p258.

Airport codes...

✈ = Airport codes...
ARL = Stockholm
BGO = Bergen
GSE = Gothenburg
HEL = Helsinki Vantaa
KRN = Kiruna
KTT = Kittilä
OSD = Östersund
OSL = Oslo
VST = Västerås

Star resorts...

2 Talma With 55 m of vertical drop and a longest run of around 600 m, Helsinki's satellite resort is an unlikely training ground for the world's best freestyle riders ► p246.

4 Hemsedal Don't expect to rock up and hit the massive Burton kickers, but there's some amazing freeriding and a predictably excellent park in the heartland of Norwegian snowboarding ► p250.

6 Stryn The original northern hemisphere summer snowboarding hideout, Stryn epitomizes the beauty of the Norwegian landscape. It's not half bad in winter either ► p254

8 Riksgränsen The world's most northerly resort is 300 km inside the Arctic Circle and has six lifts, making for an otherworldly experience ► p258.

Scandinavia occupies a peculiar place in the snowboarding firmament. There probably isn't another snowboarding region on the planet so full of paradoxes. It has produced many of the world's best riders and has one of the world's most rabid snowboarding scenes, yet the mountains are pretty flat and there's no real industry to speak of. The situation is epitomized by Talma – in scale it equates to little more than a couple of indoor snow slopes, yet it has produced many of the most progressive riders on the planet.

A lot of this is obviously to do with the fact that Scandinavia has a very strong winter sports culture. Skiing is thought to have originated in Norway: kids learn ski jumping at school; *langlauf* (cross-country skiing) is a very common activity; and kids are all hugely into skateboarding. Perhaps it was only natural that snowboarding would take off here so spectacularly. Above all, the Scandinavians adopted snowboarding in a very organic fashion – unlike other European countries, who viewed it with suspicion and only ended up begrudgingly providing shred-specific facilities after years of stubborn resistance.

So look beyond the fact that the mountains are relatively flat and lack the grandeur of the Rockies and the Alps. The parks and facilities are great, and in reality it's not *that* much more expensive than what most westerners are used to. Above all, a trip to Scandinavia, with snowboarding now part of the very fabric, offers something of real substance for the visiting snowboarder. If you're really passionate about riding, you'll never regret checking out one of snowboarding's most northerly outposts.

Scandinavia rating

Value for money
★★☆☆☆

Nightlife
★★★☆☆

Freestyle
★★★★★

Freeride
★★★☆☆

Essentials

Getting there
Finland Finland's major airport is Helsinki, and Talma is a short distance from there. Carriers to Helsinki include **SAS** (flysas.co.uk), **British Airways** (ba.com), **Finnair** (finnair.com) and **KLM** (klm.com). Levi is around 15 km from Kittila airport, so fly to Helsinki then get an internal flight with **Finnair** (finnair.com). There are also charter flights direct from the UK available from ski-flights.com.

Norway Oslo is Norway's major airport, and Lillehammer and Geilo are both nearby. Carriers include **Lufthansa** (lufthansa.com), **British Airways** (ba.com), **British Midland** (flybmi.com), **SAS** (flysas.com), **KLM** (klm.com) and **Ryanair** (ryanair.com). There are also charter flights direct to Fagernes (around 100 km from Geilo) from the UK available from ski-flights.com. There's a daily bus service from Oslo to Stryn called the **Moreekspressen**, run by Fjord1 (fjord1.no), which takes about five hours. Bergen is the nearest airport to Hemsedal – **SAS** fly direct from the UK, or you can get a domestic flight from Oslo.

Sweden Sweden's major airports are Stockholm and Gothenburg, and carriers include **SAS** (flysas.com), **Air France** (airfrance.com), **British Airways** (ba.com), **KLM** (klm.com) and **Ryanair** (ryanair.com). Riksgränsen is in the far north of Sweden so you can either fly to Kiruna airport, or take the overnight train from Stockholm or Gothenburg. This is run by **Connex** (connex.se) and goes direct to Riksgränsen. Ostersund airport is 81 km from Åre, and you can get internal flights from **SAS** (flysas.com) or charter flights direct from the UK from ski-flights.com. See skistar.com for details of transfers to the resort. There are also trains from Gothenburg and Stockholm which run direct to Åre – visit sj.se for details.

Red tape
Norway is the only country of the three to remain outside the EU (though funnily enough it has adopted more EU legislation into domestic law than any other EU country besides Denmark). In most cases (European and North American countries) a valid passport is all that's required to enter Norway, Finland or Sweden for stays of up to three months. Note that in Sweden, if you are travelling with children other than your own you should have a letter of consent from the child's parent or guardian.

Scandinavia price guide (in €)					@		
Finland	2,00	5,00	8,00	0,87	5,00	4,00	1,60
Norway	2,50	6,30	8,20	0,90	1,90	3,80	1,40
Sweden	2,70	4,40	4,00	0,77	2,10	2,20	1,30

Getting around
Car hire is easy enough to organize but it expensive. Each of these countries take drink driving very seriously, and there are harsh prison sentences for offenders – be warned. Legal limits are lower than in Western Europe. Other points to note are that headlights are mandatory at all times of the day in all three countries, and snow tyres are required by law during the months of winter. Beware of collisions with elk and reindeer!

Car hire Most major hire car companies (easycar.com, hertz.com, avis.com) have offices in airports and cities. Usual age restrictions apply.

R: DAN WAKEHAM   L: NARVIK   P: NIKE ACG

> Our mountains are smaller, they receive less snow than the Alps and it's both darker and colder. Powder, as we know it and take it for granted in central Europe, is a rare luxury up here. Same goes for sunshine. On the other hand, in many places you can ride from November to May, which makes the season considerably longer than down south. In the Alps, many riders stay home unless it's sunny and fresh tracks are up for grabs.

Jan Prokes, Volcom team manager

Public transport

Public transport is comfortable and well organized throughout Scandinavia, though it's also pretty expensive. Finland has a good network of trains (vr.fi) and buses (matkahuolto.fi). Internal flights are good but costly. Thanks to Norway's craggy coastline, roads and trains can be quite slow so internal flights are a good option. They're reasonably priced by Norwegian standards, which for the rest of the world means they're still pretty costly. Norway also has a good network of trains (nsb.no) and buses (nbe.no, timekspressen.no) connecting major towns and cities. Public transport in Sweden is excellent, particularly the trains. Planning any travel is easy here –

there's a national public transport authority with an online timetable called Resplus (resplus.se). You can buy Scanrail card (scanrail.com) for cheap rail travel throughout all the Scandinavian countries. Car hire is expensive across the board.

Opening hours and tradition

Shops in Norway generally open from 1000-1700 on weekdays, and from 1000-1500 on Saturdays. Food stores are normally open from 0900-2000 or even 2100. Larger shopping centres tend to open until 2000 on weekdays, and 1800 on Saturdays. Most towns have late shopping on Thursday when the shops stay open until 1900. Shops are closed on Sundays. Shops in Finland and Sweden share a common 0900-1800 opening on weekdays, and 0900-1300/1600 on Saturday (generally 1500 in Finland). Some larger Swedish department stores stay open until 2000/2200, and open on Sundays from 1200-1600.

Finnish supermarkets tend to open 0900-2100 on weekdays, closing at 1800 on Saturdays. Most shops are closed on Sundays, though many smaller grocery shops remain open.

All three countries observe regular European national holiday occasions such as Easter, Christmas and New Year's Day.

→ **Fact file**

Finland
Currency: Euro (€)
Exchange rate:
  US$1 = €0.78
Time zone: GMT +2
Country code: +358
Ambulance: T112
Police: T112
Fire: T112

Norway
Currency: Norwegian
  Kroner (NOK)
Exchange rate:
  €1 = NOK 7.91
Time zone: GMT +1
Country code: +47
Ambulance: T113
Police: T112
Fire: T110

Sweden
Currency: Swedish
  Kronor (SEK)
Exchange rate:
  €1 = SEK 9.12
Time zone: GMT +1
Country code: +46
Ambulance: T112
Police: T112
Fire: T112

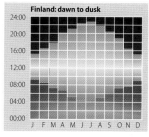

Finland: dawn to dusk

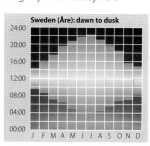

Sweden (Åre): dawn to dusk

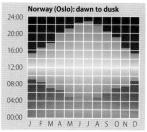

Norway (Oslo): dawn to dusk

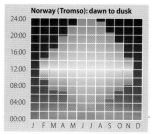

Norway (Tromso): dawn to dusk

JESSICA AND FRIEND P: SHAMUS KING

LAPLAND P: FINLAND TOURISM

Key phrases (Finnish)

Yes *kyllä*
No *ei*
Please *olkaa hyvä*
Thank you *kiitos*
Sorry *anteeksi*
Hello *terve*
Goodbye *näkemiin*
I don't understand *minä en ymmärrä*
Do you speak English? *puhutteko englantia?*

Numbers

1 *yksi*
2 *kaksi*
3 *kolme*
4 *neljä*
5 *viisi*
6 *kuusi*
7 *seitsemän*
8 *kahdeksan*
9 *yhdeksän*
10 *kymmenen*

Days *päivä*
Monday *maanantai*
Tuesday *tiistai*
Wednesday *keskiviikko*
Thursday *orstai*
Friday *perjantai*
Saturday *lauantai*
Sunday *sunnuntai/pyhä*

Key phrases (Norwegian)

Yes *jau*
No *nei*
Please *ver så snill*
Thank you *takk*
Sorry *beklager (excuse me: unnskyld)*
Hello *hallo*
Goodbye *ha det bra (informal: ha det)*
I don't understand *jeg forstår ikke*
Do you speak English? *talar du engelsk?*

Numbers

1 *én/ett*
2 *to*
3 *tre*
4 *fire*
5 *fem*
6 *seks*
7 *syv/sju*
8 *åtte*
9 *ni*
10 *ti*

Days *dag*
Monday *mandag*
Tuesday *tirsdag*
Wednesday *onsdag*
Thursday *torsdag*
Friday *fredag*
Saturday *lørdag*
Sunday *søndag*

Key phrases (Swedish)

Yes *ja*
No *nej*
Please *snälla/vänligen*
Thank you *tack*
Sorry *förlåt (excuse me: Ursäkta mig)*
Hello *hej*
Goodbye *hej då*
I don't understand *jog förstår inte*
Do you speak English? *talar du engelska?*

Numbers

1 *ett*
2 *två*
3 *tre*
4 *fyra*
5 *fem*
6 *sex*
7 *sjö*
8 *åtta*
9 *nio*
10 *tio*

Days *dar*
Monday *måndag*
Tuesday *tisdag*
Wednesday *onsdag*
Thursday *torsdag*
Friday *fredag*
Saturday *lördag*
Sunday *söndag*

Eating

Scandinavian cuisine tends to make very creative use of potatoes, and has more focus on that which can be trapped, shot or hauled out of the sea. Game (elk, reindeer and fowl) and fish (herring, sardines, salmon, cod, sardines and mackerel) are typical Scandinavian ingredients, with smoked salmon being Norway's most notable

P. SIAN HUGHES

contribution to dinner tables around the world.

Pickling is a characteristic Scandinavian pursuit – Sweden and Norway share some very similar traditional dishes made of pickled or fermented fish, some of them such as the Swedish *surströmming* (fermented Baltic herring) being notoriously offensive to the non-Scandinavian nose. *Gravlax* (*gravlaks* in Norwegian) is also very well known – it consists of salmon cured in salt, sugar and dill brine.

To brighten up the otherwise heavy cuisine, the Swedish use traditional conserves such as lingonberry and cloudberry jam. The former will be familiar to anyone who has eaten *köttbullar* (Swedish meatballs).

Breads, cheeses and jams are typical breakfast items, with *knäckebröd* (a kind of crisp, flat bread) being very common in Sweden. Yoghurt and fermented milk (such as the Swedish *filmjölk*) are also likely to be at hand. If you're in Finland then expect to eat lots of the delicious *ruisleipä* (a dark, traditional rye bread). Other traditional Finnish dishes include *kaalikääryleet* (boiled cabbage leaves filled with rice and minced meat, then covered with dark syrup and oven baked, commonly eaten with boiled potatoes and lingonberry jam), *mykyrokka* (a meaty soup with dumplings) and *mustamakkara* (a type of blood sausage). The Finnish even have a dish called *kalakukko*. It is very similar to the Cornish pasty.

Drinking is notably different in these three countries than in the rest of Europe. Aside from licensed premises such as pubs and restaurants, sales of alcohol are monopolized by government owned enterprises. In Sweden it's *Systembolaget*, in Finland it's *Alko* and in Norway it's *Vinmonopolet*. Other retailers are allowed to sell very weak alcoholic drinks such as certain beer or cider (ie in Sweden you can buy beer of up to 3.5% alcohol in shops).

Scandinavians absolutely love drinking coffee, and rank among the biggest coffee drinkers in the world. Tipping is not customary – usually, a small service charge is automatically added to hotel or restaurant bills. And bizarrely for a country renowned the world over for being expensive, mountain restaurants in Norway are in fact cheaper than they are in France. Though perhaps this says more about France than it does about Norway.

Language

Swedish and Norwegian both belong to the North Germanic group of languages, and are mutually intelligible to a certain degree. Thanks to an excellent education system, most Norwegians and Swedes speak a very high standard of English (and often French and German too), so it's easy for most foreigners to get by. Though Finland is officially bilingual (in Swedish and Finnish), the vast majority of the population (around 93%) count Finnish as their mother tongue. Unlike Swedish and Norwegian, it's difficult to learn. It's impossible to guess what a Finnish word might mean, so getting around can be difficult. But don't worry – as in the rest of Scandinavia, the overwhelming majority of Finns speak English remarkably well.

Crime/safety

Scandinavia must rank as one of the safest and most crime free areas of the world to visit. Petty crime such as pickpocketing does occur, though on a much smaller scale than the rest of Europe. As with any other country, the risk increases in busier areas in the larger cities, particularly during the tourist-heavy summer months.

Health

The Scandinavian standard of healthcare is very high, particularly in Norway. EU citizens should obtain a European Health Insurance Card (EHIC), which entitles them to emergency medical treatment on the same terms as Finnish, Norwegian or Swedish nationals. This doesn't cover non-urgent medical treatment or repatriation so having additional comprehensive medical insurance is highly recommended.

Lift chat

The Talma scene

Just over 5.2 million people live in Finland, around 515,000 of those in Helsinki, the Finnish capital. Finland, then, is really a pretty small country, which is puzzling when you consider the number of pro snowboarders to come out of the place. Of all the men's halfpipe finalists at the Turin Olympics, three of them were Finnish, which would appear to be wildly disproportionate with the amount of people there must be in Finland who snowboard.

So what gives? Are the Finns simply better than the rest of the world at snowboarding? Well, in many respects, yes. And that's largely thanks to a small resort near Helsinki called Talma, where the bulk of Finnish snowboarders cut their teeth.

Talma might well be the perfect training ground for freestyle riding. With a vertical drop of only 55 m and a longest run of only 600 m, it consists of little more than a funpark with a series of jumps, hips, a pipe and some rails. Riding at Talma consists of hitting jumps, getting on the lift, then hitting more jumps, run after run after run. The limited nature of the terrain and the high repeat factor encourages a large bag of tricks, and a dogged consistency in landing them. Furthermore, thanks to the cold and rainy local climate the snow is often very firm, if not bulletproof ice. As Finnish über-pro Joni Malmi says, "Talma is as close to as skatepark as a snowpark gets".

So when it comes to learning to snowboard in Talma only the very hardy prevail. This has two noticeable effects: firstly, the Finns learn incredible edge control right from day one. And secondly, they're not at all intimidated by a massive, icy park jump (and in a sport where people are hell bent on jumping off massive, icy park jumps, you'll consent that this is a considerable boon). Rain in Talma, according to Finnish pro Aleksi Vanninen, is "kind of like the Finnish equivalent to a powder day. Kids go nuts when it gets soft and slushy".

When the Finns travel to mountains abroad, they must think the rest of the world don't know how good they've got it. But next time you see one of them stomp a switch 1080 on an icy, uninviting looking park jump, just remember that they've probably done the same trick a thousand times on a far icier and even less inviting kicker in Talma.

R: UNKNOWN P: NATALIE MAYER

Snowboarding Scandinavia

'Norway has a lot of nice, steep and pretty big mountains, but there are no really good lifted resorts. There are a bunch of small resorts that are good, but no big mountain resorts – well, maybe two that are almost there, but not really. I think there are plans to build a gondola on a big mountain close to Molde – a lot of people already hike it, and it works pretty well. I think more foreigners than local people use the mountains – most of the guys here in Norway don't know what's in their backyard. It's the west coast and the northern parts of Norway that have the best peaks, but following storms the snow is not always good. It's very difficult to get a heli and a snowmobile permit in Norway. As King Harald says: the walks are the second best thing about it!' Terje Haakonsen, pro snowboarder

For people used to the steeps of Switzerland, the scale of France or the powder of Canada, Scandinavia isn't the most obvious place to go on a snowboarding trip. But when you actually sit down and look at the facts it's puzzling why this should be so. Finland, Norway and Sweden all have a long tradition of alpine sports; each country has long, harsh winters; and each country has produced some of the best snowboarders the world has ever seen. And here's the point: if Scandinavia has a stronghold on the sport on an international level, then surely it must have some good places to go riding? Well, yes. And while it's often said that the only reason the Finns, Norwegians and Swedes are so good at freestyle riding is because they don't have any decent mountains to ride, it's simply not true. This is a myth that anyone who has ever ridden at Riksgränsen or Hemsedal will be able to quickly dispel. True, they're low, and neither of them can even come near the vertical drop of most of the Alpine resorts, but their

Finland has a lot of small but good resorts that are mainly designed for snowboarders these days, with loads of rails and good jumps. Talma is my favourite – you take one lap in one minute so you get to practise a lot in one day. And if you are into street handrails and stuff, Finland is the place to go. Cops take pictures of us shredding rather than kick us out. And we have rails all over the place. Helsinki has over 100 legit handrails!

Eero Ettala, pro snowboarder

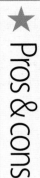

northerly latitudes mean they enjoy high snowfall and a low snowline, and there are some surprisingly large areas with some surprisingly fun terrain. However, it *is* true to say that they ride a lot of park here, and

R: AL BLACKSHAW L: ÅRE P: JAMES MCPHAIL

R: MATTY HARRIS L: ÅRE P: JAMES MCPHAIL

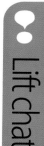

Long live the king

In 1998, with snowboarding about to debut at the winter Olympics in Nagano, Norwegian rider Terje Haakonsen announced his boycott of the games, citing corruption in the International Olympic Committee as his reason.

At the time, Haakonsen was unquestionably the best snowboarder in the world. Other competitors admitted that to win the halfpipe title in Nagano would be a hollow victory with the world's best rider not in attendance. To take such a stand while at the height of your career would be – for most people – unthinkable. Not for Terje.

Terje is one of snowboarding's quirkier characters. Private, unpredictable and notoriously difficult to interview, he's a rider who has always let his talent speak for him. And it speaks pretty loudly: not only has he won pretty much every contest he's ever entered, but he's considered by the majority of his peers to be the best snowboarder who ever lived. The anecdote about the infamous Mount Baker Banked Slalom event is instructive. Terje was penalized for turning up late by being forced to ride his qualifying heat switch. He won this, then went on to win the overall title by a margin of over two seconds on a course where tenths of a second count. When asked about the craziest thing he'd ever seen on a snowboard, Shaun Palmer unhesitatingly replied "the time that Haakon won the Baker Slalom switch".

As if everyone weren't in awe enough of Terje's riding, along came 1996's *Subjekt: Haakonsen*, a 20-minute movie devoted entirely to Terje and friends. This contained footage of the man not only ruling the pipe as expected, but tearing up the whole mountain in a way which had never been seen before, picking insane lines with cutting-edge freestyle thrown effortlessly into the mix. Watching someone ride with that level of control, balance and skill was frankly awe-inspiring. It was a display of supreme confidence from start to finish, and it still stands up to this day.

Since then Terje has gone on to wow people with standout freeride sections in every movie he appears in. Fashion comes and goes, and styles of riding become dated. But while Terje's style may no longer be popular among the sport's style police, his riding has yet to date because it has yet to be surpassed.

R: TERJE HAAKONSEN P: DEAN 'BLOTO' GRAY 2007 BURTON SNOWBOARDS

when you consider the extent of the facilities they have it's not surprising. Even Talma manages to get together a park good enough to shame pretty much any park in France. And it's this forward-looking attitude to snowboarding that explains why the Scandinavians remain at the top of their game.

Conditions

Scandinavia experiences long, harsh winters though since the resorts span a huge longitudinal distance there are correspondingly large regional variations in weather. The main factor here is the daylight – during mid winter sunlight is a scarce commodity, and many people find this off-putting. As Volcom team manager Jan Prokes points out, "Scandos are used to flat light and icy conditions. Anything better than that is a bonus".

When to go

Unfortunately it's the dark months of mid winter when Scandinavia gets the best snow, but if you're into slushy park riding then spring is an ideal time to visit – the parks begin to come into their own, and there are long hours of daylight, particularly in far northerly resorts such as Riksgransen. This is when all the Hemsedal super sessions take place. Riksgränsen is open year round – midnight sun riding at its finest.

Ingemar's air

While the progression of snowboarding over the years has been characterized by slow, steady advances, there have been various pivotal moments where the standard has lurched violently forward. Every so often, someone comes along and does something that, at the time, no one else thought was possible: Johan Olofsson's crazy descent in the movie *TB5*, Terje Haakonsen winning his heat riding switch at the Mount Baker Banked Slalom, or – perhaps most memorably of all – Ingemar Backman's monstrous backside air.

Yes, *that* air. The scene was Riksgränsen, in the summer of 1996. At the time Riksgränsen was one of the main summer snowboarding destinations, which all the pros would converge on each year. Ingemar's feat had such a huge impact that even now, a decade later, it's still simply referred to as 'Ingemar's air'. Looking at it in today's context, it still looks absolutely massive. So massive, in fact, that it wasn't topped for another five years, when Heikki Sorsas sailed comfortably into the record books with a whopping 9.5-m air on the quarterpipe at the 2001 Arctic Challenge in Norway.

But even so, it's worth remembering that Heikki did this on a perfectly shaped quarter with an enormous transition, in a world where people knew that airs this big were – at least in theory – possible. What Ingemar did on that small, hand-shaped quarter in Riksgränsen was so far beyond its time that it still stands out as one of the craziest things ever to be done on a snowboard. He was literally flying into the unknown.

Norway is basically a pretty harsh country during the winter. We have a lot of bad weather and bad light conditions. Luckily, bad weather provides a lot of snow. And a lot of resorts have night riding. This makes most Norwegian snowboarders unspoiled, creative and highly motivated. From Easter onwards it's a blast. Just look at any of the photos from the Hemsedal sessions. I think that Norway is one of the best places to go snowboarding, because we are forced to be creative, and we learn to work hard for the shots we get. Take a walk on the wild side, and explore the many secret areas we have here. Because it is truly the best when the weather is on our side.

Preben Stene Larsen, Norwegian local

L: HEMSEDAL PARK P: HEMSEDAL TOURISM

L: NORTHERN FINLAND P: CHRIS MORAN/HOTSHITPICTURES.COM

Well the most important thing to know is how good it is. Plus, all the mountains/hills are so small that you can take over a hundred runs per day in the slope. Another good thing – besides the gorgeous women – is that the standard of the parks is really good, people speak English and in general they're pretty helpful.

Anders Neuman, Editor in Chief, Transition

Off-piste policy

Refreshingly for anyone used to the restrictive policies of Canadian or North American resorts, you can pretty much go where you want here. You're on your own if you venture off the beaten track though – make sure you're prepared with all the relevant safety equipment, and know how to use it.

Secret spots

Most of the resorts are comparatively small, with a large number of very good riders, so competition can be high. Many of the resorts have a lot of local riders that live there year round – genuine locals. Some people, particularly younger riders, can become a bit testy on occasion, although that said you'll also meet people who literally can't wait to show you around. It's the old tried and tested formula: be nice to people, and you'll reap the rewards.

Freestyle

Freestyle riding is massive in Scandinavia, and the standard is high. Many of the resorts work closely with pro riders to make sure that their parks are cutting edge, and this is something they take great pride in. They're also very supportive of snowboarding events, such as The

Arctic Challenge in Norway or *The Battle* in Sweden. Mountains such as Talma (essentially one large funpark) ensure that Finland keeps knocking out world class pros on a regular basis.

The scene

Unlike in the rest of Europe, pro snowboarders have some degree of celebrity in Scandinavian countries – Terje Haakonsen is frequently in the Norwegian papers, and Heikki Sorsa is one of the most famous people in Finland.

There are prominent Scandinavians everywhere you look in the sport: Swede Mads Jonsson made history by airing a 40-m tabletop at Hemsedal in 2005; Heikki Sorsa holds the record for the highest ever air (9.5 m) on a quarter pipe; Terje is widely considered the best snowboarder ever; Eero Ettala and Jussi Oksanen are at the forefront of handrail and kicker riding today; and Johan Olofsson is considered one of the best freeriders ever.

The industry

There are several Scandinavian magazines such as *Playboard* (playboard.no), *Ultrasport* (ultrasport.no) and *Fri Flyt* (friflyt.no) in Norway, *Transition* (transition.se) in Sweden and *Slammer* in Finland. *Playboard* also has an online forum which a lot of the Norwegian riders use, while www.tacky.no and www.tackyworld.com are good sources of local scene info. Scandinavia is home to some massively prestigious contests such as The Arctic Challenge (t-a-c.no) and The Battle, as well as many unheard of ones where the standard of riding is absolutely mind blowing. Rather surprisingly for an area of such stature in the snowboarding world, there are comparatively few snowboard manufacturers – Sweden has **Allian** (alliansnowboards.com), Finland has **Icon** (iconsnowboards.com) and Norway has **Bataleon** (bataleon.com). All the brands are of the smaller, rider-driven type and have big name riders such as Ingemar Backman and Tapio Kuusakoski behind them. Ingemar Backman's clothing label **We** is perhaps the most internationally recognizable Scandinavian snowboard related brand.

....

Scandinavia: a brief history of snowboarding

1988 → Craig Kelly discovers Terje Haakonsen during a summer trip to Stryn. **1990s** → Jakob Wilhelmson comes to prominence through riding at Stryn. His dad was the local cat driver. **1993** → Terje Haakonsen wins the world halfpipe championships. **1995** → Terje Haakonsen wins the world halfpipe championships again. **1996** → Filmmaker Dave Seaone releases *Subjekt: Haakonsen*, a groundbreaking short film featuring the riding of Terje and friends such as Sebu Kulberg and Daniel Franck. The world looks on in amazement. **1996** → Terje qualifies for the Mount Baker Banked Slalom riding switch. He then wins it overall riding forwards. Shaun Palmer later calls this the most impressive thing he's ever seen on a snowboard. **1996** → Ingemar Backman makes history with a 7.5-m backside air at Riksgränsen. Rumours have it that he was heavily hungover and didn't realize how fast he was going. **1996** → Johan Olofsson has what becomes known as 'the Ballistic' section in Standard Films' *TB5* movie. It gets voted 'the most influential snowboard part ever'. **1997** → Terje Haakonsen wins the world halfpipe championships yet again. It's getting embarrassing now. **1998** – Terje Haakonsen boycotts the Nagano Olympics in protest of corruption in the IOC. Daniel Franck goes and wins the silver medal. **1998** → Norwegian rider Jorgen Karlsen patents Triple Base Technology, which he is convinced will prove to be a revolution in snowboard design. He goes on to found **Bataleon** snowboards. **1999** → Dave Seaone releases *The Haakonsen Faktor*, a follow up to *Subjekt: Haakonsen*. **1999** → Rumours begin circulating about a Finnish rider called Jussi Oksanen who snowboards regular but skateboards goofy. He's said to be the next big name. **2000** → Terje Haakonsen and Daniel Franck start The Arctic Challenge, which immediately becomes the world's most prestigious snowboarding competition. **2000** – Jarkko Kauranen launches Icon Snowboards. The brand is a hit in Finland and goes on to become a big seller in the UK. **2001** → Heikki Sorsa breaks Ingemar Backman's highest air record with a 9.3-m effort at The Arctic Challenge. **2005** → On 9 May, Mads Jonsson breaks the record for the world's largest air with a solo session on a 40-m kicker at Hemsedal. He stomps a backside 180 and a frontside 360, clearing a distance of 57 m. **2005** → Antti Autti wins the Super Pipe at the X-Games, defeating Andy Finch, Danny Kass and current Olympic gold medallist Shaun White. He is the first non-American to win it.

Levi, Finland

Classic Finnish snowboarding comfortably situated within the Lappish Arctic Circle. This hugely enjoyable little resort is extremely cold, predominantly mellow, and equipped with a great fun park.

If you like this ...
... try Bansko ▸▸p100, Breckenridge ▸▸p356, or Keystone ▸▸p364.

The Town

With roots in Lapland, 'home of Santa Claus' winter wonderland and reputation as a great base from which to see the Northern Lights, there's a otherworldly vibe about Levi. Although it would be a mistake to call the place a town (it's too remote, and is really a small centre clustered around the lifts) Levi is Finland's flagship resort and as such blends those Lappish roots with the needs and facilities of a modern snowboarding resort very successfully.

Sleeping Try leviski.fi for cheap places. Their central booking office has a wide range of accommodation across the resort. UK operator **Inghams** (inghams.co.uk) are worth looking at as one of the easiest and cheapest ways to sort accommodation in Levi . The four-star **Hotel Levitunturi** has plenty of facilities and comfortable rooms right near the hill.

Eating Try the reindeer pasta at the **Arran Bar and Restaurant**, or head slightly upmarket and take on a Lappish feast at **Kammi**. Take care of fast food fixes at the **Kebab shop** or **Mega Burger** in the Levitunturi.

Bars and clubs Start at the **Panimo** for darts, local ale and a welcome from the usually drunk locals. Then

P. CHRIS MORAN/HOTSHITPICTURES.COM

> Although it's cold and flat all around, the mountain is one of the biggest in Finland. In the spring they get light 24 hours a day. I've had some good trips there over the years – good stuff.
>
> *Nick Hamilton, photo editor,*
> *Transworld Snowboarding*

head to the **Cantina** before ending the night at the legendary **Hullu Pollo** (Crazy Reindeer) club. Hectic.

Shopping Levi suffers somewhat from its purpose-built feel here, although there are three supermarkets, a liquor store and a post office scattered around.

Health Head 10 minutes out of town to **Taivaanvalkeat** for a *kota sauna* – a sauna followed by an ice swim.

Internet The **Levitunturi** has an internet café with laptop points, wireless and terminals.

Transfer options One of Levi's real pluses is its closeness to the airport. It's 15 km from Kittila, meaning the transfer is quick and simple. Shuttle buses run from the airport to meet the daily flights – check finnair.fi for flights and levi.fi for bus times.

Local partners None.

☺ OPENING TIMES
Early Nov to mid-May: 1000-2000

⊙ RESORT PRICES
Week pass (6 days): €117
Day pass: €28,50
Season pass: €320

① DIRECTORY
Tourist office: T16 641246
Medical centre: T16 648630
Pisteurs: T16 641246
Taxi: T16 106441
Local radio: None
Website: levi.fi

The Mountain

Levi isn't the most demanding ski resort in the world in terms of steep, epic freeriding. Still, with 45 well-groomed pistes (15 of them floodlit), a park and a pipe, a little time in Levi quickly shows why those pesky Finns are so damned good at freestyle snowboarding. Still, with the temperature below freezing much of the time, giving the snow no chance to settle into the 'thaw/freeze' cycle that wreaks havoc in normal resort conditions, it's great fun shredding the resort's glistening pistes.

Beginners With no chairlifts and a great big T-bar taking you up the beginner slope, Levi isn't ideal for complete first-timers. Those linking turns will enjoy the resort's wide, well-groomed pistes though. Being so small, the place is pretty easy to negotiate, so a good day would be spent making your way over to the eastern pistes at the back of the slope, before taking the meandering green run that leads back down to the village.

Intermediate Levi is great for intermediates, with easily accessed stashes off the sides of most runs, and wide groomers to boot down. Take a run through the park and then head down to the gondola. At the top, head towards the eastern pistes and cut off the sides of the slope for some mellow powder gradients. Later, go back to the park and get into the gully over on skier's right.

Advanced For advanced riders, it's all about the park here. There are two: a mellow number right by the bottom T-bar, and a whopping, well maintained special that contains a huge number of jumps, as well as a great pipe. Warm up with a few leg burners down the piste, and head in and start hucking. Then join everyone else finding fun lines in the gully.

Kids Kids under seven with a parent (and wearing a helmet) go free, and there's a Kids' Land to get them started. There are also 10 free kids' lifts.

Flat light days There's a lot of traditional Lappish fun to have on flat light days. Try snow-mobiling with arcticsafaris.fi or dog sledding with **Wingren's Farm** (nic.fi/-wingren/). Highly recommended.

☺ LOCALS DO
- Wear a neckwarmer. It's cold.
- Talk to anybody. There's not much else to do round here, making for a very friendly place.
- Ride the park. Well.

☹ LOCALS DON'T
- Go out before 2300. The Crazy Reindeer's infamous karaoke doesn't get going till midnight. Worth visiting Levi for this alone.
- Forget to take a clear lens riding. Chances are visibility will be slight.

✔ PROS
- Brilliant for freestylers.
- The snow stays pristine.
- Amazing nightlife.

✖ CONS
- No chairlifts.
- Small area.
- No freeriding.

♥ NOT TO MISS
The natural gully on skier's right of the main park is a real must-do, with its stashes, hips and transfers. Small lines, infinite trick possibilities.

ⓘ REMEMBER TO AVOID
The World Cup run will give beginners nightmares. It's Levi's steepest run and is usually pretty icy.

❄ SNOW DEPTH

✦ RELIVE A FAMOUS MOMENT
Levi is bang in the middle of Santa Claus terrain. Take a beard and a red coat and relive any present giving moment you like.

206 m	TOWN ALTITUDE
15 km	KM TO AIRPORT
KTT	AIRPORT
★★☆	VEGETARIAN RATING
★★☆	INTERNET CAFES
★★★	RIDE IN/RIDE OUT
531 m	HIGHEST LIFT
325 m	VERTICAL DROP
250	RIDEABLE AREA (IN ACRES)
runs not measured	KM OF PISTES
10	NURSERY AREAS
18/22/4	RUNS: BEG/INTER/ADV
0/0	FUNICULAR/CABLE CARS
1/0	GONDOLAS/CHAIRS
15	DRAGS
yes	NIGHT RIDING
2	PARKS
2	PIPE
no	SUMMER AREAS
★★★ ★★★	ENVIRONMENTAL RATING
	COST INDICATOR

SCANDINAVIA
LEVI

The Town

Scandinavia meets the Baltics in Helsinki. Though the winter streets can appear quiet and the Finns reserved, lurking behind the imposing architecture is a city with an impressive energy. Nose around, get talking to people, and enjoy the novelty of walking to the train station in the morning carrying a board and in full riding getup, surrounded by smartly dressed commuters, with not a mountain in sight.

Sleeping Eurohostel (eurohostel.fi) has clean communal kitchens and saunas in addition to bargain dorm rooms, while the amazing breakfast buffets of the centrally located **Sokos** chain (sokoshotels.fi) will set you up for a week. Sleep in swanky style at the feted **Klaus K** (klauskhotel.com).
Eating Try the **Unicafe** chain (unicafe.fi) for bargain meals, the

Seahorse (seahorse.fi) for traditional Finnish dishes and the **Silvoplee** (T9726 0900) if you're a veggie looking to escape all the meat. You could also try the excellent **Zuccini** (T9622 2907) in Helsinki.
Bars and clubs Uudenmaankatu is the most notorious street for clubs, though Helsinki has no shortage of good but scarily expensive bars. Shoot pool or, if you time it right, catch a premiere of one of this year's new snowboard epics at the **Mockba/Corona/ Dubrovnik** complex (T964 2002); contest and premiere afterparties often seem to end up at **We Got Beef** (T967 9268).
Shopping Stock up on salty licorice and more substantial snacks in the giant **K-Supermarket** in the basement of Kamppi shopping centre. Visit **Lamina** (lamina.fi) upstairs for snow and skate gear.
Health Brave the traditional sauna scrub down at **Kotiharju Sauna** (T9753 1535).
Internet Free wireless and pay PCs at

I've decided that it's pointless to go to the Alps at the start of the season. When Talma opens, it only takes a day to get your riding back.

Eero Ettala, pro snowboarder

mBar (mbar.fi), open practically 24/7 and right between Kamppi and the main train station in the centre of town.
Transfer options It's a 20-minute train journey from Helsinki to Kerava station (€4,50), then a taxi (around €10) or the free ski bus for the 10-minute journey to Talma. Check the timetable on the website – it varies throughout the season.
Local partners None. Most other Finnish ski areas are up north.
Flat light days Get some culture in you at Kiasma, the progressive and architecturally- intriguing Museum of Contemporary Art.

Minuscule in size, mighty in stature, this hill outside Helsinki is the place to learn tricks with tomorrow's stars of snowboarding. Park life by day, Scandi city by night: a win-win combination.

If you like this ...
... try *Snow Park* ▸▸p230, *Big Bear* ▸▸p352, or *Mammoth* ▸▸p366.

P: NATALIE MAYER

The Mountain

'Altitude: 5500cm'. Talma locals are very good-natured about the size of their local hill. After all, it has almost everything you might need on a dark afternoon after work or school: a mellow nursery slope, a short stretch for cruising (okay, straightlining), a pipe, hits of all sizes, a handful of jibs – even a very small mogul patch. There's no need for a trail map. You won't get lost!

Beginners Though there's a perfectly good, wide nursery meadow, learning to ride here is really only worth it if you happen to be in Helsinki for some other reason. Decent equipment – including gloves and goggles – can be rented at reasonable rates.

Intermediate So long as you're all about parks, it's well worth the visit. The kickers are constructed so well that you'll be flying down the smaller line on the front face in no time, and tackling the small jibs.

Advanced More kicker heavy than jibtastic. Lower level advanced riders will progress, but those looking for monster tables and a wide selection of jibs might be disappointed.

Kids The six year olds here are better – and better dressed – than you. Rental gear to fit the smallest rider – though lessons are designed for regulars rather than tourists.

Flat light days Makes no difference – just wait for the lights to come on.

☺ OPENING TIMES

Early Jan to Feb: 1300-2100
Feb to May: 1000-2100

⊙ RESORT PRICES

Week pass: No discount
Day pass: from €18
Season pass: €300

⊙ DIRECTORY

Tourist office: T9169 3757
Medical centre: T9310 6611
Pisteurs: T9274 5410
Taxi: T0100 0700
Local radio: Radio Helsinki, 95.2 FM
Website: talmaski.fi

R: UNKNOWN P: NATALIE MAYER

R: LAURA HILL P: NATALIE MAYER

☺ LOCALS DO

- Ride early during the day if they're past school age: far less crowded.
- Warm up regularly in the family-run cafeteria.
- Keep at it for hours. No wonder they rule the world.

☹ LOCALS DON'T

- Unstrap on the speedy draglifts. Remember to hit the gate as you pass.
- Dress badly: low-key style is the norm.
- Show fear. It's all about the *sisu* (spirit of determination).

✔ PROS

- You'll hit the kickers more in a couple of hours than you would in a week at a larger resort.
- Short tables, long landings; ideal for progression
- No need for early doors – the lifts don't shut until 2100.

✖ CONS

- Dark midwinter. And cold in general. Bring a down jacket.
- Less a resort than an after-school club.
- No freeriding.

⊙ NOT TO MISS

The reindeer over in the trees near the bottom of the nursery slope. Not your average mountain creature.

⊙ REMEMBER TO AVOID

The weekend – at least until you've got used to the park. Swamped with everyone from ex-pros to kindergarteners, the atmosphere is buzzing but the line-up is ridiculous.

⊙ SNOW DEPTH

Figures not available

⊙ RELIVE A FAMOUS MOMENT

Good Old Talma – watch the extras on *Lame* before shredding.

20 m	TOWN ALTITUDE
20 km	KM TO AIRPORT
HEL	AIRPORT
★★★	VEGETARIAN RATING
★★☆	INTERNET CAFES
★☆☆	RIDE IN/RIDE OUT
55 m	HIGHEST LIFT
35 m	VERTICAL DROP
62	RIDEABLE AREA (IN ACRES)
runs not measured	KM OF PISTES
1	NURSERY AREAS
1/8/0	RUNS: BEG/INTER/ADV
0/0	FUNICULAR/CABLE CARS
0/0	GONDOLAS/CHAIRS
6	DRAGS
yes	NIGHT RIDING
2	PARKS
1	PIPE
no	SUMMER AREAS
figures not available	ENVIRONMENTAL RATING
	COST INDICATOR

SCANDINAVIA
TALMA

The Town

Like many of the Scandinavian resorts, Geilo has an almost otherworldly beauty when the light is right. It's also one of the oldest winter destinations in Norway. Today, it's a popular resort among locals with a lot to offer riders of all levels, as well as the home of the Norwegian college for their top riders. Clearly it has some pedigree. As far as the numbers go, it's not the hugest place in our guide. The two main riding areas come down into Geilo, and there are only 20 lifts. That said, in classic Scandi style there are three parks. Overall, this is great place to razz around and work on your freestyle riding – Norwegian snowboarding in a nutshell.

Sleeping Built in 1909 and with a spa and a couple of pools, **Dr Holms Hotel** is one of the more traditional hotels in Geilo, although if self catering and keeping the cost down is a priority, try the **Geilo Apartments** which are within walking distance of the slopes and have free internet. Even cheaper is the **Oen turistssenter/Geilo**

Vandrerhjem, 2 km east of the centre and linked by bus.

Eating Try Halligstuene (T3209 5640) for gourmet local specialities or **Peppes Pizza** (pepper.no) for an informal alternative. **Sofias Café and bar** (geilo.no) has great cakes and pastries.

Bars and clubs Lille Blaa is good for après and has a nightclub for the younger crowd. The other big place is the **Recepten club** in Dr Holms's Hotel. The crowd is a bit older but it's always rammed especially during the holidays.

Shopping Geilo has two sports shops where you get a wide variety of sport goods, including skis, boards and winter clothing.

Health The spa at **Dr Holms Hotel** is the only Shisheido-spa in Scandinavia. Who'd have thought it?

Internet Lille Blaa Café has internet, and so have several hotels.

Transfer options Bergensbanen, the railway between Oslo and Bergen, stops in Geilo. Check nsb.no for details. You can also take a taxi in the town. Buses leave every day: check out nor-way.no for more information.

Local partners None.

⊙ OPENING TIMES

Early Dec to early Jan: 0930-1330
Early Jan to early Feb: 0930-1600
Early Feb to late Apr: 0930-1700

⊙ RESORT PRICES

Week pass (6 days): NOK 1310
Day pass: NOK 295
Season pass: NOK 3570

⊙ DIRECTORY

Tourist office: T32 095900
Medical centre: T32 092250
Pisteurs: No tel number
Taxi: T32 091000
Website: geilo.no

> Geilo is beautiful, and it's a great family spot. Plus, everything is well groomed, and there are three parks to keep up the variety.
>
> *Martine Remsoi, Geilo local*

P: CHRIS MORAN

One of the oldest resorts in Norway, offering great riding, a lot of activities and three good snowparks.

P: CHRIS MORAN

❉ *If you like this …*
… try Alts Bandai ▸▸p206, or Hemsedal ▸▸p250.

P: CHRIS MORAN

P: GEILO TOURISM

The Mountain

Let's be honest, Geilo is not going to make the executives at Vail Resorts lose any sleep. In essence, it is a typical family resort with varied but not extreme terrain. The hill is split between two riding areas – one on either side of the valley – and has a lot of well thought out facilities for visitors, including those parks and a lot of options for families.

Beginners There are a good variety of green and blue runs to the right hand side of the resort. Take the big chairlift from the car park to access this area and wind your way down the slopes. Avoid taking the two man chairlift until you're ready as it leads to some steeper terrain. Make it a goal for the rest of the week.

Intermediate Start the morning by taking the big chair from the base and ride down from the top to Havsdalen. There's a lift here that leads you to the top area of the hill. In the afternoon, head to one of the parks or ask a local to show you some of the safer and mellower off-piste areas.

Advanced Advanced riders are pretty limited unless you want to spend your days lapping the park with the locals. If you do, you're in luck as there are three of them to play in. A good day would be to spend the morning shredding the trails and covering some ground before heading to the park in the afternoon. Again, if there is snow the best option it to hook up with a local to find the goods. They'll certainly be there before you …

Kids The children's area is situated in the lower part of the slopes, and within walking distance to the cafeterias. They have a school for kids, where you can drop them off if you would like to take a ride on your own.

Flat light days Pack the skates, and spend the day marvelling at how much the better the locals are at skating as well as snowboarding in the indoor skate hall.

☺ LOCALS DO
- Ride in the weekdays.
- Bring their own lunch to the slopes, as the cafeterias are a bit pricey.
- Go out on Thursdays and Saturdays.

☹ LOCALS DON'T
- Go out to the clubs as much during the big holidays.
- Wear leather knee-pants, which many of the upper-class tourists wear.
- Strip naked at the after-riding sessions like some tourists do.

✔ PROS
- Thanks to the train stopping at Geilo, it's easy to get to.
- Long winter, stable conditions.
- Well groomed parks.

✖ CONS
- The slopes are good, but a bit short.
- Expensive.
- Bad for freeriding.

♥ NOT TO MISS
The after-riding session at the Recepten pub should really be experienced for the full Scandinavian drinking experience.

ⓘ REMEMBER TO AVOID
The school holidays – it can be very crowded.

❄ SNOW DEPTH

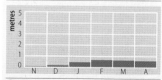

♻ RELIVE A FAMOUS MOMENT
1986's classic *The Flight of the Navigator* – featuring a young Sarah Jessica Parker – has scenes filmed not too far from Geilo.

800 m	TOWN ALTITUDE
230 km	KM TO AIRPORT
OSL	AIRPORT
★★☆	VEGETARIAN RATING
★★★	INTERNET CAFES
★★☆	RIDE IN/RIDE OUT
1178 m	HIGHEST LIFT
378 m	VERTICAL DROP
area not measured	RIDEABLE AREA (IN ACRES)
34 km	KM OF PISTES
4	NURSERY AREAS
19/16/5	RUNS: BEG/INTER/ADV
0/0	FUNICULAR/CABLE CARS
0/6	GONDOLAS/CHAIRS
14	DRAGS
yes	NIGHT RIDING
3	PARKS
1	PIPE
no	SUMMER AREAS
★★★ / ★★★	ENVIRONMENTAL RATING
💲💲💲	COST INDICATOR

SCANDINAVIA
GEILO

Hemsedal, Norway

Easily Norway's most famous snowboarding resort.

⏩ **If you like this . . .**
. . . try *La Clusaz* ▶▶*p132, Happo One* ▶▶*p208*, or *Mammoth* ▶▶*p366*.

The Town 🖥💊🖥

Until 2000, Hemsedal was just another resort that few had heard of outside Norway. Then Burton Snowboards decided to hold the annual Spring Sessions there, inviting the world's top riders and photographers to ride some absolutely enormous park jumps. Suddenly, Hemsedal – a low, generally flat hill a few hours north of Oslo, albeit one with a thriving snowboarding scene – was one of the world's most famous riding resorts. So does it deserve the reputation? Well, sort of. But even if you don't like freestyle riding, there is a lot here to keep interest levels high. Hemsedal is basically a classic Scandinavian hill – pretty flat, astonishingly beautiful, expensive and with a full-on après party scene, as well as some great snowboarding spread over a long season. Here's how to do it.

Sleeping ski-norway.co.uk is a good option for groups looking for flexibility or slightly involved travel arrangements. They can also sort out transfers and standalone accommodation. Hemsedal is a generally small place. The cheapest accommodation (and the place where the locals stay) is at **Moen camping**. Other options are the **Skarsnuten Hotel** (skarsnutenhotel.no) and the **Hemsedal Café Skiers Lodge** (gohemsedal.com). Look at hemsedal.skistar.com for online booking. **Eating** Hemsedal is pretty expensive, but the Hemsedal **Oxen Bar and Grill** is popular and damned tasty. If you're on a budget, get used to the **Experten Sports Bar** and its breakfast, lunch and dinner buffets. In the village, the **Hemsedal Café** and **Pepe's Pizza** are the ones.

Bars and clubs It's all about after-riding in Hemsedal. Try **Hemsedal Café** (gohemsedal.com), **Garasjen** (garasjen.no), **Loftet** and **Hemsen**, described by locals as the 'got to be' place.

Shopping Rimi and Coop are the two local grocery stores.

Health There's a small hospital in Gol, about an hour away. There's also a medical centre in the village with excellent facilities.

Internet Check your mail at **Hemsedal Café** (gohemsedal.com) downtown. Wireless is also available at the **Tourist Office**, **Experten Sportsbar** and the **Welcome Centre**.

Transfer options ski-norway.co.uk

Hemsedal is a dream resort for a photographer. They have the best park, and some great backcountry to work with. They are one for the first resorts to open, and the last one to close for the season. The short distance by car from Oslo makes it an easy access. For me Hemsedal is the best resort in Norway.

Espen Lystad, photographer

arranges transfers from any airport. **Local partners** Hemsedal is a **Ski Star** resort, who also run Salen, Vemdalen, Trysil and Åre.

P: MATT BARR P: JAMES MCPHAIL

☺ **OPENING TIMES**
Mid-Nov to early May:
0900-1630

💲 **RESORT PRICES**
Week pass: NOK 1450
Day pass: NOK 320
Season pass: NOK 4295

ℹ **DIRECTORY**
Tourist office: T32 055030
Medical centre: T31 408900
Pisteurs: T32 055309
Taxi: T32 062112
Local radio: None
Website: hemsedal.com

P: HEMSEDAL TOURISM

The Mountain

Hemsedal is almost comically beautiful. The light here seems to cleanse the air, especially in the early winter, when the sun's low ambit gently works the daylight into various maudlin hues. There are three broad peaks to ride, with well-groomed pistes and quick lifts making it easy to razz around. Off-piste is also pretty easy to get to, and it's fun here to just ride around between the trails, experimenting with the nooks and gullies between the runs.

It goes without saying that the fun park facilities are amazing in Hemsedal, with two parks for expert riders and those just getting to grips with jumps. Above all, Hemsedal's layout and vibe make it a very social mountain for riders of differing abilities. It's great for groups in that way – beginners, intermediates and experts can all go off and ride, and meet at the Ski Stua café at the base for lunch or an après beer and swap stories. And look out for the local pro riders – Mikkel Bang and Mads Jonsson call the place home.

Beginners There's a beginner section at the bottom of the hill, right next to the **Experten Sports Bar**. It's drag accessed, which might be a problem for complete first-timers, but as the longest run is only about 190 m a short hike might be the alternative. Later, you can get on the upper section to work on your turns. Take the long green (11) accessed by the chair. It's a 4-km run and links with some blues as well, so you can get some metres under your board.

Intermediate For intermediates, this is pretty much the perfect mountain. If you like, you can cruise all day long,

and if you want to try the park, you can head into the learner park, which was recently made a kilometre longer and has more lines than you'll ever get to grips with – like a small quarterpipe. If it snows, head to the Tinden area for some amazing, easy to get to powder runs.

Advanced If it isn't snowing, you'll be in the park – considered to be one of the best in Europe. Watch the locals and learn – they all rip! If it snows, you've got a number of options. Take the drag to Totten Bowl, the highest rideable peak in Scandinavia and head skier's left for a nice open bowl. Another very good area is the Totten Skogen (forest) with some sweet tree runs.

Kids Children under six ride for free – nice touch. Then there's an on-slope kindergarten (Trollia) and special family weeks – check the site.

Flat light days There are a lot of trees here, so it's not really a problem.

P: JAMES MCPHAIL

R: ELLIOT NEAVE P: JAMES MCPHAIL

☺ LOCALS DO
- Enjoy a drink. There's a boozy scene here.
- Wake up early to check the weather.
- Ride from Monday to Friday.

☹ LOCALS DON'T
- Give away their secret spots.
- Ride slowly. Everyone is really good here, but the vibe is friendly.
- Party if it's really good on the mountain.

✔ PROS
- Great scene, from nightlife to funpark.
- Extremely beautiful part of the world.
- Good for freestyle.

✘ CONS
- Sometimes icy.
- Not amazing for freeriders used to long, steep faces.

❂ NOT TO MISS
A real powder turn in the rubber forest. Ask the locals...

❶ REMEMBER TO AVOID
It's worth noting that Norway is very expensive, particularly when it comes to alcohol. Take as much duty free in as you can!

❄ SNOW DEPTH
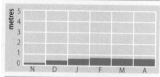

✪ RELIVE A FAMOUS MOMENT
Mads Jonsson's 187-ft frontside 360 is considered one of snowboarding's greatest feats. Recreating it might be a different matter ...

625 m
TOWN ALTITUDE

225 km
KM TO AIRPORT

OSL
AIRPORT

★★☆
VEGETARIAN RATING

★★★
INTERNET CAFES

★★☆
RIDE IN/RIDE OUT

1920 m
HIGHEST LIFT

1295 m
VERTICAL DROP

area not measured
RIDEABLE AREA (IN ACRES)

43 km
KM OF PISTES

1
NURSERY AREAS

19/21/8
RUNS: BEG/INTER/ADV

0/0
FUNICULAR/CABLE CARS

0/6
GONDOLAS/CHAIRS

15
DRAGS

yes
NIGHT RIDING

1
PARKS

2
PIPE

no
SUMMER AREAS

★★☆
★★☆
ENVIRONMENTAL RATING

COST INDICATOR

SCANDINAVIA
HEMSEDAL

The Town

Lillehammer is a small and cosy town situated near Norway's biggest lake, Mjosa. The city has kept its small-town charm, with small shops and cafés, although it has all the facilities of a bigger city. Lillehammer has four alpine ski resorts within one hour of travel time, and the closest of these is Hafjell, a 15-minute drive away.

Sleeping Nordlia cabins and apartments offer housing from six to 16 persons. It's ride in, ride out, located on the north side of the Hafjell Alpine Center. For apartments, **Gaiastova Hafjelltoppen Apartments** are located 950 m above sea level at the top of Hafjell. A good compromise might be the **Hotel Illsetra**, which has apartments with two bedrooms. They serve breakfast and dinner, and lunch on request. Contact Hafjell Booking for different options, or book online at hafjell.no.

Bars and clubs Again, after-riding is when it goes off. **Gaiastova**, at the top of the hill, has a relaxed vibe, while at the base **Ryk og Reis** has live music and 'a happy vibe'. Then there's the **Brenneriet** nightclub, one of the biggest nightclubs in Norway, and the hippest club in Lillehammer.

Shopping Lillehammer has got a very charming main street, with many small cafés and restaurants, and a variety of small shops that ranges from arts and crafts to sports equipment.

Internet There's a wireless connection in the café in the base area. In Lillehammer City you have internet at **Café Banken**, and several hotels.

Transfer options Trains from Oslo and the airport run direct to Lillehammer several times a day, and the train stops in the city centre, check nsb.no for details. Buses go by daily, check out nor-way.no for details.

Lillehammer hosted the Winter Olympics in 1994. The city and the surrounding area is now one of Norway's most popular winter sport's regions.

If you like this ...
... try *Silvretta Nova* ➤➤*p52, Kimberley* ➤➤*p82, or Big Bear* ➤➤*p352.*

OPENING TIMES

Early Dec to late Apr: 0930-1630

RESORT PRICES

Week pass (6 days): NOK 1250
Day pass: NOK 265
Season pass: NOK 2900

DIRECTORY

Tourist office: T6128 9800
Medical centre: T6127 8279
Pisteurs: T6128 9800
Local Radio: P4
Taxi: T6122 2020
Website: hafjell.no, lillehammer.com

66 99

The planning of the Winter Olympics had already started when they built Hafjell Skicenter. They have proved that they did not have the Olympics as a final goal, and have since 1994 continued to invest in the mountain and terrain park. This makes Hafjell a good place to grow up and develop your riding.

Roger Hjelmstadstuen,
pro snowboarder and local

OLYMPIC TORCH RUNNER P: HAFJELL CENTRE

The Mountain

Hafjell is cast from the same mould as the majority of Norwegian and Scandinavian resorts. Given its small area and relatively rolling terrain, they've got to make the best of what they've got. Which is why, as you might imagine, the onus is on parks, and perfect 'intermediate and families' terrain. Specifically, Hafjell's terrain gets flatter at the top of the riding area and gradually steepens as the runs reach the base. That said, it never really gets particularly steep, so it's great fun for a day of shooting around the trails.

Beginners As the terrain flattens out at the summit, much of the beginner runs are at the top of the resort. So take the chair from the base area and then the second chair to the top. These runs tend to be uncrowded and nice and wide, so you can get to grips with the basics.

Intermediate Mid level riders will probably really enjoy Hafjell, as the undulations of the place mean you can cruise around without really worrying about getting into any areas you don't want to be. A good starting point would be to take the two chairs to the top and then take the blue to the left. Follow this to another chair, from where you should keep left until you reach the Marsteinschussen.

Advanced As we've seen, the steeper slopes are lower down, but really advanced riders will be in the park. It's well kitted out, with a wide variety of jumps, rails and a pipe. The big jump is called 'Rogern' – nice touch. If there is any snow, your best bet is to hook up with a local and hope they're feeling kind.

Kids The kids' area is situated in the lower part of the resort. You can safely leave your kid in the nursery area, or with a responsible and qualified member of staff. The school is also good for kids.

Flat light days It's not amazing for flat light riding, so go sightseeing in Lillehammer, or try out the bob and luge track.

☺ LOCALS DO
- Go out in Lillehammer on Thursdays. It's a big night for local students!
- Always hit the slopes early, when they are well-groomed.
- Drink cheap Irish coffee at Bryggeri-kjelleren on Thursdays.

☹ LOCALS DON'T
- Go out to party before 0100.
- Ride in the deck or landing area of a jump. It's a local pet hate.
- Explore the less easily accessible slopes to avoid the big queues that can develop.

✓ PROS
- Direct access by train and car, as it's not far from Oslo.
- Pretty empty.
- Easy, playful slopes.

✗ CONS
- The slopes are not very challenging for advanced riders.
- The park gets crowded during the big holidays.
- Can get a bit icy after a period of mild weather, before the next snowfall.

⊙ NOT TO MISS
On the mountain, it's the park. But Lillehammer itself is beautiful.

ⓘ REMEMBER TO AVOID
Norwegian holidays in mid-February.

❄ SNOW DEPTH
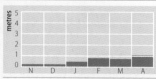

☼ RELIVE A FAMOUS MOMENT
The Heroes of Telemark, starring Kirk Douglas and Richard Harris was filmed around Lillehammer's hills in 1965.

195 m
TOWN ALTITUDE

145 km
KM TO AIRPORT

OSL
AIRPORT

★★☆
VEGETARIAN RATING

★★★
INTERNET CAFES

★★☆
RIDE IN/RIDE OUT

1030 m
HIGHEST LIFT

835 m
VERTICAL DROP

area not measured
RIDEABLE AREA (IN ACRES)

33 km
KM OF PISTES

1
NURSERY AREAS

18/6/4
RUNS: BEG/INTER/ADV

0/0
FUNICULAR/CABLE CARS

1/3
GONDOLAS/CHAIRS

12
DRAGS

yes
NIGHT RIDING

1
PARKS

2
PIPE

no
SUMMER AREAS

★★★
★★★
ENVIRONMENTAL RATING

$$$
COST INDICATOR

SCANDINAVIA
LILLEHAMMER

The Town ⊜⊘⊜

There is a town named Stryn – a beautiful Norwegian village with a decent swimming complex and some supermarkets – but it is around 30 km away from the snow and the lifts and is unlikely to be your point of call. Instead, most people who come here stay at the fantastic Folven Camping Site, around 10 km from the slopes and nestled in a staggeringly beautiful part of the Stryn Valley. It has a pub, a hotel, several cabins and a Stat-Oil petrol station, which serves as the local grocers. In 2005 it merged with the ski area to offer complete 'package' deals.

Sleeping Folven (T57 877900, strynefjellet.com) has several levels of camping from tent pitches (NOK50 per person per night) upwards. For the full experience however, stay in a cabin. The cheapest are NOK600 per night and sleep four. For one with en suite bathroom add another NOK200 per night, and an eight-person cabin with kitchen is NOK1600 per night. Where else could advertise a really battered caravan for NOK2500 for the season?

Eating The **Folven** café serves pizzas and other standards, plus, there's a free kitchen on site. Most people though tend to go for BBQs around a fire.

Bars and clubs The **Folven Pub** or the nearest campfire are the usual drinking dens, but the truly adventurous can head into Stryn for some proper small town nightclub action. Not recommended for the faint-hearted.

Shopping The local **Stat-Oil** garage is the place to buy all groceries. Note that glass bottles and plastic crates can be returned for a part refund and Norway is very recycling conscious.

Health There's a good spa around one hour's drive from Folven, but most people head to the river, the fjord or one of the nearby waterfalls for some refreshing natural cleansing. You couldn't ask for a more beautiful setting.

Internet The **Folven** café is a Wi-Fi hotspot. And it's free too.

Transfer options The **Moreekspressen** (T70 07 47 00, fjord1.no/en/) operated by Fjord1 runs from Oslo to Stryn every day. Expect to pay around NOK300 for a return ticket for the 5-hour journey.

Local partners None.

☺ OPENING TIMES
Mid-May to late Aug: 1000-1600

⦿ RESORT PRICES
Week pass (6 days): NOK1200
Day pass: NOK265
Season pass: NOK3100

ⓘ DIRECTORY
Tourist office: T57 875474
Medical centre: T57 876990
Pisteurs: No tel number
Taxi: T57 872350
Local radio: None
Website: strynefjellet.com

Arguably Europe's coolest summer snowboarding destination. Fantastic park, high snowfall, good party scene and incredible views. Plus it has some summer freeriding too – an unexpected bonus.

L: STRYN SUMMER 2006 P: TORREL KAROLUSSEN

⥁ If you like this . . .
. . . try Les Deux Alpes (in the summer) ⟶p144, Snow Park ⟶p230, or Les Diablerets ⟶p322.

The Mountain

Strynefjellet (the official name for the rideable area) has been operating since 1940. Its attractions are long daylight hours, indescribable views, amazing funpark terrain and the chance to do some summer freeriding. Stryn is one of the reasons that early Scandinavian riders rose to such prominence. It was here in '88 that Craig Kelly discovered Terje, and where Jakob Wilhelmson honed his skills in the mid-'90s – his dad used to be the cat driver for the park. Both riders still drop by if you're lucky and it's definitely the place to scope the new crop of Scandi rippers. Either way, you're sure to find a top-notch park.

Beginners With only two lifts there's a paucity of good beginner terrain, but if you're comfortable with riding cat tracks, there's a great run that snakes down the mountain and has tons of little frontside and backside hits dug into the side. Perfect for building up to your first tries in a halfpipe. It's not hard to find as you'll go straight above it on the first (and only) chairlift.

Intermediate Head to the top of the chair, then ride down to the drag, and up to the top. From the top head skier's right and you'll find yourself in possibly the best summer park in the northern hemisphere. Try out every obstacle, then hit the main café (at the bottom of the hill) for lunch and head back up for round two in the afternoon.

Advanced You're here for the park really, but if you get to the top of the drag, then head skier's left, there's a run that can take you all the way back to the deserted hotel (you'll have passed it on the road up to the mountain). If you don't want to go that far, head back towards the road at any point and you should be able to route-find your way to a car. You'll have to hitch back, but in Norway this is usually no problem at all.

Kids The ski school (strynefjellet.com) can take kids over five for NOK1190 (including liftpass) per day, but otherwise the resort isn't particularly suited to under eights.

Flat light days With no trees the resort can be a nightmare in flat light. However, the area around Folven is perfect for hiking. There's even surf if you head 1½ hours to the coast.

> 66 99
> I've had some of my best snowboard memories in Stryn. It's such as laid-back place.
> *Aleksi Vanninen, snowboard legend*

☺ LOCALS DO
- Take the bus up the mountain (get a 20% discount on your pass for being environmentally friendly!).
- Pick hitchhikers up.
- Join other campfires and like to talk.

☹ LOCALS DON'T
- Buy more than a few pints at the pub prices. Most people drink *Hembrent* – a local moonshine.
- Go to bed early. Expect there to be a campfire to sit around 24/7.

✔ PROS
- Unique, beautiful scenery in an unspoilt corner of the world.
- Great park, normally very slushy.
- Normally the friendliest atmosphere of any snowboard destination.

✘ CONS
- Need a car if you want genuine flexibility.
- Weather can be bad for long stretches.
- Norway is very expensive. Very.

☺ NOT TO MISS
The drive to Stryn town follows a staggeringly beautiful fjord. See it at dusk for the perfect mirror image of the mountains.

ⓘ REMEMBER TO AVOID
Don't head skier's right as you approach the road and café near the bottom as there's a lake under the snow.

❄ SNOW DEPTH

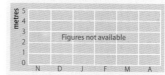
Figures not available

☺ RELIVE A FAMOUS MOMENT
Jamie Lynn got the cover of *Transworld* jumping the resort access road a few years ago. And there's a picture of someone backflipping it in 1954 on the Stryn site.

200 m	TOWN ALTITUDE
480 km	KM TO AIRPORT
OSL	AIRPORT
★☆☆	VEGETARIAN RATING
★★☆	INTERNET CAFES
★☆☆	RIDE IN/RIDE OUT
1600 m	HIGHEST LIFT
580 m	VERTICAL DROP
area not measured	RIDEABLE AREA (IN ACRES)
8 km	KM OF PISTES
1	NURSERY AREAS
1/4/1	RUNS: BEG/INTER/ADV
0/0	FUNICULAR/CABLE CARS
0/1	GONDOLAS/CHAIRS
1	DRAGS
no	NIGHT RIDING
1	PARKS
1	PIPE
yes	SUMMER AREAS
★★★☆	ENVIRONMENTAL RATING
💲💲💲	COST INDICATOR

SCANDINAVIA
STRYN

L-FOLVEN CAMPING P-STU BRASS

Åre, Sweden

Sweden's biggest and most varied resort, with one of the country's best snowparks.

If you like this ...
... try *Méribel* ▸▸*p146*, *Hemsedal* ▸▸*p250*, or *Leysin* ▸▸*p324*.

The Town

Although this is Sweden's most advanced resort in terms of infrastructure, it retains a mellow, friendly feel. The town is situated above the train station, making for easy access, and most accommodation is close to the lifts, and only a short walk from the station and centre. Unlike some other Swedish resorts Åre has a good variety of bars, shops and restaurants, and is scenically perched along the Åresjon Lake.

Sleeping For self catering and smaller budget options contact **Ski Star** (skistar.com). They look after a wide variety of properties including the **Åre Fjallby** and **Brunkulla** apartments which are convenient, modern and well located. A cheaper yet very nice hotel is the **Diplomat Ski Lodge** (diplomathotel.com). The **Tott Hotel** (totthotell.com) is a ride in/ride out luxury hotel that has extensive spa, gym and pool facilities, for those with bigger budgets.

Eating **Broken** serves Tex-Mex or try **TT's** next door. For a quick cheap breakfast get a pastry and coffee at the kiosk next to the Olympia lift.

Bars and clubs Tuesday is the big local night at **Bygget** nightclub. On Thursdays visit the sophisticated booths of **Dippan**, part of the Diplomat Ski Lodge. Check out the **Broken Bar** for laid-back beers, while the **Wersens** is also worth a look-in.

Shopping The main **ICA Are** supermarket is up a flight of stairs off the main Åre square. There is a cash point just below the stairs.

Health The best facilities are found at the **Tott Hotel** spa and gym. Non guests can to use it for a daily fee.

Internet Wireless internet is available in practically all the apartments and hotels. Ask for details at the reception. Otherwise the **Telia** on Åre square or **Zebra Café** both have access.

Transfer options You can take a taxi, but there are no official transfer companies. Trains from Gothenburg and Stockholm run direct to Åre and are a great way to travel. Check sj.se for details. skistar.com have details of transfers from nearby Ostersund airport.

Local partners None.

I like Åre cause in the wintertime I can snowboard with my friends when I am home without driving for hours. It's a beautiful place with good people living there, and nice with the mountain and the lake.

Jakob Wilhelmson, pro snowboarder
and Åre local

☺ OPENING TIMES
Early Dec to early Feb: 0900-1500
Early Feb to May: 0900-1600

☻ RESORT PRICES
Week pass (6 days): SEK1532
Day pass: SEK310
Season pass: SEK3557

ℹ DIRECTORY
Tourist office: T064 717712
Medical centre: T064 716600
Pisteurs: No tel number
Taxi: T064 710022
Local radio: Radio Rix 96.9 FM
Website: skistar.com

R. STUART EDWARDS P: NATALIE MAYER

P: TIM WARWOOD

The Mountain

The terrain in Åre isn't extremely challenging on piste, but rather pleasantly scenic and rolling, making for an ideal family resort. Experts will find some good challenging terrain by traversing and finding the steeper runs the resort has to offer, such as the natural gullies and trees towards the bottom of the mountain. The snowpark team have been developing a good park too, which consists of an intermediate and expert line, each littered with kickers, rails, boxes and a half pipe.

Beginners There is a good variety of green and blue runs to the right hand side of the resort. Take the Tottliften to access this area and wind your way down the trees. Avoid taking the big gondola or Kabinbanan as you will be forced to come down the steeper bits of the resort.

Intermediate Take the Kabinbanan to the top area of the mountain. The whole top section of the mountain is best suited for intermediates with a wealth of red runs. If you are feeling adventurous, cut left down the Traningsbacken run. To your left you will see wide and steep open fields full of good terrain.

Advanced Book a guide and explore the back of the mountain for untracked powder and the most challenging terrain. The intermediate line described above will also keep most experts entertained, as the further you traverse the steeper the terrain gets. There are tight turns and gullies in the trees below Areomradet which will test your legs.

Kids The Bjornen area is really good for kids. They have a day care centre and an area with talking animals amongst other entertaining distractions for children. There is also a BBQ area for families to enjoy with the kids.

Flat light days If riding in the trees doesn't tickle your fancy, the **Holiday Club** (holidayclub.se) is a hub of entertainment with a waterpark, bowling alley and games centre.

☺ LOCALS DO
- Party at Bygget on Tuesday nights.
- Go night riding as it's less crowded.
- Use *Snuss* instead of smoking.

☹ LOCALS DON'T
- Go to aprés-ski.
- Go out on Wednesdays.
- Call the resort 'Are'. It's pronounced 'Oar-Ah'.

✔ PROS
- One of the best funparks in Sweden.
- Very good infrastructure for all types of people and families.
- Wide variety of terrain for all levels.

✘ CONS
- Can get very windswept.
- The park gets crowded on the weekends.
- You must have ID to purchase any form of alcohol. They are strict.

☾ NOT TO MISS
If the weather is good, walk to the small cottage at the very top of the mountain accessible by the Kabinbanan gondola, where they serve coffee in front of stunning views of the valley.

ⓘ REMEMBER TO AVOID
The end of February, as this is the school holiday time in Stockholm and the resort gets very crowded.

❄ SNOW DEPTH

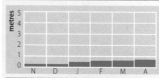

★ RELIVE A FAMOUS MOMENT
Tomas Brolin, Mel C and the Swedish Royal Family are among the stellar celebs to regularly visit Åre.

R: STUART EDWARDS P: NATALIE MAYER

372 m	TOWN ALTITUDE
100 km	KM TO AIRPORT
OSE	AIRPORT
★☆☆	VEGETARIAN RATING
★★☆	INTERNET CAFES
★★☆	RIDE IN/RIDE OUT
1420 m	HIGHEST LIFT
1048 m	VERTICAL DROP
area not measured	RIDEABLE AREA (IN ACRES)
101 km	KM OF PISTES
6	NURSERY AREAS
51/42/5	RUNS: BEG/INTER/ADV
1/1	FUNICULAR/CABLE CARS
1/9	GONDOLAS/CHAIRS
32	DRAGS
yes	NIGHT RIDING
3	PARKS
1	PIPE
no	SUMMER AREAS
★★★	ENVIRONMENTAL RATING
💲💲💲	COST INDICATOR

SCANDINAVIA
ÅRE

The Town

A cluster of buildings would be better to describe this tiny northern settlement scenically located in the midst of jagged cliffs and wild Arctic tundra. Not surprisingly there is a real secluded northern feel to this town, which is a friendly place with a village atmosphere. If you want to escape for a few days and taste a sample of true Lapland this is the place to be. It is real sledhead and powder dog country, as the constant hum of snowmobile engines reminds you.

Sleeping Everything centres around the main **Riksgränsen Ski and Spa** resort (Riksgransen.nu) which is the only real hotel here and the largest building in the town. You can choose between a luxury or standard 'skier' hotel room or self-catered apartments which come with all the trimmings.

Eating The **Ski and Spa** hotel's own restaurant, the **Laplandia**, serves traditional Swedish cuisine which is excellent if relatively pricey. For smaller snacks, go to the hotel bar and club, the **Matsal**.

Bars and clubs The hotel bar and club **Matsal** is surprisingly big and hosts live music but is reputed to be the fourth most expensive club in Sweden. The **MTR Ski Lodge** also has a small bar.

Shopping Two supermarkets double as all round convenience stores. Bring your own booze – it's pricey here.

Health The pool, gym and spa in the **Ski and Spa** hotel are open to the public. Before 1700 there is a fee of €16,50, and after 1700 this goes down to €11,00.

Internet The hotel has a small internet café where you can either you use one of their terminals or buy a code for wireless access.

Transfer options Rent a car from Kiruna airport, but a better option is taking the overnight train from Stockholm or Gothenburg which goes direct to Riksgränsen (connex.se).

Local partners An Arctic pass is available which gives access to partnering resorts of Narvik, Bjorkliden, Abisko and the Nuolia backcountry. Speak to the reception about the details, as you'll need a guide for many of the excursions.

☺ OPENING TIMES

Winter: Mid-Feb to late Jun
Summer: Late Jun to late Sep: 0900-1600
Midnight sun riding: Late May to late Jun: 2000-0030

ⓢ RESORT PRICES

Week pass (6 days): SEK1532
Day pass: SEK296
Season pass: SEK3265

ⓘ DIRECTORY

Tourist office: T098 040200
Medical centre: T098 073000
Pisteurs: T098 040080
Taxi: T098 018600
Local radio: None
Website: Riksgränsen.com

Some 300 km north of the Arctic Circle, Riksgränsen is the most northerly resort in the world and boasts some of the best backcountry riding anywhere. A late starting season means you can ride all the way up until July under the midnight sun.

❍ *If you like this . . .*
. . . try St Foy ▸▸p150, Cardrona ▸▸p228, or Levi ▸▸p244.

SCANDINAVIA
RIKSGRÄNSEN

P: SIAN HUGHES

The Mountain

The actual lift and piste system here are relatively limited with only six lifts and 17 pistes. But the reason to come here is for the endless backcountry opportunities. Whether you choose to hike for five minutes or five hours, there is a wealth of opportunity to find fresh snow, steep lines and natural hits. Snowmobiles and guides are also commonplace, and enable you to reap the benefits of this natural playground.

Beginners Head to the top of the mountain and then take the Blabarsbacken blue run down to the Nordalsliften for a nice open area. The Apelsinklyftan is a mellow blue run that will take you all the way down to the bottom chairlift. If you have the time there are various green runs that bring you down to the next village over Katterjakk, but you'll need to take the train back for one stop.

Intermediate At the top of the Ovre Stolliften cut right and hike for 10 minutes towards the little hut situated at the crest of the hill. This is effectively the Norwegian border. Keep traversing east and drop in wherever you feel for nice open powder fields, not too steep or rocky, weather conditions permitting. Once you reach the train tracks, it is a short walk back along the tracks to the bottom chairlift.

Advanced Take the Ovre Stolliften chairlift to the top and ride down the backside of the Riksgränsfjallet. There is a half-an-hour hike up the Nordalsfjall face which is directly behind. You are practically assured fresh lines and steeper terrain here. It is wise to ask a local or a guide to show you the best route the first time you ascend.

This is possibly one of the most photogenic places I've ever been to.

Natalie Mayer, snowboard photographer

Kids There is a tiny kids' area cordoned off next to Solliften poma lift. Kids can learn as they glide through the little animal slalom gates they have set up here.

Flat light days Hit the spa or go for a day trip to visit the Fjords of Narvik only an hour away by train. There is a brand new skate park in Kiruna, which is definitely worth a visit if you have the chance.

P: STROMMA

R: MIKE AUSTIN P: JAMES MCPHAIL

😊 LOCALS DO
- Hike to find the best powder.
- Ride Midnight Sun.
- Have no qualms about showing you their spots, so ask!

😠 LOCALS DON'T
- Go out during the week. It's not a resort for nightlife.
- Go up if it's windy. It's just not worth it.
- Worry about trends, this is pure snowboarding.

✅ PROS
- Some of the world's best backcountry.
- A long season (February-July) with light past midnight towards the end of the season.
- Never crowded.

❌ CONS
- A remote resort to get to.
- No cash points. And it's expensive.
- Quite volatile weather. Can be windswept for days.

☀ NOT TO MISS
The Northern Lights. Enough said.

ℹ REMEMBER TO AVOID
As this is quite wild and craggy terrain avoid dropping into anything that you haven't scoped out from underneath or seen an exit out of.

❄ SNOW DEPTH

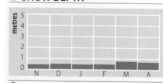

⊕ RELIVE A FAMOUS MOMENT
'Ingemar's Air', snowboarding's most famous backside method, was stomped in Riksgränsen.

504 m	TOWN ALTITUDE
137 km	KM TO AIRPORT
KRN	AIRPORT
★☆☆	VEGETARIAN RATING
★★★	INTERNET CAFES
★★★	RIDE IN/RIDE OUT
909 m	HIGHEST LIFT
405 m	VERTICAL DROP
104	RIDEABLE AREA (IN ACRES)
19 km	KM OF PISTES
1	NURSERY AREAS
4/12/1	RUNS: BEG/INTER/ADV
0/0	FUNICULAR/CABLE CARS
0/2	GONDOLAS/CHAIRS
4	DRAGS
yes	NIGHT RIDING
1	PARKS
0	PIPE
yes	SUMMER AREAS
★★★☆ ★☆☆	ENVIRONMENTAL RATING
💲💲💲	COST INDICATOR

SCANDINAVIA
RIKSGRÄNSEN

R: EWAN WALLACE L: LAS LEÑAS P: JAMES MCPHAIL

A nice reward after three days spent sitting in a condo waiting for the weather to clear. It may have been windy, but, my oh my, was it fun …

South America

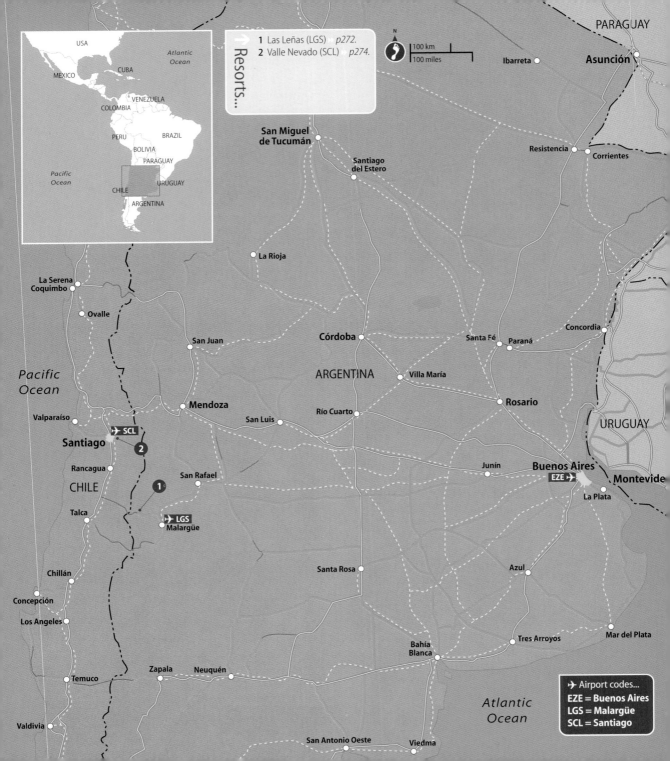

PARAGUAY

USA

Atlantic
Ocean

MEXICO

CUBA

VENEZUELA

COLOMBIA

PERU   BRAZIL

BOLIVIA

PARAGUAY

Pacific
Ocean

CHILE   URUGUAY

ARGENTINA

Resorts...

1 Las Leñas (LGS)   p272.
2 Valle Nevado (SCL)   p274.

N

100 km
100 miles

Asunción

Ibarreta

San Miguel
de Tucumán

Resistencia   Corrientes

Santiago
del Estero

La Rioja

Concordia

La Serena
Coquimbo

Ovalle

San Juan   Córdoba   Santa Fé   Paraná

Pacific
Ocean   ARGENTINA   Villa María

Valparaíso   Mendoza   Rosario

✈ SCL   San Luis   Río Cuarto   URUGUAY

Santiago   2

Junín   Buenos Aires

Rancagua   San Rafael   EZE ✈   Montevide

CHILE   1

La Plata

Talca   ✈ LGS
Malargüe

Santa Rosa   Azul

Chillán

Concepción

Los Angeles   Bahía   Tres Arroyos   Mar del Plata
Blanca

Zapala   Neuquén

Temuco

Atlantic
Ocean

Valdivia

✈ Airport codes...
EZE = Buenos Aires
LGS = Malargüe
SCL = Santiago

San Antonio Oeste   Viedma

It may seem obvious, but a snowboarding trip to South America is a different proposition from a fortnight in, say, Zillertal. For a start, the time and effort involved in travelling there makes the journey a real undertaking – and that's before you consider that the only time you can go is in the northern hemisphere summer, between the months of June and October. Throw in the cost of the flight, and you can see why resorts such as this tend to be filed in the drawer marked 'niche' for most northern hemisphere snowboarders.

South America has also suffered from the recent boom in popularity of New Zealand. True, there are a couple of obvious reasons why NZ should be so popular: the freestyle facilities are world class, the country is beautiful and everyone speaks English. But equally, South America has some major strings to its bow: the mountains are much larger with far superior vertical drop, the snowfall is better, and – crucially to the majority of the world's snowboarding population – it doesn't suffer from the crushing time difference from Europe and North America that NZ does.

So while there may be nothing to compare to Snow Park in terms of progressive freestyle facilities, this is more than compensated for by the incredible freeriding terrain of the Andes, and the fact that compared to the Alps, it's practically deserted. Add to this a rich and inviting Latin culture, the relatively low cost of living and that crazy late-night party scene and South America begins to take on a whole new dimension.

Chile has several good resorts, but we picked Valle Nevado as it's very close to Santiago and has the best infrastructure. There's also some good and relatively cheap heliboarding on offer. Argentina also has several decent resorts, and though Las Leñas is a long way from Buenos Aires and can't match Valle Nevado for convenience, it's probably the best southern hemisphere freeriding spot on the planet – on its day.

South America rating

Value for money
★★★★☆

Nightlife
★★★★★

Freestyle
★★★☆☆

Freeride
★★★★☆

Essentials

Getting there
Argentina Buenos Aires is Argentina's main airport. Carriers include **Aerolineas Argentinas** (aerolineas.com/ar), **American Airlines** (aa.com), **Lufthansa** (lufthansa.com), **Air France**, **British Airways** (ba.com) and **KLM** (klm.com). Las Leñas is a long way from Buenos Aires, so a good option is to get a flight to Malargüe or Mendoza (450 km), from where you can get a bus to the resort. Domestic flights are quite expensive in Argentina, though if you've flown into the country with **Aerolineas Argentinas** then you'll get a discount.

Chile Chile's major airport is Santiago. Carriers include **LAN** (lan.com), **Iberia** (iberia.com), **Air France** (airfrance.com) and **British Airways** (ba.com). Valle Nevado is a short distance from Santiago, so from here you can either take a taxi or get one of the cheap and frequent bus transfers.

Red tape
Most nationalities can enter Chile and Argentina without a visa for stays of less than 90 days.

Getting around
Hiring a car is easy in Chile and Argentina, though it's a relatively expensive way to get around. It can also be quite chaotic, particularly in Argentina where speed limits, lane markings and red lights are routinely ignored. In Chile the situation is much better, though most foreign visitors are likely to find it slightly worrying. Taxis are a realistic option; they're cheap, plentiful and take the responsibility out of your hands. Drink driving is very severely punished in Chile.

Car hire Most of the main international companies have offices at major airports and city centres. Usual age restrictions apply. Generally, valid driving licences from foreign nationals are sufficient for driving in either country.

Public transport
Bus is the most popular means of transport in Chile and Argentina. Argentina in particular has an outstanding network and it's by far the cheapest way to get around the country. Many buses have seats that

Top tips

- Go for more than a week if you can – the Andes are susceptible to bad weather and it's a long way to go to sit in an apartment looking out at clouds. Two weeks will give you a better window for sunshine.

- Take the opportunity to spend a few days in Buenos Aires or Santiago. They're beautiful cities that offer a unique blend of Latin American culture and European influence.

- Go heliboarding in Valle Nevado. It's relatively cheap, and the terrain you can access is incredible.

- Learn a few words of Spanish, but be aware it's a different dialect than that spoken in Spain.

- Make sure you're fit. Resorts here are higher and you can find yourself hiking a lot to reach the good stuff. It's a little different from sitting on a chair lapping the park.

recline into beds, and on journeys of more than 200 km they normally serve food. For detailed information check tebasa.com.ar.

Opening hours and traditions
Chile and Argentina share the Latin approach to opening hours, with a lunchtime respite of three hours (typically from 1200-1500). Shops tend to stay open until 1900-2000, and many supermarkets open until 2200. Shops are open until early afternoon on Saturday, and generally closed on Sunday. Banks open only from 0900-1400 in Chile, and 1000-1500 in Argentina.

Eating
Chile and Argentina share a predominantly Mediterranean diet, in that they consume a lot of fruit, vegetables, olive oil, bread, cereals and dairy.

Beef is of course Argentina's most famous food, and it's one that locals and visitors alike eat a lot of. Argentine beef is produced from herds of cattle that roam the vast *pampas*, and as such the beef is leaner and said to be tastier than that of other regions of the world. Many different cuts of meat are eaten, and the best way to experience them is by having a *parrilla* – various courses of meat (including offal),

South America price guide (in US$)							
	☕	🍴	📰	🎬	@	🍞	🔋
Argentina	1.30	3.00	1.30	0.70	Free	0.50	0.40
Chile	1.25	1-1.80	2.00	1.20	0.90	1-3.00	0.70

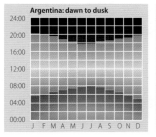

Argentina: dawn to dusk

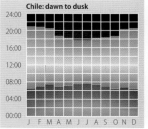

Chile: dawn to dusk

Any life is made up of a single moment, the moment in which a man finds out, once and for all, who he is.

Jorge Luis Borges, Argentine novelist

→ Fact file

Argentina	Chile
Currency: Argentine Peso (ARS)	**Currency**: Chilean Peso (CLP)
Exchange rate: US$1 = ARS 3.08	**Exchange rate**: US$1 = CLP 542.50
Time zone: GMT -3	**Time zone**: GMT -4
Country code: +54	**Country code**: +56
Ambulance: T107	**Ambulance**: T131
Police: T101	**Police**: T133
Fire: T10	**Fire**: T132

all cooked on a grill or open fire. Other common Argentine dishes include pastas and pizza, both quite different from their Italian ancestors, with *polenta* and *sorrentino* (a type of ravioli stuffed with cottage cheese, mozzarella, basil and tomato sauce) also figuring highly.

Chilean and Argentine breakfasts are very similar to Mediterranean ones, consisting of bread with jam and butter, croissants, brioches, *tostados* (grilled sandwiches filled with ham and cheese), orange juice and coffee (*espresso* or *café con leche*). In Argentina, there will also invariably be *mate cocida*, a refined version of the Argentine national drink *mate*. This is a bitter, caffeinated drink made from the leaves of the *yerba mate* plant, very similar to green tea but served in a hollowed out gourd and sipped through a *bombilla* (metal straw). It's of great cultural significance and massively popular throughout the country.

Chile has over 5000 km of coastline, so fish and seafood is of great importance in the Chilean diet. As in Argentina, barbecued meat is also very common. Traditional dishes include *empanada de pino* (a type of pastie filled with ground beef, onion, raisins, a piece of boiled egg and an olive), *pastel de choclo* (corn casserole filled with ground beef, chicken, onions, raisins, hardboiled egg and olives) and *porotos granados* (a stew of onions, fresh beans, squash, corn and basil). Sandwiches are widely eaten in Chile, with avocado being a common ingredient.

Lunch is a very large meal in Chile and Argentina, largely because dinner isn't taken until very late at night, normally around 2300 or 2400. Outside these times, most restaurants will only serve snacks such as *tostados* or the delicious *lomito* (steak sandwich). Both countries share a fondness for *dulce de leche*, a traditional sweet made from sugar and milk. Both also share the Latin approach to alcohol, in that they drink socially rather than to excess. Though this makes the Argentine habit of partying until 0600 very difficult to explain for someone from northern Europe.

Language

Spanish is the official language of Argentina and Chile. See the Spain chapter for some useful words and phrase (page 282).

Crime/safety

Most parts of Chile and Argentina are very safe to travel in, though the usual precautions against mugging and pick-pocketing should be taken in large cities. Popular demonstrations – *piqueteros* – are very common in Buenos Aires, and attract a huge armed police presence. Though they don't often turn violent they're probably best avoided by tourists. Both countries punish drug offences quite severely.

Health

Chile and Argentina have a reasonably good standard of healthcare, though having comprehensive travel and medical insurance is strongly recommended. It's safe to drink the tap water, though in Argentina it's heavily chlorinated so it tastes pretty unpleasant. Air pollution in the major cities is likely to be the major cause of complaint in both countries, so people with respiratory ailments should be aware.

P: JAMES MCPHAIL

P: MATT BARR

P: JAMES MCPHAIL

Snowboarding South America

"The riding in South America is second to none. Fewer riders than Europe or North America means small or no lift lines, giving a great pow-to-rider ratio. Several resorts are close to Santiago and the Pan American highway south along the route of the Andes, so they're easily accessible. Where else can you ride pow on volcanoes in our summer months?" Richard Dass, Snoventures.com

One thing you realize the more you go snowboarding around the world is that resorts are basically islands for rich people. Whilst this is true the world over, nowhere is it more apparent than in poorer countries such as Chile and Argentina.

Chile and Argentina are relatively well developed in terms of infrastructure, but their struggling economies lump them in with the Third World. Though the definition of the term is hazy, what it means in real terms is a frivolous pursuit such as snowboarding is an unattainable luxury for the vast majority of the population. The result is that the people who use the resorts are either tourists or extremely wealthy locals, such as famous actors and – symptomatic of the corruption found in the politics of the region – politicians.

Particularly in Argentina, the divide is quite pronounced. In terms of how this makes you feel as a visitor, it's very different to France or Canada. The facilities are in line with the more developed ski regions of the world, but they'll cost you a fraction of the price. Whilst this presents a moral dilemma for the thinking traveller, you can't deny that it gives you access to some amazing mountains.

Conditions

The Andes are the world's longest mountain range, spanning over 7000 km from Venezuela right down to the southern tip of the

The home of the condor, contrary to belief, has modern lift systems in the more popular resorts. In the case of Las Leñas they give access to 300 couloirs sporting 1000 m-plus steep powder faces. Las Leñas and its neighbouring resorts in the Chilean Andes are most popular with 'gringos', but you can go further south, to Pucón with its rideable volcanoes in the Chilean lake district and Bariloche in Patagonia. They are becoming regular stopovers on specialized snowboard tours such as those organized by SnowboardSouthAmerica.com. It's best to go on an organized tour to get what you want from your holiday as you're likely to have little time and high expectations. If you don't know what you're doing, the simplest of operations can take forever, especially if you 'no hablo Castellano'!

Dan Evans, Buenos Aires resident, snowboarding local

continent. They're also one of the world's highest mountain ranges, with an average height of over 4000 m. The proximity to the Pacific Ocean means that weather conditions can be very unpredictable, so in terms of conditions a trip to Las Leñas or Valle Nevado is vastly more hit and miss that a trip to, say, Mammoth. Thanks to the lofty altitude, snowfall tends to be high, with the snow itself often being light and dry – in short, perfect powder conditions. On the flip side, it's all way above the treeline, and since Andean weather patterns indicate that there's a good chance of storms in the southern

L: VALLE NEVADO P: NATALIE MAYER

L: VALLE NEVADO P: NATALIE MAYER

Pros & cons

Pros …

- Southern hemisphere riding, but without the jet lag.
- Healthy dash of Latin American culture.
- Incredible mountains, with some of the world's best freeriding terrain.
- Cheap.
- Friendly people, and a great party scene. Don't expect to get to bed before 0600.

… and cons

- Very little to do in Las Leñas on bad weather days, which are unfortunately pretty frequent.
- Freestyle facilities leave a lot to be desired.
- Resorts are very spread out, meaning that if you go then you're only realistically going to visit one of them.
- Long journey times for most visitors.
- The Andes can be prone to bad weather – storms frequently come in and sit there for days at a stretch.

hemisphere spring, particularly in Las Leñas, this can often shut riding down altogether.

When to go

Opening times are generally from mid-June until October. Generally, the best riding is to be had in high season, July and August. By September it's spring in the southern hemisphere, so you're looking at the rough equivalent of March and April in the Alps.

Lift chat

Las Leñas' legendary snowed-in lift

Many legends surround the Argentine resort of Las Leñas, from the amount of snow that falls, to whether Burton pro Dave Downing really did 50-50 down the cable of the chairlift during an infamous shoot there a few years back. Of them all though, the one about the place getting so much snow that they have to dig the Marte chairlift out each year is probably the most notorious. The thing is though, it's actually true. And in this case, truth is even stranger than fiction.

It's the Marte that gives Las Leñas its mystique within the winter sports world. It rises to well over 3000 m and accesses the steep terrain that makes the place unique. The first time we caught it, we were naturally nervous about what we'd be coming down. We were also intrigued – would they really have had to dig the thing out? There didn't seem to be that much snow. Then, as we came up over a rise, we saw them – gangs of bare-chested locals hacking away with shovels at a height of over 2500 m, clearing a 100-m-long channel out for the chair to travel through. As we glided past them, cheerily waving, the surrealism increased. Later, a local told us that they were prisoners from the local jail. As somebody said at the time, you don't get that in France.

James McPhail

EWAN WALLACE MAKING THE TRAIN TRACK TO THE GOOD STUFF L: LAS LENAS   P: MATT BARR

Off-piste policy

South American ski patrol isn't what it is in some of the more developed snowboarding regions, so don't rely on the pisteurs. In Las Leñas you'll need to sign a disclaimer before going off-piste, and you'll need to have all the relevant safety equipment. After that, you're on your own. It's genuine big mountain terrain in the Andes, so it pays to be well versed in the ways of avalanche rescue.

Secret spots

Locals tend to be very friendly, and will generally be only too happy to show foreign visitors around.

Freestyle

Freestyle facilities in South American resorts aren't the best, so if you're coming here to ride parks then don't bother – South America is all about the freeriding. Valle Nevado is host to a leg of the ISF World Cup meaning there's an ISF standard pipe there, but it's not well maintained outside competition periods.

The scene

The marked divide between rich and poor in Chile and Argentina ensures that no real scene has developed in either country. To date there have been no Chilean or Argentine snowboarders of any international renown; the lack of any decent parks and the relative expense of travelling abroad as a Chilean or Argentine national being two possible explanations. The region is popular with travelling foreign pro riders looking for some good summer riding, with legendary freeriders such as Serge Cornillat calling Las Leñas home each southern hemisphere winter. Burton snowboards used Las Leñas as the location for their brochure shoot for many years (this is where the famous shot of US pro Dave Downing sliding the chairlift cable was taken) so in terms of photos the region is quite well exposed in the world snowboarding media.

The industry

Neither Chile nor Argentina has their own snowboarding brands, relying instead on imports from the northern hemisphere.

Lift chat

Going to extremes

Make no mistake – it's a mission getting to Las Leñas. So much so that by the time we arrived, we were beginning to wonder if a week on resort hadn't been just a little bit optimistic. Certainly the locals we met on the lift those first few days thought we were insane travelling that distance for six days on the hill. Taking a look at the snow conditions, I half agreed with them. And then it started to snow.

It snowed and howled for three days, and at one point we thought it was destined to clear on the day our flight was due to leave for Buenos Aires. But then, unbelievably, it cleared, on our last morning. We were up at six, wolfed breakfast down and practically ran to the lift queue to make our way up the Marte. There was only one problem. Due to the high winds that often bedevil the resort, the Marte was going to be closed until the middle of next week. At first we were flustered, but soon we joined everyone else and took the chairs as far as we could, to about the halfway stage. Then we began hiking. Soon after, we saw a skier standing at the top of a massive cliff.

Las Leñas is one of those resorts that attracts the type of rider for whom 'extreme' is actually a fitting epithet. They range from the ice-axe wielding, swallowtail riding, po-faced powder lovers who make up Las Leñas' seasonaire community to the pro skiers and snowboarders who travel there each year to huck themselves off and down the many cliffs and chutes that litter the resort.

The guy we were now watching, along with everybody else breaking the boot trail up towards the summit, clearly belonged to the latter category. That much was clear from the conversation that began to drift into earshot as we approached. "I don't know", we heard him shout distantly, "...it's huge!" "Yeah", averred the photographer, "...but *you're* huge!" I guess it's the kind of logic that appears faultless to a man preparing to backflip off a 60-ft cliff onto a flat landing, because, seconds later, Bryce the skier – we later found out that was his name – launched himself off the thing. The entire valley held its breath as he landed on his side with an extremely audible "Ooofff!" Then he simply scurried back to the top, hucked himself again and landed it to wild applause from the watching tourists at the top of the nearby chair, before casually skiing away. Everybody else shrugged before continuing on up the boot pack. So did we. It's that type of place.

Riders' tales
Backcountry safety

There's no doubt that the mountains are a very dangerous place. In time past, these were dangers experienced by only the brave and the foolhardy – climbers, mountaineers and extreme skiers. Now that snowboarding has seen a massive boom in popularity, it's we snowboarders who are amongst those most at risk from the mountains and their primary killer: avalanche.

Avalanches occur when a layer of snow comes loose from the layers beneath it, and begins to slide. There are many different kinds of avalanche ranging from the relatively harmless sluff avalanche (where the loose snow on the surface of the snowpack slides) to the full blown slab avalanche, where an entire slab of snow often tens or even hundreds of metres wide and up to several metres deep breaks off and slides.

It's very easy to be blasé about avalanche hazard. The common assumption is that it's something that only concerns advanced riders who venture far off-piste, but in fact nothing could be further from the truth. The very nature of snowboarding means that even total beginners can find themselves in avalanche danger spots without even realising it. The dangers are insidious, and it's often the most innocuous looking of slopes (from gradients of as little as 22°) that can be the potential killers. Unlike with related sports such as surfing, snowboarding's rapid rate of progression leaves experience desperately struggling to keep up with ability, with the result that many riders lack the know-how to keep themselves out of trouble.

We can never eliminate the risks of avalanche, only minimize them, but the first step to this is an understanding of why avalanches occur, where they're likely to happen and in what conditions they're most likely to happen. There are numerous factors at play: wind, temperature change, type of snow crystals, aspect, gradient – the list goes on. There are many good books on backcountry safety so it's worth reading up on, but there's no substitute for local knowledge. If the locals don't ride somewhere because they say it's prone to avalanche, then pay heed.

So, if you go snowboarding and you venture off piste, you will be at risk of avalanche. Since that probably includes about 95% of the world's snowboarding population, it follows that we should all know something of the hazards, and we should all have avalanche safety gear and know how to use it effectively.

Using the safety equipment is something that responsible mountain users practice extensively. Fortunately modern transceivers are very easy to use, but in a real avalanche situation it's never as simple as it is when searching in your back garden. There are techniques and procedures to follow which will make your searching quicker, and speed is of the essence. The chances of surviving burial in an avalanche are 90% if uncovered within 15 minutes, dropping to less than 50% after 30 minutes.

The best thing you can do is go on an avalanche safety course, and learn the stuff firsthand. There are various ones taking place across snowy regions of the globe, but UK backcountry experts *Facewest* (facewest.co.uk) do a good one. They're also a good place to kit yourself out with all the necessary gear. The bare minimum is as follows:

Transceiver
This is a beacon that you wear strapped to your body, for locating people and being located. It transmits a signal at the standard frequency of 457kHz which other transceivers can pick up, and can be switched into receive mode when you need to search. In most developed countries the ski patrol are equipped with transceivers, so make sure you are too.

Shovel
A shovel is the next must have in your safety gear arsenal, as it's no use knowing where someone is buried if you can't dig them out. Lightweight, portable 2/3-piece shovels are readily available, sometimes with a probe built into the shaft. Only a good, sturdy shovel will do, as during an avalanche friction can warm up the snow, and when it comes to rest the snow refreezes and can set extremely hard. These double as handy kicker building tools.

Probe
Snow can build up pretty deep, so your transceiver is only ever going to give an estimate of where to dig. Being able to pinpoint exactly where your friend is buried can save precious minutes of digging time, and this is where your probe comes in. Probes start at 4 m in length, and they're extendable, lightweight and easy to stow in your pack. They're also very handy when checking potential jump landings for rocks.

Backpack
Obviously you're going to need something to put your shovel and

probe in, so make sure you get one that's big enough to accommodate them comfortably. While you're at it, get one you can strap your board to, which will make those long hikes easier. Other things you should have in your backpack include a first aid kit, spare hat, an extra layer of clothing and some food and water.

Mobile phone

This is the quickest and easiest way of getting in touch with the rescue services in an emergency. Make sure you have their number in there as a matter of course (where possible, we've included them in the Directory for each resort). Don't ride with it switched on, as mobile phones can interfere with your transceiver.

Unfortunately, with all the safety measures in the world, even the most experienced of us aren't safe. While we were writing this book, we were deeply saddened to hear of the death of Austrian rider Tommy Brunner. He was killed in an avalanche near Bella Coola, Canada, in April 2006.

Tommy was one of the world's best freeriders, born and bred in the Austrian Alps. It would be difficult to think of someone more experienced. Tommy was swept into a crevasse and buried under several metres of snow. His group had all the proper equipment and found him quickly, but it took a number of hours to dig him out, by which time it was too late.

The sobering fact is that stories like this are not uncommon. In the past 10 years, many prominent snowboarders have been killed in avalanches, including Craig Kelly, Jamil Khan, Tristan Picot and Tommy himself. But though it's a constant risk that every snowboarder who ventures off-piste has to take very seriously indeed, the vast majority of snowboarders are fortunate enough to continue having great experiences in the mountains without incident.

R: MARK KENT P: ANDREW HINGSTON

Las Leñas, Argentina

The southern hemisphere's best freeriding.

☼ *If you like this ...*
... *try Shemshak ▸▸p104, Tignes ▸▸p154, or Arcalis ▸▸p288.*

The Town

Las Leñas was designed by the same people who were responsible for Les Arcs in France – and it shows. The town is far from picturesque, and has a certain frontier feel about it. It really is in the middle of nowhere, and it's hard to shake the feeling that you're not in Argentina proper as the place is fairly costly even by European standards. The riding, however, is amongst the best in the world, and makes the trip worthwhile.

Sleeping The five-star **Picis** and four-star **Aires** hotels are sumptuous, but if you're on a tighter budget then plump for one of the self-catered 'apart hotels' such as **Villa Capricornio** or **Atenas**. There are also a few self-catered 'dormy houses' and a selection of budget hostel-style apartments. Book through snoventures.com.

Eating Try the steaks at **Las Cuatro Estaciones** in the **Hotel Picis**, and the snacks in the **Innsbruck** on the edge of the piste at the main lift area during the day.

Bars and clubs Start your night at a bar called the **BU bar**, above the **Corona** club, and then head on over to the two nightclubs in town: **Ku** and **UFO** – both open till 0500.

Shopping There's a well-stocked supermarket at the bottom of the settlement – you'll meet all the other gringos in there.

Health The Tauros Hotel has a health club and spa with heated indoor/outdoor swimming pool, jacuzzi, sauna and Turkish bath.

Internet Some wireless access.

Transfer options By far the best plan is to jump on a charter flight to Malargüe (aerolineas.com.ar). From there, Las Leñas is an hour's bus journey away. The next nearest airport is at Mendoza, at 450 km or five hours transfer time. For those not afraid to rough it there's also an overnight coach available from Buenos Aires.

Local partners None.

☺ OPENING TIMES
Mid-Jun to early Oct: 0900-1600

ⓢ RESORT PRICES (in Arg pesos)
Week pass (6 days): $431-657
Day pass: $90-138
Season pass: $2247

ⓘ DIRECTORY
Tourist office: T02627 471100
Medical centre: T02627 471100
Pisteurs: No tel number
Taxi: No taxi service. Free regular shuttle buses throughout the resort
Local radio: None
Website: laslenas.com

> The length and steepness of the terrain on offer is unbelievable. Every serious freerider should take a trip here at least once in their lives.
>
> *Ryan Davis, pro snowboarder*

R: EWAN WALLACE P: JAMES MCPHAIL

The Mountain

Las Leñas is considered the best resort in South America. Although there are plenty of pistes, ultimately Las Leñas is all about freeriding, and more specifically the Marte chairlift right at the end of the valley. This is the sole means of access to the incredible steeps for which the resort is renowned, including the Las Vegas couloir. It's with some frustration that you learn, then, that high winds and heavy snow frequently shut the chair down, resulting in a perpetual battle by the resort to keep it running.

Beginners The best fun to be had is by taking the Venus and then Neptuno chairlifts, which accesses a long run on some wide and friendly pistes, and you could spend days exploring the terrain off to the right-hand side.

Intermediate Take the Marte chairlift and follow the run down to skier's right to where you catch the snowcat – it costs $25 and can be found at the first aid hut on the edge of the Apollo piste. This is the only means of accessing the other side of the resort that you see from the top of the Marte chair. After lunch, head up for a few quick runs on the Vulcano chair, then spend the remainder of the day sessioning the park.

Advanced There is terrain here to challenge the most experienced of freeriders. Head up the Marte chairlift. From here you can take on the infamous Las Vegas couloir, one of the steepest and most prolonged pitches you'll find in any resort in the world. Next head round to the Vulcano chairlift, then head off into the off-piste on the skier's left of the chair. Have a couple of runs there, then head further left and follow the fall line right back down to the road, from where it's an easy hitch back up to town.

Kids Kids up to five ride for free. The green runs accessed by the Venus 1 chair are the best to learn on.

Flat light days Since it is entirely above the treeline, Las Leñas probably numbers amongst the worst resorts in the world on bad weather days, which, unfortunately, are pretty frequent. Expect hitherto unimagined levels of cabin fever.

P: MATT BARR

R: RYAN DAVIS P: JAMES MCPHAIL

😊 LOCALS DO
- Ride with full avalanche kit.
- Hike when the Marte is closed.
- Go self-catering – it's expensive eating out each night.

☹ LOCALS DON'T
- Forget to sign an off-piste disclaimer.
- Go out on the town before 0100.
- Forget to take DVDs and books for the many bad weather days.

✓ PROS
- Incredible freeriding.
- Friendly locals.
- Uncrowded.

✗ CONS
- Frequent bad weather.
- No trees.
- Slow lifts.

☺ NOT TO MISS
A decent day sessioning the runs on the Marte chairlift. It's frequently closed thanks to heavy snowfall and high winds, but the terrain you access from the top is about the best, and steepest, you'll find in the southern hemisphere.

ⓘ REMEMBER TO AVOID
Going out of bounds without signing the necessary disclaimer. This is the fastest way to anger the piste patrollers and get your lift-pass confiscated.

❄ SNOW DEPTH

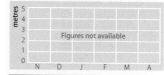

Figures not available

☻ RELIVE A FAMOUS MOMENT
Burton snowboards used Las Leñas as a location for their brochure photo shoot for many years. Reconstruct the famous chairlift cable 50-50 by Dave Downing which the company ran as an ad some years ago.

2240 m	TOWN ALTITUDE
69 km	KM TO AIRPORT
LGS	AIRPORT
★☆☆	VEGETARIAN RATING
★★☆	INTERNET CAFES
★★★	RIDE IN/RIDE OUT
3430 m	HIGHEST LIFT
1230 m	VERTICAL DROP
area not measured	RIDEABLE AREA (IN ACRES)
64 km	KM OF PISTES
2	NURSERY AREAS
16/11/ unmarked	RUNS: BEG/INTER/ADV
0/0	FUNICULAR/CABLE CARS
0/7	GONDOLAS/CHAIRS
6	DRAGS
no	NIGHT RIDING
1	PARKS
0	PIPE
no	SUMMER AREAS
figures not available	ENVIRONMENTAL RATING
💲💲💲	COST INDICATOR

Valle Nevado, Chile

Snowboarding in the summer, Chilean style: an isolated, idyllic setting, few lift queues and plenty of powder and steeps.

☾ *If you like this* …
… *try Krasnaya Poliana* ▸▸*p108, or Las Leñas* ▸▸*p272.*

The Town ◉ ♪ ⊖

Snowboarding doesn't come much more adventurous than Valle Nevado. Set in the middle of the largest skiable domain in the southern hemisphere, Valle Nevado is the Chilean resort that the cognoscenti acknowledge as the most progressive in the area. Snow is all but assured by the height of the resort and its enormous skiable area. With Santiago only 40-odd miles away and South America's wider cultural diversity to consider as another obvious attraction, Valle Nevado could be the place for that once in a lifetime summer powder fix.

Sleeping It's more suitable for holidaymakers than seasonaires as there is no cheap accommodation. In Valle Nevado, three hotels are available: the **Hotel Tres Puntas**, **Hotel Puerta del Sol** and the upmarket **Hotel Valle Nevado**. Book through snoventures.com.

Eating Snack style food is available from **Slalom**, in the **Hotel Valle Nevado**, while for good Italian cuisine head to **Don Giovanni**, also in the **Hotel Valle Nevado**. Reservations are obligatory.

Bars and clubs The liveliest bar in

R: MADS JONSSON P: DEAN 'BLOTO' GRAY 2007 BURTON SNOWBOARDS

❝ ❞

The best and most important all-round resort in Chile. It has a good snow record, great general infrastructure and is the most advanced ski area in the country.
Richard Dass, Valle Nevado local

the resort is probably the **Pub Tres Puntas**, which is a lovely spot from which to watch the sun go down. Open Thursdays, Fridays and Saturday, the **Puerta del Sol** carries on late, as do the **Bar Valle Lounge** and the **Valle Dance**.

Health Fitness facilities are available in the hotel packages, with the **Puerta del Sol** and **Valle Nevado** having pools. Massages are available for extra with a small local charge.

Internet One internet café, some wireless access.

Transfer options The best transfer option is to book one through snoventures.com. Prices for the 1½-hour journey from airport to resort start at $25,000.

Local partners Seasonaires stay in Farellones and ski from nearby El Colorado. Most spend their time in El Colorado with the occasional day in Valle Nevado.

☺ **OPENING TIMES**
Mid-Jun to early Oct: 0830-1600

⊖ **RESORT PRICES (in Chilean pesos)**
Week pass (6 days): $142,000
Day pass: $23,500
Season pass: $299,000

ⓘ **DIRECTORY**
Tourist office: T02 477 7000
Medical centre: T02 477 7086
Pisteurs: No tel number
Website: vallenevado.com
Self-contained resort with no taxis or local radio.

The Mountain

Although it could justly claim to be the biggest rideable area in the southern hemisphere (accessible terrain rather than pistes), Valle Nevado's 37 km of pistes mean it is equally suitable for snowboarders who just want to get some runs under their belts, while links to nearby El Colorado and La Parva have led to the wider area being labelled the 'Three Valleys of the Andes'. But it's the freeriding on hand that has really given the place its impressive reputation. With a huge area to explore and reliably high levels of snowfall, the place has quickly cultivated a reputation as one of the continent's best powder stashes. At the moment, Valle Nevado competes with resorts such as Las Leñas for the title of South America's best freeriding resort and is worthy if you include the accessible terrain utilizing the helicopter.

Beginners The lower slopes are the best for beginners. Try the four lifts, gradually dropping down beneath the Base Prado chair. There are many interesting runs in this front bowl.

Intermediate The whole resort is really on if you've got a handle on your turns, but the runs heading in all directions from the Andes Express high speed chair are all worth your time and exploration, in particular the back bowl, accessed by heading straight forward as you exit the chair.

Advanced That same back bowl is a good place to start exploring the off-piste Valle Nevado has to offer. The Santa Teresita and Valle Olímpico areas are other good places to look. The place is chock full of chutes, steeps and bowls though, so get exploring. Expert freestylers are going to love the place, with its super pipe and park.

Kids There's a 'snow garden' by the hotels to get them used to waddling around with a board on their feet.

Flat light days Perhaps the one drawback of the height of the resort and the Andes' generally barren nature is that there are no trees here. Most riders head for the park and pipe on flat light days.

☺ LOCALS DO
- Get up in a helicopter.
- Explore Valle Olímpico – it's a must.
- Extend their pass to explore the whole area of the Three Valleys with El Colorado and La Parva.

☹ LOCALS DON'T
- Attempt Santa Teresita unless they're with a guide or local.
- Turn up on the off chance – accommodation will be fully booked.
- Get tempted by the off-piste behind the Hotel Valle Nevado – it's a long hike back!

✔ PROS
- Largest skiable domain in South America.
- Close to international airport.
- Good climate, with lots of sunny days and a great snow record.

✗ CONS
- Only three hotels and a limited number of apartments, so it can fill up quickly.
- Close to Santiago so can be busy on holidays and weekends.
- Limited off-mountain entertainment.

⚑ NOT TO MISS
The great heliboarding facilities in Valle Nevado.

ⓘ REMEMBER TO AVOID
Don't venture too far into the back bowl on poor weather days in case the lifts need to close early.

❄ SNOW DEPTH

Figures not available

☺ RELIVE A FAMOUS MOMENT
Relive the end section from 1993's *Riders on the Storm* – Chris Roach, Terje Haakonsen and 3 ft of fresh South American powder. Just don't forget to learn how to triple-poke your melancholies before you go.

3025 m	TOWN ALTITUDE
54 km	KM TO AIRPORT
SCL	AIRPORT
★★☆	VEGETARIAN RATING
★★☆	INTERNET CAFES
★★★	RIDE IN/RIDE OUT
3670 m	HIGHEST LIFT
810 m	VERTICAL DROP
area not measured	RIDEABLE AREA (IN ACRES)
37 km	KM OF PISTES
1	NURSERY AREAS
14/14/4	RUNS: BEG/INTER/ADV
0/0	FUNICULAR/CABLE CARS
0/4	GONDOLAS/CHAIRS
7	DRAGS
no	NIGHT RIDING
1	PARKS
1	PIPE
no	SUMMER AREAS
figures not available	ENVIRONMENTAL RATING
	COST INDICATOR

SOUTH AMERICA
VALLE NEVADO

P: NATALIE MAYER

R: DAVID LOPEZ   L: SIERRA NEVADA   P: ANDONI EPELDE

David Lopez riding towards the sunset looking like a western film star.

Spain and Andorra

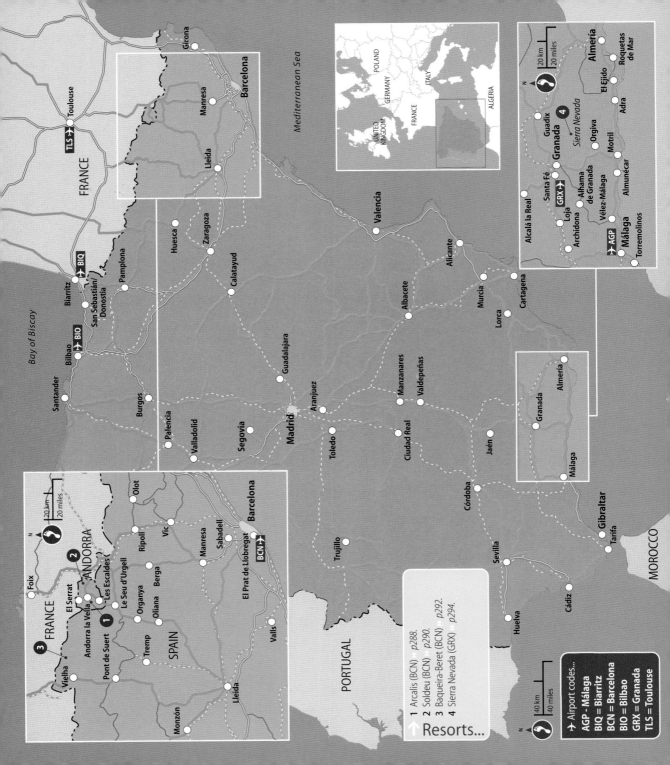

Snowboarding in Spain? The uninitiated might baulk at the prospect, but there is some serious riding to be found in this neglected corner of the European scene. True, the Spanish resorts of the Pyrenees are generally less celebrated than those of their distinctly more snowy-sounding neighbour Andorra, but they share many similarities. The main one is obviously their position on the flanks of the Pyrenees, a range actually older than the Alps and, if possible, more rugged in appearance. Both are blessed with plenty of snow and lots of sunshine, and have local snowboarding cultures that thrive in their own petri dish-like environments, miles from the mainstream. As part of the Iberian Peninsula, resorts such as Baqueira and Soldeu are subject to the same climate and thus, pretty much the same conditions. These riding areas are separated by language and custom only. In terms of geography, they are basically the same place.

And then there's Sierra Nevada, Europe's most southerly winter sports outpost, sitting proud in the province of Andalucía. The sheer cultural difference of a trip here alone is enough to warrant inclusion in the guide. Sure, going snowboarding in Spain in sight of Africa might sound daring or even slightly risky, when you're all but guaranteed snow and crazy nightlife in the familiar surroundings of somewhere like Méribel or St Anton, but isn't that what the spirit of snowboarding travel is all about?

Due to the recent amalgamation of Andorra's resorts to form the Vall Nord and Gran Valira areas, we picked Soldeu and Arcalis as most representative of that country's scene. Spain is, surprisingly, peppered with resorts, particularly in the Pyrenees, but we chose Baqueira, easily the country's best, and Sierra Nevada, Europe's most southerly resort – closer to Africa than to the rest of the European mainland.

Spain & Andorra rating

Value for money
★★★★★

Nightlife
★★★★☆

Freestyle
★★☆☆☆

Freeride
★★★☆☆

Essentials

Getting there

One of the best things about doing a trip to Spain or Andorra is the opportunity it affords to spend some time in one of the great Spanish cities. For Spain and Andorra, the handiest point of entry is Barcelona. Carriers to Barcelona include **easyJet** (Easyjet.com), **Swiss Air** (swiss.com), **KLM** (klm.com), **Air France** (airfrance.com), **Lufthansa** (lufthansa.com), **Iberia** (Iberia.com) and **British Airways** (ba.com). Another option is to fly into Bilbao and spend some time in San Sebastián before heading into the mountains. Airlines flying into Bilbao include **easyJet**, **British Airways**, **Alitalia** (alitalia.com), **Air France** and **Lufthansa**. Other airport options include Biarritz (**easyJet**, **Air France**, **BMI.com**, **BA** and **Lufthansa**) and Toulouse (**BA**, **KLM**, **Air France**, **Alitalia**).

Red tape

Spain is an EU member, so member nationals only need a valid passport to travel to and from the country. Other foreign nationals can stay for 90 days on a valid passport. A few exceptions require a visa – check spain.info for more information. Andorra is not a member of the European Union, but in most cases a valid passport is enough to gain entry.

Getting around

Although there are public transport facilities (see below) driving is probably the easiest way of making this trip. The Spanish and Andorrans drive on the right, and a full driving licence (photo type or International Driving Permit) is required plus liability insurance – you need a 'green card' certificate to prove this. You also need to carry two warning triangles by law and it's worth noting that there is a new law in effect that requires all drivers to have a reflective vest in their cars, which should be donned every time one leaves the car whilst on a highway. Fines for not having one are steep, so all rental companies now provide one. In

LAS RAMBLAS ENTERTAINMENT P: CHRIS MORAN

Spain and Andorra price guide

	☕	🍴	🍕	🎧	@	🥪	🛏
In €	1,00	3,00	4,00	0,60	5,00	3,00	0,80

Top tips

- Dive into the tapas culture, and don't be afraid to eat somewhere new every night. It's cheap and a great way of getting into the rhythm of the place.

- Visit Caldea in Andorra on a down day. It is one of the best spa complexes in Europe.

- Take advantage of Andorra's lax duty-free regulations.

- Make sure you spend a night either side of your riding time in Barcelona or San Sebastián.

- Speak to the locals. They're incredibly friendly, and surprisingly helpful when it comes to pointing out spots.

Spain, roads are generally good. New and improved road links are opening regularly, and the motorway network is expanding rapidly right across the country. Make sure your papers are in order, because unless your Spanish is top notch you're going to have a hard time understanding what is going on should you be pulled over.

Car hire Most major hire car companies (easycar.com, hertz.com, avis.com) have offices in airports and cities. Usual age restrictions apply.

Public transport

Public transport is possible – to get to Andorra, try novatel@andorrabybus.com, who run bus services from Barcelona and Toulouse. **Eurolines** also run services from Barcelona airport to Andorra (info@autocars-nadal.ad). Once in Andorra La Vella, buses run across the principality – check the andorra.ad/ang/transports/index site for more on each of these options. In Spain, the rail network is worth a look, although they are likely to charge for board carriage.

P: MIKE WEYERHAUESER/JDP

P: MATT BARR

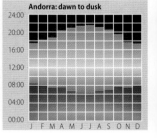

Andorra: dawn to dusk

RENFE (renfe.es) is useful for major routes. Try euskotren.es for options from the Basque country.

Opening hours and traditions
Everything grinds to a halt at lunchtime in Spain, which typically lasts for a few hours from 1400 till 1700. Shops tend to close around 2000, and are open from Monday to Saturday. Larger supermarkets have longer opening hours. Andorran shops follow similar opening hours.

Eating
Eating in Spain is a huge social occasion, and one of the main draws for any rider thinking of making the trip. Tapas (pintxos in Euskadi) culture rules across Spain, and it's a cheap, social way of taking care of the after-riding munchies and the evening meal. The bustling tapas bars fill up with families and locals in the early evening, and it's a great experience to get stuck in with a glass of vino tinto and a plateful of these tasty nibbles. Dishes range from tortilla – a potato and egg omelette – to more local delicacies of which seafood is a primary ingredient. Grab a plate from the barman, load it up and either make a note of how many you've taken or ask him to tot it up for you. In the Pyrenees, the local cuisine is an even more mouth-watering prospect, and in the Val D'Aran in particular it is almost impossible to get a bad meal. A good rule of thumb when it comes to choosing a restaurant is that if there are locals present, dive in. Be warned though – locals here share the worldwide Latin habit of dining late, meaning most

Fact file

Currency	Euro (€)
Time zone	GMT +1
Country code	+34 (Spain) +376 (Andorra)
Emergency numbers	
Ambulance:	T112 (Spain) T118 (Andorra)
Police:	T092 (Spain) T110 (Andorra)
Fire:	T112 (Spain) T118 (Andorra)

P: JAMES MCPHAIL

Lift chat

The time the board bags actually flew off the roof onto the motorway

I don't care who you are, when you are travelling to a new resort and the forecast is saying that it's dumping even the most placid of characters will start frothing at the mouth. This is exactly what happened when our crew flew into Barcelona in March '04. CNN were calling it one of Spain's worst ever snowstorms and as we left Barcelona in two tiny hatchback hire cars under black skies, anticipation was at fever pitch. Each car was packed with people, which meant that the budget roof racks hired from Euro Car were stacked with board bags. Unfortunately for our car, I was the proud owner of a TSA Danny Wheeler pro double bag, a beast that has been praised and condemned in equal measure. Because of its sheer size you can live out of it for two months straight, but for the same reason it is an endless headache at airports and for travelling in general. Because of the lashing rain I had opted to pull out the rain cover for the Wheeler, but unbeknownst to me what this did was double the already huge size of the Wheeler bag to parachute-like proportions. The promise of powder had got my foot glued to the floor and at 140 kph it was pretty obvious to photographer James McPhail in the car behind that something had to give. In that very instant the Wheeler launched itself skyward off the back of the car, taking with it the two other board bags on the racks.

In the car behind, a mixture of confusion and horror reigned. Somehow, McPhail managed to swerve round the flying coffins as they started bouncing around the three-lane motorway. One bag hit the central reservation and came to a halt, while the other one found its way to the hard shoulder. And then there was the Wheeler, straddling the middle lane of a Spanish motorway at the height of rush hour.

Somehow we managed to recover all the bags quickly, and on close inspection found that the worst injuries were friction burns to bags, a base grind for one board and even a detune for another (which was a result as it actually saved us a job once we got to the resort). At the time we were all buzzing on adrenaline and it wasn't until we got back in the cars that we realized how lucky we were not to have caused a massive pile up and to have recovered the bags without getting run over ourselves. Good job the trip that followed was one of the best ever. Bottomless powder all week, magic …

Ed Leigh

Key phrases

Key words and phrases		Numbers	
Yes	sí	0	cero
No	no	1	uno
Please	por favor	2	dos
Thank you	gracias	3	tres
Sorry	perdon	4	quatro
Hello	hola	5	cinco
Goodbye	adios	6	seis
Good	bueno	7	siete
Bad	mal	8	ocho
I don't understand	no entiendo	9	nueve
		10	diez
I'd like…	queria…	11	once
Do you have…	tienes/tiene usted?	12	doce
		13	trece
How much is it?	cuanto es?	14	catorce
Where is…?	donde está…?	15	quince
Mens	caballeros	16	dieciseis
Ladies	señoras	17	diecisiete
Left	a la izquierda	18	dieciocho
Right	a la derecha	19	diecinueve
Straight on	todo recto	20	veinte
Night	noche	21	veintiuno
Room	habitación	22	vientidos
Pitch	espacio	30	treinta
Shower	ducha	40	cuarenta
Toilet	servicio	50	cincuenta
The bill	la cuenta	60	sesenta
White coffee	café con leche	70	setenta
Beer	cerveza	80	ochenta
Red wine/white wine	vino tinto/vino blanco	90	noventa
		100	cien
Mineral water (still/sparkling)	agua mineral (sin/con gas)	200	doscientos
		1000	mil
Orange juice	zumo de naranja		
Sandwich	bocadillo	**Days of the week**	
Ham	jamon	Monday	lunes
Cheese	queso	Tuesday	martes
Help!	socorro	Wednesday	miercoles
North	norte	Thursday	juves
South	sur	Friday	viernes
East	este	Saturday	sabado
West	oeste	Sunday	domingo

I really like how the scene is evolving in Spain. There has been an explosion of parks and lots of girls getting involved in the last three years. The level of riding is insane right now but the best thing about Spain for me is the lifestyle, the food, the people and the partying. It's the quality of life.

Igor Domínguez, Spanish pro snowboarder and founder of Landing Snowboard Camps

Andorra, though most natives speak Spanish as well. While many people in the tiny Pyrenean state understand English relatively well, in Spain it is not widely spoken, so make an effort to learn some key phrases. In the Basque area of Spain (known as Euskadi), Euskara is also spoken and written down as well as Spanish. It's also worth noting that Catalonia is a largely autonomous region, proud of its language and culture, and not that happy to be lumped in with the rest of Spain.

Crime/safety

Crime is not really a massive problem in either Andorra or Spain, although there are a few precautions worth taking. In a European context, Spain has suffered from a higher than average level of terrorist activity. In popular cities such as Barcelona and San Sebastián, tourists are targeted by street criminals fairly regularly. In both Spanish and Andorran resorts, board theft from outside restaurants or apartment balconies is on the increase, so keep an eye on your set-up or use a lock if you're super paranoid. In Spain, report anything lost or stolen to the Policia Nacional, who handle urban crimes. The Guardia Civil handle roads, borders and law and order away from towns, while the Policia Local/Municipal also deal with some criminal investigations. In Euskadi, nationalistic sentiments run high so be sensitive to this situation when interacting with locals. Drunkenly singing 'Y Viva Espana' in the street is unlikely to go down well. This also applies to the Catalonians, who are equally anti-Madrid and hate being lumped in with the Castilians.

Health

Spain is governed by European health standards, so EU residents should carry a European Health Insurance Card (EHIC), which replaces the old E1-11 form. In Spanish resorts or towns, try to find an on-call pharmacy, which will be open round the clock. Health insurance is highly recommended for any trip as an additional safety net. Andorra is not an EU member so the EHIC is not valid for health cover while in the country. Health insurance is pretty much obligatory if you're going to make the trip.

restaurants only get going at around 2200, or even later. Only breakfast lets the side down somewhat, thanks to the puzzling Iberian predilection for liberally dousing their pastries in sugar and extremely sweet chocolate. In Andorra, it's pretty much the same story, although in the larger resort areas the British angle is well taken care of with fry-ups, roast dinners and other UK mainstays available in the expat bars – although that would be to miss the point somewhat. If you're serious about food, check out Iberia.

Language

Spanish is the main language in Spain. Catalan is more widely spoken in

Snowboarding Spain and Andorra

"I have been riding in so many different mountains across the world, and the more I travel the more I realize that I have as many epic days in my own backyard." Iker Fernández, Spanish pro rider.

Spain and Andorra might share the same environment, but they are very different places and the development of their snowboarding scenes has unfolded along sharply contrasting lines. Andorra has long been known as king of the budget package holiday, especially among snowboarders attracted by its cheapness and suitability for beginners – a kind of proto-Bulgaria, if you like. As a result, Andorra's profile has benefited greatly from this popularity, and the resorts themselves have responded by investing heavily in their infrastructures and marketing – as seen by the establishment of the Gran Valira and Vall Nord areas over the last two seasons. In turn, this has meant the development of a strong, freestyle-savvy local scene, with locals such as Tyler Chorlton and Jamie Phillp recent testament to the particular incubatory benefits of the Andorran scene. Spain, in

Pros ...

- Friendly locals, great nightlife.
- As you'd expect, it's generally sunnier here than in the rest of the mainland, so pack some mirrored lenses.
- Mix in a city break and make the trip more unusual.
- The food! It's one of the main reasons for visiting.
- Cheaper than the rest.

... and cons

- Check the snow before you go. Late season in particular is a bit of a lottery.
- Freestylers should choose their spot carefully. Good parks do exist, but they are by no means widespread.
- It's busy – with tourists, snowboarders, skiers and locals.
- Some antiquated lift systems, although this part of the world is catching up quickly.

contrast, rarely appears on the mainstream snowboarding radar. Think Spain and, understandably, the immediate connotations are beaches and surf rather than mountains and powder. Nevertheless, it is home to a rabid scene of snowboarders who celebrate the sport with admirable creativity and forthrightness. Iker Fernández is easily

R: JONNY BARR L: BAQUEIRA P: JAMES MCPHAIL

L: SIERRA NEVADA P: DAN MILNER.COM

R: IKER FERNÁNDEZ L: BAQUEIRA P: ANDONI EPELDE

Spanish snowboarding is probably the least known in Europe. People who think of Spain usually think of bulls and parties and miss the incredible mountains to ride. There's a good reason why Spanish snowboarders like to stay at home – the lifestyle, the women, the food, the relaxing life and the parties of the south of the Pyrenees all keep us here. Then there's the heliboarding, the possibility of using sleds and the fact there are over 30 resorts.

Andoni Epelde, Spanish photographer

Spain's most famous rider, but there are others coming up, like David Lopez and Cuca Aranda. And in Baqueria, the Spanish have a resort unique among its European peers. The other hugely appealing aspect of any riding trip to Spain is the chance to combine it with a city break or a surf trip. The surf breaks of the Basque country are among the best in Europe, and this bounty is all confined to a relatively small area. With some flexibility and a hire car, those 'ride in the morning, surf in the afternoon' clichés can become a reality here.

Above all, Iberian snowboarding offers a different take on an old theme. As Thomaz Garcia, editor of the Spanish *Snow Planet* magazine says, "…while the more celebrated Alps might be described as quaint, Pyrenean mountain culture is definitely rougher round the edges. Ancient villages, whose inhabitants haven't changed their lifestyle in centuries, dot the mountainside". Away from the Alpine heartland, with its predominantly Franco-German culture, there's a freshness about a trip to Spain and Andorra that causes you to re-evaluate the old lazy associations you might have begun to foster. Tapas after riding instead of tartiflette or fondue? Such a simple difference changes the context entirely. Consider the amazing riding as well, and you've got quite a trip.

Conditions
The Pyrenean resorts are subject to weather systems coming in from the sea. This humidity can bring huge amounts of snow in a short period of time – but it also means the resulting cover can melt quickly, and the area is characterized by a melting cycle far more rapid than that which takes place in the Alps. The moral is to make sure you're up early on a powder day to take quick advantage of it. Sierra Nevada is even more of a paradox, managing to combine limitless sunshine (it's often touted as Europe's 'sunniest' resort) with a long lasting base,

much of it due to the resort's height and a slick snow-making system. Unsurprisingly, the spring conditions here are pretty amazing. And look out for the snow taking on a reddish tint – the result of sand blowing over from the Sahara. You don't get *that* in Vail.

When to go
Thanks to an obvious difference in latitude, Iberia is subject to slightly warmer temperatures than the other main European riding centres, even if the resorts tend to have similar opening times (Sierra Nevada, for example, stayed open until the beginning of May during the 2005-2006 season). As with the other European countries, January and February are the best months to go for guaranteed snow and low temperatures, but early March is probably the best time to go if you're planning a city break as well. By this time of the year, the temperature is pleasantly rising in the cities and along the coast, while there is still plenty of snow in the mountains.

Off-piste policy
Perhaps the main thing to say is that heliboarding and snowmobiling are legal here, unlike in France. Immediately, this opens up plenty of options for riders prepared to pay the money to experience real Pyrenean backcountry conditions. That said, private sled rentals and private heli ops are the norm, so speak to some locals to find out more.

In resorts, everything is on limits to inquisitive riders, although it goes without saying that the same dangers are very prevalent and you should make sure you're fully kitted out with full avalanche equipment. Resort boundaries are well defined, but there is plenty of scope for exploration, particularly in Baqueira and Andorra's Arcalis.

Secret spots
Andorra and particularly Spain's slightly isolated position in the snowboarding world means that the resorts don't have as huge an influx of foreign riders as the French and Austrian ones do. As such, the atmosphere here is one of inquisitive friendliness rather than the hostility that can arise in France when it comes to the vexed subject of local powder rights.

Freestyle
Freestyle is huge in both countries, with local riders tending to come to prominence because of their freestyle abilities. In Spain, Thomaz Garcia puts this down to "a significant lack of any Alpine culture, which meant that those who picked up snowboarding came from a surfing and skateboarding background". Andorra's resorts have been investing in good fun parks for years now, and German photographer Hansi Herbig rates the parks of Gran Valira as "…definitely one of the best and most well maintained parks I have seen in Europe". The Spanish also have a long freestyle pedigree, and resorts such as Astun and Boi Taull have good park facilities. Local scenes are very organized and are generally happy to welcome foreign riders.

The scene

Snowboarding gained a foothold in Spain in the early '90s, thanks to pioneers such as Richard Fernández and scenes based in the Basque, Catalan and Sierra Nevada areas of the country. Later, riders such as Iker Fernández, Sergio Bartrina and Cuca Aranda began to gain Europe-wide acceptance. At the moment, Spanish snowboarding seems poised at an important crossroads, with the scene yet to make the jump into the industry mainstream and develop to the extent that Spanish pros can make a decent living. As Iker Fernández explains, "The fact that we are so far away from the main hubs of snowboarding keeps the spirit of fun alive in Spain. People may not be so focused on being professional and getting work done, but there is a carefree, almost cavalier attitude I don't see anywhere else in the world".

In Andorra, there's an equally proactive scene based around the main resorts and shops such as Tyler Chorlton's **Loaded**. The UK expat community in Andorra is influential, as is an upcoming number of Argentine riders who spend their winters in Andorra and their summers in the Andes.

The industry

The Iberian industries are developing but are still far from the main industry. Shops such as **Free Sports**, **ERT** and **Surfin** were instrumental in establishing the sport in Spain, and still support the scene today. Top Spanish riders of the moment include Peio Mongelos, Gerard Freixes, Jorge Burillo, Igor Domínguez, Konrad Lindner, David Gutiérrez, Dani Sastre and David Pujol. Magazines such as *Method Mag* are influential, but the main printed flag wavers are the influential *Snow Planet* magazine, steered by respected snowboard writer Thomaz Autran Garcia, and *Surfer Rule Snowboard* and *Solo Snowboard*. The main website in Spain is called canalsnowboard.com, although you should also check out snowpla.net. In Andorra, Tyler Chorlton, Merlin Balfour and Tessa Phillp are a few of the locals ruling at the moment. For the best source of English language information on Sierra Nevada, UK expat Giles Birch runs the sierranevada.co.uk site, as well as local snowboard school out there.

....

Spain: a brief history of snowboarding

Mid- to late 1980s → First snowboards appear in Spain. Burton, Sims, Hooger Booger, Crazy Banana and Heavy Tools are the main brands. **Late '80s** → Resorts such as Astun and Sierra Nevada allow snowboarders onto their slopes. The scene 'de la Sierra' begins to grow, while Richard Fernández leads in the Pyrenees.
1988-1989 → First Spanish snowboarding contests organized. **Early 1990s** → Ballantines' contest circuit established in Spain, and the first serious amount of money is brought into the Spanish scene. Later, AES (Asociacion Espanola de Snowboard) founded. Surfing mags *360* and *Surfer Rule* run first snowboarding stories. **Mid-1990s** → Iker Fernández makes it onto the Burton team and gets a section on *Subjekt: Haakonsen*. Sergio Bartrina gets pro model on Nidecker.
1998 → Iker Fernández and Sergio Bartrina represent Spain at the 1998 Olympics.
2001-2002 → Snowpark Division established to build good parks in Pyrenees.
2004-2005 → Spanish resorts begin to gain widespread notoriety, with foreign magazines such as *White Lines* and *Transworld* publishing articles revealing Spain's unique scene to the rest of the world.

Lift chat

The money shot

The cover picture for this guide was taken on a perfect bluebird powder day in the Spanish resort of Baqueira. It was our first day riding the mountain and we got lucky with a freshly laid blanket of snow and an empty resort. I spotted this line as we got off the top chairlift. It was just sitting there asking to be hit up. Ed Leigh, the cover star, was chomping at the bit to get some powder under his board and was hiking round the ridge to drop in before anybody else could call it.

Getting a successful line shot like this involves good communication between the rider and photographer. The first consideration is always safety. In this case, we discussed the line beforehand and came up with possible exit plans in case it slid. The snow pack seemed stable though, and the exit to the couloir opened up nicely which would spread the slide debris and give Ed a fighting chance of staying ahead of any danger.

I got myself into position on an opposite ridge and set up for the shot. Ed radioed in to check his landmarks before dropping in. Riding a line like this requires you to be able to visualize what the slope looks like from above. The view from where I was standing was very different from the 'blind' drop in that Ed was standing on top of.

You've got to be fully ready to shoot the action as it unfolds because it doesn't last long. "Dropping in five" crackled over my radio and 20 seconds later Ed was cranking his way out the bottom of his line. With the shot in the bag I got to cash in on the benefits of my job – an untouched powder face between me and the valley floor!

James McPhail

Riders' tales
Finding natural jumps

Snowboarding movies are the sport's opinion leaders, and anyone who has been closely watching the snowboarding movies over the past couple of years may have noticed a few emerging trends.

Until about three years ago, movies were full of bewilderingly technical tricks being put down on big park jumps. The size of the jumps grew to the point that a trick wouldn't make it into a movie unless it was done on an outrageously large jump. After a year or so of this we began to see less park and more powder kickers, as landing a trick in powder is much, much more difficult than it is on a park jump. Powder kickers then begun to get bigger and bigger, culminating in the ridiculous session at the 120-ft Chad's Gap in Grizzly Gulch, Utah, with Travis Rice and Romain de Marchi, featured in Absinthe's *Pop* movie from the winter of 2004-2005.

But rather than this trend for increasing size continuing unchecked, snowboarding has taken off in a very interesting direction of late, spearheaded by riders such as Nicolas Muller, Freddie Kalbermatten and Gigi Ruff and inspired by visionaries such as Terje Haakonsen and Michi Albin.

Nicolas Muller is considered by those in the know to be the best snowboarder in the world at the moment, yet if you watch any of his movie parts you'll see comparatively few park kickers in there. Neither will you see too much in the way of death-defyingly large gaps. What you will see are some of the most technical tricks in the book being done first-hit off totally natural terrain, and this seems to be where the cutting edge of snowboarding is at the moment. "It should be more about style and more about creativity", says Nicolas, "and I think you can do that in the backcountry more."

So, whilst park kickers are great, it's often more challenging and thus more rewarding to take freestyle to the backcountry, and hit up natural jumps. It's also enormously good fun, and that's one great reason why we should all get involved.

Natural hits are more difficult for a number of reasons. Firstly, on any one park kicker, the transition never changes from jump to jump (save for the snow getting softer or harder as the day goes on) so once you're used to the way the jump feels, you know exactly what you're going to get. But on a natural hit you must first work out what the jump is going to be like – which is difficult because it's going to change each time you go off it. Secondly, you have to contend with the unpredictability of powder snow. Powder is more changeable than groomed snow, and it presents a much bigger range of challenges to your edge control and weight distribution. It's way harder to ride and land in powder than it is on piste, but that makes the feeling of stomping a trick down miles better.

Finding good natural jumps is all about being creative. There's a massive variety of things that can put you in the air – cliffs, rollers, step-ups, step-downs, cat tracks, small bumps, windlips – and anything is fair game. With a bit of experience your 'eye' will develop to the point where you can pick out the best ones immediately, and you'll know how best to ride them. There's nothing quite so satisfying as spotting a jump, thinking about how best to go off it, then hitting it and finding that it worked out just right. It's also an amazing feeling when you do a trick you learned in the park off a natural jump, and you land it.

Learning to ride natural terrain well is obviously a lifetime project, but here are a few general rules to follow that should help you steer clear of trouble:

▶▶ The golden rule is that you should never jump off anything without knowing what's on the other side. There could be a barely submerged rock, a hole, some trees, a massive cliff, anything. Always check out your landing first, or have a trusted friend spot it for you. Jump it next time round if need be. This is never more true than for hitting rollers on the piste, when you simply don't know if there's a person standing right underneath, or even a ski instructor with a massive string of children in tow. There's no excuse for crashing into people on the hill, and it's always your responsibility to avoid those further down the mountain than yourself.

▶▶ Steer clear of flat landings. These are the quickest way to ruin your back, your knees and your ankles. When there's a bit of powder about you can get away with landing a bit flatter, but if the snow's firm then it's a definite no.

▶▶ Think about your run out – it's the most important thing! It's often the case that you'll come out of a jump with loads more speed than you thought, and if the run out is short or bumpy (or worse, is full of those nasty frozen traverse lines) then it's a good idea to give it a miss.

▶▶ Always look for drops where the landing is steeper than the take-off. If the take-off is steeper than the landing, you're likely to put your knees through your head. Even when you see the likes of Mikey Le Blanc taking on inner city flat landings in the movies (such as *91 Words For Snow*), if you watch carefully you'll see they never jump off anything that's steeper than their landing.

▶▶ Learn to read transitions. The gradient of a jump or lip is what decides your trajectory, and judging the tightness of a transition is the first step to judging how fast you'll be able to go off it. If you hit a whippy (short and tight) transition with too much speed, you'll get thrown in the backseat and you'll be wildly out of control. Remember the sensation of finding that a jump has flung us violently into an involuntary half backflip? We've all been there. When a transition is whippy, the way to tackle it is to approach it with much less speed,

and ollie more. Similarly, we're all familiar with the sensation of charging at a jump or roller to discover that we've barely got any air at all. Usually, a flat transition is to blame. If a transition is flat then it has no inbuilt pop of its own, so the only way you're going to get any air is by taking loads of speed (think ski jumper, or downhill skier flying off a roller) or by really popping an ollie as you go off. With a good, powerful ollie you'll get way more air than someone who goes slightly faster but doesn't pop as much.

There are other obvious pointers to keep you on the straight and narrow. Don't land in your mate's bomb-hole off a cliff. If a jump appears to be okay, but every other rider that has gone off it has twatted themselves, then it's probably not quite so okay after all. Saying that, these are things that come with experience, and learning the hard way is often great for comedy value. Now, get out there . . .

R: NICOLAS MULLER P: JEFF CURTES/BURTON SNOWBOARDS 2007

Arcalis, Andorra

The Town

Arcalis is the undiscovered gem of Andorra, and the people working at Vallnord (the company who look after the three resorts in the north west of Andorra – Arinsal, Pal and Arcalis) want to keep it that way. You won't find any enormous hotels, housing developments or large shops here. Indeed, there isn't much of a village in Arcalis, just a couple of shops and the self-service restaurant at the base, as well as an abundance of car parking.

Sleeping There is very little in the way of accommodation at Arcalis. The **La Neu Aparthotel and Apartments** (T850750) is the closest accommodation available and is a ten-minute drive down the valley. A better option is to head down the valley to the Andorran capital of Andorra La Vella. The four-star **Fenix** (T760760) is reasonable, but remember that four stars in Andorra is probably worth three stars elsewhere.

Eating Andorra La Vella has an abundance of pizzerias, and there's a great tapas restaurant called **Mama Maria** (T869996) which is really popular with the locals and serves great food.

Bars and clubs You'll find plenty of bars and a couple of nightclubs in Andorra La Vella. The **Sports Bar** just off the high street is usually rammed.

Shopping Andorra La Vella is full of shops selling absolutely everything you're going to need – the place is basically a large duty-free store!

Health The **Caldea Spa** in Andorra La Vella has a large thermal pool and is one of Europe's best spas.

Internet There are a couple of internet cafés scattered around Andorra La Vella. Several of the larger hotels have free Wi-Fi access in the lobby, including the **Fenix**.

Transfer options Hiring a car at Barcelona airport is the best option as the transfer is a speedy two hours straight down the highway. Otherwise the Novatel bus runs four times a day. Check andorrabybus.com for more information.

Local partners Arcalis recently linked up to Arinsal and Pal to form the massive Vallnord area. Your pass is valid in both resorts.

Andorra's own freeriding secret. When it's on, expect hidden, steep pockets of incredible powder, with perfect cliff lines and tree routes, all within easy reach of the pistes.

◗ If you like this you ...
... try Jasper/Marmot Basin ▸▸p76, Bansko ▸▸p100, or Levi ▸▸p244.

R: NELSON PRATT P: MIKE WEYERHAEUSER/IDP

The Mountain

Arcalis is a surprisingly versatile resort, with terrain that belies Andorra's traditional status as beginner- and intermediate-only zone. True, there are plenty of long, easy runs that are perfect for beginners and some steeper stuff for intermediates, but there's also a significant amount of freeriding on offer – especially if you're prepared to hike a little. The locals reckon it to be the best freeriding in Andorra. Better yet, Arcalis is relatively quiet, although weekend trippers from Spain and France swell the numbers a little.

Beginners The lifts around the base of Arcalis are perfect for beginners. Once you've mastered the basics, take the La Basera chairlift up to the top of Les Portelles and ride the three easy blue runs – Els Terragalls, El Tunel and La Coma – down to the restaurant and bar at La Coma for lunch before following the green La Basera run back down to the base in the afternoon.

Intermediate Take the La Basera chairlift up to the top of Les Portelles and ride the red runs – La Portella Del Mig and Les Tartares – a few times.

⊙ OPENING TIMES

Mid-Dec to late Apr: 0830-1600

⊙ RESORT PRICES

Week pass (5 days):
€149 high season, €125 low season
Day pass: €25
Season pass: €450

⊙ DIRECTORY

Tourist office: T739600
Medical centre: T890570
Pisteurs: T737622
Taxi: T383081
Local Radio: Andorra FM 89.0
Website: vallnord.com

This place reminds me of Verbier but in miniature. It's so out of keeping with the rest of Andorra. Hopefully no-one will believe me.
Mike Weyerhaueser, snowboard photographer

Head left off these and get a few powder lines in the designated Free Ride Area before heading to base camp for lunch. Take the La Basera chairlift and head left down to La Coma and then up the Creussans chairlift to take in that view.

Advanced Get a guide and your gear in order and head to the La Coma valley for some freeriding action and heli-boarding if you're that way inclined. The view mentioned should whet your appetite sufficiently to get your juices flowing. Heli-boarding is also, like most things in Andorra, much cheaper than you expect - €150 per person, per run is the going rate.

Kids There's a really popular school, but not a lot else, other than the beginner facilities mentioned above.

Flat light days Spend the day at the spa in Andorra La Vella – an absolute must.

P: MIKE WEYERHAUESER/IDP

☺ LOCALS DO

⊙ Queue up for the lifts to open on a powder day.
⊙ Ride the bottom chair line back to the car park. One of the best tree runs in the world.
⊙ Ride powder boards.

☹ LOCALS DON'T

⊗ Come here for the nightlife.
⊗ Or the food.
⊗ Go too high if the wind is up.

⊙ PROS

⊙ The best freeriding in Andorra.
⊙ Ridiculously quiet and empty on a weekday.
⊙ Big, wide, easy runs - great for beginners.

⊗ CONS

⊗ Not much in the way of amenities: most stay elsewhere.
⊗ Due to the dual aspect you get a few white-out days as the cloud sits in the valley.
⊗ There are bigger resorts in Andorra with more to offer the whole family.

☺ NOT TO MISS

The view over the back of Arcalis from the top of the Creussans chairlift.

ⓘ REMEMBER TO AVOID

Plenty of flat spots, so beginners will have to learn to 'read' terrain and do some strategic straight-lining if they're to avoid walking some sections.

☺ SNOW DEPTH

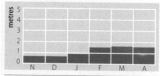

☺ RELIVE A FAMOUS MOMENT

Head to Andorra via Bilbao and visit Frank Gehry's Guggenheim Museum, a beautiful bit of architecture which also makes a cameo appearance in *The World is Not Enough*.

1940 m	TOWN ALTITUDE
140 km	KM TO AIRPORT
BCN	AIRPORT
★★☆	VEGETARIAN RATING
★★☆	INTERNET CAFES
★☆☆	RIDE IN/RIDE OUT
2625 m	HIGHEST LIFT
700 m	VERTICAL DROP
1092	RIDEABLE AREA (IN ACRES)
24 km	KM OF PISTES
1	NURSERY AREAS
12/11/2	RUNS: BEG/INTER/ADV
0/0	FUNICULAR/CABLE CARS
0/5	GONDOLAS/CHAIRS
7	DRAGS
no	NIGHT RIDING
0	PARKS
0	PIPE
no	SUMMER AREAS
★★☆ ★★☆	ENVIRONMENTAL RATING
	COST INDICATOR

SPAIN & ANDORRA
ARCALIS

Soldeu, Andorra

Andorra's most progressive freestyle resort. It's had a well-maintained fun park since the mid-nineties, and a thriving crew of loyal locals to go with it.

If you like this ...
... try *Méribel* »p146,
Les Diablerets »p322, or
Keystone »p364.

The Town

Soldeu is just one part of the much larger Andorran resort of Grand Valira, which is made up of six resorts linked by the mountain roads below. These are Pas de la Casa, Grau Roig, Soldeu, El Tarter, Canillo and Encamp. The general feel of the entire Grand Valira resort is one of fun and friendliness, which really feels a million miles away from the resorts of France or Switzerland. Everybody here, it seems, just wants to have fun.

Sleeping There are some good accommodation choices in Soldeu, ranging from the top of the line **Sport Hotel Village** (T870500) to the **Hotel Piolets** (T872787).

Eating The best of the restaurants are probably in Andorra La Vella, but locally there's **Fat Albert's** serving local cuisine, or British-run **Slim Jim's**. A little further up the price scale is **Borda del Rector** (T852606) serving fantastic traditional local cuisine.

Bars and clubs Soldeu is famed for its nightlife, and there's a distinctly British feel to the whole affair. Many resort workers and staff (including the authors of this guide) prefer to spend their time at **Fat Albert's**, **The Pussycat** or **The Aspen** – all very British affairs.

Shopping Head down to Andorra La Vella for any shopping needs. Look out for British-run snowboard shop **Loaded**, run by Brit pro Tyler Chorlton.

Health The **Calbo Thermal Leisure Centre** (T870500) is a fantastic place to recharge your batteries after a few days battering yourself on the pistes and off.

Internet For a small town Soldeu has good web facilities. **Slim Jim's** has good access.

Transfer options As with Arcalis, hiring a car in Barcelona is quick and simple. There are also bus options from Barcelona and Toulouse in France – check andorrabybus.com.

Local partners Soldeu is partnered with the other five resorts that make up Grand Valira – Pas de la Casa, Grau Roig, El Tarter, Canillo and Encamp.

> " "
>
> Apart from the nightlife here in Soldeu, the riding is actually pretty sick! Grand Valira has tons of shredding plus El Tarter has the best park in the Pyrenees and is only a couple minutes ride from Soldeu!
>
> *Tyler Chorlton, Andorra local and UK pro rider*

P: J MCNAMARA

P: J MCNAMARA

R: RHYS CRABTREE P: MIKE WEYERHAUSER/IDP

P: CHRIS MORAN/HOTSHITPICTURES.COM

⏱ OPENING TIMES
Late Nov to late Apr: 0830-1600

💲 RESORT PRICES
Week pass (6 days): €180
Day pass: €34,50
Season pass: €485-628

ⓘ DIRECTORY
Tourist office: T801060
Medical centre: T890570
Pisteurs: T808900
Taxi: T863000
Local Radio: Andorra FM 89.0
Website: grandvalira.com

The Mountain

Since Pas de la Casa agreed to amalgamate with Grau Roig and Soldeu El Tarter in 2003, Grand Valira has become the biggest area in Andorra – so you're guaranteed to find something that suits you. There are three parks ranging from total beginner to highly advanced that are all superb and well maintained. The facilities on the mountain are among the best we've seen on our travels around the world – completely contrary to what we were expecting. The people are polite and friendly and the overall vibe is that of fun and enjoyment that seems at odds with many resorts we've visited.

Beginners As a beginner just coming to Soldeu/Grand Valira is a big day out in itself, especially considering the amount of terrain that is available to you. Every resort within Grand Valira has areas that have been especially designed to cater for newbies, with wide, open, uncrowded blue runs that aren't intersected by others. Canillo is the best area for learning as it has the easiest lifts.
Intermediate Get an early start to

the day at Soldeu and head over towards Pas de la Casa in the far west. You can then head over to Encamp in the far east of the slope map and ride the entire resort from end to end inside a day and get back in time for the last lifts to take you home. Obviously make sure you keep track of the time though, and leave yourself a good seven hours or so to do the whole resort and have lunch. A great first day to get your bearings, provided the weather is good and you can see where you're going. Don't get lost though!
Advanced Hitting the parks is probably the best fun you can have here. The expert level snow park in the El Tarter sector is the best – there are several kickers of varying sizes and gaps, a selection of rails and boxes, a quarter pipe, a hip and last, but definitely not least, the 120-m half pipe. All are usually in immaculate condition and there's a button lift that allows you to jump off at the top of the park, so you're basically all set for a day of killing everything in sight.
Kids There are four fully equipped nurseries for children aged up to three across Grand Valira. For older children (four to six) there are five snow gardens (where they can take lessons in safety).
Flat light days Time to visit Calbo.

☺ LOCALS DO
- ➤ Ride the El Tarter park. It rules.
- ➤ Make non-locals welcome. This is a friendly place.
- ➤ Visit either Caldea or Calbo for the full spa experience.

☹ LOCALS DON'T
- ➤ Get lost – although you might.
- ➤ Get in the way – brush up on your park etiquette.
- ➤ Forget to hike to the top for the best freeriding.

✔ PROS
- ➤ Great for beginners, intermediate and families.
- ➤ Cheap.
- ➤ Great nightlife.

✘ CONS
- ➤ Limited choice of mountain restaurants.
- ➤ Some lift queues in places, but Grand Valira are working on it.
- ➤ Cheap drinks and lots of Brits mean it can get rowdy.

☀ NOT TO MISS
At the top of the El Tarter chairlift, find the Mickey Snow Club, which is a nice easy run for children and their parents to use. It's decorated with various Disney characters with piped Disney music to complete the feel!

ⓘ REMEMBER TO AVOID
Some of the links are often uphill! It's also easy to get lost here due to the sheer size, so keep a map handy.

❄ SNOW DEPTH

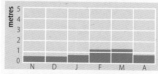

☆ RELIVE A FAMOUS MOMENT
Head to Andorra via Barcelona and you might be able to spot streets from Matt Damon's *The Bourne Identity*.

1800 m	TOWN ALTITUDE
180 km	KM TO AIRPORT
BCN	AIRPORT
★★☆	VEGETARIAN RATING
★★★	INTERNET CAFES
★★☆	RIDE IN/RIDE OUT
2640 m	HIGHEST LIFT
1710 m	VERTICAL DROP
4848	RIDEABLE AREA (IN ACRES)
193 km	KM OF PISTES
5	NURSERY AREAS
56/32/22	RUNS: BEG/INTER/ADV
1/3	FUNICULAR/CABLE CARS
55	GONDOLAS/CHAIRS
5	DRAGS
no	NIGHT RIDING
4	PARKS
1	PIPE
no	SUMMER AREAS
★★★ ★★★	ENVIRONMENTAL RATING
Ⓢ Ⓢ Ⓢ	COST INDICATOR

FIGURES COVER THE GRAN VALIRA AREA

SPAIN & ANDORRA
SOLDEU

P: JAMES MCPHAIL

Spain's best resort, offering history, great riding, delicious local food and a warm welcome.

◑ If you like this...
... try *La Tania* ▸▸p140, *Canazei* ▸▸p172, or *Cardrona* ▸▸p228.

The Town ⊟🚹⊟

Given the popularity of nearby Andorra among snowboarders, it comes as a shock to realize that the Val D'Aran in Spain is one of the few hidden gems left in Europe when it comes to snowboarding. Outstandingly beautiful, blessed with bountiful sunshine and snow – it doesn't even merit a 'Here Be Monsters' reference on most people's winter map. The resort of Baqueira-Beret sits at the head of the valley, although you can stay in a number of hamlets and towns further away – Salardu, Arties and Vielha. It means you need a car, but it also mean you get to explore the real beauty of this valley, which gives up its charms by degrees. It has enough art, culture and history to practically qualify it as a World Heritage Site – and the snowboarding is pretty incredible as well.

Sleeping In Salardu, the **Hotel Lacreu** (T973 644222) offers two-star accommodation and a great atmosphere. A little further away, **Hotel Valarties** (valarties@aranweb.com) also offers the homely Val D'Aran welcome, while the newly opened **La Pleta** (lapleta.com) is Baqueira's grandest hotel and spa.

Eating One of the main reasons for visiting the valley is the incredible food – there are hundreds of great tapas bars and restaurants. Look out for **Tammaro** in Baqueira, **Urtau** in Arties and **El Viellito** at Vielha.

Bars and clubs In Baqueira, the main club in town is **Pacha** – yes, that's right, like the Ibizan superclub. **La Luna** in Arties is pretty lively, as is the main square in Salardu.

Shopping There are two supermarkets in Baqueira – **Beso** and **Multipropiedad**. Bigger and cheaper stores are down the valley in Vielha.

Health La Pleta's spa, **Occitania** (slh.com) is the real deal. There are also thermal baths in Banys de Tredos and Baronia de Les.

Internet There's an internet café just off the main square in Vielha, and some hotels have wireless access.

Transfer options Try **Alsina Graells** (alsinagraells.com) for bus transfers.

Local partners The pass covers the Baqueira, Beret and Bonaguia areas of the resort.

⊙ OPENING TIMES

Early Dec to late Mar: 0845-1645

🟢 RESORT PRICES

Week pass (6 days): €196
Day pass: €39
Season pass: €810

🟡 DIRECTORY

Tourist office: T973 639010
Medical centre: T973 645107
Pisteurs: T973 639025
Taxi: T649 987319
Local radio: None
Website: baqueira.es

R: ED LEIGH P: JAMES MCPHAIL

The Mountain ◑❄⊛☺

Baqueira-Beret is justifiably considered the best resort in Spain, especially for snowboarders. Much of this is to do with its peculiar location. It faces the Atlantic, which means the resort gets a good share of snowfall and sunshine. Better yet, the terrain means every rider will find something to get stuck into. The only downside is a lack of decent freestyling facilities, which means experts will struggle if there is a lack of snow, although this is unlikely. Baqueira has three main areas: Baqueira proper is basically the front face as you look at the resort; while Bonaigua is the backside; over to skier's right, accessed either by car or a linking chair, is the Beret area, which has predominantly mellower slopes. Taken together, these areas form a true snowboarder's playground, with great freeriding among a beautiful, soulful mountain environment.

P: JAMES MCPHAIL

It's beautiful, unspoilt and has terrain for everyone. It is relaxed, uncrowded and has serious potential.

Ed Leigh, broadcaster

Beginners The front of Baqueira has some mellower runs at the top of the Bosque lift and the new gondola from town, called the pasture. Complete newcomers will lap the Rabada drag lift, but the best beginner terrain is really over in Beret. Here, the Pla de Beret chair offers mellow starter slopes, while the larger Clot der Os and dera Reina chairs have some nice long runs to get to grips with. Later in the week, navigate your way over to the Argulls side for some good runs.

Intermediate If it snows, you're going to have a lot of fun. A good day would be the morning in Beret, blasting the front, before heading over to Teso dera Mina chair and spending the afternoon working your way along the ridge underneath the chair. You'll get a lot of lines in, and it's all pretty safe.

Advanced Again, there is a lot of scope. If hiking is your thing, there are infinite roadside options. In resort, the steepest terrain can be accessed by taking the Mirador right to the top. Where the Manaud splits, there's a big open face but it can be dangerous. Similarly, going skier's right off the Guineu red opens up a lot of steep options for confident freeriders.

Kids Special classes for children older than five, and free passes for kids under six. Ages six to 11 get special prices as well.

Flat light days Take the opportunity to explore some of the history and beautiful architecture in the valley. Val D'Aran is full of Romanesque religious buildings.

☺ LOCALS DO
- Stay down the valley – it's cheaper.
- Afford visitors an incredibly friendly welcome.
- Eat tapas – get a plate, load it, show it to the barman and tuck in.

☹ LOCALS DON'T
- Drive over the Bonaguia pass in the middle of winter. Take the tunnel through Vielha instead.
- Lie in on a powder day – it's relatively low, so you need to make the most of it.

✔ PROS
- Time capsule valley.
- Versatile resort.
- Incredible food.

✘ CONS
- Snow at end of season can be unreliable.
- Need a car to really get the most out of the valley.
- Increasing in popularity, so might not be a well kept secret for much longer.

◉ NOT TO MISS
Although it's easy to stay in Baqueira itself, it's very worth exploring Bonaigua and Beret as well. Both have some great riding, and the park is in Bonaigua.

ⓘ REMEMBER TO AVOID
It's a compact resort, but be careful you don't get stranded in Baqueira at the end of the day if you've parked your car in Beret, or vice-versa.

◈ SNOW DEPTH
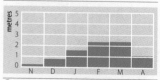

◉ RELIVE A FAMOUS MOMENT
You'll need some cash to do this properly, but you could try holidaying in Baqueira in the manner of King Juan Carlos. It's his favourite resort.

1500 m	TOWN ALTITUDE
340 km	KM TO AIRPORT
BCN	AIRPORT
★★☆	VEGETARIAN RATING
★☆☆	INTERNET CAFES
★★☆	RIDE IN/RIDE OUT
2510 m	HIGHEST LIFT
1100 m	VERTICAL DROP
4749	RIDEABLE AREA (IN ACRES)
104 km	KM OF PISTES
4	NURSERY AREAS
41/25/6	RUNS: BEG/INTER/ADV
0/0	FUNICULAR/CABLE CARS
1/20	GONDOLAS/CHAIRS
5	DRAGS
no	NIGHT RIDING
1	PARKS
0	PIPE
no	SUMMER AREAS
★★★	ENVIRONMENTAL RATING
ⓢⓢⓢ	COST INDICATOR

SPAIN & ANDORRA
BAQUEIRA-BERET

Sierra Nevada, Spain

The Town

If you stay in Granada (which we recommend) there is endless exploring to be done. Obviously the first thing to check out is the Alhambra Palace. Dating back to as early as 1238, built by the Nasrites and then taken over by the Christians when they conquered the city in 1492, it is breathtaking and totally dominates the city's architecture and makes for one hell of a backdrop. There are numerous great bars and tapas restaurants to sample and a few nightclubs to get your groove on. Sierra itself, 30-odd km up the road, is also a far cry from the usual resort experience thanks to a crazy party scene, a super-fun mountain and those incredible views over to Africa.

Sleeping If you do choose to stay down in Granada there are numerous B&Bs – most of them pretty basic but great value (as little as €15 per person/per night). Victors B&B is one example (granadahomestay.com). Apartments are also available for hire at (vivegranada.com). If you opt for staying in the resort of Sierra Nevada, which is basically a purpose-built ski village, you could try **Hotel GHM Monachil** (T958 481450). It's right in the main town square, a short walk from the Parador chair.

Eating One of the main reasons for visiting – try the Moorish cuisine at **Arrayanes** (rest-arrayanes.com) in Granada, or the **Huerto de Juan Ranas** (restaurantejuanranas.com). Up at the resort you'll find a number of cafés, fast food and mountain restaurants – on the whole all pretty good value.

Bars and clubs In Granada the nightlife is based around tapas and discos. The two main party streets are Calle Navas and Calle Elviria and they have plenty of both. In the resort itself, **El Golpe** and **Soho Bar de Copas** seem to be the most popular.

Shopping Shop in Granada – it's a big city with great value supermarkets and shops. In the resort, there are two branches of **Rio Sport**.

Health A number of the hotels in the resort offer in-house spa facilities.

Internet There are at least five internet cafés in the centre of traveller-friendly Granada. In resort, the **Explora 2** café is located at the **Hotel Ziryab** in the main square.

Transfer options RyanAir now offer budget flights to Granada Airport, 17 km from the city. Take the bus outside arrivals into Granada, although a car is probably easiest for the 37-km drive to the resort each day.

Local partners None.

> " The combination of riding powder in the morning whilst overlooking Morocco's Atlas mountains, then heading down to Granada in the afternoon is hard to beat – Sierra Nevada offers a refreshing break from the norm.
>
> *Marcus Chapman, ex-editor,* Snowboard UK

Fancy laying out some powder turns in the morning and then checking out Granada's Alhambra Palace in the afternoon? Sierra Nevada is a truly unique snowboarding trip.

⟡ If you like this . . .
. . . try Zakopane ⟩⟩p106.

P: DANMILNER.COM

The Mountain

When you drive up to Sierra Nevada the first thing you notice about the resort is the lack of trees – the ski area is almost entirely above the treeline and rises to an altitude of over 3000 m. The second thing everybody notices is the unique dome-shaped terrain of the mountain. Because of this, conditions can get icy if the wind is up. Make sure you check the weather before heading up in the morning. New for 2005 was the Sulayr snowboard park consisting of a halfpipe, kickers and rails. This is serviced by its own lift, which saves the hike. If freeriding is your thing then head to the Laguna de Yeguas area for natural ridges, gullies and cliff drops.

Beginners For total beginners and those linking basic turns this is a pretty perfect resort. There are plenty of mellow green runs at the base of resort, and two conveyor belts

making life easier. You'll also find a good snowboard school should you want lessons. The **Ski Centre Ski School**, T646 178406, set up by an English couple, offer superb tuition.
Intermediate Sierra Nevada has plenty to keep the intermediate rider occupied as well: there are great rollers to float off, ridges and gullies to explore and the snowboard park to check out. The runs are nice and wide and well groomed by the piste machines. Basically, the whole place is open to you, so get a piste map and make your way across the whole area.
Advanced In the morning head to the Laguna de Yeguas area for some powder turns then when the snow softens in the afternoon, hit the kickers and rails in the Sulayr snowpark. If you've still got energy in your legs throw yourself down the bordercross in the Borrequiles zone.
Kids There are two crèches at the resort. You'll find one in the Burreguiles main ski area and the other at the base of the Al-Andulas gondola. Call direct on T958 481081.
Flat light days When a storm rolls in to Sierra Nevada the lack of trees makes for poor visibility and it can get very windy on the mountain. It's a good excuse to check out Granada city.

⊘ OPENING TIMES
Mid-Nov to late Apr: 0900-1700

⊜ RESORT PRICES
Week pass (6 days): €220
Day pass: €37
Season pass: €700

ⓘ DIRECTORY
Tourist office: T958 249100
Medical centre: T958 481149
Pisteurs: T646 178406
Taxi: T958 280654
Local radio: None
Website: None

☺ LOCALS DO
⊘ Drive like lunatics up to resort if it's a powder day.
⊘ Drink ridiculously strong coffee as if it was Ribena.
⊘ Eat tapas – they're irresistible.

⊗ LOCALS DON'T
⊗ Complain there are no trees to shred.
⊗ Visit the Alhambra Palace – but you should.

✓ PROS
⊘ A unique mix of history and snowboarding.
⊘ Cheap accommodation in Granada.
⊘ A change from the normal holiday.

✗ CONS
⊗ Can get very busy around holiday periods.
⊗ Not the biggest ski area.
⊗ Conditions can be icy after a storm.

◐ NOT TO MISS
A trip round the Alhambra Palace and gardens.

ⓘ REMEMBER TO AVOID
With only one road from Granada up to the resort, try to avoid Spanish holidays and really bad snow days. It can be total carnage and well worth remembering the snow chains.

❋ SNOW DEPTH
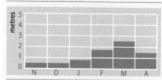

✪ RELIVE A FAMOUS MOMENT
Conan the Barbarian – starring Arnold Schwarzenegger and Gerry Lopez (yup – the pipeline surfer!) was filmed on location at Sierra Nevada. Wow!

2100 m	TOWN ALTITUDE
48 km	KM TO AIRPORT
GRX	AIRPORT
★★☆	VEGETARIAN RATING
★★☆	INTERNET CAFES
★★☆	RIDE IN/RIDE OUT
3300 m	HIGHEST LIFT
1200 m	VERTICAL DROP
area not measured	RIDEABLE AREA (IN ACRES)
84 km	KM OF PISTES
2	NURSERY AREAS
8/67/4	RUNS: BEG/INTER/ADV
0/2	FUNICULAR/CABLE CARS
0/16	GONDOLAS/CHAIRS
2	DRAGS
yes	NIGHT RIDING
1	PARKS
1	PIPE
no	SUMMER AREAS
★★★☆☆	ENVIRONMENTAL RATING
ⓢⓢⓢ	COST INDICATOR

R: MATT BURT P: DANMILNER.COM

R: HAMISH MCKNIGHT L: ZERMATT P: JAMES MCPHAIL

Switzerland

Hamish McKnight finding a small corner of Switzerland where he can yodel with delight ... Zermatt.

297

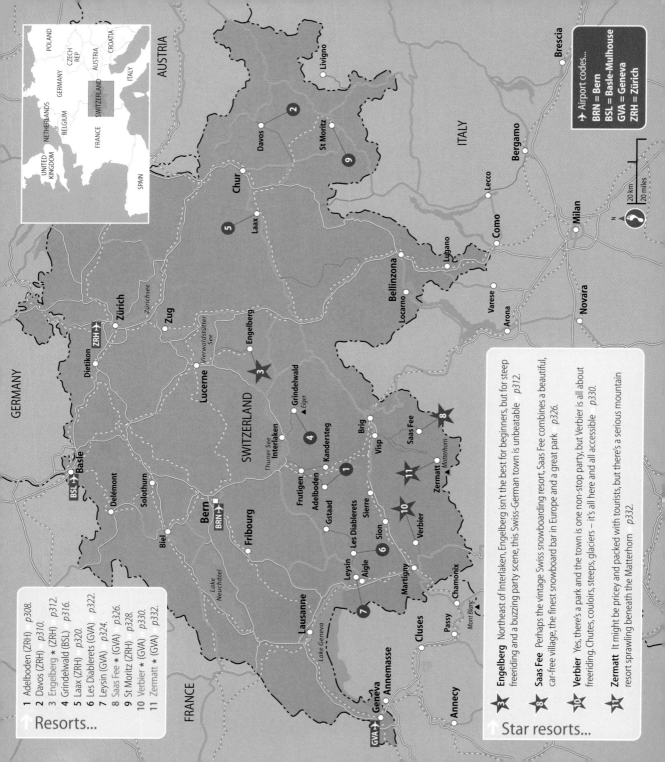

Resorts...

1 Adelboden (ZRH) → p308.
2 Davos (ZRH) p310.
3 Engelberg ★ (ZRH) → p312.
4 Grindelwald (BSL) ★ → p316.
5 Laax (ZRH) p320.
6 Les Diablerets (GVA) p322.
7 Leysin (GVA) p324.
8 Saas Fee ★ (GVA) p326.
9 St Moritz (ZRH) p328.
10 Verbier ★ (GVA) p330.
11 Zermatt ★ (GVA) p332.

Airport codes...
BRN = Bern
BSL = Basle-Mulhouse
GVA = Geneva
ZRH = Zürich

Star resorts...

3 Engelberg Northeast of Interlaken, Engelberg isn't the best for beginners, but for steep freeriding and a buzzing party scene, this Swiss-German town is unbeatable p312.

8 Saas Fee Perhaps the vintage Swiss snowboarding resort, Saas Fee combines a beautiful, car-free village, the finest snowboard bar in Europe and a great park p326.

10 Verbier Yes, there's a park and the town is one non-stop party, but Verbier is all about freeriding. Chutes, couloirs, steeps, glaciers – it's all here and all accessible → p330.

11 Zermatt It might be pricey and packed with tourists, but there's a serious mountain resort sprawling beneath the Matterhorn p332.

Introduction

For many, the Switzerland's lavish winter iconography basically defines the European Alps. The terms 'Heidi country' and 'chocolate box' are overused, and the stereotypes – ornate chalets, a quietly efficient train system wending its way through precipitous valleys and cloyingly pretty valleys overlooked by fearsome peaks – are well known. As is often the case though, the truth is a little muddier. For sure, there's *something* in each of those stereotypes (as any visit to, say, Grindelwald will illustrate) but the reality is that today Switzerland is one of the most progressive snowboarding destinations on the planet.

Unlike the French, who dallied when the sideways revolution came to town and were content with a cursory nod to our needs, the Swiss seem to have been energized by what snowboarding brought to the mountain. Today, they are enjoying the advantages of this approach and it's the resulting versatility of the place that stands out for the travelling snowboarder. For every sleepy little Les Diablerets, there's a globally famed powerhouse like Zermatt to consider. For every Engelberg, with its steep, glacial freeriding and Swedish-led party scene, there's an Adelboden, with a park rapidly gaining Europe-wide renown. And that's without even mentioning Saas Fee, Verbier or Laax: huge resorts that pretty much define the best way of providing snowboarders with cutting-edge, 21st-century facilities.

On the downside, the elephant in the room when it comes to Switzerland is always the cost: even by usual mountain standards, it's an expensive place to go riding. And some resorts suffer from a lack of any snowboarding culture. Those who rank their resorts in terms of hedonistic potential must also choose particularly carefully, as the nightlife in some towns borders on the pretentious. But for a quintessentially European experience and a winning combination of history, culture and forward-thinking facilities, Switzerland must be a serious option.

Switzerland rating

Value for money
★★☆☆☆

Nightlife
★★★☆☆

Freestyle
★★★★☆

Freeride
★★★★★

Essentials

Getting there

Geneva International airport has transformed the ease with which it's possible to reach the Swiss Alps, and it is an incredibly convenient airport for anyone heading into the west of the country to ride resorts such as Leysin, Les Diablerets, Verbier or Zermatt. Carriers to Geneva (gva.ch) include **easyJet** (easyjet.com), **British Airways** (ba.com), **Swiss Air** (swiss.com), **KLM** (KLM.com), **Alitalia** (Alitalia.com), **Lufthansa** (lufthansa.com), **BMI** (flyBMI.com), **Continental** (continental.com) and **Northwest** (nwa.com).

Switzerland's other major airport is Zurich, which is the best choice for resorts in the German-speaking part of the country such as Engelberg, Laax and Saas Fee. Carriers to Zurich include **British Airways** (ba.com), **Swiss Air** (swiss.com), **Lufthansa** (lufthansa.com), **Air France** (airfrance.com) and **American Airlines** (aa.com).

Red tape

Switzerland is not a member of the EU, but visitors from EU countries do not require a visa. Other foreigners who do not intend to work or study can stay for three months without a residence permit.

Getting around

Although we recommend using the Swiss Travel System for day-to-day travelling (see below), a car is probably the better option if you're planning a longer, multi-resort road trip. The Swiss drive on the right, and a valid UK, EU/EEA or driving license from your own country is fine. International Driving Permits are not required. People in Switzerland follow all regulations, and the police tend to enforce the law fairly strictly – particularly when it comes to the *vignette* road tax.

Mountain passes If you're planning any major mid-winter drives, check tcs.ch and mct.sbb.ch for up-to-date information on the status of local mountain passes.

VIGNETTE. P: CHRIS MORAN

P: CHRIS MORAN

Switzerland price guide							
	☕	🍴	📦	🎧	@	📚	🥤
In €	2,25	3,20	3,70	0,60	6,40	2,90	1,30

Top tips

- Choose your resort carefully. If it's nightlife you want, choose Verbier. For a romantic weekend break, Les Diablerets would be a safe bet. There are big differences between a lot of Swiss resorts.

- If you're driving, buy a *vignette*. You *will* get fined without one.

- Take lots of money. There is no escaping the fact that Switzerland is one of the most expensive locations in the world, and you don't want to spend your trip worrying about how much you're burning. Accept it, and relax.

- Make an effort to learn a few phrases of the language they speak in the part of the country you're going to be visiting.

- Try and visit as many resorts as you can. Many are close together and Switzerland is perfect road trip material.

Car hire Most major hire car companies (easycar.com, hertz.com, avis.com) have offices in airports and cities. Usual age restrictions apply.

Public transport

Once in Switzerland, the Swiss Travel System is a beautiful, green and extremely pleasant way to pass the transfer journey. Get a four-, eight-, 15-, 22-day or one-month pass for unlimited travel on trains, buses and boats. The system covers 37 cities with 50% off mountain summit trains, cable cars and funiculars. There are other options – for further information visit MySwitzerland.com/rail. For timetables have a look at sbb.ch. Buses are included, although check postbus.ch for more bus information.

Opening hours and tradition

In mountain areas, shops close on Sundays and can also close between 1200 and 1400 on weekdays, although it depends on the area. Generally speaking this isn't the case in the major cities. The Swiss also observe regular European national holiday occasions such as New Year's Day, Easter and Christmas.

Eating

The main Swiss culinary bequest to the world is, of course, the fondue: melted cheese and bread. It's followed closely by the raclette, which originally developed in the Valais and spread to the rest of the country and neighbouring France. Here, cheese is melted in front of a heat source and scraped onto a plate. Both of these dishes have their roots in Swiss diary farming, which is one of the country's main industries, and it makes sense in this context that the national dish is filling, unpretentious and takes advantage of Switzerland's range of over 200 cheeses. The result is that the fondue is nigh-on ubiquitous, and it's

Switzerland is one of the best spots for snowboarding on earth, and believe me I have been almost everywhere! The terrain goes from easy to hard, and if you're a pipe rider, a freerider or a park rider, you'll find the right spot. If you keep your eyes open there's good stuff to ride, jib, jump or cruise in every resort you go. Have fun!

Gian Simmen, 1998 Olympic Half Pipe Champion

→ **Fact file**

Currency	Swiss Franc (CHF)
Exchange rate	€1 = CHF1.56
Time zone	GMT +1
Country code	+41
Emergency numbers	
Ambulance:	T144
Police:	T117
Fire:	T118

P: CHRIS MORAN/HOTSHITPICTURES.COM

almost obligatory to sample at least a few on any trip to the country.

Breakfast in Switzerland is generally the classic continental mix of bread rolls, cheese, ham, boiled eggs, *birchermuesli* (a filling, nutritious variation of dried muesli), strong coffee and juice. Fill up or make up some extra rolls for lunch because on-mountain restaurants here are as expensive as it gets, even if the food is generally great. Another way around this, if you're on a budget, is to stock up at the local supermarkets as soon as you get into town.

In the evening, be prepared for more central European mainstays, assuming you're bored with melted cheese. Sausages, pork, veal and sundry other meats are the norm, usually with fries, potatoes or

Lift chat

Reading matter

Sun cream? Check. Passport? Check. Book? Yup – but what to choose? Before you leave for your next shred trip it might be worth leaving the airport potboiler at home for once and packing something that's both a great read *and* something that will enhance your holiday experience. Choosing a book set in the place you're going to be staying is a great way of adding to the enjoyment of reading. Not only can you look at the places being described and gain a greater understanding of the book, you can also use it as a truly alternative guidebook to help you get into the rhythm of a place your own way. Few pleasures in life beat reading, say, Heinrich Harrer's gripping account of the first ascent of the Eigerwand from the safety of a Grindelwald sun terrace.

▶▶ **Zermatt** *Killing Dragons*, Fergus Fleming
▶▶ **Queenstown** *The Colour*, Rose Tremain
▶▶ **Chamonix** *Frankenstein*, Mary Shelley
▶▶ **Shemshak** *The Road to Oxiana*, Robert Byron
▶▶ **Grindelwald** *The White Spider*, Heinrich Harrer
▶▶ **Baqueira** *Homage to Catalonia*, George Orwell
▶▶ **Davos** *The Magic Mountain*, Thomas Mann

R: LISA FILZMOSER L: LAAX P: CHRIS MORAN/HOTSHITPICTURES.COM

Key phrases

> **Swiss German dialect**
> There is no official spelling of Swiss German and there are so many regional variations that we've stuck to the 'high' German mostly. In brackets we've put words which are commonly used all over German-speaking areas of Switzerland.

Yes   *ja*
No   *nein*
Please   *bitte*
Thank you   *danke/merci*
Sorry   *Entschuldigung/ excusé/sorry*
Hello   *guten tag/grüezi/salut/ hoi (informal)*
Goodbye   *auf Wiedersehen/ uf widerluege/ciao/tschüss*
I don't understand   *ich verstehe Sie/dich nicht*
I'd like…   *ich möchte...*
How much is it?   *was kostet es?*
Where is…?   *wo ist...?*
Men   *Herren*
Ladies   *Damen*
Left   *links*
Right   *rechts*
Straight on   *gerade aus*
Night   *die Nacht*
Room   *das Zimmer*
Shower   *die Dusche*
Toilet   *die Toilette*
Bill   *die Rechnung*
White coffee   *Kaffee mit Rahm*
Beer   *das Bier*

Mineral water   *das Mineralwasser*
Orange juice   *der Orangensaft*
Sandwich   *das Sandwich*
Ham   *der Schinken*
Cheese   *der Käse*
Help!   *hilfe!*
North   *nord*
South   *süd*
East   *ost*
West   *west*

Numbers
1   *eins*
2   *zwei*
3   *drei*
4   *vier*
5   *fünf*
6   *sechs*
7   *sieben*
8   *acht*
9   *neun*
10   *zehn*
11   *elf*
20   *zwanzig*
100   *hundert*
1000   *tausend*
10000   *zehn tausend*

Days of the week
Monday   *Montag*
Tuesday   *Dienstag*
Wednesday   *Mittwoch*
Thursday   *Donnerstag*
Friday   *Freitag*
Saturday   *Samstag*
Sunday   *Sonntag*

is spoken – not 'Swiss-French', as no such dialect exists. Then there is Ticino in the south, where Italian is the official language, and the tiny 2% of the population living in the Canton of Grisons in the south-eastern corner of the country who speak the obscure Romansch. In identifying the border where Swiss-German becomes French, the Swiss speak about the 'Rösti Graben' – an imaginary border representing the change from one language to another, as well as the many cultural differences this represents.

Crime/safety

Switzerland remains one of the safest, most civil countries in Europe, although the danger obviously increases in the major cities. In most places, it is safe to leave boards on balconies and on restaurant terraces but thefts do occur, particularly in the bigger resorts such as Verbier or Laax. The Swiss police are fair, although drivers must be aware that any travel on Swiss motorways requires Swiss car tax (*vignette*), which can be bought at the border or at newsagents. Checkpoints are frequent, and large fines are common.

Health

An agreement between the EU and Switzerland came into force in June 2002, meaning that EU citizens can now use a European Health Insurance Card (EHIC) to get reduced cost healthcare while in the country. But comprehensive medical insurance is recommended for any trip to Switzerland.

L: MATTERHORN   P: JAMES MCPHAIL

vegetables on the side. But really, expect to find the usual mix of Western fusion food in most places, albeit more expensively priced. Tex-Mex, Chinese cuisine and even the 'Golden Arches' have spread, tentacle-like, into Heidi country. Vegetarians are never going to starve in Switzerland, even if they end up subsisting mainly on sauerkraut and fondue. Generally though, the choice is good for non-carnivorous types. And, as you're in Switzerland, why not sample their other notable contribution to world cuisine, and get hold of some Swiss chocolate? Apparently, the Swiss eat more chocolate per head than any other nation in the world – a whopping average consumption of 12.3 kg in 2001!

Language

For such a small country, the language situation in Switzerland is surprisingly complex. Swiss-German is a dialect of German spoken mainly in the eastern part of the country. In the west, standard French

P: ANDREW HINGSTON

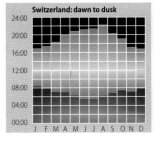

Switzerland: dawn to dusk

R: TINA BIRBAUM   P: JAMES MCPHAIL

❝❞

Swiss snowboarding is different to most other countries because people ride the whole mountain, and don't just worry about park and pipe. We grow up using the mountains for what they are and what they have to give. I think that is also why people outside of Switzerland sometimes see us as funny farmer people!

Tina Birbaum, Swiss pro snowboarder

Snowboarding Switzerland

"There are just mountains everywhere you look. If Switzerland isn't the board riding country in Europe, then I don't know what is. Being a small nation with a mere seven million inhabitants, I'm sure 60% of them are having some sort of weekend fun in the eternal white. Blessed with stunning and exciting high mountain environment Switzerland is one of the more credible places when it comes to mountain sports in general. Snowboarding is taken very seriously in our beautiful Alpine country, even though the mainstream media still fails to acknowledge the fact that it is a great industry that finds more and more recognition." Cira Riedel, Seventh Sky Magazine

The Swiss are an unlikely nation to be at the vanguard of the snowboarding revolution. There really could not be a more traditional Alpine society than this small, conservative and cash-rich country, with its unlikely dual industries of dairy farming and international banking. The advertisements for private investment banks and ridiculously expensive watches that greet the snowboarder in the arrivals area at

Pros & cons

Pros ...
- Some of Europe's best freeriding terrain in huge resort areas.
- There's a lot of Alpine culture here, making it a generally enriching experience. Few resorts can match the splendour of Zermatt.
- Watch how a Swiss resort runs, and suddenly understand where the Swiss got their reputation for efficiency.
- With Geneva in the west and Zurich in the centre, most resorts are very easy to access.
- Generally green outlook, with cars banned from many resorts.

... and cons
- Can be expensive.
- The season ends early, meaning it can be all over by April.
- It's busy – with tourists, snowboarders, skiers and locals.
- Although there are some party strongholds, Switzerland is generally calmer than its neighbours. Although that could obviously be a good thing for some.

R: MATT BURT P: DANMILNER.COM

I think riding the Alps is the best terrain in the whole world. The snow and the terrain is epic. Some places are like Alaska with chair lifts. We also have tons of fun tree runs and they are by far the best I've ridden. For example, the trees in Whistler are way too tight because the forest is too thick. In the Alps you also don't need to wake up at 6 am and wait two hours in the lift line like you have to in Squaw Valley or somewhere like that. There's power to ride for days here. Overall, it is best for filming as well as taking free runs with your friends.

Freddie Kalbermatten, pro snowboarder

Geneva airport tell that side of the tale all on their own. The casual visitor might be forgiven for thinking that the same story was carried over into the mountain communities and resorts, thanks to the schnapps 'n' fondue shtick that is the sole image of the average Swiss winter trip for so many. But we snowboarders know better. We know the truth to be that Switzerland has some of the most diverse, accessible and exciting resorts in the world. Better yet, it's underlined by a strong snowboarding culture that sees Swiss snowboarding standing proud on the world stage. Riders such as Michi Albin, Romain de Marchi, Nicolas Muller, Freddie Kalbermatten and Tina Birbaum are world renowned, while contests such as the SB Jam, Chicken Jam and Nescafé Champs are important stops on the world circuit. This top-down influence is now being felt in the resorts, which are building great parks and facilities for riders, though some are catching on more quickly than others. And that's without even mentioning the freeriding, which is some of the best in Europe and sits in some of the biggest areas. As a rule, Swiss resorts are huge – especially by North American standards. Factor in the Swiss willingness to generally maintain their resort infrastructure (they were one of the first nations in the world to catch onto electronic lift tickets, for example, and regularly upgrade their lift systems) and you're close to the reality of riding in Switzerland.

Conditions

Switzerland really is plastered with resorts, most of them curving along an imaginary meridian that links the east, south and southwest of the country. Two main weather fronts bring snow to the area, from either the north or the west. North fronts tend to predominate in the

Lift chat

Memento mori

Few resorts are as in hock to their own history as Zermatt. Even more interestingly, in Zermatt the source of much of this heritage overshadows the place, literally, in the form of the wondrous Matterhorn. In town, images of the mighty rock are inescapable.

Today the Matterhorn has been scaled in every conceivable way. People have skied the North Face, and, unbelievably, one B Brunod ascended the mountain in under three hours in 1995. But it's still the initial ascent that remains the most notorious.

By the 1860s, mountaineering's first Golden Age, the Matterhorn remained the last major peak in the Alps to be climbed. Then Britain's Edward Whymper, one of the most celebrated climbers of his generation, decided to tackle it. He left the village one morning with a party of mixed ability: Charles Hudson, Lord Francis Douglas, Douglas Hadow, Michel Croz and Peter Taugwalder, the elder and younger. Reaching the summit by the now classic Hornli route, they began to descend when tragedy struck and Hadow slipped, dragging Croz, Hudson and Douglas with him. All seven were tied together but the rope snapped, sparing Whymper and the two Taugwalders. Controversy immediately ensued as to whether the rope had been cut, and dogged them for the rest of their lives.

In his 1871 memoir *Scrambles among the Alps*, Whymper said of the incident "Every night … I see my comrades of the Matterhorn slipping on their backs, their arms outstretched, one after the other, in perfect order at equal distances – Croz the guide, first, then Hadow, then Hudson, and lastly Douglas. Yes, I shall always see them …"

The snapped rope is still preserved in Zermatt's Alpine museum.

P. ANDREW HINGSTON

earlier part of the season, while west fronts, largely affecting the southern part of the Swiss Alps, begin to take precedence from February onwards.

When to go

In common with their French and Austrian neighbours, the Swiss usually have their resorts in full swing by early December. It's a good time to visit if you're prepared to gamble on the depth of the snow base and don't mind sacrificing an old board to any potential rocks. January and February are snow-sure yet cold, so if you want powder and a goggle tan, March is probably the best month to visit – even if it is relatively expensive and more crowded. If you're planning a trip out at the beginning of April, it's essential to check conditions. Most Swiss resorts had closed by early April during the 05/06 season, although some resorts (Engelberg, Zermatt) with higher slopes were still going strong.

Off-piste policy

Along with their central European cousins, Switzerland has a pretty laid-back approach to bypassing the resort boundaries. That said, some resorts (Engelberg is one example) enforce nature areas in the resort – ride here and you might have your pass pulled or a fine issued. Check the status with the lifties if in doubt. Check slf.ch for details of any avalanche danger and meteoschweiz.ch for weather info.

Secret spots

Swiss resorts are so busy, and many of them are so enormous, that disputes over secret spots are rare indeed. Still, it can happen, mainly because of the high number of local riding communities and a generally high level of riding. But with resorts such as Verbier, Engelberg, Davos and Zermatt covering such huge areas, this is not a real concern for the average travelling rider.

Freestyle

Places such as Laax, Adelboden and Saas Fee have some of the best parks in Europe, with hordes of riders sessioning gleaming modern obstacles. Practically every resort has a strong scene, so check local snowboarding shops and bars to find out more.

The scene

Riders such as Reto Lamm, Bertrand Denervaud and Fabien Rohrer helped bring Swiss riding to the wider world's attention, while today Swiss riders like de Marchi and Müller have helped pioneer the 'take freestyle to the backcountry' school of riding and are now counted among the world's elite. Local resort scenes are strongly supported by shops such as **Stoked** (stoked.ch) in Zermatt. As Cira Riedel from *Seventh Sky* magazine explains, "the snowboarding culture is widespread and intense. There are snowboarding crews in almost every resort, which create a real underground buzz similar to the music and art scene in big cities. They are constantly working on videos, very creative contests and their riding skills."

The industry

As you'd expect, Switzerland has a strong local industry. **Nidecker** and **Rad Air** were early brand leaders and are still going, as are **Radical Snowboards** and **Kessler Snowboards**, two custom board manufacturers. **Zimstern** is a local softgoods brand, while **Seed** is a new label for girls. *Seventh Sky* is the main magazine, covering all board sports and with strong editorial and pictures. Other local magazines include the new *4 Riders* and *The Box*. After *Seventh Sky*, the most influential magazines are imports such as *OnBoard*, *Method Mag* and *Pleasure* (Germany). There are some websites too, such as **twoleftfeet.ch**, an influential community site, and **snowforce.com**.

Switzerland: a brief history of snowboarding

Late seventies → José Fernandes from Zurich brings a Winterstick back from the States, thus becoming one of Europe's first riders. **1980** → Jose and Antoine Massy establish the Hooger Booger brand and experiment with design concepts still in use today. **1986** → Other influential Franco-Swiss board companies, Swell Panick and Nidecker, begin to grow. Nidecker, in particular, is an early industry powerhouse. **1987** → Symposium in Tignes sees Antoine Massy and locals Denis Bertran, Jacques Gris and others establish Look Snowboards. Later that year, first World Championships held in Europe take place in St Moritz. **1988** → Swiss company Swatch becomes one of snowboarding's first corporate sponsors. **1989** → Swiss resorts cotton on to the potential of the sport, allowing snowboarders free reign and experimenting with pipes and funparks. **1989** → At the Kebra Classic in Tignes, Swiss riders Nicole Angelrath and Arlette Javet place well and attract attention. **1990** → Angelrath joins Burton pro team and wins World Cup pipe and mogul events. At the same time, José Fernandes wins the World Champs in Breckenridge, Colorado, on an asymmetric Hooger Booger with hiking boots on plate bindings. He meets Terry Kidwell and is one of the first riders to bring the Method Air back to Europe. Along with Antoine Massy and Phillipe Imhof, Jose also takes the honours at Euro Cup in La Plagne thanks to their sharp sidecuts and spatula boards. **1992** → Swiss rider Bertrand Denervaud takes second in halfpipe at Breckenridge, beating Craig Kelly and becoming first Euro to place on US pipe podium. He goes on to be one of most successful comp riders ever. **1993** → Rad Air board brand established. Later, Reto Lamm wins first Air and Style event in Axamer Lizum ahead of Bryan Iguchi and Shaun Palmer. **1995** → Swiss Tourism sponsors huge In The City jump contest in Covent Garden, London, attracting riders like Jamie Lynn, Brian Iguchi and Shaun Palmer. **Mid 90s** → Swiss resorts such as Laax, Les Diablerets and Saas Fee begin to develop and market their funparks as an integral part of their resorts. **1998** → Swiss rider Gian Simmen comes out of nowhere to win snowboarding's inaugural halfpipe gold medal at the 1998 Nagano Olympics. Bertrand Denervaud caps incredible career by becoming ISF President. **1999-2000** → Rene Hansen becomes Burton Team Manager from Airwalk and brings Romain de Marchi with him. De Marchi rapidly becomes one of the world's most notorious riders. **2000** → Patrick 'Brusti' Armbruster collaborates with Justin Hostenyk for the first time on *Tribal*. As *Absinthe Films*, they go on to make some of the most celebrated snowboarding films of all time. **2002** → Philipp Schoch takes gold in the Parallel GS at the Salt Lake City Olympics, while Fabienne Reuteler takes bronze in the women's pipe event. Later in the year, Nicolas Müller takes fourth at the Air and Style. **2003** → Nicolas Muller and Freddie Kalbermatten continue their rise to the top thanks to their effortless style and a string of outstanding contest placings and video parts. **2003-2004** → Swiss resorts such as Hoch Y Brig, Adelboden and Laax consolidate their park building efforts. **2003-2004** → Swiss rider Tina Birbaum establishes the Chicken Jam women-only Slopestyle event, and takes lead role in Chunky Knit's girl-only video productions. **2006** → Philipp Schoch makes it a double in the Turin Winter Olympics Parallel GS, while Daniela Meuli take the women's PGS title and Tanja Frieden wins Boardercross gold.

Adelboden

The Town

Located just west of the more famous resorts of the Jungfrau, Adelboden is a classic unsung hero of the snowboarding resort world. While it might lack the profile of Zermatt or Verbier, it is a solid, friendly place that has a better park than either of them. It's a typically beautiful Swiss resort too, with a church dating from the 15th century, a very friendly population of locals, and clued-up visitors who appreciate the slightly slower pace of life to be found here. It's this and the lack of crowds that make it a very attractive proposition for those looking for a freestyle-savvy alternative to the glitz of the Swiss über-resorts.

Adelboden provides a good mixture of riding. The Gran Masta Park has features for riders of all levels, with a selection of kickers from 3 m to 18 m and rails/boxes of all shapes and sizes.

Keith Stubbs, ochosports.com

Basically, the Swiss scene in microcosm – a brilliant park and mountain sitting above a rustic Swiss paradise.

If you like this …
… try Flachauwinkl ▸▸*p36, Seegrube/Nordpark* ▸▸*p50, or Mammoth* ▸▸*p366.*

Sleeping If you're super keen, stay in the Berghotel Hahnenmoospass, (hahnenmoos.ch) up the mountain. Probably a safer bet is to stay in Adelboden. The cheapest option is probably the **Hotel Alpenrose** (T33 673 8383), closely followed by the **Hotel Bernerhof** (bernerhof -adelboden.ch) and the **Hotel Viktoria** (viktoria-eden.ch).

Eating Take your pick from pizza at **Alfredo's** (T33 673 1940), Thai at the **Hotel Viktoria** (T33 673 8888) or the classic fondue and schnapps combo at **Restaurant Bären** (T33 673 2151).

Bars and clubs There's some good nightlife, with the **Berna Bar** being the young crowd's local. The **Alte Taverne** is usually packed out, and the **Arte Bar** and **Time Out Pub** are also popular.

Shopping The usual range of pharmacy, grocery store, bakery, hairdresser and sports shops are strung along the high street.

Health The nearest hospital is in Frutigen (16 km away) although there are doctors in town for minor problems.

Internet Kiosk Treff and Fischer IT are Adelboden's internet emporiums, although many hotels have the familiar wireless access.

Transfer options Berne is the closest airport to Adelboden, so get a Swiss Rail Card (MySwitzerland.com) and make the short 70-km trip by train.

Local partners None.

R: UNKNOWN P: ADELBODEN TOURISM

OPENING TIMES

Mid-Dec to Mid-Apr: 0900-1700

RESORT PRICES

Week pass (6 days): €163
Day pass: €37
Season pass: €531

DIRECTORY

Tourist office: T33 673 8080
Medical centre:T33 673 1348
Pisteurs: T33 673 3500
Taxi: T33 673 2848
Local radio: Radio BeO 95.7 FM
Website: adelboden.ch

P: ADELBODEN TOURISM

The Mountain

Of Adelboden's main areas, two of them – Silleren/Hahnenmoos and TschentenAlp – are accessible from the centre of town. The other two areas, Elsigenalp and Engstligenalp, are linked by a bus service, which can be inconvenient and means you need a car to really get the best out of the resort. Despite this, Adelboden is a good snowboarder's mountain. The facilities are very well thought out and there are some fun freeriding and freestyle options. The terrain generally is also solidly enjoyable, thanks to a lot of natural features to whoop and holler around, and some sure snowfall. Although serious freeriders would probably be better off in Verbier or nearby Engelberg, freestylers and general shredders will find plenty to keep them occupied here.

Beginners Some great facilities here, with the Masta Park even having its own beginner's piste. Having said that, it's probably best to start in the Geils area. You'll find some mellow blue runs here, but it requires a bus journey. Later in the week, if you're feeling adventurous, the links to Buhlberg access more undulating blues.

Intermediate It's likely you'll spend most of your time riding in the Englstligenalp and Hahnenmoos areas, although this necessitates some choice as they aren't linked. Probably a better bet in good snow is to drive or catch the bus to Engstligenalp to shred the freeride area. If not, take the Sillerenbuhl cable car and head down to Hahnenmoospass. It's where you'll find the park, as well as plenty of fun pistes to blast around.

Experts Adelboden hasn't got the world's steepest terrain, but there is some great riding here. Expert riders will also want to head over to Englistligenalp for freeriding, as well as spend much of their time frequenting the park. It is a paradise for the jib kids, with kickers, rails, boardercross, test centre and a dedicated bar, grill and permanent DJ. Check out realboarder.ch/gmp for more info.

Kids There's a dedicated **Snow Kids World** at the Geils area.

Flat light days Silleren and Berglager have the best wooded runs to get out of the flat light on bad days.

☺ LOCALS DO
- Go to the Gran Masta Park.
- Check out the bands in the Alte Taverne.
- Chill in the Berna Bar.

☹ LOCALS DON"T
- Stay in the Hotel Schönegg.
- Stay just in the Hahnenmoos – explore the other areas.

✔ PROS
- Big variety with five areas to ride.
- Never need to ride crowded slopes.
- Good public transport.

✖ CONS
- Not incredibly steep.
- You're going to need a car for true convenience.
- Not great for nightlife.

❂ NOT TO MISS
It has to be the park. It's the perfect place to work on your progression. That said there's some great freeriding as well.

① REMEMBER TO AVOID
It can get crowded on a sunny weekend during high season in the area of Lavey-Silleren.

❄ SNOW DEPTH

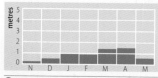

☺ RELIVE A FAMOUS MOMENT
Adelboden was the first destination of package tour pioneer Sir Henry Lunn in 1903.

1353 m	TOWN ALTITUDE
68 km	KM TO AIRPORT
ZRH	AIRPORT
★★☆	VEGETARIAN RATING
★★★	INTERNET CAFES
★☆☆	RIDE IN/RIDE OUT
2375 m	HIGHEST LIFT
1022 m	VERTICAL DROP
area not measured	RIDEABLE AREA (IN ACRES)
185 km	KM OF PISTES
5	NURSERY AREAS
39/51/15	RUNS: BEG/INTER/ADV
0/8	FUNICULAR/CABLE CARS
3/10	GONDOLAS/CHAIRS
36	DRAGS
yes	NIGHT RIDING
3	PARKS
0	PIPE
no	SUMMER AREAS
★★★ ★★☆	ENVIRONMENTAL RATING
$$$	COST INDICATOR

SWITZERLAND
ADELBODEN

P: ADELBODEN TOURISM

Davos

The Town

Like a lot of Swiss resorts, Davos has roots. Compared to many North American resorts, its history makes it practically pre-Cambrian, and it continues to dine out on this heritage today. Initially famed as a sanatorium, then as a resort, it's been written about by Conan Doyle and Thomas Mann and popular for well over a hundred years. Even today, the associations are many – from the World Economic Forum (Davos hosts the symposium each year) to its (false) claim to be the highest city in the world. And that's without even mentioning the six riding areas, two parks, great restaurants and more smoke-filled bars than Casablanca. Clearly, Snow Park this ain't.

Sleeping Stay at the heart of the action at the **Bolgenschanze** (bolgenschanze.ch), 'Davos rider's hotel and bar'. The **Sportshotel Montana** (hotels-and-more .ch) is simpler, next to the railway station, while the **Snowboarder's Palace** (T81 414 9020) is a cheaper hostel option.

Eating Padrinos (T81 413 3895) do cheap pizzas, while **Parma** (T81 413 4866) is a slightly posher, authentic Italian. And if you fancy trying the Swiss Alpine take on Indian, it's all about **Kairali** (T81 416 5726).

Bars and clubs The Bolgenschanze is definitely the social hub of the snowboarding scene. **Villa Palatina** has some full-on house nights, and La Onda is also popular with the locals.

Shopping The wonderful **Migros** chain takes care of cheap food, while **Denner** sorts out the budget booze. **Top Secret** is the best local snowboard shop.

Health When in Davos . . . **Eau-La-La Hallenbad** (T081 413 6463) has indoor pools, saunas, whirlpools and a steam bath.

Internet Villa Palatini has good internet access as well as being a wireless hotspot. Almost every hotel has free internet access, as does the **Davos Tourism** office.

Transfer Options From Zurich, use the Swiss Travel System to go to Lanquart, then Davos. From Basel, it's Chur then Davos.

Local partners Davos and Klosters are linked to form one huge area. You can also buy a TopCard that gives you access to Laax and Lenzerheide Valbella as well (davosklosters.ch).

The highest city in Europe offers the best of both worlds – world-class snowboarding and all-night partying.

🌙 *If you like this . . .*
. . . try Whistler ⇒*p86, Chamonix* ⇒*p128, or Vail* ⇒*p376.*

R: DANNY WHEELER P: DANMILNER.COM

OPENING TIMES
Mid-Nov to late Apr: 0830-1630

RESORT PRICES
Week pass (6 days): CHF316
Day pass: CHF61
Season pass: CHF900

DIRECTORY
Tourist office: T81 415 2121
Medical centre: T81 414 8888
Taxi: T81 416 7373
Local radio: Radio Grischa 106.7 FM
Website: davos.ch

The Mountain ❄ ☺

There are six areas in Davos, and each one has a unique flair to it. The main hill is Jakobshorn – the biggest area – rising right from Davos-Platz via a two-stage tram, a plethora of high-speed chairlifts to the park and the world-famous pipe. Parsenn is a big, modern area with funiculars and lifts galore, but can often be crowded. Pischa and Rinerhorn both sit about 10 minutes outside of town and offer no-frills riding – just T-bars and a plethora of wild backcountry access. The beauty of this set-up is the diversity it offers. You can ride a different area each day each with its own unique terrain, from low-angle, meticulously groomed pistes to 1000-m-plus backcountry descents – snowboarders of all levels are going to find something.

Beginners For those just learning to ride, the best bet is to head to Jakobshorn and get a lesson with the **Top Secret** snowboard school. 'J-horn' has great slopes for beginners, and comfortable chairlifts to rest your weary bones on the lift back up.

Intermediates Riders that have a grip on the pistes and are ready to step it up will have one breakthrough day after the next in this place. The 'Big Day Out' may best be had at Pischa, where the morning session

Davos is like a playground. There are lots of hikes that take you to some sick runs and drops, pillow lines and tree runs. For freeriding it's pretty much the cream of the crop. And when everything is tracked out, you can always go and hit the superpipe at the valley station. Just remember to be nice to the locals if you want to find the spots.

Michi Albin, local pro snowboarder

will consist of multiple off-piste powder runs, the day being rounded off with some rails and kickers in the park later on.

Advanced Expert riders can expect an epic day of backcountry riding at Rinerhorn. Some of the lines in the Raetian Alps rival heliboarding; it's just a matter of knowing when and where to go. Give a call to local freeride guide Tom Elias (T79 455 7826) and he will be sure to show you the secret goods.

Kids Parents who ride should look no further than Pischa. **Kinderland**, on the sunny upper slopes above the mid-mountain restaurant, is a paradise for snow tots. Here, they can take a ski or snowboard lesson, sled down a hill or play with other rugrats in the toy-laden 'Kinder Teepee'. Day care and babysitting is also available.

Flat light days Every mountain has great forest riding, but be sure to check for the 'nature reserve areas'. Gotshna in Klosters (accessible from Parsenn) has pistes back into town through the forest, while the steep trees in Madrisa are a must for expert powder riders.

☺ LOCALS DO
- Party all-night if tomorrow will be icy.
- See a HCD (Hockey Club Davos) pro hockey match before going out all night.
- Ride all six areas.

☹ LOCALS DON'T
- Party all-night when tomorrow will be a powder morning.
- Get too drunk and get beat up at the hockey match.
- Ride out-of-bounds when the avalanche hazard is high. (Check slf.ch for any details.)

✔ PROS
- Never a dull moment.
- Lots of bars, restaurants and atypical resort town scenes.
- Lots of snow between December and April.

✖ CONS
- Crowded buses and stuffy bars.
- Need to book restaurants.
- Dangerous avalanche conditions often.

☺ NOT TO MISS
The SB Jam takes place every season in Davos on New Year's Eve. The world's best pipe riders boost into next year and the outdoor party with fireworks and DJs is legendary.

ⓘ REMEMBER TO AVOID
Parsenn and Gotscha have some great terrain and long, long runs. But on weekends during the high-season, the lift lines are endless.

❄ SNOW DEPTH

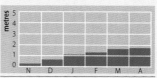

☺ RELIVE A FAMOUS MOMENT
You'll have to ride pretty well to relive Terje Haakonson winning his first ISF World Championship Title in the Davos halfpipe in 1995, but it's worth a shot.

1560 m	TOWN ALTITUDE
150 km	KM TO AIRPORT
ZRH	AIRPORT
★☆☆	VEGETARIAN RATING
★★★	INTERNET CAFES
★★☆	RIDE IN/RIDE OUT
3146 m	HIGHEST LIFT
2030 m	VERTICAL DROP
area not measured	RIDEABLE AREA (IN ACRES)
311 km	KM OF PISTES
3	NURSERY AREAS
29/47/34	RUNS: BEG/INTER/ADV
3/9	FUNICULAR/CABLE CARS
5/9	GONDOLAS/CHAIRS
27	DRAGS
yes	NIGHT RIDING
3	PARKS
2	PIPE
no	SUMMER AREAS
★★★ ★★★	ENVIRONMENTAL RATING
$$$	COST INDICATOR

SWITZERLAND
DAVOS

Engelberg

Steep, serious freeriding, a huge party scene and a picturesque Swiss village: how about 'best-kept secret in the Swiss Alps'?

☼ *If you like this...*
... try *Seegrube/Nordpark*
▶▶*p50, Banff/Sunshine*
▶▶*p70, or Les Arcs* ▶▶*p142.*

The Town ⊟⊘⊟

Although it's hugely popular among local Swiss shredders and a thriving population of transient Scandinavians, Engelberg has a relatively small profile compared to some of its giant resort neighbours. Why this should be the case is something of a mystery. The mountain is a freeriding classic and the town, with its historic ambience and relentlessly friendly party scene, is a little gem. From what we've seen, it can only be a matter of time before this emerging resort challenges the bigger and better known resorts in Switzerland.

Sleeping Three **Juhui** hostels (unterkunft.ch), owned by the same family, are perfect for the budget crew. Slightly more expensive is the **Hotel Belle Vue** (bellevue-engelberg.ch), which is popular with the snowboarding crowd and is central. Or try some old sanatorium glitz at the slightly fading **Hotel Europe** (hoteleurope.ch).
Eating Yucatán (yucatan.ch) is that old faithful – the resort Tex-Mex restaurant. Elsewhere, the **Alpen Club** serves traditional Swiss food, while the **Schweizer Haus** is the oldest place in town. Deal with the munchies at the little pizza place 100 m from the **Hotel Europe**.
Bars and clubs It goes off here. **The Yucatan** is permanently packed, while the **Eden Lounge** has a laid-back Swiss crowd. Everyone usually ends up in the **Spindle** club.
Shopping Try the **Co-op** and the **Migros**, both near the tourist office.
Health There's a swimming pool at **Sonnenberg**, and spas at the **Hotel Waldegg** and the **Ramada**.
Internet Wireless at the hotels

⊘ OPENING TIMES
Mid-Nov to late May: 0830-1700

Ⓢ RESORT PRICES
Week pass (6 days): CHF250
Day pass: CHF52
Season pass: CHF790

ⓘ DIRECTORY
Tourist office: T41 639 7777
Medical centre: T41 637 0030
Pisteurs: T41 639 5050
Taxi: T78 666 5757
Local radio: None
Website: engelberg.ch

❝❞

Epic freeriding in this town, and the party scene rocks. It'd be a great, unusual place to do a season.

Hamish McKnight, pro snowboarder

Ramada and **Europe**, and an internet café at the **Okay** freeride shop.
Transfer options Again, get a Swiss Rail Card and take to the rails. Connect from Zurich, Geneva and Basel to Luzern, then to Engelberg.
Local partners None.

R: MATT BARR P: JAMES MCPHAIL

The Mountain

Like many Swiss hills, Engelberg is divided into three distinct (and separate) areas. Brunni, south facing, gets the sun and has mellower slopes. With its one lift, Fuerenalp, at the head of the valley, is an insider's tip for hiking and freeriding that requires a bit more effort. But it's really the Titlis side that attracts most riders. It has the lot: steeps, a huge glacier complete with crevasse-strewn runs, cliffs (lots of them), a park

and long, long top-to-bottom runs. Throw in some classic freeriding runs, easy to get to, and you've got a blinder of a resort for all levels.

Beginners Complete beginners should head to the Klostermatte area in the village, which is lit and has mellow slopes. However, a surplus of T-bars and drags means Engelberg isn't ideal for real beginners, with the Gerschnialp plateau below Trubsee a case in point. You'll be better off spending the day on the Brunni side in the sun, stopping off at the **Brunnihutte** for lunch.

Intermediate It's all about the Titlis side here, so start the day over at the Jochstick chair. There are more snowboarders here, maybe because of the park. Ride these runs and those on the nice and wide Engstlealp side. After lunch at the restaurant at the top of Jochpass, take the Stand cable car and spend the afternoon lapping the super-fun front pistes back down to Trubsee.

Advanced Where to start? If the snow is good, take the classic Engelberg run – the 'Laub' down the Trubsee front face – by taking an early Stand cable car up. Stop for lunch at the **Ritz**, then head back up for some runs on the glacier – the Steinberg is the classic, but watch out for those crevasses. Later, take the Jochstock Express and then the very short skier's right traverse into the back valley, leading back to the foot of the Steinberg glacier run.

Kids There's a little park on the Brunni side as well as the Klostermatte in town. Children under six ride for free while there are various reductions for those up to 15.

Flat light days Head for the Brunni side, where there are more trees. It's more likely to be open in bad weather.

☺ LOCALS DO
⦿ Ride the Laub and stop at the Ritz for food. It's *the* classic run in town.
⦿ Happy hour at Yucatan. It's legendary – two drinks for the price of one between 5 and 6 every day.
⦿ Get to the car park early on Saturday to get a parking space.

☹ LOCALS DON'T
⊗ Ride through the nature reserves - lifties wait at the bottom to dish out fines.
⊗ Take the home run in the spring. It's too flat.
⊗ Forget about Fuerenalp for some secret pow stashes mid-winter.

✓ PROS
⦿ Friendly, up for it party scene.
⦿ Amazing freeriding.
⦿ Great town.

✗ CONS
⊗ Not good for beginners.
⊗ Long time to get up the hill.
⊗ Not great for flat light riding.

☺ NOT TO MISS
Engelberg is home to the world's only revolving cable car: the slightly pointless 'Rotair'. Avoid with hangovers.

ⓘ REMEMBER TO AVOID
The Rotegg run, from the Rotair, links the glacier to the rest of mountain and is mogully and steep. If you're not sure, take the Ice Flyer back up and descend in the Stand cable car.

❋ SNOW DEPTH

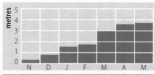

☺ RELIVE A FAMOUS MOMENT
Oscar nominated *Lagaan* is perhaps the most famous Bollywood epic filmed in town, but there have been so many that Engelberg is now on the Indian tourist trail.

1050 m	TOWN ALTITUDE
90 km	KM TO AIRPORT
ZRH	AIRPORT
★★☆	VEGETARIAN RATING
★★☆	INTERNET CAFES
★★☆	RIDE IN/RIDE OUT
3020 m	HIGHEST LIFT
1970 m	VERTICAL DROP
area not measured	RIDEABLE AREA (IN ACRES)
82 km	KM OF PISTES
3	NURSERY AREAS
8/12/3	RUNS: BEG/INTER/ADV
0/2	FUNICULAR/CABLE CARS
7/8	GONDOLAS/CHAIRS
7	DRAGS
yes	NIGHT RIDING
1	PARKS
0	PIPE
no	SUMMER AREAS
★★★ / ★★★	ENVIRONMENTAL RATING
ⓢ ⓢ ⓢ	COST INDICATOR

SWITZERLAND
ENGELBERG

Switzerland.
get natural.

Our stop light.

MySwitzerland.com

Rediscover nature – by watching the Alpine sunset as you swish down through the powder snow. Followed by a cosy fondue in your mountain hideaway. You'll find the best of Switzerland in our new Winter brochure and at www.MySwitzerland.com. Or book now by calling free: 00800 100 200 30*.

*Find information and make reservations at the Swiss holiday specialists: Switzerland Travel Centre Ltd

10 Reasons to go snowboarding in Switzerland

❶ History Zurich's Jose Fernandes was one of Europe's first snowboarders, riding a Winterstick he brought back from the States way back in 1978.

❷ Innovation In 1980, Jose started Hooger Booger, one of the world's first board brands.

❸ Competition The first European snowboard competitions kicked off in 1986 with the Swiss Championships in St Moritz.

❹ Record-breaking Early Swiss snowboard pioneer Reto Lamm decided to ride down an Olympic bobsleigh in 1998. Filming for the German show Guinness – Die Show Der Rekorde (the Guinness Record Show) he rode his snowboard at a measured speed of 80 kilometres per hour (49.7mph) before falling off and sliding a long, long, long way …

❺ Freestyle Swiss resorts such as Saas Fee, Laax and Les Diablerets were among the first resorts in the world to provide snowboarders with cutting edge funparks.

❻ Pioneering Gian Simmen, winner of the first ever men's Halfpipe Gold medal at the 1998 Olympic Games, keeps his prized possession in the safe at his local bank in Arosa, Switzerland. "I last got it out and looked at it two months ago" he confessed in a recent interview.

❼ Variety Engelberg might be one of Europe's best-kept freeriding secrets.

❽ Variety Quaint Saas Fee is the quintessential Swiss freestyle destination.

❾ Variety Popcorn in Saas Fee and the Lobby Bar at Laax's Rider's Palace are two of the hottest nights out in snowboarding.

❿ Cost The old preconceptions about Switzerland being expensive are ready for an overhaul. Isn't it time you went and checked it out for yourself?

Grindelwald

Pretty much defining the term 'chocolate box', the slopes around pretty Grindelwald provide a mellow counterpoint to the fearsome Eiger looking over the village. Links to Wengen and Murren help warrant its inclusion in the guide.

***

🌓 *If you like this* …
… try *Jasper/Marmot Basin* ▸▸*p76, Soldeu* ▸▸*p290, or Keystone* ▸▸*p364.*

The Town 🖥️💶📺

Overlooked as it is by the Jungfrau and the Eiger, two Swiss peaks steeped in modern and ancient folklore, Grindelwald should perhaps be in the same rarefied league as Zermatt or Chamonix. In common with the rest of the Berner Oberland area of the country, in which it sits, Grindelwald is the epitome of 'Heidi country'. Whether you find this atmosphere cloying or calming is a matter of personal preference, but we think this looming Alpine history gives the resort more interest than the average shred town. Secondly, the area that lies beneath these fearsome peaks has some versatile, fun riding that combines to form some of Switzerland's most characterful snowboarding.

Sleeping Plenty of low-end hostels and dorms in town, but the **Mountain Hostel** (mountainhostel.ch) is well situated, across the road from the Mannlichen gondola. In town, the mid-range **Downtown Lodge** (downtown-lodge.ch) has rooms for eight people. The more expensive **Eiger** (eiger-grindelwald.ch) and the

Spinne (spinee.grindelwald.com) hotels are perfect for nightlife.

Eating As well as the best views of the Eiger, the **Central Hotel Wolter** (T33 854 3333) serves vegetarian options. The **Spinne** is also a renowned culinary junction, with an international menu of kangaroo, moose and other strange meats. Try **C and M** for snacks.

Bars and clubs Head to the 'Bermuda Triangle' area of town, where clubs and bars centred around the **Spinne** and **Eiger** hotels go right off.

Shopping As well as a surplus of shops selling Swiss Army knives and chocolate, there's a **Co-op** located centrally.

Health A large sports centre with great facilities sits right by the tourist office. Try **Christine Sigrit** (T79 417 1672) for massages.

❝❞

Would you be surprised to see the Von Trapp family yodelling their way down the high street on a herd of Milka cows in this town? I think not.

James McPhail, snowboarding photographer

Internet Although Grindelwald is due to become a 'wireless village', at the moment there is only internet access at the **Photo Shop** and wireless at the sports centre and some hotel lobbies.

Transfer options Buy a Swiss Rail Card through myswitzerland.com. Grindelwald is linked to Geneva, Zurich and Basel.

Local partners Linked over the valley to Wengen, with the Murren/Schilthorn also accessible (although this means a full day as you have to get the train over).

P: UNKNOWN P: GRINDELWALD TOURISM

P: GRINDELWALD TOURISM

⊙ **OPENING TIMES**
Early Dec to mid-Apr: 0830-1545

⑤ **RESORT PRICES**
Week pass (6 days): CHF288
Day pass: CHF56
Season pass: CHF820

① **DIRECTORY**
Tourist office: T33 854 1212
Medical centre: T33 854 1010
Pisteurs: T33 854 5050
Taxi: T33 853 1177
Local radio: TBC
Website: grindelwald.com

The Mountain

Many resorts in Switzerland suffer from a lack of height, but Grindelwald gets around such problems thanks to the fact that a majority of the in-resort runs pass through the treeline. It makes for diverse territory, with the better snow up high, and a high number of lower slope tree runs adding variety. Another plus is the fact that there are some long valley runs, perfect for intermediate cruisers. Add in the Wengen side on the same pass and the steep freeriding of the Schilthorn area over at Murren, and you've got some absorbing snowboarding possibilities to explore during a week's holiday.

Beginners Beginners get a specific area – Bodmi – right in the centre of the town, although it's accessed by a double poma. Confident riders should head up to the Oberjoch on the Grindelwald side, where the runs tend to be wider and more open. In the afternoon, ride the Mannlichen, which is also good for weaker riders. Finish the day with some drinks at the

trendy **Bort** bar – Grindelwald's premier 'Alpine chic' on-hill spot.

Intermediate Pretty much a perfect resort for the competent cruiser. An obvious option is to head over to Wengen via the Arven chair. Have some lunch in Wengen, then get the cable car back over to the Mannlichen area and spend the rest of the afternoon checking the runs here. Later in the week, head up to the Schilthorn area to push things a little on the steeper terrain here.

Advanced Many possibilities. A day at Schilthorn is pretty much obligatory, as it has the steepest freeriding on the lift ticket, but for day-to-day Grindelwald riding, the Eigergletscher area is about the most challenging terrain in resort. Also worth checking out are the Oberjoch area, which holds fresh snow for longer, and the terrain off the Schilt lift. Fallboden and Wixi also lead to some famous freeriding routes.

Kids As well as the Bodmi area, there's also a kids' area on Mannlichen. Many cheap pass options – check the site for details.

Flat light days As noted, with a lot of trees the resort is especially suited for flat light, especially on the Kleine Schiedegg side. Basically, keep low.

☺ LOCALS DO

☺ Ride at Murren but it's a full day as you've got to drive or take the train.
☺ Head to the top of Schilthorn for good freeriding.
☺ Eat at the Mongolian barbecue at the Eiger hotel – all you can eat for CHF30.

☹ LOCALS DON'T

☹ Stop riding at 1200-1400 when the slopes and queues are quiet.
☹ Ride that many black runs. It's primarily a red run town.
☹ Stop riding when it's flat light. Stay low!

✔ PROS

✔ Good for families.
✔ And intermediates.
✔ Rich history to dip into.

✘ CONS

✘ Not for freestylers, and it isn't that steep generally.
✘ Familiar Swiss T-bar predilection.
✘ Lack of snowboarding culture.

☀ NOT TO MISS

The Jungfraujoch station, Europe's highest indoor train station, with it's incredible views of the Eiger and Jungfrau. Take your stick and ride down!

ⓘ REMEMBER TO AVOID

Over on the Grindelwald-First side, you've got to take the bus back into town, so watch the busy peak times.

❄ SNOW DEPTH

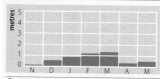

⟳ RELIVE A FAMOUS MOMENT

Take a huge, white cat and head to the Schilthorn Restaurant at the top of nearby Murren's slopes across the valley. The hilltop building was the female-assassin training camp ran by James Bond's arch nemesis Ernst Blofeld.

1050 m	TOWN ALTITUDE
195 km	KM TO AIRPORT
BSL	AIRPORT
★☆☆	VEGETARIAN RATING
★★★	INTERNET CAFES
★★☆	RIDE IN/RIDE OUT
2473 m	HIGHEST LIFT
1528 m	VERTICAL DROP
area not measured	RIDEABLE AREA (IN ACRES)
230 km	KM OF PISTES
3	NURSERY AREAS
15/28/8	RUNS: BEG/INTER/ADV
2/1	FUNICULAR/CABLE CARS
2/11	GONDOLAS/CHAIRS
7	DRAGS
yes	NIGHT RIDING
1	PARKS
1	PIPE
no	SUMMER AREAS
★★★ / ★★☆	ENVIRONMENTAL RATING
$$$	COST INDICATOR

SWITZERLAND
GRINDELWALD

Riders' tales
Making movies

With recent advances in technology, DV cameras are now more affordable than ever before. This, of course, has caused a massive upsurge in the popularity of filming amongst snowboarders.

So what's the appeal? Well, filming your mates snowboarding is simply one of the most fun things you can do. Coming home and gathering round the camera to check out the day's haul adds a whole new dimension to riding. Seeing yourself on film can also be great for your technique and style, as it can be very instructive to see how you actually look whilst on a snowboard. There's often a bit of a gap between our perceived snowboarding ability and the reality, and where a photo can lie, a bit of video footage never does.

This goes some way to explaining the massive success of Robotfood's 2002 movie *Afterbang*. Though the movie starred the world's best riders such as Jussi Oksanen and David Benedek et al, the overall feel was one of a group of friends heading out and simply filming whatever it is that they get up to during a day's riding. Of course, for Benedek and friends this meant feats such as stomping switch backside 900s into powder, but there were also numerous shots of the stars fooling around the piste and having a laugh, just as the majority of us recreational snowboarders like to do. For many people, it was great to see what extraordinary riders can do on the sort of ordinary jumps you'd find on the side of the piste, and this was pretty much carte blanche to anyone with a camera to get out there and start filming as much as they possibly could. Certainly, pretty much every snowboarding movie to come out since, no matter how big or how small, has owed a massive debt to *Afterbang*. It depicted people having fun, and since that's the reason we all go snowboarding in the first place then it was only natural that it should strike a chord.

Over the past few years there has been a glut of snowboarding movies appearing all over the world, from the highest level right down. The affordability of computers and decent editing packages has had a massive part to play in this. It's one thing to watch yourself on video, but laying down clips of yourself and your mates to some music is an amazingly good feeling. It all looks so much more authentic on a computer screen, or better still, a TV. As one renowned film maker and 16 mm cameraman said, "iMovie was the best thing that ever happened to snowboard bums."

Take, for example, UK pro riders Adam Gendle and Tim Warwood. They started filming back in 1999, whilst doing a winter season in Vail. "I didn't think anything would ever come of it," says Adam, "we just did it for fun". For him and Tim, the obvious goal was to try to put together their own movie, and that winter they produced the very low budget *Carry on up the Chairlift*. "It was pretty basic, but it kept us amused and we learned loads from the process." Six years down the line they run their own movie production company **Lockdown Projects** and have produced several high profile UK snowboarding movies such as *Bad Ass Big Airs*, *Proper* and *Updog*.

So how do you go about making a movie yourself? Well, all you need is a camera and some friends to go riding with. If you're to get up a good filming momentum, the most important thing is that you share responsibility for filming. Everyone likes seeing themselves on screen, but not everyone's quite so ready to make the effort to get the footage. Swap around, making sure that everyone in your group knows how to use the camera – there's nothing worse than doing a really nice trick or line and getting home to discover that you can't see it because the camera was too zoomed out, or it's totally out of focus. Spend the time to learn the rudimentary skills.

As for the rudimentary skills themselves, it might seem pretty obvious, but Lockdown's Tim Warwood advises, "Read your camera manual: understand how your camera works and learn to expose your footage properly. Be comfortable with your camcorder, shoot often, and view results frequently." Aside from the basic operation of the camera, there are a few other obvious pointers. "Make sure your lens is clean and free from dust", says Tim. "This is so simple, and yet so many people fall into the jaw of the dirty lens. Get yourself a lens cleaning kit (you can get them from any camera shop). And keep a goggle bag to hand too!"

At some point you'll probably want to get some followcam (riding close behind your mate holding the camera as steady as possible) footage, and for this you'll need a wide-angle lens to keep the subject in shot. These can be bought reasonably cheaply and either screw on to the front of your camera or replace the existing lens. "When shooting with a wide-angle lens, don't use your steadycam (digital image stabilizer)", Tim advises. "By doing this you'll eliminate the 'bouncing lens ring' syndrome. Also, when you're using a wide-angle lens zoom in a touch to eliminate the black corners and edges."

The great thing is that – as with snowboarding itself – the learning curve is pretty steep. With only a little practice it won't be long before you start to get some really good results, and you'll be amazed how satisfying this can be.

Of course filming is not without its drawbacks. Where there was once a time when we could all go out and have a good day's riding for the sake of it, it can now be the case that a nicely stomped trick with no one around to witness it is not the goal of a day's riding, but a missed filming opportunity. It can also be pretty disappointing to see that that absolutely massive air you did off that kicker wasn't *quite* as big as it felt. This, however, can spur you on to go bigger next time, and progression is what snowboarding is all about.

Lockdown's forthcoming movie *Showoffs* will be available from October 2006. Check out lockdownprojects.com for more information.

ADAM GENDLE DIRECTING P: ANDREW HINGSTON

Laax

The Town ⬛🔵🟢

Accommodation for the ski area is available either in the attractive lakeside village of Laax Dorf, or further up the hill at Laax 1100, a lively conglomeration of apartments, hotels and bars. Nearby Flims and Falera are also linked into the same ski area and provide a bigger selection of shops and services.

Sleeping The **Hotel Capricorn** (T81 921 2120) is a budget hotel/youth hostel with a range of private and dorm rooms, free wireless internet access and great home-cooked vegetarian meals. A more expensive but equally popular choice is the large, modern **Riders Palace** (T81 927 9700), an über-trendy converted car park that houses hotel rooms, hostel style dorms, a bar and a nightclub. Be warned – rooms are equipped with DVD players and Playstations, but not kettles or kitchens, making a stay here expensive.

Eating For a fresh pizza you can't beat the large and friendly **Pizzeria Cristallina** (T81 921 2252), which is a close as you get to a bargain in Laax. For traditional Swiss fondue book a place at **Restaurant Muhbarack** (T81 927 9940).

Bars and clubs For an après drink, the **Crap Bar** (T81 927 9945) at the bottom of the slopes is unbeatable for convenience and jugs of cold beer. For night-time happenings, the **Lobby Bar** and **Palace Club** in the **Riders Palace** are the most popular party venues.

Shopping The **Volg** supermarket in Flims and Laax 1100 are both shut on Sundays in low season.

Health Massage treatments from **Adrian Caduff** (T79 222 0311).

Internet **Lobby Bar** at the **Riders Palace**.

Transfer options Fly to Zurich and then catch the train to Chur, from there you can catch the regular PostAuto bus up to Flims and Laax (T81 256 3166).

⊙ **OPENING TIMES**
Late Oct to mid-Apr: 0830-1500

⊙ **RESORT PRICES**
Week pass (7 days): CHF336
Day pass: CHF62
Season pass: CHF1050

ℹ **DIRECTORY**
Tourist office: T81 920 8181
Medical centre: T81 921 4848
Pisteurs: No tel number
Taxi: T81 941 2222
Local radio: None
Website: laax.com

Local partners Linked to nearby Flims, although getting back there can be tricky for the uninitiated.

P: CHRIS MORAN

High mountains, consistent snow, super-good funparks and good, old-fashioned Swiss hospitality. If you are looking for a week of guaranteed snow, impressive mountains and fantastic facilities, this is one of Europe's top snowboarding resorts.

🌓 **If you like this . . .**
. . . try **Morzine** ▶▶p148, or **Verbier** ▶▶p330.

P: CHRIS MORAN/HOTSHITPICTURES.COM

The Mountain

As well as being set in a stunningly beautiful mountain range, the resort of Laax has been excellently planned and groomed to ensure the various peaks link smoothly and snowboarders of all standards are well catered for. There are great facilities for children, beginners and intermediate snowboarders, while advanced riders are spoilt for choice between the 'Mini Alaska' of the Cassons Mountain and a selection of intermediate and advanced snowparks and halfpipes. One of Europe's most advanced and well maintained mountain resorts, Laax is guaranteed to please even the pickiest snowboarder.

Beginners As a total beginner it is probably advisable to spend a morning in 'Kinderland Laax' located in Laax 1100. Once your confidence is up, take the X-Box lift up to Crap Sogn Gion, from there make your way to the aptly named Crap lift, a very slow, user-friendly mellow T-bar that services a short, wide, rolling piste, perfect for beginners.

Intermediate On a good weather day intermediate riders should head straight up to the glacier to check out the views and enjoy the big wide runs and fresh powder. After, head to the summit La Siala and work your way around the various blue and red runs that lead down to Flims Dorf.

Advanced Early risers head straight to the Cassons summit. From this peak there are various free routes to be had, so you can lap the Cable Car lift, spotting your next lines during each ride. Finish your day with a session in the

If Laax was a tennis event, it would be Wimbledon.

Gary Greenshields, pro snowboarder

snowpark or halfpipe at Crap Sogn Gion, before making your way through the trees back down to Laax 1100.

Kids Kids under six ski for free, Laax and Flims also provide special snowboard courses for young children and a day nursery for parents looking for some time out (T81 927 7155).

Flat light days There's a huge choice of trees to ski in on all the lower sections of the mountain ensuring however bad the weather is there's always somewhere good to ride. The Laax 1100 gondola is always a good spot to get good lines in even the poorest light conditions.

R: UNKNOWN P: JAMES MCPHAIL

☺ LOCALS DO
- Ride the backside of the Vorab Gletsche on a powder day.
- Buy the cheaper 'park pass' for days spent in the snowpark and pipe.
- Ride down to the supermarkets in Flims or Laax 1100 for a cheap lunch.

☹ LOCALS DON'T
- Head to the lift lines at 0900 when the ski schools start and the queues are at their biggest.
- Ride off-piste without checking avalanche conditions.
- Do big shops in the local Volg: the Co-op in Flims is far cheaper.

✓ PROS
- Parks and pistes are arguably some of the best in Europe.
- A good variety and extensive amount of terrain.
- Popular location for big competitions and events.

✗ CONS
- Small and slightly dispersed town, Laax 1100 lacks a pedestrian centre.
- Not cheap by any means.
- Exposed high terrain is hard to navigate or even closed in bad weather.

☺ NOT TO MISS
Being in Laax for any of the big competitions.

ℹ REMEMBER TO AVOID
On weekends and holidays the Sattel bowl on the Vorab Glacier can get crowded and tracked out.

❄ SNOW DEPTH

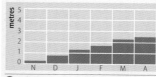

☺ RELIVE A FAMOUS MOMENT
Check out 'Das Elephant' Restaurant under Crap Masegn, and find out all about the local legend who rode an elephant up the mountain many years ago ...

1100 m	TOWN ALTITUDE
153 km	KM TO AIRPORT
ZRH	AIRPORT
★☆☆	VEGETARIAN RATING
★★☆	INTERNET CAFES
★★☆	RIDE IN/RIDE OUT
3018 m	HIGHEST LIFT
1918 m	VERTICAL DROP
area not measured	RIDEABLE AREA (IN ACRES)
220 km	KM OF PISTES
3	NURSERY AREAS
63/71/46	RUNS: BEG/INTER/ADV
0/4	FUNICULAR/CABLE CARS
7/8	GONDOLAS/CHAIRS
5	DRAGS
yes	NIGHT RIDING
2	PARKS
3	PIPE
no	SUMMER AREAS
★★★	ENVIRONMENTAL RATING
$$$	COST INDICATOR
SWITZERLAND LAAX	

The Town

The phrase 'winter wonderland' might well have been coined with little Les Diablerets in mind. Sitting just on the French side of the invisible Rösti Graben 'ditch' that divides French and German-speaking Switzerland, the locals are friendly, the fondue flows freely and there's rarely an English voice to be heard. A favourite among second home owners from Geneva and Lausanne, and locals taking advantage of the 3000-m glacier that's poised ominously above the town, the result is a resort with a somnolent, time-capsule feel. Close proximity to Geneva and a world-class park on the glacier make it perfect for a quick pre- or mid-winter mission, which is why we've included it in our top 100.

Sleeping Les Diablerets has some cheap bed and breakfast options, such as **Les Muguets** (T24 492 3510). Mid-range **Mon Abri** (monabri.ch) attracts the snowboard crowd and has the **Atomix** disco underneath. The expensive **Hotel Les Sources** (hotel-les-sources.com) has wireless throughout, serves great food and is perfect for families.

Eating The **Auberge de la Poste** (T24 492 3124) takes care of the local cuisine, while **Chez Lacroix** (T24 492 3144) has a nice vibe. **L'Ormonon** (T24 492 3838) serves pizzas and Chinese and is popular with the locals.

Bars and clubs The main snowboarding bar in town is the **MTB** bar – darts, pool and a young crowd. **L'Ormonon** serves Guinness, while the after-bar crowd is split between **Atomix** and **La Pote**, at opposite ends of town.

Shopping Two supermarkets – the **Coop** on Rue de La Gare and **Satellite Denner**, round the corner.

Health There's a swimming pool open to all at **Residence Meurice** and a solarium at **Nicole Coiffure** (T24 492 2249).

Internet The cosy **La Diabletine** is the town's cyber café, while some hotels have wireless throughout.

Transfer options Swiss Rail's clean, quick and generally excellent service extends from Geneva to Les Diablerets – details at MySwitzerland.com.

Local partners Les Diablerets is linked to Villars and Gryon across the valley, and is also part of the Alpes Vaudoises network, which means Gstaad, Leysin and Les Mosses as well.

As the glacier is one of the highest in Europe they have snow all year round and they have enough to build an exceptionally good terrain park. This resort is perfect for an early season shred and great to get the legs warmed up before the season kicks off.

Scott McMorris, pro snowboarder

P: LES DIABLERETS TOURISM

Sleepy Swiss hamlet hides seriously fun and varied mountain with a massive area.

🌓 *If you like this* …
… try *Jasper/Marmot Basin* ▶▶p76, *Arcalis* ▶▶p288, or *Vail* ▶▶p376.

SWITZERLAND
LES DIABLERETS

P: LES DIABLERETS TOURISM

⏱ OPENING TIMES
Late Nov to late Apr: 0900-1630
Jul to Oct: 0900-1650

💲 RESORT PRICES
Week pass (6 days): CHF261
Day pass: CHF55
Season pass: CHF930

❶ DIRECTORY
Tourist office: T24 492 3358
Medical centre: T24 492 3041
Pisteurs: T24 492 2814
Taxi: T24 492 1313
Local radio: None
Website: diablerets.ch

The Mountain

Although it is linked to the Alpes Vaudoises area, chances are you'll spend most of your time riding Les Diableret's three broadly defined areas: Glacier 3000, Isenau and Meilleret. Meilleret, which links Les Diablerets to Villars, has mellow tree runs and some fun nooks and crannies to explore. Isenau, with its well maintained park and links to Glacier 3000, is above the treeline so has more wide, sweeping runs. Steeper slopes also make it better for more advanced riders. As for the glacier, the ride up to it is truly impressive as you head over some truly scary cliff bands. Don't get lost on the way down! Seriously.

Beginners Beginners are better off starting the day in Meilleret. Take the Vioz-Marots chair to the summit and session the mellow blue that leads back down to the Ruvine chair. After lunch in town, take the Isenau gondola up and ride the blue back down: make sure there's enough snow cover, of course. You're walking otherwise.

Intermediate Intermediates can cover some ground. In the morning, take the Meilleret chair and head into Villars, following any of the routes down. After lunch in Villars, get the lift over to Isenau and head to the top of Floriettaz before heading over to the park for a late afternoon sesh.

Advanced There are some serious freeriding routes coming down from Glacier 3000, but if it's your first time in town a local or guide is pretty much mandatory as there are lots of very dangerous cliffs and glaciated areas to negotiate. The tourist board produces a *Freeride* booklet detailing some of the more popular runs. Over on Meilleret, there are some tight, short tree runs under the Ruvine chair, but it's known to slide. The other point of interest is the park, which opens in the autumn and is one of Europe's premiere pre-season freestyle spots.

Kids Kids from four and up can get instruction at the Jardin des Neiges (diablerets.ch/skischool).

Flat light days Not the best resort for flat light, meaning a day in the trees in Meilleret is the best option.

☺ LOCALS DO
- Shred the glacier park in the autumn, to get the legs ready for the winter. It's a serious pre-season spot.
- Take part in the big end of season party at Oldenegg. It goes off.
- Ride Isenau in the spring sun.

☹ LOCALS DON'T
- Bother with the sledge run unless it's bulletproof ice.
- Forget to head to L'Ormonon for an after riding pint of Guinness.
- Miss the Flash and Fluo Jam Session on Isenau at the end of the winter. Dig out that neon...

✓ PROS
- Snow all but guaranteed thanks to the glacier.
- Great for intermediates and families.
- Winter wonderland feel.

✕ CONS
- Nightlife limited.
- A lot of drag lifts means it's not that suited for complete beginners.
- Main winter season ends early.

○ NOT TO MISS
A ride up to Glacier 3000 to check out the ridiculous views.

ⓘ REMEMBER TO AVOID
Late season generally! By April, Les Diablerets is winding down, so make it February or early March and you'll get the resort at it's best.

❄ SNOW DEPTH

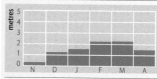

☼ RELIVE A FAMOUS MOMENT
Build something in town and you join a long list of architects to have helped Diablerets' architectural fame. Mario Botta, Switzerland's most influential designer recently added the new Botta 3000 restaurant on the glacier.

1151 m	TOWN ALTITUDE
120 km	KM TO AIRPORT
GVA	AIRPORT
★☆☆	VEGETARIAN RATING
★★★	INTERNET CAFES
★★☆	RIDE IN/RIDE OUT
2970 m	HIGHEST LIFT
1819 m	VERTICAL DROP
area not measured	RIDEABLE AREA (IN ACRES)
65 km	KM OF PISTES
1	NURSERY AREAS
14/22/1	RUNS: BEG/INTER/ADV
0/3	FUNICULAR/CABLE CARS
1/6	GONDOLAS/CHAIRS
14	DRAGS
no	NIGHT RIDING
1	PARKS
0	PIPE
yes	SUMMER AREAS
★★★	ENVIRONMENTAL RATING
$$$	COST INDICATOR
SWITZERLAND LES DIABLERETS	

Leysin

Small but perfectly formed resort with some of the most impressive views in the Alps. Versatile riding too, despite a relatively small area.

If you like this ...
... try Jasper/Marmot Basin ▸▸p76, Bansko ▸▸p100, Keystone ▸▸p364.

The Town

Compared to some of its more illustrious Swiss resort cousins such as Les Diablerets, Verbier and Zermatt, Leysin suffers from a lack of profile in the wider snowboarding world. This is a shame, because there's something about it that enables it to punch well above its weight. Somewhere between a pretty Alpine village likes Les Diablerets and a developed resort town along the lines of Morzine, Leysin is friendly, compact and has some serious snowboarding within its tight boundaries. Another trump card is its closeness to Geneva, and links to the wider Alpes Vaudoises area, making it a real option for a mid-season winter getaway.

Sleeping Best for snowboarders on a budget and for those looking for a hostel or equivalent there is the wonderfully named **Hiking Sheep** (T24 494 3535). Families or groups of friends should try the **Centrale Residence** (T24 494 1339), a classic Alpine hotel. A more upmarket shout is the four-star **Le Classic** (T24 493 0606).

Eating Eat at **Le Leysin** (leleysin.com) at least once to experience the local gastronomy. Elsewhere, the **Lynx** and the **Yeti** are recommended for cheap eats and a good atmosphere.

Bars and clubs The **Yeti Bar** is popular with the snowboarding crowd, as is **The Lynx** and **La Caleche**. Later, everyone heads to **Club 94** in **Centrale Residence**.

Shopping Leysin has a couple of supermarkets in town – the ubiquitous **Co-op** and the **Supermarket PAM**, opposite the tourist information office.

Health For a small town, Leysin has plenty of healers. Try **Britt Mollien** (T24 494 2851) for physio and commesi.ch for massage and sports therapy.

Internet There are two cyber cafés in town: the **Tea Room** (T24 494 2706) and **The Lynx** (T24 494 1532).

Transfer options From Geneva, the simplest way is by train. MySwitzerland.com has details of the Swiss Pass railcard.

Local partners If you buy the Alpes Vaudoises pass, you can ride a huge area, including Les Mosses, Les Diablerets, Villars and Gryon.

> I went to a contest in Leysin and it snowed so much that the training got cancelled. We ended up taking laps in deep powder all day long. From the top of the resort you can see Lake Geneva as well. It's an epic view.
>
> *Freddie Kalbermatten, pro snowboarder*

R: JASON HORTON P: NATALIE MAIER

OPENING TIMES

Mid-Dec to mid-Apr: 0830-1630

RESORT PRICES

Week pass (6 days): CHF261
Day pass: CHF55
Season pass: CHF930

DIRECTORY

Tourist office: T24 494 2244
Medical centre: T24 493 2929
Pisteurs: T24 494 1635
Taxi: T0800 802333
Local radio: Radio Chablais 97.1 FM
Website: leysin.ch

The Mountain

For what is seemingly a fairly tiny resort, Leysin has a hidden fund of terrain. Although much of the resort is given over to meandering, cruising pistes that lead down through some picturesque trees, there are also some short, sharp steeps. Better yet, they're all easily accessible from the top lift or by a short hike. It's not the biggest area in the world, but the scope is definitely there for some fun, creative lines, particularly if you cut off the piste over on skier's right at the top of the gondola. For its proximity to Geneva, and simple up-mountain access, we think this resort is perfect for a mid-season getaway.

Beginners Much of the beginner terrain is in the village itself, with the Valle Blanche, Plan-Praz and La Daille areas all dedicated nursery areas. Once you're up to speed, take the Tete d'Ai chair and spend the day negotiating your way back down through the resort's many meandering tree runs.

Intermediate Leysin is the kind of resort you'll know inside out by the end of the week, with its quick pitches and glade runs through the lower treeline. Start the day by heading to La Berneuse and getting your legs with a descent to the mid station of the Tete d'Ai chair. Then, head further over to the far side of the resort by heading skier's left at the top of each chair. Make your way back, and finish with some short, steep turns on the skier's right side of the Chaux-de-Mont chair.

Advanced If there's good snow cover, get your pow legs by taking the Cheaux-de-Mont chair. Over on skier's left there's an obvious traverse under the Tour d'Ai that offers some fun, short turns. Later, take the chair back up to La Berneuse. Cutting skier's right here takes you into some steep gulleys that lead back down to the central Leysin-Tete d'Ai chair.

Kids Children under nine get a free pass, and there are special rates for a child and adult.

Flat light days The lower slopes here have some tree coverage, meaning it's possible to get some turns in. But instead, pack the skateboard and head down to nearby Aigle and shred the mini-bowl skate ramp.

☺ LOCALS DO
- Chat up the students from the local international school.
- Take five minutes to look at that breathtaking view, one of the best in the Alps.
- Lap the resort top to bottom, to get the longest runs.

☹ LOCALS DON'T
- Drop the stuff in front of La Berneuse cable car. It's a restricted area.
- Forget the pipe – Leysin has a regularly well-shaped beauty.
- Just buy a Leysin pass. Buy an Alpes Vaudoises pass, and you can shred other nearby resorts once you've tired of Leysin.

✔ PROS
- Great views.
- Some good freeriding, easily accessed.
- Very quick transfer time.

✖ CONS
- It is a small resort: you'll exhaust its possibilities within a week.
- Low altitude.
- South facing - snow melts quickly.

◉ NOT TO MISS
Stop in the Kuklos restaurant for lunch at least once. It's that Alpine special, a revolving restaurant, but has great views of the area.

ⓘ REMEMBER TO AVOID
If confidence is low, stick to the lower lifts for the first day or two, as the slopes right out of La Berneuse lift are pretty steep for complete newbies.

❄ SNOW DEPTH

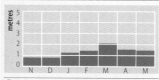

◉ RELIVE A FAMOUS MOMENT
Each January, the Nescafé Championships, a TTR event, are held in Leysin.

1263 m	TOWN ALTITUDE
100 km	KM TO AIRPORT
GVA	AIRPORT
★★☆	VEGETARIAN RATING
★★★	INTERNET CAFES
★★☆	RIDE IN/RIDE OUT
2048 m	HIGHEST LIFT
785 m	VERTICAL DROP
area not measured	RIDEABLE AREA (IN ACRES)
60 km	KM OF PISTES
4	NURSERY AREAS
12/5/2	RUNS: BEG/INTER/ADV
0/1	FUNICULAR/CABLE CARS
0/7	GONDOLAS/CHAIRS
6	DRAGS
no	NIGHT RIDING
1	PARKS
1	PIPE
no	SUMMER AREAS
★★★ ★★★	ENVIRONMENTAL RATING
$ $ $	COST INDICATOR
SWITZERLAND LEYSIN	

P: LEYSIN TOURISM

Saas Fee

The Town

Saas Fee is Swiss snowboarding perfectly encompassed in one insanely picturesque resort. Sitting in the next valley along to Zermatt, it's a traditional Swiss village with beautifully winding, car-free streets surrounded by towering 4000-m peaks such as the Allalinhorn and the Dom and a glacier that appears to hang right above the town. The snowboarding, whether freeriding or freestyle, is world class, and the nightlife manages to balance the demands of the modern, baggy-trousered snowboarding scene with the needs of fondue-supping tourists that also make up a large part of the clientele. Yes, there is a board-bag full of 'Swiss Alpine town' facilities on hand, but overall, the balance is just right.

R: FREDDIE KALBERMATTEN P: © 2006 BURTON SNOWBOARDS

P: TIM WARWOOD

One of Switzerland's most important snowboarding resorts, Saas Fee is also one of the best in Europe.

If you like this ...
... try Zillertal ▶p56, Morzine ▶p148, or Baker ▶p350.

SWITZERLAND
SAAS FEE

Sleeping Happily for cash-strapped snowboarders, Saas Fee has many self-catering apartments. A lot of the accommodation in town is family owned and rented out through the tourist board, so contact them on saas-fee.ch to secure a booking.

Eating The pizzeria in the Ferienart-Walliserhof (T27 958 1902) is reputedly one of the best in the Alps and has an amazing salad bar. A slightly cheaper Italian option can be found at the **Spaghetteria** (T27 957 1526), underneath the Hotel Brittania. Elsewhere, the **Hotel Dom** (T27 957 5101) is good for traditional Swiss food.

Bars and clubs **Popcorn** could be Europe's greatest snowboarding bar. Either way, this shop that turns into a bar each evening is packed every night with locals, bands and DJs. **The Happy Bar** is also popular, and is a little cheaper and quieter, as is **The Lounge/Living Room**, above Popcorn.

Shopping **Popcorn** is the main snowboarding shop in town, while the **Spar, Migros** and **Co-op** take care of groceries.

Health There are spa and massage facilities in the **Hotel Ferienart-Wallserhof** (ferienart.ch), although it's a little pricey. Alternatively, try the pool and sauna by the car park.

Internet There's an internet café close to the **Migros** supermarket, and wireless in many hotels. If all else fails you can also get online in the **Hotel Dom** (uniquedom.com).

Transfer options It's easy to get to Saas Fee – use the Swiss Travel System to get the train and then bus from Geneva. Check out MySwitzerland.com for full details.

Local partners Saas Fee passes work in the Saas-Fee, Saas-Grund, Saas-Almagell and Saas-Balen riding areas. You can also buy a pass that works in Zermatt.

The Mountain

For many, Saas Fee defines what is good about Swiss snowboarding. As Dan Caruso, local Swiss mountain guide and snowboarder puts it, "To my mind, Freddie Kalbermatten is the best all-round rider on the planet right now. As a product of his environment, it just shows the insane potential of Saas Fee, with great freeriding and year-round snowboarding thanks to that glacier." The only note of caution to sound about Saas Fee is for complete beginners who are uncomfortable with lots of T-bars. It's also generally north facing and guarded from the mid-winter sun by that impressive ring of peaks. This is great for serious freeriders who only care about riding soft, steep faces, but not so great for learners in January, when the place only gets a couple of hours of sun every day. Everyone else is going to love the place and its variety.

Beginners Complete beginners should start at the Staffelwald and Kalbermatten lifts in the village, but be warned – like most of Saas Fee, these slopes are T-bar accessed. Later in the week, or if you've already got

My favourite run in Saas Fee is Plattjen, and the best time to go is around Christmas. There are just so many tree runs, powder days, pillow lines and cliff drops. And the riding zone for beginners is one of the best in Europe.

Freddie Kalbermatten, pro snowboarder and Saas Fee local

your turns down, take either the Felskinn or Alpin Express from the village up to the Morenia area. There are plenty of blues to keep you busy round about here.

Intermediates Most of the mountain is good fun for cruising around, but pay particular attention to the Plattjen side, where there is some fun freeriding and a lot of great top-to-bottom runs on which to work out routes and hits. The National piste (skier's right through the woods), accesses some fun runs. It's the same story over on the Spielboden side, which you can hit up in the afternoon after lunch in town.

Advanced Obviously, for many riders the main attraction in Saas Fee is the park, so a good day's riding would be to warm up with some runs on the Plattjen before heading over to the park over on the Morenia side. It's a great park, massive and well shaped, with two kicker lines, a quarter and a corner. Then there is a multitude of rails options, as well as couches, music and the rest of the modern snowpark chilling area.

Kids There's a children's fun park, with a magic carpet, and the **Murmeli** day care centre for even younger children.

Flat light days Early season, Saas Fee can seem to suffer from predominantly flat light as it's mainly north facing. Stay low, away from the glacier.

☺ OPENING TIMES

Nov to May: 0830-1600
Jun to Oct: 0730-1400

⑤ RESORT PRICES

Week pass (6 days): CHF356
Day pass: CHF63
Season pass: CHF950

ⓘ DIRECTORY

Tourist office: T27 958 1858
Medical centre: T27 957 5859
Taxi: T27 957 3344
Local radio: None
Website: saasfee.ch

☺ LOCALS DO

- Shred the Plattjen.
- Stay off the glacier in winter - the terrain lower down is way better.
- Meet at the Number 1 bar for after riding drinks.

☹ LOCALS DON'T

- Drive. Cars are banned in resort. Take your ticket to the hotel and get a reduction on parking rates.
- Worry about a goggle tan until spring.
- Forget to ride in October. Saas Fee is a legendary pre-season warm-up spot.

✓ PROS

- No cars make for a peaceful valley.
- A cheaper alternative to next door Zermatt. Not as grand, but better value.
- Everyone speaks English.

✗ CONS

- Minimal sun until February.
- Lot of T-bars.
- Glacier can be dangerous.

☺ NOT TO MISS

A night in the Popcorn bar. It goes right off in here.

ⓘ REMEMBER TO AVOID

A car-free village, drivers must park at the end of the village and then make their own way to their hotel or apartment. Find out where you are beforehand and if necessary, book a taxi. Some hotels can be fifteen minutes walk away from the car park – a nightmare with lots of bags.

❄ SNOW DEPTH

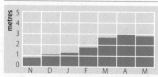

☺ RELIVE A FAMOUS MOMENT

Ken Russell's first feature film *Women in Love* starring Oliver Reed and Glenda Jackson was filmed in town.

1800 m	TOWN ALTITUDE
230 km	KM TO AIRPORT
GVA	AIRPORT
★☆☆	VEGETARIAN RATING
★★★	INTERNET CAFES
★★☆	RIDE IN/RIDE OUT
3600 m	HIGHEST LIFT
1800 m	VERTICAL DROP
area not measured	RIDEABLE AREA (IN ACRES)
100 km	KM OF PISTES
2	NURSERY AREAS
13/14/5	RUNS: BEG/INTER/ADV
1/5	FUNICULAR/CABLE CARS
2/1	GONDOLAS/CHAIRS
16	DRAGS
yes	NIGHT RIDING
2	PARKS
2	PIPE
yes	SUMMER AREAS
★★★	ENVIRONMENTAL RATING
$ $ $	COST INDICATOR

SWITZERLAND
SAAS FEE

St Moritz

The Town

Perhaps the most famous of Swiss ski resorts, St Moritz was the first town in the world to officially register its name as a trademark, back in 1986. 'St Moritz TOP OF THE WORLD' takes itself pretty seriously then as resorts go. The town has been welcoming winter tourism for over 150 years, and mostly the rich and famous at that. The small main street manages to squeeze more designer boutiques than you could shake a Manolo Blahnik stiletto at, featuring Cartier, Gucci, Versace et al. In the trendy bars and nightclubs you'll find a mix of fashionable young Swiss things visiting from Zurich, and a fair few extremely wealthy older clients as well.

Sleeping Hardly on the backpacking trail, over half the hotels in St Moritz are four or five star. Even the **Youth Hostel Stille** (youthhostel.ch/st.moritz) charges CHF60 per night. The **Hotel Laudinella** (laudinella.ch) will provide good rooms and a hearty breakfast from CHF80 in a twin room. For the full pampering experience head to the five-star **Kempinski** (kempinski-stmoritz.ch).

Eating The **Hotel Laudinella** houses six different restaurants ranging from **Zeit's** take away to classic fondue to seriously good Thai at **The Siam Wind**. Book ahead for a table at über-trendy sushi restaurant **NOBU** at Badrutt's Palace Hotel (T81 837 1000).

Bars and clubs Drink at the **Post Haus**, designed by Lord Foster (of Gherkin fame), dance at **Diamond** and gamble (or spectate) at the **Ivory Ball Lounge Bar** at the Kempinski.

Shopping Stock up on muesli and Lindt chocolate at the sizeable **Co-op**.

Health Most of the hotels offer spa facilities to paying non-guests.

Internet The easiest option is to go for a coffee at one of the bigger hotels and make the most of their wireless.

Transfer options From Milan, companies such as **ATS** (A-T-S.net) operate for around €85 return. From Zurich the train is a must. Breathtaking views and at 3½ hours it doesn't take much longer than driving. It's cheaper too. (Sbb.ch).

Local partners None

One of the top dogs of the resort world, counting itself an equal of Chamonix, Kitzbühel and Zermatt, St Moritz combines one of Europe's glitziest towns with a serious snowboarding stronghold of a mountain.

66 99

St Moritz is a freerider's paradise – but you'll also find lots of fancy people hanging out in the restaurant pretending to be little snowbunnies. The good thing about it is that they stay on the slopes – or even just in the restaurant – so all the good spots and the freeriding stays untouched for those who appreciate it. And at night you can still try to hook up with one of the fancy snowbunnies.

Alexeja Pozzoni, St Moritz local

❄ *If you like this* ...
... *try Kitzbühel* ➤p42,
Chamonix ➤p128, *or
Cortina* ➤p176.

The Mountain

St Moritz is part of the largest linked snowsports area in the country – Engadin/St Moritz, the largest snowsports region in Switzerland, with over 350 km of runs spreading through nine areas. Snow is guaranteed from November until May thanks to some state-of-the-art snowmaking kit. Although the fur-clad, knees-together skiing crew are well represented, you won't be the only one sliding sideways. Engadin market their area as 'the Hawaii of snowboarding' and count riders like Michi Albin as locals. The park at Corviglia is well maintained and hosts annual contests such as the Roxy Chicken Jam every April, when the best female riders in the world battle it out of the kickers and rails for two days. When the DJ and ladies pack up, you can have a go.

Beginners Stick to the home runs from Corviglia down to either Celerina or St Moritz Bad, where you'll find a combination of wide, mellow pistes and gentle narrower cat tracks on which to practise your straightlining away from the crowds – until about 1500 that is. Make sure you're back up at the top of Corviglia by 1600 when the piste-bashers come out.

Intermediate Head up the Trais Fluors Chair and take the wide blue down the back for some carving practice and 180 challenges coming out of the natural quarterpipe to the left of the main piste, followed by ollie-ing the gaps between the slushy moguls in the gully back to the bottom of the chair. After lunch, test your skills in the park, which has mini rails, mini boardercross and mini kickers as well as the full-scale versions if you're getting a bit cocky.

Advanced The advantage of the high proportion of skiers in the area is that even a week or two after snowfall there's a fair few pockets of untouched powder. Check out the face to the right of the Trais Fluors Chair, it's not the easiest traverse from the top but well worth it. Also the 10-km-long Morteratsch/Isla Persa glacier run in the Diavolezza Bernina area is a must.

Kids The Suvretta Snowsports School (T81 836 3600) will take them off your hands.

Flat light days As the town is above 1800 m, there's very little in the way of tree-lined runs, but as some lifts take you well over 3000 m you may find yourself above the clouds. Failing that book a passenger ride on the Olympic Bob track (olympia- bobrun.ch) and reach speeds of up to 135 kph.

OPENING TIMES
Mid-Nov to early May: 0830-1600

RESORT PRICES
Week pass (6 days): CHF296
Day pass: CHF57
Season pass: CHF1200

DIRECTORY
Tourist Office: T81 837 3333
Medical Centre: T81 833 1414
Pisteurs: T122
Taxi: T81 833 7272
Local radio: Radio Engiadina 97.0 FM
Website: stmoritz.ch

CHERYL MAAS CHICKEN RUN P: CHRIS MORAN

LOCALS DO
- Go out on Thursdays to Pontresina for live music.
- Freeride at Diavolezza.
- Ride the Davos pipe when there's nothing on in St. Moritz.

LOCALS DON'T
- Go on Corviglia during Christmas and New Year. Too many people.
- Hike too much to get the good runs.

PROS
- The St Tropez of Alpine resorts.
- Good restaurants and nightlife.
- Empty pistes while the rich swig Veuve Clicquot from 1200 to 1500.

CONS
- Expensive.
- The sunshine can leave many pistes vulnerable to moguls.
- Expensive.

NOT TO MISS
The good people of Engadin/St Moritz send the piste-bashers out at 1600 everyday. Lie in wait at the top of your favourite run, and then just relax as you glide effortlessly down through the fresh corduroy.

REMEMBER TO AVOID
The driver of the aforementioned piste-basher at the bottom.

SNOW DEPTH
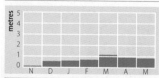

RELIVE A FAMOUS MOMENT
The legendary Errol Flynn proved himself to be a total chicken by recording the slowest ever time down the 'Cresta Run' bobsleigh track, letting out a 'high-pitched' scream all the way down. Try and beat his time and boast about it in the pub later.

1822 m	TOWN ALTITUDE
211 km	KM TO AIRPORT
ZRH	AIRPORT
★★☆	VEGETARIAN RATING
★★★	INTERNET CAFES
★★☆	RIDE IN/RIDE OUT
3303 m	HIGHEST LIFT
1481 m	VERTICAL DROP
area not measured	RIDEABLE AREA (IN ACRES)
350 km	KM OF PISTES
3	NURSERY AREAS
18/61/9	RUNS: BEG/INTER/ADV
3/7	FUNICULAR/CABLE CARS
1/18	GONDOLAS/CHAIRS
27	DRAGS
yes	NIGHT RIDING
2	PARKS
1	PIPE
no	SUMMER AREAS
★★★	ENVIRONMENTAL RATING
$$$	COST INDICATOR

SWITZERLAND
ST MORITZ

Verbier

The Town

Verbier is pretty, with low, angled roofs that layer up with each snowfall. Development is ever-present though, as cranes and concrete edge up the hillside each winter to meet the demand. Make no mistake – while Verbier might have lost some of its society status lately, it is still a place to be seen, and Dior sunglasses and Prada are still very prevalent. Thankfully, the hardcore element is just as visible, with backpacks, transceivers and long, wide snowboards considered essential. In terms of the snow that attracts this diverse crowd, Verbier never gets really massive amounts but with the bottom station at 1550 m and extensive use of snow cannons, snow stays in town for most of the season. Higher up, it's a different story.

Sleeping Real budget accommodation at **The Bunker** (thebunker.ch) and **Hotel les Touristes** (T27 771 2147) is another cheap, friendly option. Recommended for self-catering is quaint **Chalet Oliquin** (chaletoliquin .com), but be sure to book well in advance. **Hotel Garbo** (hotelgarbo .com) is at the more luxurious end.

Eating En Bas at the **Pub Mont Fort** (T27 771 1834) is cheap and caters well for vegetarians. **Al Capone's** (27 771 6774) is open for great pizza for lunch and dinner. **Le Hameau** (T27 771 4580) does an unbeatable CHF25 midday menu with a salad. If you are after a good veggie, you won't go wrong at **The Farinet** (T27 771 6626).

Bars and clubs The **Pub Mont Fort** has a tasty snack menu, while **Le Farinet** has a sun deck and a lounge bar. **Wonderbar** is relaxed, while **Le Fer a Cheval** is reliably busy. Later, **Le Casbah** is always busy.

Shopping Buy groceries at **Migros** and alcohol at **Denner**. **No Bounds** and **Hardcore** are the main snowboard shops.

Health Manouka (T27 771 3606) offers massages and various different body treatments.

Internet Check your emails in **Harold's**, **Pub Mont Fort**, **Verbier Beach** and the **Wonderbar**.

Transfer options Take the train (myswitzerland .com) or try Alpine Express (alpineexpress .com).

Local partners The 4 valleys/Mont Fort Pass includes Thyon, Veysonnaz, Siviez and Nendaz, on the same lift system.

> You find two sorts of people in Verbier. The rich, there to enjoy the beautiful chalets and the hospitable atmosphere, and the real mountain goats. They're the tough guys and girls who push their limits every day and walk a fine line between extreme pleasure and fast, painful death.
>
> *Cira Riedel*, Seventh Sky

OPENING TIMES
Early Nov to late Apr: 0830-1630

RESORT PRICES
Week pass (6 days): CHF369
Day pass: CHF63
Season pass: CHF1292

DIRECTORY
Tourist office: T27 775 3888
Medical centre: T27 771 7020
Pisteurs: T27 775 2511
Taxi: T79 332 4545
Local radio: 103.3 Rhone FM
Website: verbier.ch

One of Europe's best: a steep, sunny, internationally renowned freeride resort that's popular with the well to do and core riders alike.

If you like this . . .
. . . try *Krasnaya Poliana* ▶▶p108, *Engelberg* ▶▶p312, or *Jackson Hole* ▶▶p362.

R: MATT BURT P: DANMILNER.COM

The Mountain

Verbier consists of three main areas: Verbier/Mont Fort, Savoleyres and Bruson. Verbier is the main sector, topping out at 3330 m. This whole area is popular because of its height and because there are a lot of easily visible runs, faces, drops and couloirs to check out. Locals put in lines everywhere, and those unfamiliar with Verbier's off-piste can just copy what they see. Get to Savoleyres by taking any of the free buses, but the gondola up is slow. It's not as steep as the rest of Verbier, but is often clearer on cloudy days and has some decent lines through the trees. Bruson is worthwhile but requires taking a gondola, an infrequent bus, two chairlifts and a T-bar before doing any real riding. Hence it only really gets busy when everything else is shut from avalanche risk. But the tree riding here is world-class and a little hiking turns an area with few lifts into an expansive playground.

Beginners Les Esserts is the place for total beginners, but watch out for the draglift. It's a separate slope on the No 2 bus route, surrounded by chalets at the top of the town. A cheaper, separate ski pass is available for here and Le Rouge, which is close by and a possible next step. An alternative next step is up to Savoleyres to perfect turns on the long blue run down to the Le Taillay chair.

Intermediate Free reign at Savoleyres. Literally, go anywhere apart from the tight trees on skier's right down the Etablons chair. Attelas all the way down to Medran is great for various different lines in fresh snow, steadily further away from the motorway piste. Alternatively, when everything's tracked, Lac de Vaux and La Chaux are fun places to cruise around, with little drop-offs, and the park at La Chaux is fun to lap in the afternoon.

Advanced Head up to Mont Fort as early as possible and drop a couple of runs down the front face, skier's right, before it gets really busy. With experience and someone with local knowledge, hike up past the cross at Mont Fort and drop off the backside down the Poubelle leading you back to Siviez. Ride the lifts back up to Chassoure, then hike the ridge of the Mont Gelee – it takes about 25 minutes when the boot pack is laid. Drop the Lac de Vaux face right down into Vallon d'Arbi, and catch the gondola at La Tzoumaz, wondering how much bread and cheese you can pile into your goulash soup at the top.

Kids Under fives are free. There is a Kid's Club at Les Moulins (part of the crèche) for the smallest ones. Les Esserts is the next step.

Flat light days Bruson is the first place to go when everything else is shut down. Make sure you're early for the Poste bus from le Chable as it gets full and there's only one an hour.

☺ LOCALS DO
- Hike to out of the way spots.
- Carry avalanche gear.
- Ask about conditions from the patrollers based in the Freeride Huts.

☹ LOCALS DON'T
- Eat a lot in the mountain restaurants.
- Get many early nights.
- Take a day off because it's snowing.

✓ PROS
- Recent investment in fast lifts.
- Loads of off-piste terrain.
- Banging nightlife.

✗ CONS
- Mont Gelee lift is almost always shut.
- Not cheap.
- No pipe.

◉ NOT TO MISS
Sledging at Savoleyres. Crashing is inevitable!

ⓘ REMEMBER TO AVOID
Having a long lunch and returning too late from the 4 Valleys to connect back to Verbier and finding you have a CHF200 taxi ride home.

❄ SNOW DEPTH
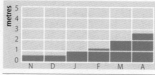

☺ RELIVE A FAMOUS MOMENT
Princes William and Harry, the Beckhams, Philip Schofield, James Blunt, Rick Astley, Ruby Wax and Les Dennis all holiday here. Yes!

1500 m	TOWN ALTITUDE
170 km	KM TO AIRPORT
GVA	AIRPORT
★★★	VEGETARIAN RATING
★★★	INTERNET CAFES
★★☆	RIDE IN/RIDE OUT
3330 m	HIGHEST LIFT
1830 m	VERTICAL DROP
2236	RIDEABLE AREA (IN ACRES)
192 km	KM OF PISTES
2	NURSERY AREAS
12/18/3	RUNS: BEG/INTER/ADV
0/5	FUNICULAR/CABLE CARS
9/24	GONDOLAS/CHAIRS
46	DRAGS
no	NIGHT RIDING
3	PARKS
0	PIPE
no	SUMMER AREAS
★★☆	ENVIRONMENTAL RATING
$$$	COST INDICATOR

SWITZERLAND
VERBIER

Zermatt

The Town

Sitting right beneath the Europe's most iconic mountain, the Matterhorn, Zermatt is one of the winter sports world's major players – and it shows. Alpine history seeps from every pore, and the place buzzes with mountaineers, skiers, tourists and snowboarders. If the town itself is impressive, the mountain is even more so, with links to Italy and five distinct riding areas on the Swiss side. But it's the Matterhorn, looming over the village, that really raises Zermatt above and beyond its 'resort' status. It is truly an awe-inspiring sight. Factor in a legendary party scene, and you have a resort to be filed in the drawer marked 'must visit'.

Sleeping Zermatt's **Youth Hostel** (youthhostel.ch/zermatt) is clean, architecturally impressive – and predictably busy and expensive. At around CHF70 a night, the one-star **Hotel Weisshorn** (holidaynet.ch /weisshorn) is about as cheap and cheerful as Zermatt gets.

Eating If **McDonald's** (reputedly the most expensive in Europe!) won't suffice, the **Pizzeria Broken** at the **Hotel Post** (hotelpost.ch) is a better option. **The Pipe**, known locally as the 'Surfer's Cantina' is also good for a sit-down meal. Locals swear by the **North Wall Bar**. Try **Green Dinner** (T27 966 5666) if you fancy a veggie.

Bars and clubs **Grampi's Pub** on the high street is expensive but worth checking out for the piano man who plays twice a night as well as the food and drinks. Other ports of call to check out are the **Papperia Pub** and the **Brown Cow Snack Bar**.

Shopping There's a **Co-op** by the main station, and a smaller supermarket by the church in the main town square.

Health Refloxology, massage, hydrotherapy – its all here. Try **Integral Wellness Therapies** (gesundheit-zermatt.ch).

Internet The wonderfully named **Stoked** (stoked.ch) is as good as they get. Terminals and laptop points are in the basement.

Transfer options As with most Swiss resorts, the train is the most efficient way of getting into town. Get a Swiss Rail Card – more details from MySwitzerland.com.

Local partners Cervinia and Valtourneche on the Italian side are all linked to form one enormous area.

With incredible views, a huge riding area, a cosmopolitan town and a mixture of modern and Victorian lift facilities, Zermatt could be the quintessential Swiss resort.

⟫ If you like this . . .
. . . try Whistler ⟫p86, Chamonix ⟫p128, or Verbier ⟫p330.

R: JAMES STENTIFORD P: JAMES MCPHAIL

P: JAMES MCPHAIL

The Mountain

Like Whistler, Chamonix or any of the other 'brand name' resorts in the world, Zermatt is absolutely huge. So huge in fact, that riders spending a week here are going to struggle to even scratch the surface of what's on offer. Parks? There's one on the glacier. Steep freeriding? Many of the lifts here head up into the high 3000 m, meaning you can get yourself in a lot of trouble if you want to. Mileage? You could spend a season here and still find a new piste to shred. Summer riding? The glacier park is a pre-season stop-off for some of the best in the world. So where to start? Here's what we reckon.

Beginners Complete beginners and unconfident riders should spend their time in one of Zermatt's five learner parks: Blauherd, Sunnegga, Riffelberg, Schwarzsee Paradise or Trockener Steg. Of the main areas, either the top of the main glacier or the blue runs from Gorenrgrat to Riffelberg will keep the blood pumping.

Intermediate Spend any time riding

OPENING TIMES

Open every day year round
Nov to May: 0830-1650
Jun to Oct: 0730-1500

RESORT PRICES

Week pass (6 days): CHF430
Day pass: CHF76
Season pass: CHF1530

DIRECTORY

Tourist office: T27 966 8100
Medical centre: T27 967 1188
Pisteurs: T27 966 0101
Taxi: T0848 11 1212
Local radio: Radio Rottu
	Oberwallis 97.8 FM
Website: zermatt.ch

> Zermatt is very much promoted as a family resort, which is good for freeriders. There are some gems if you look around and walk for a bit. The family mellow-style pistes are good fun for jibbing as well.
>
> *Scott Nixon, pro snowboarder*

Zermatt and you're going to get some miles under your base. But to really get a feel for the sheer size of the area, head up the glacier and descend in the sun to Cervinia. Have some pasta for lunch, head back up in the afternoon when Zermatt gets the sun, and end the day with some fondue to finish a truly cosmopolitan day's riding with a cracking set of goggle marks.

Advanced If the sun is out, Zermatt comes into its own. Take the Gornergrat funicular to the top station and spend half an hour ogling the incredible views. From here you've got three options: take the cable car over to the next peak and shred the open face that you pass on the way over, drop the stuff that heads to the Rosenritz ridge, or keep going to the summit of the Stockhorn. Each route takes you back to the Riffelap station of the funicular. After lunch, follow the signs to Furi and head up to the glacier to session the park in the afternoon.

Kids Children up to the age of nine get a free lift ticket. For lessons, try the versatile **Stoked** shop (stoked.ch) and **Snowflakes Kids Club**.

Flat light days The one area in which Zermatt suffers due to its sheer height and glacial coverage – bad weather comes with the territory. Spend the day in town, checking out the Alpine museum.

LOCALS DO

- Ride the home runs - they stay open right to the end of the season and are amazing fun.
- Go to the North Wall Bar for a low-priced pizza and a few beers.
- Respect this riding area. There are serious dangers here, so be safe.

LOCALS DON'T

- Ever seem to track this place out. It's simply too big.
- Drive. Cars are banned in Zermatt. Park at Tasch, further down the valley, and catch the train up.
- Take the back train on the Gornergrat funicular in the morning - it stops at every station on the way. Take the front one instead.

PROS

- Absolutely massive area.
- Height of resort means snow stays good longer.
- Some of the most awe-inspiring views in the Alps.

CONS

- Expensive.
- And busy.
- Not the best flat light area.

NOT TO MISS

The view from the Gornergrat station on a clear day, with Monte Rosa, the Matterhorn and Breithorn in sharp relief. Breathtaking.

REMEMBER TO AVOID

Beginners should avoid the Stockhorn area. It's steep, scary and intimidating.

SNOW DEPTH

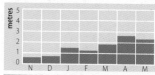

RELIVE A FAMOUS MOMENT

Edward Whymper's controversial first ascent of the Matterhorn in 1865 shook the world after local guides died on the descent (see page 305).

1620 m	TOWN ALTITUDE
244 km	KM TO AIRPORT
GVA	AIRPORT
★★★	VEGETARIAN RATING
★★☆	INTERNET CAFES
★★☆	RIDE IN/RIDE OUT
3899 m	HIGHEST LIFT
2279 m	VERTICAL DROP
area not measured	RIDEABLE AREA (IN ACRES)
313 km	KM OF PISTES
5	NURSERY AREAS
29/72/27	RUNS: BEG/INTER/ADV
2/12	FUNICULAR/CABLE CARS
6/20	GONDOLAS/CHAIRS
20	DRAGS
no	NIGHT RIDING
1	PARKS
2	PIPE
yes	SUMMER AREAS
★★★	ENVIRONMENTAL RATING
$$$	COST INDICATOR

SWITZERLAND
ZERMATT

R: JONNY BARR L: ALASKA P: DANMILNER.COM

Jonny Barr, living his dream in Alaska. See page 340 for what he thought of this turn.

USA

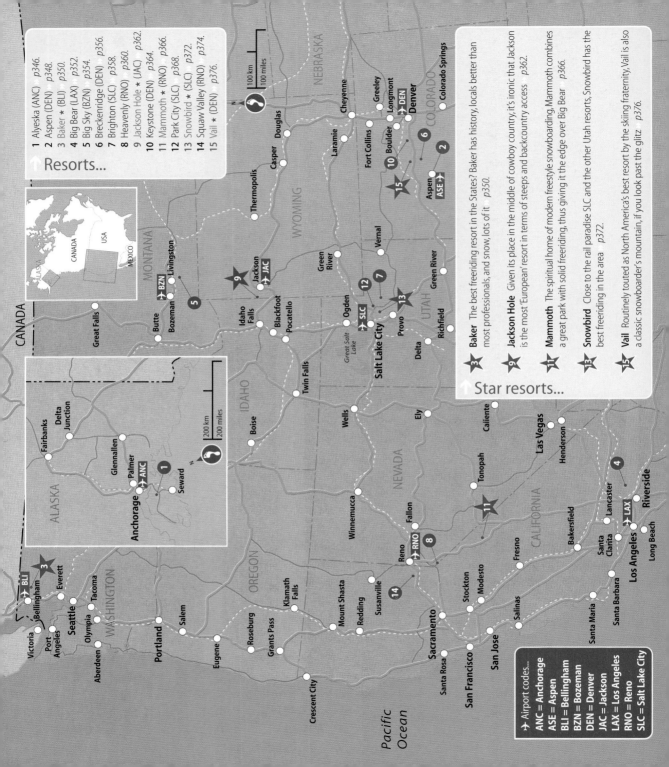

Resorts...

1 Alyeska (ANC) → p346.
2 Aspen (DEN) → p348.
3 Baker ★ (BLI) → p350.
4 Big Bear (LAX) → p352.
5 Big Sky (BZN) → p354.
6 Breckenridge (DEN) → p356.
7 Brighton (SLC) → p358.
8 Heavenly (RNO) → p360.
9 Jackson Hole ★ (JAC) → p362.
10 Keystone (DEN) → p364.
11 Mammoth ★ (RNO) → p366.
12 Park City (SLC) → p368.
13 Snowbird ★ (SLC) → p372.
14 Squaw Valley (RNO) → p374.
15 Vail ★ (DEN) → p376.

Star resorts...

Baker The best freeriding resort in the States? Baker has history, locals better than most professionals, and snow, lots of it   p350.

Jackson Hole Given its place in the middle of cowboy country, it's ironic that Jackson is the most 'European' resort in terms of steeps and backcountry access   p362.

Mammoth The spiritual home of modern freestyle snowboarding, Mammoth combines a great park with solid freeriding, thus giving it the edge over Big Bear   p366.

Snowbird Close to the rail paradise SLC and the other Utah resorts, Snowbird has the best freeriding in the area   p372.

Vail Routinely touted as North America's best resort by the skiing fraternity, Vail is also a classic snowboarder's mountain, if you look past the glitz   p376.

Airport codes...
ANC = Anchorage
ASE = Aspen
BLI = Bellingham
BZN = Bozeman
DEN = Denver
JAC = Jackson
LAX = Los Angeles
RNO = Reno
SLC = Salt Lake City

Introduction

The country that gave us snowboarding continues to lead from the front today. Think 'US snowboarding' and the resulting associations will encompass every aspect of our sport, from Shaun White's recent glitzy Olympic triumph to the hazy heritage of Sherman Poppen's 'Snurfer', the toy that started the whole thing back in the late sixties.

This sprawling, diverse contribution to the evolution of snowboarding is reflected neatly in the huge number of options available to any visitor heading to the States. If you want to ride it, you'll find it here, from the mellow groomers of Colorado to the fearsome steeps of Alaska, via some of the best parks and slickly run winter towns on the planet.

In other ways, too, a trip to the States is a winner. Flights, hotels and car rentals are cheaper than ever, and their in-resort infrastructure is easily the best in the world. Lifts work and queues move swiftly. People hand you bars of chocolate as you unstrap for the last time each day. Perhaps fittingly for these kings of convenience, it's all just strangely easy here.

True, some riders will visit the States determined not to enjoy themselves, convinced the place is too homogenized, too sanitized and there are times when riding here does have a peculiarly fixed-grin quality, particularly when it comes to the off-piste policies of some resorts or the sometimes cloying nature of the service culture. But in the main, these oft-quoted clichés are wide of the mark, as they usually are. Most people you meet here will be genuinely friendly, the beer will be cold, the mountains will be groomed to perfection and that breakfast buffet will be big enough to keep you going for most of the day. Just don't mention the war …

USA rating

Value for money
★★★★☆

Nightlife
★★★☆☆

Freestyle
★★★★★

Freeride
★★★★☆

Essentials

"The US is snowboarding. It's the birthplace, the progression forum, the media spotlight and the buffet bar of resorts and backcountry spots. There are killer parks back east, steeps out west, champagne powder in the Rockies. Don't come expecting to find one thing, expect to find everything, as long as you're willing to travel."

Jen Sherowski, Transworld Snowboarding

Getting there

Flights to the States are cheaper than they've ever been, and there are five main points of entry for the resorts featured in this guide. For Anchorage (Alaska) carriers include **American Airlines** (aa.com), **Delta** (delta.com), **British Airways** (ba.com) and **United** (united.com). For Denver (Colorado), try **Northwest Airlines** (nwa.com), **Continental** (continental.com), **American Airlines** (aa.com), Delta, **Air Canada** (aircanada.com) or **British Airways**. For the Californian resorts, points of entry are Reno or LAX and carriers include **American**, **Delta**, **United**, **BA**, **Air New Zealand** (airnewzealand.com), **Virgin** (virgin-atlantic.com), American and Northwest, while for Salt Lake City (Utah) try **Continental**, **NWA**, **AA** or **Delta**.

Red tape

US entry requirements are among the most stringent in the world. Any foreign citizen wishing to enter the US must obtain a visa beforehand – non-immigrant for a temporary stay, immigrant for permanent residence. How easy it is to obtain a non-immigrant visa depends on your country of origin, so check travel.state.gov/visa for more information. In the aftermath of 9/11, visitors to any American airport or public building are subject to stringent, often invasive security checks.

Top tips

- Take ID you don't mind using losing, such as an International Driving Permit, for entry into bars and nightclubs. EVERYBODY gets checked in the States.

- Drivers are allowed to turn right on a red light, so don't be surprised if people beep you from behind if you're sitting at the lights.

- Carry cash for tips. Tipping culture is endemic here.

- Don't make any jokes about bombs or terrorism while going through customs. That's when Americans really don't understand irony.

- Talk to people. Americans love foreigners, especially Brits and Irish.

Getting around

Driving The USA has an agreement with most countries that means the renter's full national driving licence may be used for a period of up to one year in the USA. Provisional licences are not acceptable. International Driving Permits are generally not required in the USA but they are valid in conjunction with a full national driving licence. Americans drive on the right.

Car hire Car hire companies require a full licence for a year, regardless of age. The minimum age for renting a car is usually 21, although it can be as high as 25. Additional charges can be levied on drivers under 25 years of age. Most of the major car hire companies (hertz.com, avis.com) have offices in airports and cities.

Public transport

In the States it's almost heresy not to travel by car, and a good indicator of social status. Still, the trans-continental and inter-city train

USA price guide							
In US$	1.25	5.00	6.00	0.40	8.00	6.00	1.50

Some 473 years after Columbus discovered America, Americans discovered snowboarding. Riding in America isn't one big, shared experience. Riders on the east coast make the best of small and often icy hills and either aspire to move to the west or develop a fierce case of east coast pride. Riders on the west coast have pretty much got it made, but in completely different ways. Utah gets dry snow over huge mountain chains; storms sit over Tahoe and drop feet of heavy snow before the sun comes out; and riders in the northwest live for greybird days riding the wet stuff. Don't think for a minute that because you've ridden Tahoe that you know what Baker is like – or Big Bear. California might as well be another planet when compared to the snowy slopes of Big Sky, Montana. So much diversity – but isn't that what America is all about?

Annie Fast, Transworld Snowboarding

→ **Fact file**

Currency US Dollar ($)
Exchange rate €1 = US$1.28
Time zone Eastern (GMT +4), Central (GMT +5), Mountain (GMT +6), Pacific (GMT +7), Alaska (GMT +8)
Country code +1
To place a call out of US dial 011 plus country code.
Emergency numbers
  Ambulance: T911
  Police: T911
  Fire: T911

that it's easy to fuel up for the day ahead. American breakfasts are particularly prized, with their gargantuan array of cereals, pastries, cooked courses and coffees, while lunch on the hill is also pretty reasonably priced if you don't mind burgers, fries or sandwich variations such as the Reuben. It's the same story during the evening, with most resorts riffing away on the same gastronomic themes – Italian, Tex-Mex, burgers, Chinese, Thai or French bistro. Whatever the

service run by **Amtrak** (amtrak.com) is a great way of seeing the country. If funds are really tight, try the **Greyhound** network (greyhound.com) but it is slow and uncomfortable, if cheap.

Opening hours and traditions

Shops in the States have longer opening hours than their European counterparts, with many city outlets staying open seven days a week from 0800-2100. American holidays worth keeping an eye out for include Washington's Birthday (the third Monday in February) and Martin Luther King day (the third Monday in January).

Eating

Depending on your viewpoint, a trip to America is either going to be a grease-dipped nightmare or something approaching food heaven. Think American food and you're likely to find yourself thinking of hamburgers, hot dogs, McDonald's, steaks and all-you-can-eat buffets. The reality is pretty close and it's easy to lose yourself in the frenzy of consumption that characterizes middle-class life in the States. It's cheap to eat here, and the portions are generally huge, with meat being the primary ingredient. And greasily delicious though the food can be, after a prolonged stay, it can get a bit too much. It's sometimes possible to feel your very cells yearning for fruit or some other wholesome source of vitamins and minerals.

Of course, the upside of this culinary boon for the snowboarder is

P: ADAM GENDLE

Northern exposure

The first time I went to Alaska to film and shoot pictures was in 1999. This shot [our USA chapter opener] was taken on our first day shooting. I think it was the first turn down the mountain.

It was a massive field, consistently about 40 degrees, so it was quite steep and quite open. We hacked down as a team – me, James (Stentiford), Romain Carlier and Tom Burt, who was our guide that day. That was mad – I mean, f****** hell, for us he was like one of the biggest legends in extreme snowboarding so we were like, "Ah, OK Tom". Anyway, he asked us what we wanted, then took us to the goods. So we were just hacking down and then Dan yelled at us to stop. He wanted to take some individual shots and he took mine perfectly.

It's the most published shot I've ever had. I've had one front cover, three posters, three double page shots and then it's been used in ads, quarter pages and all sorts. Why do I think it's so popular? I think it's because it expresses what snowboarding is all about. You can see a lot of snow, the background is very picturesque – and then there's the way that Dan Milner pushed it. It's one of his favourite shots snowboarding, and he pushed it a lot. Everyone who's seen it loves it. For me, it expresses speed, powder and style all in one shot. I had it, basically!

Jonny Barr, pro snowboarder

P: CHRIS MORAN/HOTSHITPICTURES.COM

genre, the themes remain the same – plentiful courses, free refills and choice. Lots of it. And there are the fast food outlets, which almost require a chapter of their own.

Not surprisingly, things can get tricky for those who don't covet a rich, starchy diet or for any riders with strict culinary needs, such as vegetarians. Noted happy-clappy areas such as California will probably yield more options than the cowboy country of Jackson Hole.

Language

English is the main spoken language, although a large minority speak Spanish. Other ethnic groups are also widespread.

Crime/safety

America is so huge that the guidelines vary from area to area. Almost all trips to the States pass off completely uneventfully – especially in rural, mountainous areas – but it is worth noting a few points. Crime is an issue in America, especially in major cities where street and car crime is a problem. At the time of writing, the US domestic threat level in relation to terrorism stood at 'elevated', and foreign nationals were advised to be on their guard. In resort, board theft does occur. The US police are fair but very strict, and there are severe penalties for drug or violent crime. Check fema.gov for up-to-date information on the current situation in the States.

Health

Fully comprehensive health insurance is absolutely essential for any trip to the United States. Medical treatment is good but very expensive, and there are no special arrangements between the US and other nations for healthcare. Cover up to US$1 million, including hospital treatment and medical evacuation if necessary, is advisable.

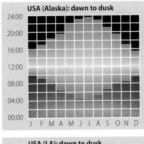

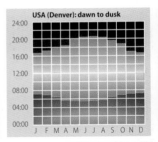

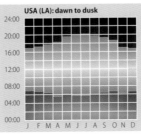

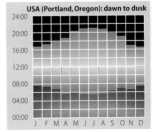

Snowboarding USA

"Snowboarding was an unexpected love child, born out of the cement trenches and wave-rich landscape of 1970s American skate and surf culture. After the world reeled in shock from this new sideways approach to sliding down mountains, millions strapped in. In the three decades since, whether it's on nearly vertical Alaskan peaks, a 25-stair handrail in New York City or a perfectly cut superpipe at Breckenridge, riding in America is still fuelled by a simple founding principle: snowboarding is what you make it. And American riders continue to make snowboarding impossible to ignore." Scooter Leonard, editor, Snowboard Journal

American snowboarding is huge in every sense. They have the largest number of riders, a huge number of resorts, the most popular magazines and videos and by far the biggest influence on snowboarding culture of any nation. It is big business, with the

Pros & cons

Pros ...

- Convenience, pure and simple. Everything works here.
- Huge variety of options for snowboarding, from rail specific city trips to SLC to heliboarding in AK.
- That service culture. It can be cloying at first, but you'll soon get used to everybody being nice to you.
- Friendly locals. They truly love snowboarding in the States and after a while it becomes infectious.
- Incredible freestyle facilities. And they make it look easy. Certain European resorts (stand up Chamonix) could do with taking notes.

... and cons

- Restrictive out of bounds policy, which will be quite alien to most Europeans.
- Resorts are quite spread out, making multi-resort road trips quite an undertaking. Though often that's exactly the point.
- You'll need to choose your resort carefully if you're after steep freeriding. Overall, the vertical drops here aren't that great.
- Strong litigious culture in the States means some resorts have frustrating restrictions – huge slow zones, limited backcountry access.
- It's pretty expensive – and lift tickets in particular can be shockingly pricey compared to Europe.

companies that make the kit enjoying huge turnovers and almost every resort in America embracing snowboarding enthusiastically in some way. The result is that the States is now the most snowboard friendly destination on the planet.

Perhaps an even more telling indicator of the sport's popularity is the way that snowboarding culture has infiltrated the mainstream.

R: BEN KILNER L: ASPEN SNOWMASS P: JAMES MCPHAIL

JUSTIN TIMBERLAKE AND FRIENDS P: HILARY NUTTING

Heliboarding Alaska

Russia, Asia and the Middle East might be the latest big mountain stars of magazines and movies, but Alaska is home to the heliboarding phenomenon, and still arguably the best choice for the average rider looking to get heli time. With a good choice of dependable guide services, reliably heavy snowfall and terrain that ranges from mellow powder bowls to gnarly vertical spines, you're unlikely to shell out for a trip that disappoints.

Different operators suit different clients. Some specialize in all-inclusive trips well-suited to wealthy holidaymakers with less experience, while others operate more as a mountain taxi-service, with a mandatory guide to show the way. Lodge or no lodge, helitime package or pay-per-day, the company of older skiers or pros on a hectic filming schedule: a little bit of web surfing should make it pretty obvious which place will suit your style, your ability and your budget. Below, we've listed three operators particularly popular with riders, one for each heli hotspot.

At the heart of the Chugach Range, Valdez is the most famous of the Alaskan heli towns. Advantages include the proximity to Anchorage and a large selection of guides to choose from; the big disadvantage is that you'll be jockeying for flight time with all the groups, particularly if the weather is bad. Points North, based in Cordova, and Chugach Powder Guides, based at Alyeska resort, also fly into the Chugach, but are well out of the Valdez crush, while Out of Bounds, in the southeast of the state, are close to the Canadian Yukon border.

Helitime is either priced by number of runs and/or guaranteed vertical feet per day, or according to the Hobbs (airtime) meter in the helicopter. Riders can join a group or book their own heli for the day; prepaid packages guarantee a seat, but as the guide service must reserve helicopters for the season, pay pilots' wages and fork out on insurance whether the heli flies or not, full refunds on pre-pay are rare. If possible, aim to spend at least twice as many days in Alaska as you'd like to fly, to allow for down days. March and April are the most popular months. February is dark and cold; by May corn snow is the norm.

Cordova

Points North Heli-Adventures, T877 787-6784, alaskaheliski.com, are based in the small cannery town of Cordova, south of Valdez and accessible only by plane or boat. Their comfortable, well-equipped main lodge is located in the converted Orca Cannery; they've also just opened a new cabin on the remote Tahneta Pass, and even offer private heliski cruises on the 85-ft *Maritime Maid*. On down days riders can sea kayak, ice climb or head to the local ski hill, Mount Eyak, which operates one creaky single chair to coastal-dump wonderland. Rates start at US$160 per night for lodging, meals and transport; expect to pay around US$900 a day for about 20,000-25,000 vertical feet.

Haines

Out of Bounds, Haines, T1800 HELL-YEA, alaskaheliskiing.com, down in southeastern Alaska, operates in the vast expanses of the Chilkat, Takshunuk, and Takhinsha Mountains. A large proportion of the clients are filmmakers, photographers and pros; one-horse Haines is a regular stop on the Absinthe filming schedule. Consequently, the guides specialize in big mountain riding without the handholding, though they'll help with in-town lodging and grey day activities if you need suggestions. They also run a guide school each spring. Daily rates average US$500, depending on the number of descents.

Valdez

While most of the guide services out of Valdez are full-service operations catering to skiers with money to burn, Alaska Backcountry Adventures, T907 835-5608, alaskabackcountry.com, still maintains an RV camp by the Worthington Airstrip, 29 miles (46 km) out of town. Riders can opt for a week-long, all-inclusive package (starting at US$3564 for five full days of helitime) or book a motorhome for a week (from US$189) and then pay for a day, half-day or even a single drop (from US$109), space and weather depending.

Tam Leach

P. JAMES MCPHAIL

Here, pro riders such as Shaun White have the status and influence of rock stars, as the groups of snowboarders riding around wearing face masks in emulation of their hero testifies. Yet beyond the glitz and the behemoth-like stature of the industry, the grassroots are still discernable. The underground America that dragged snowboarding by the scruff of the neck into the future and helped develop the sport as we enjoy it today is still going strong. The powder chargers of Baker, SLC's jib kids, the park rats of Mammoth and the heli hell-men of AK – each has a claim to be one authentic aspect of riding in the States. And as snowboarding continues to grow, the essence of what it means to be a snowboarder in America will remain refreshingly difficult to pin down.

Conditions

American riding areas are situated in three distinct areas: the east coast, the west coast and the Rocky Mountains. The west coast (roughly, Alaska down to California) is affected by storms from the Pacific, which drop vast falls of heavy snow. The Rocky Mountain range is affected by a different range of conditions, mainly due to their vast scale. But generally speaking, the Rocky climate is cooler, making for lighter and drier snow. In contrast, the east coast, being flatter and subject to sub-Arctic systems, is generally far colder and icier.

When to go

As befits a country that is in reality a continent, opening times in US resorts vary depending on the location. Many Rocky Mountain resorts opening in early November, while some of the Californian resorts stay open until May (Squaw) and even July (Mammoth) if the season is particularly strong. In between these extremes, usual northern hemisphere trends are to be expected. December, January and February see low temperatures, heavy snowfalls and a dearth of sunny days, while March is usually a good bet for a mix of good snowy conditions and bluebird days. By April, most resorts see full spring conditions, although late season snowfalls are not uncommon.

Off-piste policy

A quick round-up of US resorts reveals that this is a confusing nation when it comes to off-piste riding. Modern America is a litigious nation indeed, and to avoid being sued in the event of an accident many resorts simply ban out-of-bounds riding altogether.

Secret spots

Much filming for the big budget films takes place in the States, and the search for new terrain goes hand in hand with progression in this part of the world, whether it's the huge scale of modern backcountry

kickers or pioneering new ways of reaching the goods. Although this isn't of much concern to the average snowboarder, be aware that tensions do exist. Your best bet, as always in an environment with a high number of snowboarders, is to try and befriend the locals.

Freestyle

The Americans have been pushing the boundaries of freestyle snowboarding since Mark Anolik found the sport's first halfpipe in 1979 at Lake Tahoe. In the interim, every spike of progression on the snowboarding timeline has some kind of American involvement, and the names say it all: Terry Kidwell, Craig Kelly, Damien Sanders, Shaun Palmer, Jamie Lynn, JP Walker, Jeremy Jones, Danny Kass, Shaun White. The most exciting development in modern freestyle, the all-mountain funpark, also has its roots in America. Most resorts here have funparks and pipes that put Europe to shame, and they are constantly seeking to improve upon their existing facilities.

R: SI BRASS L: MAMMOTH P: CHRIS MORAN

R: SI BRASS L: MAMMOTH P: DANMILNER.COM

Lift chat

Up against the best

I'd wanted to ride Mount Baker for years but never realistically entertained any thoughts of riding in the banked slalom – until I won a starting place in the entrants' lottery. I was stoked. I was going to race against the best in the world in one of the oldest and most unique contests in snowboarding.

I was quietly confident that I could do well in my class. I'm no freestyler but I reckon I can get down a hill faster than most. The racecourse is exactly as it sounds: a slalom down a big natural halfpipe. How hard could it be? But, after two thigh pulverizing runs, I'd failed (by miles) to make the cut for the finals. The hardest thing was knowing I wouldn't get another shot on the course. That, and watching Tom Burt take 20 seconds off my time riding a 20-year-old board ...

Paul McConnell

MOUNT BAKER BANKED SLALOM P: MIKE WEYERHAEUSER/IDP

The scene

Really, the entire snowboarding scene comes from the States. American riders such as Milovich, Burton and Sims developed the first boards and established the first companies. From this beginning, the influence of snowboarding on American resorts has become pervasive. It isn't just the numbers (although there are a lot of riders on these shores) – more the fact that snowboarding's entire culture is more part of the mainstream in America than in any other country in the world. So the riding standard is usually incredibly high, with local riders avid followers of the magazines and videos that do so much to influence the way normal riders snowboard and even dress. One look at the hordes of mini Shaun White clones riding around the average American hill is one indication of how far snowboarding has come in a few short years.

The industry

Even at a grassroots level, American riding evolves quickly, with strong local scenes developing around supportive resorts such as Mammoth and Aspen. Shops, local 'zines and scene films are common ways of promoting local scenes, and this web-like network helps bring talented riders to the fore very quickly.

At the other extreme, the USA is the home of the snowboarding industry, with the major magazines such as *Transworld Snowboarding* and *Snowboarder* based in southern California along with many of the major crossover brands and production companies. These are easily the most influential in the sport, and have helped to make rock stars out of top riders, many of whom also hold American passports. Other less glitzy industry centres include Vermont, home of **Burton Snowboards**, Colorado, Utah and Oregon, home of the Mount Baker Banked Slalom.

Lift chat

Heli drops with Mike Basich

Throughout snowboarding's short history, unusual characters have always stood out. And in today's scene, few riders stand out as much as Mike Basich. Mike is one of the world's strongest freeriders, and highly competent in every other area of snowboarding. He's also a gifted snowboarding photographer whose work appears in magazines worldwide. But while the majority of the snowboarding world frets about learning all four 900s or how their arms look in the air, Basich has always done his own thing.

This ridiculous shot is a perfect example. Mike had set out to create something that looked impossible – a shot of him in the air with nothing else around, prompting the obvious question 'how on earth did he get there?' In the end things worked out a little differently – the shot looked so incredible that magazines worldwide ran it without cropping the heli out, partly because of the fact he thought the drop was much smaller than the whopping 120-odd feet it actually turned out to be.

Absolute insanity though this shot may be, perhaps the most amazing thing about it is that it's a self portrait. Mike set up a camera on a remote, and as he dropped out of the helicopter he had to focus not only on getting his grab and dealing with the presumably fraught sensation of having that amount of air between him and the ground, but on pressing the trigger switch. Good job he got it first time, as even he would presumably have baulked at going for this a second time...

As well as snowboarding and shooting photos at the top level, Mike has his own snowboarding shop in Truckee, California, and his own clothing brand 241 (Two-for-one, 241-USA.com), which he tests and produces in Japan, with the goal of making the most unique, artistic and functional clothing he can. For an illuminating insight into his unusual existence check out the movie *91 Words For Snow*.

R: MIKE BASICH P: MIKE BASICH

Alyeska

The Town

Originally a mining settlement, 'Girdweed', as the locals call it, is a sleepy, Bohemian hamlet, only really coming to life at the weekends, when Anchorage folk head down to their cabins in the spruce. Midweek in winter, it's a quiet, quiet place. If you'd like something to do at night other than watching the Northern Lights, consider basing yourself an hour up the road in Anchorage.

Sleeping The **Alyeska Hostel** (alyeskahostel.com) has eight dorm beds. Five minutes from the slopes, **Winner Creek** (alyeskawinnercreek. com) is an impressive log cabin B&B, while the five-star **Alyeska Prince** (alyeskaresort.com) can be a bargain midweek when empty.
Eating Stop at the excellent **Bake Shop** for inexpensive sandwiches and pancake breakfasts. **Chair 5** is the local's stop after a day on the hill while the **Double Musky** is upscale Alaska.
Bars and clubs The **Sitzmark** sees the occasional DJ but you're looking

at a drive into Anchorage. Grab a copy of the free weekly, *The Anchorage Press*, for gig and club night listings.
Shopping Stock up on groceries in Anchorage at the **New Sagaya City Markets**.
Health Holistic chiro and massage at **Girdwood Chiropractic Clinic**.
Internet **Kaladi Brothers** or **Dark Horse Coffee** in Anchorage.
Transfer options The **Magic Bus** (themagicbus.com) is the on-demand service. Far cheaper is the ski shuttle which runs from Anchorage.
Local Partners No local partners.

> ❝❞
>
> This super-fun little mountain in the back of beyond is the ideal warm-up for heliboarders en route to the interior, and a great alternative to most American resorts.
>
> *Tam Leach, snowboard journalist*

Blasted with ridiculous amounts of snow and refreshingly different from the average resort.

⟫ If you like this . . .
. . . try Val d'Isère ➤➤*p158, or Verbier* ➤➤*p330.*

⊛ **OPENING TIMES**
Late Nov to late May: Sun-Thu 1030-1730; Fri-Sun 1030-2130

⑤ **RESORT PRICES**
Week pass: No discount
Day pass: US$52
Season pass: US$1049

ⓘ **DIRECTORY**
Tourist office: T907 222 7682
Medical centre: T907 783 1355
Pisteurs: T907 754 7669
Taxi: None
Local radio: Glacier City Radio, 88.9 FM
Website: alyeskaresort.com

The Mountain

Though small in area, riding at Alyeska is a blast. The mountain is littered with gullies and natural hits, and much of the lift-accessed inbounds terrain is ungroomed. Freeriders will find steeps aplenty, with untracked chutes stretched out along the summit ridge. Bizarrely for those used to the altitudes of the Alps, the base of the mountain is practically at sea level, bordered by ocean inlets. Yet despite the altitude, it dumps here – more than twice the average in Colorado. Bleak in midwinter, by February temperatures are warming up. Come mid-March and the sun is still high when the lifts close at 1730. March is also prime viewing time for the Northern Lights.

Beginners Complete 'never-evers' should head for the day lodge; others head via Chair 4 to the upper

mountain cruisers: avoid achingly slow Chair 1. The lodge itself is often closed midweek out of peak season, making it necessary to rent beginner gear elsewhere. Stop at **Boarderline** (boarderlinealaska.com) in Anchorage.

Intermediate After a ride on the speedy tram, drop down to Chair 6 and start lapping, taking full advantage of the rolling terrain and numerous cat tracks en route. Leave the small, rail-heavy terrain park until a little later in the day, when the sun hits Prince Run and the ride back up the cable car is a welcome break.

Advanced If the snow's fresh and the sky clear, stumble onto the first tram at 1030. Drop straight off the backside onto the ungroomed North Face for a few powder laps. If it gets chopped, take Chair 6 and start hiking: the spines and chutes off the summit of Mount Alyeska are worth the trek. After a few shots at Glacier Bowl and Headwall, test your calf muscles on the long traverse to the steeps and shrubs of Max's Mountain.

Kids Most of the programmes here are geared towards Anchorage kids, but basic two-hour lift, lesson and rental packages are available on a daily basis for US$55-60. Child day ticket rates are US$34 for 14-17 year-olds and US$26 for 8-13 year-olds. Under-eights are free when skiing with a paying adult (US$10 if not).

Flat light days Whale-watching and iceberg cruises depart daily from Seward, two hours south of Girdwood. **Renown** (T1800 6553806) is the only year-round operator.

☺ LOCALS DO
- Ride the park jibs late in the day.
- Go for a post-ride pizza at Chair 5.
- Return to Anchorage at night.

☹ LOCALS DON'T
- Eat at any of the Prince Hotel restaurants, including those on-mountain.
- Head up early – cold temperatures mean it's bulletproof until midday.
- Stay in Girdwood, unless they have a weekend cabin.

✔ PROS
- Pre-heli trip acclimatization.
- Consistently amazing snow.
- Unique.

✖ CONS
- Hours from anywhere else.
- Small area.
- Less a resort than a country village.

♥ NOT TO MISS
Chugach Powder Guides is the local heliboarding outfit (chugachpowderguides.com), running snowcat trips close to the resort and heli trips further inland in the Chugach Range.

ℹ REMEMBER TO AVOID
Taking the tram around the lunchtime peak, when the queue is swelled with sightseers just up for the view.

❅ SNOW DEPTH
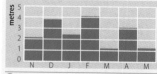

☺ RELIVE A FAMOUS MOMENT
Stumble into any restaurant for a sudden immersion into a scene straight from cult mid-nineties TV show *Northern Exposure*.

P: ALYESKA TOURISM

---

76 m
TOWN ALTITUDE

64 km
KM TO AIRPORT

ANC
AIRPORT

 ★☆☆
VEGETARIAN RATING

 ★★★
INTERNET CAFES

 ★★★
RIDE IN/RIDE OUT

1200 m
HIGHEST LIFT

760 m
VERTICAL DROP

1000
RIDEABLE AREA (IN ACRES)

area not measured
KM OF PISTES

1
NURSERY AREAS

3/14/10
RUNS: BEG/INTER/ADV

1/0
FUNICULAR/CABLE CARS

6/0
GONDOLAS/CHAIRS

2
DRAGS

yes
NIGHT RIDING

1
PARKS

1
PIPE

yes
SUMMER AREAS

★★★
★★★
ENVIRONMENTAL RATING

 $$$
COST INDICATOR

USA
ALYESKA

Aspen

The Town

This high-profile Colorado classic is many things to many riders. It is the full package resort, referred to as 'The Power of Four'. These four distinct mountains are Aspen Mountain, Aspen Highlands, Buttermilk and Snowmass, and they have distinct characters. Go to Aspen to be seen or ride steep trees, be like a local and hike the bowl of Highlands, spin and jib on the X-Games park at Buttermilk, or enjoy the variety of terrain that family-friendly Snowmass (3100-plus acres) has to offer. Aspen the town is over 100 years old, but has been tastefully restored over the years. It has the feeling of old world charm with all the luxurious amenities anyone could ever imagine. This is a place where athletes, artists, intellectuals, billionaires, snowboard bums, and your average tourist can all rub shoulders. Although wealth is abundant here it is extremely casual making it such a nice synergy of both fashion and function. Whether you think referring to your area as 'The Power of Four' is insufferably pompous or forward-thinking will probably decide how you see Aspen.

Sleeping See aspensnowmass.com/intown/lodging/lodging.cfm for an in-depth explanation of the lodging options. Lodging starts out very basic at the St Moritz for US$60 and goes up to the exquisite five-star lodgings of the Little Nell. Renting a condo at the Mountain House or Gant and splitting it amongst fellow travellers is a good value option. Although Aspen has the best of the best there are still deals out there for the budget traveller.

Eating There are too many to list here but some of the locals favourites are Jimmy's Steakhouse (T970 925 6020), Takah Sushi (T970 925 8588) and The Blue Maize (T970 925 6698). Be warned though – dining here is expensive. Try the bar menus at upscale restaurants for the best deals. For a quick affordable bite check out Johnny McGuires (T970 920 9255), they make awesome sandwiches. Another healthy budget option is Clark's Market (T970 925 8046).

Bars and clubs Don't miss Eric's for youth-inspired rabble rousing and beautiful women shooting pool. The Belly Up is an amazing venue to see live music – don't miss it! For nightly dancing with different ambience and DJs there's the Chelsea Club and Lava Room.

Shopping Again, check Clark's Market for healthy, budget food. The boutique-style snowboard stores here offer street clobber at a fraction of high street prices (once you've maxed out your credit card buying that US$9000 bronzed cougar for your home). **Health** The Aspen Health Club and Spa (aspenspa.com) and Remede spa at the St Regis (stregisaspen.com) will not disappoint, or be cheap.

Internet There's a café next to the City Market, although free wireless is available throughout most of the town.

Transfer options From Denver, CME (Colorado Mountain Express) is a good option if you don't want to rent a car. Upon arrival in the Aspen Valley area there are free bus shuttles that run between the different mountains and around town.

Local partners None.

> Life is full of trade-offs, compromises and sacrifices. When I am on vacation I want to have my cake and be able to eat it too. I feel fortunate to live here. Where else can you have it all?
>
> *Jay Tierney, Aspen local*

P: JAMES MCPHAIL

One of the most famous 'name' resorts in the world, Aspen delivers thanks to four great mountains and a cosmopolitan – if pricey – town.

If you like this ...
... try Ischgl ▸▸p38, St Anton ▸▸p48, Whistler ▸▸p86, or Val d'Isère ▸▸p158.

OPENING TIMES
Mid-Nov to late Apr: 0900-1530

RESORT PRICES
Week pass (6 days): US$525
Day pass: US$75
Season pass: US$1879

DIRECTORY
Tourist office: T970 925 1220
Medical centre: T970 453 1010
Pisteurs: T970 925 1211
Taxi: T970 975 8484
Local radio: None
Website: aspensnowmass.com

USA
ASPEN

The Mountain

The four ski areas that comprise Aspen/Snowmass are all located in the White River National Forest. They are all accessible on the same lift ticket and are connected via free shuttle. It is very plausible to enjoy one of the four in the morning and another in the afternoon. Each of the four hills has similar facilities (in other words it's all world class) and very different characteristics. The best option is to choose your spot and base yourself accordingly. Of the individual hills, Aspen Mountain (Ajax to the locals) is in town and thus is the most 'in-use'. Aspen Highlands is quieter and highly rated among the locals for its steeper slopes and off-piste access in the Highland and Olympic Bowls and Steeplechase. Highlands also has some good beginner and intermediate slopes. Again, it is versatile, with great family and beginner facilities and the small matter of the X Games park to shred. It doesn't get any better for freestyle devotees. And there's Snowmass, which is big and well rounded and also very diverse, with park and the best freeriding terrain of the four. Overall, this is slick American riding at its best. If you can afford it, you'll go home happy.

Beginners Beginners should think about Snowmass or Aspen for getting the turns down. Snowmass has some wide, mellow slopes lower down that make it really easy to get to grips with it. Slightly more advanced riders should think about the mid-mountain beginner terrain on Aspen, which also gives you good access to this mountain's more challenging terrain.
Intermediate Buttermilk would be a good option for a couple of solid days.

The runs are all groomed to perfection, and there's a beginner park as well as the X Games bad boy to tackle. Later on in the week, explore Snowmass's upper slopes to check out some of the area's freeriding options.
Advanced The area generically known as 'Aspen' has the best freeriding terrain in Highlands and Snowmass. The Highland Bowl in particular is up there with Vail's Back Bowls in terms of its legendary and/or over-hyped status. If you've got to pick a destination for a powder day, it could be Snowmass which has some pretty serious cliffs and chutes to check out. Of course, if you're of a freestyle persuasion, you'll be in Buttermilk's X Games park all day long, and good luck to you!
Kids Aspen's children's facilities are predictably great. As well as a huge programme of lessons at the Ski and Snowboard School, Snowmass has a family zone and there are great babysitting facilities. See the site for more.
Flat light days Hit up Snowmass, preferably with a local. There are some incredible tree runs here, although you won't find the best ones by accident.

R: BEN KILNER P: TIM WARWOOD

☺ LOCALS DO
- Work two or three jobs to live in the area.
- Party as hard as they ride.
- Pay homage to the shrines located amongst the four mountains.

☹ LOCALS DON'T
- Hang around in the off-season.
- Own homes in the valley because of inflated prices.
- Ever come just for one season.

✓ PROS
- Variety of terrain.
- Not crowded compared to other large resorts.
- World-class parks, pipes and nightlife.

✗ CONS
- Average of 762 cm in a year.
- Dangerous out of bounds avalanche prone areas due to Colorado conditions.
- Expensive resort prices.

⊙ NOT TO MISS
Snowmass has some pretty serious freeriding, if you know where to look. Take the top drag and try and make some friends with the locals while you're all hiking up and admiring the view.

ⓘ REMEMBER TO AVOID
Aspen, Buttermilk and Snowmass – if you want to avoid your fellow tourists. For the locals, it's Highlands all the way…

❄ SNOW DEPTH

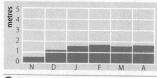

♻ RELIVE A FAMOUS MOMENT
Hunter S Thompson's 'Owl Farm' residence is still in Aspen. Sadly, he passed away recently and was blasted into the stars on the back of a rocket, but you can still go and pay tribute to the great man.

2410 m	TOWN ALTITUDE
5 km	KM TO AIRPORT
DEN	AIRPORT
★★☆	VEGETARIAN RATING
★★★	INTERNET CAFES
★☆☆	RIDE IN/RIDE OUT
3813 m	HIGHEST LIFT
1343 m	VERTICAL DROP
5206	RIDEABLE AREA (IN ACRES)
478 km	KM OF PISTES
0	NURSERY AREAS
79/42/37	RUNS: BEG/INTER/ADV
0/0	FUNICULAR/CABLE CARS
2/44	GONDOLAS/CHAIRS
0	DRAGS
no	NIGHT RIDING
2	PARKS
4	PIPE
no	SUMMER AREAS
★★★ ★★★	ENVIRONMENTAL RATING
$ $ $	COST INDICATOR
USA	
ASPEN	

Baker

This low-profile northwest gem is the locus of steep, deep and dark dreams of hard-core powder and freeriding. Everything you've heard about Baker is true. Yes it's crazy, and yes you just might need a snorkel.

◗ If you like this . . .
. . . try *Kicking Horse* ▸▸*p80.*

USA
BAKER

The Town

The resort of Mount Baker sits alone at the terminus of a cul-de-sac, and the closest thing to a 'town' is Glacier, some 30 minutes back down the road. If you blink while driving you might miss this moss-covered hamlet. Regardless of its size, Glacier contains sleeping, eating, drinking, and houses most of the locals, who might give you the hairy eyeball when you step into the tavern, but after a few beers are otherwise friendly creatures.

Sleeping See mtbaker.us/info/accommodations.html for an in-depth listing of Glacier-area rental accommodations. Most of these are condo or cabin rentals, suitable for multiple people, and vary in price from US$55 per person a night, upwards into the hundreds for upscale accommodations.
Eating If you're driving up from Bellingham, the **Maple Falls** grocery store and gas station makes a mean bagel sandwich. **Graham's** is Glacier's full-service restaurant/bar/grocery/breakfast store. **Milano's** (T360 599 2863) across the street offers fine Italian and vegetarian dishes.

Bars and clubs As mentioned above, **Graham's** is the only spot in Glacier to get a drink, unless you sneak into some hot tub with a six-pack.
Shopping Due to the lack of eateries, it's a fine idea to either stock up in Bellingham.
Health There are plenty of massage establishments in nearby Bellingham (comevisitbellingham.com/massage).

Internet Glacier is both an internet and mobile black hole, but Baker itself has free Wi-Fi.
Transfer options Bellair Baker Shuttle (airporter.com/baker-shuttle) runs a service from Bellingham to Glacier and on to Baker weekends and selected holidays. Otherwise it's almost all driving or hitchhiking in the Bellingham/Glacier/Baker area.
Local partners None.

⊙ OPENING TIMES

Late Nov to early Apr: 0900-1330 (Weekends only to late Apr)

⑤ RESORT PRICES

Week pass: No discount
Day pass: US$40
Season pass: US$660

⊙ DIRECTORY

Tourist office: T360 734 6080
Medical centre: T360 671 6350
Taxi: No tel number
Local radio: None
Website: mtbaker.us

R: JESSE HUFFMAN P: MIKE YOSHIDA

The Mountain ⛰❄😊

Baker's popularity and continued success lies in its stock of steep and challenging in-bounds terrain, plentiful and easy access to backcountry terrain and abundant snowfall (a world record breaking 28,956 cm in the '98-99 season). For families there are several mellow-grade beginner/intermediate runs, but a lack of grooming leaves these bumpy and rugged more often that not. Not that the place is intimidating, but the main clientele are intermediate to advanced snowboarders who don't care for resort amenities or niceties and would rather just ride Baker's legendary bulk. The mountain sits smack in the centre of the Mount Baker-Snoqualmie National Forest, and the peaks surrounding the resort provide an almost unlimited amount of terrain beyond the resort's boundaries.

Beginners After signing up for a lesson, head to the rope tow on the mellow slope right in front of the **White Salmon Day Lodge**, or over to Chair 2. **Baker Instruction** offers a 'Best for Beginners' package that includes rentals and lessons for those completely new to the mountain experience.

Intermediate Lap Chair 7 a few times, then try a few runs underneath Chair 8. Session the natural halfpipe to the west of Chair 5, which has endless wall-hits and banks to slash. The woods off Chair 7 offer a mellow pitch to build up confidence at tree riding. End up the day with a quick hike to the east of Chair 1, where you'll be rewarded with steeper tree shots and wide-open bowls.

Advanced Behold! Baker is your playground. Go straight to Chair 5,

> Mount Baker's terrain ranges from mellow pow runs to challenging Tarzan courses billy-goated by only the best. The resort has evolved into a breeding ground for some of the most talented and humble riders in the world.
>
> *John Laing, Baker local*

where you can spot your line from the chair and plot your descent down the funnest in-bounds terrain in the northwest: cliffs, chutes, jumps and steep, steep pitch. After a few laps (on a good day you could be here till closing), head over to Chair 1, where after a leisurely shred down the front bowl, the hill funnels into a glorious array of even more chutes and cliffs. In bounds, it's pretty much fair game: if you can spot it, you can drop it. But beware following people's tracks – there are plenty of features that cliff out.

Kids Check into **Baker Instruction** for their comprehensive kids learning programme.

Flat light days Baker's notoriety for snowfall is also synonymous with flat light. Almost all the terrain in bounds has plenty of trees around for contrast, especially under Chair 5. And who cares what it looks like if your tracks fill in after one run?

R: JESSE HUFFMAN P: MIKE YOSHIDA

☺ LOCALS DO
- Get to the hill early.
- Drive down to Bellingham to do a big grocery shop and hit the bars.
- Ride the backcountry with full kit and knowledge.

☹ LOCALS DON'T
- Rock the latest Polo gear in the lodge après.
- Duck ropes without proper gear and a partner.
- Have to sleep in Glacier – don't be afraid to sleep in your car overnight!

✔ PROS
- Possibly the most concentrated amount of freeriding terrain in America.
- Cheap tickets and no crowds.
- The most snow in the world.

✖ CONS
- No village means limited nightlife and eating options.
- Lack of grooming and mellow terrain means it's shocking without fresh powder.
- Poor park and pipe programme.

☺ NOT TO MISS
In Glacier, you have to check out the Mt Baker Snowboard Shop, with signed pictures of shred legends past, present and future plastered up on the walls.

ⓘ REMEMBER TO AVOID
On powder days, get up early. Baker is not a crowded place, but tends to get tracked fast, and the resulting bumps can render your legs jelly-like by noon.

❄ SNOW DEPTH
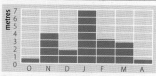

☺ RELIVE A FAMOUS MOMENT
The Baker Banked Slalom (mtbaker.us) is the event of choice for hardcore snowboarders.

1066 m	TOWN ALTITUDE
90 km	KM TO AIRPORT
BLI	AIRPORT
★★★	VEGETARIAN RATING
★★☆	INTERNET CAFES
★☆☆	RIDE IN/RIDE OUT
1551 m	HIGHEST LIFT
485 m	VERTICAL DROP
1000	RIDEABLE AREA (IN ACRES)
runs not measured	KM OF PISTES
0	NURSERY AREAS
6/16/9	RUNS: BEG/INTER/ADV
0/0	FUNICULAR/CABLE CARS
0/7	GONDOLAS/CHAIRS
1	DRAGS
no	NIGHT RIDING
1	PARKS
1	PIPE
no	SUMMER AREAS
★★★	ENVIRONMENTAL RATING
★☆☆	
💲💲💲	COST INDICATOR

USA
BAKER

Big Bear

Twin peaks above Los Angeles with over 200 jumps and jibs between them, for riding day and night. Molehills in size but mighty in stature – so long as you like parks.

☼ If you like this . . .
. . . *try, Snow Park* ▸▸*p230, Laax* ▸▸*p320, or Mammoth* ▸▸*p366.*

The Town ⬛ ⚡ ⬛

Clusters of wooden cabins, tumbledown motels, diners and weekend homes sprawl along the south shore of Big Bear Lake, a year-round country retreat for harassed southern Californians for over a century. Yet despite the weekend crowds, the place feels sleepy and suburban once the last of the SUVs has departed down valley – more an annex of LA than a stand-alone resort.

Sleeping It's all about **The Block** (theblockatbigbear.com), Marc Frank Montoya's latest hotel venture (the first is in South Lake Tahoe). If sponsor-decorated bedrooms are too hectic, try elegant B&B at the historic **Gold Mountain Manor** (T909 585 6997). Eating Bypass the strip mall fast food and hit up **El Jacalito** (T909 878 2131) for super cheap, authentic burritos and tacos. Fill up on a breakfast of champions at the **Grizzly Manor Café** (T909 866 6226) and splurge at **Sushi Ichiban** (T909 866 6413). Good veggie options are available everywhere.

⊙ **OPENING TIMES**
Mid-Nov to mid-May: Mon-Fri 0800-1600; Sat and Sun 0800-1800

Ⓢ **RESORT PRICES**
Week pass: No discount
Day pass: US$49-62
Season pass: US$349-549 (limited number available)

Ⓓ **DIRECTORY**
Tourist office: T909 866 5766
Medical centre: T909 866 6501
Pisteurs: T909 866 5766
Taxi: T909 866 8294
Local radio: 93.3 KBHR
Website: bigbearmountainresorts .com

Bars and clubs Sunny afternoon partying goes down at the base of both resorts both weekends, but those left in town after sundown may find it a little dead. The Block-owned **Log Cabin** (T909 866 3667) is SoCal scene-central following any event, while **Chad's Place** (T909 866 2161) has pool and weekly live bands.

Shopping At the eastern end of Big Bear Boulevard is a large **Vons** supermarket handily located close to the crew at the **Real Deal Ride Shop** (T909 878 5935).

Health There's a full range of spa treatments at the mountain hippy-style **Believe In Magic** (T909 653 5094).

Internet Free access at the library (T909 866 5571) on Garstin Drive.

Transfer options You *can* buck the LA trend by taking a Metrolink train out to San Bernardino (metrolinktrains.com) and picking up the local **MARTA** bus (T909 584 1111); it'll take a few hours and cost around US$15 each way. More direct are the weekend bus trips run by many LA ski and snowboard stores.

Local partners Bear Mountain and Snow Summit came under joint ownership in 2002. Though 2 miles

You get to ride at two separate mountains for the price of one and the sun is always shining. The park is always groomed and there are jibs for everybody. Come during the week as it's always slower. On the weekend the LA crowds come up which can be fun for people watching. You never know who you're going to meet!

Jon Nutting, Big Bear local

apart, both are covered by the same ticket and linked by a frequent free shuttle service.

P: BIG BEAR MOUNTAIN RESORT

P: BIG BEAR MOUNTAIN RESORT

The Mountain

Two hours' drive from LA and San Diego, Southern Californian families flock to Big Bear every weekend, when it's quite normal for tickets to sell out (book in advance on the website if you feel like braving the crowds). And so influential is the surf/skate/snow triptych over young SoCal minds that the powers that be decided to pass on the pistes and turn all of Bear Mountain into a terrain park – leaving Snow Summit as a refuge for beginners, recreational skiers, and park novices. It hasn't hurt their ticket sales one little bit.

Beginners Though both mountains have large beginner areas and a wide range of lessons to choose from, slightly more sedate Summit is a less intimidating place to find your feet. When happily linking turns on cruisers like Mainstream and Eastway, scoot over to the Family Park, where mellow bumps and rollers serve as an introduction to airtime.

Intermediate Start the day at Summit, warming up on the cruisers before tacking the beginner-to-intermediate jib and table lines in Westridge, the mile-long, top-to-bottom park that first brought Big Bear fame. In the afternoon, take the bus over to Bear Mountain and start working your way up their menu of obstacles.

Advanced Hit Bear mid-morning: no need for an early start when the entire mountain is a park. After shutting down the superpipe, exhibitionists can work 'The Scene' in the afternoon, a collection of jibs right by the base area. Come nightfall and it's time to head over to Summit, where the Westridge hits are groomed every Friday, Saturday and holiday afternoon in time for a session under the lights.

Kids Bear Moutain is so popular with young riders that Burton has deemed this micro-resort worthy of a Kid's Method Centre, where kids as young as five are guaranteed the right equipment to get their future extreme careers off to a raging start.

Flat light days Though it can get icy occasionally, all the slopes at Big Bear are flanked by trees, and flat light is seldom an issue. Check out Bear Mountain's base area jibs first if in doubt.

EVEN THE TREES ARE PART OF THE FUN PARK IN BIG BEAR. P: BIG BEAR MOUNTAIN RESORT

☺ LOCALS DO
- Ride midweek for cheaper tickets and quiet slopes.
- Take Highway-38 instead of the I-10 route at the weekends, to beat the traffic.
- Ride free on their birthday: just show the ticket office ID.

☹ LOCALS DON'T
- Pay attention to trail classification. The so-called black runs here just aren't.
- Often wear jackets. T-shirts and hoodies are the norm.
- Drive anywhere in weekend rush hour. The out-of-town traffic is a nightmare.

✔ PROS
- Perfect slopes for beginners.
- Jibs and hits in all sizes: progress your park riding.
- Inexpensive and quiet midweek.

✘ CONS
- Low on resort ambience.
- Seriously crowded at the weekend.
- Lack of natural snow and natural terrain.

☺ NOT TO MISS
Bear's recognizable signature hits and jibs: keep an eye out for the inanimate stars of countless ads and photo shoots.

ⓘ REMEMBER TO AVOID
Summit Run, the top-to-bottom highway at Snow Summit. It's a minefield of out-of-control weekend warriors and shakily snaking beginners.

❄ SNOW DEPTH

Figures not available

✪ RELIVE A FAMOUS MOMENT
Justin Timberlake, Shaun White and Tom Cruise all have season passes at Big Bear.

2177 m	TOWN ALTITUDE
183 km	KM TO AIRPORT
LAX	AIRPORT
★★☆	VEGETARIAN RATING
★★☆	INTERNET CAFES
★☆☆	RIDE IN/RIDE OUT
2684 m	HIGHEST LIFT
507 m	VERTICAL DROP
438	RIDEABLE AREA (IN ACRES)
27 km	KM OF PISTES
1	NURSERY AREAS
19/39/19	RUNS: BEG/INTER/ADV
0/0	FUNICULAR/CABLE CARS
0/20	GONDOLAS/CHAIRS
6	DRAGS
yes	NIGHT RIDING
1	PARKS
2	PIPE
no	SUMMER AREAS
figures not available	ENVIRONMENTAL RATING
$ $ $	COST INDICATOR

USA
BIG BEAR

Big Sky

The Town

It's time to get away from it all. It's time for Montana: land of big skies, cowboys, pickup trucks, domestic beers … and lots and lots of wide-open land. And this is exactly what you're going to find on the slopes of Big Sky. The nearest town is Bozeman, 39 miles (62 km) to the north, a college town full of everything from sushi and wine bars to excellent dive bars. In the winter, locals divide their snowboarding time between the community-owned Bridger Bowl Ski Area and the destination resort of Big Sky. The life force of the town is snow. A small blue light on the tallest building on Main Street flashes to alert residents when there's fresh snow – on those days, appointments get rescheduled and classes are cancelled.

Sleeping Big Sky is a scenic hour's drive south along the Gallatin River from the airport and the hip college town of Bozeman (population 75,000). Lodging options start in the Gallatin Canyon at **Bucks T4 Lodge** (buckst4.com). It's a good option for delicious food and a happening bar, but is a shuttle ride from the slopes. There're plenty of lodging and condo options at Big Sky. **The Mountain Inn** is the cheapest option and within walking distance of the slopes and bars (themountaininn.com). Big Sky operates the **Huntley Lodge**, also slopeside, and the swanky **Summit At Big Sky** (bigskyresort.com).

Eating On the slopes, **The Timbers** (T406 995 7777) in Moonlight Basin Lodge offers good barbeque, deli food and sit-down dining. Over at Big Sky, grab a slice of pizza at **Mountain Top Pizza** (T406 995 4646). Down in the meadow, stop by **Milkie's Pizza & Pub** (T406 995 2900). If it's within budget, make reservations and indulge at the **Rainbow Ranch** (T406 995 4132) an award-winning restaurant, or grab a burger at the rowdy local's favourite **The Corral** (T406 995 4249) both located in Gallatin Canyon.

Bars and clubs Locals can be found après on the sundeck or at **The Alpine Lounge** in the Mountain Mall. Check out **The Black Bear** for live music and more locals putting 'em back. DJs light up the dancefloor at **The Bambu Bar** in the slopeside Arrowhead Mall. **Chet's Bar & Grill** in the Huntley Lodge is where vacationers hang. The **Half Moon Saloon**, down in the canyon, has occasional live music.

> If you don't like wide open fast turns and gut churning drop-ins, then Big Sky isn't for you.
>
> *Korey Kaczmarek, pro snowboarder*

Shopping Bozeman is home to World Boards Snowboard shop (T406 587 1707). Stop in before you head up to Big Sky.

Health The Huntley Lodge has a pool, fitness centre, and offers yoga and stretching classes.

Internet Wireless access is available in the lobby of the Huntley Lodge.

Transfer options Snow Express circulates the meadow, mountain, and canyon areas every 30 minutes for free (T406 995 6BUS).

Local partners Moonlight Basin (moonlightbasin.com) is accessible with a Big Sky ticket. High rollers should look into home ownership at the private Yellowstone Club Ski Area (yellowstoneclub.com).

Frontier snowboarding in Big Sky country.

⟫ If you like this …
… try *Fernie* ⟫*p74*, *Chamonix* ⟫*p128*, or *Jackson Hole* ⟫*p362*.

⊘ OPENING TIMES
Late Nov to mid-Apr: 0900-1600

⊙ RESORT PRICES
Week pass (7 days): US$443
Day pass: US$69
Season pass: US$1060

ⓘ DIRECTORY
Tourist office: T1-800-VISITMT
Medical centre: T406 995 2797, docsky.us
Pisteurs: T406 995 5880
Taxi: T1-800 423 4742
Local radio: KGLT 91.9
Website: bigskyresort.com

P: DANMILNER.COM

The Mountain

Big Sky has always been a haven for uncrowded riding, but in 2005 the resort merged with neighbouring Moonlight Basin and additionally expanded its terrain access off the backside of the summit, wrapping its snowy fist almost completely around the A-shaped 3398-m mountain. The merge established Big Sky as the resort with the second biggest vertical descent in the US and a massive 5300 rideable acres. When you consider that the entire state of Montana has a population of 6.2 people for every square mile, you might consider bringing a friend – it can get lonely. The terrain truly has something for everyone from precariously steep tram-accessed summit to the mellow groomers and tree runs of adjoining Andesite Mountain.

Beginners Lower Mr K is accessed by its own beginner chairlift, Explorer. It's a consistent pitch all the way down to hot chocolate in the base lodge. Once you master Mr K, the whole mountain is open to you … well, actually the whole of Andesite Mountain. The mountain saddles up to the southern flank of the massive Lone Peak and will serve you well as the training grounds from beginner to intermediate. You can even safely dip in and out of fresh powder on the sides of the groomers.

Intermediate Plan ahead. If it's a powder day, do you: a) head over to Challenger and get some steep arcing turns down the face and through the Moonlight trees; b) do laps on the Lone Peak Triple into the bowl and jump on the tram when it opens (one run down Lenin or Marx will make your day); or c) head over to Andesite and sneak around in the trees off Thunder High Speed Quad – it'll probably be just you and your friends. Decisions, decisions, decisions.

Advanced This is serious. Big Sky has expert terrain that allows you to push yourself to the very limit. The hazards include steep pitches, unmarked cliffs, and most importantly, lots of sharp rocks hiding just below the surface. See that narrow dog-leg shoot below the tram? That's Big Couloir. Sign out with the ski patrol to shred it, or hike from the top of Challenger to any one of the A-Z chutes dropping into the bowl. From the backside of Lone Peak, follow the Yeti Traverse around to the frontside to get to the Gullies – be ready for the steepest turns you'll probably ever make. Hold that edge!

Kids Big Sky offers kids 10 and under free skiing and free lodging in the Huntley Lodge. It also has a snowsports school teaching the fundamentals of pizza and French fries. The resort hosts a free Kids Club everyday from 1530-1800 for kids four years and up.

Flat light days Head over to the trees off Andesite and Challenger or just do laps on the Swift Current Quad down Rice Bowl and Lobo.

R: UNKNOWN P: DANMILNER.COM

☺ LOCALS DO
- Wear helmets.
- Head straight to the tram on powder days.
- Drink two-dollar tall boys from C&P Grocery on the sundeck at the end of the day.

☹ LOCALS DON'T
- Take the easy way down – don't follow the guys in the full-face helmets.
- Ever leave.

✔ PROS
- It's steep.
- Uncrowded.
- 3600 acres of terrain.

✖ CONS
- Unexciting nightlife.
- No village.
- Hard to get here.

❂ NOT TO MISS
Head over to Moonlight Basin with your dual-mountain ticket. The terrain is a mix of empty winding groomers and insane black diamond chutes. It's a whole different vibe over there.

ⓘ REMEMBER TO AVOID
The jagged Andesite rocks covering the mountain. Keep this in mind before you throttle into an 'untouched' powder field.

❄ SNOW DEPTH

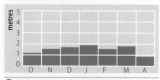

☼ RELIVE A FAMOUS MOMENT
Robert Redford's *A River Runs Through It* was filmed nearby, while Steven Seagal's *The Patriot* used Montana's backdrop for an environmentally sub-plotted turkey.

2286 m	TOWN ALTITUDE
63 km	KM TO AIRPORT
BZN	AIRPORT
★★☆	VEGETARIAN RATING
★★☆	INTERNET CAFES
★★☆	RIDE IN/RIDE OUT
3399 m	HIGHEST LIFT
1326 m	VERTICAL DROP
3600	RIDEABLE AREA (IN ACRES)
runs not measured	KM OF PISTES
1	NURSERY AREAS
27/33/95	RUNS: BEG/INTER/ADV
0/1	FUNICULAR/CABLE CARS
1/12	GONDOLAS/CHAIRS
3	DRAGS
no	NIGHT RIDING
1	PARKS
1	PIPE
no	SUMMER AREAS
★★★☆	ENVIRONMENTAL RATING
$$$	COST INDICATOR
USA	
BIG SKY	

The Town

Breckenridge manages to have its cake and eat it. In US terms, Breckenridge the town and nearby Frisco, about 9 miles (14 km) down the road, count as historical artefacts of Stonehenge-style significance, thanks to their mining heritage. Then there is the mountain, which is at the forefront of the US snowboarding scene and has one of the best parks (one of five!) in the world. This, and the fact that it is generally cheaper than, say, nearby Vail, is a winning combination that has made it one of America's most popular resorts. It attracts a regular clientele of local families, loyal returnees and snowboard fanatics attracted by Breck's strong showing in the international media. Thanks to this perceived grassroots involvement, there's a general air of snow-boarding get-up-and-go about the place. If you're into the

The beating heart of the US freestyle snowboarding scene? Breck has roots and still leads from the front today.

If you like this . . .
. . . try Zillertal ▶▶p56, Morzine ▶▶p148, or Saas Fee ▶▶p326.

66 99

If you're into freestyle snowboarding, it just doesn't get any better.

Nate Kern, Breckenridge local and pro snowboarder

snowboarding mags and videos, you're going to love this place.

Sleeping Try the **Fireside Inn** (firesideinn.com) for cheap accommodation in town, or there's a **Best Western** in Frisco (lakedillonlodge.com). More capacious budgets should consider the **Beaver Run Resort**, a plush slopeside hotel (beaverun.com).
Eating Downstairs at **Eric's** has the best burgers and pizzas in Breckenridge at cheap prices, while **Bubba Gump's Shrimp company** is good for American-style seafood and a thriving happy hour. Take on the classic American breakfast at **Daylight Donuts**. Check out the excellent

R. NATE KERN P. AARONDODDSPHOTO.COM

⊚ **OPENING TIMES**
Mid-Nov to late Apr: 0830-1600
$ **RESORT PRICES**
Week pass (6 days): US$525
Day pass: US$75
Season pass: No discount
ⓘ **DIRECTORY**
Tourist office: T970 453 2913
Medical centre: T970 453 1010
Pisteurs: T1-800 789 7669
Taxi: T970 468 2266
Local radio: Krystal 93.9FM
Website: breckenridge.com

Rasta Pasta (T970 453 7467) if you're after a veggie option.
Bars and clubs Breck's nightlife is pretty outstanding. **Sherpa and Yetis** always has live bands and is highly recommended, while **Salt Creek** is a locals' spot. **Cecilia's Bar** is usually where everyone ends up.
Shopping Wal-Mart in Frisco to really join the US consumer revolution, or **City Market** in Breckenridge. **Big Hit** and **Mountain Wave** are the local snowboard shops.
Health Mountain Sanctuary Holistic Spa (T970 547 1610) on Main Street has the lot.
Internet Try Gourmet Cabby, Alpine Internet and The Crown Café to log on.
Transfer options Colorado Mountain Express (ridecme .com) is the most efficient option from any airport.
Local partners Your pass also works in nearby Arapahoe Basin, Keystone, Beaver Creek and Vail.

The Mountain

As with most resorts in this area, Breckenridge should really be filed under 'classic Americana'. It's not that it has the steepest or best freeriding on the planet (it's not as steep as nearby Vail), more that there is something for every standard of rider: plenty of trees, five parks, runs groomed to within an inch of their lives and a supremely slick lift service combine to make riding here an extremely enjoyable experience, especially for intermediates and freestylers, who will spend much of the time exploring the five parks. There are four distinct parts to the mountain, based around Peaks 7 to 10. A new chair accessing the top of Peak 8, the Imperial Express Superchair, is the highest in North America and has opened up a lot of freeriding terrain. The announcement of a new gondola from town should also improve access up the hill.

Beginners Although the whole mountain is very beginner friendly, Peaks 8 and 9 are going to keep beginners very occupied. All terrain on the lower front of Peak 8 is wide, groomed, mellow and very easily accessed. Start the week with Chair 7 on Peak 8, and, as confidence grows, get acquainted with Chair 5 and the Colorado Super Chair, also on Peak 8. You can take these at any speeds you like. Later, head on over to Peak 9 and work out a circuit between Chair A and the Quicksilver Super Chair.

Intermediate Really, this is a mountain made for intermediates. Everything here is amazing fun, but think about the Mercury Super Chair, Beaver Run Super Chair and Rocky Mountain Super Chair on Peak 9, and the Independence Super Chair on Peak 7. A good day can be spent just linking all four peaks. And check out the parks! If Freeway is too much, there are four others to work your way up, with amazing kickers and rails.

Advanced On the piste, this place is straightline heaven although it is speed controlled in busy areas so keep a look out for that. If there is snow, try Breck's relatively meagre freeriding by taking the Imperial Express Superchair to the top of Peak 8. It's likely though that you'll spend morning, noon and if possible night in the Freeway park on Peak 8. Take Chair 5, follow everyone else and prepare to learn and be amazed at how much better than you everyone is. Amazing.

Kids There is a dizzying amount of facilities for children in Breckenridge, including a ski and ride school, and a 5-6-year-old Burton Learn to Ride programme. Check the website.

Flat light days Like all the Colorado resorts, Breckenridge is great in flat light. The Chair 6 freeway rails runs, Duke Trees and Super Connect trees are popular among the locals.

R: NATE KERN P: AARONDOODSPHOTO.COM

☺ LOCALS DO

● Hit up Chair 6, Imperial Express and Contest Bowl on powder days.
● Head to Keystone for night riding.
● Go to Salt Creek on Tuesdays and Thursdays for cheap wings and skins and happy hour.

☹ LOCALS DON'T

✗ Stay here to ride powder – it's too flat.
✗ Eat out on Fridays and Saturdays – too busy.
✗ Dress like a gaper – the US term for punter!

✓ PROS

● Excellent free bus system running late.
● Awesome nightlife with top artists playing every week.
● The best terrain parks from beginning to expert.

✗ CONS

✗ Flat terrain for advanced freeriders.
✗ Spring break is absolutely packed.
✗ Liquor stores close on Sundays.

ⓘ REMEMBER TO AVOID

Many of the chairs on Peak 8 have long lift queues, particularly Colorado Super Chair. Beaver Run Super Chair on Peak 9 also gets clogged.

◉ NOT TO MISS

Ever wonder how, say, Chad Otterstrom got so good? Breck's incredible park should provide a few answers.

❄ SNOW DEPTH

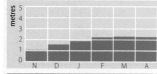

◉ RELIVE A FAMOUS MOMENT

Classic '90s comedy *Dumb and Dumber* was filmed in Breckenridge, not Aspen as was claimed in the film. Apparently it was cheaper in Breck.

2926 m	TOWN ALTITUDE
160 km	KM TO AIRPORT
DEN	AIRPORT
★★★	VEGETARIAN RATING
★★★	INTERNET CAFES
★★☆	RIDE IN/RIDE OUT
3963 m	HIGHEST LIFT
1037 m	VERTICAL DROP
5456	RIDEABLE AREA (IN ACRES)
runs not measured	KM OF PISTES
22	NURSERY AREAS
49/29/47	RUNS: BEG/INTER/ADV
0/0	FUNICULAR/CABLE CARS
0/16	GONDOLAS/CHAIRS
12	DRAGS
no	NIGHT RIDING
5	PARKS
2	PIPE
no	SUMMER AREAS
★★★ ★★★	ENVIRONMENTAL RATING
$ $ $	COST INDICATOR

USA
BRECKENRIDGE

The Town

As the first resort to open in Utah and one of the first in the area to actively encourage snowboarding, Brighton practically qualifies as 'grassroots' in the North American scheme of things. Today, it enjoys a reputation as a classic snowboarder's hill, thanks to a modern lift-system, some varied terrain, 1200-1300 cm of snow a year and an ongoing willingness to embrace snowboarding's freestyle and freeriding possibilities. This, as well as its proximity to Salt Lake City, means that today the place attracts a wildly diverse crowd, from top pros who have chosen to chase a career in the area to local families. With Brighton's 'town' really just a base lodge and a few restaurants and cafés, most will choose to stay in nearby Salt Lake City, about 30 minutes' drive away down beautiful Big Cottonwood Canyon.

Sleeping Those completely skint can check out a **Super 8** motel in SLC (super8saltlake.com) – as cheap and cheerful as it gets in the States, and on the way up to the resort. Further up the scale, try **Wasatch Front Ski Accommodations** (wfsa.com) for a range of condos, apartments and houses to rent. Look for something in Sandy or Murray, near the resort access road. Bigger budgets can stay at the slopeside **Brighton Lodge** (brightonresort.com). Hot tubs, kids under 10 stay free and it's at the base.

Eating In Brighton there are the usual base lodge options, but try the **Silver Fork Lodge** for locally tipped dining. In SLC there are almost too many options, but the **Rio Grande Café** serves great Mexican. **La Caille**, on Little Cottonwood Canyon, serves swanky French cuisine. A good vegetarian is **Brighton Base Lodge**.

Bars and clubs **Molly Green's**, a 'private club for members' (you'll need to become a member temporarily, in common with many bars in Utah), is Brighton's main spot. In SLC, **Brewvies** shows independent films and serves beer and pizza, while the **Squatters Pub** is a popular microbrewery.

Shopping Head down into SLC for groceries and also any liquor you're thinking of buying. It's a city of one million, so there are plenty of supermarkets and shops.

Health As befits a big city, plenty of options, from the **Kura Door Holistic Japanese Spa** (thekuradoor.com) to a 24-hour gym (24hourfitness.com).

Internet Almost every hotel in Salt Lake is wireless enabled, and many of them offer free access.

Transfer options In SLC you can take the Utah light railway (UTA TRAX) and from there a UTA ski bus to the resort. To really explore this area though, the car is king.

Local partners Solitude.

> The best part of riding there is the access to out of bounds. It's more of a European-type attitude, where if you feel like going out there and dying, no one is going to get in your way. Once you're out there, it is like riding through a museum of snowboarding's 'greatest hits'. Cliff, jumps, rollers, cornices, tree runs and chutes that have been splashed across the pages of magazines and screens of videos for years. It's not big by any means – in fact it's quite small – But it's the density of terrain all packed together that makes Brighton so awesome.
>
> *Andy Wright, Brighton local and snowboard photographer*

Managing to be both rootsy and progressive, Brighton sits at the heart of one of US snowboarding's real core scenes.

☼ *If you like this*...
... *try Banff/Sunshine*
▸▸*p70.*

R: BEN KILNER P: JAMES MCPHAIL

R: LAURA BERRY P: JAMES MCPHAIL

The Mountain

It might not have the steeps of Alaska or the Banked Slalom of Baker to its credit, but in its own way Brighton is an important US snowboarding heartland, right at the centre of the Utah scene. Its early acceptance of the sideways creed means it enjoys a certain pedigree, since underlined by the sheer amount of serious terrain there is to be explored here. In other ways, too, its seemingly small size belies its versatility. Mellow glade runs take care of things for beginners, while intermediate and advanced riders have a whopping three parks and acres of backcountry terrain to explore.

Beginners Complete beginners should try the Burton Learn-to-Ride programme in resort, as it's a great introduction. Those linking turns have options, but taking the Explorer and Majestic lifts and spending the day riding the wide, flat runs accessed from these lifts would be a good start to the week. By the end, think about Crest Express and tackling the beginners' park.

Intermediate Start the day with some warm up laps off the Crest Express run before heading over to the Millicent chair. From here you can access the terrain that has made the resort famous, and take it is easy or as serious as you see fit. Later in the afternoon, head over towards the other side of the resort, and either ride the super fun middle line through the park or take the Great Western and charge the Aspen Glow and Golden Needle runs.

Advanced Freestylers are going to spend the whole day in the park, which has a ridiculous number of rails, kickers, pipes and boxes for all

standards. The locals rip too. Freeriders have almost too much to check out, but start by taking the Millicent chair and traversing skier's right towards the obvious cliff band, as seen in many, many films and shoots. Afterwards…well, where to start? The top of Mount Millicent, with its cliffs and steeps? Over to the Great Western, to traverse right and ride pow down to the roads? Or out of bounds, to hike as long as your legs will last? Pack a transceiver.

Kids Kids under 10 ride free. Brighton also runs Just For Kids daily programmes as well as other learning options.

Flat light days With a lot of terrain below the tree line, it's still on during cloudy weather. Pioneer Peak trees are a good pow day stash.

⏱ OPENING TIMES
Late Oct to late Apr: 0900-1600

💲 RESORT PRICES
Week pass: No discount
Day pass: US$44
Season pass: US$925

📖 DIRECTORY
Tourist office: T1-800 873 5512
Medical centre: T435 655 3205
Pisteurs: T1-800 873 5512
Taxi: T1-800 255 1841
Local Radio: None
Website: brightonresort.com

☺ LOCALS DO
- Hike – there is a lot of terrain out the back of this resort.
- Ride the park.
- Wear some daft riding outfits in the name of shred fashion.

☹ LOCALS DON'T
- Stop riding at night; 20 trails are lit Monday-Saturday.
- Stop having fun. There's a great snowboarding vibe on this hill.

✔ PROS
- Over 1200 cm of snow a year.
- Good for families.
- Strong snowboarding culture in the resort.

✖ CONS
- Long daily commute if you're on a budget and stay in SLC.
- Strict liquor laws mean weak beer.
- Hiring a car is pretty much essential.

◐ NOT TO MISS
A hike to the summit of Mount Millicent to see what Brighton really has to offer.

ⓘ REMEMBER TO AVOID
The Millicent chair is the slowest in resort, so try to avoid it during busy periods if you want to maximize runs.

❄ SNOW DEPTH

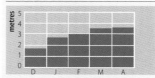

☺ RELIVE A FAMOUS MOMENT
Jeremy Jones' backflip to couloir from *The Resistance* was filmed in Brighton. Spot it from the Crest Express and Majestic chairs.

2669 m	TOWN ALTITUDE
56 km	KM TO AIRPORT
SLC	AIRPORT
★★★	VEGETARIAN RATING
★★★	INTERNET CAFES
★☆☆	RIDE IN/RIDE OUT
3200 m	HIGHEST LIFT
531 m	VERTICAL DROP
1050	RIDEABLE AREA (IN ACRES)
runs not measured	KM OF PISTES
1	NURSERY AREAS
13/26/27	RUNS: BEG/INTER/ADV
0/0	FUNICULAR/CABLE CARS
0/7	GONDOLAS/CHAIRS
0	DRAGS
yes	NIGHT RIDING
3	PARKS
1	PIPE
no	SUMMER AREAS
figures not available	ENVIRONMENTAL RATING
💲💲💲	COST INDICATOR

USA
BRIGHTON

Heavenly

Straddling glitzy Nevada and laid-back California, Heavenly boasts progressive parks and miles of rolling cruisers along with a suitably schizophrenic healthy-living meets casino-nights resort vibe.

◑ *If you like this* ...
... try *Zillertal* ➠*p56, Big White* ➠*p72, or La Rosière* ➠*p138.*

The Town

Not your average ski resort, South Lake (California) and Stateline (Nevada) sprawl seamlessly along the south shore of Lake Tahoe, one long messy street of motels, marinas, strip malls and casinos. The recent addition of a gondola and pedestrian village is just the first step in a resort revitalization plan, but it's the idiosyncrasies that make the town interesting: quickie wedding chapels and fruit machines, old-school diners and New Age health food.

Sleeping Bargain lift and lodging packages are offered at high-rise casinos such as **Harrah's** (harrahs.com), while the **Marriot Timber Lodge** (marriot.com) has swish apartments at the base of the gondola. **The Block** (theblockattahoe.com) motel is owned by pro Marc Frank Montoya.

Eating A vast choice. The best rice bowls, stuffed bagels and healthy burritos are served at **Sprouts** (T530 541 6969). The stylish **Naked Fish** (T530 541 3474) does great sushi, while little **Café Fiore** (T530 541 2908) is fine Italian dining, cozy Cali-style.

Bars and clubs Cabo Wabo Cantina, inside Harvey's casino, sets the south shore tone: brash and loud. Check out the band schedule for **Whiskey Dicks** or retreat to **Turn 3** for peanuts and punk karaoke with the locals.

Shopping Drive along Lake Tahoe Boulevard for a selection of large 24-hour supermarkets: **Safeways**, **Albertsons** and **Raley's**. South Lake has many snowboard shops, but well-stocked **Shoreline** (T888 877 7669) was the pioneer.

Health For sports massage and other spa services, visit **A Massage For All Seasons** (T530 541 1525).

Internet The Village Hotspot offers access right at the base of the gondola, but it's free at the local library. Many coffee shops and hotels have free or cheap wireless.

Transfer options Running 11 services a day to and from Reno, the **South Tahoe Express** (T775 325 8944) costs a US$38 roundtrip.

Local partners Heavenly is part of the Vail Resorts group – check vailresorts.com for more info. Not linked but worth a visit is Kirkwood, 45 minutes away (kirkwood.com).

My favourite aspect of riding Heavenly is hitting the little windlips... they are so fun to play around on! When I'm not riding in the powder, I always have a really good park ride, and it's getting better every year.

Andreas Wiig, pro snowboarder

R: UNKNOWN P: HEAVENLY MOUNTAIN RESORT

The Mountain

Heavenly is criss-crossed by an extensive network of confidence-building cruisers, rolling blue runs groomed twice daily, flanked by trees and with views of the sparkling lake below. Ideal for families and once-a-year skiers, it's the Tahoe resort most popular with out-of-state visitors. Yet when snow conditions are good, tricky chutes and wide glades beckon local freeriders. And Vail Resorts has been the pumping money in since they took control in 2002, resulting in a major upgrade to the mountain's parks.

Beginners Not the best place for first-timers, with limited terrain. The top of the gondola has the better of the nursery slopes, being slightly more secluded. Once you're linking turns, scoot down to the Dipper Express and spend the afternoon lapping all the different blues, with the option of heading all the way down to the Nevada base if you feel up to testing your legs.

Intermediate Warm up with a cruise down Ridge Run, the Tahoe lakeview postcard classic. If snow conditions are good, duck into Skiways Glades: mellow, widely spaced powder caches. Hit up the Nevada side for some early afternoon speed runs, then cross back to the top of the California tram for a jib-about in the Low Roller terrain park.

Advanced On a powder day, drop through the Dipper Woods and get to the Mott Canyon chutes early. You can then lap the Canyon lift until they get tracked out, or hike up to Killbrew for more of the same. After a caffeine break at the **East Peak Lodge**, cruise back over to California to the High Roller park and superpipe, home of the annual South Shore Soldiers camp.

Kids Snowboard lessons are offered for kids aged seven and above, with three different nursery areas to choose from. Kids not ready for a full day of shredding can go sledging or tubing at Adventure Peak, located at the top of the gondola.

Flat light days Choose from a ton of tree areas, from California's steep East Bowl woods to Nevada's wide Stagecoach glades. If snow conditions are bad, wait until nightfall and hit up the Night Roller park (Thursday-Saturday).

P: HEAVENLY MOUNTAIN RESORT

☺ LOCALS DO
- Ride Sierra often, even if they have Heavenly season passes.
- Download into California. Most of Heavenly is invisible from the base areas.
- Score cheap drinks at the casinos' midweek locals' nights (and no, they don't check).

☹ LOCALS DON'T
- Cross the ski area boundary: for backcountry, head towards Kirkwood.
- Get day passes at full value – better deals are available online, even for visitors.

✔ PROS
- One of North America's largest mountains.
- South Lake lodging and dining cheap by US standards.
- Intermediates' nirvana.

✖ CONS
- Can get busy.
- Mountain tough to navigate at first.
- Sprawling town rather than a compact resort.

◉ NOT TO MISS
Stuff yourself at the Forest Buffet, on the top floor of 18-storey Hurrah's. Best views of the lake while overeating American-style.

ℹ REMEMBER TO AVOID
The slopes directly above the California Lodge, if you're a beginner or intermediate. Just looking at the low-altitude, patchily-covered blacks is enough to put you off.

❄ SNOW DEPTH

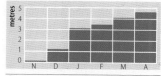

☺ RELIVE A FAMOUS MOMENT
Drive up the scenic west side of the lake. The Fleur du Lac Estates in Homewood was used for the grand opening scenes in *The Godfather II*.

1908 m	TOWN ALTITUDE
91 km	KM TO AIRPORT
RNO	AIRPORT
★★★	VEGETARIAN RATING
★★★	INTERNET CAFES
★★☆	RIDE IN/RIDE OUT
3060 m	HIGHEST LIFT
1067 m	VERTICAL DROP
4800	RIDEABLE AREA (IN ACRES)
runs not measured	KM OF PISTES
4	NURSERY AREAS
21/44/7	RUNS: BEG/INTER/ADV
0/1	FUNICULAR/CABLE CARS
1/18	GONDOLAS/CHAIRS
10	DRAGS
yes	NIGHT RIDING
4	PARKS
2	PIPE
no	SUMMER AREAS
★★★	ENVIRONMENTAL RATING
	COST INDICATOR
USA	
HEAVENLY	

The Town 📶🌐💬

Jackson is an international destination in its own right. It's located on the southern border of Yellowstone National Park, with the immediately recognizable jagged Tetons to the west. The Exum mountain school draws Chamonix-esque mountaineers, and the combination of Yellowstone park, the wildlife and Jackson Hole resort entices visitors all year round.

Sleeping You have three choices of where to stay. Teton Village is at the base of **Jackson Hole Resort**, which is 12 miles (19 km) from Jackson the town. At about the halfway mark is the town of Wilson at the base of Teton Pass. All three are good choices, but opt for the resort if you don't have a car. **Hostel X** (hostelx.com) is slopeside at Jackson Hole; bunk up for only US$68 for four people. **Jackson Hole Resort** (jhrl.com) also offers condo packages with lift tickets – a good option for groups. If you're looking for in-town accommodation close to the bustling town square, stay at the ski hill **Snow King Resort** (snowking.com).

Eating The Village Café (T307 732 2375) under the old tram dock at the resort is the best quick stop-in for breakfast (upstairs) and pizza slices, sandwiches and beers downstairs. **Mizu Sushi** (T307 734 5205) and **Calico Italian Restaurant** (T307 733 2460) will cost you, but are both worth it. **Snake River Brewing Company**, in town at 84 East Broadway (T307 739 2337), is a locals' hot spot, and the **Cadillac Grille** (T307 733 3279) on the town square has the best counter-service all-American cheeseburgers. **Harvest Bakery and Café** (T208 733 5418) is a good veggie choice.

Bars and clubs The **Mangy Moose** at the resort is the spot for après and for late-night live music. Head to the **Stagecoach** in Wilson and blend in with the locals. In town, hit up the **Log Cabin Saloon** on Cache Street, or head downtown and saddle up at the **Million Dollar Cowboy Bar** – just don't talk back to the cowboys . . . unless you want to get thrown through the swinging doors old-west style.

Shopping Stop by **Hole in the Wall Snowboard Shop** in Teton Village or the **Illuminati Board Shop** in town to update your snowboarding kit.

Health The **Recreation Center** (T307 739 6789) is located two blocks north of the town square on 155 East Gill; US$6 will get you access to the pools, jacuzzi, sauna and much more.

Internet The **Hole Internet Zone**, on 140 West Broadway on town square, has dozens of computer stations and remote workstations.

Transfer options START bus (startbus.com) offers service around Jackson (free) and to and from Teton Village (US$3).

Local partners Grand Targhee (grandtarghee.com) and Snow King (snowking.com) are two other nearby riding options. Guiding is offered locally by **Exum Mountain Guides** (exumguides.com).

Wild West terrain – saddle up!

❄ **If you like this** . . .
. . . try **Chamonix** ➤➤p128, or **Big Sky** ➤➤p354.

R: STU BRASS P: NICK HAMILTON

The Mountain

Jackson is celebrated for its steepness – top to bottom it's a 1261-m vertical drop with the greatest continuous rise in the United States to the 3,185-m summit. This alone separates it from most North American resorts, but it's also the open boundaries access that keep locals firmly rooted. The backcountry gates access over 3000 acres of additional terrain. The big story is that 2006 was the last year for Jackson Hole's legendary tram – it has been 'decommissioned'. A new double chairlift to the summit is the substitute until the tram is replaced.

Beginners Jackson actually consists of two mountains: Rendezvous and Apres Vous. Only 10% of the mountain is truly for beginners, all of which is found on the wide-open groomers of Apres Vous, accessed by the Teewinot quad chair and the Eagle's Rest double. The Jackson Hole Mountain School offers the Burton Learn-To-Ride programme – a deal of US$95 for full day lesson, lift ticket, and rental.

Intermediate Jackson isn't a mountain of groomed runs – we're heading into the powder fields now. Head up the Gondola and start off with some hot laps down what locals call 'The Track', hit some lips, jump the cat tracks, and make your way through Dicks Ditch, the site of the annual Banked Slalom. Repeat, but jump on the Thunder Quad and find your way into those chutes and trees below the lift.

Advanced If the avalanche conditions permit, get a partner, beacon and shovel, and head up the Sublette Chair to the new Eastridge chair up to the summit. Have a peek into Corbett's Couloir and ride past it to either of the two backcountry access gates. Rock Springs is filled with deep light powder, cliffs, and tons of cool terrain features. For straight epic pow turns, head down Rendezvous Bowl – hoot if you feel the need. Look for Travis Rice, Bryan Iguchi, and the TGR (Teton Gravity Research) crews gettin' 'er done out here.

Kids Daycare and snowboard lessons start at US$85 for a half-day, but kids can ride the beginner lifts for free and adults for US$15 per day.

Flat light days Jackson experiences frequent weather inversions, with clouds in the valley and brilliant blue skies on the top of the mountain. Check that web cam, it might be sunny up top. If not, stay in the trees below the Thunder quad and watch out for cliff signs.

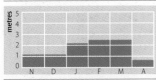

> I went to Jackson before I turned pro and I still think about the experience. The locals are not going to like this, but … it is one of the steepest mountains in America. You feel like you are somewhere special, and don't have to share the mountain with the rest of the world.
>
> *Lukas Huffman, professional snowboarder*

⚙ OPENING TIMES
Early Dec to early Apr: 0900-1600

$ RESORT PRICES
Week pass (6 days): US$360
Day pass: US$70
Season pass: US$1595

✆ DIRECTORY
Tourist office: T307 733 2292
Medical centre: T307 733 3636
Backcountry guides: Exum Mountaineering, T307 733 2297
Taxi: T307 690 0887
Local radio: 90.3 KUWJ
Website: jacksonhole.com

☺ LOCALS DO
◉ Wake up extremely early on powder days and only stop long enough to grab a slice at the Village Café.
◉ Do laps in the backcountry at Teton Pass throughout the winter.
◉ Try to beat Rob Kingwell in the Dick's Ditch Banked Slalom. It's usually the last weekend in February.

☹ LOCALS DON'T
◉ Wear 'I skied Corbett's Couloir' shirts.
◉ Talk about their snowboard prowess on the mountain.
◉ Take kindly to tourists following them out of the backcountry gates. Chances are that their idea of a 'line down' isn't the same as yours.

✓ PROS
◉ Open-boundaries.
◉ Great local vibe.
◉ Scenery and wildlife.

✗ CONS
◉ Hard to get here.
◉ Really, really cold.
◉ When the snow conditions are bad, they're bad.

☺ NOT TO MISS
Spend a day on a guided snowmobile tour, soak in the hot springs, check out the buffalo in Yellowstone Park, and see Old Faithful firing.

ⓘ REMEMBER TO AVOID
Moose!

❄ SNOW DEPTH

(chart: metres 0–5 over months N D J F M A)

↺ RELIVE A FAMOUS MOMENT
Johan Olofsson moved to Jackson for a season and laid down some heavy lines in-bounds. Check out TB5 and then take a look at those cliffs under the Thunder chair.

1924 m	TOWN ALTITUDE
14 km	KM TO AIRPORT
JAC	AIRPORT
★★★	VEGETARIAN RATING
★★☆	INTERNET CAFES
★★☆	RIDE IN/RIDE OUT
3185 m	HIGHEST LIFT
1261 m	VERTICAL DROP
2500	RIDEABLE AREA (IN ACRES)
runs not measured	KM OF PISTES
1	NURSERY AREAS
1/11/44	RUNS: BEG/INTER/ADV
0/0	FUNICULAR/CABLE CARS
1/10	GONDOLAS/CHAIRS
1	DRAGS
no	NIGHT RIDING
2	PARKS
1	PIPE
no	SUMMER AREAS
★★★	ENVIRONMENTAL RATING
$ $ $	COST INDICATOR
USA	JACKSON HOLE

The Town ◒❶◓

If Colorado – all groomed slopes, slick, man-made villages and undulating, freestyle-heavy terrain – defines middle ground North American snowboarding, then Keystone is basically Colorado in miniature. The base village is that classic American imagining of what 'ye olde' Alpine ski town should look like and the overall impression is of a resort that sees the mountain as something to be wrought into suitable shapes. Witness the fervour with which trails are groomed, and the recent decision to change the name of the mountain from Keystone to 'Dercum' after the people who decided to build a ski resort there

way back in 1970. The stamp of Vail Resorts, the current owners, is all over this place. So why is it in the guide? Put simply, riding here is fun. Intermediates, beginners and freestyle obsessives will love it, mainly for those groomed slopes, the imaginative parks and the great night riding facilities, which count as one of Keystone's must-dos.

Sleeping Keystone sprawls along the Snake River and has seven different areas, each varying in expense. Mountain House and River Run are probably the best bets, with outer suburbs such as West Keystone and Keystone Ranch being more expensive. Check out keystone.snow.com for the interactive accommodation finder.

Eating Inxpot (inxpot.com) is pretty irresistible, a coffee shop, bar and bookstore in the middle of the village that also serves great food. **Fritz Alpine Bistro** (fritzalpinebistro. com) is good for breakfast, while the **Bighorn Steakhouse** (T970 496 4386) takes care of the meat lovers.

Bars and clubs The Goat is Keystone's 'underground' bar, while the **Snake River Saloon** is vintage Americana. Club-wise, the **Green Light** is the must-head-to after-hours bar.

Shopping Keystone Grocery and **Rock n R Ranch** are in Keystone, but you'd be best heading to nearby Silverthorne, just down the road, to take care of groceries. For snowboard spares and rentals, try **Keystone Sports** (T970 496 4619).

Health Keystone Lodge Spa (keystone.snow.com/info/spa) takes care of massages, facials, body wraps – you name it.

Internet Starbucks and most hotels have wireless. If you're still plugging in, head to the **Keystone Lodge**.

Transfer options Try our old friends at **Colorado Mountain Express** (cme.com) and use the complimentary bus services to get around the resort. They're frequent and very handy.

Local partners As this is a member of the Vail Resorts group, your pass works in nearby Vail, Breckenridge, Beaver Creek and A-Basin.

Neat, well-kept and with a strong park – Keystone is basically Vail's little brother.

❂ *If you like this* ...
... *try Ischgl* ▸▸*p38,
La Clusaz* ▸▸*p132, or
Les Diablerets* ▸▸*p322.*

The Mountain

Serious freeriders would do well to turn around and head to Vail or, better yet, Utah, as Keystone is primarily a hill best enjoyed for cruising and freestyle. It's pretty flat and consists of a lot of groomed terrain, but there are some interesting features to check out. There are three hills – Dercum Mountain, North Peak and Outback. Dercum is the focal point, and has the mellower stuff, while the other two have what counts for Keystone's freeriding terrain. What saves the place for experts is the amazing park and the well-run catboarding facilities. It's a blend that makes Keystone pretty perfect for a mixed ability group.

Keystone is super good fun. The park is well maintained, and you can ride at night which is wicked. And then they've got the 'buck fiddy' rail, which you could spend all day trying to take on.

James Carr, pro snowboarder

Beginners The Yanks know how to run a mellow mountain for beginners, and Keystone is especially well suited to first-timers. Dercum Mountain's lower slopes are perfect, so take the Peru Express and get yourself onto Schoolmarm, which is quintessential Keystone – groomed, mellow and wide. If confidence is high, head up to **Outpost Lodge** for lunch and then ride down Prospector afterwards.

Intermediate You're basically going to spend your time riding around between all three mountains, getting a real feel for the area, and dabbling in the park. This mountain is so well groomed that gunning around all over the place is extremely good fun, but moguls do develop so keep your eyes peeled for them. After lunch at **Outpost Lodge**, head to the park and build up to that rail...

Advanced Advanced riders should head straight to the A51 park in the day, which is one of those parks that they build so well over here, with more lines, jumps, rails and interesting features than you could possible get bored of. Oh yeah, and a superpipe. If it snows, you've got two choices: head to The Windows area (not the longest pitches in the world); a better bet is probably to try catboarding with **Keystone Adventure Tours** for a proper day out. Finally, Keystone has extensive night riding facilities. Plan the week well, and you'll have a right old time.

Kids As this is America, there are a bewildering number of options for the youngsters, from 'Snow Play' for pre-schoolers to the Keystone Kroozers programme for five to 15-year-olds. Check the site.

Flat light days Pretty much all of Keystone is below the snowline, but check out The Grizz, Badger and Wolverine for advanced to intermediate riders. Beginners should stick to Spring Dipper and Schoolmarm.

OPENING TIMES
Early Nov to mid-Apr: 0900-1600; Wed-Sat mid-season

RESORT PRICES
Week pass: No discount
Day pass: US$45-75
Season pass: See website

DIRECTORY
Tourist office: T970 496 4FUN
Medical centre: T970 468 6677
Snow conditions: T1800 468 5004
Taxi: T970 496 4200
Local radio: 93.1 Krystal
Website: keystone-snow.com

LOCALS DO
- Ride the park – and rip with it.
- Hang out in Inxpot for after-riding coffee and brownies.
- Ride at night. Keystone is open till 2100 most nights mid-season.

LOCALS DON'T
- Expect Chamonix-style steeps. They're not here.
- Duck the ropes – the patrol are pretty on it here.
- Forget that the weather can come in quickly here. It's high.

PROS
- Amazing park.
- Close to other good resorts.
- Friendly, efficient – all the good parts of US riding.

CONS
- Flat for freeriders.
- Pretty homogenized town.
- Tame nightlife.

NOT TO MISS
The funpark, especially the mad obstacles they build – like the quarterpipe bowl with through tunnel of seasons past. And pray the 'buck fiddy' rail is still there.

REMEMBER TO AVOID
Thanks to the slow zones in place, lower slopes can be crowded. Make sure to avoid Mozart at the end of the day if that's a problem for you.

SNOW DEPTH

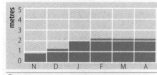

RELIVE A FAMOUS MOMENT
It's the 'buck fiddy' rail – reputedly the longest in the world. You could spend the day trying to 50-50 it to the end and never get bored. Amazing fun.

2829 m	TOWN ALTITUDE
144 km	KM TO AIRPORT
DEN	AIRPORT
★★☆	VEGETARIAN RATING
★★★	INTERNET CAFES
★★☆	RIDE IN/RIDE OUT
3782 m	HIGHEST LIFT
963 m	VERTICAL DROP
2870	RIDEABLE AREA (IN ACRES)
runs not measured	KM OF PISTES
4	NURSERY AREAS
14/39/63	RUNS: BEG/INTER/ADV
0/0	FUNICULAR/CABLE CARS
2/12	GONDOLAS/CHAIRS
5	DRAGS
yes	NIGHT RIDING
1	PARKS
1	PIPE
no	SUMMER AREAS
★★★☆	ENVIRONMENTAL RATING
$$$	COST INDICATOR
USA	KEYSTONE

Mammoth

Early and late season spot of choice for the world's current crop of freestyle pros, this sleeping volcano above the California desert is more than the sum of its parks. Consistently heavy snowfall, blue skies and miles of mellow groomers keep the crowds returning.

❖ *If you like this ...*
... try *Zillertal* ▸▸*p56*, *Laax* ▸▸*p320*, *Big Bear* ▸▸*p352*, or *Squaw Valley* ▸▸*p374*.

The Town

It wouldn't be overstating things to say that Mammoth is a place of pilgrimage for riders of a freestyle persuasion. It's a proper snowboarding town, attracting pro riders, pro spotters and those keen on pushing their riding in an almost laboratory-like atmosphere of progression. The resort is a classic American standalone, meaning that everybody stays in nearby Mammoth Lakes, a few miles down the road. Again, this is a typically spread-out American settlement with no real focal point, but plenty of facilities. There is some nightlife here, but not along European lines. Instead, locals tend to hold house parties and 'gatherings', so befriend some if you're looking for to get right amongst it. But you're here for the park jumps, right? If so, jump in your car or get the free bus to the resort and join the rest of the hordes.

Sleeping A step up from the town's generic motels – try **Motel 6** (motel6.com) for low rates – is the cutesy **Mammoth Country Inn B&B** (mammothcountryinn.com). However, it's really all about the condo in Mammoth. For apartments

6699

Mammoth is amazing. There are endless runs on powder days. I've been here six years and am still finding new stashes. The other best part is the fact that their park is one of the best in the world and open into June and sometimes July. Spring park riding in Mammoth are the funnest days I've ever had.

Eddie Wall, pro snowboarder, Mammoth local

in the slick new resort-owned Village, book at mammothmountain.com.
Eating Chow down on great breakfasts, sandwiches and salads at the veggie-friendly **Good Life Café** (T760 934 1734). **Bergers** (T760 934 6622) serves good value homestyle American cooking. A good vegetarian is **The Alpenrose** (T760 934 3077) is . Splash out on Italian at **Cervinos** (T760 934 4734) or sushi at the new **Sand Dollar Sushi** (T760 934 5282).
Bars and clubs There's no Euro-style party scene, but occasionally things go off. Lurk at **Lakanuki Tiki bar**, rock out at **Whisky Creek** or retreat to the **Clock Tower** for pool and a quiet pint.
Shopping Wave Rave (T760 934 2471) is the first place to look for gear, either to rent or buy, while giant **Vons** supermarket takes care of

the groceries.
Health Sports massage, deep tissue work and other spa services are available at the well-equipped **SnowCreek Athletic Club** (T760 934 8511).
Internet The Looney Bean (T760 934 1345) is the local quality coffee stalwart, while most other cafés and hotels offer wireless, usually at a price.
Transfer options It only runs three days a week, and at such awkward times that an overnight in a Reno casino may be necessary, but at least the regional **CREST** bus (T760 872 1901) from Reno-Tahoe International is cheap: US$23 each way.
Local partners June Mountain (junemountain.com).

☺ OPENING TIMES
Early Oct to early May: 0830-1600; from late May to early Jul: 0700-1400

ⓢ RESORT PRICES
Week pass (5 days): US$244
Day pass: US$70 weekends, US$61 Mon-Fri
Season pass: US$1500

ⓘ DIRECTORY
Tourist office: T760 934 2712
Medical centre: T760 934 3311
Pisteurs: T760 934 0745
Taxi: T760 924 8294
Local radio: KMMT 106.5 FM
Website: mammothmountain.com

P: JAMES MCPHAIL

The Mountain

Although not huge by European standards, those initially wowed by Mammoth's park reputation are often surprised to learn that there's a pretty big mountain here. There are some fun cruisers and the freeriding is good, but with predominantly rolling terrain, those looking to tear up the steeps all day would be better staying in Europe. Instead, this place is pretty much defined by the fun park, which is easily one of the best in the world. Most people come here to ride with the pros and push themselves as hard as they can. One other rarely mentioned fact about Mammoth is that it stays open so late closing in July. If you're looking to spend the season in Mammoth, look out for their 'Early Bird' pass deals. It can be possible to pick up a season pass for a couple of hundred dollars or less if you get in early.

Beginners Ask about the limited access beginner tickets – they're not always advertised. Though busy, Canyon Lodge is a good place to get going: more sheltered than the Main Lodge nursery slopes, not as frustratingly flat as Little Eagle. From the wide open bunny slope, move up to the trails through the trees off Schoolyard Express. Once confident linking turns, have a go at Canyon's micro-jibs and baby pipe.

Intermediate Take the bus all the way to Main Lodge and warm up on the wide Broadway and Stump Alley groomers. If there's fresh, head way over to Chair 9 for powder turns and small natural hits in widely spaced glades. If not, lap the small tables and mini-jibs on Forest Trail, then take some speed runs back in the Outpost.

Advanced On a powder morning, work the trees and small drops under Chair 27; keep an eye out for handmade kickers. As the snow settles, take some runs through SouthPark; don't miss Jibs Galore, slightly hidden over to rider's left. Move onto Main Park in the afternoon, where you can tackle the bigger hits or lap the SuperDuper pipe. Hiking is unnecessary – the park has its own fast-moving chairlift.

Kids Excellent lessons for mini-rippers, with micro parks and pipes close to both Canyon and Main lodge and a large, well-equipped kids' centre by the Main Lodge gondola – Woollywood (named for Woolly, Mammoth's namesake).

Flat light days Stay away from the upper slopes and Main Lodge. Either play in the mellow glades above Little Eagle, or lap South Park.

R: STU EDWARDS P: JAMES MCPHAIL
JP CHALLINOR P: DANMILNER.COM

😊 LOCALS DO
✓ Get off the bus early and hit up the softer South Park first thing.
✓ Ride neighbouring June at the weekends and over the holidays, when Mammoth is heaving.
✓ Head into the backcountry through the Hole in the Wall: ask around.

😠 LOCALS DON'T
✗ Leave sheltered South Park when it's windy.
✗ Ride Eagle Lodge in hot weather – the snow becomes boggy.
✗ Ride in super deep pow: the lower slopes are too flat and the upper ones usually closed.

✓ PROS
✓ Some of the world's best parks.
✓ Lots of snow and sun from November through to May or June.
✓ Good terrain mix and lift layout for mixed ability groups.

✗ CONS
✗ Expensive daily and weekly tickets.
✗ The sprawling town feels more like a suburb of LA.
✗ Long transfers with limited connections on public transport.

😊 NOT TO MISS
The new Volcom Brother's Skatepark, created in memory of local pro Jeff Anderson.

ⓘ REMEMBER TO AVOID
Canyon lifts on weekend/holiday mornings, and Mill Café lifts at weekend/holiday lunch.

❄ SNOW DEPTH

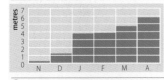

☺ RELIVE A FAMOUS MOMENT
The skydive/raft sequence in *Indiana Jones and the Temple of Doom* was filmed on location at Mammoth.

2377 m	TOWN ALTITUDE
265 km	KM TO AIRPORT
RNO	AIRPORT
★★★	VEGETARIAN RATING
★★★	INTERNET CAFES
★☆☆	RIDE IN/RIDE OUT
3369 m	HIGHEST LIFT
945 m	VERTICAL DROP
3500	RIDEABLE AREA (IN ACRES)
runs not measured	KM OF PISTES
3	NURSERY AREAS
19/63/53	RUNS: BEG/INTER/ADV
0/0	FUNICULAR/CABLE CARS
3/23	GONDOLAS/CHAIRS
2	DRAGS
no	NIGHT RIDING
3	PARKS
2	PIPE
no	SUMMER AREAS
★★★☆	ENVIRONMENTAL RATING
💲💲💲	COST INDICATOR
USA	
MAMMOTH	

Park City

Stylishly renovated Victorian mining-turned-tourist town lying at the heart of Utah riding country, with runs from the eponymously named mountain curling right down to Main Street, and seven other resorts a short bus ride away.

➲ *If you like this ...*
... try Whistler ➼p86, Breckenridge ➼p356, or Vail ➼p376.

The Town

Easy on the eye, ringed by resorts and always bustling with activity, Park City is a classic American ski town. Don't believe the Mormon hype: this is partyville, and the state's alcohol restrictions might as well not exist. A free bus service links the old town with more affordable suburbs; Kimball Junction, in particular, is the shopping hub for locals.

Sleeping Try the barrack-like dorms at the **Chateau Apres** (chateauapres .com). Budget private rooms are also available. Up a notch are B&Bs like the comfy **Old Town Guesthouse** (oldtownguesthouse.com), but the best value-for-money option in pricey Park City is renting a condo; booking agencies and individual properties are listed on the Park City website (parkcityinfo.com).

Eating There are over 100 restaurants, from taco stands to a Viking yurt, and plenty of it affordable. Load up on a full American breakfast at the **Eating Establishment** (T435 649 8284), grab an overstuffed sandwich to go at **Leger's** (T435 649 5678) and sit down for dinner at the **Good Karma** curry house (T801 787 5907). Spend a bit more at **Bangkok Thai** (T435 649 8424), splash out at **Flying Sumo** (T435 649 5522) or do the Sundance thing at Monsieur Redford's very own **Zoom** (T435 649 9108).

Bars and clubs Hit **Rum Bunnies** (T435 615 8852) for drinks specials and **Mulligan's** (T435 658 0717) for pool. **Suade** (T435 658 2665) hosts big-name bands, usually in the blues/funk/old-school hip hop vein; for nightlife with a bit more punch, head down to SLC.

Shopping **Smith's** (T435 649 7278) is the 24/7 budget supermarket; **Wild Oats** (T435 575 0200) the impressive organic version. Both are out at Kimball Junction. For gear, rentals and the bro-down, it's got to be **The Click** (T435 940 9004).

Health In a town of exclusive spas, private home visits and even canine masseurs, **Knead a Massage** (T435 613 8440) is proudly affordable.

OPENING TIMES
Late Nov to late Apr: 0900-1600

RESORT PRICES
Week pass (6 days): US$402
Day pass: US$73
Season pass: US$1095

DIRECTORY
Tourist Office: parkcityinfo.com
Medical Centre: T435 649 7690
Pisteurs: Ski patrol at Park City Mountain Resort
Taxi: T435 647 3999
Local radio: KPCW 91.9 FM
Website: parkcitymountain.com or pcride.com

Like Aspen, Breckenridge, Telluride and Truckee, Park City is more than just a resort: you can see why people would actually want to set up home here. Easy living topped off with the lightest powder in the Rockies.

Tam Leach, snowboarding journalist

Internet Access is free at the library (T435 615 5600), hooked-up or wireless.

Transfer options Expect to pay around $30-$35 one way for a shared shuttle bus from SLC; if there are at least three of you, it can work out less to book a private one. **Powder For The People** (T435 649 6648) is one of the cheapest; the tourist office site (parkcityinfo.com) lists others.

Local partners Only available through tour operators, the Silver Passport covers Park City and immediate neighbour The Canyons.

P: JAMES MCPHAIL

The Mountain ◔❄☻☺

Crowned with bowls, glades and chutes, there's way more to Park City Mountain Resort than its reputed cruisers and terrain parks, though of Utah's 13 resorts it's certainly one of the most manicured, tourist-oriented – and expensive. To experience the famous Utah freeriding stomping grounds you'll need to travel over to cheaper Brighton, Snowbird and Solitude.

Beginners Start out at First Time lift, moving higher up to the greens and easy blues off Bonanza and Pioneer when you get bored. If all goes well, by the end of the day you'll be able to tackle Quit n' Time, the long cruising blue which winds back right into the centre of town.

Intermediate Race the blues off King Con as a warm-up, then move up to Silverlode to duck in and out of the trees. For more freeriding, head over to Blueslip Bowl and then across to the glades off McConkey's: cruise down Tycoon and drop in low to avoid the upper bowl. Time for the park? The ride-on rails and kickers of Jonesy's are decently sized, so that you'll progress rather than get it all done first run.

Advanced Want to warm up on natural terrain? The bowls, glades and chutes of Blueslip and McConkey's are the most accessible should you be itching to move on to the parks regularly voted best in the US. Begin on the boxes and hits of Pick n' Shovel before stepping up to King's Crown and the immaculately groomed Eagle superpipe, home to the Park City All-Stars (Shaun White, Jeremy Jones, MFM et al). Darkness brings no respite: the smaller rails and boxes along PayDay are lit until 1930.

Kids The Kid's Mountain School offers snowboard lessons from beginner to park ripper, for ages 7-13; there are a number of childcare providers in town. Six and unders ski free with a paying adult.

Flat Light Days Even if it's mid-season and the humungous Park City skatepark is filled with snow, it's likely that the plethora of concrete parks down in the flatlands will be dry. Besides, you need the excuse to check out the towering Mormon temple in Salt Lake, right? Check concretedisciples.com for listings.

P: JAMES CARR P: JAMES MCPHAIL

P: JAMES MCPHAIL

P: JAMES MCPHAIL

☺ LOCALS DO
☺ Pre-purchase lift tickets for the best rates.
☺ Queue up at least an hour before Sundance screenings for Wait List tickets.

☹ LOCALS DON'T
☹ Ride Alta or Deer Valley: still snobbishly skiers only.
☹ Drive home drunk: call for the free Taxi Against Drunk Driving (T435 647 3999).
☹ Stay downtown late during Sundance: taxis are booked, there's nowhere to park and you can't get home.

✔ PROS
☺ A town proper, with lots going on: other Utah resorts have little to offer in comparison.
☺ Great parks and a world of freeriding less than an hour away.
☺ Easy access from the airport and to other resorts.

✖ CONS
✖ Expensive rooms and lift passes.
✖ Can feel touristy.
✖ The downside of 'champagne powder': icy parks during dry periods.

☺ NOT TO MISS
When conditions are right, forget the parks and hike up Jupiter Peak or out along Pinecone Ridge: a little bit of time and effort means a lot of unpoached fresh.

ⓘ REMEMBER TO AVOID
Thaynes Canyon – hell for those who haven't yet got the knack for keeping their speed on the flat.

❄ SNOW DEPTH

Figures not available

(metres, axis 0–5, months N D J F M A)

☺ RELIVE A FAMOUS MOMENT
Ski Patrol, a classic goofball comedy from 1990, is set entirely in Park City.

2103 m	TOWN ALTITUDE
60 km	KM TO AIRPORT
SLC	AIRPORT
★★☆	VEGETARIAN RATING
★★★	INTERNET CAFES
★★☆	RIDE IN/RIDE OUT
3048 m	HIGHEST LIFT
945 m	VERTICAL DROP
3300	RIDEABLE AREA (IN ACRES)
runs not measured	KM OF PISTES
1	NURSERY AREAS
18/44/38	RUNS: BEG/INTER/ADV
0/0	FUNICULAR/CABLE CARS
0/14	GONDOLAS/CHAIRS
1	DRAGS
yes	NIGHT RIDING
4	PARKS
1	PIPE
no	SUMMER AREAS
★★★ ★★☆	ENVIRONMENTAL RATING
$ $ $	COST INDICATOR

USA
PARK CITY

Riders' tales
A short history of snowboarding

By the early 20th century, so many people were skiing and surfing that the idea of joining them together was bound to happen at some point. In 1914, an Austrian by the name of Toni Lenhardt invented the mono-glider, a pre-curser to the monoski, but the design didn't catch on. Neither did MJ 'Jack' Burchett's more familiar-looking board on which to stand sideways. By 1939, Vern Wicklund, who had been riding since 1917, patented what is clearly a snowboard. He even filmed himself riding down a Chicago hill. But incidents of invention were cropping up all over the place. Army privates were seen riding adopted barrels in the snow during the Second World War, people modifying sledges and skis popped up throughout the '40s and '50s and when skateboarding came on the scene at the start of the '60s, the numbers of garage-based designs making it to the snow increased. Tom Sims, for example, submitted his own 'ski board' for a school project in 1963. Putting the idea on the back burner, he went and started a skateboard business instead. Clearly, by the simple numbers of patents that were applied for, the idea of standing on a board to ride the snow was generating genuine interest amongst the people who thought they'd germinated the idea from seed. But *still* none caught on.

That all changed on Christmas Day 1965 when an engineer named Sherman Poppen looked out of his house in Muskegon, Michigan and had the same brain wave as the previous inventors. Poppen's 'Snurfer' was an instant hit, and he licensed the toy to Brunswick Manufacturing. In June of 1966 – the same month that The Beatles were getting thrown out of the Philippines for insulting Imelda Marcos – the world's first commercial snowboard came off the press. According to some reports, up to a million Snurfers were sold until its discontinuation in 1969, but it's more likely that the actual figure was in the thousands.

The Snurfer, although dead by the end of the decade, left a lasting impression on some. Dimitrije Milovich, a student and surfer from the east coast of the States living in Utah, built his own powder board with a swallowtail. He later founded Winterstick with boards that had grown in size for the adult rider, and developed bindings and shapes for use in soft snow. Pushing for a wider audience, he featured in several national magazines including *Powder*, *Playboy* and *Newsweek*. By 1977 the scene was set for other self-confessed Snurfer owners to set up their own companies. Sims and Burton both hail from the era. But if '77 was the year that snowboarding as we know it today burst

out of the workshops and onto the sales floor of sport shops, it wasn't until 1985 that snowboarding hit the mainstream when the British Secret Service got involved.

James Bond tried snowboarding when he ripped the middle steering ski off a skidoo and rode down a slope and across a lake to the sound of *The Beach Boys* in the 007 film *A View To A Kill*. Filmed on location at Glacier Lake in Iceland and Vadrietta di Scersen in Switzerland, Tom Sims and Steve Link doubled for Roger Moore. With Bond skimming effortlessly across an expanse of water, easily outwitting the black-suited skiing baddies as they sink to their deaths, snowboarding had in one swift swoop set out its stall as a younger, cooler alternative to skiing. And what a spectacular way to do it.

With snowboarding growing at a very rapid speed, it finally looked like the potential of the sport was finally coming to fruition. In Europe, meanwhile, things had taken a fairly different route. As far back as the late '70s, Henri Authier and José Fernandes had ridden in Switzerland on Wintersticks they'd bought from the States, while in 1980 a German girl by the name of Petra Mussig had begun messing around with her own binding and board combination. In the same year, Alain Gaimard, publicity director for Les Arcs resorts, invited an Australian called Paul Loxton to the Tarantaise slopes to ride his Winterstick as a publicity stunt. There he met local ski instructor Regís Rolland who fell for the sport and ended up starring in Europe's first snowboard film – *Apocalypse Snow*. As part of the 'Extreme Movement', the film went around the world turning hundreds of thousands of people onto snowboarding. From the early '90s onwards, the world knew about snowboarding, and was grappling for a piece of the action as the sport doubled in size nearly every

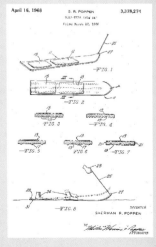

year – which is where we find ourselves now. Estimates vary, but according to the industry there are somewhere between eight and 14 million riders out there today, and it is increasing every year.

The origins of Snowboarding?

Do any instances of snowboarding exist prior to the 20th century? The answer is: *probably*. It is extremely likely that a type of snowboarding was practiced by Hawaiians as far back as the 15th century.

The sport of land surfing – or *papa holua* in the native language – was practiced on huge man-made slides constructed from rock on the slopes of the island's volcanoes. Some of the sites took hundreds of men years to build. Clearly, they were incredibly important structures. Many legends describe the rides as a ritualistic offering to the volcanic gods, presumably to placate the frequent earthquakes and tsunamis that were an inevitable part of life.

Professors at the University of Hawaii have mapped ruins of the ramps, and several are found above 9000 ft on the volcanoes of Mauna Lao and Mauna Kea, roughly the height of the snowline during the Pacific winter. Did the Hawaiians take their sleds onto the snow? Well, considering the ramps took so long to build, and that armies of men carried tons of grass to make the slides work when the contests and sacrifices were on, it would seem more ludicrous to suggest they *didn't* try their holua sleds on the snow.

Of course, there's a certain romance to this idea that makes us want to believe they were snowboarding in the dark ages, but alas it must remain in the realms of conjecture – unfortunately, the demise of Polynesian culture following the European colonization of the 16th century means we'll never know. What is clear however is that modern snowboarding - after many false starts – looks sturdy enough to survive for the foreseeable future. And while most attribute the contemporary version of the sport to Sherman Poppen's initial brainwave, it is equally obvious that without the original concept of sliding sideways on waves – invented by an unknown Polynesian genius *at least* 1000 years before him – the concept of riding a board on the snow would in all probability still be lying dormant.

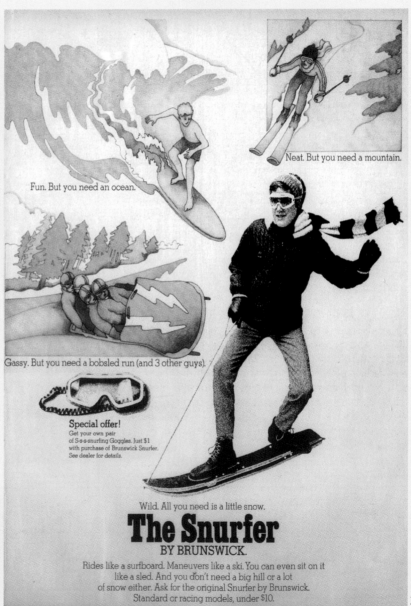

Fun. But you need an ocean.

Neat. But you need a mountain.

Gassy. But you need a bobsled run (and 3 other guys).

Special offer!
Get your own pair of S-s-s-snurfing Goggles. Just $1 with purchase of Brunswick Snurfer. See dealer for details.

Wild. All you need is a little snow.

The Snurfer
BY BRUNSWICK.

Rides like a surfboard. Maneuvers like a ski. You can even sit on it like a sled. And you don't need a big hill or a lot of snow either. Ask for the original Snurfer by Brunswick. Standard or racing models, under $10.

Snowbird

One of the best of the rich crop of high-class resorts that surround Salt Lake City.

» If you like this . . .
. . . try Whistler »p86, or Squaw Valley »p374.

The Town

In the last two years, the mountain resorts around SLC have averaged over 1500 cm of 'the best snow on earth'. Combine that with seven surrounding resorts and all the conveniences of a city, and SLC presents a tidy package that's hard to beat. Thanks to the 2002 Winter Olympics, Salt Lake City even got an updated look, transforming it from the town that Brigham Young and his Mormon pioneers established in 1847 into a 21st-century destination. The city is easy to navigate, with a grid pattern of streets centred on the Mormon Temple Square. Snowbird is off 9400 South (94 blocks south of the temple) up Little Cottonwood Canyon, 46 km from the international airport and only 20 minutes from the neighbourhoods of Sandy and Sugarhouse.

Sleeping Slopeside lodging can be found in the avalanche-proof concrete buildings around Snowbird's base area: **The Inn At Snowbird**, **The Lodge At Snowbird**, and the swanky **Cliff Lodge** (T1-800 453 3000, snowbird.com). Stay in the South Valley of SLC for more nightlife/dining options as well as quicker access to other resorts, such as Brighton. **Residence Inn Salt Lake City Cottonwood** (T801 453 0430) or **Fairfield Inn Salt Lake City South** (T801 265 9600) are both good options.

Eating Grab some pizza at **Pier49** under the tram building or a sandwich at **General Gritts** and chill on the sundeck. For après, have sushi and drinks at **The Aerie Lounge** (on the 10th floor of the Cliff Lodge) or margaritas and Mexican at **El Chanate**

Cantina (T801 933 2145). Just at the base of the canyon, there's something for every budget, from the Carne Asada burritos at **Molca Salsa** (T801 487 3850) in Sandy, to the hearty platters of exactly what you want after a day on the hill at **The Porcupine Pub & Grill** (T801 942 5555).

Bars and clubs Get ready to get frustrated with the confusing drinking laws in this great Mormon state. Down in Salt Lake, rock out at **Todd's Bar** (T801 328 8650) or get civilized at the snowboarder-owned sushi-cocktail experience at **Circle Lounge** (T801 531 5400). For a unique drinking/dining experience, check out **Brewvies** (T801 355 5500). They provide beer, pizza, and movies – you bring a date.

Shopping **Milo Sport** (T801 487 8600) is the hub of the local snowboarding scene and a good place to stock up on Coal Beanies and Holden Outerwear.

Health Snowbird Canyon Racquet & Fitness Club (T801 947 8200) or **The Cliff Spa** (T801 933 2225).

Internet Wireless is available in **The Cliff Lodge**.

Transfer options The **Utah Transit Authority** (T1-888-RIDE-UTA, rideuta.com) has bus services to Alta, Brighton, Snowbird and Solitude.

☺ OPENING TIMES
Mid-Nov to late May: 0900-1630

⊛ RESORT PRICES
Week pass: Check for specials
Day pass: US$62 (tram and chair); US$51 (chair only)
Season pass: US$1049 (unlimited tram and chair)

ⓘ DIRECTORY
Tourist office: skiutah.com
Medical centre: T1-801 933 2222
Taxi: T1-801 328 5704
Local radio: None
Website: snowbird.com

My ideal day at The Bird would involve a mid-week storm that dumps 28 inches and stays stormy-walk-on tramlines, riding with my long time Celtek Clan homies, and finishing off the day with a trip to the Cliff Lodge Spa.

Bjorn Leines, professional snowboarder

Arrange your airport transfers through Snowbird Central Reservations line (T1-800 232 9542).

Local partners Snowbird and Alta have a shared pass for US$69 – just bring some skis – snowboarding is banned at Alta!

R: ED LEIGH P: JAMES MCPHAIL

P: JAMES MCPHAIL

The Mountain

Snowbird is a freeriders' haven located next to Alta Resort in the steep confines of Little Cottonwood Canyon. The combination of steep runs, 3000 vertical foot top-to-bottom descents, an average of over 1300 cm of snowfall in the last two winters, and tram access makes 'The Bird' the jewel in the crown of Salt Lake resorts. Riders such as Marc Frank Montoya and Bjorn and Eric Leines call it home. With 2500 acres to explore and more out of the backcountry gates, you'll be hard pressed to lose interest in Snowbird. Progression for anyone who rides here is mandatory.

Beginners Start your day over at the new **Creekside Lodge** with a lesson (half day for US$70 including a lift ticket). Take it easy on the Wilbere lift working your way up to the Mid-Gad lift. If the skies are clear, head up the tram (yes, the tram) to Mineral Basin and prepare for a whole new mountain on Lupine Loop accessed through the new Peruvian Gulch tunnel. How about those views? Be sure to take
the tram back down.

Intermediate Jump on the brand new Peruvian Express quad to Mineral Basin on the backside. It gets the early morning sunshine. Have a look around and decide what you're up for: if it's powder, just find the widest open swathe of slope and open her up. Head back to the frontside and get your jib on with laps down Chips Run. Follow the locals for natural terrain kickers and drop down the steep sections to briefly sample black diamonds.

Advanced It's obvious what your mission is as you look down from the eight-minute tram ride. The Cirque needs to get tracked out. Head down the Cirque Traverse and drop in wherever looks best. The upper chutes like Great Scott and Upper Fox tend to be the gnarliest. You'll find something new each time: 45° slopes, powder, trees and rocks. Head back to Mineral Basin, skier's right. Jump on the Path to Paradise, and just when you've had enough of the cat-traffic, drop into Nash Flora Lode. Scope out some cliff drops on the Hamilton Cliffs in Mineral Basin. Oh, the glory of it all!

Kids Twelve and under ride for free (tram rides costs US$15). Snowbird offers Kids Camp and comprehensive children's learning programmes for ages three and up.

Flat light days Stay low on the frontside or head over to the park and Superpipe accessed by the Baby Thunder lift.

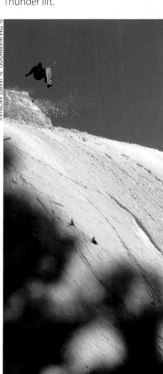

R. TIM WARWOOD P. JAMES MCPHAIL

☺ LOCALS DO

- Wake up early and stand in the tramline on powder days.
- Eat at least one meal a day at Molca Salsa.
- Consist of a Who's Who of professional snowboarders.

☹ LOCALS DON'T

- Snowboard on Sundays (if they're Mormon).
- Live at Snowbird.
- Ride the surrounding backcountry without avalanche gear or before checking the local avalanche forecast (T801 742 0830).

✔ PROS

- Marc Frank Montoya.
- 'The Best Snow On Earth'.
- 120 passenger tram.

✖ CONS

- Weekend tram lines.
- Little Cottonwood Canyon closing due to avalanches.
- Not much grooming.

☺ NOT TO MISS

Take a day and hit up nearby Brighton in Big Cottonwood Canyon for a completely different vibe. Locals pick one or the other to be faithful to – but you don't have to.

ⓘ REMEMBER TO AVOID

3.2 % beer and one-ounce martinis.

❄ SNOW DEPTH

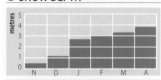

☺ RELIVE A FAMOUS MOMENT

Look out for famous kickers like Chad's Gap and the Pyramid Gap, made famous by Travis Rice in Absinthe's *Pop*.

2360 m	TOWN ALTITUDE
46 km	KM TO AIRPORT
SLC	AIRPORT
★★☆	VEGETARIAN RATING
★★☆	INTERNET CAFES
★☆☆	RIDE IN/RIDE OUT
3352 m	HIGHEST LIFT
987 m	VERTICAL DROP
2500	RIDEABLE AREA (IN ACRES)
runs not measured	KM OF PISTES
1	NURSERY AREAS
23/32/30	RUNS: BEG/INTER/ADV
0/1	FUNICULAR/CABLE CARS
0/10	GONDOLAS/CHAIRS
2	DRAGS
yes	NIGHT RIDING
2	PARKS
1	PIPE
no	SUMMER AREAS
★★★ ★★★	ENVIRONMENTAL RATING
⑤⑤⑤	COST INDICATOR

USA
SNOWBIRD

The village might be an afterthought, but at Squaw you'll get sunny days, consistently good snow and arguably the biggest and best natural terrain of any Californian resort: it's no surprise so many pros have made "Squallywood" home.

☼ *If you like this . . .*
. . . try Lake Louise ⇒p84, or Brighton ⇒p358.

The Town

Until recently little more than a parking lot amidst the log homes of surrounding Olympic Valley, the base area at Squaw is now a small corporate ski village; all swanky apartment condos and coffee bars. Yet thanks to the strong local community, it still retains an idiosyncratic, laid-back California vibe, typical of Tahoe's backwoodsy North Shore.

Sleeping The Village at Squaw Valley are the plush new condos; older, slightly more worn-in apartments are also available. Book through Central Reservations (T1-800 403 0206). The PlumpJack Inn (T530 583 1576) is the stylish hotel alternative. Motel and B&B accommodation is 15 minutes' drive away, either inTruckee or in lakeside Tahoe City.

Eating Do not miss the cinnamon rolls at the Wildflour Bakery (T530 583 1963). Dave's Deli Counter (T530 581 1085) is the local's lunch and beer pitstop, while the pricey Balboa Café

“ ”

Squaw has the famous KT 22 chair, and a lot of cliff bands. I did a trip there a while back and everyone was just throwing themselves off every cliff in sight. It's probably one of the best all-round resorts in Tahoe.

Nick Hamilton, photo editor,
Transworld Snowboarding

(T530 583 5850) brings a little SF to the mountains. Grass Roots (T383 541 7788) for good veggie.

Bars and clubs Try après-lounging rather than serious partying at the Red Dog or in the bar at the Plumpjack. Truckee and Tahoe City have a bit more going on.

Shopping Stock up on provisions at one of the big supermarkets in Truckee, and save bucks by renting gear at Dave's (T530 583 5665).

Health For sports medicine issues and physio referrals, pop into the Truckee Tahoe Medical office (T530 581 8864) at the ski area.

Internet Squaw was the first mountain to go wireless; rates start at

US$2.50 per hour, with many hotels offering free access.

Transfer options The No Stress Express (T775 333 6955, nostressexpress.com) is one of many shuttles serving Squaw from Reno-Tahoe International; single journeys start at US$47. Alternatively, gamble your first night away and catch the resort's early morning US$10 ski shuttle from the major Reno casinos to the mountain; reservations necessary (T866 769 4653).

Local partners None.

P: SQUAW VALLEY

The Mountain

Californians consider Squaw the closest thing that they have to an alpine resort. This is where you'll find the golden state's Olympic skiers and cliff-huckers lining up early on powder days to make the most of the mountain's steeps and deeps. Rock faces and mogul fields, superpipes and cornices; the host of the 1960 Olympics is a big mountain with a great variety of terrain.

Beginners Head up to High Camp in the cable car for the same views that the experts get, and a wide open plateau perfect for first turns. Move onto East Broadway and Riviera, but don't take Mountain Run back down until comfortably keeping speed in a straight line: you're likely to get stranded on the flats.

Intermediate Shirley Lake and

tougher Solitude are good confidence builders: mellow runs peppered with small natural hits and rollers, glades, powder stashes and even a baby cornice. If there's powder, head over to Broken Arrow to hit up the mellow bowl. In the afternoon, run laps at the Riviera park, a sunny, sheltered spot with a standard-size pipe and smaller hits and jibs.

Advanced First thing on a powder day you have to make the choice: get in line for the KT22 lift, which climbs straight to powdery steeps, cornices and big cliffs, or begin the long journey back towards Granite Chief, Squaw's highest peak, and hike in to an open bowl, rock drops and trees. Secluded Silverado is good for a bit of rock-hopping away from the crowds. By the afternoon, when the sun is out and the snow has settled, you'll find most locals in the Mainline park, lapping Squaw's well-maintained superpipe.

Kids 12 and unders ride for just US$5 at Squaw. At the bottom of the mountain, the Papoose nursery slopes have easy moving carpet lifts for nervous never-evers.

Flat light days Don't overlook the lower terrain off Snow King. Though heavy and wet when the temperature rises, the gentle cruisers afford stellar views of the lake sparkling below, and in powder conditions the tight trees and hidden pillow lines are epic.

☺ LOCALS DO
◉ Get in line before 0800 on a powder day.
◉ Bring swimsuits up the mountain in spring.
◉ Take advantage of the free transceiver classes held by Ski Patrol every Friday evening.

☹ LOCALS DON'T
⊗ Ride at the weekends (midweek passes are much cheaper and the lifts are swamped with city folk).
⊗ Bother much with night riding, unless they're pipe fiends.
⊗ Stop for lunch up the mountain.

✔ PROS
◉ 11-m average annual snowfall.
◉ Great spring riding, usually through till end of May.
◉ Fun, easily accessible freeriding and a well-maintained pipe.

✗ CONS
⊗ Expensive.
⊗ The village is little more than a collection of places to stay.
⊗ Need a car to make the most of North Lake Tahoe.

☺ NOT TO MISS
First tracks off Broken Arrow on a powder day, as the sun glints off the summit's red rocks.

⊙ REMEMBER TO AVOID
Mountain Run after 1500. The three-mile cat track turns into an erratically moving obstacle course as everyone takes the highway home.

❄ SNOW DEPTH

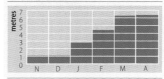

✪ RELIVE A FAMOUS MOMENT
Drive up through the back of Truckee (don't take the freeway) to Donner Pass and spot seminal early '90s snowboard movie series *Totally Board*'s secret spots.

1890 m	TOWN ALTITUDE
72 km	KM TO AIRPORT
RNO	AIRPORT
★★★	VEGETARIAN RATING
★★★	INTERNET CAFES
★☆☆	RIDE IN/RIDE OUT
2652 m	HIGHEST LIFT
869 m	VERTICAL DROP
4000	RIDEABLE AREA (IN ACRES)
runs not measured	KM OF PISTES
2	NURSERY AREAS
40/70/50	RUNS: BEG/INTER/ADV
0/1	FUNICULAR/CABLE CARS
2/26	GONDOLAS/CHAIRS
5	DRAGS
yes	NIGHT RIDING
3	PARKS
2	PIPE
no	SUMMER AREAS
★★★ / ★★★	ENVIRONMENTAL RATING
$$$	COST INDICATOR

USA
SQUAW VALLEY

R: UNKNOWN P: SQUAW VALLEY

P: SQUAW VALLEY

The Town

Vail might well define what most people think of as US snowboarding. Despite terrain that suffers in comparison to some other steeper or more powder-blessed mountains, Vail has managed to garner a reputation as the archetypal Rocky Mountain destination.

Spend a little time here and it's easy to see why Vail has such a reputation. Yes, the purpose-built, slightly sterile town looks like an Alpine mountain village designed by Walt Disney, with a motorway running through the middle of it (Interstate 70), rammed full of tourists and very expensive – but like all good shred towns, there's just something in the air in Vail. And it's the pursuit of this nameless essence that brings the people back year after year. The versatile, rewarding mountain helps, as does a local nightlife and snowboarding scene with a predominantly US and Aussie seasonaires base. But is it really the best resort in America? For many, the answer is definitely 'yes'. It'll take a visit to answer that one for yourself.

Sleeping vail.snow.com has a huge online accommodation finder for all budgets. Just a kilometre out of town, **Roost Lodge** (roostlodge.com) is pretty cheap and basic for Vail. **The Holiday Inn Apex at Vail** (T970 476 2739) would be a good top-end option, with shuttles, breakfast and in-house spa included in the price.

Eating Vail has the lot, from haute cuisine to cheaper eateries. Popular with local riders are **Vendettas** (T970 476 5070) for pizza and beers, **DJ's Diner** (T970 476 2336) for a classic breakfast and, just out of town, **Bagali's** (T970 479 9242) for Italian. Book ahead.

Bars and clubs After you've eaten that pizza, why not stay in **Vendettas** with the rest of the locals? Later, everyone heads to the **Tap Room** or the **Sanctuary**.

Shopping City Market is the

For me, it's the best resort in North America. Other resorts might have steeper terrain or better parks, but Vail has perfect terrain for all riders.

Tim Warwood, six-season Vail veteran and pro snowboarder

in-town option, while the ubiquitous (and cheap) **Wal-Mart** is just out of town.

Health There's a medical centre in town, on the bus route between Lion's Head and Vail, as well as half a dozen massage therapists in town.

Internet At least four in town, with hotels and some lift stations wireless enabled!

Transfer Options Use the super efficient **Colorado Mountain Express** (ridecme.com) for connections from any airport.

Local partners The Vail Pass also works in Beaver Creek, Breckenridge, A-Basin and Keystone, as well as at Heavenly and Lake Tahoe in California.

Colorado's finest is also one of North America's most famous snowboarding resorts. For some, one trip is all it takes to get hooked for life.

If you like this ...
... try St Anton ▸▸p48, Whistler ▸▸p86, or Val d'Isère ▸▸p158.

P: TIM WARWOOD

The Mountain

Taken as a whole, Vail Mountain is a supremely versatile snowboarders' mountain. Banks, hips, mellow powder runs, amazing funparks and, above all, great tree riding are all here and all easy to access. Roughly speaking, there are three areas to explore: Frontside (where the majority of tree riding is to be found), the famous Vail back bowls and, lastly, Blue Sky Basin. For some, the terrain just won't be steep and long enough. Then again, if you want to ride big, open powder faces, you're probably better off riding in Europe. But most riders will revel in the tree runs, the mountain's sheer variety and the fact that they know everything here is safe. If you can see it, chances are somebody has been down it before you. Overall, this is quintessential American snowboarding, as slick and enjoyable as it comes.

Beginners Complete beginners should take lessons at **Vail Ski School**, which has an excellent programme. Once you're linking turns, Vail is a great riding experience. Golden Peak has good starter facilities, but you should really take advantage of the beginner area at the top of Eagle Bahn gondola, which has some amazing views of the entire riding area as well as mellow runs to get you started.

Intermediate Ride everything and go everywhere. Northwoods would be a good area to start, particularly around Lift 11 (locals tend to refer to lifts by number in Vail), so spend the morning here, stop for lunch at one of the on-hill stands and then head back up to spend the afternoon riding the baby funpark on the Born Free run, under the gondola.

Advanced Head straight to the top of Lift 4 and ride the run called Windows. Next, go through the gate and take the tree run in the Back Bowls. It's usually avoided by tourists put off by the trees and steepness. More fool them – it opens out into a big bowl. Head to the WFO trees next before stopping for lunch. In the afternoon, if your legs can take it, head to the park and pipe. Locals rate the pipe as the best in Colorado.

Kids Kids registered for Vail's ski and snowboard school get tickets free as part of the package.

Flat light days Vail is among the best in the world for tree riding. Get wrapped up and ride the front face all day.

☺ LOCALS DO
- Go to the Tap Room on a Monday night for 25-cent beers.
- Avoid President's Day weekend. It's so busy season passes don't work on the lifts!
- Get a City Market discount card, and save money on groceries.

☺ LOCALS DON'T
- Pay full price for food on mountain restaurants
- Ride the moguls underneath the gondola on the Frontside.
- Just head straight for the Back Bowls on a powder day. Everyone has the same idea.

✔ PROS
- Trees.
- Friendliness.
- Sunny.

✖ CONS
- Expensive.
- Not amazingly steep.
- Short runs.

☺ NOT TO MISS
At least once, try and take the first groomed run down Northwoods from top to bottom. You can absolutely fly down it.

ⓘ REMEMBER TO AVOID
The three-man Chair 5 on a powder day. It's a notorious queuing spot. Avoid at all costs!

❄ SNOW DEPTH

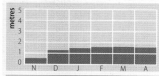

☺ RELIVE A FAMOUS MOMENT
Clint Eastwood is a Vail fanatic, and regularly visits for the America Ski Classic weekend, usually at the end of March.

☺ OPENING TIMES
Mid-Nov to mid-Apr: 0900-1600

ⓢ RESORT PRICES
Week pass (6 days): US$413
Day pass: US$59
Season pass: see website

ⓘ DIRECTORY
Tourist office: T877 204 7881
Medical centre: T970 479 5119
Pisteurs: T970 476 4888
Taxi: T877 829 8294
Local radio: 93.1 FM
Website: vail.snow.com

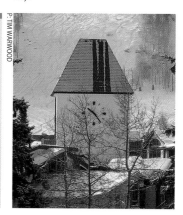

P: TIM WARWOOD

2475 m	TOWN ALTITUDE
161 km	KM TO AIRPORT
DEN	AIRPORT
★★★	VEGETARIAN RATING
★★★	INTERNET CAFES
★★☆	RIDE IN/RIDE OUT
3427 m	HIGHEST LIFT
1052 m	VERTICAL DROP
5289	RIDEABLE AREA (IN ACRES)
317 km	KM OF PISTES
1	NURSERY AREAS
22/61/80	RUNS: BEG/INTER/ADV
0	FUNICULAR/CABLE CARS
1/23	GONDOLAS/CHAIRS
10	DRAGS
yes	NIGHT RIDING
4	PARKS
1	PIPE
no	SUMMER AREAS
★★★☆	ENVIRONMENTAL RATING
$$$	COST INDICATOR

Directory

Snowboarding is not a real sport..."
Steve Cram, BBC Sport

It's better than running.

www.whitelines.com

whitelines
snowboard magazine

Index

Bold italic entries denote resorts. Countries are indicated in brackets: **And** = Andorra; **Arg** = Argentina; **Aus** = Austria; **Bul** = Bulgaria; **Can** = Canada; **Chi** = Chile; **Fin** = Finland; **Fr** = France; **Ira** = Iran; **It** = Italy; **Jpn** = Japan; **NZ** = New Zealand; **Nor** = Norway; **Pol** = Poland; **Rus** = Russia; **Sp** = Spain; **Swe** = Sweden;**Swi** = Switzerland and **USA** = USA.

Riders pictured

Riders' tales and lift chat

Credits

Footprint credits

Text editor: Alan Murphy
Map editor: Sarah Sorensen
Layout and production: Patrick Dawson
Proof reader: Stephanie Lambe

Publisher: Patrick Dawson
Editorial: Sophie Blacksell,
Felicity Laughton, Nicola Jones
Cartography: Angus Dawson, Robert Lunn, Kevin Feeney
Graphs: Joe Copestake
Design: Mytton Williams
Sales and marketing: Andy Riddle
Advertising: Debbie Wylde
Finance and administration: Elizabeth Taylor

Photography credits

Title page: danmilner.com (Johno Verity, Scandinavia)
Front cover: James McPhail (Ed Leigh, Baquiera-Beret)
Back cover: Chris Moran/hotshitpictures.com (Niseko, Japan)

Print

Manufactured in Italy by EuroGrafica
Pulp from sustainable forests

Footprint feedback

We try as hard as we can to make each Footprint guide
as up to date as possible but, of course, things always change.
If you want to let us know about your experiences – good, bad
or ugly – then don't delay, go to www.footprintbooks.com
and send in your comments.

Every effort has been made to ensure that the facts in this
guidebook are accurate. However, travellers should still
obtain advice from consulates, airlines etc about travel and
visa requirements before travelling. The authors and
publishers cannot accept responsibility for any loss, injury
or inconvenience however caused.

Publishing information

Footprint Snowboarding the World
1st edition
© Footprint Handbooks Ltd
September 2006

ISBN 1 904777 78 3
CIP DATA: A catalogue record for this book is
available from the British Library

® Footprint Handbooks and the Footprint mark are
a registered trademark of Footprint Handbooks Ltd

Published by Footprint

6 Riverside Court
Lower Bristol Road
Bath BA2 3DZ, UK
T +44 (0)1225 469141
F +44 (0)1225 469461
discover@footprintbooks.com
www.footprintbooks.com

Distributed in the USA by

Publishers Group West

The colour maps are not intended to have any political
significance.